FEDERAL RULES OF CIVIL PROCEDURE
with Resources for Study
2008-2009

PJ: Long Arm statutes NY §§ 301, 302
12(b)2 lack of PJ defense
12(h)1 waiving 12 defense

SMJ: Federal Question Jurisdiction
28 USC 1331 - Federal Question: const, laws, treaties
1337 - commerce + anti trust regulations
1338 - patent, copyright, unfair competition
1343 - civil rights, elective franchise
1345 - US as a Π
1346 - US as a Δ

Diversity Jurisdiction
28 USC 1332 (a-c) - Diversity + Amount ⊗

Removal
28 USC
1441 Removal Generally
1443 Civil Rights cases
1446 Procedure for Removal
1447 Procedure after Removal
1448 Process after Removal

FRCP 18 Simple Joinder

28 USC 1367 Supplement Jurisdiction
a - qualify
b - disqualifying
c - discretion

Res judicata
Restatment Judgments §17 → generally (221)
§ 24 → same claim
§ 20 → final judgment on merits

Joinder
FRCP 20 - permissive
FRCP 19 - required

Class Action
FRCP 23

ASPEN PUBLISHERS

FEDERAL RULES
OF CIVIL PROCEDURE
WITH RESOURCES FOR STUDY
2008-2009

EDITED BY

STEPHEN N. SUBRIN
NORTHEASTERN UNIVERSITY SCHOOL OF LAW

MARTHA L. MINOW
HARVARD LAW SCHOOL

MARK S. BRODIN
BOSTON COLLEGE SCHOOL OF LAW

THOMAS O. MAIN
UNIVERSITY OF THE PACIFIC
McGEORGE SCHOOL OF LAW

Wolters Kluwer
Law & Business

AUSTIN   BOSTON   CHICAGO   NEW YORK   THE NETHERLANDS

To contact Customer Care, e-mail customer.care@aspenpublishers.com,
call 1-800-234-1660, fax 1-800-901-9075, or mail correspondence to:

Aspen Publishers
Attn: Order Department
PO Box 990
Frederick, MD 21705

Printed in the United States of America.

1 2 3 4 5 6 7 8 9 0

ISBN 978-0-7355-7214-0

ISSN 1550-4425

About Wolters Kluwer Law & Business

Wolters Kluwer Law & Business is a leading provider of research information and workflow solutions in key specialty areas. The strengths of the individual brands of Aspen Publishers, CCH, Kluwer Law International and Loislaw are aligned with Wolters Kluwer Law & Business to provide comprehensive, in-depth solutions and expert-authored content for the legal, professional and education markets.

CCH was founded in 1913 and has served more than four generations of business professionals and their clients. The CCH products in the Wolters Kluwer Law & Business group are highly regarded electronic and print resources for legal, securities, antitrust and trade regulation, government contracting, banking, pension, payroll, employment and labor, and healthcare reimbursement and compliance professionals.

Aspen Publishers is a leading information provider for attorneys, business professionals and law students. Written by preeminent authorities, Aspen products offer analytical and practical information in a range of specialty practice areas from securities law and intellectual property to mergers and acquisitions and pension/benefits. Aspen's trusted legal education resources provide professors and students with high-quality, up-to-date and effective resources for successful instruction and study in all areas of the law.

Kluwer Law International supplies the global business community with comprehensive English-language international legal information. Legal practitioners, corporate counsel and business executives around the world rely on the Kluwer Law International journals, loose-leafs, books and electronic products for authoritative information in many areas of international legal practice.

Loislaw is a premier provider of digitized legal content to small law firm practitioners of various specializations. Loislaw provides attorneys with the ability to quickly and efficiently find the necessary legal information they need, when and where they need it, by facilitating access to primary law as well as state-specific law, records, forms and treatises.

Wolters Kluwer Law & Business, a unit of Wolters Kluwer, is headquartered in New York and Riverwoods, Illinois. Wolters Kluwer is a leading multinational publisher and information services company.

- TRADITIONAL CONCEPTION of PJ -

Pennoyer: 4 grounds to exercise personal jurisdiction: Resident, consent, presence + service, property in the state (recover value of that property)
: Article IV → full faith & credit for valid judgments

Harris + Balk: Quasi in Rem debt follows a person & is subject to attachment

Tauza v. Susquehanna Coal: Δ corp was in the state & ∴ Δ corp. was "here"

Hess v. Pawloski: (PA resident in MA accident) Long arm statutes valid under Pennoyer;
: By using a MA highway, non-resident motorists constructivly appoint a state officer to except service for them

- MODERN CONCEPTION of PJ -

International Shoe: (DE incorp. MI primary place of buisness WA sues for non-payment unemployment comp tax)
: Δ must have minimum contacts with the forum state such that the maintenance of the suit does not offend traditional notions of fair play & substantial justice
: Nature of contacts → systematic & continious or isolated
: Relationship → related to the cause of action or unrelated
→ Catagory 1 = systematic & continious + related COA → International Shoe ⟩ general
→ Catagory 2 = systematic & continious + unrelated COA → Tauza
→ Catagory 3 = isolated + related COA → Hess / McGee ⟩ specific
→ Catagory 4 = isolated + unrelated COA → Helicoptoros

McGee v. International Life: (Insurance comp in Cali)
: Solicitation in CA + interest in protecting its residents
: Δ defalted believing no PJ, then when δ collaterially attached judgment when brought to Δ's state for enforcement PJ was found ∴ Δ was issue percluded from litigating on merits

Hanson v. Denckla: (DA trust case)
: Purposeful availment is a factor in minimum contacts
: Δ had a deliberate choice to relate to the state invoking privilages + benefits of the law

Helicopteros: (IV-K signing)
: Catagory IV here insufficient to satisfy DP of 14th amendment

- LONG ARM STATUTES -

LAS: provide PJ over non-residents who could not be served in forum state
1) Does the LAS apply? READ IT 2) Is it w/in Shoe's minimum contact test?
NY CPLR §§ 301, 302

PJ in Federal Courts: FRCP 4(k)(1)(a)₂ – 4(k)(2) = exception
: PJ of federal DC is equal to jurisdictional reach of trial courts in the state + 100 miles for joinder
: Exception: fed courts can exercise jurisdiction over a Δ who is not subject to the jurisdiction of the courts of general jurisdiction of any state when claim arises under federal law + is consistent w/ DP.

Gray v. American Radiator: (out of state manufactor defective safety valve)
: Tort cannot be seperated from the injury
: Look @ action / business & does it fit in w/ LAS?

- MINIMUM CONTACT OPERATION -

World Wide Volks v. Woodson: (driving to new home; en route accident)
: Forum injury is not enough. Foreseeability of being hauled into court → purposeful availment to forum state: sell products / advertisement (not enough to foresee product ending up there)

Calder v. Jones: (National Enquirer Defamation)
: B/c Δ targetted forum state it was reasonable to foresee hauling into court there
: Even though Δ outside the state Δ's contact's w/ state caused injury

Kulko v. Supenor Court (Divorce case)
: Isolated contacts, unrelated COA, no availment to forum state ∴ no jurisdiction (IV)

Asahi Metal v. Supenor court: (products liabily; tire on motorcycle)
: Balancing Convience (5 justices agreed it over came sovergnity)
: Need to establish minimum contacts
: O'Connor = targeting / purposeful availment (4); or
Brennan = mere awareness; plus
Stevens = awareness plus → volume, value, hazardous character

Burger King: (K negotiations in MI; signing in FL; forum selection clause)
: forum clause not enough but a factor when considering foreseeability / availment
: foreseeability applies but OBS disagree about what it is

ALS Scan v. Digital Services: (internet case)
: passive activity / transmission not enough; look for interactivity / commerzial nature of online transmissions

Shaffer v. Heitner: modern quasi in rem must satisfy minimum contacts too.

Burnham v. Supenor Court: tag jurisdiction is not dead
: presence + service enough but no agreement why.
: Scali → tradition Brennan → fairness

Consent Carnival Cruise
Special appearance: challenging jurisdiction
Limited appearance: defending property; limited to in Rem
General appearance: appear ∴ subject to in persona jurisdiction
FRCP 12(h)(1) Appearance w/ failure to assert timely objection to PJ waives PJ objection
Notice Mollane
Standard for notice = reasonably calculated to give actual notice/ best notice not required
FRCP 4(m)
CPLR 308: ranking

CONTENTS

FEDERAL RULES OF CIVIL PROCEDURE

Contents

RESOURCES FOR STUDY

The Choice of an Appropriate Court: SMJ + Removal

Federal Question Jurisdiction + Diversity Jurisdiction

Article III §2 + 28 USC 1332: Fed Court limited parameters ∴ parties may challenge it @ anytime
and courts required to sua sponte when litigants don't
: Parties invoking fed jurisdiction have burden to prove entitlement

1. Federal Question: 1331→ dc have original jurisdiction of fed question; 1337→ anti-trust;
1338→ patents; 1345 US as π; 1346 US as Δ
: Fed law creates the COA; constitutional interpretation; Fed statute
application, fed law permeates the area

Louisville RR v. Mottley: (π settle claim in exchange for life RR passes)
: A potential federal question / anticipation of use of defence
Presenting a federal issue ≠ enough

TB Harms v. Eliscu : (dispute over copyright ownership) : Federal Question must appear in a "well pleaded complaint"
: look @ what is the dispute: violation of copyright law = fed question BUT
who owns the copyright = state K case

Merrell Dow v. Thompson: look @ issue. federal issue (violation of FDCA act) in state claim (negligence)
: congress intend to leave remedy open to states? Intend to occupy entire field?

2. Diversity Jurisdiction: 28 USC § 1332 (a-c)
: to eliminate bias against foreigners
: Amount in controversy =/+ 75,000 + π show good faith estimate
: Δ wishing to remove must show w/ legal certainty claim is less than 7500
: may aggregate amount but cant add interest + court costs

Ochoa v. PV Holding (Katrina Domicile)
: Domicile= where one's state citizenship is; fixed permenate residence;
ones life and home
: must have one and only one; get rid of old must establish a new one
: must show 1) intent 2) residence w/ burden on party invoking

1332 (a-c) : France v. England→ no; NY v. CT→ yes; US citizen domicile in Eng v. NY→ no;
: must show 2 different states; corp = incorporated + principal place of business
: divorce, probate, Family law = State only
: Diversity is considered @ beginning of action; no same citizenship on both sides of "v."

3. Removal: 28 USC 1441: Δ may remove to federal court if dc has original jurisdiction
look @ facts @ time notice was filed 1441 Removal Generally
1443: civil actions / criminal proceedings that may be removed
1446: procedure for removal; 1447: procedure after removal; 1448 process
after removal. = Filing notice in state court perfects removal;
π would have to go to fed court w/ motion to remand or fed; can
remand on its own; only Δ may remove + can't if resident
of state action was brought + 1332 claim (diversity)
: FRCP: 12(h)(1)(2)(3)

Burnett v. Board of Ed : 1441 (c) remand clause allows remand of entire case or
the dc could the federal question & remand state claim
: Protects Δ's from π's tacking on non-removal state claims to
federal claim to avoid federal court.

Joinder FRCP 18/ Keara v. Philly: May join as many claims so long as same transaction
or occurance
: FRCP does not confer SMJ or PJ: still must evaluate
and court may sever.

4. Supplemental Jurisdiction: 28 USC § 1367
: Every claim has to have a ticket to get into federal court &
Supplemental Jurisdiction = the companion ticket

Pendent Jurisdiction: π tool: ct extended jurisdiction from freestanding claim to
otherwise insufficient claim —convience—

Ancillary Jurisdiction: Δ tool: ct extend jurisdiction from freestanding claim to
otherwise insufficient claim

1367 : codified pendent + ancillary into supplemental jurisdiction

United Mine Workers v. Gibbs: (Pendent jurisdiction case that congress codified (1367) afterwards)
: Federal courts have the power to decide a non-federal
claim whenever it is so related to the federal claim
that it is 1 constitutional case.
: transaction test
: when federal claim no longer stands it is courts descretion
to finish hearing the state claim; jury confusion; state law dominate @

1367 (a): Qualifying: same
1367 (b): Dis-Qualifying: cuts off π's trying to evade 1332 reqs.
1367 (c): Descretion: factors / compelling reason

Executive Software v. US DC: (modifies Gibbs): default is to take the state claim
unless 1367(c) factors (state claim dominates, jury confussion,
before trial fed claims dismissed, exceptional circumstances)

1. const. power to hear the claim? SMJ/PJ + same nexus of common fact.
Run through 1367 a, b, c

PREFACE AND ACKNOWLEDGMENTS

This book was prepared as a resource to supplement any civil procedure course. In addition to the usual fare of Federal Rules, Committee Notes, the U.S. Constitution, and U.S. Code provisions, this supplement includes examples of state long-arm and venue statutes, as well as excerpts from the Restatement (Second) of Judgments and the American Law Institute/UNIDROIT Rules of Transnational Civil Procedure. Inclusion of these materials reflects not only our teaching preferences but also our thoughts about the contours of this rewarding field of study. Space constraints present difficult editorial choices, and we have focused here on the core procedure courses. We welcome any editorial suggestions that you may have for future editions of this supplement.

In this supplement we have integrated into the text of the Federal Rules useful cross-references to relevant external materials—Forms, Advisory Committee Notes, Restatement sections, and Transnational Rules. These cross-references appear in bold with the designation: "For further study, see." We intend this cross-referencing method to help students explore the larger context of each Federal Rule without having to significantly interrupt the presentation of the Federal Rules themselves.

We also recommend that students frequent the federal judiciary's web site at *www.uscourts.gov*. The rulemaking link on that site provides access to national and local rules currently in effect in the federal courts, contextual information about the rulemaking process, and the status of all pending and proposed procedural rules and legislation.

The authors are grateful to Jack Schroeder and the librarians at the University of the Pacific McGeorge School of Law for their assistance in producing this book.

S.N.S.
M.L.M.
M.S.B.
T.O.M.

Choice of Federal or State Law: Erie Doctrine

Erie RR v. Tompkins: (RR hits person → trespasser?) (overrules Swift v Tyson)
- There is no federal general law
- Except in matters relation to Constitution (Supremecy Clause)
- the law to be applied is the law of the state.
- purpose: stop forum shopping, uniformity, fairness

Guaranty Trust v. York: (SOL → Fed or state) (How to Apply Erie)
- State Law
- outcome determinitive test: Apply state law when conflicting fed law would sign. effect outcome of litigation
- problem: no limit FRCP have no weight

Byrd v. Blue Ridge: (judge or jury decision)
- SC relaxes the outcome determinitive test → a factor now
- Now balance federal & state concern
1) State's interest: goes to the heart of the rights & obligations of state citizens then state law must be applied
2) Big Federal Deal: Federal policy may outweigh outcome determination
3) Strong likelihood of a different result through outcome determination —only—
   Should State procedure outweigh federal

Hanna v. Plumber: (service of process) (Rules Enabling Act Approach)
- FRCP is a BFD
- when FRCP directly clashes w/ state rule FRCP wins - Supremecy clause
- twin Aims → Forum shoping + unequitable justice

Walker v. Armco Steel: (Fed Statute in conflict w/ state statute)
- If no direct conflict fed statute + state statute may both apply
- FRCP interpreted narrowly to avoid infringment on state rights
- SOL: Sub. State Law b/c sub. due process right

Stewart Organization v. Ricoh (fed statute in conflict w/ state statute)
- FRCP read for plain meaning
- Federal Statutes have wider interpetation
- Federal courts are bound to follow rules enacted by congress if act of congress = Federal procedural issue then federal courts will adhere to that act - Supremecy clause - even if outcome determinitive

Sources of Federal Rule in Conflict w/ State Law:
- Constitution → fed governs
- Acts of Congress - if federal rule is procedural /BFD → fed governs
- FRCP → governs unless violates §2072 or Const.

Gasperini v. Center for Humanities (both sub. + pro. law)
- State causes of action NO BFD; but who determines is a BFD
- back to Byrd

Presomption: State law governs. BFD → Byrd balancing rebut this presomption
- How fed courts are run = a BFD
- Method of Service = a BFD FRCP 4(d)(1)
- Federal Rules = a BFD → supremecy clause
- Constitutional Statute = a BFD / Federal Statue = a BFD
- Fed + State clash (direct collision) on procedural law = BFD
- SOL = no BFD

FEDERAL RULES OF CIVIL PROCEDURE
FOR THE UNITED STATES DISTRICT COURTS

I. Scope of Rules; Form of Action

RULE 1. SCOPE AND PURPOSE

These rules govern the procedure in all civil actions and proceedings in the United States district courts, except as stated in Rule 81. They should be construed and administered to secure the just, speedy, and inexpensive determination of every action and proceeding.

> **For further study, see:** 1938 Advisory Committee Notes at 111; 1993 Advisory Committee Notes at 159; and Transnational Rule 3 at 279.

RULE 2. ONE FORM OF ACTION

There is one form of action—the civil action.

> **For further study, see:** Transnational Rule 11 at 279.

II. Commencing an Action; Service of Process, Pleadings, Motions, and Orders

RULE 3. COMMENCING AN ACTION

A civil action is commenced by filing a complaint with the court.

> **For further study, see:** Transnational Rule 11 at 279.

RULE 4. SUMMONS

(a) CONTENTS; AMENDMENTS

   (1) Contents. A summons must:

      (A) name the court and the parties;

      (B) be directed to the defendant;

      (C) state the name and address of the plaintiff's attorney or—if unrepresented—of the plaintiff;

      (D) state the time within which the defendant must appear and defend;

      (E) notify the defendant that a failure to appear and defend will result in a default judgment against the defendant for the relief demanded in the complaint;

      (F) be signed by the clerk; and

      (G) bear the court's seal.

   (2) Amendments. The court may permit a summons to be amended.

(b) ISSUANCE

On or after filing the complaint, the plaintiff may present a summons to the clerk for signature and seal. If the summons is properly completed, the clerk must sign, seal, and issue it to the plaintiff for service on the defendant. A summons—or a copy of a summons that is addressed to multiple defendants—must be issued for each defendant to be served.

(c) SERVICE

(1)   In General. A summons must be served with a copy of the complaint. The plaintiff is responsible for having the summons and complaint served within the time allowed by Rule 4(m) and must furnish the necessary copies to the person who makes service.

(2)   By Whom. Any person who is at least 18 years old and not a party may serve a summons and complaint.

(3)   By a Marshall or Someone Specially Appointed. At the plaintiff's request, the court may order that service be made by a United States marshal or deputy marshal or by a person specially appointed by the court. The court must so order if the plaintiff is authorized to proceed in forma pauperis under 28 U.S.C. § 1915 or as a seaman under 28 U.S.C. § 1916.

(d) WAIVING SERVICE

(1)   Requesting a Waiver. An individual, corporation, or association that is subject to service under Rule 4(e), (f), or (h) has a duty to avoid unnecessary expenses of serving the summons. The plaintiff may notify such a defendant that an action has been commenced and request that the defendant waive service of a summons. The notice and request must:

(A) be in writing and be addressed:

    (i)   to the individual defendant; or

    (ii)   for a defendant subject to service under Rule 4(h), to an officer, a managing or general agent, or any other agent authorized by appointment or by law to receive service of process;

(B) name the court where the complaint was filed;

(C) be accompanied by a copy of the complaint, two copies of a waiver form, and a prepaid means for returning the form;

(D) inform the defendant, using text prescribed in Form 5, of the consequences of waiving and not waiving service;

(E) state the date when the request is sent;

(F) give the defendant a reasonable time of at least 30 days after the request was sent — or at least 60 days if sent to the defendant outside any judicial district of the United States — to return the waiver; and

(G) be sent by first-class mail or other reliable means.

(2)   Failure to Waive. If a defendant located within the United States fails, without good cause, to sign and return a waiver requested by a plaintiff located within the United States, the court must impose on the defendant:

(A) the expenses later incurred in making service; and

(B) the reasonable expenses, including attorney's fees, of any motion required to collect those service expenses.

(3)   Time to Answer After a Waiver. A defendant who, before being served with process, timely returns a waiver need not serve an answer to the complaint until 60 days after the request was sent — or until 90 days after it was sent to the defendant outside any judicial district of the United States.

(4)   Results of Filing a Waiver. When the plaintiff files a waiver, proof of service is not required and these rules apply as if a summons and complaint had been served at the time of filing the waiver.

(5) *Jurisdiction and Venue Not Waived.* Waiving service of a summons does not waive any objection to personal jurisdiction or to venue.

(e) SERVING AN INDIVIDUAL WITHIN A JUDICIAL DISTRICT OF THE UNITED STATES

Unless federal law provides otherwise, an individual—other than a minor, an incompetent person, or a person whose waiver has been filed—may be sued in a judicial district of the United States by:

(1) following state law for serving a summons in an action brought in courts of general jurisdiction in the state where the district court is located or where service is made; or

(2) doing any of the following:

> (A) delivering a copy of the summons and of the complaint to the individual personally;
>
> (B) leaving a copy of each at the individual's dwelling or usual place of abode with someone of suitable age and discretion who resides there; or
>
> (C) delivering a copy of each to an agent authorized by appointment or by law to receive service of process.

(f) SERVING AN INDIVIDUAL IN A FOREIGN COUNTRY

Unless federal law provides otherwise, an individual—other than a minor, an incompetent person, or a person whose waiver has been filed—may be served at a place not within any judicial district of the United States:

(1) by any internationally agreed means of service that is reasonably calculated to give notice, such as those authorized by the Hague Convention on the Service Abroad of Judicial and Extrajudicial Documents;

(2) if there is no internationally agreed means, or if an international agreement allows but does not specify other means, by a method that is reasonably calculated to give notice:

> (A) as prescribed by the foreign country's law for service in that country in an action in its courts of general jurisdiction;
>
> (B) as the foreign authority directs in response to a letter rogatory or letter of request; or
>
> (C) unless prohibited by the foreign country's law, by:
>
> > (i)   delivering a copy of the summons and of the complaint to the individual personally; or
> >
> > (ii) using any form of mail that the clerk addresses and sends to the individual and that requires a signed receipt; or

(3) by other means not prohibited by international agreement, as the court orders.

(g) SERVING A MINOR OR AN INCOMPETENT PERSON

A minor or an incompetent person in a judicial district of the United States must be served by following state law for serving a summons or like process on such a defendant in an action brought in the courts of general jurisdiction of the state where service is made. A minor or an incompetent person who is not within any judicial district of the United States must be served in the manner prescribed by Rule 4(f)(2)(A), (f)(2)(B), or (f)(3).

(h) SERVING A CORPORATION, PARTNERSHIP, OR ASSOCIATION

Unless federal law provides otherwise or the defendant's waiver has been filed, a domestic or foreign corporation, or a partnership or other unincorporated association that is subject to suit under a common name, must be served:

    (1)   in a judicial district of the United States:

        (A) in the manner prescribed by Rule 4(e)(1) for serving an individual; or

        (B) by delivering a copy of the summons and of the complaint to an officer, a managing or general agent, or any other agent authorized by appointment or by law to receive service of process and — if the agent is one authorized by statute and the statute so requires — by also mailing a copy of each to the defendant; or

    (2)   at a place not within any judicial district of the United States, in any manner prescribed by Rule 4(f) for serving an individual, except personal delivery under (f)(2)(C)(i).

(i) SERVING THE UNITED STATES AND ITS AGENCIES, CORPORATIONS, OFFICERS, OR EMPLOYEES

    (1)   United States. To serve the United States, a party must:

        (A)

            (i)   deliver a copy of the summons and of the complaint to the United States attorney for the district where the action is brought — or to an assistant United States attorney or clerical employee whom the United States attorney designates in a writing filed with the court clerk — or

            (ii) send a copy of each by registered or certified mail to the civil-process clerk at the United States attorney's office;

        (B) send a copy of each by registered or certified mail to the Attorney General of the United States at Washington, D.C.; and

        (C) if the action challenges an order of a nonparty agency or officer of the United States, send a copy of each by registered or certified mail to the agency or officer.

    (2)   Agency; Corporation; Officer or Employee Sued in an Official Capacity. To serve a United States agency or corporation, or a United States officer or employee sued only in an official capacity, a party must serve the United States and also send a copy of the summons and of the complaint by registered or certified mail to the agency, corporation, officer, or employee.

    (3)   Officer or Employee Sued Individually. To serve a United States officer or employee sued in an individual capacity for an act or omission occurring in connection with duties performed on the United States' behalf (whether or not the officer or employee is also sued in an official capacity), a party must serve the United States and also serve the officer or employee under Rule 4(e), (f), or (g).

    (4)   Extending Time. The court must allow a party a reasonable time to cure its failure to:

        (A) serve a person required to be served under Rule 4(i)(2), if the party has served either the United States attorney or the Attorney General of the United States; or

        (B) serve the United States under Rule 4(i)(3), if the party has served the United States officer or employee.

(j) SERVING A FOREIGN, STATE, OR LOCAL GOVERNMENT

    (1)   Foreign State. A foreign state or its political subdivision, agency, or instrumentality must be served in accordance with 28 U.S.C. § 1608.

(2)   State or Local Government. A state, a municipal corporation, or any other state-created governmental organization that is subject to suit must be served by:

> (A) delivering a copy of the summons and of the complaint to its chief executive officer; or
>
> (B) serving a copy of each in the manner prescribed by that state's law for serving a summons or like process on such a defendant.

(k) TERRITORIAL LIMITS OF EFFECTIVE SERVICE

(1)   In General. Serving a summons or filing a waiver of service establishes personal jurisdiction over a defendant:

> (A) who is subject to the jurisdiction of a court of general jurisdiction in the state where the district court is located; *PJ For federal courts*
>
> (B) who is a party joined under Rule 14 or 19 and is served within a judicial district of the United States and not more than 100 miles from where the summons was issued; or
>
> (C) when authorized by a federal statute.

(2)   Federal Claim Outside State-Court Jurisdiction. For a claim that arises under federal law, serving a summons or filing a waiver of service establishes personal jurisdiction over a defendant if:

> (A) the defendant is not subject to jurisdiction in any state's courts of general jurisdiction; and
>
> (B) exercising jurisdiction is consistent with the United States Constitution and laws.

(l) PROVING SERVICE

(1)   Affidavit Required. Unless service is waived, proof of service must be made to the court. Except for service by a United States marshal or deputy marshal, proof must be made by the server's affidavit.

(2)   Service Outside the United States. Service not within any judicial district of the United States must be proved as follows:

> (A) if made under Rule 4(f)(1), as provided in the applicable treaty or convention; or
>
> (B) if made under Rule 4(f)(2) or (f)(3), by a receipt signed by the addressee, or by other evidence satisfying the court that the summons and complaint were delivered to the addressee.

(3)   Validity of Service; Amending Proof. Failure to prove service does not affect the validity of service. The court may permit proof of service to be amended.

(m) TIME LIMIT FOR SERVICE

If a defendant is not served within 120 days after the complaint is filed, the court—on motion or on its own after notice to the plaintiff—must dismiss the action without prejudice against that defendant or order that service be made within a specified time. But if the plaintiff shows good cause for the failure, the court must extend the time for service for an appropriate period. This subdivision (m) does not apply to service in a foreign country under Rule 4(f) or 4(j)(1).

(n) ASSERTING JURISDICTION OVER PROPERTY OR ASSETS

(1)   Federal Law. The court may assert jurisdiction over property if authorized by a federal statute. Notice to claimants of the property must be given as provided in the statute or by serving a summons under this rule.

(2)   State Law. On a showing that personal jurisdiction over a defendant cannot be obtained in the district where the action is brought by reasonable efforts to serve a summons under this rule, the court may assert jurisdiction over the defendant's assets found in the district. Jurisdiction is acquired by seizing the assets under the circumstances and in the manner provided by state law in that district.

> **For further study, see**: Fed. R. Civ. P. Forms 2-6 at 95; 1993 Advisory Committee Notes at 159; and Transnational Rule 7 at 281.

RULE 4.1. SERVING OTHER PROCESS

(a) IN GENERAL

Process — other than a summons under Rule 4 or a subpoena under Rule 45 — must be served by a United States marshal or deputy marshal or by a person specially appointed for that purpose. It may be served anywhere within the territorial limits of the state where the district court is located and, if authorized by a federal statute, beyond those limits. Proof of service must be made under Rule 4(l).

(b) ENFORCING ORDERS: COMMITTING FOR CIVIL CONTEMPT

An order committing a person for civil contempt of a decree or injunction issued to enforce federal law may be served and enforced in any district. Any other order in a civil-contempt proceeding may be served only in the state where the issuing court is located or elsewhere in the United States within 100 miles from where the order was issued.

> **For further study, see**: 1993 Advisory Committee Notes at 165.

RULE 5. SERVING AND FILING PLEADINGS AND OTHER PAPERS

(a) SERVICE: WHEN REQUIRED

(1)   In General. Unless these rules provide otherwise, each of the following papers must be served on every party:

  (A) an order stating that service is required;

  (B) a pleading filed after the original complaint, unless the court orders otherwise under Rule 5(c) because there are numerous defendants;

  (C) a discovery paper required to be served on a party, unless the court orders otherwise;

  (D) a written motion, except one that may be heard ex parte; and

  (E) a written notice, appearance, demand, or offer of judgment, or any similar paper.

(2)   If a Party Fails to Appear. No service is required on a party who is in default for failing to appear. But a pleading that asserts a new claim for relief against such a party must be served on that party under Rule 4.

(3)   Seizing Property. If an action is begun by seizing property and no person is or need be named as a defendant, any service required before the filing of an appearance, answer, or claim must be made on the person who has custody or possession of the property when it was seized.

(b) SERVICE: HOW MADE

(1)   Serving an Attorney. If a party is represented by an attorney, service under this rule must be made on the attorney unless the court orders service on the party.

(2)   Service in General. A paper is served under this rule by:

(A) handing it to the person;

(B) leaving it:

    (i)   at the person's office with a clerk or other person in charge or, if no one is in charge, in a conspicuous place in the office; or

    (ii) if the person has no office or the office is closed, at the person's dwelling or usual place of abode with someone of suitable age and discretion who resides there;

(C) mailing it to the person's last known address—in which event service is complete upon mailing;

(D) leaving it with the court clerk if the person has no known address;

(E) sending it by electronic means if the person consented in writing—in which event service is complete upon transmission, but is not effective if the serving party learns that it did not reach the person to be served; or

(F) delivering it by any other means that the person consented to in writing—in which event service is complete when the person making service delivers it to the agency designated to make delivery.

(3)   Using Court Facilities. If a local rule so authorizes, a party may use the court's transmission facilities to make service under Rule 5(b)(2)(E).

(c) SERVING NUMEROUS DEFENDANTS

(1)   In General. If an action involves an unusually large number of defendants, the court may, on motion or on its own, order that:

(A) defendants' pleadings and replies to them need not be served on other defendants;

(B) any crossclaim, counterclaim, avoidance, or affirmative defense in those pleadings and replies to them will be treated as denied or avoided by all other parties; and

(C) filing any such pleading and serving it on the plaintiff constitutes notice of the pleading to all parties.

(2)   Notifying Parties. A copy of every such order must be served on the parties as the court directs.

(d) FILING

(1)   Required Filings; Certificate of Service. Any paper after the complaint that is required to be served—together with a certificate of service—must be filed within a reasonable time after service. But disclosures under Rule 26(a)(1) or (2) and the following discovery requests and responses must not be filed until they are used in the proceeding or the court orders filing: depositions, interrogatories, requests for documents or tangible things or to permit entry onto land, and requests for admission.

(2)   How Filing Is Made—In General. A paper is filed by delivering it:

(A) to the clerk; or

(B) to a judge who agrees to accept it for filing, and who must then note the filing date on the paper and promptly send it to the clerk.

(3)   Electronic Filing, Signing, or Verification. A court may, by local rule, allow papers to be filed, signed, or verified by electronic means that are consistent with any technical standards established by the Judicial Conference of the United States. A local rule may require electronic

filing only if reasonable exceptions are allowed. A paper filed electronically in compliance with a local rule is a written paper for purposes of these rules.

(4) *Acceptance by the Clerk.* The clerk must not refuse to file a paper solely because it is not in the form prescribed by these rules or by a local rule or practice.

> **For further study, see:** 1970 Advisory Committee Notes at 125; 1980 Advisory Committee Notes at 143; 2000 Advisory Committee Notes at 186; and Transnational Rule 7 at 281.

RULE 5.1. CONSTITUTIONAL CHALLENGE TO A STATUTE—NOTICE, CERTIFICATION, AND INTERVENTION

(a) NOTICE BY A PARTY

A party that files a pleading, written motion, or other paper drawing into question the constitutionality of a federal or state statute must promptly:

(1) file a notice of constitutional question stating the question and identifying the paper that raises it, if:

    (A) a federal statute is questioned and the parties do not include the United States, one of its agencies, or one of its officers or employees in an official capacity; or

    (B) a state statute is questioned and the parties do not include the state, one of its agencies, or one of its officers or employees in an official capacity; and

(2) serve the notice and paper on the Attorney General of the United States if a federal statute is questioned—or on the state attorney general if a state statute is questioned—either by certified or registered mail or by sending it to an electronic address designated by the attorney general for this purpose.

(b) CERTIFICATION BY THE COURT

The court must, under 28 U.S.C. § 2403, certify to the appropriate attorney general that a statute has been questioned.

(c) INTERVENTION; FINAL DECISION ON THE MERITS

Unless the court sets a later time, the attorney general may intervene within 60 days after the notice is filed or after the court certifies the challenge, whichever is earlier. Before the time to intervene expires, the court may reject the constitutional challenge, but may not enter a final judgment holding the statute unconstitutional.

(d) NO FORFEITURE

A party's failure to file and serve the notice, or the court's failure to certify, does not forfeit a constitutional claim or defense that is otherwise timely asserted.

RULE 5.2. PRIVACY PROTECTION FOR FILINGS MADE WITH THE COURT

(a) REDACTED FILINGS

Unless the court orders otherwise, in an electronic or paper filing with the court that contains an individual's social-security number, taxpayer-identification number, or birth date, the name of an individual known to be a minor, or a financial-account number, a party or nonparty making the filing may include only:

(1) the last four digits of the social-security number and taxpayer-identification number;

(2) the year of the individual's birth;

    (3)   the minor's initials; and

    (4)   the last four digits of the financial-account number.

(b) EXEMPTIONS FROM THE REDACTION REQUIREMENT

The redaction requirement does not apply to the following:

    (1)   a financial-account number that identifies the property allegedly subject to forfeiture in a forfeiture proceeding;

    (2)   the record of an administrative or agency proceeding;

    (3)   the official record of a state-court proceeding;

    (4)   the record of a court or tribunal, if that record was not subject to the redaction requirement when originally filed;

    (5)   a filing covered by Rule 5.2(c) or (d); and

    (6)   a pro se filing in an action brought under 28 U.S.C. §§ 2241, 2254, or 2255.

(c) LIMITATIONS ON REMOTE ACCESS TO ELECTRONIC FILES; SOCIAL-SECURITY APPEALS AND IMMIGRATION CASES

Unless the court orders otherwise, in an action for benefits under the Social Security Act, and in an action or proceeding relating to an order of removal, to relief from removal, or to immigration benefits or detention, access to an electronic file is authorized as follows:

    (1)   the parties and their attorneys may have remote electronic access to any part of the case file, including the administrative record;

    (2)   any other person may have electronic access to the full record at the courthouse, but may have remote electronic access only to:

        (A) the docket maintained by the court; and

        (B) an opinion, order, judgment, or other disposition of the court, but not any part of the case file or the administrative record.

(d) FILINGS MADE UNDER SEAL

The court may order that a filing be made under seal without redaction. The court may later unseal the filing or order the person who made the filing to file a redacted version for the public record.

(e) PROTECTIVE ORDERS

For good cause, the court may by order in a case:

    (1)   require redaction of additional information; or

    (2)   limit or prohibit a nonparty's remote electronic access to a document filed with the court.

(f) OPTION FOR ADDITIONAL UNREDACTED FILING UNDER SEAL

A person making a redacted filing may also file an unredacted copy under seal. The court must retain the unredacted copy as part of the record.

(g) OPTION FOR FILING A REFERENCE LIST

A filing that contains redacted information may be filed together with a reference list that identifies each item of redacted information and specifies an appropriate identifier that uniquely corresponds to each item listed. The list must be filed under seal and may be amended as of right. Any reference in the case to a listed identifier will be construed to refer to the corresponding item of information.

(h) WAIVER OF PROTECTION OF IDENTIFIERS

A person waives the protection of Rule 5.2(a) as to the person's own information by filing it without redaction and not under seal.

RULE 6. COMPUTING AND EXTENDING TIME; TIME FOR MOTION PAPERS

(a) COMPUTING TIME

The following rules apply in computing any time period specified in these rules or in any local rule, court order, or statute:

 (1)　Day of the Event Excluded. Exclude the day of the act, event, or default that begins the period.

 (2)　Exclusions from Brief Periods. Exclude intermediate Saturdays, Sundays, and legal holidays when the period is less than 11 days.

 (3)　Last Day. Include the last day of the period unless it is a Saturday, Sunday, legal holiday, or—if the act to be done is filing a paper in court—a day on which weather or other conditions make the clerk's office inaccessible. When the last day is excluded, the period runs until the end of the next day that is not a Saturday, Sunday, legal holiday, or day when the clerk's office is inaccessible.

 (4)　"Legal Holiday" Defined. As used in these rules, "legal holiday" means:

  (A) the day set aside by statute for observing New Year's Day, Martin Luther King Jr.'s Birthday, Washington's Birthday, Memorial Day, Independence Day, Labor Day, Columbus Day, Veterans' Day, Thanksgiving Day, or Christmas Day; and

  (B) any other day declared a holiday by the President, Congress, or the state where the district court is located.

(b) EXTENDING TIME

 (1)　In General. When an act may or must be done within a specified time, the court may, for good cause, extend the time:

  (A) with or without motion or notice if the court acts, or if a request is made, before the original time or its extension expires; or

  (B) on motion made after the time has expired if the party failed to act because of excusable neglect.

 (2)　Exceptions. A court must not extend the time to act under Rules 50(b) and (d), 52(b), 59(b), (d), and (e), and 60(b), except as those rules allow.

(c) MOTIONS, NOTICES OF HEARING, AND AFFIDAVITS

 (1)　In General. A written motion and notice of the hearing must be served at least 5 days before the time specified for the hearing, with the following exceptions:

  (A) when the motion may be heard ex parte;

  (B) when these rules set a different time; or

  (C) when a court order—which a party may, for good cause, apply for ex parte—sets a different time.

(2) Supporting Affidavit. Any affidavit supporting a motion must be served with the motion. Except as Rule 59(c) provides otherwise, any opposing affidavit must be served at least 1 day before the hearing, unless the court permits service at another time.

(d) ADDITIONAL TIME AFTER CERTAIN KINDS OF SERVICE

When a party may or must act within a specified time after service and service is made under Rule 5(b)(2)(C), (D), (E) or (F), 3 days are added to the period.

For further study, see: 2001 Advisory Committee Notes at 190; and Transnational Rules 11 & 13 at 281.

III. Pleadings and Motions

RULE 7. PLEADINGS ALLOWED; FORM OF MOTIONS AND OTHER PAPERS

(a) PLEADINGS

Only these pleadings are allowed:

(1) a complaint;

(2) an answer to a complaint;

(3) an answer to a counterclaim designated as a counterclaim;

(4) an answer to a crossclaim;

(5) a third-party complaint;

(6) an answer to a third-party complaint; and

(7) if the court orders one, a reply to an answer.

(b) MOTIONS AND OTHER PAPERS

(1) In General. A request for a court order must be made by motion. The motion must:

(A) be in writing unless made during a hearing or trial;

(B) state with particularity the grounds for seeking the order; and

(C) state the relief sought.

(2) Form. The rules governing captions and other matters of form in pleadings apply to motions and other papers.

For further study, see: Transnational Rule 11 at 369.

RULE 7.1. DISCLOSURE STATEMENT

(a) WHO MUST FILE; CONTENTS

A nongovernmental corporate party must file two copies of a disclosure statement that:

(1) identifies any parent corporation and any publicly held corporation owning 10% or more of its stock; or

(2) states that there is no such corporation.

(b) TIME TO FILE; SUPPLEMENTAL FILING

A party must:

(1) file the disclosure statement with its first appearance, pleading, petition, motion, response, or other request addressed to the court; and

(2) promptly file a supplemental statement if any required information changes.

RULE 8. GENERAL RULES OF PLEADING

(a) CLAIM FOR RELIEF

A pleading that states a claim for relief must contain:

(1)   a short and plain statement of the grounds for the court's jurisdiction, unless the court already has jurisdiction and the claim needs no new jurisdictional support;

(2)   a short and plain statement of the claim showing that the pleader is entitled to relief; and

(3)   a demand for the relief sought, which may include relief in the alternative or different types of relief.

(b) DEFENSES; ADMISSIONS AND DENIALS

(1)   In General. In responding to a pleading, a party must:

(A) state in short and plain terms its defenses to each claim asserted against it; and

(B) admit or deny the allegations asserted against it by an opposing party.

(2)   Denials—Responding to the Substance. A denial must fairly respond to the substance of the allegation.

(3)   General and Specific Denials. A party that intends in good faith to deny all the allegations of a pleading—including the jurisdictional grounds—may do so by a general denial. A party that does not intend to deny all the allegations must either specifically deny designated allegations or generally deny all except those specifically admitted.

(4)   Denying Part of an Allegation. A party that intends in good faith to deny only part of an allegation must admit the part that is true and deny the rest.

(5)   Lacking Knowledge or Information. A party that lacks knowledge or information sufficient to form a belief about the truth of an allegation must so state, and the statement has the effect of a denial.

(6)   Effect of Failing to Deny. An allegation—other than one relating to the amount of damages—is admitted if a responsive pleading is required and the allegation is not denied. If a responsive pleading is not required, an allegation is considered denied or avoided.

(c) AFFIRMATIVE DEFENSES

(1)   In General. In responding to a pleading, a party must affirmatively state any avoidance or affirmative defense, including:

- accord and satisfaction;
- arbitration and award;
- assumption of risk;
- contributory negligence;
- discharge in bankruptcy;
- duress;
- estoppel;
- failure of consideration;
- fraud;
- illegality;
- injury by fellow servant;
- laches;

- license;
- payment;
- release;
- res judicata;
- statute of frauds;
- statute of limitations; and
- waiver

(2)   Mistaken Designation. If a party mistakenly designates a defense as a counterclaim, or a counterclaim as a defense, the court must, if justice requires, treat the pleading as though it were correctly designated, and may impose terms for doing so.

(d) PLEADING TO BE CONCISE AND DIRECT; ALTERNATIVE STATEMENTS; INCONSISTENCY

(1)   In General. Each allegation must be simple, concise, and direct. No technical form is required.

(2)   Alternative Statements of a Claim or Defense. A party may set out two or more statements of a claim or defense alternatively or hypothetically, either in a single count or defense or in separate ones. If a party makes alternative statements, the pleading is sufficient if any one of them is sufficient.

(3)   Inconsistent Claims or Defenses. A party may state as many separate claims or defenses as it has, regardless of consistency.

(e) CONSTRUING PLEADINGS

Pleadings must be construed so as to do justice.

> **For further study, see:** Fed. R. Civ. P. Forms 7-31 at 98; 2007 Advisory Committee Notes at 209; and Transnational Rules 11-13 at 281.

RULE 9. PLEADING SPECIAL MATTERS

(a) CAPACITY OR AUTHORITY TO SUE; LEGAL EXISTENCE

(1)   In General. Except when required to show that the court has jurisdiction, a pleading need not allege:

(A) a party's capacity to sue or be sued;

(B) a party's authority to sue or be sued in a representative capacity;

(C) the legal existence of an organized association of persons that is made a party.

(2)   Raising Those Issues. To raise any of those issues, a party must do so by a specific denial, which must state any supporting facts that are peculiarly within the party's knowledge.

(b) FRAUD OR MISTAKE; CONDITION OF MIND

In alleging fraud or mistake, a party must state with particularity the circumstances constituting fraud or mistake. Malice, intent, knowledge, and other conditions of a person's mind may be alleged generally.

(c) CONDITIONS PRECEDENT

In pleading conditions precedent, it suffices to allege generally that all conditions precedent have occurred or been performed. But when denying that a condition precedent has occurred or been performed, a party must do so with particularity.

(d) OFFICIAL DOCUMENT OR ACT

In pleading an official document or official act, it suffices to allege that the document was legally issued or the act legally done.

(e) JUDGMENT

In pleading a judgment or decision of a domestic or foreign court, a judicial or quasi-judicial tribunal, or a board or officer, it suffices to plead the judgment or decision without showing jurisdiction to render it.

(f) TIME AND PLACE

An allegation of time or place is material when testing the sufficiency of a pleading.

(g) SPECIAL DAMAGES

If an item of special damage is claimed, it must be specifically stated.

(h) ADMIRALTY OR MARITIME CLAIM

(1) How Designated. If a claim for relief is within the admiralty or maritime jurisdiction and also within the court's subject-matter jurisdiction on some other ground, the pleading may designate the claim as an admiralty or maritime claim for purposes of Rules 14(c), 38(e), and 82 and the Supplemental Rules for Admiralty or Maritime Claims and Asset Forfeiture Actions. A claim cognizable only in the admiralty or maritime jurisdiction is an admiralty or maritime claim for those purposes, whether or not so designated.

(2) Designation for Appeal. A case that includes an admiralty or maritime claim within this subdivision (h) is an admiralty case within 28 U.S.C. § 1292(a)(3).

For further study, see: Fed. R. Civ. P. Forms 7-31 at 98; and Transnational Rules 11-13 at 281.

RULE 10. FORM OF PLEADINGS

(a) CAPTION; NAMES OF PARTIES

Every pleading must have a caption with the court's name, a title, a file number, and a Rule 7(a) designation. The title of the complaint must name all the parties; the title of other pleadings, after naming the first party on each side, may refer generally to other parties.

(b) PARAGRAPHS; SEPARATE STATEMENTS

A party must state its claims or defenses in numbered paragraphs, each limited as far as practicable to a single set of circumstances. A later pleading may refer by number to a paragraph in an earlier pleading. If doing so would promote clarity, each claim founded on a separate transaction or occurrence — and each defense other than a denial — must be stated in a separate count or defense.

(c) ADOPTION BY REFERENCE; EXHIBITS

A statement in a pleading may be adopted by reference elsewhere in the same pleading or in any other pleading or motion. A copy of a written instrument that is an exhibit to a pleading is a part of the pleading for all purposes.

For further study, see: Fed. R. Civ. P. Form 1-31 at 95.

RULE 11. SIGNING PLEADINGS, MOTIONS, AND OTHER PAPERS; REPRESENTATIONS TO THE COURT; SANCTIONS

(a) SIGNATURE

Every pleading, written motion, and other paper must be signed by at least one attorney of record in the attorney's name—or by a party personally if the party is unrepresented. The paper must state the signer's address, e-mail address, and telephone number. Unless a rule or statute specifically states otherwise, a pleading need not be verified or accompanied by an affidavit. The court must strike an unsigned paper unless the omission is promptly corrected after being called to the attorney's or party's attention.

(b) REPRESENTATIONS TO THE COURT

By presenting to the court a pleading, written motion, or other paper—whether by signing, filing, submitting, or later advocating it—an attorney or unrepresented party certifies that to the best of the person's knowledge, information, and belief, formed after an inquiry reasonable under the circumstances:

(1)   it is not being presented for any improper purpose, such as to harass, cause unnecessary delay, or needlessly increase the cost of litigation;

(2)   the claims, defenses, and other legal contentions are warranted by existing law or by a nonfrivolous argument for extending, modifying, or reversing existing law or for establishing new law;

(3)   the factual contentions have evidentiary support or, if specifically so identified, will likely have evidentiary support after a reasonable opportunity for further investigation or discovery; and

(4)   the denials of factual contentions are warranted on the evidence or, if specifically so identified, are reasonably based on belief or a lack of information.

(c) SANCTIONS

(1)   In General. If, after notice and a reasonable opportunity to respond, the court determines that Rule 11(b) has been violated, the court may impose an appropriate sanction on any attorney, law firm, or party that violated the rule or is responsible for the violation. Absent exceptional circumstances, a law firm must be held jointly responsible for a violation committed by its partner, associate, or employee.

(2)   Motion for Sanctions. A motion for sanctions must be made separately from any other motion and must describe the specific conduct that allegedly violates Rule 11(b). The motion must be served under Rule 5, but it must not be filed or be presented to the court if the challenged paper, claim, defense, contention, or denial is withdrawn or appropriately corrected within 21 days after service or within another time the court sets. If warranted, the court may award to the prevailing party the reasonable expenses, including attorney's fees, incurred for the motion.

(3)   On the Court's Initiative. On its own, the court may order an attorney, law firm, or party to show cause why conduct specifically described in the order has not violated Rule 11(b).

(4)   Nature of a Sanction. A sanction imposed under this rule must be limited to what suffices to deter repetition of the conduct or comparable conduct by others similarly situated.

The sanction may include nonmonetary directives; an order to pay a penalty into court; or, if imposed on motion and warranted for effective deterrence, an order directing payment to the movant of part or all of the reasonable attorney's fees and other expenses directly resulting from the violation.

(5) Limitations on Monetary Sanctions. The court must not impose a monetary sanction:

(A) against a represented party for violating Rule 11(b)(2); or

(B) on its own, unless it issued the show-cause order under Rule 11(c)(3) before voluntary dismissal or settlement of the claims made by or against the party that is, or whose attorneys are, to be sanctioned.

(6) Requirements for an Order. An order imposing a sanction must describe the sanctioned conduct and explain the basis for the sanction.

(d) INAPPLICABILITY TO DISCOVERY

This rule does not apply to disclosures and discovery requests, responses, objections, and motions under Rules 26 through 37.

> **For further study, see**: 1983 Advisory Committee Notes at 144; 1993 Advisory Committee Notes at 165; 2007 Advisory Committee Notes at 210; and Transnational Rules 12, 16, 20 & 35 at 282.

RULE 12. DEFENSES AND OBJECTIONS: WHEN AND HOW PRESENTED; MOTION FOR JUDGMENT ON THE PLEADINGS; CONSOLIDATING MOTIONS; WAIVING DEFENSES; PRETRIAL HEARING

(a) TIME TO SERVE A RESPONSIVE PLEADING

(1) In General. Unless another time is specified by this rule or a federal statute, the time for serving a responsive pleading is as follows:

(A) A defendant must serve an answer:

(i) within 20 days after being served with the summons and complaint; or

(ii) if it has timely waived service under Rule 4(d), within 60 days after the request for a waiver was sent, or within 90 days after it was sent to the defendant outside any judicial district of the United States.

(B) A party must serve an answer to a counterclaim or crossclaim within 20 days after being served with the pleading that states the counterclaim or crossclaim.

(C) A party must serve a reply to an answer within 20 days after being served with an order to reply, unless the order specifies a different time.

(2) United States and Its Agencies, Officers, or Employees Sued in an Official Capacity. The United States, a United States agency, or a United States officer or employee sued only in an official capacity must serve an answer to a complaint, counterclaim, or crossclaim within 60 days after service on the United States attorney.

(3) United States Officers or Employees Sued in an Individual Capacity. A United States officer or employee sued in an individual capacity for an act or omission occurring in connection with duties performed on the United States' behalf must serve an answer to a complaint, counterclaim, or crossclaim within 60 days after service on the officer or employee or service on the United States attorney, whichever is later.

(4) Effect of a Motion. Unless the court sets a different time, serving a motion under this rule alters these periods as follows:

> (A) if the court denies the motion or postpones its disposition until trial, the responsive pleading must be served within 10 days after notice of the court's action; or
>
> (B) if the court grants a motion for a more definite statement, the responsive pleading must be served within 10 days after the more definite statement is served.

(b) HOW TO PRESENT DEFENSES

Every defense to a claim for relief in any pleading must be asserted in the responsive pleading if one is required. But a party may assert the following defenses by motion:

(1) lack of subject-matter jurisdiction; ✕

(2) lack of personal jurisdiction; ✕

(3) improper venue;

(4) insufficient process;

(5) insufficient service of process;

(6) failure to state a claim upon which relief can be granted; and

(7) failure to join a party under Rule 19.

A motion asserting any of these defenses must be made before pleading if a responsive pleading is allowed. If a pleading sets out a claim for relief that does not require a responsive pleading, an opposing party may assert at trial any defense to that claim. No defense or objection is waived by joining it with one or more other defenses or objections in a responsive pleading or in a motion.

(c) MOTION FOR JUDGMENT ON THE PLEADINGS

After the pleadings are closed—but early enough not to delay trial—a party may move for judgment on the pleadings.

(d) RESULT OF PRESENTING MATTERS OUTSIDE THE PLEADINGS

If, on a motion under Rule 12(b)(6) or 12(c), matters outside the pleadings are presented to and not excluded by the court, the motion must be treated as one for summary judgment under Rule 56. All parties must be given a reasonable opportunity to present all the material that is pertinent to the motion.

(e) MOTION FOR A MORE DEFINITE STATEMENT

A party may move for a more definite statement of a pleading to which a responsive pleading is allowed but which is so vague or ambiguous that the part cannot reasonably prepare a response. The motion must be made before filing a responsive pleading and must point out the defects complained of and the details desired. If the court orders a more definite statement and the order is not obeyed within 10 days after notice of the order or within the time the court sets, the court may strike the pleading or issue any other appropriate order.

(f) MOTION TO STRIKE

The court may strike from a pleading an insufficient defense or any redundant, immaterial, impertinent, or scandalous matter. The court may act:

(1) on its own; or

(2) on motion made by a party either before responding to the pleading or, if a response is not allowed, within 20 days after being served with the pleading.

(g) JOINING MOTIONS

(1)   Right to Join. A motion under this rule may be joined with any other motion allowed by this rule.

(2)   Limitation on Further Motions. Except as provided in Rule 12(h)(2) or (3), a party that makes a motion under this rule must not make another motion under this rule raising a defense or objection that was available to the party but omitted from its earlier motion.

(h) WAIVING AND PRESERVING CERTAIN DEFENSES

(1)   When Some Are Waived. A party waives any defense listed in Rule 12(b)(2)-(5) by:

(A) omitting it from a motion in the circumstances described in Rule 12(g)(2); or

(B) failing to either

(i)   make it by motion under this rule; or

(ii) include it in a responsive pleading or in an amendment allowed by Rule 15(a)(1) as a matter of course.

(2)   When to Raise Others. Failure to state a claim upon which relief can be granted, to join a person required by Rule 19(b), or to state a legal defense to a claim may be raised:

(A) in any pleading allowed or ordered under Rule 7(a);

(B) by a motion under Rule 12(c); or

(C) at trial.

(3)   Lack of Subject-Matter Jurisdiction. If the court determines at any time that it lacks subject matter jurisdiction, the court must dismiss the action.

(i) HEARING BEFORE TRIAL

If a party so moves, any defense listed in Rule 12(b)(1)-(7) — whether made in a pleading or by motion — and a motion under Rule 12(c) must be heard and decided before trial unless the court orders a deferral until trial.

> **For further study, see**: Fed. R. Civ. P. Forms 30-40 at 104; 1966 Advisory Committee Notes at 115; 1993 Advisory Committee Notes at 169; and Transnational Rules 13, 14, 15 & 19 at 282.

RULE 13. COUNTERCLAIM AND CROSS-CLAIM

(a) COMPULSORY COUNTERCLAIM

(1)   In General. A pleading must state as a counterclaim any claim that — at the time of its service — the pleader has against an opposing party if the claim:

(A) arises out of the transaction or occurrence that is the subject matter of the opposing party's claim; and

(B) does not require adding another party over whom the court cannot acquire jurisdiction.

(2)   Exceptions. The pleader need not state the claim if:

(A) when the action was commenced, the claim was the subject of another pending action; or

(B) the opposing party sued on its claim by attachment or other process that did not establish personal jurisdiction over the pleader on that claim, and the pleader does not assert any counterclaim under this rule.

(b) PERMISSIVE COUNTERCLAIM

A pleading may state as a counterclaim against an opposing party any claim that is not compulsory.

(c) RELIEF SOUGHT IN A COUNTERCLAIM

A counterclaim need not diminish or defeat the recovery sought by the opposing party. It may request relief that exceeds in amount or differs in kind from the relief sought by the opposing party.

(d) COUNTERCLAIM AGAINST THE UNITED STATES

These rules do not expand the right to assert a counterclaim—or to claim a credit—against the United States or a United States officer or agency.

(e) COUNTERCLAIM MATURING OR ACQUIRED AFTER PLEADING

The court may permit a party to file a supplemental pleading asserting a counterclaim that matured or was acquired by the party after serving an earlier pleading.

(f) OMITTED COUNTERCLAIM

The court may permit a party to amend a pleading to add a counterclaim if it was omitted through oversight, inadvertence, or excusable neglect or if justice so requires.

(g) CROSSCLAIM AGAINST A COPARTY

A pleading may state as a crossclaim any claim by one party against a coparty if the claim arises out of the transaction or occurrence that is the subject matter of the original action or of a counterclaim, or if the claim relates to any property that is the subject matter of the original action. The crossclaim may include a claim that the coparty is or may be liable to the crossclaimant for all or part of a claim asserted in the action against the crossclaimant.

(h) JOINING ADDITIONAL PARTIES

Rules 19 and 20 govern the addition of a person as a party to a counterclaim or crossclaim.

(i) SEPARATE TRIALS; SEPARATE JUDGMENTS

If the court orders separate trials under Rule 42(b), it may enter judgment on a counterclaim or crossclaim under Rule 54(b) when it has jurisdiction to do so, even if the opposing party's claims have been dismissed or otherwise resolved.

For further study, see: Fed. R. Civ. P. Form 30-31 at 104; 1948 Advisory Committee Notes at 112; 1966 Advisory Committee Notes at 116; Restatement (Second) of Judgments § 22 at 231; and Transnational Rules 5 & 13 at 280.

RULE 14. THIRD-PARTY PRACTICE

(a) WHEN A DEFENDING PARTY MAY BRING IN A THIRD PARTY

(1) Timing of the Summons and Complaint. A defending party may, as third-party plaintiff, serve a summons and complaint on a nonparty who is or may be liable to it for all or part of the claim against it. But the third-party plaintiff must, by motion, obtain the court's leave if it files the third-party complaint more than 10 days after serving its original answer.

(2) Third-Party Defendant's Claims and Defenses. The person served with the summons and third-party complaint—the "third-party defendant":

   (A) must assert any defense against the third-party plaintiff's claim under Rule 12;

   (B) must assert any counterclaim against the third-party plaintiff under Rule 13(a), and may assert any counterclaim against the third-party plaintiff under Rule 13(b) or any crossclaim against another third-party defendant under Rule 13(g);

   (C) may assert against the plaintiff any defense that the third-party plaintiff has to the plaintiff's claim; and

   (D) may also assert against the plaintiff any claim arising out of the transaction or occurrence that is the subject matter of the plaintiff's claim against the third-party plaintiff.

(3) Plaintiff's Claims Against a Third-Party Defendant. The plaintiff may assert against the third-party defendant any claim arising out of the transaction or occurrence that is the subject matter of the plaintiff's claim against the third-party plaintiff. The third-party defendant must then assert any defense under Rule 12 and any counterclaim under Rule 13(a), and may assert any counterclaim under Rule 13(b) or any crossclaim under Rule 13(g).

(4) Motion to Strike, Sever or Try Separately. Any party may move to strike the third-party claim, to sever it, or to try it separately.

(5) Third-Party Defendant's Claim Against a Nonparty. A third-party defendant may proceed under this rule against a non-party who is or may be liable to the third-party defendant for all or part of any claim against it.

(6) Third-Party Complaint In Rem. If it is within the admiralty or maritime jurisdiction, a third-party complaint may be in rem. In that event, a reference in this rule to the "summons" includes the warrant of arrest, and a reference to the defendant or third-party plaintiff includes, when appropriate, a person who asserts a right under Supplemental Rule C(6)(a)(i) in the property arrested.

(b) WHEN A PLAINTIFF MAY BRING IN A THIRD PARTY

When a claim is asserted against a plaintiff, the plaintiff may bring in a third party if this rule would allow a defendant to do so.

(c) ADMIRALTY OR MARITIME CLAIM

(1) Scope of Impleader. If a plaintiff asserts an admiralty or maritime claim under Rule 9(h), the defendant or a person who asserts a right under Supplemental Rule C(6)(a)(i) may, as a third-party plaintiff, bring in a third-party defendant who may be wholly or partly liable—either to the plaintiff or to the third-party plaintiff—for remedy over, contribution, or otherwise on account of the same transaction, occurrence, or series of transactions or occurrences.

(2) Defending Against a Demand for Judgment for the Plaintiff. The third-party plaintiff may demand judgment in the plaintiff's favor against the third-party defendant. In that event, the third-party defendant must defend under Rule 12 against the plaintiff's claim as well as the

third-party plaintiff's claim; and the action proceeds as if the plaintiff had sued both the third-party defendant and the third-party plaintiff.

For further study, see: Fed. R. Civ. P. Forms 4,16 at 96; 1948 Advisory Committee Notes at 112; 1966 Advisory Committee Notes at 116; and Transnational Rules 5 & 13 at 280.

RULE 15. AMENDED AND SUPPLEMENTAL PLEADINGS

(a) AMENDMENTS BEFORE TRIAL

(1)   Amending as a Matter of Course. A party may amend its pleadings once as a matter of course:

(A) before being served with a responsive pleading; or

(B) within 20 days after serving the pleading if a responsive pleading is not allowed and the action is not yet on the trial calendar.

(2)   Other Amendments. In all other cases, a party may amend its pleading only with the opposing party's written consent or the court's leave. The court should freely give leave when justice so requires.

(3)   Time to Respond. Unless the court orders otherwise, any required response to an amended pleading must be made within the time remaining to respond to the original pleading or within 10 days after service of the amended pleading, whichever is later.

(b) AMENDMENTS DURING AND AFTER TRIAL

(1)   Based on an Objection at Trial. If, at trial, a party objects that evidence is not within the issues raised in the pleadings, the court may permit the pleadings to be amended. The court should freely permit an amendment when doing so will aid in presenting the merits and the objecting party fails to satisfy the court that the evidence would prejudice that party's action or defense on the merits. The court may grant a continuance to enable the objecting party to meet the evidence.

(2)   For Issues Tried by Consent. When an issue not raised by the pleadings is tried by the parties' express or implied consent, it must be treated in all respects as if raised in the pleadings. A party may move—at any time, even after judgment—to amend the pleadings to conform them to the evidence and to raise an unpleaded issue. But failure to amend does not affect the result of the trial of that issue.

(c) RELATION BACK OF AMENDMENTS

(1)   When an Amendment Relates Back. An amendment to a pleading relates back to the date of the original pleading when:

(A) the law that provides the applicable statute of limitations allows relation back;

(B) the amendment asserts a claim or defense that arose out of the conduct, transaction, or occurrence set out—or attempted to be set out—in the original pleading; or

(C) the amendment changes the party or the naming of the party against whom a claim is asserted, if Rule 15(c)(1)(B) is satisfied and if, within the period provided by Rule 4(m) for serving the summons and complaint, the party to be brought in by amendment:

(i)   received such notice of the action that it will not be prejudiced in defending on the merits; and

(ii) knew or should have known that the action would have been brought against it, but for a mistake concerning the proper party's identity.

21

(2)   Notice to the United States. When the United States or a United States officer or agency is added as a defendant by amendment, the notice requirements of Rule 15(c)(1)(C)(i) and (ii) are satisfied if, during the stated period, process was delivered or mailed to the United States attorney or the United States attorney's designees, to the Attorney General of the United States, or to the officer or agency.

(d) SUPPLEMENTAL PLEADINGS

On motion and reasonable notice, the court may, on just terms, permit a party to serve a supplemental pleading setting out any transaction, occurrence, or event that happened after the date of the pleading to be supplemented. The court may permit supplementation even though the original pleading is defective in stating a claim or defense. The court may order that the opposing party plead to the supplemental pleading within a specified time.

> **For further study, see:** 1963 Advisory Committee Notes at 114; 1966 Advisory Committee Notes at 116; 1991 Advisory Committee Notes at 153; 2007 Advisory Committee Notes at 211; and Restatement (Second) of Judgments § 25 at 237; and Transnational Rules 14 & 19 at 283.

RULE 16. PRETRIAL CONFERENCES; SCHEDULING; MANAGEMENT

(a) PURPOSES OF A PRETRIAL CONFERENCE

In any action, the court may order the attorneys and any unrepresented parties to appear for one or more pretrial conferences for such purposes as:

(1)   expediting disposition of the action;

(2)   establishing early and continuing control so that the case will not be protracted because of lack of management;

(3)   discouraging wasteful pretrial activities;

(4)   improving the quality of the trial through more thorough preparation; and

(5)   facilitating settlement.

(b) SCHEDULING

(1)   Scheduling Order. Except in categories of actions exempted by local rule, the district judge — or a magistrate judge when authorized by local rule — must issue a scheduling order:

    (A) after receiving the parties' report under Rule 26(f); or

    (B) after consulting with the parties' attorneys and any unrepresented parties at a scheduling conference or by telephone, mail, or other means.

(2)   Time to Issue. The judge must issue the scheduling order as soon as practicable, but in any event within the earlier of 120 days after any defendant has been served with the complaint or 90 days after any defendant has appeared.

(3)   Contents of the Order

    (A) Required Contents. The scheduling order must limit the time to join other parties, amend the pleadings, complete discovery, and file motions.

    (B) Permitted Contents. The scheduling order may:

        (i)   modify the timing of disclosures under Rules 26(a) and 26(e)(1);

        (ii)   modify the extent of discovery;

        (iii) provide for the disclosure or discovery of electronically stored information;

        (iv)   include any agreements the parties reach for asserting claims of privilege or of protection as trial-preparation material after information is produced;

(v)   set dates for pretrial conferences and for trial; and

(vi) include other appropriate matters.

(4)   Modifying a Schedule. A schedule may be modified only for good cause and with the judge's consent.

(c) ATTENDANCE AND MATTERS FOR CONSIDERATION AT A PRETRIAL CONFERENCE

(1)   Attendance. A represented party must authorize at least one of its attorneys to make stipulations and admissions about all matters that can reasonably be anticipated for discussion at a pretrial conference. If appropriate, the court may require that a party or its representative be present or reasonably available by other means to consider possible settlement.

(2)   Matters for Consideration. At any pretrial conference, the court may consider and take appropriate action on the following matters:

(A) formulating and simplifying the issues, and eliminating frivolous claims or defenses;

(B) amending the pleadings if necessary or desirable;

(C) obtaining admissions and stipulations about facts and documents to avoid unnecessary proof, and ruling in advance on the admissibility of evidence;

(D) avoiding unnecessary proof and cumulative evidence, and limiting the use of testimony under Federal Rule of Evidence 702;

(E) determining the appropriateness and timing of summary adjudication under Rule 56;

(F) controlling and scheduling discovery, including orders affecting disclosures and discovery under Rule 26 and Rules 29 through 37;

(G) identifying witnesses and documents; scheduling the filing and exchange of any pretrial briefs, and setting dates for further conferences and for trial;

(H) referring matters to a magistrate judge or a master;

(I) settling the case and using special procedures to assist in resolving the dispute when authorized by statute or local rule;

(J) determining the form and content of the pretrial order;

(K) disposing of pending motions;

(L) adopting special procedures for managing potentially difficult or protracted actions that may involve complex issues, multiple parties, difficult legal questions, or unusual proof problems;

(M) ordering a separate trial under Rule 42(b) of a claim, counterclaim, crossclaim, third-party claim, or particular issue;

(N) ordering the presentation of evidence early in the trial on a manageable issue that might, on the evidence, be the basis for a judgment as a matter of law under Rule 50(a) or a judgment on partial findings under Rule 52(c);

(O) establishing a reasonable limit on the time allowed to present evidence; and

(P) facilitating in other ways the just, speedy, and inexpensive disposition of the action.

(d) PRETRIAL ORDERS

After any conference under this rule, the court should issue an order reciting the action taken. This order controls the course of the action unless the court modifies it.

(e) FINAL PRETRIAL CONFERENCES AND ORDERS

The court may hold a final pretrial conference to formulate a trial plan, including a plan to facilitate the admission of evidence. The conference must be held as close to the start of trial as is reasonable, and must be attended by at least one attorney who will conduct the trial for each party and by any unrepresented party. The court may modify the order issued after a final pretrial conference only to prevent manifest injustice.

(f) SANCTIONS

(1) In General. On motion or on its own, the court may issue any just orders, including those authorized by Rule 37(b)(2)(A)(ii)-(vii), if a party or by its attorney:

(A) fails to appear at a scheduling or other pretrial conference;

(B) is substantially unprepared to participate—or does not participate in good faith—in the conference; or

(C) fails to obey a scheduling or other pretrial order.

(2) Imposing Fees and Costs. Instead of or in addition to any other sanction, the court must order the party, its attorney, or both to pay the reasonable expenses—including attorney's fees—incurred because of any noncompliance with this rule, unless the noncompliance was substantially justified or other circumstances make an award of expenses unjust.

> **For further study, see**: 1983 Advisory Committee Notes at 146; 1993 Advisory Committee Notes at 169; and Transnational Rules 16 & 18 at 284.

IV. Parties

RULE 17. PLAINTIFF AND DEFENDANT; CAPACITY; PUBLIC OFFICERS

(a) REAL PARTY IN INTEREST

(1) Designation in General. An action must be prosecuted in the name of the real party in interest. The following may sue in their own names without joining the person for whose benefit the action is brought:

(A) an executor;

(B) an administrator;

(C) a guardian;

(D) a bailee;

(E) a trustee of an express trust;

(F) a party with whom or in whose name a contract has been made for another's benefit; and

(G) a party authorized by statute.

(2) Action in the Name of the United States for Another's Use or Benefit. When a federal statute so provides, an action for another's use or benefit must be brought in the name of the United States.

(3) Joinder of the Real Party in Interest. The court may not dismiss an action for failure to prosecute in the name of the real party in interest until, after an objection, a reasonable time has been allowed for the real party in interest to ratify, join, or be substituted into the action. After ratification, joinder, or substitution, the action proceeds as if it had been originally commenced by the real party in interest.

(b) CAPACITY TO SUE OR BE SUED

Capacity to sue or be sued is determined as follows:

(1) for an individual who is not acting in a representative capacity, by the law of the individual's domicile;

(2) for a corporation, by the law under which it was organized; and

(3) for all other parties, by the law of the state where the court is located, except that:

(A) a partnership or other unincorporated association with no such capacity under that state's law may sue or be sued in its common name to enforce a substantive right existing under the United States Constitution or laws; and

(B) 28 U.S.C. §§ 754 and 959(a) govern the capacity of a receiver appointed by a United States court to sue or be sued in a United States court.

(c) MINOR OR INCOMPETENT PERSON

(1) With a Representative. The following representatives may sue or defend on behalf of a minor or an incompetent person:

(A) a general guardian;

(B) a committee;

(C) a conservator; or

(D) a like fiduciary.

(2) Without a Representative. A minor or an incompetent person who does not have a duly appointed representative may sue by a next friend or by a guardian ad litem. The court must appoint a guardian ad litem—or issue another appropriate order—to protect a minor or incompetent person who is unrepresented in an action.

(d) PUBLIC OFFICER'S TITLE AND NAME

A public officer who sues or is sued in an official capacity may be designated by official title rather than by name, but the court may order that the officer's name be added.

For further study, see: Fed. R. Civ. P. Form 9 at 98; and 1966 Advisory Committee Notes at 117.

RULE 18. JOINDER OF CLAIMS

(a) IN GENERAL

A party asserting a claim, counterclaim, crossclaim, or third-party claim may join, as independent or alternative claims, as many claims as it has against an opposing party.

(b) JOINDER OF CONTINGENT CLAIMS

A party may join two claims even though one of them is contingent on the disposition of the other; but the court may grant relief only in accordance with the parties' relative substantive rights. In particular, a plaintiff may state a claim for money and a claim to set aside a conveyance that is fraudulent as to that plaintiff, without first obtaining a judgment for the money.

For further study, see: 1966 Advisory Committee Notes at 118; Restatement (Second) of Judgments § 24 at 233; and Transnational Rule 5 at 280.

RULE 19. REQUIRED JOINDER OF PARTIES

(a) PERSONS REQUIRED TO BE JOINED IF FEASIBLE

(1)   Required Party. A party who is subject to service of process and whose joinder will not deprive the court of subject-matter jurisdiction must be joined as a party if:

    (A) in that person's absence, the court cannot accord complete relief among existing parties; or

    (B) that person claims an interest to the subject of the action and is so situated that disposing of the action in the person's absence may:

        (i)   as a practical matter impair or impede the person's ability to protect the interest; or

        (ii)   leave an existing party subject to a substantial risk of incurring double, multiple, or otherwise inconsistent obligations because of the interest.

(2)   Joinder by Court Order. If a person has not been joined as required, the court must order that the person be made a party. A person who refuses to join as a plaintiff may be made either a defendant or, in a proper case, an involuntary plaintiff.

(3)   Venue. If a party objects to venue and the joinder would make venue improper, the court must dismiss that party.

(b) WHEN JOINDER IS NOT FEASIBLE

If a person who is required to be joined if feasible cannot be joined, the court must determine whether the action should proceed among the existing parties or should be dismissed. The factors for the court to consider include:

(1)   the extent to which a judgment rendered in the person's absence might prejudice that person or the existing parties;

(2)   the extent to which any prejudice could be lessened or avoided by:

    (A) protective provisions in the judgment;

    (B) shaping the relief; or

    (C) other measures;

(3)   whether a judgment rendered in the person's absence would be adequate; and

(4)   whether the plaintiff would have an adequate remedy if the action were dismissed for nonjoinder.

(c) PLEADING THE REASONS FOR NONJOINDER

When asserting a claim for relief, a party must state:

(1)   the name, if known, of any person who is required to be joined if feasible but is not joined; and

(2)   the reasons for not joining that person.

(d) EXCEPTION FOR CLASS ACTIONS

This rule is subject to Rule 23.

For further study, see: Fed. R. Civ. P. Form 8 at 98; 1966 Advisory Committee Notes at 118; 2007 Advisory Committee Notes at 212; and Transnational Rule 5 at 280.

1) Is absent party connected?
2) can we get him? PJ + SMJ
3) can we go on w/o him?
    Indispensible?

RULE 20. PERMISSIVE JOINDER OF PARTIES

(a) PERSONS WHO MAY JOIN OR BE JOINED

    (1)   Plaintiffs. Persons may join in one action as plaintiffs if:

        (A) they assert any right to relief jointly, severally, or in the alternative with respect to or arising out of the same transaction, occurrence, or series of transactions or occurrences; and

        (B) any question of law or fact common to all plaintiffs will arise in the action.

    (2)   Defendants. Persons—as well as a vessel, cargo, or other property subject to admiralty process in rem—may be joined in one action as defendants if:

        (A) any right to relief is asserted against them jointly, severally, or in the alternative with respect to or arising out of the same transaction, occurrence, or series of transactions or occurrences; and

        (B) any question of law or fact common to all defendants will arise in the action.

    (3)   Extent of Relief. Neither a plaintiff nor a defendant need be interested in obtaining or defending against all the relief demanded. The court may grant judgment to one or more plaintiffs according to their rights, and against one or more defendants according to their liabilities.

(b) PROTECTIVE MEASURES

The court may issue orders—including an order for separate trials—to protect a party against embarrassment, delay, expense, or other prejudice that arises from including a person against whom the party asserts no claim and who asserts no claim against the party.

    For further study, see: Transnational Rules 5 & 18 at 280.

RULE 21. MISJOINDER AND NONJOINDER OF PARTIES

Misjoinder of parties is not a ground for dismissing an action. On motion or on its own, the court may at any time, on just terms, add or drop a party. The court may also sever any claim against a party.

    For further study, see: Transnational Rule 5 at 280.

RULE 22. INTERPLEADER

(a) GROUNDS

    (1)   By a Plaintiff. Persons with claims that may expose a plaintiff to double or multiple liability may be joined as defendants and required to interplead. Joinder for interpleader is proper even though:

        (A) the claims of the several claimants, or the titles on which their claims depend, lack a common origin or are adverse and independent rather than identical; or

        (B) the plaintiff denies liability in whole or in part to any or all of the claimants.

    (2)   By a Defendant. A defendant exposed to similar liability may seek interpleader through a crossclaim or counterclaim.

(b) RELATION TO OTHER RULES AND STATUTES

This rule supplements—and does not limit—the joinder of parties allowed by Rule 20. The remedy this rule provides is in addition to—and does not supersede or limit—the remedy provided by 28 U.S.C. §§ 1335, 1397, and 2361. An action under those statutes must be conducted under these rules.

For further study, see: Fed. R. Civ. P. Forms 20 & 31 at 103.

RULE 23. CLASS ACTIONS

(a) PREREQUISITES

One or more members of a class may sue or be sued as representative parties on behalf of all members only if:

    (1)   the class is so numerous that joinder of all members is impracticable;

    (2)   there are questions of law or fact common to the class;

    (3)   the claims or defenses of the representative parties are typical of the claims or defenses of the class; and

    (4)   the representative parties will fairly and adequately protect the interests of the class.

(b) TYPES OF CLASS ACTIONS

A class action may be maintained if Rule 23(a) is satisfied and if:

    (1)   prosecuting separate actions by or against individual class members would create a risk of:

        (A) inconsistent or varying adjudications with respect to individual class members that would establish incompatible standards of conduct for the party opposing the class; or

        (B) adjudications with respect to individual class members that, as a practical matter, would be dispositive of the interests of the other members not parties to the individual adjudications or would substantially impair or impede their ability to protect their interests;

    (2)   the party opposing the class has acted or refused to act on grounds that apply generally to the class, so that final injunctive relief or corresponding declaratory relief is appropriate respecting the class as a whole; or

    (3)   the court finds that the questions of law or fact common to class members predominate over any questions affecting only individual members, and that a class action is superior to other available methods for fairly and efficiently adjudicating the controversy. The matters pertinent to these findings include:

        (A) the class members' interests in individually controlling the prosecution or defense of separate actions;

        (B) the extent and nature of any litigation concerning the controversy already begun by or against class members;

        (C) the desirability or undesirability of concentrating the litigation of the claims in the particular forum; and

        (D) the likely difficulties in managing a class action.

(c) CERTIFICATION ORDER; NOTICE TO CLASS MEMBERS; JUDGMENT; ISSUES CLASSES; SUBCLASSES

    (1) Certification Order

        (A) Time to Issue. At an early practicable time after a person sues or is sued as a class representative, the court must determine by order whether to certify the action as a class action.

        (B) Defining the Class; Appointing Class Counsel. An order that certifies a class action must define the class and the class claims, issues, or defenses, and must appoint class counsel under Rule 23(g).

        (C) Altering or Amending the Order. An order that grants or denies class certification may be altered or amended before final judgment.

    (2) Notice

        (A) For (b)(1) or (b)(2) Classes. For any class certified under Rule 23(b)(1) or (b)(2), the court may direct appropriate notice to the class.

        (B) For (b)(3) Classes. For any class certified under Rule 23(b)(3), the court must direct to class members the best notice that is practicable under the circumstances, including individual notice to all members who can be identified through reasonable effort. The notice must clearly and concisely state in plain, easily understood language:

            (i) the nature of the action;

            (ii) the definition of the class certified;

            (iii) the class claims, issues, or defenses;

            (iv) that a class member may enter an appearance through an attorney if the member so desires;

            (v) that the court will exclude from the class any member who requests exclusion;

            (vi) the time and manner for requesting exclusion; and

            (vii) the binding effect of a class judgment on members under Rule 23(c)(3).

    (3) Judgment. Whether or not favorable to the class, the judgment in a class action must:

        (A) for any class certified under Rule 23(b)(1) or (b)(2), include and describe those whom the court finds to be class members; and

        (B) for any class certified under Rule 23(b)(3), include and specify or describe those to whom the Rule 23(c)(2) notice was directed, who have not requested exclusion, and whom the court finds to be class members.

    (4) Particular Issues. When appropriate, an action may be brought or maintained as a class action with respect to particular issues.

    (5) Subclasses. When appropriate, a class may be divided into subclasses that are each treated as a class under this rule.

(d) CONDUCTING THE ACTION

    (1) In General. In conducting an action under this rule, the court may issue orders that:

        (A) determine the course of proceedings or prescribe measures to prevent undue repetition or complication in presenting evidence or argument;

        (B) require — to protect class members and fairly conduct the action — giving appropriate notice to some or all class members of:

            (i) any step in the action;

            (ii) the proposed extent of the judgment; or

     (iii) the members' opportunity to signify whether they consider the representation fair and adequate, to intervene and present claims or defenses, or to otherwise come into the action;

  (C) impose conditions on the representative parties or on intervenors;

  (D) require that the pleadings be amended to eliminate allegations about representation of absent persons and that the action proceed accordingly; or

  (E) deal with similar procedural matters.

    (2) Combining and Amending Orders. An order under Rule 23(d)(1) may be altered or amended from time to time and may be combined with an order under Rule 16.

(e) SETTLEMENT, VOLUNTARY DISMISSAL, OR COMPROMISE

The claims, issues, or defenses of a certified class may be settled, voluntarily dismissed, or compromised only with the court's approval. The following procedures apply to a proposed settlement, voluntary dismissal, or compromise:

    (1) The Court must direct notice in a reasonable manner to all class members who would be bound by the proposal.

    (2) If the proposal would bind class members, the court may approve it only after a hearing and on finding that it is fair, reasonable, and adequate.

    (3) The parties seeking approval must file a statement identifying any agreement made in connection with the proposal.

    (4) If the class action was previously certified under Rule 23(b)(3), the court may refuse to approve a settlement unless it affords a new opportunity to request exclusion to individual class members who had an earlier opportunity to request exclusion but did not do so.

    (5) Any class member may object to the proposal if it requires court approval under this subdivision (e); the objection may be withdrawn only with the court's approval.

(f) APPEALS

A court of appeals may permit an appeal from an order granting or denying class-action certification under this rule if a petition for permission to appeal is filed with the circuit clerk within 10 days after the order is entered. An appeal does not stay proceedings in the district court unless the district judge or the court of appeals so orders.

(g) CLASS COUNSEL

    (1) Appointing Class Counsel. Unless a statute provides otherwise, a court that certifies a class must appoint class counsel. In appointing class counsel, the court:

  (A) must consider:

    (i)   the work counsel has done in identifying or investigating potential claims in this action;

    (ii) counsel's experience in handling class actions, other complex litigation, and the type of claims asserted in the action;

    (iii) counsel's knowledge of the applicable law; and

    (iv) the resources that counsel will commit to representing the class;

  (B) may consider any other matter pertinent to counsel's ability to fairly and adequately represent the interests of the class;

  (C) may order potential class counsel to provide information on any subject pertinent to the appointment and to propose terms for attorney's fees and nontaxable costs;

(D) may include in the appointing order provisions about the award of attorney's fees or nontaxable costs under Rule 23(h); and

(E) may make further orders in connection with the appointment.

(2) Standard for Appointing Class Counsel. When one applicant seeks appointment as class counsel, the court may appoint that applicant only if the applicant is adequate under Rule 23(g)(1) and (4). If more than one adequate applicant seeks appointment, the court must appoint the applicant best able to represent the interests of the class.

(3) Interim Counsel. The court may designate interim counsel to act on behalf of a putative class before determining whether to certify the action as a class action.

(4) Duty of Class Counsel. Class counsel must fairly and adequately represent the interests of the class.

(h) ATTORNEY'S FEES AND NONTAXABLE COSTS

In a certified class action, the court may award reasonable attorney's fees and nontaxable costs that are authorized by law or by the parties' agreement. The following procedures apply:

(1) A claim for an award must be made by motion under Rule 54(d)(2), subject to the provisions of this subdivision (h), at a time the court sets. Notice of the motion must be served on all parties and, for motions by class counsel, directed to class members in a reasonable manner.

(2) A class member, or a party from whom payment is sought, may object to the motion.

(3) The court may hold a hearing and must find the facts and state its legal conclusions under Rule 52(a).

(4) The court may refer issues related to the amount of the award to a special master or a magistrate judge, as provided in Rule 54(d)(2)(D).

> **For further study, see**: 1938 Advisory Committee Notes at 111; 1966 Advisory Committee Notes at 119; 2003 Advisory Committee Notes at 191; and Transnational Rule 5 at 280.

RULE 23.1. DERIVATIVE ACTIONS

(a) PREREQUISITES

This rule applies only when one or more shareholders or members of a corporation or an unincorporated association bring a derivative action to enforce a right that the corporation or association may properly assert but has failed to enforce. The derivative action may not be maintained if it appears that the plaintiff does not fairly and adequately represent the interests of shareholders or members who are similarly situated in enforcing the right of the corporation or association.

(b) PLEADING REQUIREMENTS

The complaint must be verified and must:

(1) allege that the plaintiff was a shareholder or member at the time of the transaction complained of, or that the plaintiff's share or membership later devolved on it by operation of law;

(2) allege that the action is not a collusive one to confer jurisdiction that the court would otherwise lack; and

(3) state with particularity:

   (A) any effort by the plaintiff to obtain the desired action from the directors or comparable authority and, if necessary, from the shareholders or members; and

   (B) the reasons for not obtaining the action or not making the effort.

(c) SETTLEMENT, DISMISSAL, AND COMPROMISE

A derivative action may be settled, voluntarily dismissed, or compromised only with the court's approval. Notice of a proposed settlement, voluntary dismissal, or compromise must be given to shareholders or members in the manner that the court orders.

For further study, see: 1966 Advisory Committee Notes at 122.

RULE 23.2. ACTIONS RELATING TO UNINCORPORATED ASSOCIATIONS

This rule applies to an action brought by or against the members of an unincorporated association as a class by naming certain members as representative parties. The action may be maintained only if it appears that those parties will fairly and adequately protect the interests of the association and its members. In conducting the action, the court may issue any appropriate orders corresponding with those in Rule 23(d), and the procedure for settlement, voluntary dismissal, or compromise must correspond with the procedure in Rule 23(e).

For further study, see: 1966 Advisory Committee Notes at 123.

RULE 24. INTERVENTION

(a) INTERVENTION OF RIGHT

On timely motion, the court must permit anyone to intervene who:

(1) is given an unconditional right to intervene by a federal statute; or

(2) claims an interest relating to the property or transaction that is the subject of the action, and is so situated that disposing of the action may as a practical matter impair or impede the movant's ability to protect its interest, unless existing parties adequately represent that interest.

(b) PERMISSIVE INTERVENTION

(1) In General. On timely motion, the court may permit anyone to intervene who:

   (A) is given a conditional right to intervene by a federal statute; or

   (B) has a claim or defense that shares with the main action a common question of law or fact.

(2) By a Government Officer or Agency. On timely motion, the court may permit a federal or state governmental officer or agency to intervene if a party's claim or defense is based on:

   (A) a statute or executive order administered by the officer or agency; or

   (B) any regulation, order, requirement, or agreement issued or made under the statute or executive order.

(3) Delay or Prejudice. In exercising its discretion, the court must consider whether the intervention will unduly delay or prejudice the adjudication of the original parties' rights.

(c) NOTICE AND PLEADING REQUIRED

A motion to intervene must be served on the parties as provided in Rule 5. The motion must state the grounds for intervention and be accompanied by a pleading that sets out the claim or defense for which intervention is sought.

> **For further study, see**: Fed. R. Civ. P. Form 42 at 106; 1966 Advisory Committee Notes at 123; and Transnational Rule 5 at 280.

RULE 25. SUBSTITUTION OF PARTIES

(a) DEATH

(1)   Substitution if the Claim is Not Extinguished. If a party dies and the claim is not extinguished, the court may order substitution of the proper party. A motion for substitution may be made by any party or by the decedent's successor or representative. If the motion is not made within 90 days after service of a statement noting the death, the action by or against the decedent must be dismissed.

(2)   Continuation Among the Remaining Parties. After a party's death, if the right sought to be enforced survives only to or against the remaining parties, the action does not abate, but proceeds in favor of or against the remaining parties. The death should be noted on the record.

(3)   Service. A motion to substitute, together with a notice of hearing, must be served on the parties as provided in Rule 5 and on nonparties as provided in Rule 4. A statement noting death must be served in the same manner. Service may be made in any judicial district.

(b) INCOMPETENCY

If a party becomes incompetent, the court may, on motion, permit the action to be continued by or against the party's representative. The motion must be served as provided in Rule 25(a)(3).

(C) TRANSFER OF INTEREST

If an interest is transferred, the action may be continued by or against the original party unless the court, on motion, orders the transferee to be substituted in the action or joined with the original party. The motion must be served as provided in Rule 25(a)(3).

(d) PUBLIC OFFICERS; DEATH OR SEPARATION FROM OFFICE

An action does not abate when a public officer who is a party in an official capacity dies, resigns, or otherwise ceases to hold office while the action is pending. The officer's successor is automatically substituted as a party. Later proceedings should be in the substituted party's name, but any misnomer not affecting the parties' substantial rights must be disregarded. The court may order substitution at any time, but the absence of such an order does not affect the substitution.

> **For further study, see**: Fed. R. Civ. P. Form 9 at 98; 1963 Advisory Committee Notes at 114; and Transnational Rule 5 at 280.

V. Disclosures and Discovery

RULE 26. DUTY TO DISCLOSE; GENERAL PROVISIONS GOVERNING DISCOVERY

(a) REQUIRED DISCLOSURES

 (1) Initial Disclosure

  (A) In General. Except as exempted by Rule 26(a)(1)(B) or as otherwise stipulated or ordered by the court, a party must, without awaiting a discovery request, provide to the other parties:

   (i) the name and, if known, the address and telephone number of each individual likely to have discoverable information—along with the subjects of that information—that the disclosing party may use to support its claims or defenses, unless the use would be solely for impeachment;

   (ii) a copy—or a description by category and location—of all documents, electronically stored information, and tangible things that the disclosing party has in its possession, custody, or control and may use to support its claims or defenses, unless the use would be solely for impeachment;

   (iii) a computation of each category of damages claimed by the disclosing party—who must also make available for inspection and copying as under Rule 34 the documents or other evidentiary material, unless privileged or protected from disclosure, on which each computation is based, including materials bearing on the nature and extent of injuries suffered; and

   (iv) for inspection and copying as under Rule 34, any insurance agreement under which an insurance business may be liable to satisfy all or part of a possible judgment in the action or to indemnify or reimburse for payments made to satisfy the judgment.

  (B) Proceedings Exempt from Initial Disclosure. The following proceedings are exempt from initial disclosure:

   (i) an action for review on an administrative record;

   (ii) a petition for habeas corpus or any other proceeding to challenge a criminal conviction or sentence;

   (iii) an action brought without an attorney by a person in the custody of the United States, a state, or a state subdivision;

   (iv) an action to enforce or quash an administrative summons or subpoena;

   (v) an action by the United States to recover benefit payments;

   (vi) an action by the United States to collect on a student loan guaranteed by the United States;

   (vii) a proceeding ancillary to a proceeding in another court; and

   (viii) an action to enforce an arbitration award.

  (C) Time for Initial Disclosures—In General. A party must make the initial disclosures at or within 14 days after the parties' Rule 26(f) conference unless a different time is set by stipulation or court order, or unless a party objects during the conference that initial disclosures are not appropriate in this action and states the objection in the proposed discovery plan. In ruling on the objection, the court must determine what disclosures, if any, are to be made and must set the time for disclosure.

  (D) Time for Initial Disclosures—For Parties Served or Joined Later. A party that is first served or otherwise joined after the Rule 26(f) conference must make the initial disclosures within 30 days after being served or joined, unless a different time is set by stipulation or court order.

(E) Basis for Initial Disclosure; Unacceptable Excuses. A party must make its initial disclosures based on the information then reasonably available to it. A party is not excused from making its disclosures because it has not fully investigated the case or because it challenges the sufficiency of another party's disclosures or because another party has not made its disclosures.

(2) Disclosure of Expert Testimony

(A) In General. In addition to the disclosures required by Rule 26(a)(1), a party must disclose to the other parties the identity of any witness it may use at trial to present evidence under Federal Rule of Evidence 702, 703, or 705.

(B) Written Report. Unless otherwise stipulated or ordered by the court, this disclosure must be accompanied by a written report—prepared and signed by the witness—if the witness is one retained or specially employed to provide expert testimony in the case or one whose duties as the party's employee regularly involve giving expert testimony. The report must contain:

(i)   a complete statement of all opinions the witness will express and the basis and reasons for them;

(ii) the data or other information considered by the witness in forming them;

(iii) any exhibits that will be used to summarize or support them;

(iv) the witness's qualifications, including a list of all publications authored in the previous ten years;

(v)   a list of all other cases in which, during the previous four years, the witness testified as an expert at trial or by deposition; and

(vi) a statement of the compensation to be paid for the study and testimony in the case.

(C) Time to Disclose Expert Testimony. A party must make these disclosures at the times and in the sequence that the court orders. Absent a stipulation or a court order, the disclosures must be made:

(i)   at least 90 days before the date set for trial or for the case to be ready for trial; or

(ii) if the evidence is intended solely to contradict or rebut evidence on the same subject matter identified by another party under Rule 26(a)(2)(B), within 30 days after the other party's disclosure.

(D) Supplementing the Disclosure. The parties must supplement these disclosures when required under Rule 26(e).

(3) Pretrial Disclosures

(A) In General. In addition to the disclosures required by Rule 26(a)(1) and (2), a party must provide to the other parties and promptly file the following information about the evidence that it may present at trial other than solely for impeachment:

(i)   the name and, if not previously provided, the address and telephone number of each witness—separately identifying those the party expects to present and those it may call if the need arises;

(ii) the designation of those witnesses whose testimony the party expects to present by deposition and, if not taken stenographically, a transcript of the pertinent parts of the deposition; and

      (iii) an identification of each document or other exhibit, including summaries of other evidence—separately identifying those items the party expects to offer and those it may offer if the need arises.

    (B) Time for Pretrial Disclosures; Objections. Unless the court orders otherwise, these disclosures must be made at least 30 days before trial. Within 14 days after they are made, unless the court sets a different time, a party may serve and promptly file a list of the following objections: any objections to the use under Rule 32(a) of a deposition designated by another party under Rule 26(a)(3)(A)(ii); and any objection, together with the grounds for it, that may be made to the admissibility of materials identified under Rule 26(a)(3)(A)(iii). An objection not so made—except for one under Federal Rule of Evidence 402 or 403—is waived unless excused by the court for good cause.

  (4) Form of Disclosures. Unless the court orders otherwise, all disclosures under Rule 26(a) must be in writing, signed, and served.

(b) DISCOVERY SCOPE AND LIMITS

  (1) Scope in General. Unless otherwise limited by court order, the scope of discovery is as follows: Parties may obtain discovery regarding any nonprivileged matter that is relevant to any party's claim or defense—including the existence, description, nature, custody, condition, and location of any documents or other tangible things and the identify and location of persons who know of any discoverable matter. For good cause, the court may order discovery of any matter relevant to the subject matter involved in the action. Relevant information need not be admissible at the trial if the discovery appears reasonably calculated to lead to the discovery of admissible evidence. All discovery is subject to the limitations imposed by Rule 26(b)(2)(C).

  (2) Limitations on Frequency and Extent

    (A) When Permitted. By order, the court may alter the limits in these rules on the number of depositions and interrogatories or on the length of depositions under Rule 30. By order or local rule, the court may also limit the number of requests under Rule 36.

    (B) Specific Limitations on Electronically Stored Information. A party need not provide discovery of electronically stored information from sources that the party identifies as not reasonably accessible because of undue burden or cost. On motion to compel discovery or for a protective order, the party from whom discovery is sought must show that the information is not reasonably accessible because of undue burden or cost. If that showing is made, the court may nonetheless order discovery from such sources if the requesting party shows good cause, considering the limitations of Rule 26(b)(2)(C). The court may specify conditions for the discovery.

    (C) When Required. On motion or on its own, the court must limit the frequency or extent of discovery otherwise allowed by these rules or by local rule if it determines that:

      (i) the discovery sought is unreasonably cumulative or duplicative, or can be obtained from some other source that is more convenient, less burdensome, or less expensive;

      (ii) the party seeking discovery has had ample opportunity to obtain the information by discovery in the action; or

        (iii) the burden or expense of the proposed discovery outweighs its likely benefit, considering the needs of the case, the amount in controversy, the parties' resources, the importance of the issues at stake in the action, and the importance of the discovery in resolving the issues.

(3) Trial Preparation; Materials

    (A) Documents and Tangible Things. Ordinarily, a party may not discover documents and tangible things that are prepared in anticipation of litigation or for trial by or for another party or its representative (including the other party's attorney, consultant, surety, indemnitor, insurer, or agent). But, subject to Rule 26(b)(4), those materials may be discovered if:

        (i) they are otherwise discoverable under Rule 26(b)(1); and

        (ii) the party shows that it has substantial need for the materials to prepare its case and cannot, without undue hardship, obtain their substantial equivalent by other means.

    (B) Protection Against Disclosure. If the court orders discovery of those materials, it must protect against disclosure of the mental impressions, conclusions, opinions, or legal theories of a party's attorney or other representative concerning the litigation.

    (C) Previous Statement. Any party or other person may, on request and without the required showing, obtain the person's own previous statement about the action or its subject matter. If the request is refused, the person may move for a court order, and Rule 37(a)(5) applies to the award of expenses. A previous statement is either:

        (i) a written statement that the person has signed or otherwise adopted or approved; or

        (ii) a contemporaneous stenographic, mechanical, electrical, or other recording—or a transcription of it—that recites substantially verbatim the person's oral statement.

(4) Trial Preparation; Experts

    (A) Expert Who May Testify. A party may depose any person who has been identified as an expert whose opinions may be presented at trial. If Rule 26(a)(2)(B) requires a report from the expert, the deposition may be conducted only after the report is provided.

    (B) Expert Employed Only for Trial Preparation. Ordinarily, a party may not, by interrogatories or deposition, discover facts known or opinions held by an expert who has been retained or specially employed by another party in anticipation of litigation or to prepare for trial and who is not expected to be called as a witness at trial. But a party may do so only:

        (i) as provided in Rule 35(b); or

        (ii) on showing exceptional circumstances under which it is impracticable for the party to obtain facts or opinions on the same subject by other means.

    (C) Payment. Unless manifest injustice would result, the court must require that the party seeking discovery:

        (i) pay the expert a reasonable fee for time spent in responding to discovery under Rule 26(b)(4)(A) or (B); and

        (ii) for discovery under (B), also pay the other party a fair portion of the fees and expenses it reasonably incurred in obtaining the expert's facts and opinions.

(5) Claiming Privilege or Protecting Trial-Preparation Materials

(A) Information Withheld. When a party withholds information otherwise discoverable by claiming that the information is privileged or subject to protection as trial-preparation material, the party must:

(i) expressly make the claim; and

(ii) describe the nature of the documents, communications, or things not produced or disclosed—and do so in a manner that, without revealing information itself privileged or protected, will enable other parties to assess the claim.

(B) Information Produced. If information produced in discovery is subject to a claim of privilege or of protection as trial-preparation material, the party making the claim may notify any party that received the information of the claim and the basis for it. After being notified, a party must promptly return, sequester, or destroy the specified information and any copies it has; must not use or disclose the information until the claim is resolved; must take reasonable steps to retrieve the information if the party disclosed it before being notified; and may promptly present the information to the court under seal for a determination of the claim. The producing party must preserve the information until the claim is resolved.

(c) PROTECTIVE ORDERS

(1) In General. A party or any person from whom discovery is sought may move for a protective order in the court where the action is pending—or as an alternative on matters relating to a deposition, in the court for the district where the deposition will be taken. The motion must include a certification that the movant has in good faith conferred or attempted to confer with other affected parties in an effort to resolve the dispute without court action. The court may, for good cause, issue an order to protect a party or person from annoyance, embarrassment, oppression, or undue burden or expense, including one or more of the following:

(A) forbidding the disclosure or discovery;

(B) specifying terms, including time and place, for the disclosure or discovery;

(C) prescribing a discovery method other than the one selected by the party seeking discovery;

(D) forbidding inquiry into certain matters, or limiting the scope of disclosure or discovery to certain matters;

(E) designating the persons who may be present while the discovery is conducted;

(F) requiring that a deposition be sealed and opened only on court order;

(G) requiring that a trade secret or other confidential research, development, or commercial information not be revealed or be revealed only in a specified way; and

(H) requiring that the parties simultaneously file specified documents or information in sealed envelopes, to be opened as the court directs.

(2) Ordering Discovery. If a motion for a protective order is wholly or partly denied, the court may, on just terms, order that any party or person provide or permit discovery.

(3) Awarding Expenses. Rule 37(a)(5) applies to the award of expenses.

(d) TIMING AND SEQUENCE OF DISCOVERY

(1)　Timing. A party may not seek discovery from any source before the parties have conferred as required by Rule 26(f), except in a proceeding exempted from initial disclosure under Rule 26(a)(1)(B), or when authorized by these rules, by stipulation, or by court order.

(2)　Sequence. Unless, on motion, the court orders otherwise for the parties' and witnesses' convenience and in the interest of justice:

(A) methods of discovery may be used in any sequence; and

(B) discovery by one party does not require any other party to delay its discovery.

(e) SUPPLEMENTING DISCLOSURES AND RESPONSES

(1)　In General. A party who has made a disclosure under Rule 26(a) — or who has responded to an interrogatory, request for production, or request for admission — must supplement or correct its disclosure or response:

(A) in a timely manner if the party learns that in some material respect the disclosure or response is incomplete or incorrect, and if the additional or corrective information has not otherwise been made known to the other parties during the discovery process or in writing; or

(B) as ordered by the court.

(2)　Expert Witness. For an expert whose report must be disclosed under Rule 26(a)(2)(B), the party's duty to supplement extends both to information included in the report and to information given during the expert's deposition. Any additions or changes to this information must be disclosed by the time the party's pretrial disclosures under Rule 26(a)(3) are due.

(f) CONFERENCE OF THE PARTIES; PLANNING FOR DISCOVERY

(1)　Conference Timing. Except in a proceeding exempted from initial disclosure under Rule 26(a)(1)(B) or when the court orders otherwise, the parties must confer as soon as practicable — and in any event at least 21 days before a scheduling conference is to be held or a scheduling order is due under Rule 16(b).

(2)　Conference Content; Parties' Responsibilities. In conferring, the parties must consider the nature and basis of their claims and defenses and the possibilities for promptly settling or resolving the case; make or arrange for the disclosures required by Rule 26(a)(1); discuss any issues about preserving discoverable information; and develop a proposed discovery plan. The attorneys of record and all unrepresented parties that have appeared in the case are jointly responsible for arranging the conference, for attempting in good faith to agree on the proposed discovery plan, and for submitting to the court within 14 days after the conference a written report outlining the plan. The court may order the parties or attorneys to attend the conference in person.

(3)　Discovery Plan. A discovery plan must state the parties' views and proposals on:

(A) what changes should be made in the timing, form, or requirement for disclosures under Rule 26(a), including a statement of when initial disclosures were made or will be made;

(B) the subjects on which discovery may be needed, when discovery should be completed, and whether discovery should be conducted in phases or be limited to or focused on particular issues;

(C) any issues about disclosure or discovery of electronically stored information, including the form or forms in which it should be produced;

(D) any issues about claims of privilege or of protection as trial-preparation materials, including—if the parties agree on a procedure to assert these claims after production—whether to ask the court to include their agreement in an order;

(E) what changes should be made in the limitations on discovery imposed under these rules or by local rule, and what other limitations should be imposed; and

(F) any other orders that the court should issue under Rule 26(c) or under Rule 16(b) and (c).

(4) Expedited Schedule. If necessary to comply with its expedited schedule for Rule 16(b) conferences, a court may by local rule:

(A) require the parties' conference to occur less than 21 days before the scheduling conference is held or a scheduling order is due under Rule 16(b); and

(B) require the written report outlining the discovery plan to be filed less than 14 days after the parties' conference, or excuse the parties from submitting a written report and permit them to report orally on their discovery plan at the Rule 16(b) conference.

(g) SIGNING DISCLOSURES AND DISCOVERY REQUESTS, RESPONSES, AND OBJECTIONS

(1) Signature Required; Effect of Signature. Every disclosure under Rule 26(a)(1) or (a)(3) and every discovery request, response, or objection must be signed by at least one attorney of record in the attorney's own name—or by the party personally, if unrepresented—and must state the signer's address, e-mail address, and telephone number. By signing, an attorney or party certifies that to the best of the person's knowledge, information, and belief formed after a reasonable inquiry:

(A) with respect to a disclosure, it is complete and correct as of the time it is made; and

(B) with respect to a discovery request, response, or objection, it is:

 (i) consistent with these rules and warranted by existing law or by a nonfrivolous argument for extending, modifying, or reversing existing law, or for establishing new law;

 (ii) not interposed for any improper purpose, such as to harass, cause unnecessary delay, or needlessly increase the cost of litigation; and

 (iii) neither unreasonable nor unduly burdensome or expensive, considering the needs of the case, prior discovery in the case, the amount in controversy, and the importance of the issues at stake in the action.

(2) Failure to Sign. Other parties have no duty to act on an unsigned disclosure, request, response, or objection until it is signed, and the court must strike it unless a signature is promptly supplied after the omission is called to the attorney's or party's attention.

(3)   Sanction for Improper Certification. If a certification violates this rule without substantial justification, the court, on motion or on its own, must impose an appropriate sanction on the signer, the party on whose behalf the signer was acting, or both. The sanction may include an order to pay the reasonable expenses, including attorney's fees, caused by the violation.

> **For further study, see**: Fed. R. Civ. P. Forms 50-52 at 106; 1938 Advisory Committee Notes at 111; 1948 Advisory Committee Notes at 113; 1970 Advisory Committee Notes at 125, 127; 1980 Advisory Committee Notes at 143; 1983 Advisory Committee Notes at 149; 1993 Advisory Committee Notes at 170; 2000 Advisory Committee Notes at 186; 2006 Advisory Committee Notes at 203; and Transnational Rules 18-23 at 287.

RULE 27. DEPOSITIONS TO PERPETUATE TESTIMONY

(a) BEFORE AN ACTION IS FILED

(1)   Petition. A person who wants to perpetuate testimony about any matter cognizable in a United States court may file a verified petition in the district court for the district where any expected adverse party resides. The petition must ask for an order authorizing the petitioner to depose the named persons in order to perpetuate their testimony. The petition must be titled in the petitioner's name and must show:

    (A) that the petitioner expects to be a party to an action cognizable in a United States court but cannot presently bring it or cause it to be brought;

    (B) the subject matter of the expected action and the petitioner's interest;

    (C) the facts that the petitioner wants to establish by the proposed testimony and the reasons to perpetuate it;

    (D) the names or a description of the persons whom the petitioner expects to be adverse parties and their addresses, so far as known; and

    (E) the name, address, and expected substance of the testimony of each deponent.

(2)   Notice and Service. At least 20 days before the hearing date, the petitioner must serve each expected adverse party with a copy of the petition and a notice stating the time and place of the hearing. The notice may be served either inside or outside the district or state in the manner provided in Rule 4. If that service cannot be made with reasonable diligence on an expected adverse party, the court may order service by publication or otherwise. The court must appoint an attorney to represent persons not served in the manner provided in Rule 4 and to cross-examine the deponent if an unserved person is not otherwise represented. If any expected adverse party is a minor or is incompetent, Rule 17(c) applies.

(3)   Order and Examination. If satisfied that perpetuating the testimony may prevent a failure or delay of justice, the court must issue an order that designates or describes the persons whose depositions may be taken, specifies the subject matter of the examinations, and states whether the depositions will be taken orally or by written interrogatories. The depositions may then be taken under these rules, and the court may issue orders like those authorized by Rules 34 and 35. A reference in these rules to the court where an action is pending means, for purposes of this rule, the court where the petition for the deposition was filed.

(4)   Using the Deposition. A deposition to perpetuate testimony may be used under Rule 32(a) in any later-filed district-court action involving the same subject matter if the deposition

either was taken under these rules or, although not so taken, would be admissible in evidence in the courts of the state where it was taken.

(b) PENDING APPEAL

(1)   In General. The court where a judgment has been rendered may, if an appeal has been taken or may still be taken, permit a party to depose witnesses to perpetuate their testimony for use in the event of further proceedings in that court.

(2)   Motion. The party who wants to perpetuate testimony may move for leave to take the depositions, on the same notice and service as if the action were pending in the district court. The motion must show:

    (A) the name, address, and expected substance of the testimony of each deponent; and

    (B) the reasons for perpetuating the testimony.

(3)   Court Order. If the court finds that perpetuating the testimony may prevent a failure or delay of justice, the court may permit the depositions to be taken and may issue orders like those authorized by Rules 34 and 35. The depositions may be taken and used as any other deposition taken in a pending district-court action.

(c) PERPETUATION BY AN ACTION

This rule does not limit a court's power to entertain an action to perpetuate testimony.

For further study, see: 1970 Advisory Committee Notes at 125.

RULE 28. PERSONS BEFORE WHOM DEPOSITIONS MAY BE TAKEN

(a) WITHIN THE UNITED STATES

(1)   In General. Within the United States or a territory or insular possession subject to United States jurisdiction, a deposition must be taken before:

    (A) an officer authorized to administer oaths either by federal law or by the law in the place of examination; or

    (B) a person appointed by the court where the action is pending to administer oaths and take testimony.

(2)   Definition of "Officer." The term "officer" in Rules 30, 31, and 32 includes a person appointed by the court under this rule or designated by the parties under Rule 29(a).

(b) IN A FOREIGN COUNTRY

(1)   In General. A deposition may be taken in a foreign country:

    (A) under an applicable treaty or convention;

    (B) under a letter of request, whether or not captioned a "letter rogatory";

    (C) on notice, before a person authorized to administer oaths either by federal law or by the law in the place of examination; or

    (D) before a person commissioned by the court to administer any necessary oath and take testimony.

(2)   Issuing a Letter of Request or a Commission. A letter of request, a commission, or both may be issued:

    (A) on appropriate terms after an application and notice of it; and

    (B) without a showing that taking the deposition in another manner is impracticable or inconvenient.

(3) Form of a Request, Notice, or Commission. When a letter of request or any other device is used according to a treaty or convention, it must be captioned in the form prescribed by that treaty or convention. A letter of request may be addressed "To the Appropriate Authority in [name of country]." A deposition notice or a commission must designate by name or descriptive title the person before whom the deposition is to be taken.

(4) Letter of Request—Admitting Evidence. Evidence obtained in response to a letter of request need not be excluded merely because it is not a verbatim transcript, because the testimony was not taken under oath, or because of any similar departure from the requirements for depositions taken within the United States.

(c) DISQUALIFICATION

A deposition must not be taken before a person who is any party's relative, employee, or attorney; who is related to or employed by any party's attorney; or who is financially interested in the action.

> **For further study, see**: 1963 Advisory Committee Notes at 114; 1970 Advisory Committee Notes at 125; and 1993 Advisory Committee Notes at 181.

RULE 29. STIPULATIONS ABOUT DISCOVERY PROCEDURE

Unless the court orders otherwise, the parties may stipulate that:

(a) a deposition may be taken before any person, at any time or place, on any notice, and in the manner specified—in which event it may be used in the same way as any other deposition; and

(b) other procedures governing or limiting discovery be modified—but a stipulation extending the time for any form of discovery must have court approval if it would interfere with the time set for completing discovery, for hearing a motion, or for a trial.

> **For further study, see**: 1970 Advisory Committee Notes at 125, 134; and 1993 Advisory Committee Notes at 182.

RULE 30. DEPOSITIONS BY ORAL EXAMINATION

(a) WHEN A DEPOSITION MAY BE TAKEN

(1) Without Leave. A party may, by oral questions, depose any person, including a party, without leave of court except as provided in Rule 30(a)(2). The deponent's attendance may be compelled by subpoena under Rule 45.

(2) With Leave. A party must obtain leave of court, and the court must grant leave to the extent consistent with Rule 26(b)(2):

 (A) if the parties have not stipulated to the deposition and:

   (i) the deposition would result in more than 10 depositions being taken under this rule or Rule 31 by the plaintiffs, or by the defendants, or by the third-party defendants;

   (ii) the deponent has already been deposed in the case; or

   (iii) the party seeks to take the deposition before the time specified in Rule 26(d), unless the party certifies in the notice, with supporting facts, that the deponent is expected to leave the United States and be unavailable for examination in this country after that time; or

 (B) if the deponent is confined in prison.

(b) NOTICE OF THE DEPOSITION; OTHER FORMAL REQUIREMENTS

(1) **Notice in General.** A party who wants to depose a person by oral questions must give reasonable written notice to every other party. The notice must state the time and place of the deposition and, if known, the deponent's name and address. If the name is unknown, the notice must provide a general description sufficient to identify the person or the particular class or group to which the person belongs.

(2) **Producing Documents.** If a subpoena duces tecum is to be served on the deponent, the materials designated for production, as set out in the subpoena, must be listed in the notice or in an attachment. The notice to a party deponent may be accompanied by a request under Rule 34 to produce documents and tangible things at the deposition.

(3) **Method of Recording**

    (A) **Method Stated in the Notice.** The party who notices the deposition must state in the notice the method for recording the testimony. Unless the court orders otherwise, testimony may be recorded by audio, audiovisual, or stenographic means. The noticing party bears the recording costs. Any party may arrange to transcribe a deposition.

    (B) **Additional Method.** With prior notice to the deponent and other parties, any party may designate another method for recording the testimony in addition to that specified in the original notice. That party bears the expense of the additional record or transcript unless the court orders otherwise.

(4) **By Remote Means.** The parties may stipulate — or the court may on motion order — that a deposition be taken by telephone or other remote means. For the purpose of this rule and Rules 28(a), 37(a)(2), and 37(b)(1), the deposition takes place where the deponent answers the questions.

(5) **Officer's Duties**

    (A) **Before the Deposition.** Unless the parties stipulate otherwise, a deposition must be conducted before an officer appointed or designated under Rule 28. The officer must begin the deposition with an on-the-record statement that includes:

        (i) the officer's name and business address;

        (ii) the date, time, and place of the deposition;

        (iii) the deponent's name;

        (iv) the officer's administration of the oath or affirmation to the deponent; and

        (v) the identity of all persons present.

    (B) **Conducting the Deposition: Avoiding Distortion.** If the deposition is recorded nonstenographically, the officer must repeat the items in Rule 30(b)(5)(A)(i)-(iii) at the beginning of each unit of the recording medium. The deponent's and attorneys' appearance or demeanor must not be distorted through recording techniques.

    (C) **After the Deposition.** At the end of each deposition, the officer must state on the record that the deposition is complete and must set out any stipulations made by the attorneys about custody of the transcript or recording and of the exhibits, or about any other pertinent matters.

(6) **Notice or Subpoena Directed to an Organization.** In its notice or subpoena, a party may name as the deponent a public or private corporation, a partnership, an association, a governmental agency, or other entity and must describe with reasonable particularity the matters for examination. The named organization must then designate one or more officers, directors, or managing agents, or designate other persons who consent to testify on its behalf; and it may

set out the matters on which each person designated will testify. A subpoena must advise a nonparty organization of its duty to make this designation. The persons designated must testify about information known or reasonably available to the organization. This paragraph (6) does not preclude a deposition by any other procedure allowed by these rules.

(c) EXAMINATION AND CROSS-EXAMINATION; RECORD OF THE EXAMINATION; OBJECTIONS; WRITTEN QUESTIONS

(1) Examination and Cross-Examination. The examination and cross-examination of a deponent proceed as they would at trial under the Federal Rules of Evidence, except Rules 103 and 615. After putting the deponent under oath or affirmation, the officer must record the testimony by the method designated under Rule 30(b)(3)(A). The testimony must be recorded by the officer personally or by a person acting in the presence and under the direction of the officer.

(2) Objections. An objection at the time of the examination—whether to evidence, to a party's conduct, to the officer's qualifications, to the manner of taking the deposition, or to any other aspect of the deposition—must be noted on the record, but the examination still proceeds; the testimony is taken subject to any objection. An objection must be stated concisely in a nonargumentative and nonsuggestive manner. A person may instruct a deponent not to answer only when necessary to preserve a privilege, to enforce a limitation ordered by the court, or to present a motion under 30(d)(3).

(3) Participating Through Written Questions. Instead of participating in the oral examination, a party may serve written questions in a sealed envelope on the party noticing the deposition, who must deliver them to the officer. The officer must ask the deponent these questions and record the answers verbatim.

(d) DURATION; SANCTION; MOTION TO TERMINATE OR LIMIT

(1) Duration. Unless otherwise stipulated or ordered by the court, a deposition is limited to 1 day of 7 hours. The court must allow additional time consistent with Rule 26(b)(2) if needed to fairly examine the deponent or if the deponent, another person, or any other circumstance impedes or delays the examination.

(2) Sanction. The court may impose an appropriate sanction—including the reasonable expenses and attorney's fees incurred by any party—on a person who impedes, delays, or frustrates the fair examination of the deponent.

(3) Motion to Terminate or Limit

(A) Grounds. At any time during a deposition, the deponent or a party may move to terminate or limit it on the ground that it is being conducted in bad faith or in a manner that unreasonably annoys, embarrasses, or oppresses the deponent or party. The motion may be filed in the court where the action is pending or the deposition is being taken. If the objecting deponent or party so demands, the deposition must be suspended for the time necessary to obtain an order.

(B) Order. The court may order that the deposition be terminated or may limit its scope and manner as provided in Rule 26(c). If terminated, the deposition may be resumed only by order of the court where the action is pending.

(C) Award of Expenses. Rule 37(a)(5) applies to the award of expenses.

(e) REVIEW BY THE WITNESS; CHANGES

(1) *Review; Statement of Changes.* On request by the deponent or a party before the deposition is completed, the deponent must be allowed 30 days after being notified by the officer that the transcript or recording is available in which:

> (A) to review the transcript or recording; and
>
> (B) if there are changes in form or substance, to sign a statement listing the changes and the reasons for making them.

(2) *Changes Indicated in the Officer's Certificate.* The officer must note in the certificate prescribed by Rule 30(f)(1) whether a review was requested and, if so, must attach any changes the deponent makes during the 30-day period.

(f) CERTIFICATION AND DELIVERY; EXHIBITS; COPIES OF THE TRANSCRIPT OR RECORDING; FILING

(1) *Certification and Delivery.* The officer must certify in writing that the witness was duly sworn and that the deposition accurately records the witness's testimony. The certificate must accompany the record of the deposition. Unless the court orders otherwise, the officer must seal the deposition in an envelope or package bearing the title of the action and marked "Deposition of [witness's name]" and must promptly send it to the attorney who arranged for the transcript or recording. The attorney must store it under conditions that will protect it against loss, destruction, tampering, or deterioration.

(2) *Documents and Tangible Things*

> (A) *Originals and Copies.* Documents and tangible things produced for inspection during a deposition must, on a party's request, be marked for identification and attached to the deposition. Any party may inspect and copy them. But if the person who produced them wants to keep the originals, the person may:
>
> > (i)   offer copies to be marked, attached to the deposition, and then used as originals — after giving all parties a fair opportunity to verify the copies by comparing them with the originals; or
> >
> > (ii)   give all parties a fair opportunity to inspect and copy the originals after they are marked — in which event the originals may be used as if attached to the deposition.
>
> (B) *Order Regarding the Originals.* Any party may move for an order that the originals be attached to the deposition pending final disposition of the case.

(3) *Copies of the Transcript or Recording.* Unless otherwise stipulated or ordered by the court, the officer must retain the stenographic notes of a deposition taken stenographically or a copy of the recording of a deposition taken by another method. When paid reasonable charges, the officer must furnish a copy of the transcript or recording to any party or the deponent.

(4) *Notice of Filing.* A party who files the deposition must promptly notify all other parties of the filing.

(g) FAILURE TO ATTEND A DEPOSITION OR SERVE A SUBPOENA; EXPENSES

A party who, expecting a deposition to be taken, attends in person or by an attorney may recover reasonable expenses for attending, including attorney's fees, if the noticing party failed to:

(1)   attend and proceed with the deposition; or

(2)   serve a subpoena on a nonparty deponent, who consequently did not attend.

For further study, see: 1970 Advisory Committee Notes at 125, 134; 1971 Advisory Committee Notes at 142; 1993 Advisory Committee Notes at 182; and 2000 Advisory Committee Notes at 189.

RULE 31. DEPOSITIONS BY WRITTEN QUESTIONS

(a) WHEN A DEPOSITION MAY BE TAKEN

(1)   Without Leave. A party may, by written questions, depose any person, including a party, without leave of court except as provided in Rule 31(a)(2). The deponent's attendance may be compelled by subpoena under Rule 45.

(2)   With Leave. A party must obtain leave of court, and the court must grant leave to the extent consistent with Rule 26(b)(2):

   (A) if the parties have not stipulated to the deposition and:

   (i)   the deposition would result in more than 10 depositions being taken under this rule or Rule 30 by the plaintiffs, or by the defendants, or by the third-party defendants;

   (ii)   the deponent has already been deposed in the case; or

   (iii) the party seeks to take a deposition before the time specified in Rule 26(d); or

   (B) if the deponent is confined to prison.

(3)   Service; Required Notice. A party who wants to depose a person by written questions must serve them on every other party, with a notice stating, if known, the deponent's name and address. If the name is unknown, the notice must provide a general description sufficient to identify the person or the particular class or group to which the person belongs. The notice must also state the name or descriptive title and the address of the officer before whom the deposition will be taken.

(4)   Questions Directed to an Organization. A public or private corporation, a partnership, an association, or a governmental agency may be deposed by written questions in accordance with Rule 30(b)(6).

(5)   Questions from Other Parties. Any questions to the deponent from other parties must be served on all parties as follows: cross-questions, within 14 days after being served with the notice and direct questions; redirect questions, within 7 days after being served with cross-questions; and recross-questions, within 7 days after being served with redirect questions. The court may, for good cause, extend or shorten these times.

(b) DELIVERY TO THE OFFICER; OFFICER'S DUTIES

The party who noticed the deposition must deliver to the officer a copy of all the questions served and of the notice. The officer must promptly proceed in the manner provided in Rule 30(c), (e), and (f) to:

(1)   take the deponent's testimony in response to the questions;

(2)   prepare and certify the deposition; and

(3)   send it to the party, attaching a copy of the questions and of the notice.

(c) NOTICE OF COMPLETION OR FILING

(1) **Completion.** The party who noticed the deposition must notify all other parties when it is completed.

(2) **Filing.** A party who files the deposition must promptly notify all other parties of the filing.

For further study, see: 1970 Advisory Committee Notes at 125.

RULE 32. USING DEPOSITIONS IN COURT PROCEEDINGS

(a) USING DEPOSITIONS

(1) **In General.** At a hearing or trial, all or part of a deposition may be used against a party on these conditions:

(A) the party was present or represented at the taking of the deposition or had reasonable notice of it;

(B) it is used to the extent it would be admissible under the Federal Rules of Evidence if the deponent were present and testifying; and

(C) the use is allowed by Rule 32(a)(2) through (8).

(2) **Impeachment and Other Uses.** Any party may use a deposition to contradict or impeach the testimony given by the deponent as a witness, or for any other purpose allowed by the Federal Rules of Evidence.

(3) **Deposition of Party, Agent, or Designee.** An adverse party may use for any purpose the deposition of a party or anyone who, when deposed, was the party's officer, director, managing agent, or designee under Rule 30(b)(6) or 31(a)(4).

(4) **Unavailable Witness.** A party may use for any purpose the deposition of a witness, whether or not a party, if the court finds:

(A) that the witness is dead;

(B) that the witness is more than 100 miles from the place of hearing or trial or is outside the United States, unless it appears that the witness's absence was procured by the party offering the deposition;

(C) that the witness cannot attend or testify because of age, illness, infirmity, or imprisonment;

(D) that the party offering the deposition could not procure the witness's attendance by subpoena; or

(E) on motion and notice, that exceptional circumstances make it desirable—in the interest of justice and with due regard to the importance of live testimony in open court—to permit the deposition to be used.

(5) **Limitations on Use**

(A) **Deposition Taken on Short Notice.** A deposition must not be used against a party who, having received less than 11 days' notice of the deposition, promptly moved for a protective order under Rule 26(c)(1)(B) requesting that it not be taken or be taken at a different time or place—and this motion was still pending when the deposition was taken.

(B) **Unavailable Deponent; Party Could Not Obtain an Attorney.** A deposition taken without leave of court under the unavailability provision of Rule 30(a)(2)(A)(iii) must not be used against a party who shows that, when served with the notice, it could not, despite diligent efforts, obtain an attorney to represent it at the deposition.

(6) Using Part of a Deposition. If a party offers in evidence only part of a deposition, an adverse party may require the offeror to introduce other parts that in fairness should be considered with the part introduced, and any party may itself introduce any other parts.

(7) Substituting a Party. Substituting a party under Rule 25 does not affect the right to use a deposition previously taken.

(8) Deposition Taken in an Earlier Action. A deposition lawfully taken and, if required, filed in any federal- or state-court action may be used in a later action involving the same subject matter between the same parties, or their representatives or successors in interest, to the same extent as if taken in the later action. A deposition previously taken may also be used as allowed by the Federal Rules of Evidence.

(b) OBJECTIONS TO ADMISSIBILITY

Subject to Rules 28(b) and 32(d)(3), an objection may be made at a hearing or trial to the admission of any deposition testimony that would be inadmissible if the witness were present and testifying.

(c) FORM OF PRESENTATION

Unless the court orders otherwise, a party must provide a transcript of any deposition testimony the party offers, but may provide the court with the testimony in nontranscript form as well. On any party's request, deposition testimony offered in a jury trial for any purpose other than impeachment must be presented in nontranscript form, if available, unless the court for good cause orders otherwise.

(d) WAIVER OF OBJECTIONS

(1) To the Notice. An objection to an error or irregularity in a deposition notice is waived unless promptly served in writing on the party giving the notice.

(2) To the Officer's Qualification. An objection based on disqualification of the officer before whom a deposition is to be taken is waived if not made:

(A) before the deposition begins; or

(B) promptly after the basis for disqualification becomes known or, with reasonable diligence, could have been known.

(3) To the Taking of the Deposition

(A) Objection to Competence, Relevance, or Materiality. An objection to a deponent's competence — or to the competence, relevance, or materiality of testimony — is not waived by a failure to make the objection before or during the deposition, unless the ground for it might have been corrected at that time.

(B) Objection to an Error or Irregularity. An objection to an error or irregularity at an oral examination is waived if:

(i)   it relates to the manner of taking the deposition, the form of a question or answer, the oath or affirmation, a party's conduct, or other matters that might have been corrected at that time; and

(ii)   it is not timely made during the deposition.

(C) Objection to a Written Question. An objection to the form of a written question under Rule 31 is waived if not served in writing on the party submitting the question within the time for serving responsive questions or, if the question is a recross-question, within 5 days after being served with it.

(4) To Completing and Returning the Deposition. An objection to how the officer transcribed the testimony—or prepared, signed, certified, sealed, endorsed, sent, or otherwise dealt with the deposition—is waived unless a motion to suppress is made promptly after the error or irregularity becomes known or, with reasonable diligence, could have been known.

For further study, see: 1970 Advisory Committee Notes at 125.

RULE 33. INTERROGATORIES TO PARTIES

(a) IN GENERAL

(1) Number. Unless otherwise stipulated or ordered by the court, a party may serve on any other party no more than 25 written interrogatories, including all discrete subparts. Leave to serve additional interrogatories may be granted to the extent consistent with Rule 26(b)(2).

(2) Scope. An interrogatory may relate to any matter that may be inquired into under Rule 26(b). An interrogatory is not objectionable merely because it asks for an opinion or contention that relates to fact or the application of law to fact, but the court may order that the interrogatory need not be answered until designated discovery is complete, or until a pretrial conference or some other time.

(b) ANSWERS AND OBJECTIONS

(1) Responding Party. The interrogatories must be answered:

(A) by the party to whom they are directed; or

(B) if that party is a public or private corporation, a partnership, an association, or a governmental agency, by any officer or agent, who must furnish the information available to the party.

(2) Time to Respond. The responding party must serve its answers and any objections within 30 days after being served with the interrogatories. A shorter or longer time may be stipulated to under Rule 29 or be ordered by the court.

(3) Answering Each Interrogatory. Each interrogatory must, to the extent it is not objected to, be answered separately and fully in writing under oath.

(4) Objections. The grounds for objecting to an interrogatory must be stated with specificity. Any ground not stated in a timely objection is waived unless the court, for good cause, excuses the failure.

(5) Signature. The person who makes the answers must sign them, and the attorney who objects must sign any objections.

(c) USE

An answer to an interrogatory may be used to the extent allowed by the Federal Rules of Evidence.

(d) OPTION TO PRODUCE BUSINESS RECORDS

If the answer to an interrogatory may be determined by examining, auditing, compiling, abstracting, or summarizing a party's business records (including electronically stored information), and if the burden of deriving or ascertaining the answer will be substantially the same for either party, the responding party may answer by

(1)   specifying the records that must be reviewed, in sufficient detail to enable the interrogating party to locate and identify them as readily as the responding party could; and

(2)   giving the interrogating party a reasonable opportunity to examine and audit the records and to make copies, compilations, abstracts, or summaries.

For further study, see: 1970 Advisory Committee Notes at 125, 136; 1980 Advisory Committee Notes at 143; and 1993 Advisory Committee Notes at 183.

RULE 34. PRODUCING DOCUMENTS, ELECTRONICALLY STORED INFORMATION, AND TANGIBLE THINGS, OR ENTERING ONTO LAND, FOR INSPECTION AND OTHER PURPOSES

(a) IN GENERAL

A party may serve on any other party a request within the scope of Rule 26(b):

(1)   to produce and permit the requesting party or its representative to inspect, copy, test, or sample the following items in the responding party's possession, custody, or control:

(A) any designated documents or electronically stored information—including writings, drawings, graphs, charts, photographs, sound recordings, images, and other data or data compilations—stored in any medium from which information can be obtained either directly or, if necessary, after translation by the responding party into a reasonably usable form; or

(B) any designated tangible things; or

(2)   to permit entry onto designated land or other property possessed or controlled by the responding party, so that the requesting party may inspect, measure, survey, photograph, test, or sample the property or any designated object or operation on it.

(b) PROCEDURE

(1)   Contents of the Request. The request:

(A) must describe with reasonable particularity each item or category of items to be inspected;

(B) must specify a reasonable time, place, and manner for the inspection and for performing the related acts; and

(C) may specify the form or forms in which electronically stored information is to be produced.

(2)   Responses and Objections

(A) Time to Respond. The party to whom the request is directed must respond in writing within 30 days after being served. A shorter or longer time may be stipulated to under Rule 29 or be ordered by the court.

(B) Responding to Each Item. For each item or category, the response must either state that inspection and related activities will be permitted as requested or state an objection to the request, including the reasons.

(C) Objections. An objection to part of a request must specify the part and permit inspection of the rest.

(D) Responding to a Request for Production of Electronically Stored Information. The response may state an objection to a requested form for producing electronically stored information. If the responding party objects to a requested form—or if no form was specified in the request—the party must state the form or forms it intends to use.

    (E) *Producing the Documents or Electronically Stored Information.* Unless otherwise stipulated or ordered by the court, these procedures apply to producing documents or electronically stored information:

        (i)   A party must produce documents as they are kept in the usual course of business or must organize and label them to correspond to the categories in the request;

        (ii)   If a request does not specify a form for producing electronically stored information, a party must produce it in a form or forms in which it is ordinarily maintained or in a reasonably usable form or forms; and

        (iii) A party need not produce the same electronically stored information in more than one form.

(c) NONPARTIES

As provided in Rule 45, a nonparty may be compelled to produce documents and tangible things or to permit an inspection.

> **For further study, see**: Fed. R. Civ. P. Form 50 at 106; 1948 Advisory Committee Notes at 113; 1970 Advisory Committee Notes at 125, 137; 1980 Advisory Committee Notes at 143; and 2006 Advisory Committee Notes at 207.

RULE 35. PHYSICAL AND MENTAL EXAMINATIONS

(a) ORDER FOR AN EXAMINATION

    (1)   *In General.* The court where the action is pending may order a party whose mental or physical condition—including blood group—is in controversy to submit to a physical or mental examination by a suitably licensed or certified examiner. The court has the same authority to order a party to produce for examination a person who is in its custody or under its legal control.

    (2)   *Motion and Notice; Contents of the Order.* The order:

        (A) may be made only on motion for good cause and on notice to all parties and the person to be examined; and

        (B) must specify the time, place, manner, conditions, and scope of the examination, as well as the person or persons who will perform it.

(b) EXAMINER'S REPORT

    (1)   *Request by the Party or Person Examined.* The party who moved for the examination must, on request, deliver to the requester a copy of the examiner's report, together with like reports of all earlier examinations of the same condition. The request may be made by the party against whom the examination order was issued or by the person examined.

    (2)   *Contents.* The examiner's report must be in writing and must set out in detail the examiner's findings, including diagnoses, conclusions, and the results of any tests.

    (3)   *Request by the Moving Party.* After delivering the reports, the party who moved for the examination may request—and is entitled to receive—from the party against whom the examination order was issued like reports of all earlier or later examinations of the same condition. But those reports need not be delivered by the party with custody or control of the person examined if the party shows that it could not obtain them.

    (4)   *Waiver of Privilege.* By requesting and obtaining the examiner's report, or by deposing the examiner, the party examined waives any privilege it may have—in that action or any other

action involving the same controversy—concerning testimony about all examinations of the same condition.

(5)   Failure to Deliver a Report. The court on motion may order—on just terms—that a party deliver the report of an examination. If the report is not provided, the court may exclude the examiner's testimony at trial.

(6)   Scope. The subdivision (b) applies also to an examination made by the parties' agreement, unless the agreement states otherwise. This subdivision does not preclude obtaining an examiner's report or deposing an examiner under other rules.

> **For further study, see**: 1970 Advisory Committee Notes at 125, 138; and 1991 Advisory Committee Notes at 153.

RULE 36. REQUESTS FOR ADMISSION

(a) SCOPE AND PROCEDURE

(1)   Scope. A party may serve on any other party a written request to admit, for purposes of the pending action only, the truth of any matters within the scope of Rule 26(b)(1) relating to:

    (A) facts, the application of law to fact, or opinions about either; and

    (B) the genuineness of any described document.

(2)   Form; Copy of a Document. Each matter must be separately stated. A request to admit the genuineness of a document must be accompanied by a copy of the document unless it is, or has been, otherwise furnished or made available for inspection and copying.

(3)   Time to Respond; Effect of Not Responding. A matter is admitted unless, within 30 days after being served, the party to whom the request is directed serves on the requesting party a written answer or objection addressed to the matter and signed by the party or its attorney. A shorter or longer time for responding may be stipulated to under Rule 29 or be ordered by the court.

(4)   Answer. If a matter is not admitted, the answer must specifically deny it or state in detail why the answering party cannot truthfully admit or deny it. A denial must fairly respond to the substance of the matter; and when good faith requires that a party qualify an answer or deny only a part of a matter, the answer must specify the part admitted and qualify or deny the rest. The answering party may assert lack of knowledge or information as a reason for failing to admit or deny only if the party states that it has made reasonable inquiry and that the information it knows or can readily obtain is insufficient to enable it to admit or deny.

(5)   Objections. The grounds for objecting to a request must be stated. A party must not object solely on the ground that the request presents a genuine issue for trial.

(6)   Motion Regarding the Sufficiency of an Answer or Objection. The requesting party may move to determine the sufficiency of an answer or objection. Unless the court finds an objection justified, it must order that an answer be served. On finding that an answer does not comply with this rule, the court may order either that the matter is admitted or that an amended answer be served. The court may defer its final decision until a pretrial conference or a specified time before trial. Rule 37(a)(5) applies to an award of expenses.

(b) EFFECT OF AN ADMISSION; WITHDRAWING OR AMENDING IT

A matter admitted under this rule is conclusively established unless the court, on motion, permits the admission to be withdrawn or amended. Subject to Rule 16(e), the court may permit withdrawal or amendment if it would promote the presentation of the merits of the action and if the court is not persuaded that it would prejudice the requesting party in maintaining or defending the action on the merits. An admission under this rule is not an admission for any other purpose and cannot be used against the party in any other proceeding.

For further study, see: Fed. R. Civ. P. Form 51 at 107; and 1970 Advisory Committee Notes at 125, 138.

RULE 37. FAILURE TO MAKE DISCLOSURES OR TO COOPERATE IN DISCOVERY; SANCTIONS

(a) MOTION FOR AN ORDER COMPELLING DISCLOSURE OR DISCOVERY

(1)   In General. On notice to other parties and all affected persons, a party may move for an order compelling disclosure or discovery. The motion must include a certification that the movant has in good faith conferred or attempted to confer with the person or party failing to make disclosure or discovery in an effort to obtain it without court action.

(2)   Appropriate Court. A motion for an order to a party must be made in the court where the action is pending. A motion for an order to a nonparty must be made in the court where the discovery is or will be taken.

(3)   Specific Motions

(A) To Compel Disclosure. If a party fails to make a disclosure required by Rule 26(a), any other party may move to compel disclosure and for appropriate sanctions.

(B) To Compel a Discovery Response. A party seeking discovery may move for an order compelling an answer, designation, production, or inspection. This motion may be made if:

(i)   a deponent fails to answer a question asked under Rule 30 or 31;

(ii)   a corporation or other entity fails to make a designation under Rule 30(b)(6) or 31(a)(4);

(iii)   a party fails to answer an interrogatory submitted under Rule 33; or

(iv)   a party fails to respond that inspection will be permitted—or fails to permit inspection—as requested under Rule 34.

(C) Related to a Deposition. When taking an oral deposition, the party asking a question may complete or adjourn the examination before moving for an order.

(4)   Evasive or Incomplete Disclosure, Answer, or Response. For purposes of this subdivision (a), an evasive or incomplete disclosure, answer, or response must be treated as a failure to disclose, answer, or respond.

(5)   Payment of Expenses; Protective Orders

(A) If the Motion Is Granted (or Disclosure or Discovery Is Provided After Filing). If the motion is granted—or if the disclosure or requested discovery is provided after the motion was filed—the court must, after giving an opportunity to be heard, require the party or deponent whose conduct necessitated the motion, the party or attorney advising that conduct, or both to pay the movant's reasonable expenses incurred in making the motion, including attorney's fees. But the court must not order this payment if:

(i)   the movant filed the motion before attempting in good faith to obtain the disclosure or discovery without court action;

(ii)   the opposing party's nondisclosure, response, or objection was substantially justified; or

(iii)   other circumstances make an award of expenses unjust.

(B) If the Motion is Denied. If the motion is denied, the court may issue any protective order authorized under Rule 26(c) and must, after giving an opportunity to be heard, require the movant, the attorney filing the motion, or both to pay the party or deponent who opposed the motion its reasonable expenses incurred in opposing the motion, including attorney's fees. But the court must not order this payment if the motion was substantially justified or other circumstances make an award of expenses unjust.

(C) If the Motion is Granted in Part and Denied in Part. If the motion is granted in part and denied in part, the court may issue any protective order authorized under Rule 26(c) and may, after giving an opportunity to be heard, apportion the reasonable expenses for the motion.

(b) FAILURE TO COMPLY WITH A COURT ORDER

(1) Sanctions in the District Where the Deposition Is Taken. If the court where the discovery is taken orders a deponent to be sworn or to answer a question and the deponent fails to obey, the failure may be treated as contempt of court.

(2) Sanctions in the District Where the Action Is Pending

(A) For Not Obeying a Discovery Order. If a party or a party's officer, director, or managing agent — or a witness designated under Rule 30(b)(6) or 31(a)(4) — fails to obey an order to provide or permit discovery, including an order under Rule 26(f), 35, or 37(a), the court where the action is pending may issue further just orders. They may include the following:

(i) directing that the matters embraced in the order or other designated facts be taken as established for purposes of the action, as the prevailing party claims;

(ii) prohibiting the disobedient party from supporting or opposing designated claims or defenses, or from introducing designated matters in evidence;

(iii) striking pleadings in whole or in part;

(iv) staying further proceedings until the order is obeyed;

(v) dismissing the action or proceeding in whole or in part;

(vi) rendering a default judgment against the disobedient party; or

(vii) treating as contempt of court the failure to obey any order except an order to submit to a physical or mental examination.

(B) For Not Producing a Person for Examination. If a party fails to comply with an order under Rule 35(a) requiring it to produce another person for examination, the court may issue any of the orders listed in Rule 37(b)(2)(A)(i)-(vi), unless the disobedient party shows that it cannot produce the other person.

(C) Payment of Expenses. Instead of or in addition to the orders above, the court may order the disobedient party, the attorney advising that party, or both to pay the reasonable expenses, including attorney's fees, caused by the failure, unless the failure was substantially justified or other circumstances make an award of expenses unjust.

(c) FAILURE TO DISCLOSE, TO SUPPLEMENT AN EARLIER RESPONSE, OR TO ADMIT

(1) Failure to Disclose or Supplement. If a party fails to provide information or identify a witness as required by Rule 26(a) or (e), the party is not allowed to use that information or witness to supply evidence on a motion, at a hearing, or at a trial, unless the failure was

substantially justified or is harmless. In addition to or instead of this sanction, the court, on motion and after giving an opportunity to be heard:

    (A) may order payment of the reasonable expenses, including attorney's fees, caused by the failure;

    (B) may inform the jury of the party's failure; and

    (C) may impose other appropriate sanctions, including any of the orders listed in Rule 37(b)(2)(A)(i)-(vi).

(2) *Failure to Admit.* If a party fails to admit what is requested under Rule 36 and if the requesting party later proves a document to be genuine or the matter true, the requesting party may move that the party who failed to admit pay the reasonable expenses, including attorney's fees, incurred in making that proof. The court must so order unless:

    (A) the request was held objectionable under Rule 36(a);

    (B) the admission sought was of no substantial importance;

    (C) the party failing to admit had a reasonable ground to believe that it might prevail on the matter; or

    (D) there was other good reason for the failure to admit.

(d) PARTY'S FAILURE TO ATTEND ITS OWN DEPOSITION, SERVE ANSWERS TO INTERROGATORIES, OR RESPOND TO A REQUEST FOR INSPECTION

    (1) In General

        (A) *Motion; Ground for Sanctions.* The court where the action is pending may, on motion, order sanctions if:

            (i)   a party or a party's officer, director, or managing agent—or a person designated under Rule 30(b)(6) or 31(a)(4)—fails, after being served with proper notice, to appear for that person's deposition; or

            (ii) a party, after being properly served with interrogatories under Rule 33 or a request for inspection under Rule 34, fails to serve its answers, objections, or written response.

        (B) *Certification.* A motion for sanctions for failing to answer or respond must include a certification that the movant has in good faith conferred or attempted to confer with the party failing to act in an effort to obtain the answer or response without court action.

(2) *Unacceptable Excuse for Failing to Act.* A failure described in Rule 37(d)(1)(A) is not excused on the ground that the discovery sought was objectionable, unless the party failing to act has a pending motion for a protective order under Rule 26(c).

(3) *Types of Sanctions.* Sanctions may include any of the orders listed in Rule 37(b)(2)(A)(i)-(vi). Instead of or in addition to these sanctions, the court must require the party failing to act, the attorney advising that party, or both to pay the reasonable expenses, including attorney's fees, caused by the failure, unless the failure was substantially justified or other circumstances make an award of expenses unjust.

(e) FAILURE TO PROVIDE ELECTRONICALLY STORED INFORMATION

Absent exceptional circumstances, a court may not impose sanctions under these rules on a party for failing to provide electronically stored information lost as a result of the routine, good-faith operation of an electronic information system.

(f) FAILURE TO PARTICIPATE IN FRAMING A DISCOVERY PLAN

If a party or its attorney fails to participate in good faith in developing and submitting a proposed discovery plan as required by Rule 26(f), the court may, after giving an opportunity to be heard, require that party or attorney to pay to any other party the reasonable expenses, including attorney's fees, caused by the failure.

> **For further study, see**: 1970 Advisory Committee Notes at 125, 140; 1980 Advisory Committee Notes at 143; 1993 Advisory Committee Notes at 184; 2000 Advisory Committee Notes at 190; 2006 Advisory Committee Notes at 208; 2007 Advisory Committee Notes at 212; and Transnational Rules 20-23 at 377-379.

VI. Trials

RULE 38. RIGHT TO A JURY TRIAL; DEMAND

(a) RIGHT PRESERVED

The right of trial by jury as declared by the Seventh Amendment to the Constitution—or as provided by a federal statute—is preserved to the parties inviolate.

(b) DEMAND

On any issue triable of right by a jury, a party may demand a jury trial by:

(1)   serving the other parties with a written demand—which may be included in a pleading—no later than 10 days after the last pleading directed to the issue is served; and

(2)   filing the demand in accordance with Rule 5(d).

(c) SPECIFYING ISSUES

In its demand, a party may specify the issues that it wishes to have tried by a jury; otherwise, it is considered to have demanded a jury trial on all the issues so triable. If the party has demanded a jury trial on only some issues, any other party may—within 10 days after being served with the demand or within a shorter time ordered by the court—serve a demand for a jury trial on any other or all factual issues triable by jury.

(d) WAIVER; WITHDRAWAL

A party waives a jury trial unless its demand is properly served and filed. A proper demand may be withdrawn only if the parties consent.

(e) ADMIRALTY AND MARITIME CLAIMS

These rules do not create a right to a jury trial on issues in a claim that is an admiralty or maritime claim under Rule 9(h).

> **For further study, see**: 1938 Advisory Committee Notes at 111.

RULE 39. TRIAL BY JURY OR BY THE COURT

(a) WHEN A DEMAND IS MADE

When a jury trial has been demanded under Rule 38, the action must be designated on the docket as a jury action. The trial on all issues so demanded must be by jury unless:

(1)   the parties or their attorneys file a stipulation to a nonjury trial or so stipulate on the record; or

(2)   the court, on motion or on its own, finds that on some or all of those issues there is no federal right to a jury trial.

(b) WHEN NO DEMAND IS MADE

Issues on which a jury trial is not properly demanded are to be tried by the court. But the court may, on motion, order a jury trial on any issue for which a jury might have been demanded.

(c) ADVISORY JURY; JURY TRIAL BY CONSENT

In an action not triable of right by a jury, the court, on motion or on its own:

(1)   may try any issue with an advisory jury; or

(2)   may, with the parties' consent, try any issue by a jury whose verdict has the same effect as if a jury trial had been a matter of right, unless the action is against the United States and a federal statute provides for a nonjury trial

RULE 40. SCHEDULING CASES FOR TRIAL

Each court must provide by rule for scheduling trials. The court must give priority to actions entitled to priority by a federal statute.

RULE 41. DISMISSAL OF ACTIONS

(a) VOLUNTARY DISMISSAL

    (1)   By the Plaintiff

        (A) Without a Court Order. Subject to Rules 23(e), 23.1(c), 23.2, and 66 and any applicable federal statute, the plaintiff may dismiss an action without a court order by filing:

           (i)   a notice of dismissal before the opposing party serves either an answer or a motion for summary judgment; or

           (ii)   a stipulation of dismissal signed by all parties who have appeared.

        (B) Effect. Unless the notice or stipulation states otherwise, the dismissal is without prejudice. But if the plaintiff previously dismissed any federal- or state-court action based on or including the same claim, a notice of dismissal operates as an adjudication on the merits.

    (2)   By Court Order; Effect. Except as provided in Rule 41(a)(1), an action may be dismissed at the plaintiff's request only by court order, on terms that the court considers proper. If a defendant has pleaded a counterclaim before being served with the plaintiff's motion to dismiss, the action may be dismissed over the defendant's objection only if the counterclaim can remain pending for independent adjudication. Unless the order states otherwise, a dismissal under this paragraph (2) is without prejudice.

(b) INVOLUNTARY DISMISSAL; EFFECT

If the plaintiff fails to prosecute or to comply with these rules or a court order, a defendant may move to dismiss the action or any claim against it. Unless the dismissal order states otherwise, a dismissal under this subdivision (b) and any dismissal not under this rule—except one for lack of jurisdiction, improper venue, or failure to join a party under Rule 19—operates as an adjudication on the merits.

(c) DISMISSING A COUNTERCLAIM, CROSSCLAIM, OR THIRD-PARTY CLAIM

This rule applies to a dismissal of any counterclaim, crossclaim, or third-party claim. A claimant's voluntary dismissal under Rule 41(a)(1)(A)(i) must be made:

(1)   before a responsive pleading is served; or

(2)   if there is no responsive pleading, before evidence is introduced at a hearing or trial.

(d) COSTS OF A PREVIOUSLY DISMISSED ACTION

If a plaintiff who previously dismissed an action in any court files an action based on or including the same claim against the same defendant, the court:

(1)   may order the plaintiff to pay all or part of the costs of that previous action; and

(2)   may stay the proceedings until the plaintiff has complied.

> **For further study, see**: Restatement (Second) of Judgments §§ 19 and 20 at 225; and Transnational Rule 15 at 284.

RULE 42. CONSOLIDATION; SEPARATE TRIALS

(a) CONSOLIDATION

If actions before the court involve a common question of law or fact, the court may:

(1)   join for hearing or trial any or all matters at issue in the actions;

(2)   consolidate the actions; or

(3)   issue any other orders to avoid unnecessary cost or delay.

(b) SEPARATE TRIALS

For convenience, to avoid prejudice, or to expedite and economize, the court may order a separate trial of one or more separate issues, claims, crossclaims, counterclaims, or third-party claims. When ordering a separate trial, the court must preserve any federal right to a jury trial.

> **For further study, see**: Transnational Rules 5 & 18 at 280.

RULE 43. TAKING TESTIMONY

(a) IN OPEN COURT

At trial, the witnesses' testimony must be taken in open court unless a federal statute, the Federal Rules of Evidence, these rules, or other rules adopted by the Supreme Court provide otherwise. For good cause in compelling circumstances and with appropriate safeguards, the court may permit testimony in open court by contemporaneous transmission from a different location.

(b) AFFIRMATION INSTEAD OF AN OATH

When these rules require an oath, a solemn affirmation suffices.

(c) EVIDENCE ON A MOTION

When a motion relies on facts outside the record, the court may hear the matter on affidavits or may hear it wholly or partly on oral testimony or on depositions.

(d) INTERPRETER

The court may appoint an interpreter of its choosing; fix reasonable compensation to be paid from funds provided by law or by one or more parties; and tax the compensation as costs.

RULE 44. PROVING AN OFFICIAL RECORD

(a) MEANS OF PROVING

(1)   Domestic Record. Each of the following evidences an official record—or an entry in it—that is otherwise admissible and is kept within the United States, any state, district, or commonwealth, or any territory subject to the administrative or judicial jurisdiction of the United States:

    (A) an official publication of the record; or

    (B) a copy attested by the officer with legal custody of the record—or by the officer's deputy—and accompanied by a certificate that the officer has custody. The certificate must be made under seal:

        (i)   by a judge of a court of record in the district or political subdivision where the record is kept; or

        (ii) by any public officer with a seal of office and with official duties in the district or political subdivision where the record is kept.

(2)   Foreign Record

    (A) In General. Each of the following evidences a foreign official record—or an entry in it—that is otherwise admissible:

        (i)   an official publication of the record; or

        (ii) the record—or a copy—that is attested by an authorized person and is accompanied either by a final certification of genuineness or by a certification under a treaty or convention to which the United States and the country where the record is located are parties.

    (B) Final Certification of Genuineness. A final certification must certify the genuineness of the signature and official position of the attester or of any foreign official whose certificate of genuineness relates to the attestation or is in a chain of certificates of genuineness relating to the attestation. A final certification may be made by a secretary of a United States embassy or legation; by a consul general, vice consul, or consular agent of the United States; or by a diplomatic or consular official of the foreign country assigned or accredited to the United States.

    (C) Other Means of Proof. If all parties have had a reasonable opportunity to investigate a foreign record's authenticity and accuracy, the court may, for good cause, either:

        (i)   admit an attested copy without final certification; or

        (ii) permit the record to be evidenced by an attested summary with or without a final certification.

(b) LACK OF A RECORD

A written statement that a diligent search of designated records revealed no record or entry of a specified tenor is admissible as evidence that the records contain no such record or entry. For domestic records, the statement must be authenticated under Rule 44(a)(1). For foreign records, the statement must comply with (a)(2)(C)(ii).

(c) OTHER PROOF

A party may prove an official record—or an entry or lack of an entry in it—by any other method authorized by law.

RULE 44.1. DETERMINING FOREIGN LAW

A party who intends to raise an issue about a foreign country's law must give notice by a pleading or other writing. In determining foreign law, the court may consider any relevant material or source, including testimony, whether or not submitted by a party or admissible under the Federal Rules of Evidence. The court's determination must be treated as a ruling on a question of law.

For further study, see: 1966 Advisory Committee Notes at 124.

RULE 45. SUBPOENA

(a) IN GENERAL

   (1) Form and Contents

      (A) Requirements—In General. Every subpoena must:

         (i)   state the court from which it issued;

         (ii) state the title of the action, the court in which it is pending, and its civil-action number;

         (iii) command each person to whom it is directed to do the following at a specified time and place: attend and testify; produce designated documents, electronically stored information, or tangible things in that person's possession, custody, or control; or permit the inspection of the premises; and

         (iv) set out the text of Rule 45(c) and (d).

      (B) Command to Attend a Deposition—Notice of the Recording Method. A subpoena commanding attendance at a deposition must state the method for recording the testimony.

      (C) Combining or Separating a Command to Produce or to Permit Inspection; Specifying the Form for Electronically Stored Information. A command to produce documents, electronically stored information, or tangible things or to permit the inspection of premises may be included in a subpoena commanding attendance at a deposition, hearing, or trial, or may be set out in a separate subpoena. A subpoena may specify the form or forms in which electronically stored information is to be produced.

      (D) Command to Produce; Included Obligations. A command in a subpoena to produce documents, electronically stored information, or tangible things requires the responding party to permit inspection, copying, testing, or sampling of the materials.

   (2) Issued from Which Court. A subpoena must issue as follows:

      (A) for attendance at a hearing or trial, from the court for the district where the hearing or trial is to be held;

      (B) for attendance at a deposition, from the court for the district where the deposition is to be taken; and

      (C) for production or inspection, if separate from a subpoena commanding a person's attendance, from the court for the district where the production or inspection is to be made.

(3) *Issued by Whom.* The clerk must issue a subpoena, signed but otherwise in blank, to a party who requests it. That party must complete it before service. An attorney also may issue and sign a subpoena as an officer of:

> (A) a court in which the attorney is authorized to practice; or
>
> (B) a court for a district where a deposition is to be taken or production is to be made, if the attorney is authorized to practice in the court where the action is pending.

(b) SERVICE

(1) *By Whom; Tendering Fees; Serving a Copy of Certain Subpoenas.* Any person who is at least 18 years old and not a party may serve a subpoena. Serving a subpoena requires delivering a copy to the named person and, if the subpoena requires that person's attendance, tendering the fees for 1 day's attendance and the mileage allowed by law. Fees and mileage need not be tendered when the subpoena issues on behalf of the United States or any of its officers or agencies. If the subpoena commands the production of documents, electronically stored information, or tangible things or the inspection of premises before trial, then before it is served, a notice must be served on each party.

(2) *Service in the United States.* Subject to Rule 45(c)(3)(A)(ii), a subpoena may be served at any place:

> (A) within the district of the issuing court;
>
> (B) outside that district but within 100 miles of the place specified for the deposition, hearing, trial, production, or inspection;
>
> (C) within the state of the issuing court if a state statute or court rule allows service at that place of a subpoena issued by a state court of general jurisdiction sitting in the place specified for the deposition, hearing, trial, production, or inspection; or
>
> (D) that the court authorizes on motion and for good cause, if a federal statute so provides.

(3) *Service in a Foreign Country.* 28 U.S.C. § 1783 governs issuing and serving a subpoena directed to a United States national or resident who is in a foreign country.

(4) *Proof of Service.* Proving service, when necessary, requires filing with the issuing court a statement showing the date and manner of service and the names of the persons served. The statement must be certified by the server.

(c) PROTECTING A PERSON SUBJECT TO A SUBPOENA

(1) *Avoiding Undue Burden or Expense; Sanctions.* A party or attorney responsible for issuing and serving a subpoena must take reasonable steps to avoid imposing an undue burden or expense on a person subject to the subpoena. The issuing court must enforce this duty and impose an appropriate sanction—which may include lost earnings and reasonable attorney's fees—on a party or attorney who fails to comply.

(2) *Command to Produce Materials or Permit Inspection*

> (A) *Appearance Not Required.* A person commanded to produce designated documents, electronically stored information, or tangible things, or to permit the inspection of premises, need not appear in person at the place of production or inspection unless also commanded to appear for a deposition, hearing, or trial.
>
> (B) *Objections.* A person commanded to produce designated materials or to permit inspection may serve on the party or attorney designated in the subpoena a written objection to inspecting, copying, testing, or sampling any or all of the designated materials or to inspecting the premises—or to producing electronically stored

information in the form or forms requested. The objection must be served before the earlier of the time specified for compliance or 14 days after the subpoena is served. If an objection is made, the following rules apply:

(i)   At any time, on notice to the commanded person, the serving party may move the issuing court for an order compelling production or inspection.

(ii)   These acts may be required only as directed in the order, and the order must protect a person who is neither a party nor a party's officer from significant expense resulting from compliance.

(3) Quashing or Modifying a Subpoena

(A) When Required. On timely motion, the issuing court must quash or modify a subpoena that:

(i)   fails to allow a reasonable time to comply;

(ii)   requires a person who is neither a party not a party's officer to travel more than 100 miles from where that person resides, is employed, or regularly transacts business in person—except that, subject to Rule 45(c)(3)(B)(iii), the person may be commanded to attend a trial by traveling from any such place within the state where the trial is held;

(iii)   requires disclosure of privileged or other protected matter, if no exception or waiver applies; or

(iv)   subjects a person to undue burden.

(B) When Permitted. To protect a person subject to or affected by a subpoena, the issuing court may, on motion, quash or modify the subpoena if it requires:

(i)   disclosing a trade secret or other confidential research, development, or commercial information;

(ii)   disclosing an unretained expert's opinion or information that does not describe specific occurrences in dispute and results from the expert's study that was not requested by a party; or

(iii)   a person who is neither a party nor a party's officer to incur substantial expenses to travel more than 100 miles to attend trial.

(C) Specifying Conditions as an Alternative. In the circumstances described in Rule 45(c)(3)(B), the court may, instead of quashing or modifying a subpoena, order appearance or production under specified conditions if the serving party:

(i)   shows a substantial need for the testimony or material that cannot be otherwise met without undue hardship; and

(ii)   ensures that the subpoenaed person will be reasonably compensated.

(d) DUTIES IN RESPONDING TO A SUBPOENA

(1) Producing Documents or Electronically Stored Information. These procedures apply to producing documents or electronically stored information:

(A) Documents. A person responding to a subpoena to produce documents must produce them as they are kept in the ordinary course of business or must organize and label them to correspond to the categories in the demand.

(B) Form for Producing Electronically Stored Information Not Specified. If a subpoena does not specify a form for producing electronically stored information, the person responding must produce it in a form or forms in which it is ordinarily maintained or in a reasonably usable form or forms.

(C) Electronically Stored Information Produced in Only One Form. The person responding need not produce the same electronically stored information in more than one form.

(D) Inaccessible Electronically Stored Information. The person responding need not provide discovery of electronically stored information from sources that the person identifies as not reasonably accessible because of undue burden or cost. On motion to compel discovery or for a protective order, the person responding must show that the information is not reasonably accessible because of undue burden or cost. If that showing is made, the court may nonetheless order discovery from such sources if the requesting party shows good cause, considering the limitations of Rule 26(b)(2)(C). The court may specify conditions for the discovery.

(2) Claiming Privilege or Protection.

(A) Information Withheld. A person withholding subpoenaed information under a claim that it is privileged or subject to protection as trial-preparation material must:

(i) expressly assert the claim; and

(ii) describe the nature of the withheld documents, communications, or things in a manner that, without revealing information itself privileged or protected, will enable the parties to assess the claim.

(B) Information Produced. If information produced in response to a subpoena is subject to a claim of privilege or of protection as trial-preparation material, the person making the claim may notify any party that received the information of the claim and the basis for it. After being notified, a party must promptly return, sequester, or destroy the specified information and any copies it has; must not use or disclose the information until the claim is resolved; must take reasonable steps to retrieve the information if the party disclosed it before being notified; and may promptly present the information to the court under seal for a determination of the claim. The person who produced the information must preserve the information until the claim is resolved.

(e) CONTEMPT

The issuing court may hold in contempt a person who, having been served, fails without adequate excuse to obey the subpoena. A nonparty's failure to obey must be excused if the subpoena purports to require the nonparty to attend or produce at a place outside the limits of Rule 45(c)(3)(A)(ii).

For further study, see: 1991 Advisory Committee Notes at 154; and Transnational Rule 20 at 289.

RULE 46. OBJECTING TO A RULING OR ORDER

A formal exception to a ruling or order is unnecessary. When the ruling or order is requested or made, a party need only state the action that it wants the court to take or objects to, along with the grounds for the request or objection. Failing to object does not prejudice a party who had no opportunity to do so when the ruling or order was made.

RULE 47. SELECTING JURORS

(a) EXAMINING JURORS

The court may permit the parties or their attorneys to examine prospective jurors or may itself do so. If the court examines the jurors, it must permit the parties or their attorneys to make any further inquiry it considers proper, or must itself ask any of the additional questions it considers proper.

(b) PEREMPTORY CHALLENGES

The court must allow the number of peremptory challenges provided by 28 U.S.C. § 1870.

(c) EXCUSING A JUROR

During trial or deliberation, the court may excuse a juror for good cause.

> **For further study, see**: 1991 Advisory Committee Notes at 156.

RULE 48. NUMBER OF JURORS; VERDICT

A jury must initially have at least 6 and no more than 12 members, and each juror must participate in the verdict unless excused under Rule 47(c). Unless the parties stipulate otherwise, the verdict must be unanimous and be returned by a jury of at least 6 members.

> **For further study, see**: 1991 Advisory Committee Notes at 157.

RULE 49. SPECIAL VERDICT; GENERAL VERDICT AND QUESTIONS

(a) SPECIAL VERDICT

(1) In General. The court may require a jury to return only a special verdict in the form of a special written finding on each issue of fact. The court may do so by:

(A) submitting written questions susceptible of a categorical or other brief answer;

(B) submitting written forms of the special findings that might properly be made under the pleadings and evidence; or

(C) using any other method that the court considers appropriate.

(2) Instructions. The court must give the instructions and explanations necessary to enable the jury to make its findings on each submitted issue.

(3) Issues Not Submitted. A party waives the right to a jury trial on any issue of fact raised by the pleadings or evidence but not submitted to the jury unless, before the jury retires, the party demands its submission to the jury. If the party does not demand submission, the court may make a finding on the issue. If the court makes no finding, it is considered to have made a finding consistent with its judgment on the special verdict.

(b) GENERAL VERDICT WITH ANSWERS TO WRITTEN QUESTIONS

(1) In General. The court may submit to the jury forms for a general verdict, together with written questions on one or more issues of fact that the jury must decide. The court must give the instructions and explanations necessary to enable the jury to render a general verdict and answer the questions in writing, and must direct the jury to do both.

(2) Verdict and Answers Consistent. When the general verdict and the answers are consistent, the court must approve, for entry upon Rule 58, an appropriate judgment on the verdict and answers.

(3) *Answers Inconsistent with the Verdict.* When the answers are consistent with each other but one or more is inconsistent with the general verdict, the court may:

    (A) approve, for entry under Rule 58, an appropriate judgment according to the answers, notwithstanding the general verdict;

    (B) direct the jury to further consider its answers and verdict; or

    (C) order a new trial.

(4) *Answers Inconsistent with Each Other and the Verdict.* When the answers are inconsistent with each other and one or more is also inconsistent with the general verdict, judgment must not be entered; instead, the court must direct the jury to further consider its answers and verdict, or must order a new trial.

RULE 50. JUDGMENT AS A MATTER OF LAW IN A JURY TRIAL; RELATED MOTION FOR A NEW TRIAL; CONDITIONAL RULING

(a) JUDGMENT AS A MATTER OF LAW

(1) *In General.* If a party has been fully heard on an issue during a jury trial and the court finds that a reasonable jury would not have a legally sufficient evidentiary basis to find for the party on that issue, the court may:

    (A) resolve the issue against the party; and

    (B) grant a motion for judgment as a matter of law against the party on a claim or defense that, under the controlling law, can be maintained or defeated only with a favorable finding on that issue.

(2) *Motion.* A motion for judgment as a matter of law may be made at any time before the case is submitted to the jury. The motion must specify the judgment sought and the law and facts that entitle the movant to the judgment.

(b) RENEWING THE MOTION AFTER TRIAL; ALTERNATIVE MOTION FOR A NEW TRIAL

If the court does not grant a motion for judgment as a matter of law made under Rule 50(a), the court is considered to have submitted the action to the jury subject to the court's later deciding the legal questions raised by the motion. No later than 10 days after the entry of judgment—or if the motion addresses a jury issue not decided by a verdict, no later than 10 days after the jury was discharged—the movant may file a renewed motion for judgment as a matter of law and may include an alternative or joint request for a new trial under Rule 59. In ruling on the renewed motion, the court may:

    (1) allow judgment on the verdict, if the jury returned a verdict;

    (2) order a new trial; or

    (3) direct the entry of judgment as a matter of law.

(c) GRANTING THE RENEWED MOTION; CONDITIONAL RULING ON A MOTION FOR NEW TRIAL

(1) *In General.* If the court grants a renewed motion for judgment as a matter of law, it must also conditionally rule on any motion for a new trial by determining whether a new trial should be granted if the judgment is later vacated or reversed. The court must state the grounds for conditionally granting or denying the motion for a new trial.

(2) *Effect of a Conditional Ruling.* Conditionally granting the motion for a new trial does not affect the judgment's finality; if the judgment is reversed, the new trial must proceed unless the appellate court orders otherwise. If the motion for a new trial is conditionally denied, the appellee may assert error in that denial; if the judgment is reversed, the case must proceed as the appellate court orders.

(d) TIME FOR A LOSING PARTY'S NEW-TRIAL MOTION

Any motion for a new trial under Rule 59 by a party against whom judgment as a matter of law is rendered must be filed no later than 10 days after the entry of the judgment.

(e) DENYING THE MOTION FOR JUDGMENT AS A MATTER OF LAW; REVERSAL ON APPEAL

If the court denies the motion for judgment as a matter of law, the prevailing party may, as appellee, assert grounds entitling it to a new trial should the appellate court conclude that the trial court erred in denying the motion. If the appellate court reverses the judgment, it may order a new trial, direct the trial court to determine whether a new trial should be granted, or direct the entry of judgment.

> **For further study, see**: 1991 Advisory Committee Notes at 157; 2006 Advisory Committee Notes at 209; 2007 Advisory Committee Notes at 214; and Transnational Rule 15 & 19 at 284.

RULE 51. INSTRUCTIONS TO THE JURY; OBJECTIONS; PRESERVING A CLAIM FOR ERROR

(a) REQUESTS

(1)   Before or at the Close of the Evidence. At the close of the evidence or at any earlier reasonable time that the court orders, a party may file and furnish to every other party written requests for the jury instructions it wants the court to give.

(2)   After the Close of the Evidence. After the close of the evidence a party may:

   (A) file requests for instructions on issues that could not reasonably have been anticipated by an earlier time that the court set for requests; and

   (B) with the court's permission, file untimely requests for instructions on any issue.

(b) INSTRUCTIONS

The court:

(1)   must inform the parties of its proposed instructions and proposed action on the requests before instructing the jury and before final jury arguments;

(2)   must give the parties an opportunity to object on the record and out of the jury's hearing before the instructions and arguments are delivered; and

(3)   may instruct the jury at any time before the jury is discharged.

(c) OBJECTIONS

(1)   How to Make. A party who objects to an instruction or the failure to given an instruction must do so on the record, stating distinctly the matter objected to and the grounds for the objection.

(2)   When to Make. An objection is timely if:

   (A) a party objects at the opportunity provided under Rule 51(b)(2); or

   (B) a party was not informed of an instruction or action on a request before that opportunity to object, and the party objects promptly after learning that the instruction or request will be, or has been, given or refused.

(d) ASSIGNING ERROR; PLAIN ERROR

(1)   Assigning Error. A party may assign as error:

(A) an error in an instruction actually given, if that party properly objected; or

(B) a failure to give an instruction, if that party properly requested it and—unless the court rejected the request in a definitive ruling on the record—also properly objected.

(2)   Plain Error. A court may consider a plain error in the instructions that has not been preserved as required by Rule 51(d)(1) if the error affects substantial rights.

For further study, see: 1987 Advisory Committee Notes at 153; and 2003 Advisory Committee Notes at 197.

RULE 52. FINDINGS AND CONCLUSIONS BY THE COURT; JUDGMENT ON PARTIAL FINDINGS

(a) FINDINGS AND CONCLUSIONS

(1)   In General. In an action tried on the facts without a jury or with an advisory jury, the court must find the facts specially and state its conclusions of law separately. The findings and conclusions may be stated on the record after the close of the evidence or may appear in an opinion or a memorandum of decision filed by the court. Judgment must be entered under Rule 58.

(2)   For an Interlocutory Injunction. In granting or refusing an interlocutory injunction, the court must similarly state the findings and conclusions that support its action.

(3)   For a Motion. The court is not required to state findings or conclusions when ruling on a motion under Rule 12 or 56 or, unless these rules provide otherwise, on any other motion.

(4)   Effect of a Master's Findings. A master's findings, to the extent adopted by the court, must be considered the court's findings.

(5)   Questioning the Evidentiary Support. A party may later question the sufficiency of the evidence supporting the findings, whether or not the party requested findings, objected to them, moved to amend them, or moved for partial findings.

(6)   Setting Aside the Findings. Findings of fact, whether based on oral or other evidence must not be set aside unless clearly erroneous, and the reviewing court must give due regard to the trial court's opportunity to judge the witnesses' credibility.

(b) AMENDED OR ADDITIONAL FINDINGS

On a party's motion filed no later than 10 days after the entry of judgment, the court may amend its findings—or make additional findings—and may amend the judgment accordingly. The motion may accompany a motion for a new trial under Rule 59.

(c) JUDGMENT ON PARTIAL FINDINGS

If a party has been fully heard on an issue during a nonjury trial and the court finds against the party on that issue, the court may enter judgment against the party on a claim or defense that, under the controlling law, can be maintained or defeated only with a favorable finding on that issue. The court may, however, decline to render any judgment until the close of the evidence. A judgment on partial findings must be supported by findings of fact and conclusions of law as required by Rule 52(a).

For further study, see: Fed. R. Civ. P. Forms 70 & 71 at 109; 1985 Advisory Committee Notes at 151; 1991 Advisory Committee Notes at 158; and Transnational Rule 15 & 19 at 284.

RULE 53. MASTERS

(a) APPOINTMENT

(1) Scope. Unless a statute provides otherwise, a court may appoint a master only to:

  (A) perform duties consented to by the parties;

  (B) hold trial proceedings and make or recommend findings of fact on issues to be decided without a jury if appointment is warranted by:

    (i) some exceptional condition; or

    (ii) the need to perform an accounting or resolve a difficult computation of damages; or

  (C) address pretrial and posttrial matters that cannot be effectively and timely addressed by an available district judge or magistrate judge of the district.

(2) Disqualification. A master must not have a relationship to the parties, attorneys, action, or court that would require disqualification of a judge under 28 U.S.C. § 455, unless the parties, with the court's approval, consent to the appointment after the master discloses any potential grounds for disqualification.

(3) Possible Expense or Delay. In appointing a master, the court must consider the fairness of imposing the likely expenses on the parties and must protect against unreasonable expense or delay.

(b) ORDER APPOINTING A MASTER

(1) Notice. Before appointing a master, the court must give the parties notice and an opportunity to be heard. Any party may suggest candidates for appointment.

(2) Contents. The appointing order must direct the master to proceed with all reasonable diligence and must state:

  (A) the master's duties, including any investigation or enforcement duties, and any limits on the master's authority under Rule 53(c);

  (B) the circumstances, if any, in which the master may communicate ex parte with the court or a party;

  (C) the nature of the materials to be preserved and filed as the record of the master's activities;

  (D) the time limits, method of filing the record, other procedures, and standards for reviewing the master's orders, findings, and recommendations; and

  (E) the basis, terms, and procedure for fixing the master's compensation under Rule 53(g).

(3) Issuing. The court may issue the order only after:

  (A) the master files an affidavit disclosing whether there is any ground for disqualification under 28 U.S.C. § 455; and

  (B) if a ground is disclosed, the parties, with the court's approval, waive the disqualification.

(4) Amending. The order may be amended at any time after notice to the parties and an opportunity to be heard.

(c) MASTER'S AUTHORITY

(1)   In General. Unless the appointing order directs otherwise, a master may:

   (A) regulate all proceedings;

   (B) take all appropriate measures to perform the assigned duties fairly and efficiently; and

   (C) if conducting an evidentiary hearing, exercise the appointing court's power to compel, take, and record evidence.

(2)   Sanctions. The master may by order impose on a party any noncontempt sanction provided by Rule 37 or 45, and may recommend a contempt sanction against a party and sanctions against a nonparty.

(d) MASTER'S ORDERS

A master who issues an order must file it and promptly serve a copy on each party. The clerk must enter the order on the docket.

(e) MASTER'S REPORTS

A master must report to the court as required by the appointing order. The master must file the report and promptly serve a copy on each party, unless the court orders otherwise.

(f) ACTION ON THE MASTER'S ORDER, REPORT, OR RECOMMENDATIONS

(1)   Opportunity for a Hearing; Action in General. In acting on a master's order, report, or recommendations, the court must give the parties notice and an opportunity to be heard; may receive evidence; and may adopt or affirm, modify, wholly or partly reject or reverse, or resubmit it to the master with instructions.

(2)   Time to Object or Move to Adopt or Modify. A party may file objections to — or a motion to adopt or modify — the master's order, report, or recommendations no later than 20 days after a copy is served, unless the court sets a different time.

(3)   Reviewing Factual Findings. The court must decide de novo all objections to findings of fact made or recommended by a master, unless the parties, with the court's approval, stipulate that:

   (A) the findings will be reviewed for clear error; or

   (B) the findings of a master appointed under Rule 53(a)(1)(A) or (C) will be final.

(4)   Reviewing Legal Conclusions. The court must decide de novo all objections to conclusions of law made or recommended by a master.

(5)   Reviewing Procedural Matters. Unless the appointing order establishes a different standard of review, the court may set aside a master's ruling on a procedural matter only for an abuse of discretion.

(g) COMPENSATION

(1)   Fixing Compensation. Before or after judgment, the court must fix the master's compensation on the basis and terms stated in the appointing order, but the court may set a new basis and terms after giving notice and an opportunity to be heard.

(2)   Payment. The compensation must be paid either:

   (A) by a party or parties; or

   (B) from a fund or subject matter of the action within the court's control.

(3) *Allocating Payment.* The court must allocate payment among the parties after considering the nature and amount of the controversy, the parties' means, and the extent to which any party is more responsible than the other parties for the reference to a master. An interim allocation may be amended to reflect a decision on the merits.

(h) APPOINTING A MAGISTRATE JUDGE

A magistrate judge is subject to this rule only when the order referring a matter to the magistrate judge states that the reference is made under this rule.

> **For further study, see**: Fed. R. Civ. P. Forms 80-82 at 109; 2003 Advisory Committee Notes at 199; and Transnational Rule 18 at 287.

VII. Judgment

RULE 54. JUDGMENT; COSTS

(a) DEFINITION; FORM

"Judgment" as used in these rules includes a decree and any order from which an appeal lies. A judgment should not include recitals of pleadings, a master's report, or a record of prior proceedings.

(b) JUDGMENT ON MULTIPLE CLAIMS OR INVOLVING MULTIPLE PARTIES

When an action presents more than one claim for relief—whether as a claim, counterclaim, crossclaim, or third-party claim—or when multiple parties are involved, the court may direct entry of a final judgment as to one or more, but fewer than all, claims or parties only if the court expressly determines that there is no just reason for delay. Otherwise, any order or other decision, however designated, that adjudicates fewer than all the claims or the rights and liabilities of fewer than all the parties does not end the action as to any of the claims or parties and may be revised at any time before the entry of a judgment adjudicating all the claims and all the parties' rights and liabilities.

(c) DEMAND FOR JUDGMENT; RELIEF TO BE GRANTED

A default judgment must not differ in kind from, or exceed in amount, what is demanded in the pleadings. Every other final judgment should grant the relief to which each party is entitled, even if the party has not demanded that relief in its pleadings.

(d) COSTS; ATTORNEY'S FEES

(1) *Costs Other Than Attorney's Fees.* Unless a federal statute, these rules, or a court order provides otherwise, costs—other than attorney's fees—should be allowed to the prevailing party. But costs against the United States, its officers, and its agencies may be imposed only to the extent allowed by law. The clerk may tax costs on 1 day's notice. On motion served within the next 5 days, the court may review the clerk's action.

(2) Attorney's Fees

(A) *Claim to Be by Motion.* A claim for attorney's fees and related nontaxable expenses must be made by motion unless the substantive law requires those fees to be proved at trial as an element of damages.

    (B) Timing and Content of the Motion. Unless a statute or a court order provides otherwise, the motion must:

        (i)   be filed no later than 14 days after the entry of judgment;

        (ii)   specify the judgment and the statute, rule, or other grounds entitling the movant to the award;

        (iii)   state the amount sought or provide a fair estimate of it; and

        (iv)   disclose, if the court so orders, the terms of any agreement about fees for the services for which the claim is made.

    (C) Proceedings. Subject to Rule 23(h), the court must, on a party's request, give an opportunity for adversary submissions on the motion in accordance with Rule 43(c) or 78. The court may decide issues of liability for fees before receiving submissions on the value of services. The court must find the facts and state its conclusions of law as provided in Rule 52(a).

    (D) Special Procedures by Local Rule; Reference to a Master or a Magistrate Judge. By local rule, the court may establish special procedures to resolve fee-related issues without extensive evidentiary hearings. Also, the court may refer issues concerning the value of services to a special master under Rule 53 without regard to the limitations of Rule 53(a)(1), and may refer a motion for attorney's fees to a magistrate judge under Rule 72(b) as if it were a dispositive pretrial matter.

    (E) Exceptions. Subparagraphs (A)-(D) do not apply to claims for fees and expenses as sanctions for violating these rules or as sanctions under 28 U.S.C. § 1927.

      For further study, see: Fed. R. Civ. P. Forms 70 & 71 at 109; Restatement (Second) of Judgment § 25 at 237; and Transnational Rules 15, 19 & 34 at 284.

RULE 55. DEFAULT; DEFAULT JUDGMENT

(a) ENTERING A DEFAULT

When a party against whom a judgment for affirmative relief is sought has failed to plead or otherwise defend, and that failure is shown by affidavit or otherwise, the clerk must enter the party's default.

(b) ENTERING A DEFAULT JUDGMENT

    (1)   By the Clerk. If the plaintiff's claim is for a sum certain or a sum that can be made certain by computation, the clerk—on the plaintiff's request, with an affidavit showing the amount due—must enter judgment for that amount and costs against a defendant who has been defaulted for not appearing and who is neither a minor nor an incompetent person.

    (2)   By the Court. In all other cases, the party must apply to the court for a default judgment. A default judgment may be entered against a minor or incompetent person only if represented by a general guardian, conservator, or other like fiduciary who has appeared. If the party against whom a default judgment is sought has appeared personally or by a representative, that party or its representative must be served with written notice of the application at least 3 days before the hearing. The court may conduct hearings or make referrals—preserving any federal statutory right to a jury trial—when, to enter or effectuate judgment, it needs to:

        (A) conduct an accounting;

        (B) determine the amount of damages;

        (C) establish the truth of any allegation by evidence; or

        (D) investigate any other matter.

(c) SETTING ASIDE A DEFAULT OR A DEFAULT JUDGMENT

The court may set aside an entry of default for good cause, and it may set aside a default judgment under Rule 60(b).

(d) JUDGMENT AGAINST THE UNITED STATES

A default judgment may be entered against the United States, its officers, or its agencies only if the claimant establishes a claim or right to relief by evidence that satisfies the court.

> **For further study, see**: Restatement (Second) of Judgments § 68 at 265; and Transnational Rules 13, 14, 15 & 34 at 282.

RULE 56. SUMMARY JUDGMENT

(a) BY A CLAIMING PARTY

A party claiming relief may move, with or without supporting affidavits, for summary judgment on all or part of the claim. The motion may be filed at any time after:

(1)   20 days have passed from commencement of the action; or

(2)   the opposing party serves a motion for summary judgment.

(b) BY A DEFENDING PARTY

A party against whom relief is sought may move at any time, with or without supporting affidavits, for summary judgment on all or part of the claim.

(c) SERVING THE MOTION; PROCEEDINGS

The motion must be served at least 10 days before the day set for the hearing. An opposing party may serve opposing affidavits before the hearing day. The judgment sought should be rendered if the pleadings, the discovery and disclosure materials on file, and any affidavits show that there is no genuine issue as to any material fact and that the movant is entitled to judgment as a matter of law.

(d) CASE NOT FULLY ADJUDICATED ON THE MOTION

(1)   Establishing Facts. If summary judgment is not rendered on the whole action, the court should, to the extent practicable, determine what material facts are not genuinely at issue. The court should so determine by examining the pleadings and evidence before it and by interrogating the attorneys. It should then issue an order specifying what facts—including items of damages or other relief—are not genuinely at issue. The facts so specified must be treated as established in the action.

(2)   Establishing Liability. An interlocutory summary judgment may be rendered on liability alone, even if there is a genuine issue on the amount of damages.

(e) AFFIDAVITS; FURTHER TESTIMONY

(1)   In General. A supporting or opposing affidavit must be made on personal knowledge, set out facts that would be admissible in evidence, and show that the affiant is competent to testify on the matters stated. If a paper or part of a paper is referred to in an affidavit, a sworn or certified copy must be attached to or served with the affidavit. The court may permit an affidavit to be supplemented or opposed by depositions, answers to interrogatories, or additional affidavits.

(2)   Opposing Party's Obligation to Respond. When a motion for summary judgment is properly made and supported, an opposing party may not rely merely on allegations or denials

in its own pleading; rather, its response must—by affidavits or as otherwise provided in this rule—set out specific facts showing a genuine issue for trial. If the opposing party does not so respond, summary judgment should, if appropriate, be entered against that party.

(f) WHEN AFFIDAVITS ARE UNAVAILABLE

If a party opposing the motion shows by affidavit that, for specified reasons, it cannot present facts essential to justify its opposition, the court may:

(1)   deny the motion;

(2)   order a continuance to enable affidavits to be obtained, depositions to be taken, or other discovery be undertaken; or

(3)   issue any other just order.

(g) AFFIDAVIT SUBMITTED IN BAD FAITH

If satisfied that an affidavit under this rule is submitted in bad faith or solely for delay, the court must order the submitting party to pay the other party the reasonable expenses, including attorney's fees, it incurred as a result. An offending party or attorney may also be held in contempt.

> **For further study, see**: 1938 Advisory Committee Notes at 112; 1948 Advisory Committee Notes at 113; 1963 Advisory Committee Notes at 115; Restatement (Second) of Judgments § 19 at 225; and Transnational Rules 15 & 19 at 284.

RULE 57. DECLARATORY JUDGMENT

These rules govern the procedure for obtaining a declaratory judgment under 28 U.S.C. § 2201. Rules 38 and 39 govern a demand for a jury trial. The existence of another adequate remedy does not preclude a declaratory judgment that is otherwise appropriate. The court may order a speedy hearing of a declaratory-judgment action.

> **For further study, see**: 1938 Advisory Committee Notes at 112.

RULE 58. ENTERING JUDGMENT

(a) SEPARATE DOCUMENT

Every judgment and amended judgment must be set out in a separate document, but a separate document is not required for an order disposing of a motion:

(1)   for judgment under Rule 50(b);

(2)   to amend or make additional findings under Rule 52(b);

(3)   for attorney's fees under Rule 54;

(4)   for a new trial, or to alter or amend the judgment, under Rule 59; or

(5)   for relief under Rule 60.

(b) ENTERING JUDGMENT

(1)   Without the Court's Direction. Subject to Rule 54(b) and unless the court orders otherwise, the clerk must, without awaiting the court's direction, promptly prepare, sign, and enter the judgment when:

(A) the jury returns a general verdict;

(B) the court awards only costs or a sum certain; or

(C) the court denies all relief.

(2) Court's Approval Required. Subject to Rule 54(b), the court must promptly approve the form of the judgment, which the clerk must promptly enter, when:

> (A) the jury returns a special verdict or a general verdict with answers to written questions; or
>
> (B) the court grants other relief not described in this subdivision (b).

(c) TIME OF ENTRY

For purposes of these rules, judgment is entered at the following times:

(1) if a separate document is not required, when the judgment is entered in the civil docket under Rule 79(a); or

(2) if a separate document is required, when the judgment is entered in the civil docket under Rule 79(a) and the earlier of these events occurs:

> (A) it is set out in a separate document; or
>
> (B) 150 days have run from the entry in the civil docket.

(d) REQUEST FOR ENTRY

A party may request that judgment be set out in a separate document as required by Rule 58(a).

(e) COST OR FEE AWARDS

Ordinarily, the entry of judgment may not be delayed, nor the time for appeal extended, in order to tax costs or award fees. But if a timely motion for attorney's fees is made under Rule 54(d)(2), the court may act before a notice of appeal has been filed and become effective to order that the motion have the same effect under Federal Rule of Appellate Procedure 4(a)(4) as a timely motion under Rule 59.

> **For further study, see**: Fed. R. Civ. P. Forms 70 & 71 at 109; 2002 Advisory Committee Notes at 190; and Transnational Rule 35 at 292.

RULE 59. NEW TRIAL; ALTERING OR AMENDING A JUDGMENT

(a) IN GENERAL

(1) Grounds for New Trial. The court may, on motion, grant a new trial on all or some of the issues—and to any party—as follows:

> (A) after a jury trial, for any reason for which a new trial has heretofore been granted in an action at law in federal court; or
>
> (B) after a nonjury trial, for any reason for which a rehearing has heretofore been granted in a suit in equity in federal court.

(2) Further Action After a Nonjury Trial. After a nonjury trial, the court may, on motion for a new trial, open the judgment if one has been entered, take additional testimony, amend findings of fact and conclusions of law or make new ones, and direct the entry of a new judgment.

(b) TIME TO FILE A MOTION FOR A NEW TRIAL

A motion for a new trial must be filed no later than 10 days after the entry of judgment.

(c) TIME TO SERVE AFFIDAVITS

When a motion for a new trial is based on affidavits, they must be filed with the motion. The opposing party has 10 days after being served to file opposing affidavits; but that period may be extended for up to 20 days, either by the court for good cause or by the parties' stipulation. The court may permit reply affidavits.

(d) NEW TRIAL ON THE COURT'S INITIATIVE OR FOR REASONS NOT IN THE MOTION

No later than 10 days after the entry of judgment, the court, on its own, may order a new trial for any reason that would justify granting one on a party's motion. After giving the parties notice and an opportunity to be heard, the court may grant a timely motion for a new trial for a reason not stated in the motion. In either event, the court must specify the reasons in its order.

(e) MOTION TO ALTER OR AMEND A JUDGMENT

A motion to alter or amend a judgment must be filed no later than 10 days after the entry of the judgment.

For further study, see: Restatement (Second) of Judgments § 71 at 271; and Transnational Rule 34 at 292.

RULE 60. RELIEF FROM A JUDGMENT OR ORDER

(a) CORRECTIONS BASED ON CLERICAL MISTAKES; OVERSIGHTS AND OMISSIONS

The court may correct a clerical mistake or a mistake arising from oversight or omission whenever one is found in a judgment, order, or other part of the record. The court may do so on motion or on its own, with or without notice. But after an appeal has been docketed in the appellate court and while it is pending, such a mistake may be corrected only with the appellate court's leave.

(b) GROUNDS FOR RELIEF FROM A FINAL JUDGMENT, ORDER, OR PROCEEDING

On motion and just terms, the court may relieve a party or its legal representative from a final judgment, order, or proceeding for the following reasons:

(1)   mistake, inadvertence, surprise, or excusable neglect;

(2)   newly discovered evidence that, with reasonable diligence, could not have been discovered in time to move for a new trial under Rule 59(b);

(3)   fraud (whether previously called intrinsic or extrinsic), misrepresentation, or misconduct by an opposing party;

(4)   the judgment is void;

(5)   the judgment has been satisfied, released or discharged; it is based on an earlier judgment that has been reversed or vacated; or applying it prospectively is no longer equitable; or

(6)   any other reason that justifies relief.

(c) TIMING AND EFFECT OF THE MOTION

(1)   Timing. A motion under Rule 60(b) must be made within a reasonable time—and for reasons (1), (2), and (3) no more than a year after the entry of the judgment or order or the date of the proceeding.

(2)   Effect on Finality. The motion does not affect the judgment's finality or suspend its operation.

(d) OTHER POWERS TO GRANT RELIEF

This rule does not limit a court's power to:

(1) entertain an independent action to relieve a party from a judgment, order, or proceeding;

(2) grant relief under 28 U.S.C. § 1655 to a defendant who was not personally notified of the action; or

(3) set aside a judgment for fraud on the court.

(e) BILLS AND WRITS ABOLISHED

The following are abolished: bills of review, bills in the nature of bills of review, and writs of coram nobis, coram vobis, and audita querela.

> **For further study, see**: Restatement (Second) of Judgments §§ 65-74 at 261; and Transnational Rule 15 & 34 at 284.

RULE 61. HARMLESS ERROR

Unless justice requires otherwise, no error in admitting or excluding evidence—or any other error by the court or a party—is ground for granting a new trial, for setting aside a verdict, or for vacating, modifying, or otherwise disturbing a judgment or order. At every stage of the proceeding, the court must disregard all errors and defects that do not affect any party's substantial rights.

RULE 62. STAY OF PROCEEDINGS TO ENFORCE A JUDGMENT

(a) AUTOMATIC STAY; EXCEPTIONS FOR INJUNCTIONS, RECEIVERSHIPS, AND PATENT ACCOUNTINGS

Except as stated in this rule, no execution may issue on a judgment, nor may proceedings be taken to enforce it, until 10 days have passed after its entry. But unless the court orders otherwise, the following are not stayed after being entered, even if an appeal is taken:

(1) an interlocutory or final judgment in an action for an injunction or a receivership; or

(2) a judgment or order that directs an accounting in an action for patent infringement.

(b) STAY PENDING THE DISPOSITION OF A MOTION

On appropriate terms for the opposing party's security, the court may stay the execution of a judgment—or any proceedings to enforce it—pending disposition of any of the following motions:

(1) under Rule 50, for judgment as a matter of law;

(2) under Rule 52(b), to amend the findings or for additional findings;

(3) under Rule 59, for a new trial or to alter or amend a judgment; or

(4) under Rule 60, for relief from a judgment or order.

(c) INJUNCTION PENDING AN APPEAL

While an appeal is pending from an interlocutory order or final judgment that grants, dissolves, or denies an injunction, the court may suspend, modify, restore, or grant an injunction on terms for bond or other terms that secure the opposing party's rights. If the judgment appealed from is rendered by a statutory three-judge district court, the order must be made either:

(1) by that court sitting in open session; or

(2) by the assent of all its judges, as evidenced by their signatures.

(d) STAY WITH BOND ON APPEAL

If an appeal is taken, the appellant may obtain a stay by supersedeas bond, except in an action described in Rule 62(a)(1) or (2). The bond may be given upon or after filing the notice of appeal or after obtaining the order allowing the appeal. The stay takes effect when the court approves the bond.

(e) STAY WITHOUT BOND ON AN APPEAL BY THE UNITED STATES, ITS OFFICERS, OR ITS AGENCIES

The court must not require a bond, obligation, or other security from the appellant when granting a stay on an appeal by the United States, its officers, or its agencies or on an appeal directed by a department of the federal government.

(f) STAY IN FAVOR OF A JUDGMENT DEBTOR UNDER STATE LAW

If a judgment is a lien on the judgment debtor's property under the law of the state where the court is located, the judgment debtor is entitled to the same stay of execution the state court would give.

(g) APPELLATE COURT'S POWER NOT LIMITED

This rule does not limit the power of the appellate court or one of its judges or justices:

(1) to stay proceedings—or suspend, modify, restore, or grant an injunction—while an appeal is pending; or

(2) to issue an order to preserve the status quo or the effectiveness of the judgment to be entered.

(h) STAY WITH MULTIPLE CLAIMS OR PARTIES

A court may stay the enforcement of a final judgment entered under Rule 54(b) until it enters a later judgment or judgments, and may prescribe terms necessary to secure the benefit of the stayed judgment for the party in whose favor it was entered.

For further study, see: Transnational Rule 35 at 292.

RULE 63. JUDGE'S INABILITY TO PROCEED

If a judge conducting a hearing or trial is unable to proceed, any other judge may proceed upon certifying familiarity with the record and determining that the case may be completed without prejudice to the parties. In a hearing or a nonjury trial, the successor judge must, at a party's request, recall any witness whose testimony is material and disputed and who is available to testify again without undue burden. The successor judge may also recall any other witness.

VIII. Provisional and Final Remedies

RULE 64. SEIZING A PERSON OR PROPERTY

(a) REMEDIES UNDER STATE LAW — IN GENERAL

At the commencement of and throughout an action, every remedy is available that, under the law of the state where the court is located, provides for seizing a person or property to secure satisfaction of the potential judgment. But a federal statute governs to the extent it applies.

(b) SPECIFIC KINDS OF REMEDIES

The remedies available under this rule include the following — however designated and regardless of whether state procedure requires an independent action:

- arrest;
- attachment;
- garnishment;
- replevin;
- sequestration; and
- other corresponding or equivalent remedies.

For further study, see: Transnational Rule 17 & 20 at 286.

RULE 65. INJUNCTIONS AND RESTRAINING ORDERS

(a) PRELIMINARY INJUNCTION

(1) Notice. The court may issue a preliminary injunction only on notice to the adverse party.

(2) Consolidating the Hearing with the Trial on the Merits. Before or after beginning the hearing on a motion for a preliminary injunction, the court may advance the trial on the merits and consolidate it with the hearing. Even when consolidation is not ordered, evidence that is received on the motion and that would be admissible at trial becomes part of the trial record and need not be repeated at trial. But the court must preserve any party's right to a jury trial.

(b) TEMPORARY RESTRAINING ORDER

(1) Issuing Without Notice. The court may issue a temporary restraining order without written or oral notice to the adverse party or its attorney only if:

(A) specific facts in an affidavit or a verified complaint clearly show that immediate and irreparable injury, loss, or damage will result to the movant before the adversary party can be heard in opposition; and

(B) the movant's attorney certifies in writing any efforts made to give notice and the reasons why it should not be required.

(2) Contents; Expiration. Every temporary restraining order issued without notice must state the date and hour it was issued; describe the injury and state why it is irreparable; state why the order was issued without notice; and be promptly filed in the clerk's office and entered in the record. The order expires at the time after entry — not to exceed 10 days — that the court sets, unless before that time the court, for good cause, extends it for a like period or the adverse party consents to a longer extension. The reasons for an extension must be entered in the record.

(3)   Expediting the Preliminary-Injunction Hearing. If the order is issued without notice, the motion for a preliminary injunction must be set for hearing at the earliest possible time, taking precedence over all other matters except hearings on older matters of the same character. At the hearing, the party who obtained the order must proceed with the motion; if the party does not, the court must dissolve the order.

(4)   Motion to Dissolve. On 2 days' notice to the party who obtained the order without notice—or on shorter notice set by the court—the adverse party may appear and move to dissolve or modify the order. The court must then hear and decide the motion as promptly as justice requires.

(c) SECURITY

The court may issue a preliminary injunction or a temporary restraining order only if the movant gives security in an amount that the court considers proper to pay the costs and damages sustained by any party found to have been wrongfully enjoined or restrained. The United States, its officers, and its agencies are not required to give security.

(d) CONTENTS AND SCOPE OF EVERY INJUNCTION AND RESTRAINING ORDER

(1)   Contents. Every order granting an injunction and every restraining order must:

(A) state the reasons why it issued;

(B) state its terms specifically; and

(C) describe in reasonable detail—and not by referring to the complaint or other document—the act or acts restrained or required.

(2)   Persons Bound. The order binds only the following who receive actual notice of it by personal service or otherwise:

(A) the parties;

(B) the parties' officers, agents, servants, employees, and attorneys; and

(C) other persons who are in active concert or participation with anyone described in Rule 65(d)(2)(A) or (B).

(e) OTHER LAWS NOT MODIFIED

These rules do not modify the following:

(1)   any federal statute relating to temporary restraining orders or preliminary injunctions in actions affecting employer and employee;

(2)   28 U.S.C. § 2361, which relates to preliminary injunctions in actions of interpleader or in the nature of interpleader; or

(3)   28 U.S.C. § 2284, which relates to actions that must be heard and decided by a three-judge district court.

(f) COPYRIGHT IMPOUNDMENT

This rule applies to copyright-impoundment proceedings.

For further study, see: 1966 Advisory Committee Notes at 125; and Transnational Rule 17 & 20 at 286.

RULE 65.1. PROCEEDINGS AGAINST A SURETY

Whenever these rules (including the Supplemental Rules for Admiralty or Maritime Claims and Asset Forfeiture actions) require or allow a party to give security, and security is given through a bond or other undertaking with one or more sureties, each surety submits to the court's jurisdiction and irrevocably appoints the court clerk as its agent for receiving service of any papers that affect its liability on the bond or undertaking. The surety's liability may be enforced on motion without an independent action. The motion and any notice that the court orders may be served on the court clerk, who must promptly mail a copy of each to every surety whose address is known.

RULE 66. RECEIVERS

These rules govern an action in which the appointment of a receiver is sought or a receiver sues or is sued. But the practice in administering an estate by a receiver or a similar court-appointed officer must accord with the historical practice in federal courts or with a local rule. An action in which a receiver has been appointed may be dismissed only by court order.

RULE 67. DEPOSIT INTO COURT

(a) DEPOSITING PROPERTY

If any part of the relief sought is a money judgment or the disposition of a sum of money or some other deliverable thing, a party—on notice to every other party and by leave of court—may deposit with the court all or part of the money or thing, whether or not that party claims any of it. The depositing party must deliver to the clerk a copy of the order permitting deposit.

(b) INVESTING AND WITHDRAWING FUNDS

Money paid into court under this rule must be deposited and withdrawn in accordance with 28 U.S.C. §§ 2041 and 2042 and any like statute. The money must be deposited in an interest-bearing account or invested in a court-approved, interest-bearing instrument.

RULE 68. OFFER OF JUDGMENT

(a) MAKING AN OFFER; JUDGMENT ON AN ACCEPTED OFFER

More than 10 days before the trial begins, a party defending against a claim may serve on an opposing party an offer to allow judgment on specified terms, with the costs then accrued. If, within 10 days after being served, the opposing party serves written notice accepting the offer, either party may then file the offer and notice of acceptance, plus proof of service. The clerk must then enter judgment.

(b) UNACCEPTED OFFER

An unaccepted offer is considered withdrawn, but it does not preclude a later offer. Evidence of an unaccepted offer is not admissible except in a proceeding to determine costs.

(c) OFFER AFTER LIABILITY IS DETERMINED

When one party's liability to another has been determined but the extent of liability remains to be determined by further proceedings, the party held liable may make an offer of judgment. It must be served within a reasonable time—but at least 10 days—before a hearing to determine the extent of liability.

(d) PAYING COSTS AFTER AN UNACCEPTED OFFER

If the judgment that the offeree finally obtains is not more favorable than the unaccepted offer, the offeree must pay the costs incurred after the offer was made.

For further study, see: Transnational Rule 16 at 284.

RULE 69. EXECUTION

(a) IN GENERAL

(1)   Money Judgment; Applicable Procedure. A money judgment is enforced by a writ of execution, unless the court directs otherwise. The procedure on execution—and in proceedings supplementary to and in aid of judgment or execution—must accord with the procedure of the state where the court is located, but a federal statute governs to the extent it applies.

(2)   Obtaining Discovery. In aid of the judgment or execution, the judgment creditor or a successor in interest whose interest appears of record may obtain discovery from any person—including the judgment debtor—as provided in these rules or by the procedure of the state where the court is located.

(b) AGAINST CERTAIN PUBLIC OFFICERS

When a judgment has been entered against a revenue officer in the circumstances stated in 28 U.S.C. § 2006, or against an officer of Congress in the circumstances stated in 2 U.S.C. § 118, the judgment must be satisfied as those statutes provide.

For further study, see: 1970 Advisory Committee Notes at 142; and Transnational Rule 20 & 35 at 289.

RULE 70. ENFORCING A JUDGMENT FOR A SPECIFIC ACT

(a) PARTY'S FAILURE TO ACT; ORDERING ANOTHER TO ACT

If a judgment requires a party to convey land, to deliver a deed or other document, or to perform any other specific act and the party fails to comply within the time specified, the court may order the act to be done—at the disobedient party's expense—by another person appointed by the court. When done, the act has the same effect as if done by the party.

(b) VESTING TITLE

If the real or personal property is within the district, the court—instead of ordering a conveyance—may enter a judgment divesting any party's title and vesting it in others. That judgment has the effect of a legally executed conveyance.

(c) OBTAINING A WRIT OF ATTACHMENT OR SEQUESTRATION

On application by a party entitled to performance of an act, the clerk must issue a writ of attachment or sequestration against the disobedient party's property to compel obedience.

(d) OBTAINING A WRIT OF EXECUTION OR ASSISTANCE

On application by a party who obtains a judgment or order for possession, the clerk must issue a writ of execution or assistance.

(e) HOLDING IN CONTEMPT

The court may also hold the disobedient party in contempt.

For further study, see: Transnational Rule 20 & 35 at 289.

RULE 71. ENFORCING RELIEF FOR OR AGAINST A NONPARTY

When an order grants relief for a nonparty or may be enforced against a nonparty, the procedure for enforcing the order is the same as for a party.

For further study, see: Transnational Rule 20 & 35 at 289.

IX. Special Proceedings

RULE 71.1. CONDEMNING REAL OR PERSONAL PROPERTY

(a) APPLICABILITY OF OTHER RULES

These rules govern proceedings to condemn real and personal property by eminent domain, except as this rule provides otherwise.

(b) JOINDER OF PROPERTIES

The plaintiff may join separate pieces of property in a single action, no matter whether they are owned by the same persons or sought for the same use.

(c) COMPLAINT

(1)   Caption. The complaint must contain a caption as provided in Rule 10(a). The plaintiff must, however, name as defendants both the property — designated generally by kind, quantity, and location — and at least one owner of some part or interest in the property.

(2)   Contents. The complaint must contain a short and plain statement of the following:

   (A) the authority for the taking;

   (B) the uses for which the property is to be taken;

   (C) a description sufficient to identify the property;

   (D) the interests to be acquired; and

   (E) for each piece of property, a designation of each defendant who has been joined as an owner or owner of an interest in it.

(3)   Parties. When the action commences, the plaintiff need join as defendants only those persons who have or claim an interest in the property and whose names are then known. But before any hearing on compensation, the plaintiff must add as defendants all those persons who have or claim an interest and whose names have become known or can be found by a reasonably diligent search of the records, considering both the property's character and value and the interests to be acquired. All others may be made defendants under the designation "Unknown Owners."

(4)   Procedure. Notice must be served on all defendants as provided in Rule 71.1(d), whether they were named as defendants when the action commenced or were added later. A defendant may answer as provided in Rule 71.1(e). The court, meanwhile, may order any distribution of a deposit that the facts warrant.

(5)   Filing; Additional Copies. In addition to filing the complaint, the plaintiff must give the clerk at least one copy for the defendants' use and additional copies at the request of the clerk or a defendant.

(d) PROCESS

(1)   Delivering Notice to the Clerk. On filing a complaint, the plaintiff must promptly deliver to the clerk joint or several notices directed to the named defendants. When adding defendants, the plaintiff must deliver to the clerk additional notices directed to the new defendants.

(2) Contents of the Notice

    (A) Main Contents. Each notice must name the court, the title of the action, and the defendant to whom it is directed. It must describe the property sufficiently to identify it, but need not describe any property other than that to be taken from the named defendant. The notice must also state:

        (i)　that the action is to condemn property;

        (ii)　the interest to be taken;

        (iii)　the authority for the taking;

        (iv)　the uses for which the property is to be taken;

        (v)　that the defendant may serve an answer on the plaintiff's attorney within 20 days after being served with the notice;

        (vi)　that the failure to so serve an answer constitutes consent to the taking and to the court's authority to proceed with the action and fix the compensation; and

        (vii)　that a defendant who does not serve an answer may file a notice of appearance.

    (B) Conclusion. The notice must conclude with the name of the plaintiff's attorney and an address within the district in which the action is brought where the attorney may be served.

(3) Serving the Notice

    (A) Personal Service. When a defendant whose address is known resides within the United States or a territory subject to the administrative or judicial jurisdiction of the United States, personal service of the notice (without a copy of the complaint) must be made in accordance with Rule 4.

    (B) Service by Publication

        (i)　A defendant may be served by publication only when the plaintiff's attorney files a certificate stating that the attorney believes the defendant cannot be personally served, because after diligent inquiry within the state where the complaint is filed, the defendant's place of residence is still unknown or, if known, that it is beyond the territorial limits of personal service. Service is then made by publishing the notice—once a week for at least three successive weeks—in a newspaper published in the county where the property, is located or, if there is no such newspaper, in a newspaper with general circulation where the property is located. Before the last publication, a copy of the notice must also be mailed to every defendant who cannot be personally served but whose place of residence is then known. Unknown owners may be served by publication in the same manner by a notice addressed to "Unknown Owners."

        (ii)　Service by publication is complete on the date of the last publication. The plaintiff's attorney must prove publication and mailing by a certificate, attach a printed copy of the published notice, and mark on the copy the newspaper's name and the dates of publication.

(4) Effect of Delivery and Service. Delivering the notice to the clerk and serving it have the same effect as serving a summons under Rule 4.

(5) Proof of Service; Amending the Proof or Notice. Rule 4(l) governs proof of service. The court may permit the proof or the notice to be amended.

(e) APPEARANCE OR ANSWER

(1) **Notice of Appearance.** A defendant that has no objection or defense to the taking of its property may serve a notice of appearance designating the property in which it claims an interest. The defendant must then be given notice of all later proceedings affecting the defendant.

(2) **Answer.** A defendant that has an objection or defense to the taking must serve an answer within 20 days after being served with the notice. The answer must:

  (A) identify the property in which the defendant claims an interest;

  (B) state the nature and extent of the interest; and

  (C) state all the defendant's objections and defenses to the taking.

(3) **Waiver of Other Objections and Defenses; Evidence on Compensation.** A defendant waives all objections and defenses not stated in its answer. No other pleading or motion asserting an additional objection or defense is allowed. But at the trial on compensation, a defendant—whether or not it has previously appeared or answered—may present evidence on the amount of compensation to be paid and may share in the award.

(f) AMENDING PLEADINGS

Without leave of court, the plaintiff may—as often as it wants—amend the complaint at any time before the trial on compensation. But no amendment may be made if it would result in a dismissal inconsistent with Rule 71.1(i)(1) or (2). The plaintiff need not serve a copy of an amendment, but must serve notice of the filing, as provided in Rule 5(b), on every affected party who has appeared and, as provided in Rule 71.1(d), on every affected party who has not appeared. In addition, the plaintiff must give the clerk at least one copy of each amendment for the defendants' use, and additional copies at the request of the clerk or a defendant. A defendant may appear or answer in the time and manner and with the same effect as provided in Rule 71.1(d)(3).

(f) SUBSTITUTING PARTIES

If a defendant dies, becomes incompetent, or transfers an interest after being joined, the court may, on motion and notice of hearing, order that the proper party be substituted. Service of the motion and notice on a nonparty must be made as provided in Rule 71.1(d)(3).

(h) TRIAL OF THE ISSUES

(1) **Issues Other Than Compensation; Compensation.** In an action involving eminent domain under federal law, the court tries all issues, including compensation, except when compensation must be determined:

  (A) by any tribunal specially constituted by a federal statute to determine compensation; or

  (B) if there is no such tribunal, by a jury when a party demands one within the time to answer or within any additional time the court sets, unless the court appoints a commission.

(2) Appointing a Commission; Commission's Powers and Report

(A) Reasons for Appointing. If a party has demanded a jury, the court may instead appoint a three-person commission to determine compensation because of the character, location, or quantity of the property to be condemned or for other just reasons.

(B) Alternate Commissioners. The court may appoint up to two additional persons to serve as alternate commissioners to hear the case and replace commissioners who, before a decision is filed, the court finds unable or disqualified to perform their duties. Once the commission renders its final decision, the court must discharge any alternate who has not replaced a commissioner.

(C) Examining the Prospective Commissioners. Before making its appointments, the court must advise the parties of the identity and qualifications of each prospective commissioner and alternate, and may permit the parties to examine them. The parties may not suggest appointees, but for good cause may object to a prospective commissioner or alternate.

(D) Commission's Powers and Report. A commission has the powers of a master under Rule 53(c). Its action and report are determined by a majority. Rule 53(d), (e), and (f) apply to its action and report.

(i) DISMISSAL OF THE ACTION OR A DEFENDANT

(1) Dismissing the Action

(A) By the Plaintiff. If no compensation hearing on a piece of property has begun, and if the plaintiff has not acquired title or a lesser interest or taken possession, the plaintiff may, without a court order, dismiss the action as to that property by filing a notice of dismissal briefly describing the property.

(B) By Stipulation. Before a judgment is entered vesting the plaintiff with title or a lesser interest in or possession of property, the plaintiff and affected defendants may, without a court order, dismiss the action in whole or in part by filing a stipulation of dismissal. And if the parties so stipulate, the court may vacate a judgment already entered.

(C) By Court Order. At any time before compensation has been determined and paid, the court may, after a motion and hearing, dismiss the action as to a piece of property. But if the plaintiff has already taken title, a lesser interest, or possession as to any part of it, the court must award compensation for the title, lesser interest, or possession taken.

(2) Dismissing a Defendant. The court may at any time dismiss a defendant who was unnecessarily or improperly joined.

(3) Effect. A dismissal is without prejudice unless otherwise stated in the notice, stipulation, or court order.

(j) DEPOSIT AND ITS DISTRIBUTION

(1) Deposit. The plaintiff must deposit with the court any money required by law as a condition to the exercise of eminent domain and may make a deposit when allowed by statute.

(2) Distribution; Adjusting Distribution. After a deposit, the court and attorneys must expedite the proceedings so as to distribute the deposit and to determine and pay compensation. If the compensation finally awarded to a defendant exceeds the amount distributed to that defendant, the court must enter judgment against the plaintiff for the deficiency. If the

compensation awarded to a defendant is less than the amount distributed to that defendant, the court must enter judgment against that defendant for the overpayment.

(k) CONDEMNATION UNDER A STATE'S POWER OF EMINENT DOMAIN

This rule governs an action involving eminent domain under state law. But if state law provides for trying an issue by jury—or for trying the issue of compensation by jury or commission or both—that law governs.

(l) COSTS

Costs are not subject to Rule 54(d).

> **For further study, see**: Fed. R. Civ. P. Forms 60 & 61 at 108; and Transnational Rule 35 at 292.

RULE 72. MAGISTRATE JUDGES; PRETRIAL ORDER

(a) NONDISPOSITIVE MATTERS

When a pretrial matter not dispositive of a party's claim or defense is referred to a magistrate judge to hear and decide, the magistrate judge must promptly conduct the required proceedings and, when appropriate, issue a written order stating the decision. A party may serve and file objections to the order within 10 days after being served with a copy. A party may not assign as error a defect in the order not timely objected to. The district judge in the case must consider timely objections and modify or set aside any part of the order that is clearly erroneous or is contrary to law.

(b) DISPOSITIVE MOTIONS AND PRISONER PETITIONS

(1) Findings and Recommendations. A magistrate judge must promptly conduct the required proceedings when assigned, without the parties' consent, to hear a pretrial matter dispositive of a claim or defense or a prisoner petition challenging the conditions of confinement. A record must be made of all evidentiary proceedings and may, at the magistrate judge's discretion, be made of any other proceedings. The magistrate judge must enter a recommended disposition, including, if appropriate, proposed findings of fact. The clerk must promptly mail a copy to each party.

(2) Objections. Within 10 days after being served with a copy of the recommended disposition, a party may serve and file specific written objections to the proposed findings and recommendations. A party may respond to another party's objections within 10 days after being served with a copy. Unless the district judge orders otherwise, the objecting party must promptly arrange for transcribing the record, or whatever portions of it the parties agree to or the magistrate judge considers sufficient.

(3) Resolving Objections. The district judge must determine de novo any part of the magistrate judge's disposition that has been properly objected to. The district judge may accept, reject, or modify the recommended disposition; receive further evidence; or return the matter to the magistrate judge with instructions.

> **For further study, see**: Fed. R. Civ. P. Forms 80-82 at 109; and Transnational Rule 18 at 287.

RULE 73. MAGISTRATE JUDGES; TRIAL BY CONSENT; APPEAL

(a) TRIAL BY CONSENT

When authorized under 28 U.S.C. § 636(c), a magistrate judge may, if all parties consent, conduct a civil action or proceeding, including a jury or nonjury trial. A record must be made in accordance with 28 U.S.C. § 636(c)(5).

(b) CONSENT PROCEDURE

(1)   In General. When a magistrate judge has been designated to conduct civil actions or proceedings, the clerk must give the parties written notice of their opportunity to consent under 28 U.S.C. § 636(c). To signify their consent, the parties must jointly or separately file a statement consenting to the referral. A district judge or magistrate judge may be informed of a party's response to the clerk's notice only if all parties have consented to the referral.

(2)   Reminding the Parties About Consenting. A district judge, magistrate judge, or other court official may remind the parties of the magistrate judge's availability, but must also advise them that they are free to withhold consent without adverse substantive consequences.

(3)   Vacating a Referral. On its own for good cause—or when a party shows extraordinary circumstances—the district judge may vacate a referral to a magistrate judge under this rule.

(c) APPEALING A JUDGMENT

In accordance with 28 U.S.C. § 636(c)(3), an appeal from a judgment entered at a magistrate judge's direction may be taken to the court of appeals as would any other appeal from a district-court judgment.

For further study, see: Fed. R. Civ. P. Forms 80-82 at 109; and Transnational Rule 18 at 287.

RULE 74. [ABROGATED]
RULE 75. [ABROGATED]
RULE 76. [ABROGATED]

X. District Courts and Clerks

RULE 77. CONDUCTING BUSINESS; CLERK'S AUTHORITY; NOTICE OF AN ORDER OR JUDGMENT

(a) WHEN COURT IS OPEN

Every district court is considered always open for filing any paper, issuing and returning process, making a motion, or entering an order.

(b) PLACE FOR TRIAL AND OTHER PROCEEDINGS

Every trial on the merits must be conducted in open court and, so far as convenient, in a regular courtroom. Any other act or proceeding may be done or conducted by a judge in chambers, without the attendance of the clerk or other court official, and anywhere inside or outside the district. But no hearing—other than one ex parte—may be conducted outside the district unless all the affected parties consent.

(c) CLERK'S OFFICE HOURS; CLERK'S ORDERS

(1) Hours. The clerk's office—with a clerk or deputy on duty—must be open during business hours every day except Saturdays, Sundays, and legal holidays. But a court may, by local rule or order, require that the office be open for specified hours on Saturday or a particular legal holiday other than one listed in Rule 6(a)(4)(A).

(2) Orders. Subject to the court's power to suspend, alter, or rescind the clerk's action for good cause, the clerk may:

(A) issue process;

(B) enter a default;

(C) enter a default judgment under Rule 55(b)(1); and

(D) act on any other matter that does not require the court's action.

(d) SERVING NOTICE OF AN ORDER OR JUDGMENT

(1) Service. Immediately after entering an order or judgment, the clerk must serve notice of the entry, as provided in Rule 5(b), on each party who is not in default for failing to appear. The clerk must record that service on the docket. A party also may serve notice of the entry as provided in Rule 5(b).

(2) Time to Appeal Not Affected by Lack of Notice. Lack of notice of the entry does not affect the time for appeal or relieve—or authorize the court to relieve—a party for failing to appeal within the time allowed, except as allowed by Federal Rule of Appellate Procedure 4(a).

For further study, see: 1991 Advisory Committee Notes at 158.

RULE 78. HEARING MOTIONS; SUBMISSION ON BRIEFS

(a) PROVIDING A REGULAR SCHEDULE FOR ORAL HEARINGS

A court may establish regular times and places for oral hearings on motions.

(b) PROVIDING FOR SUBMISSION ON BRIEFS

By rule or order, the court may provide for submitting and determining motions on briefs, without oral hearings.

RULE 79. RECORDS KEPT BY THE CLERK

(a) CIVIL DOCKET

(1) In General. The clerk must keep a record known as the "civil docket" in the form and manner prescribed by the Director of the Administrative Office of the United States Courts with the approval of the Judicial Conference of the United States. The clerk must enter each civil action in the docket. Actions must be assigned consecutive file numbers, which must be noted in the docket where the first entry of the action is made.

(2) Items to be Entered. The following items must be marked with the file number and entered chronologically in the docket:

(A) papers filed with the clerk;

(B) process issued, and proofs of service or other returns showing execution; and

(C) appearances, orders, verdicts, and judgments.

(3)   Contents of Entries; Jury Trial Demanded. Each entry must briefly show the nature of the paper filed or writ issued, the substance of each proof of service or other return, and the substance and date of entry of each order and judgment. When a jury trial has been properly demanded or ordered, the clerk must enter the word "jury" in the docket.

(b) CIVIL JUDGMENTS AND ORDERS

The clerk must keep a copy of every final judgment and appealable order; of every order affecting title to or a lien on real or personal property; and of any other order that the court directs to be kept. The clerk must keep these in the form and manner prescribed by the Director of the Administrative Office of the United States courts with the approval of the Judicial Conference of the United States.

(c) INDEXES; CALENDARS

Under the court's direction, the clerk must:

(1)   keep indexes of the docket and of the judgments and orders described Rule 79(b); and

(2)   prepare calendars of all actions ready for trial, distinguishing jury trials from nonjury trials.

(d) OTHER RECORDS

The clerk must keep any other records required by the Director of the Administrative Office of the United States Courts with the approval of the Judicial Conference of the United States.

RULE 80. STENOGRAPHIC TRANSCRIPT AS EVIDENCE

If stenographically reported testimony at a hearing or trial is admissible in evidence at a later trial, the testimony may be proved by a transcript certified by the person who reported it.

XI. General Provisions

RULE 81. APPLICABILITY OF THE RULES IN GENERAL; REMOVED ACTIONS

(a) APPLICABILITY TO PARTICULAR PROCEEDINGS

(1)   Prize Proceedings. These rules do not apply to prize proceedings in admiralty governed by 10 U.S.C. §§ 7651-7681.

(2)   Bankruptcy. These rules apply to bankruptcy proceedings to the extent provided by the Federal Rules of Bankruptcy Procedure.

(3)   Citizenship. These rules apply to proceedings for admission to citizenship to the extent that the practice in those proceedings is not specified in federal statutes and has previously conformed to the practice in civil actions. The provisions of 8 U.S.C. § 1451 for service by publication and for answer apply in proceedings to cancel citizenship certificates.

(4)   Special Writs. These rules apply to proceedings for habeas corpus and for quo warranto to the extent that the practice in those proceedings:

    (A) is not specified in a federal statute, the Rules Governing Section 2254 Cases, or the Rules Governing Section 2255 Cases; and

    (B) has previously conformed to the practice in civil actions.

(5)   Proceedings Involving a Subpoena. These rules apply to proceedings to compel testimony or the production of documents through a subpoena issued by a United States officer

or agency under a federal statute, except as otherwise provided by statute, by local rule, or by court order in the proceedings.

(6) *Other Proceedings.* These rules, to the extent applicable, govern proceedings under the following laws, except as these laws provide other procedures:

(A) 7 U.S.C. §§ 292, 499g(c), for reviewing an order of the Secretary of Agriculture;

(B) 9 U.S.C., relating to arbitration;

(C) 15 U.S.C. § 522, for reviewing an order of the Secretary of the Interior;

(D) 15 U.S.C. § 715d(c), for reviewing an order denying a certificate of clearance;

(E) 29 U.S.C. §§ 159, 160, for enforcing an order of the National Labor Relations Board;

(F) 33 U.S.C. §§ 918, 921, for enforcing or reviewing a compensation order under the Longshore and Harbor Workers' Compensation Act; and

(G) 45 U.S.C. § 159, for reviewing an arbitration award in a railway-labor dispute.

(b) SCIRE FACIAS AND MANDAMUS

The writs of scire facias and mandamus are abolished. Relief previously available through them may be obtained by appropriate action or motion under these rules.

(c) REMOVED ACTIONS

(1) *Applicability.* These rules apply to a civil action after it is removed from a state court.

(2) *Further Pleading.* After removal, repleading is unnecessary unless the court orders it. A defendant who did not answer before removal must answer or present other defenses or objections under these rules within the longest of these periods:

(A) 20 days after receiving — through service or otherwise — a copy of the initial pleading stating the claim for relief;

(B) 20 days after being served with the summons for an initial pleading on file at the time of service; or

(C) 5 days after the notice of removal is filed.

(3) Demand for a Jury Trial

(A) *As Affected by State Law.* A party who, before removal, expressly demanded a jury trial in accordance with state law need not renew the demand after removal. If the state law did not require an express demand for a jury trial, a party need not make one after removal unless the court orders the parties to do so within a specified time. The court must so order at a party's request and may so order on its own. A party who fails to make a demand when so ordered waives a jury trial.

(B) *Under Rule 38.* If all necessary pleadings have been served at the time of removal, a party entitled to a jury trial under Rule 38 must be given one if the party serves a demand within 10 days after:

(i) it files a notice of removal; or

(ii) it is served with a notice of removal filed by another party.

(d) LAW APPLICABLE

(1)   State Law. When these rules refer to state law, the term "law" includes the state's statutes and the state's judicial decisions.

(2)   District of Columbia. The term "state" includes, where appropriate, the District of Columbia. When these rules provide for state law to apply, in the District Court for the District of Columbia:

> (A) the law applied in the District governs; and
>
> (B) the term "federal statute" includes any Act of Congress that applies locally to the District.

RULE 82. JURISDICTION AND VENUE UNAFFECTED

These rules do not extend or limit the jurisdiction of the district courts or the venue of actions in those courts. An admiralty or maritime claim under Rule 9(h) is not a civil action for purposes of 28 U.S.C. §§ 1391-1392.

RULE 83. RULES BY DISTRICT COURTS; JUDGE'S DIRECTIVES

(a) LOCAL RULES

(1)   In General. After giving public notice and an opportunity for comment, a district court, acting by a majority of its district judges, may adopt and amend rules governing its practice. A local rule must be consistent with — but not duplicate — federal statutes and rules adopted under 28 U.S.C. § 2072 and 2075, and must conform to any uniform numbering system prescribed by the Judicial Conference of the United States. A local rule takes effect on the date specified by the district court and remains in effect unless amended by the court or abrogated by the judicial council of the circuit. Copies of rules and amendments must, on their adoption, be furnished to the judicial council and the Administrative Office of the United States Courts and be made available to the public.

(2)   Requirement of Form. A local rule imposing a requirement of form must not be enforced in a way that causes a party to lose any right because of a nonwillful failure to comply.

(b) PROCEDURE WHEN THERE IS NO CONTROLLING LAW

A judge may regulate practice in any manner consistent with federal law, rules adopted under 28 U.S.C. §§ 2072 and 2075, and the district's local rules. No sanction or other disadvantage may be imposed for noncompliance with any requirement not in federal law, federal rules, or the local rules unless the alleged violator has been furnished in the particular case with actual notice of the requirement.

> **For further study, see**: 1985 Advisory Committee Notes at 152; 1995 Advisory Committee Notes at 185; and Transnational Rule 18 at 287.

RULE 84. FORMS

The forms in the Appendix suffice under these rules and illustrate the simplicity and brevity that these rules contemplate.

RULE 85. TITLE

These rules may be cited as the Federal Rules of Civil Procedure.

RULE 86. EFFECTIVE DATES

(a) IN GENERAL

These rules and any amendments take effect at the time specified by the Supreme Court, subject to 28 U.S.C. § 2074. They govern:

    (1)   proceedings in an action commenced after their effective date; and

    (2)   proceedings after that date in an action then pending unless:

        (A) the Supreme Court specifies otherwise; or

        (B) the court determines that applying them in a particular action would be infeasible or work an injustice.

(b) DECEMBER 1, 2007 AMENDMENTS

If any provisions in Rules 1-5.1, 6-73, or 77-86 conflicts with another law, priority in time for the purpose of 28 U.S.C. § 2072(b) is not affected by the amendments taking effect on December 1, 2007.

APPENDIX OF FORMS
(See Rule 84)

FORM 1. CAPTION
(Use on every summons, complaint, answer, motion, or other document.)

United States District Court for the
_____ District of _____

A B, Plaintiff   )
)
v.   )   Civil Action No. _____
)
C D, Defendant   )
)
v.   )
)
E F, Third-Party Defendant   )
    (Use if needed.)   )

(Name of Document)

FORM 2. DATE, SIGNATURE, ADDRESS, E-MAIL ADDRESS, AND TELEPHONE NUMBER
(Use at the conclusion of pleadings and other papers that require a signature.)

Date:_____

                    _____
                    (Signature of the attorney or unrepresented party)

                    _____
                    (Printed name)

                    _____
                    (Address)

                    _____
                    (E-mail address)

                    _____
                    (Telephone number)

FORM 3. SUMMONS

(Caption—See Form 1.)

To name the defendant:

A lawsuit has been filed against you.

Within 20 days after service of this summons on you (not counting the day you received it), you must serve on the plaintiff an answer to the attached complaint or a motion under Rule 12 of the Federal Rules of Civil Procedure. The answer or motion must be served on the plaintiff's attorney, _____, whose address is _____. If you fail to do so, judgment by default will be entered against you for the relief demanded in the complaint. You also must file your answer or motion with the court.

Date:_____   _____
(Court seal)   Clerk of Court

(Use 60 days if the defendant is the United States or a United States agency, or is an officer or employee of the United States allowed 60 days by Rule 12(a)(3).)

FORM 4. SUMMONS ON A THIRD-PARTY COMPLAINT

(Caption—See Form 1.)

To name the third-party defendant:

A lawsuit has been filed against defendant _____, who as third-party plaintiff is making this claim against you to pay part or all of what [he] may owe to the plaintiff _____.

Within 20 days after service of this summons on you (not counting the day you received it), you must serve on the plaintiff and on the defendant an answer to the attached third-party complaint or a motion under Rule 12 of the Federal Rules of Civil Procedure. The answer or motion must be served on the defendant's attorney, _____, whose address is _____, and also on the plaintiff's attorney, _____, whose address is _____. If you fail to do so, judgment by default will be entered against you for the relief demanded in the third-party compalint. You also must file the answer or motion with the court and serve it on any other parties.

A copy of the plaintiff's complaint is also attached. You may—but are not required to—respond to it.

Date:_____   _____
(Court seal)   Clerk of Court

FORM 5. NOTICE OF A LAWSUIT AND REQUEST TO WAIVE SERVICE OF A SUMMONS

(Caption—See Form 1.)

To name the defendant—or if the defendant is a corporation, partnership, or association name an officer or agent authorized to receive service:

Why are you getting this?

A lawsuit has been filed against you, or the entity you represent, in this court under the number shown above. A copy of the complaint is attached.

96

This is not a summons, or an official notice from the court. It is a request that, to avoid expenses, you waive formal service of a summons by signing and returning the enclosed waiver. To avoid these expenses, you must return the signed waiver within <u>give at least 30 days or at least 60 days if the defendant is outside any judicial district of the United States</u> from the date shown below, which is the date this notice was sent. Two copies of the waiver form are enclosed, along with a stamped, self-addressed envelope or other prepaid means for returning one copy. You may keep the other copy.

What happens next?

If you return the signed waiver, I will file it with the court. The action will then proceed as if you had been served on the date the waiver is filed, but no summons will be served on you and you will have 60 days from the date this notice is sent (see the date below) to answer the complaint (or 90 days if this notice is sent to you outside any judicial district of the United States).

If you do not return the signed waiver within the time indicated, I will arrange to have the summons and complaint served on you. And I will ask the court to require you, or the entity you represent, to pay the expenses of making service.

Please read the enclosed statement about the duty to avoid unnecessary expenses.

I certify that this request is being sent to you on the date below.

(Date and sign — See Form 2.)

FORM 6. WAIVER OF THE SERVICE OF SUMMONS

(Caption — See Form 1.)

To <u>name the plaintiff's attorney or the unrepresented plaintiff</u>:

I have received your request to waive service of a summons in this action along with a copy of the complaint, two copies of this waiver form, and a prepaid means of returning one signed copy of the form to you.

I, or the entity I represent, agree to save the expense of serving a summons and complaint in this case.

I understand that I, or the entity I represent, will keep all defenses or objections to the lawsuit, the court's jurisdiction, and the venue of the action, but that I waive any objections to the absence of a summons or of service.

I also understand that I, or the entity I represent, must file and serve an answer or a motion under Rule 12 within 60 days from _____, the date when this request was sent (or 90 days if it was sent outside the United States). If I fail to do so, a default judgment will be entered against me or the entity I represent.

(Date and sign — See Form 2.)

(Attach the following to Form 6)

Duty to Avoid Unnecessary Expenses of Serving a Summons

Rule 4 of the Federal Rules of Civil Procedure requires certain defendants to cooperate in saving unnecessary expenses of serving a summons and complaint. A defendant who is located in the United States and who fails to return a signed waiver of service requested by a plaintiff located in the United States will be required to pay the expenses of service, unless the defendant shows good cause for the failure.

"Good cause" does not include a belief that the lawsuit is groundless, or that it has been brought in an improper venue, or that the court has no jurisdiction over this matter or over the defendant or the defendant's property.

If the waiver is signed and returned, you can still make these and all other defenses and objections, but you cannot object to the absence of a summons or of service.

If you waive service, then you must, within the time specified on the waiver form, serve an answer or a motion under Rule 12 on the plaintiff and file a copy with the court. By signing and returning the waiver form, you are allowed more time to respond than if a summons had been served.

FORM 7. STATEMENT OF JURISDICTION

a. For diversity-of-citizenship jurisdiction. The plaintiff is [a citizen of <u>Michigan</u>] [a corporation incorporated under the laws of <u>Michigan</u> with its principal place of business in <u>Michigan</u>]. The defendant is [a citizen of <u>New York</u>] [a corporation incorporated under the laws of <u>New York</u> with its principal place of business in <u>New York</u>]. The amount in controversy, without interests and costs, exceeds the sum or value specified by 28 U.S.C. § 1332.

b. For federal-question jurisdiction. This action arises under [the United States Constitution, <u>specify the article or amendment and the section</u>] [a United States treaty <u>specify</u>] [a federal statute, __ U.S.C. § __].

c. For a claim in the admiralty or maritime jurisdiction. This is a case of admiralty or maritime jurisdiction. <u>To invoke admiralty status under Rule 9(h) use the following:</u> This is an admiralty or maritime claim within the meaning of Rule 9(h).

FORM 8. STATEMENT OF REASONS FOR OMITTING A PARTY

(If a person who ought to be made a party under Rule 19(a) is not named, include this statement in accordance with Rule 19(c).)

This complaint does not join as a party <u>name</u> who [is not subject to this court's personal jurisdiction] [cannot be made a party without depriving this court of subject-matter jurisdiction] because <u>state the reason</u>.

FORM 9. STATEMENT NOTING A PARTY'S DEATH

(Caption—See Form 1.)

In accordance with Rule 25(a) <u>name the person</u>, who is [a party to this action] [a representative of or successor to the deceased party], notes the death during the pendency of this action of <u>name</u>, [<u>describe as party</u> in this action].

(Date and sign—See Form 2.)

FORM 10. COMPLAINT TO RECOVER A SUM CERTAIN

(Caption—See Form 1.)

1.   (Statement of Jurisdiction—See Form 7.)

Use one or more of the following as appropriate and include a demand for judgment.

(a) On a Promissory Note

2.   On date, the defendant executed and delivered a note promising to pay the plaintiff on _____ the sum of $_____ with interest at the rate of ___ percent. A copy of the note [is attached as Exhibit A] [is summarized as follows: _____].

3.   The defendant has not paid the amount owed.

(b) On an Account

2.   The defendant owes the plaintiff $_____ according to the account set out in Exhibit A.

(c) For Goods Sold and Delivered

2.   The defendant owes the plaintiff $_____ for goods sold and delivered by the plaintiff to the defendant from date to date.

(d) For Money Lent

2.   The defendant owes the plaintiff $_____ for money lent by the plaintiff to the defendant on date.

(e) For Money Paid by Mistake

2.   The defendant owes the plaintiff $_____ for money paid by mistake to the defendant on date under these circumstances: describe with particularity in accordance with Rule 9(b).

(f) For Money Had and Received

2.   The defendant owes the plaintiff $_____ for money that was received from name on date to be paid by the defendant to the plaintiff.

Demand for Judgment

Therefore, the plaintiff demands judgment against the defendant for $_____, plus interest and costs.

(Date and sign—See Form 2.)

FORM 11. COMPLAINT FOR NEGLIGENCE

(Caption—See Form 1.)

1.   (Statement of Jurisdiction—See Form 7.)

2.   On date, at place, the defendant negligently drove a motor vehicle against the plaintiff.

3.   As a result, the plaintiff was physically injured, lost wages or income, suffered physical and mental pain, and incurred medical expenses of $_____.

Therefore, the plaintiff demands judgment against the defendant for $_____, plus costs.

(Date and sign—See Form 2.)

FORM 12. COMPLAINT FOR NEGLIGENCE WHEN THE PLAINTIFF DOES NOT KNOW WHO IS RESPONSIBLE

(Caption—See Form 1.)

1. (Statement of Jurisdiction—See Form 7.)

2. On date, at place, defendant name or defendant name or both of them willfully or recklessly or negligently drove, or caused to be driven, a motor vehicle against the plaintiff.

3. As a result, the plaintiff was physically injured, lost wages or income, suffered mental and physical pain, and incurred medical expenses of $_____.

Therefore, the plaintiff demands judgment against one or both defendants for $_____, plus costs.

(Date and sign—See Form 2.)

FORM 13. COMPLAINT FOR NEGLIGENCE UNDER THE FEDERAL EMPLOYERS' LIABILITY ACT

(Caption—See Form 1.)

1. (Statement of Jurisdiction—See Form 7.)

2. At the times below, the defendant owned and operated in interstate commerce a railroad line that passed through a tunnel located at _____.

3. On date, the plaintiff was working to repair and enlarge the tunnel to make it convenient and safe for use in interstate commerce.

4. During this work, the defendant, as the employer, negligently put the plaintiff to work in a section of the tunnel that the defendant had left unprotected and unsupported.

5. The defendant's negligence caused the plaintiff to be injured by a rock that fell from an unsupported portion of the tunnel.

6. As a result, the plaintiff was physically injured, lost wages or income, suffered mental and physical pain, and incurred medical expenses of $_____.

Therefore, the plaintiff demands judgment against the defendant for $_____, and costs.

(Date and sign—See Form 2.)

FORM 14. COMPLAINT FOR DAMAGES UNDER THE MERCHANT MARINE ACT

(Caption—See Form 1.)

1. (Statement of Jurisdiction—See Form 7.)

2. At the times below, the defendant owned and operated the vessel name and used it to transport cargo for hire by water in interstate and foreign commerce.

3. On date, at place, the defendant hired the plaintiff under seamen's articles of customary form for a voyage from _____ to _____ and return at a wage of $_____ a month and found, which is equal to a shore worker's wage of $_____.

4. On date, the vessel was at sea on the return voyage. Describe the weather and the condition of the vessel.

5. Describe as in Form 11 the defendant's negligent conduct.

6. As a result of the defendant's negligent conduct and the unseaworthiness of the vessel,

the plaintiff was physically injured, has been incapable of any gainful activity, suffered mental and physical pain, and has incurred medical expenses of $_____.

Therefore, the plaintiff demands judgment against the defendant for $_____, plus costs.

(Date and sign—See Form 2.)

FORM 15. COMPLAINT FOR THE CONVERSION OF PROPERTY

(Caption—See Form 1.)

1. (Statement of Jurisdiction—See Form 7.)

2. On date, at place, the defendant converted to the defendant's own use property owned by the plaintiff. The property consists of describe.

3. The property is worth $_____.

Therefore, the plaintiff demands judgment against the defendant for $_____, plus costs.

(Date and sign—See Form 2.)

FORM 16. THIRD PARTY COMPLAINT

(Caption—See Form 1.)

1. Plaintiff name has filed against defendant name a complaint, a copy of which is attached.

2. State grounds entitling defendant's name to recover from third-party defendant's name for (all or an identified share) of any judgment for plaintiff's name against defendant's name.

Therefore, the defendant demands judgment against third-party defendant's name for all or an identified share of sums that may be adjudged against the defendant in the plaintiff's favor.

(Date and sign—See Form 2.)

FORM 17. COMPLAINT FOR SPECIFIC PERFORMANCE OF A CONTRACT TO CONVEY LAND

(Caption—See Form 1.)

1. (Statement of Jurisdiction—See Form 7.)

2. On date, the parties agreed to the contract [attached as Exhibit A] [summarize the contract].

3. As agreed, the plaintiff tendered the purchase price and requested a conveyance of the land, but the defendant refused to accept the money or make a conveyance.

4. The plaintiff now offers to pay the purchase price.

Therefore, the plaintiff demands that:

(a) the defendant be required to specifically perform the agreement and pay damages of $_____, plus interest and costs, or

(b) if specific performance is not ordered, the defendant be required to pay damages of $_____, plus interests and costs.

(Date and sign—See Form 2.)

FORM 18. COMPLAINT FOR PATENT INFRINGEMENT

(Caption—See Form 1.)

1. (Statement of Jurisdiction—See Form 7.)

2. On <u>date</u>, United States Letters Patent No. _____ were issued to the plaintiff for an invention in an <u>electric motor</u>. The plaintiff owned the patent throughout the period of the defendant's infringing acts and still owns the patent.

3. The defendant has infringed and is still infringing the Letters Patent by making, selling, and using <u>electric motors</u> that embody the patented invention, and the defendant will continue to do so unless enjoined by this court.

4. The plaintiff has complied with the statutory requirement of placing a notice of the Letters Patent on all <u>electric motors</u> it manufactures and sells and has given the defendant written notice of the infringement.

Therefore, the plaintiff demands:

(a) a preliminary and final injunction against the continuing infringement;

(b) an accounting for damages;

(c) interests and costs.

(Date and sign—See Form 2.)

FORM 19. COMPLAINT FOR COPYRIGHT INFRINGEMENT AND UNFAIR COMPETITION

(Caption—See Form 1.)

1. (Statement of Jurisdiction—See Form 7.)

2. Before <u>date</u>, the plaintiff, a United States citizen, wrote a book entitled _____.

3. The book is an original work that may be copyrighted under United States law. A copy of the book is attached as Exhibit A.

4. Between <u>date</u> and <u>date</u>, the plaintiff applied to the copyright office and received a certificate of registration dated _____ and identified as <u>date, class, number</u>.

5. Since <u>date</u>, the plaintiff has either published or licensed for publication all copies of the book in compliance with the copyright laws and has remained the sole owner of the copyright.

6. After the copyright was issued, the defendant infringed the copyright by publishing and selling a book entitled _____, which was copied largely from the plaintiff's book. A copy of the defendant's book is attached as Exhibit B.

7. The plaintiff has notified the defendant in writing of the infringement.

8. The defendant continues to infringe the copyright by continuing to publish and sell the infringing book in violation of the copyright, and further has engaged in unfair trade practices and unfair competition in connection with its publication and sale of the infringing book, thus causing irreparable damage.

Therefore, the plaintiff demands that:

(a) until this case is decided the defendant and the defendant's agents be enjoined from disposing of any copies of the defendant's book by sale or otherwise;

(b) the defendant account for and pay as damages to the plaintiff all profits and advantages gained from unfair trade practices and unfair competition in selling the defendant's book, and all profits and advantages gained from infringing the plaintiff's copyright (but no less than the statutory minimum);

(c) the defendant deliver for impoundment all copies of the book in the defendant's possession or control and deliver for destruction all infringing copies and all plates, molds, and other materials for making infringing copies;

(d) the defendant pay the plaintiff interest, costs, and reasonable attorneys' fees; and

(e) the plaintiff be awarded any other just relief.

(Date and sign—See Form 2.)

FORM 20. COMPLAINT FOR INTERPLEADER AND DECLARATORY RELIEF

(Caption—See Form 1.)

1.   (Statement of Jurisdiction—See Form 7.)

2.   On date, the plaintiff issued a life insurance policy on the life of name with name as the named beneficiary.

3.   As a condition for keeping the policy in force, the policy required payment of a premium during the first year and then annually.

4.   The premium due on date was never paid, and the policy lapsed after that date.

5.   On date, after the policy had lapsed, both the insured and the named beneficiary died in an automobile collision.

6.   Defendant name claims to be the beneficiary in place of name and has filed a claim to be paid the policy's full amount.

7.   The other two defendants are representatives of the deceased persons' estates. Each defendant has filed a claim on behalf of each estate to receive payment of the policy's full amount.

8.   If the policy was in force at the time of death, the plaintiff is in doubt about who should be paid.

Therefore, the plaintiff demands that:

(a) each defendant be restrained from commencing any action against the plaintiff on the policy;

(b) a judgment be entered that no defendant is entitled to the proceeds of the policy or any part of it, but if the court determines that the policy was in effect at the time of the insured's death, that the defendants be required to interplead and settle among themselves their rights to the proceeds, and that the plaintiff be discharged from all liability except to the defendant determined to be entitled to the proceeds; and

(c) the plaintiff recover its costs.

(Date and sign—See Form 2.)

FORM 21. COMPLAINT ON A CLAIM FOR A DEBT AND TO SET ASIDE A FRAUDULENT CONVEYANCE UNDER RULE 18(B)

(Caption—See Form 1.)

1. (Statement of Jurisdiction—See Form 7.)

2. On <u>date</u>, defendant <u>name</u> signed a note promising to pay to the plaintiff on <u>date</u> the sum of $_____ with interest at the rate of ___ percent. [The pleader may, but need not, attach a copy or plead the note verbatim.]

3. Defendant <u>name</u> owes the plaintiff the amount of the note and interest.

4. On <u>date</u>, defendant <u>name</u> conveyed all defendant's real and personal property <u>if less than all, describe it fully</u> to defendant <u>name</u> for the purpose of defrauding the plaintiff and hindering or delaying the collection of the debt.

Therefore, the plaintiff demands that:

(a) judgment for $_____, plus costs, be entered against defendant <u>name(s)</u>; and

(b) the conveyance to defendant <u>name</u> be declared void and any judgment granted be made a lien on the property.

(Date and sign—See Form 2.)

FORM 30. ANSWER PRESENTING DEFENSES UNDER RULE 12(B)

(Caption—See Form 1.)

Responding to Allegations in the Complaint

1. Defendant admits the allegations in paragraphs _____.

2. Defendant lacks knowledge or information sufficient to form a belief about the truth of the allegations in paragraphs _____.

3. Defendant admits <u>identify part of the allegation</u> in paragraph _____ and denies or lacks knowledge or information sufficient to form a belief about the truth of the rest of the paragraph.

Failure to State a Claim

4. The complaint fails to state a claim upon which relief can be granted.

Failure to Join a Required Party

5. If there is a debt, it is owed jointly by the defendant and <u>name</u> who is a citizen of _____. This person can be made a party without depriving this court of jurisdiction over the existing parties.

Affirmative Defense—Statute of Limitations

6. The plaintiff's claim is barred by the statute of limitations because it arose more than _____ years before this action was commenced.

Counterclaim

7. <u>Set forth any counterclaim in the same way a claim is pleaded in ia complaint. Include a further statement of jurisdiction if needed.</u>

Crossclaim

8.   Set forth a crossclaim against a coparty in the same way a claim is pleaded in a complaint. Include a further statement of jurisdiction if needed.

(Date and sign—See Form 2.)

FORM 31. ANSWER TO A COMPLAINT FOR MONEY HAD AND RECEIVED WITH A COUNTERCLAIM FOR INTERPLEADER

(Caption—See Form 1.)

Response to the Allegations in the Complaint

(See Form 30.)

Counterclaim for Interpleader

1.   The defendant received from name a deposit of $_____.

2.   The plaintiff demands payment of the deposit because of a purported assignment from name, who has notified the defendant that the assignment is not valid and who continues to hold the defendant responsible for the deposit.

Therefore, the defendant demands that:

(a)   name be made a party to this action;

(b)   the plaintiff and name be required to interplead their respective claims;

(c)   the court decide whether the plaintiff or name or either of them is entitled to the deposit and discharge the defendant of any liability except to the person entitled to the deposit; and

(d)   the defendant recover costs and attorney's fees.

(Date and sign—See Form 2.)

FORM 40. MOTION TO DISMISS UNDER RULE 12(B) FOR LACK OF JURISDICTION, IMPROPER VENUE, INSUFFICIENT SERVICE OF PROCESS, OR FAILURE TO STATE A CLAIM

(Caption—See Form 1.)

The defendant moves to dismiss the action because:

1.   the amount in controversy is less than the sum or value specified by 28 U.S.C. § 1332;

2.   the defendant is not subject to the personal jurisdiction of this court;

3.   venue is improper (this defendant does not reside in this district and no part of the events or omissions giving rise to the claim occurred in the district);

4.   the defendant has not been properly served, as shown by the attached affidavits of _____; or

5.   the complaint fails to state a claim upon which relief can be granted.

(Date and sign—See Form 2.)

FORM 41. MOTION TO BRING IN A THIRD-PARTY DEFENDANT

(Caption—See Form 1.)

The defendant, as third-party plaintiff, moves for leave to serve on <u>name</u> a summons and third-party complaint, copies of which are attached.

(Date and sign—See Form 2.)

FORM 42. MOTION TO INTERVENE AS A DEFENDANT UNDER RULE 24

(Caption—See Form 1.)

1.   <u>name</u> moves for leave to intervene as a defendant in this action and to file the attached answer.

<u>State grounds under Rule 24(a) or (b).</u>

2.   The plaintiff alleges patent infringement. We manufacture and sell to the defendant the articles involved, and we have a defense to the plaintiff's claim.

3.   Our defense presents questions of law and fact that are common to this action.

(Date and sign—See Form 2.)

<u>An Intervener's Answer must be attached. See Form 30.</u>

FORM 50. REQUEST TO PRODUCE DOCUMENTS AND TANGIBLE THINGS, OR TO ENTER ONTO LAND UNDER RULE 34

(Caption—See Form 1.)

The plaintiff <u>name</u> requests that the defendant <u>name</u> respond within _____ days to the following requests:

1.   To produce and permit the plaintiff to inspect and copy and to test or sample the following documents, including electronically stored information:

<u>Describe each document and the electronically stored information,</u>
<u>either individually or by category.</u>

<u>State the time, place, and manner of the inspection and any related acts.</u>

2.   To produce and permit the plaintiff to inspect and copy—and to test or sample—the following tangible things:

<u>Describe each thing, either individually or by category.</u>

<u>State the time, place, and manner of the inspection and any related acts.</u>

3.   To permit the plaintiff to enter onto the following land to inspect, photograph, test, or sample the property or an object or operation on the property.

<u>Describe the property and each object or operation.</u>

<u>State the time and manner of the inspection and any related acts.</u>

(Date and sign—See Form 2.)

FORM 51. REQUEST FOR ADMISSIONS UNDER RULE 36

(Caption—See Form 1.)

The plaintiff <u>name</u> asks the defendant <u>name</u> to respond within 30 days to these requests by admitting, for purposes of this action only and subject to objections to admissibility at trial:

1.   The genuineness of the following documents, copies of which [are attached] [are or have been furnished or made available for inspection and copying].

<u>List each document.</u>

2.   The truth of each of the following statements:

<u>List each statement.</u>

(Date and sign—See Form 2.)

FORM 52. REPORT OF THE PARTIES' PLANNING MEETING

(Caption—See Form 1.)

1.   The following persons participated in a Rule 26(f) conference on <u>date</u> by <u>state the method of conferring</u>:

<u>e.g., name</u> representing the plaintiff.

2.   Initial Disclosures. The parties [have completed] [will complete by <u>date</u>] the initial disclosures required by Rule 26(a)(1).

3.   Discovery Plan. The parties propose this discovery plan:

<u>Use separate paragraphs or subparagraphs if the parties disagree.</u>

(a)   Discovery will be needed on these subjects: <u>describe</u>.

(b)   (Dates for commencing and completing discovery, including discovery to be commenced or completed before other discovery.)

(c)   (Maximum number of interrogatories by each party to another party, along with the dates the answers are due.)

(d)   (Maximum number of requests for admission, along with the dates responses are due.)

(e)   (Maximum number of depositions by each party.)

(f)   (Limits on the length of depositions, in hours.)

(g)   (Dates for exchanging reports of expert witnesses.)

(h)   (Dates for supplementation under Rule 26(e).)

4.   Other Items:

(a)   (A date if the parties ask to meet with the court before a scheduling order.)

(b)   (Requested dates for pretrial conferences.)

(c)   (Final dates for the plaintiff to amend pleadings or to join parties.)

(d)   (Final dates for the defendant to amend pleadings or to join parties.)

(e)   (Final dates to file dispositive motions.)

(f)   (State the prospects for settlement.)

(g)   (Identify any alternative dispute resolution procedure that may enhance settlement prospects.)

(h) (Final dates for submitting Rule 26(a)(3) witness lists, designations of witnesses whose testimony will be presented by deposition, and exhibit lists.)

(i) (Final dates to file objections under Rule 26(a)(3).)

(j) (Suggested trial date and estimate of trial length.)

(k) (Other matters.)

(Date and sign—See Form 2.)

FORM 60. NOTICE OF CONDEMNATION

(Caption—See Form 1.)

To <u>name the defendant</u>.

1. A complaint in condemnation has been filed in the United States District Court for the _____ District of _____, to take property to use for <u>purpose</u>. The interest to be taken is <u>describe</u>. The court is located in the United States courthouse at this address: _____.

2. The property to be taken is described below. You have or claim an interest in it.

<u>Describe the property</u>

3. The authority for taking this property is <u>cite</u>.

4. If you want to object or present any defense to the taking you must serve an answer on the plaintiff's attorney within 20 days [after being served with this notice] [from <u>insert the date of the last publication of notice</u>]. Send your answer to this address: _____.

5. Your answer must identify the property in which you claim an interest, state the nature and extent of that interest, and state all your objections and defenses to the taking. Objections and defenses not presented are waived.

6. If you fail to answer you consent to the taking and the court will enter a judgment that takes your described property interest.

7. Instead of answering, you may serve on the plaintiff's attorney a notice of appearance that designates the property in which you claim an interest. After you do that, you will receive a notice of any proceedings that affect you. Whether or not you have previously appeared or answered, you may present evidence at a trial to determine compensation for the property and share in the overall award.

(Date and sign—See Form 2.)

FORM 61. COMPLAINT FOR CONDEMNATION

(Caption—See Form 1; name as defendants the property and at least one owner.)

1. (Statement of Jurisdiction—See Form 7.)

2. This is an action to take property under the power of eminent domain and to determine just compensation to be paid to the owners and parties in interest.

3. The authority for the taking is _____.

4. The property is to be used for _____.

5. The property to be taken is <u>describe in enough detail for identification—or attach the description and state "is described in Exhibit A, attached."</u>

6.   The interest to be acquired is _____.

7.   The persons known to the plaintiff to have or claim an interest in the property are: _____
___. For each person include the interest claimed.

8.   There may be other persons who have or claim an interest in the property and whose names could not be found after a reasonably diligent search. They are made parties under the designation "Unknown Owners."

Therefore, the plaintiff demands judgment:

(a) condemning the property;

(b) determining and awarding just compensation; and

(c) granting any other lawful and proper relief.

(Date and sign—See Form 2.)

FORM 70. JUDGMENT ON A JURY VERDICT

(Caption—See Form 1.)

This action was tried by a jury with Judge _____ presiding, and the jury has rendered a verdict.

It is ordered that:

[the plaintiff name recover from the defendant name the amount of $_____ with interest at the rate of ___ %, along with costs.]

[the plaintiff recover nothing, the action be dismissed on the merits, and the defendant name recover costs from the plaintiff name.]

Date:_____   _____
                                   Clerk of Court

FORM 71. JUDGMENT BY THE COURT WITHOUT A JURY

(Caption—See Form 1.)

This action was tried by Judge _____ without a jury and the following decision was reached:

It is ordered that [the plaintiff name recover from the defendant name the amount of $_____ _ with prejudgment interest at the rate of ___ %, along with costs.] [the plaintiff recover nothing, the action be dismissed on the merits, and the defendant name recover costs from the plaintiff name.]

Date:_____   _____
                                   Clerk of Court

FORM 80. NOTICE OF A MAGISTRATE JUDGE'S AVAILABILITY

1.   A magistrate judge is available under title 28 U.S.C. § 636(c) to conduct the proceedings in this case, including a jury or nonjury trial and the entry of final judgment. But a magistrate judge can be assigned only if all parties voluntarily consent.

2.   You may withhold your consent without adverse substantive consequences. The identity of any party consenting or withholding consent will not be disclosed to the judge to whom the case is assigned or to any magistrate judge.

3.   If a magistrate judge does hear your case, you may appeal directly to a United States court of appeals as you would if a district judge heard it.

A form called Consent to an Assignment to a United States Magistrate Judge is available from the court clerk's office.

FORM 81. CONSENT TO AN ASSIGNMENT TO A MAGISTRATE JUDGE

(Caption—See Form 1.)

I voluntarily consent to have a United States magistrate judge conduct all further proceedings in this case, including a trial, and order the entry of final judgment. (Return this form to the court clerk—not to a judge or magistrate judge.)

Date:_____

_____
Signature of the Party

FORM 82. ORDER OF ASSIGNMENT TO A MAGISTRATE JUDGE

(Caption—See Form 1.)

With the parties' consent it is ordered that this case be assigned to United States Magistrate Judge _____ of this district to conduct all proceedings and enter final judgment in accordance with 28 U.S.C. § 636(c).

Date:_____

_____
United States District Judge

ADVISORY COMMITTEE NOTES TO 1938 (ORIGINAL) RULES

RULE 1

These rules are drawn under the authority of the act of June 19, 1934, U.S.C., Title 28, formerly § 723b (now § 2072) (Rules in actions at law; Supreme Court authorized to make), and formerly § 723c (now § 2072) (Union of equity and action at law rules; power of Supreme Court) and also other grants of rule making power to the Court. *See* Clark and Moore, *A New Federal Civil Procedure – I. The Background*, 44 Yale L.J. 387, 391 (1935). Under former § 723b (now § 2072) after the rules have taken effect all laws in conflict therewith are of no further force or effect. In accordance with former § 723c (now § 2072) the Court has united the general rules prescribed for cases in equity with those in actions at law so as to secure one form of civil action and procedure for both. *See* Rule 2 (One Form of Action). For the former practice in equity and at law. *See* U.S.C., Title 28, formerly §§ 723 and 730 (now §§ 2071–2073) (conferring power on the Supreme Court to make rules of practice in equity) and the former Equity Rules promulgated thereunder; U.S.C., Title 28, former § 724 (Conformity Act): former Equity Rule 22 (Action at Law Erroneously Begun as Suit in Equity – Transfer); former Equity Rule 23 (Matters Ordinarily Determinable at Law When Arising in Suit in Equity to be Disposed of Therein); U.S.C., Title 28, former §§ 397 (Amendments to pleadings when case brought to wrong side of court), and 398 (Equitable defenses and equitable relief in actions at law).

RULE 23

This is a substantial restatement of former Equity Rule 38 (Representatives of Class) as that rule has been construed. It applies to all actions, whether formerly denominated legal or equitable. For a general analysis of class actions, effect of judgment, and requisites of jurisdiction *see* Moore, *Federal Rules of Civil Procedure: Some Problems Raised by the Preliminary Draft*, 25 Georgetown L.J. 551, 570 et seq. (1937); Moore and Cohn, *Federal Class Actions*, 32 Ill. L. Rev. 307 (1937); Moore and Cohn, *Federal Class Actions – Jurisdiction and Effect of Judgment*, 32 Ill. L. Rev. 555–567 (1938); Lesar, *Class Suits and the Federal Rules*, 22 Minn. L. Rev. 34 (1937); *cf.* Arnold and James, *Cases on Trials, Judgments and Appeals* (1936) 175; and *see* Blume, *Jurisdictional Amount in Representative Suits*, 15 Minn. L. Rev. 501 (1931).

The general test of former Equity Rule 38 (Representatives of Class) that the question should be "one of common or general interest to many persons constituting a class so numerous as to make it impracticable to bring them all before the court," is a common test. For states which require the two elements of a common or general interest and numerous persons, as provided for in former Equity Rule 38, *see* Del. Ch. R. 113; Fla. Comp. Gen. Laws Ann. (Supp., 1936) § 4918(7); Georgia Code (1933) § 37-1002, and *see* English Rules Under the Judicature Act (The Annual Practice, 1937) O. 16, r. 9. For statutory provisions providing for class actions when the question is one of common or general interest or when the parties are numerous, *see* Ala. Code Ann. (Michie, 1928) § 5701; 2 Ind. Stat. Ann. (Burns, 1933) § 2-220; NYCPA (1937) § 195; Wis. Stat. (1935) § 260.12. These statutes have, however, been uniformly construed as though phrased in the conjunctive. *See Garfein v. Stiglitz*, 260 Ky. 430, 86 S.W.2d 155 (1935). The rule adopts the test of former Equity Rule 38, but defines what constitutes a "common or general interest". Compare with code provisions which make the action dependent upon the propriety of joinder of the parties. *See* Blume, *The "Common Questions" Principle in the Code Provision for Representative Suits*, 30 Mich. L. Rev. 878 (1932). For discussion of what constitutes "numerous persons," *see* Wheaton, *Representative Suits Involving Numerous Litigants*, 19 Corn. L. Q. 399 (1934); Note, 36 Harv. L. Rev. 89 (1922).

RULE 26

While a number of states permit discovery only from parties or their agents, others either make no distinction between parties or agents of parties and ordinary witnesses, or authorize the taking of ordinary depositions, without restriction, from any persons who have knowledge of relevant facts.

While the old chancery practice limited discovery to facts supporting the case of the party seeking it, this limitation has been largely abandoned by modern legislation.

RULE 38

This rule provides for the preservation of the constitutional right of trial by jury as directed in the enabling act (act of June 19, 1934, 48 Stat 1064, U.S.C., Title 28, former § 723c (now § 2072)), and it and the next rule make definite provision for claim and waiver of jury trial, following the method used in many American states and in England and the British Dominions. Thus the claim must be made at once on initial pleading or appearance under Ill. Rev. Stat. (1937) ch 110, § 188; 6 Tenn. Code Ann. (Williams, 1934) § 8734; compare Wyo. Rev. Stat. Ann. (1931) § 89-1320 (with answer or reply); within 10 days after the pleadings are completed or the case is at issue under 2 Conn. Gen. Stat. (1930) § 5624; Hawaii Rev. Laws (1935) § 4101; 2 Mass. Gen. Laws (Ter. Ed. 1932) ch. 231, § 60; 3 Mich. Comp. Laws (1929) § 14263; Mich. Court Rules Ann. (Searl, 1933) Rule 33 (15 days); England (until 1933) O. 36, r. r. 2 and 6; and Ontario Jud. Act (1927) § 57(1) (4 days, or, where prior notice of trial, 2 days from such notice); or at a definite time varying under different codes, from 10 days before notice of trial to 10 days after notice, or, as in many, when the case is called for assignment, Ariz. Rev. Code Ann. (Struckmeyer, 1928) § 3802; Calif. Code Civ. Proc. (Deering, 1937) § 631, par. 4; Iowa Code (1935) § 10724; 4 Nev. Comp. Laws (Hillyer, 1929) § 8782; N.M. Stat. Ann. (Courtright, 1929) § 105-814; NYCPA (1937) § 426, subdivision 5 (applying to New York, Bronx, Richmond, Kings, and Queens Counties); R.I. Pub. Laws (1929), ch. 1327, amending R.I. Gen. Laws (1923) ch. 337 § 6; Utah Rev. Stat. Ann. (1933) § 104-23-6; 2 Wash. Rev. Stat. Ann. (Remington, 1932) § 316; England (4 days after notice of trial), Administration of Justice Act (1933) § 6 and amended rule under the Judicature Act (The Annual Practice, 1937), O. 36, r. 1; Australia High Court Procedure Act (1921) § 12, Rules, O. 33, r. 2; Alberta Rules of Ct. (1914) 172, 183, 184; British Columbia Sup. Ct. Rules (1925) O. 36, r. r. 2, 6, 11, and 16; New Brunswick Jud. Act (1927) O. 36, r. r. 2 and 5. *See* James, *Trial by Jury and the New Federal Rules of Procedure*, 45 Yale L.J. 1022 (1936). Rule 81(c) provides for claim for jury trial in removed actions.

RULE 56

Summary judgment procedure is a method for promptly disposing of actions in which there is no genuine issue as to any material fact. It has been extensively used in England for more than 50 years and has been adopted in a number of American states. New York, for example, has made great use of it. During the first nine years after its adoption there, the records of New York county alone show 5,600 applications for summary judgments. Report of the Commission on the Administration of Justice in New York State (1934), p. 383. *See also* Third Annual Report of the Judicial Council of the State of New York (1937), p. 30.

In England it was first employed only in cases of liquidated claims, but there has been a steady enlargement of the scope of the remedy until it is now used in actions to recover land or chattels and in all other actions at law, for liquidated or unliquidated claims, except for a few designated torts and breach of promise of marriage. English Rules Under the Judicature Act (The Annual Practice, 1937) O. 3, r. 6; Orders 14, 14A, and 15; *see also* O. 32, r. 6, authorizing an application for judgment at any time upon admissions. In Michigan (3 Comp. Laws (1929) § 14260) and Illinois (Smith-Hurd Ill. Stats. c. 110, §§ 181, 259.15, 259.16), it is not limited to liquidated demands. New York (N.Y.R.C.P. (1937) Rule 113; *see also* Rule 107) has brought so many classes of actions under the operation of the rule that the Commission on Administration of Justice in New York State (1934) recommend that all restrictions be removed and that the remedy be available "in any action" (p. 287). For the history and nature of the summary judgment procedure and citations of state statutes, *see* Clark and Samenow, *The Summary Judgment*, 38 Yale L.J. 423 (1929).

RULE 57

The fact that a declaratory judgment may be granted "whether or not further relief is or could be prayed" indicates that declaratory relief is alternative or cumulative and not exclusive or extraordinary. A declaratory judgment is appropriate when it will "terminate the controversy" giving rise to the proceeding. Inasmuch as it often involves only an issue of law on undisputed or relatively undisputed facts, it operates frequently as a summary proceeding, justifying docketing the case for early hearing as on a motion, as provided for in California (Code Civ. Proc. (Deering, 1937) § 1062a), Michigan (3 Comp. Laws (1929) § 13904), and Kentucky (Codes (Carroll, 1932) Civ. Pract. § 639a-3).

The "controversy" must necessarily be "of a justiciable nature, thus excluding an advisory decree upon a hypothetical state of facts." *Ashwander v. Tennessee Valley Authority*, 297 U.S. 288, 325 (1936). The existence or nonexistence of any right, duty, power, liability, privilege, disability, or immunity or of any fact upon which such legal relations depend, or of a status, may be declared. The petitioner must have a practical interest in the declaration sought and all parties having an interest therein or adversely affected must be made parties or be cited. A declaration may not be rendered if a special statutory proceeding has been provided for the adjudication of some special type of case, but general ordinary or extraordinary legal remedies, whether regulated by statute or not, are not deemed special statutory proceedings.

ADVISORY COMMITTEE NOTES TO 1948 AMENDMENTS

RULE 13

Subdivision (g). The amendment is to care for a situation such as where a second mortgagee is made defendant in a foreclosure proceeding and wishes to file a cross-complaint against the mortgagor in order to secure a personal judgment for the indebtedness and foreclose his lien. A claim of this sort by the second mortgagee may not necessarily arise out of the transaction or occurrence that is the subject matter of the original action under the terms of Rule 13(g).

RULE 14

The provisions in Rule 14 (a) which relate to the impleading of a third party who is or may be liable to the plaintiff have been deleted by the proposed amendment. It has been held that under Rule 14(a) the plaintiff need not amend his complaint to state a claim against such third party if he does not wish to do so.... In *Delano v. Ives*, 40 F. Supp. 672 (E.D. Pa. 1941), the court said: "... the weight of authority is to the effect that a defendant cannot compel the plaintiff, who has sued him, to sue also a third party whom he does not wish to sue, by tendering in a third party complaint the third party as an additional defendant directly liable to the plaintiff." Thus impleader here amounts to no more than a mere offer of a party to the plaintiff, and if he rejects it, the attempt is a time-consuming futility.... Moreover, in any case where the plaintiff could not have joined the third party originally because of jurisdictional limitations such as lack of diversity of citizenship, the majority view is that any attempt by the plaintiff to amend his complaint and assert a claim against the impleaded third party would be unavailing.... For these reasons therefore, the words "or to the plaintiff" in the first sentence of subdivision (a) have been removed by the amendment; and in conformance therewith the words "the plaintiff" in the second sentence of the subdivision, and the words "or to the third-party plaintiff" in the concluding sentence thereof have likewise been eliminated.

The third sentence of Rule 14(a) has been expanded to clarify the right of the third-party defendant to assert any defenses which the third-party plaintiff may have to the plaintiff's claim. This protects the impleaded third-party defendant where the third-party plaintiff fails or neglects to assert a proper defense to the plaintiff's action. A new sentence has also been inserted giving the third-party defendant the right to assert directly against the original plaintiff any claim arising out of the transaction or occurrence that is the subject matter of the plaintiff's claim against the third-party plaintiff. This permits all claims arising out of the same transaction or occurrence to be heard and determined in the same action.... Accordingly, the next to the last sentence of subdivision (a) has also been revised to make clear that the plaintiff may, if he desires, assert directly against the third-party defendant either by amendment or by a new pleading any claim he may have against him arising out of the transaction or occurrence that is the subject matter of the plaintiff's claim against the third-party plaintiff. In such a case, the third-party defendant then is entitled to assert the defenses, counter-claims and cross-claims provided in Rules 12 and 13.

RULE 26

The amendments to subdivision (b) make clear the broad scope of examination and that it may cover not only evidence for use at the trial but also inquiry into matters in themselves inadmissible as evidence but which will lead to the discovery of such evidence. The purpose of discovery is to allow a broad search for facts, the names of witnesses, or any other matters which may aid a party in the preparation or presentation of his case.... In such a preliminary inquiry admissibility at trial should not be the test as to whether the information sought is within the scope of proper examination. Such a standard unnecessarily curtails the utility of discovery practice. Of course, matters entirely without bearing either as direct evidence or as leads to evidence are not within the scope of inquiry, but to the extent that the examination develops useful information, it functions successfully as an instrument of discovery, even if it produces no testimony directly admissible.... Thus hearsay, while inadmissible itself, may suggest testimony which properly may be proved.

RULE 34

The changes in clauses (1) and (2) correlate the scope of inquiry permitted under Rule 34 with that provided in Rule 26(b), and thus remove any ambiguity created by the former differences in language. As stated in *Olson Transportation Co. v. Socony-Vacuum Oil Co.*, 8 Fed Rules Serv. 34.41, Case 2 (E.D. Wisc. 1944), "Rule 34 is a direct and simple method of discovery." At the same time the addition of the words following the term "parties" makes certain that the person in whose custody, possession, or control the evidence reposes may have the benefit of the applicable protective orders stated in Rule 30(b). This change should be considered in the light of the proposed expansion of Rule 30(b).

RULE 56

Subdivision (a). The amendment allows a claimant to move for a summary judgment at any time after the expiration of 20 days from the commencement of the action or after service of a motion for summary judgment by the adverse party. This will normally operate to permit an earlier motion by the claimant than under the original rule, where the phrase "at any time after the pleading in answer thereto has been served" operates to prevent a claimant from moving for summary judgment, even in a case clearly proper for its exercise, until a formal answer has been filed. Thus in *People's Bank v. Federal Reserve Bank of San Francisco*, 58 F. Supp. 25 (N.D. Cal. 1944), the plaintiff's countermotion for a summary judgment was stricken as premature, because the defendant had not filed an answer. Since Rule 12(a) allows at least 20 days for an answer, that time plus the 10 days required in Rule 56(c) means that under original Rule 56(a) a minimum period of 30 days necessarily has to elapse in every case before the claimant can be heard on his right to a summary judgment. An extension of time by the court or the service of preliminary motions of any kind will prolong that period even further. In many cases this merely represents unnecessary delay.... The changes are in the interest of more expeditious litigation. The 20-day period, as provided, gives the defendant an opportunity to secure counsel and determine a course of action. But in a case where the defendant himself makes a motion for summary judgment within that time, there is no reason to restrict the plaintiff and the amended rule so provides.

Subdivision (c). The amendment of Rule 56(c) ... makes clear that although the question of recovery depends on the amount of damages, the summary judgment rule is applicable and summary judgment may be granted in a proper case. If the case is not fully adjudicated it may be dealt with as provided in subdivision (d) of Rule 56, and the right to summary recovery determined by a preliminary order, interlocutory in character, and the precise amount of recovery left for trial.

Subdivision (d). Rule 54(a) defines "judgment" as including a decree and "any order from which an appeal lies." Subdivision (d) of Rule 56 indicates clearly, however, that a partial summary "judgment" is not a final judgment, and, therefore, that it is not appealable, unless in the particular case some statute allows an appeal from the interlocutory order involved. The partial summary judgment is merely a pretrial adjudication that certain issues shall be deemed established for the trial of the case. This adjudication is more nearly akin to the preliminary order under Rule 16, and likewise serves the purpose of speeding up litigation by eliminating before trial matters wherein there is no genuine issue of fact.... Since interlocutory appeals are not allowed, except where specifically provided by statute, ... this interpretation is in line with that policy.

ADVISORY COMMITTEE NOTES TO 1963 AMENDMENTS

RULE 15

Rule 15(d) is intended to give the court broad discretion in allowing a supplemental pleading. However, some cases, opposed by other cases and criticized by the commentators, have taken the rigid and formalistic view that where the original complaint fails to state a claim upon which relief can be granted, leave to serve a supplemental complaint must be denied.... Thus plaintiffs have sometimes been needlessly remitted to the difficulties of commencing a new action even though events occurring after the commencement of the original action have made clear the right to relief.

Under the amendment the court has discretion to permit a supplemental pleading despite the fact that the original pleading is defective. As in other situations where a supplemental pleading is offered, the court is to determine in the light of the particular circumstances whether filing should be permitted, and if so, upon what terms. The amendment does not attempt to deal with such questions as the relation of the statute of limitations to supplemental pleadings, the operation of the doctrine of laches, or the availability of other defenses. All these questions are for decision in accordance with the principles applicable to supplemental pleadings generally.

RULE 25

Present Rule 25(a)(1), together with present Rule 6(b), results in an inflexible requirement that an action be dismissed as to a deceased party if substitution is not carried out within a fixed period measured from the time of the death. The hardships and inequities of this unyielding requirement plainly appear from the cases. *See, e.g., Anderson v. Yungkau*, 329 U.S. 482 (1947). The amended rule establishes a time limit for the motion to substitute based not upon the time of the death, but rather upon the time information of the death is provided by means of a suggestion of death upon the record, i.e. service of a statement of the fact of the death. *Cf.* Ill. Ann. Stat., c. 110, § 54(2) (Smith-Hurd 1956). The motion may not be made later than 90 days after the service of the statement unless the period is extended pursuant to Rule 6(b), as amended.

A motion to substitute may be made by any party or by the representative of the deceased party without awaiting the suggestion of death. Indeed, the motion will usually be so made. If a party or the representative of the deceased party desires to limit the time within which another may make the motion, he may do so by suggesting the death upon the record.

A motion to substitute made within the prescribed time will ordinarily be granted, but under the permissive language of the first sentence of the amended rule ("the court may order") it may be denied by the court in the exercise of a sound discretion if made long after the death — as can occur if the suggestion of death is not made or is delayed — and circumstances have arisen rendering it unfair to allow substitution. *Cf. Anderson v. Yungkau, supra,* 329 U.S. at 485, 486, where it was noted under the present rule that settlement and distribution of the estate of a deceased defendant might be so far advanced as to warrant denial of a motion for substitution even though made within the time limit prescribed by that rule. Accordingly, a party interested in securing substitution under the amended rule should not assume that he can rest indefinitely awaiting the suggestion of death before he makes his motion to substitute.

RULE 28

The amendment of clause (1) is designed to facilitate depositions in foreign countries by enlarging the class of persons before whom the depositions may be taken on notice. The class is no longer confined, as at present, to a secretary of embassy or legation, consul general, consul, vice consul, or consular agent of the United States. In a country that regards the taking of testimony by a foreign official in aid of litigation pending in a court of another country as an infringement upon its sovereignty, it will be expedient to notice depositions before officers of the country in which the examination is taken....

Clause (2) of amended subdivision (b), like the corresponding provision of subdivision (a) dealing with depositions taken in the United States, makes it clear that the appointment of a person by commission in itself confers power upon him to administer any necessary oath.

It has been held that a letter rogatory will not be issued unless the use of a notice or commission is shown to be impossible or impractical.... The intent of the fourth sentence of the amended subdivision is to overcome this judicial antipathy and to permit a sound choice between depositions under a letter rogatory and on notice or by commission in the light of all the circumstances. In a case in which the foreign country will compel a witness to attend or testify in aid of a letter rogatory but not in aid of a commission, a letter rogatory may be preferred on the ground that it is less expensive to execute, even if there is plainly no need for compulsive process. A letter rogatory may also be preferred when it cannot be demonstrated that a witness will be recalcitrant or when the witness states that he is willing to testify voluntarily, but the contingency exists that he will change his mind at the last moment. In the latter case, it may be advisable to issue both a commission and a letter rogatory, the latter to be executed if the former fails. The choice between a letter rogatory and a commission may be conditioned by other factors, including the nature and extent of the assistance that the foreign country will give to the execution of either.

In executing a letter rogatory the courts of other countries may be expected to follow their customary procedure for taking testimony.... In many noncommon-law countries the judge questions the witness, sometimes without first administering an oath, the attorneys put any supplemental questions either to the witness or through the judge, and the judge dictates a summary of the testimony, which the witness acknowledges as correct.... The last sentence of the amended subdivision provides, contrary to the implications of some authority, that evidence recorded in such a fashion need not be excluded on that account.... The specific reference to the lack of an oath or a verbatim transcript is intended to be illustrative. Whether or to what degree the value or weight of the evidence may be affected by the method of taking or recording the testimony is left for determination according to the circumstances of the particular case...; the testimony may indeed be so devoid of substance or probative value as to warrant its exclusion altogether.

Some foreign countries are hostile to allowing a deposition to be taken in their country, especially by notice or commission, or to lending assistance in the taking of a deposition. Thus compliance with the terms of amended subdivision (b) may not in all cases ensure completion of a deposition abroad. Examination of the law and policy of the particular foreign country in advance of attempting a deposition is therefore advisable.

RULE 56

Subdivision (c). By the amendment "answers to interrogatories" are included among the materials which may be considered on motion for summary judgment. The phrase was inadvertently omitted from the rule, *see* 3 Barron & Holtzoff, *Federal Practice and Procedure* 159–60 (Wright ed. 1958), and the courts have generally reached by interpretation the result which will hereafter be required by the text of the amended rule. *See* Annot., 74 ALR2d 984 (1960).

Subdivision (e). ...The last two sentences are added to overcome a line of cases, chiefly in the Third Circuit, which has impaired the utility of the summary judgment device. A typical case is as follows: A party supports his motion for summary judgment by affidavits or other evidentiary matter sufficient to show that there is no genuine issue as to a material fact. The adverse party, in opposing the motion, does not produce any evidentiary matter, or produces some but not enough to establish that there is a genuine issue for trial. Instead, the adverse party rests on averments of his pleadings which on their face present an issue. In this situation Third Circuit cases have taken the view that summary judgment must be denied, at least if the averments are "well-pleaded," and not supposititious, conclusory, or ultimate....

The very mission of the summary judgment procedure is to pierce the pleadings and to assess the proof in order to see whether there is a genuine need for trial. The Third Circuit doctrine, which permits the pleadings themselves to stand in the way of granting an otherwise justified summary judgment, is incompatible with the basic purpose of the rule. It is hoped that the amendment will contribute to the more effective utilization of the salutary device of summary judgment. The amendment is not intended to derogate from the solemnity of the pleadings. Rather it recognizes that, despite the best efforts of counsel to make his pleadings accurate, they may be overwhelmingly contradicted by the proof available to his adversary. Nor is the amendment designed to affect the ordinary standards applicable to the summary judgment motion. So, for example:

Where an issue as to a material fact cannot be resolved without observation of the demeanor of witnesses in order to evaluate their credibility, summary judgment is not appropriate. Where the evidentiary matter in support of the motion does not establish the absence of a genuine issue, summary judgment must be denied even if no opposing evidentiary matter is presented. And summary judgment may be inappropriate where the party opposing it shows under subdivision (f) that he cannot at the time present facts essential to justify his opposition.

ADVISORY COMMITTEE NOTES TO 1966 AMENDMENTS

RULE 12

Subdivision (g). Subdivision (g) has forbidden a defendant who makes a preanswer motion under this rule from making a further motion presenting any defense or objection which was available to him at the time he made the first motion and which he could have included, but did not in fact include therein. Thus if the defendant moves before answer to dismiss the complaint for failure to state a claim, he is barred from making a further motion presenting the defense of improper venue, if that defense was available to him when he made his original motion. Amended subdivision (g) is to the same effect. This required consolidation of defenses and objections in a Rule 12 motion is salutary in that it works against piecemeal consideration of a case. For exceptions to the requirement of consolidation, *see* the last clause of subdivision (g), referring to new subdivision (h)(2).

Subdivision (h). The question has arisen whether an omitted defense which cannot be made the basis of a second motion may nevertheless be pleaded in the answer. Subdivision (h) called for waiver of "... defenses and objections which he [defendant] does not present ... by motion ... or, if he has made no motion, in his answer...." If the clause "if he has made no motion," was read literally, it seemed that the omitted defense was waived and could not be pleaded in the answer. On the other hand, the clause might be read as adding nothing of substance to the preceding words; in that event it appeared that a defense was not waived by reason of being omitted from the motion and might be set up in the answer. The decisions were divided....

Amended subdivision (h)(1)(A) eliminates the ambiguity and states that certain specified defenses which were available to a party when he made a preanswer motion, but which he omitted from the motion, are waived. The specified defenses are lack of jurisdiction over the person, improper venue, insufficiency of process, and insufficiency of service of process (*see* Rule 12(b)(2)–(5)). A party who by motion invites the court to pass upon a threshold defense should bring forward all the specified defenses he then has and thus allow the court to do a reasonably complete job. The waiver reinforces the policy of subdivision (g) forbidding successive motions.

RULE 13

Rule 13(h), dealing with the joinder of additional parties to a counterclaim or cross-claim, has partaken of some of the textual difficulties of Rule 19 on necessary joinder of parties.... Rule 13(h) has also been inadequate in failing to call attention to the fact that a party pleading a counterclaim or cross-claim may join additional persons when the conditions for permissive joinder of parties under Rule 20 are satisfied.

The amendment of Rule 13(h) supplies the latter omission by expressly referring to Rule 20, as amended, and also incorporates by direct reference the revised criteria and procedures of Rule 19, as amended. Hereafter, for the purpose of determining who must or may be joined as additional parties to a counterclaim or cross-claim, the party pleading the claim is to be regarded as a plaintiff and the additional parties as plaintiffs or defendants as the case may be, and amended Rules 19 and 20 are to be applied in the usual fashion.

RULE 14

Rule 14 was modeled on Admiralty Rule 56. An important feature of Admiralty Rule 56 was that it allowed impleader not only of a person who might be liable to the defendant by way of remedy over, but also of any person who might be liable to the plaintiff. The importance of this provision was that the defendant was entitled to insist that the plaintiff proceed to judgment against the third-party defendant. In certain cases this was a valuable implementation of a substantive right. For example, in a case of ship collision where a finding of mutual fault is possible, one shipowner, if sued alone, faces the prospect of an absolute judgment for the full amount of the damage suffered by an innocent third party; but if he can implead the owner of the other vessel, and if mutual fault is found, the judgment against the original defendant will be in the first instance only for a moiety of the damages; liability for the remainder will be conditioned on the plaintiff's inability to collect from the third-party defendant.

This feature was originally incorporated in Rule 14, but was eliminated by the amendment of 1946, so that under the amended rule a third party could not be impleaded on the basis that he might be liable to the plaintiff. One of the reasons for the amendment was that the Civil Rule, unlike the Admiralty Rule, did not require the plaintiff to go to judgment against the third-party defendant. Another reason was that where jurisdiction depended on diversity of citizenship the impleader of an adversary having the same citizenship as the plaintiff was not considered possible.

Retention of the admiralty practice in those cases that will be counterparts of a suit in admiralty is clearly desirable.

RULE 15

Rule 15(c) is amplified to state more clearly when an amendment of a pleading changing the party against whom a claim is asserted (including an amendment to correct a misnomer or misdescription of a defendant) shall "relate back" to the date of the original pleading.

The problem has arisen most acutely in certain actions by private parties against officers or agencies of the United States. Thus an individual denied social security benefits by the Secretary of Health, Education, and Welfare may secure review of the decision by bringing a civil action against that officer within sixty days. 42 U.S.C. § 405(g) (Supp. III, 1962). In several recent cases the claimants instituted timely action but mistakenly named as defendant the United States, the Department of HEW, the "Federal Security Administration" (a nonexistent agency), and a Secretary who had retired from the office nineteen days before. Discovering their mistakes, the claimants moved to amend their complaints to name the proper defendant; by this time the statutory sixty-day period had expired. The motions were denied on the ground that the amendment "would amount to the commencement of a new proceeding and would not relate back in time so as to avoid the statutory provisions ... that suit be brought within sixty days ...." *Cohn v. Federal Security Adm.*, 199 F. Supp. 884, 885 (W.D.N.Y. 1961)....

Relation back is intimately connected with the policy of the statute of limitations. The policy of the statute limiting the time for suit against the Secretary of HEW would not have been offended by allowing relation back in the situations described above. For the government was put on notice of the claim within the stated period — in the particular instances, by means of the initial delivery of process to a responsible government official (*see* Rule 4(d)(4) and (5)). In these circumstances, characterization of the amendment as a new proceeding is not responsive to the reality, but is merely question-begging; and to deny relation back is to defeat unjustly the claimant's opportunity to prove his case. *See* the full discussion by Byse, *Suing the "Wrong" Defendant in Judicial Review of Federal Administrative Action: Proposals for Reform*, 77 Harv. L. Rev. 40 (1963); *see also* Ill. Civ. P. Act § 46(4).

Much the same question arises in other types of actions against the government (*see* Byse, *supra*, at 45 n. 15). In actions between private parties, the problem of relation back of amendments changing defendants has generally been better handled by the courts, but incorrect criteria have sometimes been applied, leading sporadically to doubtful results. *See* 1A Barron & Holtzoff, *Federal Practice & Procedure* § 451 (Wright ed. 1960); 1 *id.* § 186 (1960); 2 *id.* § 543 (1961); 3 *Moore's Federal Practice*, par. 15.15 (Cum. Supp. 1962); Annot, *Change in Party After Statute of Limitations Has Run*, 8 ALR2d 6 (1949). Rule 15(c) has been amplified to provide a general solution. An amendment changing the party against whom a claim is asserted relates back if the amendment satisfies the usual condition of Rule 15(c) of "arising out of the conduct . . . set forth . . . in the original pleading," and if, within the applicable limitations period, the party brought in by amendment, first, received such notice of the institution of the action — the notice need not be formal — that he would not be prejudiced in defending the action, and second, knew or should have known that the action would have been brought against him initially had there not been a mistake concerning the identity of the proper party. Revised Rule 15(c) goes on to provide specifically in the government cases that the first and second requirements are satisfied when the government has been notified in the manner there described (*see* Rule 4(d)(4) and (5)). As applied to the government cases, revised Rule 15(c) further advances the objectives of the 1961 amendment of Rule 25(d) (substitution of public officers).

The relation back of amendments changing plaintiffs is not expressly treated in revised Rule 15(c) since the problem is generally easier. Again the chief consideration of policy is that of the statute of limitations, and the attitude taken in revised Rule 15(c) toward change of defendants extends by analogy to amendments changing plaintiffs. Also relevant is the amendment of Rule 17(a) (real party in interest). To avoid forfeitures of just claims, revised Rule 17(a) would provide that no action shall be dismissed on the ground that it is not prosecuted in the name of the real party in interest until a reasonable time has been allowed for correction of the defect in the manner there stated.

RULE 17

The rule adds to the illustrative list of real parties in interest a bailee — meaning, of course, a bailee suing on behalf of the bailor with respect to the property bailed. (When the possessor of property other than the owner sues for an invasion of the possessory interest he is the real party in interest.) The word "bailee" is added primarily to preserve the admiralty practice whereby the owner of a vessel as bailee of the cargo, or the master of the vessel as bailee of both vessel and cargo, sues for damage to either property interest or both. But there is no reason to limit such a provision to maritime situations. The owner of a warehouse in which household furniture is stored is equally entitled to sue on behalf of the numerous owners of the furniture stored. *Cf. Gulf Oil Corp. v. Gilbert*, 330 U.S. 501 (1947).

The provision that no action shall be dismissed on the ground that it is not prosecuted in the name of the real party in interest until a reasonable time has been allowed, after the objection has been raised, for ratification, substitution, etc., is added simply in the interests of justice. In its origin the rule concerning the real party in interest was permissive in purpose: it was designed to allow an assignee to sue in his own name. That having been accomplished, the modern function of the rule in its negative aspect is simply to protect the defendant against a subsequent action by the party actually entitled to recover, and to insure generally that the judgment will have its proper effect as res judicata.

This provision keeps pace with the law as it is actually developing. Modern decisions are inclined to be lenient when an honest mistake has been made in choosing the party in whose name the action is to be filed — in both maritime and nonmaritime cases. *See Levinson v. Deupree*, 345 U.S. 648 (1953); *Link Aviation, Inc. v. Downs*, 325 F.2d 613 (D.C. Cir. 1963). The provision should not be misunderstood or distorted. It is intended to prevent forfeiture when determination of the proper party to sue is difficult or when an understandable mistake has been made. It does not mean, for example, that, following an airplane crash in which all aboard were killed, an action may be filed in the name of John Doe (a fictitious person), as personal representative of Richard Roe (another fictitious person), in the hope that at a later time the attorney filing the action may substitute the real name of the real personal representative of a real victim, and have the benefit of suspension of the limitation period. It does not even mean, when an action is filed by the personal representative of John Smith, of Buffalo, in the good faith belief that he was aboard the flight, that upon discovery that Smith is alive and well, having missed the fatal flight, the representative of James Brown, of San Francisco, an actual victim, can be substituted to take advantage of the suspension of the limitation period. It is, in cases of this sort, intended to insure against forfeiture and injustice.

RULE 18

The Rules "proceed upon the theory that no inconvenience can result from the joinder of any two or more matters in the pleadings, but only from trying two or more matters together which have little or nothing in common." Sunderland, *The New Federal Rules*, 45 W. Va. L.Q. 5, 13 (1938); *see* Clark, *Code Pleading* 58 (2d ed. 1947). Accordingly, Rule 18(a) has permitted a party to plead multiple claims of all types against an opposing party, subject to the court's power to direct an appropriate procedure for trying the claims. *See* Rules 42(b), 20(b), 21.

The liberal policy regarding joinder of claims in the pleadings extends to cases with multiple parties. However, the language used in the second sentence of Rule 18(a) — "if the requirements of Rules 19 [necessary joinder of parties], 20 [permissive joinder of parties], and 22 [interpleader] are satisfied" — has led some courts to infer that the rules regulating joinder of parties are intended to carry back to Rule 18(a) and to impose some special limits on joinder of claims in multiparty cases. In particular, Rule 20(a) has been read as restricting the operation of Rule 18(a) in certain situations in which a number of parties have been permissively joined in an action. In *Federal Housing Admr. v. Christianson*, 26 F. Supp. 419 (D. Conn. 1939), the indorsee of two notes sued the three co-makers of one note, and sought to join in the action a count on a second note which had been made by two of the three defendants. There was no doubt about the propriety of the joinder of the three parties defendant, for a right to relief was being asserted against all three defendants which arose out of a single "transaction" (the first note) and a question of fact or law "common" to all three defendants would arise in the action. *See* the text of Rule 20(a). The court, however, refused to allow the joinder of the count on the second note, on the ground that this right to relief, assumed to arise from a distinct transaction, did not involve a question common to all the defendants but only two of them. For analysis of the *Christianson* case and other authorities, *see* 2 Barron & Holtzoff, *Federal Practice & Procedure*, § 533.1 (Wright ed. 1961); 3 *Moore's Federal Practice*, par. 18.04 [3] (2d ed. 1963).

If the court's view is followed, it becomes necessary to enter at the pleading stage into speculations about the exact relation between the claim sought to be joined against fewer than all the defendants properly joined in the action, and the claims asserted against all the defendants.... Thus if it could be found in the *Christianson* situation that the claim on the second note arose out of the same transaction as the claim on the first or out of a transaction forming part of a "series," and that any question of fact or law with respect to the second note also arose with regard to the first, it would be held that the claim on the second note could be joined in the complaint. *See* 2 Barron & Holtzoff, *supra*, at 199; *see also id.* at 198 n 60.4; *cf.* 3 *Moore's Federal Practice, supra*, at 1811. Such pleading niceties provide a basis for delaying and wasteful maneuver. It is more compatible with the design of the Rules to allow the claim to be joined in the pleading, leaving the question of possible separate trial of that claim to be later decided.... It is instructive to note that the court in the *Christianson* case, while holding that the claim on the second note could not be joined as a matter of pleading, held open the possibility that both claims would later be consolidated for trial under Rule 42(a). *See* 26 F. Supp. 419. Rule 18(a) is now amended not only to overcome the *Christianson* decision and similar authority, but also to state clearly, as a comprehensive proposition, that a party asserting a claim (an original claim, counterclaim, cross-claim, or third-party claim) may join as many claims as he has against an opposing party.... This permitted joinder of claims is not affected by the fact that there are multiple parties in the action. The joinder of parties is governed by other rules operating independently.

RULE 19

General Considerations. Whenever feasible, the persons materially interested in the subject of an action — see the more detailed description of these persons in the discussion of new subdivision (a) below — should be joined as parties so that they may be heard and a complete disposition made. When this comprehensive joinder cannot be accomplished — a situation which may be encountered in Federal courts because of limitations on service of process, subject matter jurisdiction, and venue — the case should be examined pragmatically and a choice made between the alternatives of proceeding with the action in the absence of particular interested persons, and dismissing the action.

Even if the court is mistaken in its decision to proceed in the absence of an interested person, it does not by that token deprive itself of the power to adjudicate as between the parties already before it through proper service of process. But the court can make a legally binding adjudication only between the parties actually joined in the action. It is true that an adjudication between the parties before the court may on occasion adversely affect the absent person as a practical matter, or leave a party exposed to a later inconsistent recovery by the absent person. These are factors which should be considered in deciding whether the action should proceed, or should rather be dismissed; but they do not themselves negate the court's power to adjudicate as between the parties who have been joined....

The Amended Rule. New subdivision (a) defines the persons whose joinder in the action is desirable. Clause (1) stresses the desirability of joining those persons in whose absence the court would be obliged to grant partial or "hollow" rather than complete relief to the parties before the court. The interests that are being furthered here are not only those of the parties, but also that of the public in avoiding repeated lawsuits on the same essential subject matter. Clause (2)(i) recognizes the importance of protecting the person whose joinder is in question against the practical prejudice to him which may arise through a disposition of the action in his absence. Clause (2)(ii) recognizes the need for considering whether a party may be left, after the adjudication, in a position where a person not joined can subject him to a double or otherwise inconsistent liability....

The subdivision (a) definition of persons to be joined is not couched in terms of the abstract nature of their interests—"joint," "united," "separable," or the like.... It should be noted particularly, however, that the description is not at variance with the settled authorities holding that a tortfeasor with the usual "joint-and-several" liability is merely a permissive party to an action against another with like liability.... Joinder of these tortfeasors continues to be regulated by Rule 20; compare Rule 14 on third-party practice.

If a person as described in subdivision (a)(1)(2) is amenable to service of process and his joinder would not deprive the court of jurisdiction in the sense of competence over the action, he should be joined as a party; and if he has not been joined, the court should order him to be brought into the action. If a party joined has a valid objection to the venue and chooses to assert it, he will be dismissed from the action.

Subdivision (b). When a person as described in subdivision (a)(1)–(2) cannot be made a party, the court is to determine whether in equity and good conscience the action should proceed among the parties already before it, or should be dismissed. That this decision is to be made in the light of pragmatic considerations has often been acknowledged by the courts.... The subdivision sets out four relevant considerations drawn from the experience revealed in the decided cases. The factors are to a certain extent overlapping, and they are not intended to exclude other considerations which may be applicable in particular situations.

The first factor brings in a consideration of what a judgment in the action would mean to the absentee. Would the absentee be adversely affected in a practical sense, and if so, would the prejudice be immediate and serious, or remote and minor? The possible collateral consequences of the judgment upon the parties already joined are also to be appraised. Would any party be exposed to a fresh action by the absentee, and if so, how serious is the threat?...

The second factor calls attention to the measures by which prejudice may be averted or lessened. The "shaping of relief" is a familiar expedient to this end. See, e.g., the award of money damages in lieu of specific relief where the latter might affect an absentee adversely....

Sometimes the party is himself able to take measures to avoid prejudice. Thus a defendant faced with a prospect of a second suit by an absentee may be in a position to bring the latter into the action by defensive interpleader. See ... *Abel v. Brayton Flying Service, Inc.*, 248 F.2d 713, 716 (5th Cir. 1957) (suggestion of possibility of counter-claim under Rule 13(h)).... So also the absentee may sometimes be able to avert prejudice to himself by voluntarily appearing in the action or intervening on an ancillary basis. The court should consider whether this, in turn, would impose undue hardship on the absentee. (For the possibility of the court's informing an absentee of the pendency of the action, *see* comment under subdivision (c) below.)

The third factor—whether an "adequate" judgment can be rendered in the absence of a given person—calls attention to the extent of the relief that can be accorded among the parties joined. It meshes with the other factors, especially the "shaping of relief" mentioned under the second factor....

The fourth factor, looking to the practical effects of a dismissal, indicates that the court should consider whether there is any assurance that the plaintiff, if dismissed, could sue effectively in another forum where better joinder would be possible.

The subdivision uses the word "indispensable" only in a conclusory sense, that is, a person is "regarded as indispensable" when he cannot be made a party and, upon consideration of the factors above mentioned, it is determined that in his absence it would be preferable to dismiss the action, rather than to retain it....

RULE 23

The amended rule describes in more practical terms the occasions for maintaining class actions; provides that all class actions maintained to the end as such will result in judgments including those whom the court finds to be members of the class, whether or not the judgment is favorable to the class; and refers to the measures which can be taken to assure the fair conduct of these actions.

Subdivision (a) states the prerequisites for maintaining any class action in terms of the numerousness of the class making joinder of the members impracticable, the existence of questions common to the class, and the desired qualifications of the representative parties.... Subdivision (b) describes the additional elements which in varying situations justify the use of a class action.

Subdivision (b)(1). The difficulties which would be likely to arise if resort were had to separate actions by or against the individual members of the class here furnish the reasons for, and the principal key to, the propriety and value of utilizing the class-action device. The considerations stated under clauses (A) and (B) are comparable to certain of the elements which define the persons whose joinder in an action is desirable as stated in Rule 19(a), as amended. *See* Hazard, *Indispensable Party: The Historical Origin of a Procedural Phantom*, 61 Colum. L. Rev. 1254, 1259–60 (1961); *cf.* 3 Moore, *supra*, par. 23.08, at 3435.

Clause (A): One person may have rights against, or be under duties toward, numerous persons constituting a class, and be so positioned that conflicting or varying adjudications in lawsuits with individual members of the class might establish incompatible standards to govern his conduct. The class action device can be used effectively to obviate the actual or virtual dilemma which would thus confront the party opposing the class. The matter has been stated thus: "The felt necessity for a class action is greatest when the courts are called upon to order or sanction the alteration of the status quo in circumstances such that a large number of persons are in a position to call on a single person to alter the status quo, or to complain if it is altered, and the possibility exists that [the] actor might be called upon to act in inconsistent ways." Louisell & Hazard, *Pleading and Procedure: State and Federal* 719 (1962); *see Supreme Tribe of Ben-Hur v. Cauble*, 255 U.S. 356, 366–67 (1921). To illustrate: Separate actions by individuals against a municipality to declare a bond issue invalid or condition or limit it, to prevent or limit the making of a particular appropriation or to compel or invalidate an assessment, might create a risk of inconsistent or varying determinations. In the same way, individual litigations of the rights and duties of riparian owners, or of landowners' rights and duties respecting a claimed nuisance, could create a possibility of incompatible adjudications. Actions by or against a class provide a ready and fair means of achieving unitary adjudication....

Clause (B): This clause takes in situations where the judgment in a nonclass action by or against an individual member of the class, while not technically concluding the other members, might do so as a practical matter. The vice of an individual action would lie in the fact that the other members of the class, thus practically concluded, would have had no representation in the lawsuit. In an action by policy holders against a fraternal benefit association attacking a financial reorganization of the society, it would hardly have been practical, if indeed it would have been possible, to confine the effects of a validation of the reorganization to the individual plaintiffs. Consequently a class action was called for with adequate representation of all members of the class. *See Supreme Tribe of Ben-Hur v. Cauble*, 255 U.S. 356 (1921); *Waybright v. Columbian Mut. Life Ins. Co.*, 30 F. Supp. 885 (W.D. Tenn. 1939); *cf. Smith v. Swormstedt*, 16 How. 288, 14 L. Ed. 942 (U.S., 1853). For much the same reason actions by shareholders to compel the declaration of a dividend, the proper recognition and handling of redemption or pre-emption rights, or the like (or actions by the corporation for corresponding declarations of rights), should ordinarily be conducted as class actions, although the matter has been much obscured by the insistence that each shareholder has an individual claim....

In various situations an adjudication as to one or more members of the class will necessarily or probably have an adverse practical effect on the interests of other members who should therefore be represented in the lawsuit. This is plainly the case when claims are made by numerous persons against a fund insufficient to satisfy all claims. A class action by or against representative members to settle the validity of the claims as a whole, or in groups, followed by separate proof of the amount of each valid claim and proportionate distribution of the fund, meets the problem. The same reasoning applies to an action by a creditor to set aside a fraudulent conveyance by the debtor and to appropriate the property to his claim, when the debtor's assets are insufficient to pay all creditors' claims.... Similar problems, however, can arise in the absence of a fund either present or potential. A negative or mandatory injunction secured by one of a numerous class may disable the opposing party from performing claimed duties toward the other members of the class or materially affect his ability to do so. An adjudication as to movie "clearances and runs" nominally affecting only one exhibitor would often have practical effects on all the exhibitors in the same territorial area.... Assuming a sufficiently numerous class of exhibitors, a class action would be advisable. (Here representation of subclasses of exhibitors could become necessary; *see* subdivision (c)(3)(B).)

Subdivision (b)(2). This subdivision is intended to reach situations where a party has taken action or refused to take action with respect to a class, and final relief of an injunctive nature or of a corresponding declaratory nature, settling the legality of the behavior with respect to the class as a whole, is appropriate. Declaratory relief "corresponds" to injunctive relief when as a practical matter it affords injunctive relief or serves as a basis for later injunctive relief. The subdivision does not extend to cases in which the appropriate final relief relates exclusively or predominantly to money damages. Action or inaction is directed to a class within the meaning of this subdivision even if it has taken effect or is threatened only as to one or a few members of the class, provided it is based on grounds which have general application to the class.

Illustrative are various actions in the civil-rights field where a party is charged with discriminating unlawfully against a class, usually one whose members are incapable of specific enumeration.... Subdivision (b)(2) is not limited to civil-rights cases. Thus an action looking to specific or declaratory relief could be brought by a numerous class of purchasers, say retailers of a given description, against a seller alleged to have undertaken to sell to that class at prices higher than those set for other purchasers, say retailers of another description, when the applicable law forbids such a pricing differential. So also a patentee of a machine, charged with selling or licensing the machine on condition that purchasers or licensees also purchase or obtain licenses to use an ancillary unpatented machine, could be sued on a class basis by a numerous group of purchasers or licensees, or by a numerous group of competing sellers or licensors of the unpatented machine, to test the legality of the "tying" condition.

Subdivision (b)(3). In the situations to which this subdivision relates, class-action treatment is not as clearly called for as in those described above, but it may nevertheless be convenient and desirable depending upon the particular facts. Subdivision (b)(3) encompasses those cases in which a class action would achieve economies of time, effort, and expense, and promote uniformity of decision as to persons similarly situated, without sacrificing procedural fairness or bringing about other undesirable results. *Cf.* Chafee, *Some Problems of Equity* 201 (1950).

The court is required to find, as a condition of holding that a class action may be maintained under this subdivision, that the questions common to the class predominate over the questions affecting individual members. It is only where this predominance exists that economies can be achieved by means of the class-action device. In this view, a fraud perpetrated on numerous persons by the use of similar misrepresentations may be an appealing situation for a class action, and it may remain so despite the need, if liability is found, for separate determination of the damages suffered by individuals within the class. On the other hand, although having some common core, a fraud case may be unsuited for treatment as a class action if there was material variation in the representations made or in the kinds or degrees of reliance by the persons to whom they were addressed. *See Oppenheimer v. F. J. Young & Co., Inc.*, 144 F.2d 387 (2d Cir. 1944); *Miller v. National City Bank of N.Y.*, 166 F.2d 723 (2d Cir. 1948); and for like problems in other contexts, *see Hughes v. Encyclopaedia Britannica*, 199 F.2d 295 (7th Cir. 1952); *Sturgeon v. Great Lakes Steel Corp.*, 143 F.2d 819 (6th Cir. 1944). A "mass accident" resulting in injuries to numerous persons is ordinarily not appropriate for a class action because of the likelihood that significant questions, not only of damages but of liability and defenses to liability, would be present, affecting the individuals in different ways. In these circumstances an action conducted nominally as a class action would degenerate in practice into multiple lawsuits separately tried. *See Pennsylvania R.R. v. United States*, 111 F. Supp. 80 (D.N.J. 1953); *cf.* Weinstein, *Revision of Procedure: Some Problems in Class Actions*, 9 Buffalo L. Rev. 433, 469 (1960). Private damage claims by numerous individuals arising out of concerted antitrust violations may or may not involve predominating common questions. *See Union Carbide & Carbon Corp. v. Nisley*, 300 F.2d 561 (10th Cir. 1961), *pet. cert. dism.*, 371 U.S. 801 (1963)....

That common questions predominate is not itself sufficient to justify a class action under subdivision (b)(3), for another method of handling the litigious situation may be available which has greater practical advantages. Thus one or more actions agreed to by the parties as test or model actions may be preferable to a class action; or it may prove feasible and preferable to consolidate actions. *Cf.* Weinstein, *supra*, 9 Buff. L. Rev. at 438–54. Even when a number of separate actions are proceeding simultaneously, experience shows that the burdens on the parties and the courts can sometimes be reduced by arrangements for avoiding repetitious discovery or the like. Currently the Coordinating Committee on Multiple Litigation in the United States District Courts (a subcommittee of the Committee on Trial Practice and Technique of the Judicial Conference of the United States) is charged with developing methods for expediting such massive litigation. To reinforce the point that the court with the aid of the parties ought to assess the relative advantages of alternative procedures for handling the total controversy, subdivision (b)(3) requires, as a further condition of maintaining the class action, that the court shall find that that procedure is "superior" to the others in the particular circumstances.

Factors (A)–(D) are listed, non-exhaustively, as pertinent to the findings. The court is to consider the interests of individual members of the class in controlling their own litigations and carrying them on as they see fit. *See Weeks v. Bareco Oil Co.*, 125 F.2d 84, 88–90, 93–94 (7th Cir. 1941) (anti-trust action); *see also Pentland v. Dravo Corp.*, 152 F.2d 851 (3d Cir. 1945), and Chafee, *supra*, at 273–75, regarding policy of Fair Labor Standards Act of 1938, § 16(b), 29 U.S.C. § 216(b), prior to amendment by Portal-to-Portal Act of 1947, § 5(a). [The present provisions of 29 U.S.C. § 216(b) are not intended to be affected by Rule 23, as amended.] In this connection the court should inform itself of any litigation actually pending by or against the individuals. The interests of individuals in conducting separate lawsuits may be so strong as to call for denial of a class action. On the other hand, these interests may be theoretical rather than practical: the class may have a high degree of cohesion and prosecution of the action through representatives would be quite unobjectionable, or the amounts at stake for individuals may be so small that separate suits would be impracticable. The burden that separate suits would impose on the party opposing the class, or upon the court calendars, may also fairly be considered. (See the discussion, under subdivision (c)(2) below, of the right of members to be excluded from the class upon their request.)

Also pertinent is the question of the desirability of concentrating the trial of the claims in the particular forum by means of a class action, in contrast to allowing the claims to be litigated separately in forums to which they would ordinarily be brought. Finally, the court should consider the problems of management which are likely to arise in the conduct of a class action.

Subdivision (c)(1). In order to give clear definition to the action, this provision requires the court to determine, as early in the proceedings as may be practicable, whether an action brought as a class action is to be so maintained. The determination depends in each case on satisfaction of the terms of subdivision (a) and the relevant provisions of subdivision (b).

An order embodying a determination can be conditional; the court may rule, for example, that a class action may be maintained only if the representation is improved through intervention of additional parties of a stated type. A determination once made can be altered or amended before the decision on the merits if, upon fuller development of the facts, the original determination appears unsound. A negative determination means that the action should be stripped of its character as a class action. *See* subdivision (d)(4). Although an action thus becomes a nonclass action, the court may still be receptive to interventions before the decision on the merits so that the litigation may cover as many interests as can be conveniently handled; the questions whether the intervenors in the nonclass action shall be permitted to claim "ancillary" jurisdiction or the benefit of the date of the commencement of the action for purposes of the statute of limitations are to be decided by reference to the laws governing jurisdiction and limitations as they apply in particular contexts....

As noted in the discussion of the latter subdivision, the interests of the individuals in pursuing their own litigations may be so strong here as to warrant denial of a class action altogether. Even when a class action is maintained under subdivision (b)(3), this individual interest is respected. Thus the court is required to direct notice to the members of the class of the right of each member to be excluded from the class upon his request. A member who does not request exclusion may, if he wishes, enter an appearance in the action through his counsel; whether or not he does so, the judgment in the action will embrace him.

The notice, setting forth the alternatives open to the members of the class, is to be the best practicable under the circumstances, and shall include individual notice to the members who can be identified through reasonable effort. (For further discussion of this notice, *see* the statement under subdivision (d)(2) below.)

Subdivision (c)(3). The judgment in a class action maintained as such to the end will embrace the class, that is, in a class action under subdivision (b)(1) or (b)(2), those found by the court to be class members; in a class action under subdivision (b)(3), those to whom the notice prescribed by subdivision (c)(2) was directed, excepting those who requested exclusion or who are ultimately found by the court not to be members of the class. The judgment has this scope whether it is favorable or unfavorable to the class. In a (b)(1) or (b)(2) action the judgment "describes" the members of the class, but need not specify the individual members; in a (b)(3) action the judgment "specifies" the individual members who have been identified and describes the others....

Although thus declaring that the judgment in a class action includes the class, as defined, subdivision (c)(3) does not disturb the recognized principle that the court conducting the action cannot predetermine the res judicata effect of the judgment; this can be tested only in a subsequent action. *See Restatement, Judgments* § 86, comment (h), § 116 (1942). The court, however, in framing the judgment in any suit brought as a class action, must decide what its extent or coverage shall be, and if the matter is carefully considered, questions of res judicata are less likely to be raised at a later time and if raised will be more satisfactorily answered. *See* Chafee, *supra*, at 294; Weinstein, *supra*, 9 Buff. L. Rev. at 460.

Subdivision (c)(4). This provision recognizes that an action may be maintained as a class action as to particular issues only. For example, in a fraud or similar case the action may retain its "class" character only through the adjudication of liability to the class; the members of the class may thereafter be required to come in individually and prove the amounts of their respective claims.

Two or more classes may be represented in a single action. Where a class is found to include subclasses divergent in interest, the class may be divided correspondingly, and each subclass treated as a class....

Subdivision (d)(2) sets out a non-exhaustive list of possible occasions for orders requiring notice to the class. Such notice is not a novel conception. For example, in "limited fund" cases, members of the class have been notified to present individual claims after the basic class decision. Notice has gone to members of a class so that they might express any opposition to the representation, ... and notice may encourage interventions to improve the representation of the class. Notice has been used to poll members on a proposed modification of a consent decree. *See* record in *Sam Fox Publishing Co. v. United States*, 366 U.S. 683 (1961).

Subdivision (d)(2) does not require notice at any stage, but rather calls attention to its availability and invokes the court's discretion. In the degree that there is cohesiveness or unity in the class and the representation is effective, the need for notice to the class will tend toward a minimum. These indicators suggest that notice under subdivision (d)(2) may be particularly useful and advisable in certain class actions maintained under subdivision (b)(3), for example, to permit members of the class to object to the representation. Indeed, under subdivision (c)(2), notice must be ordered, and is not merely discretionary, to give the members in a subdivision (b)(3) class action an opportunity to secure exclusion from the class. This mandatory notice pursuant to subdivision (c)(2), together with any discretionary notice which the court may find it advisable to give under subdivision (d)(2), is designed to fulfill requirements of due process to which the class action procedure is of course subject. *See Hansberry v. Lee*, 311 U.S. 32 (1940); *Mullane v. Central Hanover Bank & Trust Co.*, 339 U.S. 306 (1950).

RULE 23.1

A derivative action by a shareholder of a corporation or by a member of an unincorporated association has distinctive aspects which require the special provisions set forth in the new rule. The next-to-the-last sentence recognizes that the question of adequacy of representation may arise when the plaintiff is one of a group of shareholders or members....

The court has inherent power to provide for the conduct of the proceedings in a derivative action, including the power to determine the course of the proceedings and require that any appropriate notice be given to shareholders or members.

RULE 23.2

Although an action by or against representatives of the membership of an unincorporated association has often been viewed as a class action, the real or main purpose of this characterization has been to give "entity treatment" to the association when for formal reasons it cannot sue or be sued as a jural person under Rule 17(b).... Rule 23.2 deals separately with these actions, referring where appropriate to Rule 23.

RULE 24

Subdivision (a). In attempting to overcome certain difficulties which have arisen in the application of present Rule 24(a)(2) and (3), this amendment draws upon the revision of the related Rules 19 (joinder of persons needed for just adjudication) and 23 (class actions), and the reasoning underlying that revision. Rule 24(a)(3) as amended in 1948 provided for intervention of right where the applicant established that he would be adversely affected by the distribution or disposition of property involved in an action to which he had not been made a party. Significantly, some decided cases virtually disregarded the language of this provision. Thus Professor Moore states: "The concept of a fund has been applied so loosely that it is possible for a court to find a fund in almost any in personam action." 4 *Moore's Federal Practice*, par. 24.09 [3], at 55 (2d ed. 1962).... This development was quite natural, for Rule 24(a)(3) was unduly restricted. If an absentee would be substantially affected in a practical sense by the determination made in an action, he should, as a general rule, be entitled to intervene, and his right to do so should not depend on whether there is a fund to be distributed or otherwise disposed of. Intervention of right is here seen to be a kind of counterpart to Rule 19(a)(2)(i) on joinder of persons needed for a just adjudication: where, upon motion of a party in an action, an absentee should be joined so that he may protect his interest which as a practical matter may be substantially impaired by the disposition of the action, he ought to have a right to intervene in the action on his own motion. *See* Louisell & Hazard, *Pleading and Procedure: State and Federal* 749-50 (1962).

The general purpose of original Rule 24(a)(2) was to entitle an absentee, purportedly represented by a party, to intervene in the action if he could establish with fair probability that the representation was inadequate. Thus, where an action is being prosecuted or defended by a trustee, a beneficiary of the trust should have a right to intervene if he can show that the trustee's representation of his interest probably is inadequate; similarly a member of a class should have the right to intervene in a class action if he can show the inadequacy of the representation of his interest by the representative parties before the court.

Original Rule 24(a)(2), however, made it a condition of intervention that "the applicant is or may be bound by a judgment in the action," and this created difficulties with intervention in class actions. If the "bound" language was read literally in the sense of res judicata, it could defeat intervention in some meritorious cases. A member of a class to whom a judgment in a class action extended by its terms (*see* Rule 23(c)(3), as amended) might be entitled to show in a later action, when the judgment in the class action was claimed to operate as res judicata against him, that the "representative" in the class action had not in fact adequately represented him. If he could make this showing, the class-action judgment might be held not to bind him. *See Hansberry v. Lee*, 311 U.S. 32 (1940). If a class member sought to intervene in the class action proper, while it was still pending, on grounds of inadequacy of representation, he could be met with the argument: if the representation was in fact inadequate, he would not be "bound" by the judgment when it was subsequently asserted against him as res judicata, hence he was not entitled to intervene; if the representation was in fact adequate, there was no occasion or ground for intervention.... This reasoning might be linquistically justified by original Rule 24 (a)(2); but it could lead to poor results. *Compare* the discussion in *International M. & I. Corp. v. Von Clemm*, 301 F.2d 857 (2d Cir. 1962); *with Atlantic Refining Co. v. Standard Oil Co.*, 304 F.2d 387 (D.C. Cir. 1962). A class member who claims that his "representative" does not adequately represent him, and is able to establish that proposition with sufficient probability, should not be put to the risk of having a judgment entered in the action which by its terms extends to him, and be obliged to test the validity of the judgment as applied to his interest by a later collateral attack. Rather he should, as a general rule, be entitled to intervene in the action.

The amendment provides that an applicant is entitled to intervene in an action when his position is comparable to that of a person under Rule 19(a)(2)(i), as amended, unless his interest is already adequately represented in the action by existing parties. The Rule 19(a)(2)(i) criterion imports practical considerations, and the deletion of the "bound" language similarly frees the rule from undue preoccupation with strict considerations of res judicata.

The representation whose adequacy comes into question under the amended rule is not confined to formal representation like that provided by a trustee for his beneficiary or a representative party in a class action for a member of the class. A party to an action may provide practical representation to the absentee seeking intervention although no such formal relationship exists between them, and the adequacy of this practical representation will then have to be weighed....

An intervention of right under the amended rule may be subject to appropriate conditions or restrictions responsive among other things to the requirements of efficient conduct of the proceedings.

RULE 44.1

Rule 44.1 is added by amendment to furnish Federal courts with a uniform and effective procedure for raising and determining an issue concerning the law of a foreign country.

To avoid unfair surprise, the first sentence of the new rule requires that a party who intends to raise an issue of foreign law shall give notice thereof. The uncertainty under Rule 8(a) about whether foreign law must be pleaded... is eliminated by the provision that the notice shall be "written" and "reasonable." It may, but need not be, incorporated in the pleadings. In some situations the pertinence of foreign law is apparent from the outset; accordingly the necessary investigation of that law will have been accomplished by the party at the pleading stage, and the notice can be given conveniently in the pleadings. In other situations the pertinence of foreign law may remain doubtful until the case is further developed. A requirement that notice of foreign law be given only through the medium of the pleadings would tend in the latter instances to force the party to engage in a peculiarly burdensome type of investigation which might turn out to be unnecessary; and correspondingly the adversary would be forced into a possibly wasteful investigation. The liberal provisions for amendment of the pleadings afford help if the pleadings are used as the medium of giving notice of the foreign law; but it seems best to permit a written notice to be given outside of and later than the pleadings, provided the notice is reasonable.

The new rule does not attempt to set any definite limit on the party's time for giving the notice of an issue of foreign law; in some cases the issue may not become apparent until the trial, and notice then given may still be reasonable. The stage which the case has reached at the time of the notice, the reason proffered by the party for his failure to give earlier notice, and the importance to the case as a whole of the issue of foreign law sought to be raised, are among the factors which the court should consider in deciding a question of the reasonableness of a notice. If notice is given by one party it need not be repeated by any other and serves as a basis for presentation of material on the foreign law by all parties.

The second sentence of the new rule describes the materials to which the court may resort in determining an issue of foreign law. Heretofore the district courts, applying Rule 43(a), have looked in certain cases to State law to find the rules of evidence by which the content of foreign-country law is to be established. The State laws vary; some embody procedures which are inefficient, time consuming, and expensive. *See generally* Nussbaum, *Proving the Law of Foreign Countries*, 3 Am. J. Comp. L. 60 (1954). In all events the ordinary rules of evidence are often inapposite to the problem of determining foreign law and have in the past prevented examination of material which could have provided a proper basis for the determination. The new rule permits consideration by the court of any relevant material, including testimony, without regard to its admissibility under Rule 43....

In further recognition of the peculiar nature of the issue of foreign law, the new rule provides that in determining this law the court is not limited by material presented by the parties; it may engage in its own research and consider any relevant material thus found. The court may have at its disposal better foreign law materials than counsel have presented, or may wish to reexamine and amplify material that has been presented by counsel in partisan fashion or in insufficient detail. On the other hand, the court is free to insist on a complete presentation by counsel.

There is no requirement that the court give formal notice to the parties of its intention to engage in its own research on an issue of foreign law which has been raised by them, or of its intention to raise and determine independently an issue not raised by them. Ordinarily the court should inform the parties of material it has found diverging substantially from the material which they have presented; and in general the court should give the parties an opportunity to analyze and counter new points upon which it proposes to rely.... To require, however, that the court give formal notice from time to time as it proceeds with its study of the foreign law would add an element of undesirable rigidity to the procedure for determining issues of foreign law.

The new rule refrains from imposing an obligation on the court to take "judicial notice" of foreign law because this would put an extreme burden on the court in many cases; and it avoids use of the concept of "judicial notice" in any form because of the uncertain meaning of that concept as applied to foreign law.... Rather the rule provides flexible procedures for presenting and utilizing material on issues of foreign law by which a sound result can be achieved with fairness to the parties.

Under the third sentence, the court's determination of an issue of foreign law is to be treated as a ruling on a question of "law," not "fact," so that appellate review will not be narrowly confined by the "clearly erroneous" standard of Rule 52(a)....

The new rule parallels Article IV of the Uniform Interstate and International Procedure Act, approved by the Commissioners on Uniform State Laws in 1962, except that section 4.03 of Article IV states that "[t]he court, not the jury" shall determine foreign law. The new rule does not address itself to this problem, since the Rules refrain from allocating functions as between the court and the jury. *See* Rule 38(a). It has long been thought, however, that the jury is not the appropriate body to determine issues of foreign law. *See, e.g.*, Story, *Conflict of Laws* § 638 (1st ed. 1834, 8th ed. 1883); 1 Greenleaf, *Evidence*, § 468 (1st ed. 1842, 16th ed. 1899); 4 Wigmore, *Evidence* § 2558 (1st ed. 1905); 9 *id.* § 2558 (3d ed. 1940). The majority of the States have committed such issues to determination by the court. *See* Article 5 of the Uniform

Judicial Notice of Foreign Law Act, adopted by twenty-six states, 9A ULA 318 (1957) (Suppl. 1961, at 134). And Federal courts that have considered the problem in recent years have reached the same conclusion without reliance on statute.

RULE 65

Subdivision (a)(2). This new subdivision provides express authority for consolidating the hearing of an application for a preliminary injunction with the trial on the merits. The authority can be exercised with particular profit when it appears that a substantial part of the evidence offered on the application will be relevant to the merits and will be presented in such form as to qualify for admission on the trial proper. Repetition of evidence is thereby avoided. The fact that the proceedings have been consolidated should cause no delay in the disposition of the application for the preliminary injunction, for the evidence will be directed in the first instance to that relief, and the preliminary injunction, if justified by the proof, may be issued in the course of the consolidated proceedings. Furthermore, to consolidate the proceedings will tend to expedite the final disposition of the action. It is believed that consolidation can be usefully availed of in many cases.

The subdivision further provides that even when consolidation is not ordered, evidence received in connection with an application for a preliminary injunction which would be admissible on the trial on the merits forms part of the trial record. This evidence need not be repeated on the trial. On the other hand, repetition is not altogether prohibited. That would be impractical and unwise. For example, a witness testifying comprehensively on the trial who has previously testified upon the application for a preliminary injunction might sometimes be hamstrung in telling his story if he could not go over some part of his prior testimony to connect it with his present testimony. So also, some repetition of testimony may be called for where the trial is conducted by a judge who did not hear the application for the preliminary injunction. In general, however, repetition can be avoided with an increase of efficiency in the conduct of the case and without any distortion of the presentation of evidence by the parties. Since an application for a preliminary injunction may be made in an action in which, with respect to all or part of the merits, there is a right to trial by jury, it is appropriate to add the caution appearing in the last sentence of the subdivision. In such a case the jury will have to hear all the evidence bearing on its verdict, even if some part of the evidence has already been heard by the judge alone on the application for the preliminary injunction....

Subdivision (b). In view of the possibly drastic consequences of a temporary restraining order, the opposition should be heard, if feasible, before the order is granted. Many judges have properly insisted that, when time does not permit of formal notice of the application to the adverse party, some expedient, such as telephonic notice to the attorney for the adverse party, be resorted to if this can reasonably be done. On occasion, however, temporary restraining orders have been issued without any notice when it was feasible for some fair, although informal notice to be given....

Heretofore the first sentence of subdivision (b), in referring to a notice "served" on the "adverse party" on which a "hearing" could be held, perhaps invited the interpretation that the order might be granted without notice if the circumstances did not permit of a formal hearing on the basis of a formal notice. The subdivision is amended to make it plain that informal notice, which may be communicated to the attorney rather than the adverse party, is to be preferred to no notice at all.

Before notice can be dispensed with, the applicant's counsel must give his certificate as to any efforts made to give notice and the reasons why notice should not be required. This certificate is in addition to the requirement of an affidavit or verified complaint setting forth the facts as to the irreparable injury which would result before the opposition could be heard.

The amended subdivision continues to recognize that a temporary restraining order may be issued without any notice when the circumstances warrant....

ADVISORY COMMITTEE NOTES TO 1970 AMENDMENTS

RULE 5

The amendment makes clear that all papers relating to discovery which are required to be served on any party must be served on all parties, unless the court orders otherwise. The present language expressly includes notices and demands, but it is not explicit as to answers or responses as provided in Rules 33, 34, and 36. Discovery papers may be voluminous or the parties numerous, and the court is empowered to vary the requirement if in a given case it proves needlessly onerous.

EXPLANATORY STATEMENT CONCERNING RULES 26-37

This statement is intended to serve as a general introduction to the amendments of Rules 26-37, concerning discovery, as well as related amendments of other rules. A separate note of customary scope is appended to amendments proposed for each rule. This statement provides a framework for the consideration of individual rule changes.

Changes in the Discovery Rules.

The discovery rules, as adopted in 1938, were a striking and imaginative departure from tradition. It was expected from the outset that they would be important, but experience has shown them to play an even larger role than was initially foreseen. Although the discovery rules have been amended since 1938, the changes were relatively few and narrowly focused, made in order to remedy specific defects. The amendments now proposed reflect the first comprehensive review of the discovery rules undertaken since 1938. These amendments make substantial changes in the discovery rules. Those summarized here are among the more important changes

Scope of Discovery.

New provisions are made and existing provisions changed affecting the scope of discovery: (1) The contents of insurance policies are made discoverable (Rule 26(b)(2)). (2) A showing of good cause is no longer required for discovery of documents and things and entry upon land (Rule 34). However, a showing of need is required for discovery of "trial preparation" materials other than a party's discovery of his own statement and a witness' discovery of his own statement; and protection is afforded against disclosure in such documents of mental impressions, conclusions, opinions, or legal theories concerning the litigation. (Rule 26(b)(3)). (3) Provision is made for discovery with respect to experts retained for trial preparation, and particularly those experts who will be called to testify at trial. (Rule 26(b)(4)). (4) It is provided that interrogatories and requests for admission are not objectionable simply because they relate to matters of opinion or contention, subject of course to the supervisory power of the court (Rules 38(b), 36(a)). (5) Medical examination is made available as to certain nonparties. (Rule 35(a))

Mechanics of Discovery

A variety of changes are made in the mechanics of the discovery process, affecting the sequence and timing of discovery, the respective obligations of the parties with respect to requests, responses, and motions for court orders, and the related powers of the court to enforce discovery requests and to protect against their abusive use. A new provision eliminates the automatic grant of priority in discovery to one side (Rule26(d)). Another provides that a party is not under a duty to supplement his responses to requests for discovery, except as specified (Rule 26(e)).

Other changes in the mechanics of discovery are designed to encourage extrajudicial discovery with a minimum of court intervention. Among these are the following: (1) The requirement that a plaintiff seek leave of court for early discovery requests is eliminated or reduced, and motions for a court order under Rule 34 are made unnecessary. Motions under Rule 35 are continued. (2)Answers and objections are to be served together and an enlargement of the time for response is provided. (3) The party seeking discovery, rather than the objecting party, is made responsible for invoking judicial determination of discovery disputes not resolved by the parties. (4) Judicial sanctions are tightened with respect to unjustified insistence upon or objection to discovery. These changes bring Rules 33, 34, and 36 substantially into line with the procedure now provided for depositions.

Failure to amend Rule 35 in the same way is based upon two considerations. First, the Columbia Survey (described below) finds that only about 5 percent of medical examinations require court motions, of which about half result in court orders. Second and of greater importance, the interest of the person to be examined in the privacy of his person was recently stressed by the Supreme Court in *Schlagenhauf v. Holder*, 379 U.S. 104 (1964). The court emphasized the trial judge's responsibility to assure that the medical examination was justified, particularly as to its scope....

A Field Survey of Discovery Practice

Despite widespread acceptance of discovery as an essential part of litigation, disputes have inevitably arisen concerning the values claimed for discovery and abuses alleged to exist. Many disputes about discovery relate to particular rule provisions or court decisions and can be studied in traditional fashion with a view to specific amendment.

Since discovery is in large measure extrajudicial, however, even these disputes may be enlightened by a study of discovery "in the field." And some of the larger questions concerning discovery can be pursued only by a study of its operation at the law office level and in unreported cases.

The Committee, therefore, invited the Project for Effective Justice of Columbia Law School to conduct a field survey of discovery. Funds were obtained from the Ford Foundation and the Walter E. Meyer Research Institute of Law, Inc. The survey was carried on under the direction of Prof. Maurice Rosenberg of Columbia Law School. The Project for Effective Justice has submitted a report to the Committee entitled "Field Survey of Federal Pretrial Discovery" (hereafter referred to as the Columbia Survey). The Committee is deeply grateful for the benefit of this extensive undertaking and is most appreciative of the cooperation of the Project and the funding organizations. The Committee is particularly grateful to Professor Rosenberg who not only directed the survey but has given much time in order to assist the Committee in assessing the results.

The Columbia Survey concludes, in general, that there is no empirical evidence to warrant a fundamental change in the philosophy of the discovery rules. No widespread or profound failings are disclosed in the scope or availability of discovery. The costs of discovery do not appear to be oppressive, as a general matter, either in relation to ability to pay or to the stakes of the litigation. Discovery frequently provides evidence that would not otherwise be available to the parties and thereby makes for a fairer trial or settlement. On the other hand, no positive evidence is found that discovery promotes settlement.

More specific findings of the Columbia Survey are described in other Committee notes, in relation to particular rule provisions and amendments. Those interested in more detailed information may obtain it from the Project for Effective Justice.

Rearrangement of the Discovery Rules

...Under the rules as promulgated in 1938 ... each of the discovery devices was separate and self-contained. A defect of this arrangement is that there is no natural location in the discovery rules for provisions generally applicable to all discovery or to several discovery devices. From 1938 until the present, a few amendments have applied a discovery provision to several rules. For example, in 1948, the scope of deposition discovery in Rule 26(b) and the provision for protective orders in Rule 30(b) were incorporated by reference in Rules 33 and 34. The arrangement was adequate so long as there were few provisions governing discovery generally and these provisions were relatively simple.

As will be seen, however, a series of amendments are now proposed which govern most or all of the discovery devices. Proposals of a similar nature will probably be made in the future. Under these circumstances, it is very desirable, even necessary, that the discovery rules contain one rule addressing itself to discovery generally.

Rule 26 is obviously the most appropriate rule for this purpose. One of its subdivisions, Rule 26(b), in terms governs only scope of deposition discovery, but it has been expressly incorporated by reference in Rules 33 and 34 and is treated by courts as setting a general standard. By means of a transfer to Rule 26 of the provisions for protective orders now contained in Rule 30(b), and a transfer from Rule 26 of provisions addressed exclusively to depositions, Rule 26 is converted into a rule concerned with discovery generally. It becomes a convenient vehicle for the inclusion of new provisions dealing with the scope, timing, and regulation of discovery. Few additional transfers are needed....

On the other hand, the amendments now proposed will in any event require revision of texts and reference works as well as reconsideration by States following the Federal model. If these amendments are to be incorporated in an understandable way, a rule with general discovery provisions is needed. As will be seen, the proposed rearrangement produces a more coherent and intelligible pattern for the discovery rules taken as a whole. The difficulties described are those encountered whenever statutes are reexamined and revised. Failure to rearrange the discovery rules now would freeze the present scheme, making future change even more difficult.

RULE 26

Subdivision (a)—Discovery devices. This is a new subdivision listing all of the discovery devices provided in the discovery rules and establishing the relationship between the general provisions of Rule 26 and the specific rules for particular discovery devices. The provision that the frequency of use of these methods is not limited confirms existing law. It incorporates in general form a provision now found in Rule 33.

Subdivision (b)—Scope of discovery. This subdivision is recast to cover the scope of discovery generally. It regulates the discovery obtainable through any of the discovery devices listed in Rule 26(a).

All provisions as to scope of discovery are subject to the initial qualification that the court may limit discovery in accordance with these rules. Rule 26(c) (transferred from 30(b)) confers broad powers on the courts to regulate or prevent discovery even though the materials sought are within the scope of 26(b), and these powers have always been freely exercised. For example, a party's income tax return is generally held not privileged, ... and yet courts have recognized that interests in privacy may call for a measure of extra protection.... Similarly, the courts have in appropriate circumstances protected materials that are primarily of an impeaching character. These two types of materials merely illustrate the many situations, not capable of governance by precise rule, in which courts must exercise judgment. The new subsections in Rule 26(b) do not change existing law with respect to such situations.

Subdivision (b)(1)—In general. The language is changed to provide for the scope of discovery in general terms. The existing subdivision, although in terms applicable only to depositions, is incorporated by reference in existing Rules 33 and 34. Since decisions as to relevance to the subject matter of the action are made for discovery purposes well in advance of trial, a flexible treatment of relevance is required and the making of discovery, whether voluntary or under court order, is not a concession or determination of relevance for purposes of trial. Cf. 4 Moore's Federal Practice para. 26-16 [1] (2d ed. 1966).

Subdivision (b)(2)—Insurance policies. Both the cases and commentators are sharply in conflict on the question whether defendant's liability insurance coverage is subject to discovery in the usual situation when the insurance coverage is not itself admissible and does not bear on another issue in the case....

The division in reported cases is close. State decisions based on provisions similar to the federal rules are similarly divided. *See* cases collected in 2A Barron & Holtzoff, *Federal Practice and Procedure* § 647.1, nn. 45.5, 45.6 (Wright ed. 1961). It appears to be difficult if not impossible to obtain appellate review of the issue. Resolution by rule amendment is indicated. The question is essentially procedural in that it bears upon preparation for trial and settlement before trial, and courts confronting the question, however they have decided it, have generally treated it as procedural and governed by the rules.

The amendment resolves this issue in favor of disclosure. Most of the decisions denying discovery, some explicitly, reason from the text of Rule 26(b) that it permits discovery only of matters which will be admissible in evidence or appear reasonably calculated to lead to such evidence; they avoid considerations of policy, regarding them as foreclosed.... Some note also that facts about a defendant's financial status are not discoverable as such, prior to judgment with execution unsatisfied, and fear that, if courts hold insurance coverage discoverable, they must extend the principle to other aspects of the defendant's financial status. The cases favoring disclosure rely heavily on the practical significance of insurance in the decisions lawyers make about settlement and trial preparation. In *Clauss v. Danker*, 264 F. Supp. 246 (S.D.N.Y. 1967), the court held that the rules forbid disclosure but called for an amendment to permit it.

Disclosure of insurance coverage will enable counsel for both sides to make the same realistic appraisal of the case, so that settlement and litigation strategy are based on knowledge and not speculation. It will conduce to settlement and avoid protracted litigation in some cases, though in others it may have an opposite effect. The amendment is limited to insurance coverage, which should be distinguished from any other facts concerning defendant's financial status (1) because insurance is an asset created specifically to satisfy the claim; (2) because the insurance company ordinarily controls the litigation; (3) because information about coverage is available only from defendant or his insurer; and (4) because disclosure does not involve a significant invasion of privacy.

Disclosure is required when the insurer "may be liable" on part of all of the judgment. Thus, an insurance company must disclose even when it contests liability under the policy, and such disclosure does not constitute a waiver of its claim. It is immaterial whether the liability is to satisfy the judgment directly or merely to indemnify or reimburse another after he pays the judgment.

The provision applies only to persons "carrying on an insurance business" and thus covers insurance companies and not the ordinary business concern that enters into a contract of indemnification.... Thus, the provision makes no change in existing law on discovery of indemnity agreements other than insurance agreements by persons carrying on an insurance business. Similarly, the provision does not cover the business concern that creates a reserve fund for purposes of self-insurance.

For some purposes other than discovery, an application for insurance is treated as a part of the insurance agreement. The provision makes clear that, for discovery purposes, the application is not to be so treated. The insurance application may contain personal and financial information concerning the insured, discovery of which is beyond the purpose of this provision.

In no instance does disclosure make the facts concerning insurance coverage admissible in evidence.

Subdivision (b)(3) — Trial preparation: Materials. Some of the most controversial and vexing problems to emerge from the discovery rules have arisen out of requests for the production of documents or things prepared in anticipation of litigation or for trial. The existing rules make no explicit provision for such materials. Yet, two verbally distinct doctrines have developed, each conferring a qualified immunity on these materials — the "good cause" requirement in Rule 34 (now generally held applicable to discovery of documents via deposition under Rule 45 and interrogatories under Rule 33) and the work-product doctrine of *Hickman v. Taylor*, 329 U.S. 495 (1947). Both demand a showing of justification before production can be had, the one of "good cause" and the other variously described in the *Hickman* case: "necessity or justification," "denial . . . would unduly prejudice the preparation of petitioner's case," or "cause hardship or injustice" 329 U.S. at 509–510.

In deciding the *Hickman* case, the Supreme Court appears to have expressed a preference in 1947 for an approach to the problem of trial preparation materials by judicial decision rather than by rule. Sufficient experience has accumulated, however, with lower court applications of the *Hickman* decision to warrant a reappraisal.

The major difficulties visible in the existing case law are (1) confusion and disagreement as to whether "good cause" is made out by a showing of relevance and lack of privilege, or requires an additional showing of necessity, (2) confusion and disagreement as to the scope of the *Hickman* work-product doctrine, particularly whether it extends beyond work actually performed by lawyers, and (3) the resulting difficulty of relating the "good cause" required by Rule 34 and the "necessity or justification" of the work-product doctrine, so that their respective roles and the distinctions between them are understood.

Basic standard. Since Rule 34 in terms requires a showing of "good cause" for the production of all documents and things, whether or not trial preparation is involved, courts have felt that a single formula is called for and have differed over whether a showing of relevance and lack of privilege is enough or whether more must be shown. When the facts of the cases are studied, however, a distinction emerges based upon the type of materials. With respect to documents not obtained or prepared with an eye to litigation, the decisions, while not uniform, reflect a strong and increasing tendency to relate "good cause" to a showing that the documents are relevant to the subject matter of the action.... When the party whose documents are sought shows that the request for production is unduly burdensome or oppressive, courts have denied discovery for lack of "good cause", although they might just as easily have based their decision on the protective provisions of existing Rule 30(b) (new Rule 26(c))....

As to trial-preparation materials, however, the courts are increasingly interpreting "good cause" as requiring more than relevance. When lawyers have prepared or obtained the materials for trial, all courts require more than relevance; so much is clearly commanded by *Hickman*. But even as to the preparatory work of non-lawyers, while some courts ignore work-product and equate "good cause" with relevance, … the more recent trend is to read "good cause" as requiring inquiry into the importance of and need for the materials as well as into alternative sources for securing the same information. In *Guilford Nat'l Bank v. Southern Ry.*, 297 F.2d 921 (4th Cir. 1962), statements of witnesses obtained by claim agents were held not discoverable because both parties had had equal access to the witnesses at about the same time, shortly after the collision in question. The decision was based solely on Rule 34 and "good cause"; the court declined to rule on whether the statements were work-product. The court's treatment of "good cause" is quoted at length and with approval in *Schlagenhauf v. Holder*, 379 U.S. 104, 117–18 (1964).… While the opinions dealing with "good cause" do not often draw an explicit distinction between trial preparation materials and other materials, in fact an overwhelming proportion of the cases in which a special showing is required are cases involving trial preparation materials.

The rules are amended by eliminating the general requirement of "good cause" from Rule 34 but retaining a requirement of a special showing for trial preparation materials in this subdivision. The required showing is expressed, not in terms of "good cause" whose generality has tended to encourage confusion and controversy, but in terms of the elements of the special showing to be made; substantial need of the materials in the preparation of the case and inability without undue hardship to obtain the substantial equivalent of the materials by other means.

These changes conform to the holdings of the cases, when viewed in light of their facts. Apart from trial preparation, the fact that the materials sought are documentary does not in and of itself require a special showing beyond relevance and absence of privilege. The protective provisions are of course available, and if the party from whom production is sought raises a special issue of privacy (as with respect to income tax returns or grand jury minutes) or points to evidence primarily impeaching, or can show serious burden or expense, the court will exercise its traditional power to decide whether to issue a protective order. On the other hand, the requirement of a special showing for discovery of trial preparation materials reflects the view that each side's informal evaluation of its case should be protected, that each side should be encouraged to prepare independently, and that one side should not automatically have the benefit of the detailed preparatory work of the other side.…

Elimination of a "good cause" requirement from Rule 34 and the establishment of a requirement of a special showing in this subdivision will eliminate the confusion caused by having two verbally distinct requirements of justification that the courts have been unable to distinguish clearly. Moreover, the language of the subdivision suggests the factors which the courts should consider in determining whether the requisite showing has been made. The importance of the materials sought to the party seeking them in preparation of his case and the difficulty he will have obtaining them by other means are factors noted in the *Hickman* case. The courts should also consider the likelihood that the party, even if he obtains the information by independent means, will not have the substantial equivalent of the documents the production of which he seeks.

Consideration of these factors may well lead the court to distinguish between witness statements taken by an investigator, on the one hand, and other parts of the investigative file, on the other. The court in *Southern Ry. v. Lanham*, 403 F.2d 119 (5th Cir. 1968), while it naturally addressed itself to the "good cause" requirements of Rule 34, set forth as controlling considerations the factors contained in the language of this subdivision. The analysis of the court suggests circumstances under which witness statements will be discoverable. The witness may have given a fresh and contemporaneous account in a written statement while he is available to the party seeking discovery only a substantial time thereafter. *Lanham, supra* at 127–28.… Or he may be reluctant or hostile. *Lanham, supra* at 128–29.… Or he may have a lapse of memory. *Tannenbaum v. Walker*, 16 F.R.D. 570 (E.D. Pa. 1954). Or he may probably be deviating from his prior statement. *Cf. Hauger v. Chicago, R. I. & Pac. R.R.*, 216 F.2d 501 (7th Cir. 1954). On the other hand, a much stronger showing is needed to obtain evaluative materials in an investigator's reports. *Lanham, supra* at 131–33.…

Materials assembled in the ordinary course of business, or pursuant to public requirements unrelated to litigation, or for other nonlitigation purposes are not under the qualified immunity provided by this subdivision.… No change is made in the existing doctrine, noted in the *Hickman* case, that one party may discover relevant facts known or available to the other party, even though such facts are contained in a document which is not itself discoverable.

Treatment of lawyers; special protection of mental impressions, conclusions, opinions, and legal theories concerning the litigation. The courts are divided as to whether the work-product doctrine extends to the preparatory work only of lawyers. The *Hickman* case left this issue open since the statements in that case were taken by a lawyer. As to courts of appeals, *compare Alltmont v. United States*, 177 F.2d 971, 976 (3d Cir. 1949), *cert. denied*, 339 U.S. 967 (1950) (*Hickman* applied to statements obtained by FBI agents on theory it should apply to "all statements of prospective witnesses which a party has obtained for his trial counsel's use"), *with Southern Ry. v. Campbell*, 309 F.2d 569 (5th Cir. 1962) (statements taken by claim agents not work-product), and *Guilford Nat'l Bank v. Southern Ry.*, 297 F.2d 921 (4th Cir. 1962) (avoiding issue of work-product as to claim agents, deciding case instead under Rule 34 "good cause").…

129

A complication is introduced by the use made by courts of the "good cause" requirement of Rule 34, as described above. A court may conclude that trial preparation materials are not work-product because not the result of lawyer's work and yet hold that they are not producible because "good cause" has not been shown.... When the decisions on "good cause" are taken into account, the weight of authority affords protection of the preparatory work of both lawyers and nonlawyers (though not necessarily to the same extent) by requiring more than a showing of relevance to secure production. Subdivision (b)(3) reflects the trend of the cases by requiring a special showing, not merely as to materials prepared by an attorney, but also as to materials prepared in anticipation of litigation or preparation for trial by or for a party or any representative acting on his behalf. The subdivision then goes on to protect against disclosure the mental impressions, conclusions, opinions, or legal theories concerning the litigation of an attorney or other representative of a party. The *Hickman* opinion drew special attention to the need for protecting an attorney against discovery of memoranda prepared from recollection of oral interviews. The courts have steadfastly safeguarded against disclosure of lawyers' mental impressions and legal theories, as well as mental impressions and subjective evaluations of investigators and claim-agents. In enforcing this provision of the subdivision, the courts will sometimes find it necessary to order disclosure of a document but with portions deleted.

Rules 33 and 36 have been revised in order to permit discovery calling for opinions, contentions, and admissions relating not only to fact but also to the application of law to fact. Under those rules, a party and his attorney or other representative may be required to disclose, to some extent, mental impressions, opinions, or conclusions. But documents or parts of documents containing these matters are protected against discovery by this subdivision. Even though a party may ultimately have to disclose in response to interrogatories or requests to admit, he is entitled to keep confidential documents containing such matters prepared for internal use.

Party's right to own statement. An exception to the requirement of this subdivision enables a party to secure production of his own statement without any special showing. The cases are divided.... Courts which treat a party's statement as though it were that of any witness overlook the fact that the party's statement is, without more, admissible in evidence. Ordinarily, a party gives a statement without insisting on a copy because he does not yet have a lawyer and does not understand the legal consequences of his actions. Thus, the statement is given at a time when he functions at a disadvantage. Discrepancies between his trial testimony and earlier statement may result from lapse of memory or ordinary inaccuracy; a written statement produced for the first time at trial may give such discrepancies a prominence which they do not deserve. In appropriate cases the court may order a party to be deposed before his statement is produced....

Commentators strongly support the view that a party be able to secure his statement without a showing. 4 *Moore's Federal Practice* para. 26.23 [8.4] (2d ed. 1966); 2A Barron & Holtzoff, *Federal Practice and Procedure* § 652.3 (Wright ed. 1961).... The following states have by statute or rule taken the same position: Statutes: Fla. Stat. Ann. § 92.33; Ga. Code Ann. § 38-2109(b); La. Stat. Ann. R.S. 13:3732; Mass. Gen. Laws. Ann. c. 271, § 44; Minn. Stat. Ann. § 602.01; N.Y. C.P.L.R. § 3101(e). Rules: Mo. R. C. P. 56.01(a); N. Dak. R. C. P. 34(b); Wyo. R. C. P. 34(b); *cf.* Mich. G. C. R. 306.2.

In order to clarify and tighten the provision on statements by a party, the term "statement" is defined. The definition is adapted from 18 U.S.C. § 3500(e) (Jencks Act). The statement of a party may of course be that of plaintiff or defendant, and it may be that of an individual or of a corporation or other organization.

Witness' right to own statement. A second exception to the requirement of this subdivision permits a non-party witness to obtain a copy of his own statement without any special showing. Many, though not all, of the considerations supporting a party's right to obtain his statement apply also to the nonparty witness. Insurance companies are increasingly recognizing that a witness is entitled to a copy of his statement and are modifying their regular practice accordingly.

Subdivision (b)(4) — Trial preparation: Experts. This is a new provision dealing with the discovery of information (including facts and opinions) obtained by a party from an expert retained by that party in relation to litigation or obtained by the expert and not yet transmitted to the party. The subdivision deals separately with those experts whom the party expects to call as trial witnesses and with those experts who have been retained or specially employed by the party but who are not expected to be witnesses. It should be noted that the subdivision does not address itself to the expert whose information was not acquired in preparation for trial but rather because he was an actor or viewer with respect to transactions or occurrences that are part of the subject matter of the lawsuit. Such an expert should be treated as an ordinary witness.

Subsection (b)(4)(A) deals with discovery of information obtained by or through experts who will be called as witnesses at trial. The provision is responsive to problems suggested by a relatively recent line of authorities. Many of these cases present intricate and difficult issues as to which expert testimony is likely to be determinative. Prominent among them are food and drug, patent, and condemnation cases....

In cases of this character, a prohibition against discovery of information held by expert witnesses produces in acute form the very evils that discovery has been created to prevent. Effective cross-examination of an expert witness requires advance preparation. The lawyer even with the help of his own experts frequently can not anticipate the particular approach his adversary's expert will take or the data on which he will base his judgment on the stand.... A California study of discovery and pretrial in condemnation cases notes that the only substitute for discovery of experts' valuation materials is "lengthy—and often fruitless—cross-examination during trial," and recommends pretrial exchange of such material. Calif. Law Rev. Comm'n, *Discovery in Eminent Domain Proceedings* 707–10 (Jan. 1963). Similarly, effective rebuttal requires advance knowledge of the line of testimony of the other side. If the latter is foreclosed by a rule against discovery, then the narrowing of issues and elimination of surprise which discovery normally produces are frustrated.

These considerations appear to account for the broadening of discovery against experts in the cases cited where expert testimony was central to the case. In some instances, the opinions are explicit in relating expanded discovery to improved cross-examination and rebuttal at trial. On the other hand, the need for a new provision is shown by the many cases in which discovery of expert trial witnesses is needed for effective cross-examination and rebuttal, and yet courts apply the traditional doctrine and refuse disclosure....

Although the trial problems flowing from lack of discovery of expert witnesses are most acute and noteworthy when the case turns largely on experts, the same problems are encountered when a single expert testifies. Thus, subdivision (b)(4)(A) draws no line between complex and simple cases, or between cases with many experts and those with but one. It establishes by rule substantially the procedure adopted by decision of the court in *Knighton v. Villian & Fassio*, 39 F.R.D. 11 (D. Md. 1965). For a full analysis of the problem and strong recommendations to the same effect, *see* Friedenthal, *Discovery and Use of an Adverse Party's Expert Information*, 14 Stan. L. Rev. 455, 485–88 (1962). Long, *Discovery and Experts under the Federal Rules of Civil Procedure*, 38 F.R.D. 111 (1965).

Past judicial restrictions on discovery of an adversary's expert, particularly as to his opinions, reflect the fear that one side will benefit unduly from the other's better preparation. The procedure established in subsection (b)(4)(A) holds the risk to a minimum. Discovery is limited to trial witnesses, and may be obtained only at a time when the parties know who their expert witnesses will be. A party must as a practical matter prepare his own case in advance of that time, for he can hardly hope to build his case out of his opponent's experts.

Subdivision (b)(4)(A) provides for discovery of an expert who is to testify at the trial. A party can require one who intends to use the expert to state the substance of the testimony that the expert is expected to give. The court may order further discovery, and it has ample power to regulate its timing and scope and to prevent abuse. Ordinarily, the order for further discovery shall compensate the expert for his time, and may compensate the party who intends to use the expert for past expenses reasonably incurred in obtaining facts or opinions from the expert. Those provisions are likely to discourage abusive practices.

Subdivision (b)(4)(B) deals with an expert who has been retained or specially employed by the party in anticipation of litigation or preparation for trial (thus excluding an expert who is simply a general employee of the party not specially employed on the case), but who is not expected to be called as a witness. Under its provisions, a party may discover facts known or opinions held by such an expert only by a showing of exceptional circumstances under which it is impracticable for the party seeking discovery to obtain facts or opinions on the same subject by other means.

Subdivision (b)(4)(B) is concerned only with experts retained or specially consulted in relation to trial preparation. Thus the subdivision precludes discovery against experts who were informally consulted in preparation for trial, but not retained or specially employed. As an ancillary procedure, a party may on a proper showing require the other party to name experts retained or specially employed, but not those informally consulted.

These new provisions of subdivision (b)(4) repudiate the few decisions that have held an expert's information privileged simply because of his status as an expert.... They also reject as ill-considered the decisions which have sought to bring expert information within the work-product doctrine.... The provisions adopt a form of the more recently developed doctrine of "unfairness". *See e.g., United States v. 23.76 Acres of Land*, 32 F.R.D. 593, 597 (D. Md. 1963); Louisell, *supra*, 317–318; 4 *Moore's Federal Practice* para. 26.24 (2d ed. 1966).

Under subdivision (b)(4)(C), the court is directed or authorized to issue protective orders, including an order that the expert be paid a reasonable fee for time spent in responding to discovery, and that the party whose expert is made subject to discovery be paid a fair portion of the fees and expenses that the party incurred in obtaining information from the expert. The court may issue the latter order as a condition of discovery, or it may delay the order until after discovery is completed. These provisions for fees and expenses meet the objection that it is unfair to permit one side to obtain without cost the benefit of an expert's work for which the other side has paid, often a substantial sum.... On the other hand, a party may not obtain discovery simply by offering to pay fees and expenses....

In instances of discovery under subdivision (b)(4)(B), the court is directed to award fees and expenses to the other party, since the information is of direct value to the discovering party's preparation of his case. In ordering discovery under (b)(4)(A)(ii), the court has discretion whether to award fees and expenses to the other party; its decision should depend upon whether the discovering party is simply learning about the other party's case or is going beyond this to develop his own case. Even in cases where the court is directed to issue a protective order, it may decline to do so if it finds that manifest injustice would result. Thus, the court can protect, when necessary and appropriate, the interests of an indigent party.

Subdivision (c)—Protective orders. The provisions of existing Rule 30(b) are transferred to this subdivision (c), as part of the rearrangement of Rule 26. The language has been changed to give its application to discovery generally. The subdivision recognizes the power of the court in the district where a deposition is being taken to make protective orders. Such power is needed when the deposition is being taken far from the court where the action is pending. The court in the district where the deposition is being taken may, and frequently will, remit the deponent or party to the court where the action is pending.

In addition, drafting changes are made to carry out and clarify the sense of the rule. Insertions are made to avoid any possible implication that a protective order does not extend to "time" as well as to "place" or may not safeguard against "undue burden or expense."

The new reference to trade secrets and other confidential commercial information reflects existing law. The courts have not given trade secrets automatic and complete immunity against disclosure, but have in each case weighed their claim to privacy against the need for disclosure. Frequently, they have been afforded a limited protection....

The subdivision contains new matter relating to sanctions. When a motion for a protective order is made and the court is disposed to deny it, the court may go a step further and issue an order to provide or permit discovery. This will bring the sanctions of Rule 37(b) directly into play. Since the court has heard the contentions of all interested persons, an affirmative order is justified. *See* Rosenberg, *Sanctions to Effectuate Pretrial Discovery*, 58 Colum. L. Rev. 480, 492–93 (1958). In addition, the court may require the payment of expenses incurred in relation to the motion.

Subdivision (d)—Sequence and priority. This new provision is concerned with the sequence in which parties may proceed with discovery and with related problems of timing. The principal effects of the new provision are first, to eliminate any fixed priority in the sequence of discovery, and second, to make clear and explicit the court's power to establish priority by an order issued in a particular case.

A priority rule developed by some courts, which confers priority on the party who first serves notice of taking a deposition, is unsatisfactory in several important respects:

First, this priority rule permits a party to establish a priority running to all depositions as to which he has given earlier notice. Since he can on a given day serve notice of taking many depositions he is in a position to delay his adversary's taking of depositions for an inordinate time. Some courts have ruled that deposition priority also permits a party to delay his answers to interrogatories and production of documents....

Second, since notice is the key to priority, if both parties wish to take depositions first a race results. *See Caldwell-Clements, Inc. v. McGraw-Hill Pub. Co.*, 11 F.R.D. 156 (S.D.N.Y. 1951) (description of tactics used by parties). But the existing rules on notice of deposition create a race with runners starting from different positions. The plaintiff may not give notice without leave of court until 20 days after commencement of the action, whereas the defendant may serve notice at any time after commencement. Thus, a careful and prompt defendant can almost always secure priority. This advantage of defendants is fortuitous, because the purpose of requiring plaintiff to wait 20 days is to afford defendant an opportunity to obtain counsel, not to confer priority.

Third, although courts have ordered a change in the normal sequence of discovery on a number of occasions, ... and have at all times avowed discretion to vary the usual priority, most commentators are agreed that courts in fact grant relief only for "the most obviously compelling reasons." 2A Barron & Holtzoff, *Federal Practice and Procedure* 44–47 (Wright ed. 1961); *see also* Younger, *Priority of Pretrial Examination in the Federal Courts—A Comment*, 34 N.Y.U. L. Rev. 1271 (1959); Freund, *The Pleading and Pretrial of an Antitrust Claim*, 46 Corn. L.Q. 555, 564 (1964). Discontent with the fairness of actual practice has been evinced by other observers. Comment, 59 Yale L.J. 117, 134–36 (1949); Yudkin, *Some Refinements in Federal Discovery Procedure*, 11 Fed B. J. 289, 296–97 (1951); *Developments in the Law-Discovery*, 74 Harv. L. Rev. 940, 954–58 (1961).

Despite these difficulties, some courts have adhered to the priority rule, presumably because it provides a test which is easily understood and applied by the parties without much court intervention. It thus permits deposition discovery to function extrajudicially, which the rules provide for and the courts desire. For these same reasons, courts are reluctant to make numerous exceptions to the rule.

The Columbia Survey makes clear that the problem of priority does not affect litigants generally. It found that most litigants do not move quickly to obtain discovery. In over half of the cases, both parties waited at least 50 days. During the first 20 days after commencement of the action—the period when defendant might assure his priority by noticing depositions—16 percent of the defendants acted to obtain discovery. A race could not have occurred in more than 16 percent of the cases and it undoubtedly occurred in fewer. On the other hand, five times as many defendants as plaintiffs served notice of deposition during the first 19 days....

These findings do not mean, however, that the priority rule is satisfactory or that a problem of priority does not exist. The court decisions show that parties do battle on this issue and carry their disputes to court. The statistics show that these court cases are not typical. By the same token, they reveal that more extensive exercise of judicial discretion to vary the priority will not bring a flood of litigation, and that a change in the priority rule will in fact affect only a small fraction of the cases.

It is contended by some that there is no need to alter the existing priority practice. In support, it is urged that there is no evidence that injustices in fact result from present practice and that, in any event, the courts can and do promulgate local rules, as in New York, to deal with local situations and issue orders to avoid possible injustice in particular cases.

Subdivision (d) is based on the contrary view that the rule of priority based on notice is unsatisfactory and unfair in its operation. Subdivision (d) follows an approach adapted from Civil Rule 4 of the District Court for the Southern District of New York. That rule provides that starting 40 days after commencement of the action, unless otherwise ordered by the court, the fact that one party is taking a deposition shall not prevent another party from doing so "concurrently." In practice, the depositions are not usually taken simultaneously; rather, the parties work out arrangements for alteration in the taking of depositions. One party may take a complete deposition and then the other, or, if the depositions are extensive, one party deposes for a set time, and then the other....

In principle, one party's initiation of discovery should not wait upon the other's completion, unless delay is dictated by special considerations. Clearly the principle is feasible with respect to all methods of discovery other than depositions. And the experience of the Southern District of New York shows that the principle can be applied to depositions as well. The courts have not had an increase in motion business on this matter. Once it is clear to lawyers that they bargain on an equal footing, they are usually able to arrange for an orderly succession of depositions without judicial intervention. Professor Moore has called attention to Civil Rule 4 and suggested that it may usefully be extended to other areas. 4 *Moore's Federal Practice* 1154 (2d ed. 1966).

The court may upon motion and by order grant priority in a particular case. But a local court rule purporting to confer priority in certain classes of cases would be inconsistent with this subdivision and thus void.

Subdivision (e)—Supplementation of responses. The rules do not now state whether interrogatories (and questions at deposition as well as requests for inspection and admissions) impose a "continuing burden" on the responding party to supplement his answers if he obtains new information. The issue is acute when new information renders substantially incomplete or inaccurate an answer which was complete and accurate when made. It is essential that the rules provide an answer to this question. The parties can adjust to a rule either way, once they know what it is....

Arguments can be made both ways. Imposition of a continuing burden reduces the proliferation of additional sets of interrogatories. Some courts have adopted local rules establishing such a burden.... Others have imposed the burden by decision. On the other hand, there are serious objections to the burden, especially in protracted cases. Although the party signs the answers, it is his lawyer who understands their significance and bears the responsibility to bring answers up to date. In a complex case all sorts of information reaches the party, who little understands its bearing on answers previously given to interrogatories. In practice, therefore, the lawyer under a continuing burden must periodically recheck all interrogatories and canvass all new information. But a full set of new answers may no longer be needed by the interrogating party. Some issues will have been dropped from the case, some questions are now seen as unimportant, and other questions must in any event be reformulated....

Subdivision (e) provides that a party is not under a continuing burden except as expressly provided.... An exception is made as to the identity of persons having knowledge of discoverable matters, because of the obvious importance to each side of knowing all witnesses and because information about witnesses routinely comes to each lawyer's attention. Many of the decisions on the issue of a continuing burden have in fact concerned the identity of witnesses. An exception is also made as to expert trial witnesses in order to carry out the provisions of Rule 26(b)(4)....

Another exception is made for the situation in which a party or more frequently his lawyer, obtains actual knowledge that a prior response is incorrect. This exception does not impose a duty to check the accuracy of prior responses, but it prevents knowing concealment by a party or attorney. Finally, a duty to supplement may be imposed by order of the court in a particular case (including an order resulting from a pretrial conference) or by agreement of the parties. A party may of course make a new discovery request which requires supplementation of prior responses.

The duty will normally be enforced, in those limited instances where it is imposed, through sanctions imposed by the trial court, including exclusion of evidence, continuous, or other action, as the court may deem appropriate.

RULE 29

There is no provision for stipulations varying the procedures by which methods of discovery other than depositions are governed. It is common practice for parties to agree on such variations, and the amendment recognizes such agreements and provides a formal mechanism in the rules for giving them effect. Any stipulation varying the procedures may be superseded by court order, and stipulations extending the time for response to discovery under Rules 33, 34, and 36 require court approval.

RULE 30

This subdivision is further revised in regard to the requirement of leave of court for taking a deposition. The present procedure, requiring a plaintiff to obtain leave of court if he serves notice of taking a deposition within 20 days after commencement of the action, is changed in several respects. First, leave is required by reference to the time the deposition is to be taken rather than the date of serving notice of taking. Second, the 20-day period is extended to 30 days and runs from the service of summons and complaint on any defendant, rather than the commencement of the action.... Third, leave is not required beyond the time that defendant initiates discovery, thus showing that he has retained counsel. As under the present practice, a party not afforded a reasonable opportunity to appear at a deposition, because he has not yet been served with process, is protected against use of the deposition at trial against him. *See* Rule 32(a), transferred from 26(d). Moreover, he can later redepose the witness if he so desires.

The purpose of requiring the plaintiff to obtain leave of court is, as stated by the Advisory Committee that proposed the present language of Rule 26(a), to protect "a defendant who has not had an opportunity to retain counsel and inform himself as to the nature of the suit." Note to 1948 amendment of Rule 26(a), quoted in 3A Barron and Holtzoff, *Federal Practice and Procedure* 455–56 (Wright ed. 1958). In order to assure defendant of this opportunity, the period is lengthened to 30 days. This protection, however, is relevant to the time of taking the deposition, not to the time that notice is served. Similarly, the protective period should run from the service of process rather than the filing of the complaint with the court. As stated in the note to Rule 26(d), the courts have used the service of notice as a convenient reference point for assigning priority in taking depositions, but with the elimination of priority in new Rule 26(d) the reference point is no longer needed. The new procedure is consistent in principle with the provisions of Rules 33, 34, and 36 as revised.

Plaintiff is excused from obtaining leave even during the initial 30-day period if he gives the special notice provided in subdivision (b)(2). The required notice must state that the person to be examined is about to go out of the district where the action is pending and more than 100 miles from the place of trial, or out of the United States, or on a voyage to sea, and will be unavailable for examination unless deposed within the 30-day period. These events occur most often in maritime litigation, when seamen are transferred from one port to another or are about to go to sea. Yet, there are analogous situations in nonmaritime litigation, and although the maritime problems are more common, a rule limited to claims in the admiralty and maritime jurisdiction is not justified.

In the recent unification of the civil and admiralty rules, this problem was temporarily met through addition in Rule 26(a) of a provision that depositions de bene esse may continue to be taken as to admiralty and maritime claims within the meaning of Rule 9(h). It was recognized at the time that "a uniform rule applicable alike to what are now civil actions and suits in admiralty" was clearly preferable, but the de bene esse procedure was adopted "for the time being at least." *See* Advisory Committee's note in Report of the Judicial Conference: Proposed Amendments to Rules of Civil Procedure 43–44 (1966).

The changes in Rule 30(a) and the new Rule 30(b)(2) provide a formula applicable to ordinary civil as well as maritime claims. They replace the provision for depositions de bene esse. They authorize an early deposition without leave of court where the witness is about to depart and, unless his deposition is promptly taken, (1) it will be impossible or very difficult to depose him before trial or (2) his deposition can later be taken but only with substantially increased effort and expense. *Cf. S. S. Hai Chang,* 1966 AMC 2239 (S.D.N.Y. 1966), in which the deposing party is required to prepay expenses and counsel fees of the other party's lawyer when the action is pending in New York and depositions are to be taken on the West Coast. Defendant is protected by a provision that the deposition cannot be used against him if he was unable through exercise of diligence to obtain counsel to represent him.

The distance of 100 miles from place of trial is derived from the de bene esse provision and also conforms to the reach of a subpoena of the trial court, as provided in Rule 45(e). *See also* S.D.N.Y. Civ. R. 5(a). Some parts of the de bene esse provision are omitted from Rule 30(b)(2). Modern deposition practice adequately covers the witness who lives more than 100 miles away from place of trial. If a witness is aged or infirm, leave of court can be obtained....

Subdivision (b)(1). If a subpoena duces tecum is to be served, a copy thereof or a designation of the materials to be produced must accompany the notice. Each party is thereby enabled to prepare for the deposition more effectively....

Subdivision (b)(4). In order to facilitate less expensive procedures, provision is made for the recording of testimony by other than stenographic means—e.g., by mechanical, electronic, or photographic means. Because these methods give rise to problems of accuracy and trustworthiness, the party taking the deposition is required to apply for a court order. The order is to specify how the testimony is to be recorded, preserved, and filed, and it may contain whatever additional safeguards the court deems necessary.

Subdivision (b)(5). A provision is added to enable a party, through service of notice, to require another party to produce documents or things at the taking of his deposition. This may now be done as to a nonparty deponent through use of a subpoena duces tecum as authorized by Rule 45, but some courts have held that documents may be secured from a party only under Rule 34. *See* 2A Barron and Holtzoff, *Federal Practice and Procedure* § 644.1 n. 83.2, § 792 n. 16 (Wright ed. 1961). With the elimination of "good cause" from Rule 34, the reason for this restrictive doctrine has disappeared. *Cf.* N.Y. C.P.L.R. § 3111.

Whether production of documents or things should be obtained directly under Rule 34 or at the deposition under this rule will depend on the nature and volume of the documents or things. Both methods are made available. When the documents are few and simple, and closely related to the oral examination, ability to proceed via this rule will facilitate discovery. If the discovering party insists on examining many and complex documents at the taking of the deposition, thereby causing undue burdens on others, the latter may, under Rule 26(c) or 30(d), apply for a court order that the examining party proceed via Rule 34 alone.

Subdivision (b)(6). A new provision is added, whereby a party may name a corporation, partnership, association, or governmental agency as the deponent and designate the matters on which he requests examination, and the organization shall then name one or more of its officers, directors, or managing agents, or other persons consenting to appear and testify on its behalf with respect to matters known or reasonably available to the organization. *Cf.* Alberta Sup. Ct. R. 255. The organization may designate persons other than officers, directors, and managing agents, but only with their consent. Thus, an employee or agent who has an independent or conflicting interest in the litigation—for example, in a personal injury case—can refuse to testify on behalf of the organization.

This procedure supplements the existing practice whereby the examining party designates the corporate official to be deposed. Thus, if the examining party believes that certain officials who have not testified pursuant to this subdivision have added information, he may depose them. On the other hand, a court's decision whether to issue a protective order may take account of the availability and use made of the procedures provided in this subdivision.

The new procedure should be viewed as an added facility for discovery, one which may be advantageous to both sides as well as an improvement in the deposition process. It will reduce the difficulties now encountered in determining, prior to taking of a deposition, whether a particular employee or agent is a "managing agent." *See* Note, *Discovery Against Corporations Under the Federal Rules*, 47 Iowa L. Rev. 1006–16 (1962). It will curb the "bandying" by which officers or managing agents of a corporation are deposed in turn but each disclaims knowledge of facts that are clearly known to persons in the organization and thereby to it…. The provision should also assist organizations which find that an unnecessarily large number of their officers and agents are being deposed by a party uncertain of who in the organization has knowledge. Some courts have held that under the existing rules a corporation should not be burdened with choosing which person is to appear for it…. This burden is not essentially different from that of answering interrogatories under Rule 33, and is in any case lighter than that of an examining party ignorant of who in the corporation has knowledge.

Subdivision (c). A new sentence is inserted at the beginning, representing the transfer of existing Rule 26(c) to this subdivision. Another addition conforms to the new provision in subdivision (b)(4).

The present rule provides that transcription shall be carried out unless all parties waive it. In view of the many depositions taken from which nothing useful is discovered, the revised language provides that transcription is to be performed if any party requests it. The fact of the request is relevant to the exercise of the court's discretion in determining who shall pay for transcription.

Parties choosing to serve written questions rather than participate personally in an oral deposition are directed to serve their questions on the party taking the deposition, since the officer is often not identified in advance. Confidentiality is preserved, since the questions may be served in a sealed envelope.

Subdivision (d). The assessment of expenses incurred in relation to motions made under this subdivision (d) is made subject to the provisions of Rule 37(a). The standards for assessment of expenses are more fully set out in Rule 37(a), and these standards should apply to the essentially similar motions of this subdivision.

Subdivision (e). The provision relating to the refusal of a witness to sign his deposition is tightened through insertion of a 30-day time period.

Subdivision (f)(1). A provision is added which codifies in a flexible way the procedure for handling exhibits related to the deposition and at the same time assures each party that he may inspect and copy documents and things produced by a nonparty witness in response to a subpoena duces tecum. As a general rule and in the absence of agreement to the contrary or order of the court, exhibits produced without objection are to be annexed to and returned with the deposition, but a witness may substitute copies for purposes of marking and he may obtain return of the exhibits. The right of the parties to inspect exhibits for identification and to make copies is assured.

RULE 33

Subdivision (a). The mechanics of the operation of Rule 33 are substantially revised by the proposed amendment, with a view to reducing court intervention. There is general agreement that interrogatories spawn a greater percentage of objections and motions than any other discovery device. The Columbia Survey shows that, although half of the litigants resorted to depositions and about one-third used interrogatories, about 65 percent of the objections were made with respect to interrogatories and 26 percent related to depositions. *See also* Speck, *The Use of Discovery in the United States District Courts*, 60 Yale L.J. 1132, 1144, 1151 (1951); Note, 36 Minn. L. Rev. 364, 379 (1952).

The procedures now provided in Rule 33 seem calculated to encourage objections and court motions. The time periods now allowed for responding to interrogatories—15 days for answers and 10 days for objections—are too short. The Columbia Survey shows that tardy response to interrogatories is common, virtually expected. The same was reported in Speck, *supra*, 60 Yale L.J. 1132, 1144. The time pressures tend to encourage objections as a means of gaining time to answer.

The time for objections is even shorter than for answers, and the party runs the risk that if he fails to object in time he may have waived his objections.... It often seems easier to object than to seek an extension of time. Unlike Rules 30(d) and 37(a), Rule 33 imposes no sanction of expenses on a party whose objections are clearly unjustified. Rule 33 assures that the objections will lead directly to court, through its requirement that they be served with a notice of hearing. Although this procedure does not preclude an out-of-court resolution of the dispute, the procedure tends to discourage informal negotiations. If answers are served and they are thought inadequate, the interrogating party may move under Rule 37(a) for an order compelling adequate answers. There is no assurance that the hearing on objections and that on inadequate answers will be heard together.

The amendment improves the procedure of Rule 33 in the following respects: (1) The time allowed for response is increased to 30 days and this time period applies to both answers and objections, but a defendant need not respond in less than 45 days after service of the summons and complaint upon him. As is true under existing law, the responding party who believes that some parts or all of the interrogatories are objectionable may choose to seek a protective order under new Rule 26(c) or may serve objections under this rule. Unless he applies for a protective order, he is required to serve answers or objections in response to the interrogatories, subject to the sanctions provided in Rule 37(d). Answers and objections are served together, so that a response to each interrogatory is encouraged, and any failure to respond is easily noted. (2) In view of the enlarged time permitted for response, it is no longer necessary to require leave of court for service of interrogatories. The purpose of this requirement—that defendant have time to obtain counsel before a response must be made—is adequately fulfilled by the requirement that interrogatories be served upon a party with or after service of the summons and complaint upon him.

Some would urge that the plaintiff nevertheless not be permitted to serve interrogatories with the complaint. They fear that a routine practice might be invited, whereby form interrogatories would accompany most complaints. More fundamentally, they feel that, since very general complaints are permitted in present-day pleading, it is fair that the defendant have a right to take the lead in serving interrogatories. (These views apply also to Rule 36.) The amendment of Rule 33 rejects these views, in favor of allowing both parties to go forward with discovery, each free to obtain the information he needs respecting the case. (3) If objections are made, the burden is on the interrogating party to move under Rule 37(a) for a court order compelling answers, in the course of which the court will pass on the objections. The change in the burden of going forward does not alter the existing obligation of an objecting party to justify his objections.... If the discovering party asserts that an answer is incomplete or evasive, again he may look to Rule 37(a) for relief, and he should add this assertion to his motion to overrule objections. There is no requirement that the parties consult informally concerning their differences, but the new procedure should encourage consultation, and the court may by local rule require it.

The proposed changes are similar in approach to those adopted by California in 1961. *See* Calif. Code Civ. Proc. § 2030(a). The experience of the Los Angeles Superior Court is informally reported as showing that the California amendment resulted in a significant reduction in court motions concerning interrogatories. Rhode Island takes a similar approach. *See* R. 33, R.I.R. Civ. Proc. Official Draft, p. 74 (Boston Law Book Co.).

A change is made in subdivision (a) which is not related to the sequence of procedures. The restriction to "adverse" parties is eliminated. The courts have generally construed this restriction as precluding interrogatories unless an issue between the parties is disclosed by the pleadings—even though the parties may have conflicting interests. *E.g., Mozeika v. Kaufman Construction Co.* 25 F.R.D. 233 (E.D. Pa. 1960) (plaintiff and third-party defendant); *Biddle v. Hutchinson*, 24 F.R.D. 256 (M.D. Pa. 1959) (co-defendants). The resulting distinctions have often been highly technical. In *Schlagenhauf v. Holder*, 379 U.S. 104 (1964), the Supreme Court rejected a contention that examination under Rule 35 could be had only against an "opposing" party, as not in keeping "with the aims of a liberal, nontechnical application of the Federal Rules." 379 U.S. at 116. Eliminating the requirement of "adverse" parties from Rule 33 brings it into line with all other discovery rules....

Subdivision (b). There are numerous and conflicting decisions on the question whether and to what extent interrogatories are limited to matters "of fact," or may elicit opinions, contentions, and legal conclusions.... For lists of the many conflicting authorities, *see* 4 *Moore's Federal Practice* para. 33.17 (2d ed. 1966); 2A Barron & Holtzoff, *Federal Practice and Procedure* § 768 (Wright ed. 1961). Rule 33 is amended to provide that an interrogatory is not objectionable merely because it calls for an opinion or contention that relates to fact or the application of law to fact. Efforts to draw sharp lines between facts and opinions have invariably been unsuccessful, and the clear trend of the cases is to permit "factual" opinions. As to requests for opinions or contentions that call for the application of law to fact, they can be most useful in narrowing and sharpening the issues, which is a major purpose of discovery.... On the other hand, under the new language interrogatories may not extend to issues of "pure law," i.e., legal issues unrelated to the facts of the case....

Since interrogatories involving mixed questions of law and fact may create disputes between the parties which are best resolved after much or all of the other discovery has been completed, the court is expressly authorized to defer an answer. Likewise, the court may delay determination until pretrial conference, if it believes that the dispute is best resolved in the presence of the judge.

The principal question raised with respect to the cases permitting such interrogatories is whether they reintroduce undesirable aspects of the prior pleading practice, whereby parties were chained to misconceived contentions or theories, and ultimate determination on the merits was frustrated. *See* James, *The Revival of Bills of Particulars under the Federal Rules*, 71 Harv. L. Rev. 1473 (1958). But there are few if any instances in the recorded cases demonstrating that such frustration has occurred. The general rule governing the use of answers to interrogatories is that under ordinary circumstances they do not limit proof.... Although in exceptional circumstances reliance on an answer may cause such prejudice that the court will hold the answering party bound to his answer, *e.g., Zielinski v. Philadelphia Piers, Inc.* 139 F. Supp. 408 (E.D. Pa. 1956), the interrogating party will ordinarily not be entitled to rely on the unchanging character of the answers he receives and cannot base prejudice on such reliance. The rule does not affect the power of a court to permit withdrawal or amendment of answers to interrogatories.

The use of answers to interrogatories at trial is made subject to the rules of evidence. The provisions governing use of depositions, to which Rule 33 presently refers, are not entirely apposite to answers to interrogatories, since deposition practice contemplates that all parties will ordinarily participate through cross-examination. *See* 4 *Moore's Federal Practice* para. 33.29 [1] (2d ed. 1966).

Certain provisions are deleted from subdivision (b) because they are fully covered by new Rule 26(c) providing for protective orders and Rules 26(a) and 26(d). The language of the subdivision is thus simplified without any change of substance.

Subdivision (c). This is a new subdivision, adapted from Calif. Code Civ. Proc. § 2030(c), relating especially to interrogatories which require a party to engage in burdensome or expensive research into his own business records in order to give an answer. The subdivision gives the party an option to make the records available and place the burden of research on the party who seeks the information. "This provision, without undermining the liberal scope of interrogatory discovery, places the burden of discovery upon its potential benefitee," Louisell, *Modern California Discovery*, 124–125 (1963), and alleviates a problem which in the past has troubled Federal courts.... The interrogating party is protected against abusive use of this provision through the requirement that the burden of ascertaining the answer be substantially the same for both sides. A respondent may not impose on an interrogating party a mass of records as to which research is feasible only for one familiar with the records. At the same time, the respondent unable to invoke this subdivision does not on that account lose the protection available to him under new Rule 26(c) against oppressive or unduly burdensome or expensive interrogatories. And even when the respondent successfully invokes the subdivision, the court is not deprived of its usual power, in appropriate cases, to require that the interrogating party reimburse the respondent for the expense of assembling his records and making them intelligible.

RULE 34

Rule 34 is revised to accomplish the following major changes in the existing rule: (1) to eliminate the requirement of good cause; (2) to have the rule operate extrajudicially; (3) to include testing and sampling as well as inspecting or photographing tangible things; and (4) to make clear that the rule does not preclude an independent action for analogous discovery against persons not parties....

The revision of Rule 34 to have it operate extrajudicially rather than by court order, is to a large extent a reflection of existing law office practice. The Columbia Survey shows that of the litigants seeking inspection of documents or things, only about 25 percent filed motions for court orders. This minor fraction nevertheless accounted for a significant number of motions. About half of these motions were uncontested and in almost all instances the party seeking production ultimately prevailed. Although an extrajudicial procedure will not drastically alter existing practice under Rule 34—it will conform to it in most cases—it has the potential of saving court time in a substantial though proportionately small number of cases tried annually.

The inclusion of testing and sampling of tangible things and objects or operations on land reflects a need frequently encountered by parties in preparation for trial. If the operation of a particular machine is the basis of a claim for negligent injury, it will often be necessary to test its operating parts or to sample and test the products it is producing. *Cf.* Mich. Gen. Ct. R. 310.1(1) (1963) (testing authorized).

The inclusive description of "documents" is revised to accord with changing technology. It makes clear that Rule 34 applies to electronic data compilations from which information can be obtained only with the use of detection devices, and that when the data can as a practical matter be made usable by the discovering party only through respondent's devices, respondent may be required to use his devices to translate the data into usable form. In many instances, this means that respondent will have to supply a print-out of computer data. The burden thus placed on respondent will vary from case to case, and the courts have ample power under Rule 26(c) to protect respondent against undue burden or expense, either by restricting discovery or requiring that the discovering party pay costs. Similarly, if the discovering party needs to check the electronic source itself, the court may protect respondent with respect to preservation of his records, confidentiality of nondiscoverable matters, and costs....

Subdivision (c). Rule 34 as revised continues to apply only to parties. Comments from the bar make clear that in the preparation of cases for trial it is occasionally necessary to enter land or inspect large tangible things in the possession of a person not a party, and that some courts have dismissed independent actions in the nature of bills in equity for such discovery on the ground that Rule 34 is preemptive. While an ideal solution to this problem is to provide for discovery against persons not parties in Rule 34, both the jurisdictional and procedural problems are very complex. For the present, this subdivision makes clear that Rule 34 does not preclude independent actions for discovery against persons not parties.

RULE 35

Subdivision (a). Rule 35(a) has hitherto provided only for an order requiring a party to submit to an examination. It is desirable to extend the rule to provide for an order against the party for examination of a person in his custody or under his legal control. As appears from the provisions of amended Rule 37(b)(2) and the comment under that rule, an order to "produce" the third person imposes only an obligation to use good faith efforts to produce the person.

The amendment will settle beyond doubt that a parent or guardian suing to recover for injuries to a minor may be ordered to produce the minor for examination. Further, the amendment expressly includes blood examination within the kinds of examinations that can be ordered under the rule.... Provisions similar to the amendment have been adopted in at least 10 states....

The amendment makes no change in the requirements of Rule 35 that, before a court order may issue, the relevant physical or mental condition must be shown to be "in controversy" and "good cause" must be shown for the examination. Thus, the amendment has no effect on the recent decision of the Supreme Court in *Schlagenhauf v. Holder*, 379 U.S. 104 (1964), stressing the importance of these requirements and applying them to the facts of the case. The amendment makes no reference to employees of a party. Provisions relating to employees in the State statutes and rules cited above appear to have been virtually unused.

Subdivision (b)(1). This subdivision is amended to correct an imbalance in Rule 35(b)(1) as heretofore written. Under that text, a party causing a Rule 35(a) examination to be made is required to furnish to the party examined, on request, a copy of the examining physicians' report. If he delivers this copy, he is in turn entitled to receive from the party examined reports of all examinations of the same condition previously or later made. But the rule has not in terms entitled the examined party to receive from the party causing the Rule 35(a) examination any reports of earlier examinations of the same condition to which the latter may have access. The amendment cures this defect....

The amendment specifies that the written report of the examining physician includes results of all tests made, such as results of X-rays and cardiograms. It also embodies changes required by the broadening of Rule 35(a) to take in persons who are not parties.

Subdivision (b)(3). This new subdivision removes any possible doubt that reports of examination may be obtained although no order for examination has been made under Rule 35(a). Examinations are very frequently made by agreement, and sometimes before the party examined has an attorney. The courts have uniformly ordered that reports be supplied, and it appears best to fill the technical gap in the present rule.

RULE 36

Rule 36 serves two vital purposes, both of which are designed to reduce trial time. Admissions are sought, first to facilitate proof with respect to issues that cannot be eliminated from the case, and secondly, to narrow the issues by eliminating those that can be. The changes made in the rule are designed to serve these purposes more effectively. Certain disagreements in the courts about the proper scope of the rule are resolved. In addition, the procedural operation of the rule is brought into line with other discovery procedures, and the binding effect of an admission is clarified....

Subdivision (a). As revised, the subdivision provides that a request may be made to admit any matters within the scope of Rule 26(b) that relate to statements or opinions of fact or of the application of law to fact. It thereby eliminates the requirement that the matters be "of fact." This change resolves conflicts in the court decisions as to whether a request to admit matters of "opinion" and matters involving "mixed law and fact" is proper under the rule.... Not only is it difficult as a practical matter to separate "fact" from "opinion," see 4 Moore's Federal Practice para. 36.04 (2d ed. 1966); cf. 2A Barron & Holtzoff, Federal Practice and Procedure 317 (Wright ed. 1961), but an admission on a matter of opinion may facilitate proof or narrow the issues or both. An admission of a matter involving the application of law to fact may, in a given case, even more clearly narrow the issues. For example, an admission that an employee acted in the scope of his employment may remove a major issue from the trial. In McSparran v. Hanigan, [225 F. Supp. 628 (E.D. Pa. 1963),] plaintiff admitted that "the premises on which said accident occurred, were occupied or under the control" of one of the defendants, 225 F. Supp. at 636. This admission, involving law as well as fact, removed one of the issues from the lawsuit and thereby reduced the proof required at trial. The amended provision does not authorize requests for admissions of law unrelated to the facts of the case.

Requests for admission involving the application of law to fact may create disputes between the parties which are best resolved in the presence of the judge after much or all of the other discovery has been completed. Power is therefore expressly conferred upon the court to defer decision until a pretrial conference is held or until a designated time prior to trial. On the other hand, the court should not automatically defer decision; in many instances, the importance of the admission lies in enabling the requesting party to avoid the burdensome accumulation of proof prior to the pretrial conference.

Courts have also divided on whether an answering party may properly object to requests for admission as to matters which that party regards as "in dispute." ...The proper response in such cases is an answer. The very purpose of the request is to ascertain whether the answering party is prepared to admit or regards the matter as presenting a genuine issue for trial. In his answer, the party may deny, or he may give as his reason for inability to admit or deny the existence of a genuine issue. The party runs no risk of sanctions if the matter is genuinely in issue, since Rule 37(c) provides a sanction of costs only when there are no good reasons for a failure to admit.

On the other hand, requests to admit may be so voluminous and so framed that the answering party finds the task of identifying what is in dispute and what is not unduly burdensome. If so, the responding party may obtain a protective order under Rule 26(c). Some of the decisions sustaining objections on "disputability" grounds could have been justified by the burdensome character of the requests....

Another sharp split of authority exists on the question whether a party may base his answer on lack of information or knowledge without seeking out additional information. One line of cases has held that a party may answer on the basis of such knowledge as he has at the time he answers. E.g., Jackson Buff Corp. v. Marcelle, 20 F.R.D. 139 (E.D.N.Y. 1957); Sladek v. General Motors Corp., 16 F.R.D. 104 (S.D. Iowa 1954). A larger group of cases, supported by commentators, has taken the view that if the responding party lacks knowledge, he must inform himself in reasonable fashion. E.g., Hise v. Lockwood Grader Corp., 153 F. Supp. 276 (D. Neb. 1957); E. H. Tate Co. v. Jiffy Enterprises, Inc., 16 F.R.D. 571 (E.D. Pa. 1954); ... 2A Barron & Holtzoff, Federal Practice and Procedure 509 (Wright ed. 1961).

The rule as revised adopts the majority view, as in keeping with a basic principle of the discovery rules that a reasonable burden may be imposed on the parties when its discharge will facilitate preparation for trial and ease the trial process. It has been argued against this view that one side should not have the burden of "proving" the other side's case. The revised rule requires only that the answering party make reasonable inquiry and secure such knowledge and information as are readily obtainable by him. In most instances, the investigation will be necessary either to his own case or to preparation for rebuttal. Even when it is not, the information may be close enough at hand to be "readily obtainable." Rule 36 requires only that the party state that he has taken these steps. The sanction for failure of a party to inform himself before he answers lies in the award of costs after trial, as provided in Rule 37(c).

The requirement that the answer to a request for admission be sworn is deleted, in favor of a provision that the answer be signed by the party or by his attorney. The provisions of Rule 36 make it clear that admissions function very much as pleadings do. Thus, when a party admits in part and denies in part, his admission is for purposes of the pending action only and may not be used against him in any other proceeding. The broadening of the rule to encompass mixed questions of law and fact reinforces this feature. Rule 36 does not lack a sanction for false answers; Rule 37(c) furnishes an appropriate deterrent....

Subdivision (b). The rule does not now indicate the extent to which a party is bound by his admission. Some courts view admissions as the equivalent of sworn testimony.... At least in some jurisdictions a party may rebut his own testimony, e.g., Alamo v. Del Rosario, 98 F.2d 328 (D.C. Cir. 1938), and by analogy an admission made pursuant to Rule 36 may likewise be thought rebuttable.... In McSparran v. Hanigan, 225 F. Supp. 628, 636–37 (E.D. Pa. 1963), the court held that an admission is conclusively binding, though noting the confusion created by prior decisions.

The new provisions give an admission a conclusively binding effect, for purposes only of the pending action, unless the admission is withdrawn or amended. In form and substance a Rule 36 admission is comparable to an admission in pleadings or a stipulation drafted by counsel for use at trial, rather than to evidentiary admission of a party. Louisell, Modern California Discovery § 8.07 (1963); 2A Barron & Holtzoff,

Federal Practice and Procedure § 838 (Wright ed. 1961). Unless the party securing an admission can depend on its binding effect, he cannot safely avoid the expense of preparing to prove the very matters on which he has secured the admission, and the purpose of the rule is defeated....

Provision is made for withdrawal or amendment of an admission. This provision emphasizes the importance of having the action resolved on the merits, while at the same time assuring each party that justified reliance on an admission in preparation for trial will not operate to his prejudice.

RULE 37

Rule 37 provides generally for sanctions against parties or persons unjustifiably resisting discovery. Experience has brought to light a number of defects in the language of the rule as well as instances in which it is not serving the purposes for which it was designed.... In addition, changes being made in other discovery rules require conforming amendments to Rule 37. Rule 37 sometimes refers to a "failure" to afford discovery and at other times to a "refusal" to do so. Taking note of this dual terminology, courts have imported into "refusal" a requirement of "wilfullness." ... In *Societe Internationale v. Rogers,* 357 U.S. 197 (1958), the Supreme Court concluded that the rather random use of these two terms in Rule 37 showed no design to use them with consistently distinctive meanings, that "refused" in Rule 37(b)(2) meant simply a failure to comply, and that wilfullness was relevant only to the selection of sanctions, if any, to be imposed. Nevertheless, after the decision in *Societe,* the court in *Hinson v. Michigan Mutual Liability Co.,* 275 F.2d 537 (5th Cir. 1960) once again ruled that "refusal" required wilfullness. Substitution of "failure" for "refusal" throughout Rule 37 should eliminate this confusion and bring the rule into harmony with the *Societe Internationale* decision....

Subdivision (a). Rule 37(a) provides relief to a party seeking discovery against one who, with or without stated objections, fails to afford the discovery sought. It has always fully served this function in relation to depositions, but the amendments being made to Rules 33 and 34 give Rule 37(a) added scope and importance. Under existing Rule 33, a party objecting to interrogatories must make a motion for court hearing on his objections. The changes now made in Rules 33 and 37(a) make it clear that the interrogating party must move to compel answers, and the motion is provided for in Rule 37(a). Existing Rule 34, since it requires a court order prior to production of documents or things or permission to enter on land, has no relation to Rule 37(a). Amendments of Rules 34 and 37(a) create a procedure similar to that provided for Rule 33.

Subdivision (a)(1). This is a new provision making clear to which court a party may apply for an order compelling discovery. Existing Rule 37(a) refers only to the court in which the deposition is being taken; nevertheless, it has been held that the court where the action is pending has "inherent power" to compel a party deponent to answer.... In relation to Rule 33 interrogatories and Rule 34 requests for inspection, the court where the action is pending is the appropriate enforcing tribunal. The new provision eliminates the need to resort to inherent power by spelling out the respective roles of the court where the action is pending and the court where the deposition is taken. In some instances, two courts are available to a party seeking to compel answers from a party deponent. The party seeking discovery may choose the court to which he will apply, but the court has power to remit the party to the other court as a more appropriate forum.

Subdivision (a)(2). This subdivision contains the substance of existing provisions of Rule 37(a) authorizing motions to compel answers to questions put at depositions and to interrogatories. New provisions authorize motions for orders compelling designation under Rules 30(b)(6) and 31(a) and compelling inspection in accordance with a request made under Rule 34. If the court denies a motion, in whole or part, it may accompany the denial with issuance of a protective order. Compare the converse provision in Rule 26(c).

Subdivision (a)(3). This new provision makes clear that an evasive or incomplete answer is to be considered, for purposes of subdivision (a), a failure to answer. The courts have consistently held that they have the power to compel adequate answers.... This power is recognized and incorporated into the rule.

Subdivision (a)(4). This subdivision amends the provisions for award of expenses, including reasonable attorney's fees, to the prevailing party or person when a motion is made for an order compelling discovery. At present, an award of expenses is made only if the losing party or person is found to have acted without substantial justification. The change requires that expenses be awarded unless the conduct of the losing party or person is found to have been substantially justified. The test of "substantial justification" remains, but the change in language is intended to encourage judges to be more alert to abuses occurring in the discovery process.

On many occasions, to be sure, the dispute over discovery between the parties is genuine, though ultimately resolved one way or the other by the court. In such cases, the losing party is substantially justified in carrying the matter to court. But the rules should deter the abuse implicit in carrying or forcing a discovery dispute to court when no genuine dispute exists. And the potential or actual imposition of expenses is virtually the sole formal sanction in the rules to deter a party from pressing to a court hearing frivolous requests for or objections to discovery.

The present provision of Rule 37(a) that the court shall require payment if it finds that the defeated party acted without "substantial justification" may appear adequate, but in fact it has been little used. Only a handful of reported cases include an award of expenses, and the Columbia Survey found that in only one instance out of about 50 motions decided under Rule 37(a) did the court award expenses. It appears that the courts do not utilize the most important available sanction to deter abusive resort to the judiciary.

The proposed change provides in effect that expenses should ordinarily be awarded unless a court finds that the losing party acted justifiably in carrying his point to court. At the same time, a necessary flexibility is maintained, since the court retains the power to find that other circumstances make an award of expenses unjust—as where the prevailing party also acted unjustifiably. The amendment does not significantly narrow the discretion of the court, but rather presses the court to address itself to abusive practices. The present provision that expenses may be imposed upon either the party or his attorney or both is unchanged. But it is not contemplated that expenses will be imposed upon the attorney merely because the party is indigent.

Subdivision (b). This subdivision deals with sanctions for failure to comply with a court order. The present captions for subsections (1) and (2) entitled "Contempt" and "Other Consequences," respectively, are confusing. One of the consequences listed in (2) is the arrest of the party, representing the exercise of the contempt power. The contents of the subsections show that the first authorizes the sanction of contempt (and no other) by the court in which the deposition is taken, whereas the second subsection authorizes a variety of sanctions, including contempt, which may be imposed by the court in which the action is pending. The captions of the subsections are changed to reflect their contents.

The scope of Rule 37(b)(2) is broadened by extending it to include any order "to provide or permit discovery," including orders issued under Rules 37(a) and 35. Various rules authorize orders for discovery—e.g., Rule 35(b)(1), Rule 20(c) as revised, Rule 37(d).... Rule 37(b)(2) should provide comprehensively for enforcement of all these orders.... On the other hand, the reference to Rule 34 is deleted to conform to the changed procedure in that rule.

A new subsection (E) provides that sanctions which have been available against a party for failure to comply with an order under Rule 35(a) to submit to examination will now be available against him for his failure to comply with a Rule 35(a) order to produce a third person for examination, unless he shows that he is unable to produce the person. In this context, "unable" means in effect "unable in good faith." See *Societe Internationale v. Rogers*, 357 U.S. 197 (1958).

Subdivision (b)(2) is amplified to provide for payment of reasonable expenses caused by the failure to obey the order. Although Rules 37(b)(2) and 37(d) have been silent as to award of expenses, courts have nevertheless ordered them on occasion. The provision places the burden on the disobedient party to avoid expenses by showing that his failure is justified or that special circumstances make an award of expenses unjust. Allocating the burden in this way conforms to the changed provisions as to expenses in Rule 37(a), and is particularly appropriate when a court order is disobeyed....

Subdivision (c). Rule 37(c) provides a sanction for the enforcement of Rule 36 dealing with requests for admission. Rule 36 provides the mechanism whereby a party may obtain from another party in appropriate instances either (1) an admission, or (2) a sworn and specific denial, or (3) a sworn statement "setting forth in detail the reasons why he cannot truthfully admit or deny." If the party obtains the second or third of these responses, in proper from, Rule 36 does not provide for a pretrial hearing on whether the response is warranted by the evidence thus far accumulated. Instead, Rule 37(c) is intended to provide posttrial relief in the form of a requirement that the party improperly refusing the admission pay the expenses of the other side in making the necessary proof at trial. Rule 37(c), as now written, addresses itself in terms only to the sworn denial and is silent with respect to the statement of reasons for an inability to admit or deny. There is no apparent basis for this distinction, since the sanction provided in Rule 37(c) should deter all unjustified failures to admit. This omission in the rule has caused confused and diverse treatment in the courts. One court has held that if a party gives inadequate reasons, he should be treated before trial as having denied the request, so that Rule 37(c) may apply. *Bertha Bldg. Corp. v. National Theatres Corp.*, 15 F.R.D. 339 (E.D.N.Y. 1954). Another has held that the party should be treated as having admitted the request. *Heng Hsin Co. v. Stern, Morgenthau & Co.*, 20 Fed. Rules Serv. 36a.52, Case 1 (S.D.N.Y. Dec. 10, 1954). Still another has ordered a new response, without indicating what the outcome should be if the new response were inadequate. *United States Plywood Corp. v. Hudson Lumber Co.*, 127 F. Supp. 489, 497–98 (S.D.N.Y. 1954). *See generally* Finman, *The Request for Admissions in Federal Civil Procedure*, 71 Yale L.J. 371, 426–430 (1962). The amendment eliminates this defect in Rule 37(c) by bringing within its scope all failures to admit.

Additional provisions in Rule 37(c) protect a party from having to pay expenses if the request for admission was held objectionable under Rule 36(a) or if the party failing to admit had reasonable ground to believe that he might prevail on the matter. The latter provision emphasizes that the true test under Rule 37(c) is not whether a party prevailed at trial but whether he acted reasonably in believing that he might prevail.

Subdivision (d). The scope of subdivision (d) is broadened to include responses to requests for inspection under Rule 34, thereby conforming to the new procedures of Rule 34.

Two related changes are made in subdivision (d): the permissible sanctions are broadened to include such orders "as are just"; and the requirement that the failure to appear or respond be "wilful" is eliminated. Although Rule 37(d) in terms provides for only three sanctions, all rather severe, the courts have interpreted it as permitting softer sanctions than those which it sets forth…. The rule is changed to provide the greater flexibility as sanctions which the cases show is needed.

The resulting flexibility as to sanctions eliminates any need to retain the requirement that the failure to appear or respond be "wilful." The concept of "wilful failure" is at best subtle and difficult, and the cases do not supply a bright line. Many courts have imposed sanctions without referring to wilfulness. *E.g., Milewski v. Schneider Transportation Co.*, 238 F.2d 397 (6th Cir. 1956); *Dictograph Products, Inc. v. Kentworth Corp.*, 7 F.R.D. 543 (W.D. Ky. 1947). In addition, in view of the possibility of light sanctions, even a negligent failure should come within Rule 37(d). If default is caused by counsel's ignorance of Federal practice, *cf. Dunn. v. Pa R.R.*, 96 F. Supp. 597 (N.D. Ohio 1951), or by his preoccupation with another aspect of the case, *cf. Maurer-Neuer, Inc. v. United Packinghouse Workers*, 26 F.R.D. 139 (D. Kans. 1960), dismissal of the action and default judgment are not justified, but the imposition of expenses and fees may well be. "Wilfulness" continues to play a role, along with various other factors, in the choice of sanctions. Thus, the scheme conforms to Rule 37(b) as construed by the Supreme Court in *Societe Internationale v. Rogers*, 357 U.S. 197, 208 (1958).

A provision is added to make clear that a party may not properly remain completely silent even when he regards a notice to take his deposition or a set of interrogatories or requests to inspect as improper and objectionable. If he desires not to appear or not to respond, he must apply for a protective order. The cases are divided on whether a protective order must be sought. The party from whom discovery is sought is afforded, through Rule 26(c), a fair and effective procedure whereby he can challenge the request made. At the same time, the total noncompliance with which Rule 37(d) is concerned may impose severe inconvenience or hardship on the discovering party and substantially delay the discovery process….

The failure of an officer or managing agent of a party to make discovery as required by present Rule 37(d) is treated as the failure of the party. The rule as revised provides similar treatment for a director of a party. There is slight warrant for the present distinction between officers and managing agents on the one hand and directors on the other. Although the legal power over a director to compel his making discovery may not be as great as over officers or managing agents, … the practical differences are negligible. That a director's interests are normally aligned with those of his corporation is shown by the provisions of old Rule 26(d)(2), transferred to 32(a)(2) (deposition of director of party may be used at trial by an adverse party for any purpose) and of Rule 43(b) (director of party may be treated at trial as a hostile witness on direct examination by any adverse party). Moreover, in those rare instances when a corporation is unable through good faith efforts to compel a director to make discovery, it is unlikely that the court will impose sanctions.

RULE 69

The amendment assures that, in aid of execution on a judgment, all discovery procedures provided in the rules are available and not just discovery via the taking of a deposition. Under the present language, one court has held that Rule 34 discovery is unavailable to the judgment creditor. *M. Lowenstein & Sons, Inc. v. American Underwear Mfg. Co.*, 11 F.R.D. 172 (E.D. Pa. 1951). Notwithstanding the language, and relying heavily on legislative history referring to Rule 33, the Fifth Circuit has held that a judgment creditor may invoke Rule 33 interrogatories. *United States v. McWhirter*, 376 F.2d 102 (5th Cir. 1967). But the court's reasoning does not extend to discovery except as provided in Rules 26–33. One commentator suggests that the existing language might properly be stretched to all discovery, 7 *Moore's Federal Practice* para. 69.05 [1] (2d ed. 1966), but another believes that a rules amendment is needed. 3 Barron & Holtzoff, *Federal Practice and Procedure* 1484 (Wright ed. 1958). Both commentators and the court in *McWhirter* are clear that, as a matter of policy, Rule 69 should authorize the use of all discovery devices provided in the rules.

ADVISORY COMMITTEE NOTES TO 1971 AMENDMENTS

RULE 30

The subdivision permits a party to name a corporation or other form of organization as a deponent in the notice of examination and to describe in the notice the matters about which discovery is desired…. The amendment clarifies the procedure to be followed if a party desires to examine a non-party organization through persons designated by the organization. Under the rules, a subpoena rather than a notice of examination is served on a non-party to compel attendance at the taking of a deposition. The amendment provides that a subpoena may name a non-party organization as the deponent and may indicate the matters about which discovery is desired. In that event, the non-party organization must respond by designating natural persons, who are then obliged to testify as to matters known or reasonably available to the organization. To insure that a non-party organization that is not represented by counsel has knowledge of its duty to designate, the amendment directs the party seeking discovery to advise of the duty in the body of the subpoena.

ADVISORY COMMITTEE NOTES TO 1980 AMENDMENTS

RULE 5

Subdivision (d). By the terms of this rule and Rule 30(f)(1) discovery materials must be promptly filed, although it often happens that no use is made of the materials after they are filed. Because the copies required for filing are an added expense and the large volume of discovery filings presents serious problems of storage in some districts, the Committee in 1978 first proposed that discovery materials not be filed unless on order of the court or for use in the proceedings. But such materials are sometimes of interest to those who may have no access to them except by a requirement of filing, such as members of a class, litigants similarly situated, or the public generally. Accordingly, this amendment and a change in Rule 30(f)(1) continue the requirement of filing but make it subject to an order of the court that discovery materials not be filed unless filing is requested by the court or is effected by parties who wish to use the materials in the proceeding.

RULE 26

Subdivision (f). This subdivision is new. There has been widespread criticism of abuse of discovery. The Committee has considered a number of proposals to eliminate abuse, including a change in Rule 26(b)(1) with respect to the scope of discovery and a change in Rule 33(a) to limit the number of questions that can be asked by interrogatories to parties.

The Committee believes that abuse of discovery, while very serious in certain cases, is not so general as to require such basic changes in the rules that govern discovery in all cases. A very recent study of discovery in selected metropolitan districts tends to support its belief. P. Connoly, E. Holleman, & M. Kuhlman, *Judicial Controls and the Civil Litigative Process: Discovery* (Federal Judicial Center, 1978). In the judgment of the Committee abuse can best be prevented by intervention by the court as soon as abuse is threatened.

To this end this subdivision provides that counsel who has attempted without success to effect with opposing counsel a reasonable program or plan for discovery is entitled to the assistance of the court.

It is not contemplated that requests for discovery conferences will be made routinely. A relatively narrow discovery dispute should be resolved by resort to Rules 26(c) or 37(a), and if it appears that a request for a conference is in fact grounded in such a dispute, the court may refer counsel to those rules. If the court is persuaded that a request is frivolous or vexatious, it can strike it. *See* Rules 11 and 7(b)(2).

A number of courts routinely consider discovery matters in preliminary pretrial conferences held shortly after the pleadings are closed. This subdivision does not interfere with such a practice. It authorizes the court to combine a discovery conference with a pretrial conference under Rule 16 if a pretrial conference is held sufficiently early to prevent or curb abuse.

Effective date of 1980 amendments to Rule 26. Section 2 of the Order of April 29, 1980, — U.S. —, 64 L. Ed. 2d No. 2, v., — S Ct —, which adopted the 1980 amendments to this Rule, provided "That the foregoing amendments to the Federal Rules of Civil Procedure shall take effect on August 1, 1980, and shall govern all civil proceedings thereafter commenced and, insofar as just and practicable, all proceedings then pending."

RULE 33

Subdivision (c). The Committee is advised that parties upon whom interrogatories are served have occasionally responded by directing the interrogating party to a mass of business records or by offering to make all of their records available, justifying the response by the option provided by this subdivision. Such practices are an abuse of the option. A party who is permitted by the terms of this subdivision to offer records for inspection in lieu of answering an interrogatory should offer them in a manner that permits the same direct and economical access that is available to the party. If the information sought exists in the form of compilations, abstracts or summaries then available to the responding party, those should be made available to the interrogating party. The final sentence is added to make it clear that a responding party has the duty to specify, by category and location, the records from which answers to interrogatories can be derived.

RULE 34

Subdivision (b). The Committee is advised that, "It is apparently not rare for parties deliberately to mix critical documents with others in the hope of obscuring significance." *Report of the Special Committee for the Study of Discovery Abuse*, Section of Litigation of the American Bar Association (1977) 22. The sentence added by this subdivision follows the recommendation of the Report.

RULE 37

Subdivision (b)(2). New Rule 26(f) provides that if a discovery conference is held, at its close the court shall enter an order respecting the subsequent conduct of discovery. The amendment provides that the sanctions available for violation of other court orders respecting discovery are available for violation of the discovery conference order....

Subdivision (g). New Rule 26(f) imposes a duty on parties to participate in good faith in the framing of a discovery plan by agreement upon the request of any party. This subdivision authorizes the court to award to parties who participate in good faith in an attempt to frame a discovery plan the expenses incurred in the attempt if any party or his attorney fails to participate in good faith and thereby causes additional expense.

Failure of United States to Participate in Good Faith in Discovery. Rule 37 authorizes the court to direct that parties or attorneys who fail to participate in good faith in the discovery process pay the expenses, including attorneys' fees, incurred by other parties, as a result of that failure. Since attorneys' fees cannot ordinarily be awarded against the United States (28 U.S.C. § 2412), there is often no practical remedy for the misconduct of its officers and attorneys. However, in the case of a government attorney who fails to participate in good faith in discovery, nothing prevents a court in an appropriate case from giving written notification of that fact to the Attorney General of the United States and other appropriate heads of offices or agencies thereof.

ADVISORY COMMITTEE NOTES TO 1983 AMENDMENTS

RULE 11
[Text of amended Rule, indicating changes]

Every pleading, motion, and other paper of a party represented by an attorney shall be signed by at least one attorney of record in the attorney's individual name, whose address shall be stated. A party who is not represented by an attorney shall sign the party's his pleading, motion, or other paper and state the party's his address. Except when otherwise specifically provided by rule or statute, pleadings need not be verified or accompanied by affidavit. The rule in equity that the averments of an answer under oath must be overcome by the testimony of two witnesses or of one witness sustained by corroborating circumstances is abolished. The signature of an attorney or party constitutes a certificate by the signer him that the signer he has read the pleading, motion, or other paper; that to the best of the signer's his knowledge, information and belief formed after reasonable inquiry it is well grounded in fact and is warranted by existing law or a good faith argument for the extension, modification, or reversal of existing law, there is good ground to support it; and that it is not interposed for any improper purpose, such as to harass or to cause unnecessary delay or needless increase in the cost of litigation. If a pleading, motion, or other paper is not signed, it shall be stricken unless it is signed promptly after the omission is called to the attention of the pleader or movant. If a pleading, motion, or other paper or is signed with the intent to defeat the purposes in violation of this rule; the court, upon motion or upon its own initiative, it may be stricken as sham and false and the action may proceed as though the pleading had not been served. For a wilful violation of this rule, an attorney may be subjected to shall impose upon the person who signed it, a represented party, or both, an appropriate sanction, which may include an order to pay to the other party or parties the amount of the reasonable expenses incurred because of the filing of the pleading, motion, or other paper, including a reasonable attorney's fee. disciplinary action. Similar action may be taken if scandalous or indecent matter is inserted.

* * *

Since its original promulgation, Rule 11 has provided for the striking of pleadings and the imposition of disciplinary sanctions to check abuses in the signing of pleadings. Its provisions have always applied to motions and other papers by virtue of incorporation by reference in Rule 7(b)(2). The amendment and the addition of Rule 7(b)(3) expressly confirms this applicability.

Experience shows that in practice Rule 11 has not been effective in deterring abuses. See 6 Wright & Miller, *Federal Practice and Procedure: Civil* § 1334 (1971). There has been considerable confusion as to (1) the circumstances that should trigger striking a pleading or motion or taking disciplinary action, (2) the standard of conduct expected of attorneys who sign pleadings and motions, and (3) the range of available and appropriate sanctions. See Rodes, Ripple & Mooney, *Sanctions Imposable for Violations of the Federal Rules of Civil Procedure* 64–65, Federal Judicial Center (1981). The new language is intended to reduce the reluctance of courts to impose sanctions, see Moore, *Federal Practice* para. 7.05, at 1547, by emphasizing the responsibilities of the attorney and reenforcing those obligations by the imposition of sanctions.

The amended rule attempts to deal with the problem by building upon and expanding the equitable doctrine permitting the court to award expenses, including attorney's fees, to a litigant whose opponent acts in bad faith in instituting or conducting litigation.... Greater attention by the district courts to pleading and motion abuses and the imposition of sanctions when appropriate, should discourage dilatory or abusive tactics and help to streamline the litigation process by lessening frivolous claims or defenses.

The expanded nature of the lawyer's certification in the fifth sentence of amended Rule 11 recognizes that the litigation process may be abused for purposes other than delay. See, e.g., *Browning Debenture Holders' Committee v. DASA Corp.*, 560 F.2d 1078 (2d Cir. 1977).

The words "good ground to support" the pleading in the original rule were interpreted to have both factual and legal elements. See, e.g., *Heart Disease Research Foundation v. General Motors Corp.*, 15 Fed. R. Serv. 2d 1517, 1519 (S.D.N.Y. 1972). They have been replaced by a standard of conduct that is more focused.

The new language stresses the need for some prefiling inquiry into both the facts and the law to satisfy the affirmative duty imposed by the rule. The standard is one of reasonableness under the circumstances.

144

See Kinee v. Abraham Lincoln Fed. Sav. & Loan Ass'n, 365 F. Supp. 975 (E.D. Pa. 1973). This standard is more stringent than the original good-faith formula and thus it is expected that a greater range of circumstances will trigger its violation....

The rule is not intended to chill an attorney's enthusiasm or creativity in pursuing factual or legal theories. The court is expected to avoid using the wisdom of hindsight and should test the signer's conduct by inquiring what was reasonable to believe at the time the pleading, motion, or other paper was submitted. Thus, what constitutes a reasonable inquiry may depend on such factors as how much time for investigation was available to the signer; whether he had to rely on a client for information as to the facts underlying the pleading, motion, or other paper; whether the pleading, motion, or other paper was based on a plausible view of the law; or whether he depended on forwarding counsel or another member of the bar.

The rule does not require a party or an attorney to disclose privileged communications or work product in order to show that the signing of the pleading, motion, or other paper is substantially justified. The provisions of Rule 26(c), including appropriate orders after in camera inspection by the court, remain available to protect a party claiming privilege or work product protection.

Amended Rule 11 continues to apply to anyone who signs a pleading, motion, or other paper. Although the standard is the same for unrepresented parties, who are obliged themselves to sign the pleadings, the court has sufficient discretion to take account of the special circumstances that often arise in pro se situations. *See Haines v. Kerner*, 404 U.S. 519 (1972).

The provision in the original rule for striking pleadings and motions as sham and false has been deleted. The passage has rarely been utilized, and decisions thereunder have tended to confuse the issue of attorney honesty with the merits of the action. *See generally* Risinger, *Honesty in Pleading and its Enforcement: Some "Striking" Problems with Fed. R. Civ. P. 11*, 61 Minn. L. Rev. 1 (1976). Motions under this provision generally present issues better dealt with under Rules 8, 12, or 56. *See Murchison v. Kirby*, 27 F.R.D. 14 (S.D.N.Y. 1961); 5 Wright & Miller, *Federal Practice and Procedure: Civil* § 1334 (1969).

The former reference to the inclusion of scandalous or indecent matter, which is itself strong indication that an improper purpose underlies the pleading, motion, or other paper, also has been deleted as unnecessary. Such matter may be stricken under Rule 12(f) as well as dealt with under the more general language of amended Rule 11.

The text of the amended rule seeks to dispel apprehensions that efforts to obtain enforcement will be fruitless by insuring that the rule will be applied when properly invoked. The word "sanctions" in the caption, for example, stresses a deterrent orientation in dealing with improper pleadings, motions or other papers. This corresponds to the approach in imposing sanctions for discovery abuses. *See National Hockey League v. Metropolitan Hockey Club*, 427 U.S. 639 (1976) (per curiam). And the words "shall impose" in the last sentence focus the court's attention on the need to impose sanctions for pleading and motion abuses. The court, however, retains the necessary flexibility to deal appropriately with violations of the rule. It has discretion to tailor sanctions to the particular facts of the case, with which it should be well acquainted.

The reference in the former text to wilfulness as a prerequisite to disciplinary action has been deleted. However, in considering the nature and severity of the sanctions to be imposed, the court should take account of the state of the attorney's or party's actual or presumed knowledge when the pleading or other paper was signed. Thus, for example, when a party is not represented by counsel, the absence of legal advice is an appropriate factor to be considered.

Courts currently appear to believe they may impose sanctions on their own motion. *See North American Trading Corp. v. Zale Corp.*, 73 F.R.D. 293 (S.D.N.Y. 1979). Authority to do so has been made explicit in order to overcome the traditional reluctance of courts to intervene unless requested by one of the parties. The detection and punishment of a violation of the signing requirement, encouraged by the amended rule, is part of the court's responsibility for securing the system's effective operation.

If the duty imposed by the rule is violated, the court should have the discretion to impose sanctions on either the attorney, the party the signing attorney represents, or both, or on an unrepresented party who signed the pleading, and the new rule so provides. Although Rule 11 has been silent on the point, courts have claimed the power to impose sanctions on an attorney personally, either by imposing costs or employing the contempt technique. *See* 5 Wright & Miller, *Federal Practice and Procedure: Civil* § 1334 (1969); 2A Moore, *Federal Practice* para. 11.02, at 2104 n.8. This power has been used infrequently. The amended rule should eliminate any doubt as to the propriety of assessing sanctions against the attorney.

Even though it is the attorney whose signature violates the rule, it may be appropriate under the circumstances of the case to impose a sanction on the client.... This modification brings Rule 11 in line with practice under Rule 37, which allows sanctions for abuses during discovery to be imposed upon the party, the attorney, or both.

A party seeking sanctions should give notice to the court and the offending party promptly upon discovering a basis for doing so. The time when sanctions are to be imposed rests in the discretion of the trial judge. However, it is anticipated that in the case of pleadings the sanctions issue under Rule 11 normally will be determined at the end of the litigation, and in the case of motions at the time when the motion is decided or shortly thereafter. The procedure obviously must comport with due process requirements. The particular format to be followed should depend on the circumstances of the situation and the severity of the sanction under consideration. In many situations the judge's participation in the proceedings provides him with full knowledge of the relevant facts and little further inquiry will be necessary.

To assure that the efficiencies achieved through more effective operation of the pleading regimen will not be offset by the cost of satellite litigation over the imposition of sanctions, the court must to the extent possible limit the scope of sanction proceedings to the record. Thus, discovery should be conducted only by leave of the court, and then only in extraordinary circumstances.

Although the encompassing reference to "other papers" in new Rule 11 literally includes discovery papers, the certification requirement in that context is governed by proposed new Rule 26(g). Discovery motions, however, fall within the ambit of Rule 11.

RULE 16

Rule 16 has not been amended since the Federal Rules were promulgated in 1938. In many respects, the rule has been a success. For example, there is evidence that pretrial conferences may improve the quality of justice rendered in the federal courts by sharpening the preparation and presentation of cases, tending to eliminate trial surprise, and improving, as well as facilitating, the settlement process. *See* 6 Wright & Miller, *Federal Practice and Procedure: Civil* § 1522 (1971). However, in other respects particularly with regard to case management, the rule has not always been as helpful as it might have been. Thus there has been a widespread feeling that amendment is necessary to encourage pretrial management that meets the needs of modern litigation. *See Report of the National Commission for the Review of Antitrust Laws and Procedures* (1979).

Major criticism of Rule 16 has centered on the fact that its application can result in over-regulation of some cases and under-regulation of others. In simple, run-of-the-mill cases, attorneys have found pretrial requirements burdensome. It is claimed that over-administration leads to a series of mini-trials that result in a waste of an attorney's time and needless expense to a client. Pollack, *Pretrial Procedures More Effectively Handled*, 65 F.R.D. 475 (1974). This is especially likely to be true when pretrial proceedings occur long before trial. At the other end of the spectrum, the discretionary character of Rule 16 and its orientation toward a single conference late in the pretrial process has led to under-administration of complex or protracted cases. Without judicial guidance beginning shortly after institution, these cases often become mired in discovery.

Four sources of criticism of pretrial have been identified. First, conferences often are seen as a mere exchange of legalistic contentions without any real analysis of the particular case. Second, the result frequently is nothing but a formal agreement on minutiae. Third, the conferences are seen as unnecessary and time-consuming in cases that will be settled before trial. Fourth, the meetings can be ceremonial and ritualistic, having little effect on the trial and being of minimal value, particularly when the attorneys attending the sessions are not the ones who will try the case or lack authority to enter into binding stipulations....

There also have been difficulties with the pretrial orders that issue following Rule 16 conferences. When an order is entered far in advance of trial, some issues may not be properly formulated. Counsel naturally are cautious and often try to preserve as many options as possible. If the judge who tries the case did not conduct the conference, he could find it difficult to determine exactly what was agreed to at the conference. But any insistence on a detailed order may be too burdensome, depending on the nature or posture of the case.

Given the significant changes in federal civil litigation since 1938 that are not reflected in Rule 16, it has been extensively rewritten and expanded to meet the challenges of modern litigation. Empirical studies reveal that when a trial judge intervenes personally at an early stage to assume judicial control over a case and to schedule dates for completion by the parties of the principal pretrial steps, the case is disposed of by settlement or trial more efficiently and with less cost and delay than when the parties are left to their own devices. Flanders, *Case Management and Court Management in United States District Courts* 17, Federal Judicial Center (1977). Thus, the rule mandates a pretrial scheduling order. However, although scheduling and pretrial conferences are encouraged in appropriate cases, they are not mandated.

Subdivision (a); Pretrial Conferences: Objectives. The amended rule makes scheduling and case management an express goal of pretrial procedure. This is done in Rule 16(a) by shifting the emphasis away from a conference focused solely on the trial and toward a process of judicial management that embraces the entire pretrial phase, especially motions and discovery. In addition, the amendment explicitly recognizes some of the objectives of pretrial conferences and the powers that many courts already have assumed. Rule 16 thus will be a more accurate reflection of actual practice.

Subdivision (b); Scheduling and Planning. The most significant change in Rule 16 is the mandatory scheduling order described in Rule 16(b), which is based in part on Wisconsin Civil Procedure Rule 802.10. The idea of scheduling orders is not new. It has been used by many federal courts. *See, e.g.,* Southern District of Indiana, Local Rule 19.

Although a mandatory scheduling order encourages the court to become involved in case management early in the litigation, it represents a degree of judicial involvement that is not warranted in many cases. Thus, subdivision (b) permits each district court to promulgate a local rule under Rule 83 exempting certain categories of cases in which the burdens of scheduling orders exceed the administrative efficiencies that would be gained. *See* Eastern District of Virginia, Local Rule 12(1). Logical candidates for this treatment include social security disability matters, habeas corpus petitions, forfeitures, and reviews of certain administrative actions.

A scheduling conference may be requested either by the judge, a magistrate when authorized by district court rule, or a party within 120 days after the summons and complaint are filed. If a scheduling conference is not arranged within that time and the case is not exempted by local rule, a scheduling order must be issued under Rule 16(b), after some communication with the parties, which may be by telephone or mail rather than in person. The use of the term "judge" in subdivision (b) reflects the Advisory Committee's judgment that it is preferable that this task should be handled by a district judge rather than a magistrate, except when the magistrate is acting under 28 U.S.C. § 636(c). While personal supervision by the trial judge is preferred, the rule, in recognition of the impracticality or difficulty of complying with such a requirement in some districts, authorizes a district by local rule to delegate the duties to a magistrate. In order to formulate a practicable scheduling order, the judge, or a magistrate when authorized by district court rule, and attorneys are required to develop a timetable for the matters listed in Rule 16(b)(1)-(3). As indicated in Rule 16(b)(4)-(5), the order may also deal with a wide range of other matters. The rule is phrased permissively as to clauses (4) and (5), however, because scheduling these items at an early point may not be feasible or appropriate. Even though subdivision (b) relates only to scheduling, there is no reason why some of the procedural matters listed in Rule 16(c) cannot be addressed at the same time, at least when a scheduling conference is held.

Item (1) assures that at some point both the parties and the pleadings will be fixed, by setting a time within which joinder of parties shall be completed and the pleadings amended.

Item (2) requires setting time limits for interposing various motions that otherwise might be used as stalling techniques.

Item (3) deals with the problem of procrastination and delay by attorneys in a context in which scheduling is especially important—discovery. Scheduling the completion of discovery can serve some of the same functions as the conference described in Rule 26(f).

Item (4) refers to setting dates for conferences and for trial. Scheduling multiple pretrial conferences may well be desirable if the case is complex and the court believes that a more elaborate pretrial structure, such as that described in the Manual for Complex Litigation, should be employed. On the other hand, only one pretrial conference may be necessary in an uncomplicated case.

As long as the case is not exempted by local rule, the court must issue a written scheduling order even if no scheduling conference is called. The order, like pretrial orders under the former rule and those under new Rule 16(c), normally will "control the subsequent course of the action." *See* Rule 16(e). After consultation with the attorneys for the parties and any unrepresented parties—a formal motion is not necessary—the court may modify the schedule on a showing of good cause if it cannot reasonably be met despite the diligence of the party seeking the extension. Since the scheduling order is entered early in the litigation, this standard seems more appropriate than a "manifest injustice" or "substantial hardship" test. Otherwise, a fear that extensions will not be granted may encourage counsel to request the longest possible periods for completing pleading, joinder, and discovery. Moreover, changes in the court's calendar sometimes will oblige the judge or magistrate when authorized by district court rule to modify the scheduling order.

The district courts undoubtedly will develop several prototype scheduling orders for different types of cases. In addition, when no formal conference is held, the court may obtain scheduling information by telephone, mail, or otherwise. In many instances this will result in a scheduling order better suited to the individual case than a standard order, without taking the time that would be required by a formal conference. Rule 16(b) assures that the judge will take some early control over the litigation, even when its character does not warrant holding a scheduling conference. Despite the fact that the process of preparing a scheduling order does not always bring the attorneys and judge together, the fixing of time limits serves to stimulate litigants to narrow the areas of inquiry and advocacy to those they believe are truly relevant and material. Time limits not only compress the amount of time for litigation, they should also reduce the amount of resources invested in litigation. Litigants are forced to establish discovery priorities and thus to do the most important work first. *Report of the National Commission for the Review of Antitrust Laws and Procedures* 28 (1979).

Thus, except in exempted cases, the judge or a magistrate when authorized by district court rule will have taken some action in every case within 120 days after the complaint is filed that notifies the attorneys that the case will be moving toward trial. Subdivision (b) is reenforced by subdivision (f), which makes it clear that the sanctions for violating a scheduling order are the same as those for violating a pretrial order.

Subdivision (c); Subjects to be Discussed at Pretrial Conferences. This subdivision expands upon the list of things that may be discussed at a pretrial conference that appeared in original Rule 16. The intention is to encourage better planning and management of litigation. Increased judicial control during the pretrial process accelerates the processing and termination of cases....

The reference in Rule 16(c)(1) to "formulation" is intended to clarify and confirm the court's power to identify the litigable issues. It has been added in the hope of promoting efficiency and conserving judicial resources by identifying the real issues prior to trial, thereby saving time and expense for everyone.... The notion is emphasized by expressly authorizing the elimination of frivolous claims or defenses at a pretrial conference. There is no reason to require that this await a formal motion for summary judgment. Nor is there any reason for the court to wait for the parties to initiate the process called for in Rule 16(c)(1).

The timing of any attempt at issue formulation is a matter of judicial discretion. In relatively simple cases it may not be necessary or may take the form of a stipulation between counsel or a request by the court that counsel work together to draft a proposed order.

Counsel bear a substantial responsibility for assisting the court in identifying the factual issues worthy of trial. If counsel fail to identify an issue for the court, the right to have the issue tried is waived. Although an order specifying the issues is intended to be binding, it may be amended at trial to avoid manifest injustice. See Rule 16(e). However, the rule's effectiveness depends on the court employing its discretion sparingly.

Clause (6) acknowledges the widespread availability and use of magistrates. The corresponding provision in the original rule referred only to masters and limited the function of the reference to the making of "findings to be used as evidence" in a case to be tried to a jury. The new text is not limited and broadens the potential use of a magistrate to that permitted by the Magistrate's Act.

Clause (7) explicitly recognizes that it has become commonplace to discuss settlement at pretrial conferences. Since it obviously eases crowded court dockets and results in savings to the litigants and the judicial system, settlement should be facilitated at as early a stage of the litigation as possible. Although it is not the purpose of Rule 16(b)(7) to impose settlement negotiations on unwilling litigants, it is believed that providing a neutral forum for discussing the subject might foster it.... For instance, a judge to whom a case has been assigned may arrange, on his own motion or at a party's request, to have settlement conferences handled by another member of the court or by a magistrate. The rule does not make settlement conferences mandatory because they would be a waste of time in many cases. See Flanders, *Case Management and Court Management in the United States District Courts*, 39, Federal Judicial Center (1977). Requests for a conference from a party indicating a willingness to talk settlement normally should be honored, unless thought to be frivolous or dilatory.

A settlement conference is appropriate at any time. It may be held in conjunction with a pretrial or discovery conference, although various objectives of pretrial management, such as moving the case toward trial, may not always be compatible with settlement negotiations, and thus a separate settlement conference may be desirable....

In addition to settlement, Rule 16(c)(7) refers to exploring the use of procedures other than litigation to resolve the dispute. This includes urging the litigants to employ adjudicatory techniques outside the courthouse. See, for example, the experiment described in Green, Marks & Olson, *Settling Large Case Litigation: An Alternative Approach*, 11 Loyola of L.A. L. Rev. 493 (1978). Rule 16(c)(10) authorizes the use of special pretrial procedures to expedite the adjudication of potentially difficult or protracted cases. Some district courts obviously have done so for many years. See Rubin, *The Managed Calendar: Some Pragmatic Suggestions About Achieving the Just, Speedy and Inexpensive Determination of Civil Cases in Federal Courts*, 4 Just. Sys. J. 135 (1976). Clause 10 provides an explicit authorization for such procedures and encourages their use. No particular techniques have been described; the Committee felt that flexibility and experience are the keys to efficient management of complex cases. Extensive guidance is offered in such documents as the Manual for Complex Litigation.

The rule simply identifies characteristics that make a case a strong candidate for special treatment. The four mentioned are illustrative, not exhaustive, and overlap to some degree. But experience has shown that one or more of them will be present in every protracted or difficult case and it seems desirable to set them out. See Kendig, *Procedures for Management of Non-Routine Cases*, 3 Hofstra L. Rev. 701 (1975).

The last sentence of subdivision (c) is new.... It has been added to meet one of the criticisms of the present practice described earlier and insure proper preconference preparation so that the meeting is more than a ceremonial or ritualistic event. The reference to "authority" is not intended to insist upon the ability to settle the litigation. Nor should the rule be read to encourage the judge conducting the conference to compel attorneys to enter into stipulations or to make admissions that they consider to be unreasonable, that touch on matters that could not normally have been anticipated to arise at the conference, or on subjects of a dimension that normally require prior consultation with and approval from the client.

Subdivision (d); Final Pretrial Conference. This provision has been added to make it clear that the time between any final pretrial conference (which in a simple case may be the only pretrial conference) and trial should be as short as possible to be certain that the litigants make substantial progress with the case and avoid the inefficiency of having that preparation repeated when there is a delay between the last pretrial conference and trial. An optimum time of 10 days to two weeks has been suggested by one federal judge. Rubin, *The Managed Calendar: Some Pragmatic Suggestions About Achieving the Just, Speedy and Inexpensive Determination of Civil Cases in Federal Courts*, 4 Just. Sys. J. 135, 141 (1976). The Committee, however, concluded that it would be inappropriate to fix a precise time in the rule, given the numerous variables that could bear on the matter. Thus the timing has been left to the court's discretion.

At least one of the attorneys who will conduct the trial for each party must be present at the final pretrial conference. At this late date there should be no doubt as to which attorney or attorneys this will be. Since the agreements and stipulations made at this final conference will control the trial, the presence of lawyers who will be involved in it is especially useful to assist the judge in structuring the case, and to lead to a more effective trial.

Subdivision (e); Pretrial Orders. Rule 16(e) does not substantially change the portion of the original rule dealing with pretrial orders. The purpose of an order is to guide the course of the litigation and the language of the original rule making that clear has been retained. No compelling reason has been found for major revision, especially since this portion of the rule has been interpreted and clarified by over forty years of judicial decisions with comparatively little difficulty. *See* 6 Wright & Miller, *Federal Practice and Procedure: Civil* §§ 1521–30 (1971). Changes in language therefore have been kept to a minimum to avoid confusion.

Since the amended rule encourages more extensive pretrial management than did the original, two or more conferences may be held in many cases. The language of Rule 16(e) recognizes this possibility and the corresponding need to issue more than one pretrial order in a single case.

Once formulated, pretrial orders should not be changed lightly; but total inflexibility is undesirable…. The exact words used to describe the standard for amending the pretrial order probably are less important than the meaning given them in practice. By not imposing any limitation on the ability to modify a pretrial order, the rule reflects the reality that in any process of continuous management what is done at one conference may have to be altered at the next. In the case of the final pretrial order, however, a more stringent standard is called for and the words "to prevent manifest injustice," which appeared in the original rule, have been retained. They have the virtue of familiarity and adequately describe the restraint the trial judge should exercise.

Many local rules make the plaintiff's attorney responsible for drafting a proposed pretrial order, either before or after the conference. Others allow the court to appoint any of the attorneys to perform the task, and others leave it to the court…. Rule 16 has never addressed this matter. Since there is no consensus about which method of drafting the order works best and there is no reason to believe that nationwide uniformity is needed, the rule has been left silent on the point.

Subdivision (f); Sanctions. Original Rule 16 did not mention the sanctions that might be imposed for failing to comply with the rule. However, courts have not hesitated to enforce it by appropriate measures. *See, e.g., Link v. Wabash R. Co.*, 370 U.S. 628 (1962) (district court's dismissal under Rule 41(b) after plaintiff's attorney failed to appear at a pretrial conference upheld); *Admiral Theatre Corp. v. Douglas Theatre*, 585 F.2d 877 (8th Cir. 1978) (district court has discretion to exclude exhibits or refuse to permit the testimony of a witness not listed prior to trial in contravention of its pretrial order).

To reflect that existing practice, and to obviate dependence upon Rule 41(b) or the court's inherent power to regulate litigation, *cf. Societe Internationale Pour Participations Industrielles et Commerciales, S.A. v. Rogers*, 357 U.S. 197 (1958), Rule 16(f) expressly provides for imposing sanctions on disobedient or recalcitrant parties, their attorneys, or both in four types of situations. Rodes, Ripple & Mooney, *Sanctions Imposable for Violations of the Federal Rules of Civil Procedure* 65–67, 80–84, Federal Judicial Center (1981). Furthermore, explicit reference to sanctions reenforces the rule's intention to encourage forceful judicial management. Rule 16(f) incorporates portions of Rule 37(b)(2), which prescribes sanctions for failing to make discovery. This should facilitate application of Rule 16(f), since courts and lawyers already are familiar with the Rule 37 standards. Among the sanctions authorized by the new subdivision are: preclusion order, striking a pleading, staying the proceeding, default judgment, contempt, and charging a party, his attorney, or both with the expenses, including attorney's fees, caused by noncompliance. The contempt sanction, however, is only available for a violation of a court order. The references in Rule 16(f) are not exhaustive.

As is true under Rule 37(b)(2), the imposition of sanctions may be sought by either the court or a party. In addition, the court has discretion to impose whichever sanction it feels is appropriate under the circumstances. Its action is reviewable under the abuse-of-discretion standard.

RULE 26

Excessive discovery and evasion or resistance to reasonable discovery requests pose significant problems. Recent studies have made some attempt to determine the sources and extent of the difficulties. *See* Brazil, *Civil Discovery: Lawyers' Views of its Effectiveness, Principal Problems and Abuses*, American Bar Foundation (1980); Connolly, Holleman & Kuhlman, *Judicial Controls and the Civil Litigative Process: Discovery*, Federal Judicial Center (1978); Ellington, *A Study of Sanctions for Discovery Abuse*, Department of Justice (1979); Schroeder & Frank, *The Proposed Changes in the Discovery Rules*, 1978 Ariz. St. L.J. 475.

The purpose of discovery is to provide a mechanism for making relevant information available to the litigants. "Mutual knowledge of all the relevant facts gathered by both parties is essential to proper litigation." *Hickman v. Taylor*, 329 U.S. 495, 507 (1947). Thus the spirit of the rules is violated when advocates attempt to use discovery tools as tactical weapons rather than to expose the facts and illuminate the issues by overuse of discovery or unnecessary use of defensive weapons or evasive responses. All of this results in excessively costly and time-consuming activities that are disproportionate to the nature of the case, the amount involved, or the issues or values at stake.

Given our adversary tradition and the current discovery rules, it is not surprising that there are many opportunities, if not incentives, for attorneys to engage in discovery that, although authorized by the broad, permissive terms of the rules, nevertheless results in delay. *See* Brazil, *The Adversary Character of Civil Discovery: A Critique and Proposals for Change*, 31 Vand. L. Rev. 1259 (1978). As a result, it has been said that the rules have "not infrequently [been] exploited to the disadvantage of justice." *Herbert v. Lando*, 441 U.S. 153, 179 (1979) (Powell, J., concurring). These practices impose costs on an already overburdened system and impede the fundamental goal of the "just, speedy, and inexpensive determination of every action." Fed. R. Civ. P. 1.

Subdivision (a); Discovery Methods. The deletion of the last sentence of Rule 26(a)(1), which provided that unless the court ordered otherwise under Rule 26(c) "the frequency of use" of the various discovery methods was not to be limited, is an attempt to address the problem of duplicative, redundant, and excessive discovery and to reduce it. The amendment, in conjunction with the changes in Rule 26(b)(1), is designed to encourage district judges to identify instances of needless discovery and to limit the use of the various discovery devices accordingly. The question may be raised by one of the parties, typically on a motion for a protective order, or by the court on its own initiative. It is entirely appropriate to consider a limitation on the frequency of use of discovery at a discovery conference under Rule 26(f) or at any other pretrial conference authorized by these rules. In considering the discovery needs of a particular case, the court should consider the factors described in Rule 26(b)(1).

Subdivision (b); Discovery Scope and Limits. Rule 26(b)(1) has been amended to add a sentence to deal with the problem of over-discovery. The objective is to guard against redundant or disproportionate discovery by giving the court authority to reduce the amount of discovery that may be directed to matters that are otherwise proper subjects of inquiry. The new sentence is intended to encourage judges to be more aggressive in identifying and discouraging discovery overuse. The grounds mentioned in the amended rule for limiting discovery reflect the existing practice of many courts in issuing protective orders under Rule 26(c). *See e.g., Carlson Cos. v. Sperry & Hutchinson Co.*, 374 F. Supp. 1080 (D. Minn. 1974); *Dolgow v. Anderson*, 53 F.R.D. 661 (E.D.N.Y. 1971).... On the whole, however, district judges have been reluctant to limit the use of the discovery devices. *See, e.g., Apco Oil Co. v. Certified Transp., Inc.*, 46 F.R.D. 428 (W.D. Mo. 1969). *See generally* 8 Wright & Miller, *Federal Practice and Procedure: Civil* §§ 2036, 2037, 2039, 2040 (1970).

The first element of the standard, Rule 26(b)(1)(i), is designed to minimize redundancy in discovery and encourage attorneys to be sensitive to the comparative costs of different methods of securing information. Subdivision (b)(1)(ii) also seeks to reduce repetitiveness and to oblige lawyers to think through their discovery activities in advance so that full utilization is made of each deposition, document request, or set of interrogatories. The elements of Rule 26(b)(1)(iii) address the problem of discovery that is disproportionate to the individual lawsuit as measured by such matters as its nature and complexity, the importance of the issues at stake in a case seeking damages, the limitations on a financially weak litigant to withstand extensive opposition to a discovery program or to respond to discovery requests, and the significance of the substantive issues, as measured in philosophic, social, or institutional terms. Thus the rule recognizes that many cases in public policy spheres, such as employment practices, free speech, and other matters, may have importance far beyond the monetary amount involved. The court must apply the standards in an even-handed manner that will prevent use of discovery to wage a war of attrition or as a device to coerce a party, whether financially weak or affluent.

The rule contemplates greater judicial involvement in the discovery process and thus acknowledges the reality that it cannot always operate on a self-regulating basis. *See* Connolly, Holleman & Kuhlman, *Judicial Controls and the Civil Litigative Process: Discovery* 77, Federal Judicial Center (1978). In an appropriate case the court could restrict the number of depositions, interrogatories, or the scope of a production request. But the court must be careful not to deprive a party of discovery that is reasonably necessary to afford a fair opportunity to develop and prepare the case.

The court may act on motion, or its own initiative. It is entirely appropriate to resort to the amended rule in conjunction with a discovery conference under Rule 26(f) or one of the other pretrial conferences authorized by the rules.

Subdivision (g); Signing of Discovery Requests, Responses, and Objections. Rule 26(g) imposes an affirmative duty to engage in pretrial discovery in a responsible manner that is consistent with the spirit and purposes of Rules 26 through 37. In addition, Rule 26(g) is designed to curb discovery abuse by explicitly encouraging the imposition of sanctions. The subdivision provides a deterrent to both excessive discovery and evasion by imposing a certification requirement that obliges each attorney to stop and think about the legitimacy of a discovery request, a response thereto, or an objection. The term "response" includes answers to interrogatories and to requests to admit as well as responses to production requests.

If primary responsibility for conducting discovery is to continue to rest with the litigants, they must be obliged to act responsibly and avoid abuse. With this in mind, Rule 26(g), which parallels the amendments to Rule 11, requires an attorney or unrepresented party to sign each discovery request, response, or objection. Motions relating to discovery are governed by Rule 11. However, since a discovery request, response, or objection usually deals with more specific subject matter than motions or papers, the elements that must be certified in connection with the former are spelled out more completely. The signature is a certification of the elements set forth in Rule 26(g).

Although the certification duty requires the lawyer to pause and consider the reasonableness of his request, response, or objection, it is not meant to discourage or restrict necessary and legitimate discovery. The rule simply requires that the attorney make a reasonable inquiry into the factual basis of his response, request, or objection.

The duty to make a "reasonable inquiry" is satisfied if the investigation undertaken by the attorney and the conclusions drawn therefrom are reasonable under the circumstances. It is an objective standard similar to the one imposed by Rule 11. *See* the Advisory Committee Note to Rule 11.... In making the inquiry, the attorney may rely on assertions by the client and on communications with other counsel in the case as long as that reliance is appropriate under the circumstances. Ultimately, what is reasonable is a matter for the court to decide on the totality of the circumstances. Rule 26(g) does not require the signing attorney to certify the truthfulness of the client's factual responses to a discovery request. Rather, the signature certifies that the lawyer has made a reasonable effort to assure that the client has provided all the information and documents available to him that are responsive to the discovery demand. Thus, the lawyer's certification under Rule 26(g) should be distinguished from other signature requirements in the rules, such as those in Rules 30(e) and 33.

Nor does the rule require a party or an attorney to disclose privileged communications or work product in order to show that a discovery request, response, or objection is substantially justified. The provisions of Rule 26(c), including appropriate orders after in camera inspection by the court, remain available to protect a party claiming privilege or work product protection.

The signing requirement means that every discovery request, response, or objection should be grounded on a theory that is reasonable under the precedents or a good faith belief as to what should be the law. This standard is heavily dependent on the circumstances of each case. The certification speaks as of the time it is made. The duty to supplement discovery responses continues to be governed by Rule 26(e).

Concern about discovery abuse has led to widespread recognition that there is a need for more aggressive judicial control and supervision. *ACF Industries, Inc. v. EEOC*, 439 U.S. 1081 (1979) (*certiorari denied*) (Powell, J., dissenting). Sanctions to deter discovery abuse would be more effective if they were diligently applied "not merely to penalize those whose conduct may be deemed to warrant such a sanction, but to deter those who might be tempted to such conduct in the absence of such a deterrent." *National Hockey League v. Metropolitan Hockey Club*, 427 U.S. 639, 643 (1976). *See also* Note, *The Emerging Deterrence Orientation in the Imposition of Discovery Sanctions*, 91 Harv. L. Rev. 1033 (1978). Thus the premise of Rule 26(g) is that imposing sanctions on attorneys who fail to meet the rule's standards will significantly reduce abuse by imposing disadvantages therefor.

Because of the asserted reluctance to impose sanctions on attorneys who abuse the discovery rules, ... Rule 26(g) makes explicit the authority judges now have to impose appropriate sanctions and requires them to use it. This authority derives from Rule 37, 28 U.S.C. § 1927, and the court's inherent power. *See Roadway Express, Inc. v. Piper*, 447 U.S. 752 (1980); *Martin v. Bell Helicopter Co.*, 85 F.R.D. 654, 661-62 (D. Colo. 1980); Note, *Sanctions Imposed by Courts on Attorneys Who Abuse the Judicial Process*, 44 U. Chi. L. Rev. 619 (1977). The new rule mandates that sanctions be imposed on attorneys who fail to meet the standards established in the first portion of Rule 26(g). The nature of the sanction is a matter of judicial discretion to be exercised in light of the particular circumstances. The court may take into account any failure by the party seeking sanctions to invoke protection under Rule 26(c) at an early stage in the litigation.

The sanctioning process must comport with due process requirements. The kind of notice and hearing required will depend on the facts of the case and the severity of the sanction being considered. To prevent the proliferation of the sanction procedure and to avoid multiple hearings, discovery in any sanction proceeding normally should be permitted only when it is clearly required by the interests of justice. In most cases the court will be aware of the circumstances and only a brief hearing should be necessary.

ADVISORY COMMITTEE NOTES TO 1985 AMENDMENTS

RULE 52

Rule 52(a) has been amended (1) to avoid continued confusion and conflicts among the circuits as to the standard of appellate review of findings of fact by the court, (2) to eliminate the disparity between the standard of review as literally stated in Rule 52(a) and the practice of some courts of appeals, and (3) to promote nationwide uniformity....

Some courts of appeal have stated that when a trial court's findings do not rest on demeanor evidence and evaluation of a witness' credibility, there is no reason to defer to the trial court's findings and the appellate court more readily can find them to be clearly erroneous.... Others go further, holding that appellate review may be had without application of the "clearly erroneous" test since the appellate court is in as good a position as the trial court to review a purely documentary record....

A third group has adopted the view that the "clearly erroneous" rule applies in all nonjury cases even when findings are based solely on documentary evidence or on inferences from undisputed facts....

The Supreme Court has not clearly resolved the issue.... The principal argument advanced in favor of a more searching appellate review of findings by the district court based solely on documentary evidence is that the rationale of Rule 52(a) does not apply when the findings do not rest on the trial court's assessment of credibility of the witnesses but on an evaluation of documentary proof and the drawing of inferences from it, thus eliminating the need for any special deference to the trial court's findings. These considerations are outweighed by the public interest in the stability and judicial economy that would be promoted by recognizing that the trial court, not the appellate tribunal, should be the finder of the facts. To permit courts of appeals to share more actively in the fact-finding function would tend to undermine the legitimacy of the district courts in the eyes of litigants, multiply appeals by encouraging appellate retrial of some factual issues, and needlessly reallocate judicial authority.

RULE 83

Rule 83, which has not been amended since the Federal Rules were promulgated in 1938, permits each district to adopt local rules not inconsistent with the Federal Rules by a majority of the judges. The only other requirement is that copies be furnished to the Supreme Court.

The widespread adoption of local rules and the modest procedural prerequisites for their promulgation have led many commentators to question the soundness of the process as well as the validity of some rules.... Although the desirability of local rules for promoting uniform practice within a district is widely accepted, several commentators also have suggested reforms to increase the quality, simplicity, and uniformity of the local rules....

The amended Rule attempts, without impairing the procedural validity of existing local rules, to enhance the local rulemaking process by requiring appropriate public notice of proposed rules and an opportunity to comment on them. Although some district courts apparently consult the local bar before promulgating rules, many do not, which has led to criticism of a process that has district judges consulting only with each other.... The new language subjects local rulemaking to scrutiny similar to that accompanying the Federal Rules, administrative rulemaking, and legislation. It attempts to assure that the expert advice of practitioners and scholars is made available to the district court before local rules are promulgated. *See* Weinstein, *Reform of Court Rule-Making Procedures* 84-87, 127-37, 151 (1977).

The amended Rule does not detail the procedure for giving notice and an opportunity to be heard since conditions vary from district to district. Thus, there is no explicit requirement for a public hearing, although a district may consider that procedure appropriate in all or some rulemaking situations. *See generally*, Weinstein, *supra*, at 117-37, 151. The new Rule does not foreclose any other form of consultation. For example, it can be accomplished through the mechanism of an "Advisory Committee" similar to that employed by the Supreme Court in connection with the Federal Rules themselves.

The amended Rule provides that a local rule will take effect upon the date specified by the district court and will remain in effect unless amended by the district court or abrogated by the judicial council. The effectiveness of a local rule should not be deferred until approved by the judicial council because that might unduly delay promulgation of a local rule that should become effective immediately, especially since some councils do not meet frequently. Similarly, it was thought that to delay a local rule's effectiveness for a fixed period of time would be arbitrary and that to require the judicial council to abrogate a local rule within a specified time would be inconsistent with its power under 28 U.S.C. § 332 (1976) to nullify a local rule at any time. The expectation is that the judicial council will examine all local rules, including those currently in effect, with an eye toward determining whether they are valid and consistent with the Federal Rules, promote inter-district uniformity and efficiency, and do not undermine the basic objectives of the Federal Rules.

The amended Rule requires copies of local rules to be sent upon their promulgation to the judicial council and the Administrative Office of the United States Courts rather than to the Supreme Court. The Supreme Court was the appropriate filing place in 1938, when Rule 83 originally was promulgated, but the establishment of the Administrative Office makes it a more logical place to develop a centralized file of local rules. This procedure is consistent with both the Criminal and the Appellate Rules. *See* Fed. R. Crim. P. 57(a); Fed. R. App. P. 47. The Administrative Office also will be able to provide improved utilization of the file because of its recent development of a Local Rules Index.

The practice pursued by some judges of issuing standing orders has been controversial, particularly among members of the practicing bar. The last sentence in Rule 83 has been amended to make certain that standing orders are not inconsistent with the Federal Rules or any local district court rules. Beyond that, it is hoped that each district will adopt procedures, perhaps by local rule, for promulgating and reviewing single-judge standing orders....

ADVISORY COMMITTEE NOTES TO 1987 AMENDMENTS
RULE 51

Although Rule 51 in its present form specifies that the court shall instruct the jury only after the arguments of the parties are completed, in some districts (typically those in states where the practice is otherwise) it is common for the parties to stipulate to instruction before the arguments. The purpose of the amendment is to give the court discretion to instruct the jury either before or after argument. Thus, the rule as revised will permit resort to the long-standing federal practice or to an alternative procedure, which has been praised because it gives counsel the opportunity to explain the instructions, argue their application to the facts and thereby give the jury the maximum assistance in determining the issues and arriving at a good verdict on the law and the evidence. As an ancillary benefit, this approach aids counsel by supplying a natural outline so that arguments may be directed to the essential fact issues which the jury must decide. *See generally* Raymond, *Merits and Demerits of the Missouri System of Instructing Juries*, 5 St. Louis U. L.J. 317 (1959). Moreover, if the court instructs before an argument, counsel then know the precise words the court has chosen and need not speculate as to the words the court will later use in its instructions. Finally, by instructing ahead of argument the court has the attention of the jurors when they are fresh and can give their full attention to the court's instructions. It is more difficult to hold the attention of jurors after lengthy arguments.

ADVISORY COMMITTEE NOTES TO 1991 AMENDMENTS
RULE 15

The rule has been revised to prevent parties against whom claims are made from taking unjust advantage of otherwise inconsequential pleading errors to sustain a limitations defense.

Paragraph (c)(1). This provision is new. It is intended to make it clear that the rule does not apply to preclude any relation back that may be permitted under the applicable limitations law. Generally, the applicable limitations law will be state law. If federal jurisdiction is based on the citizenship of the parties, the primary reference is the law of the state in which the district court sits. *Walker v. Armco Steel Corp.*, 446 U.S. 740 (1980). If federal jurisdiction is based on a federal question, the reference may be to the law of the state governing relations between the parties. *E.g., Board of Regents v. Tomanio*, 446 U.S. 478 (1980). In some circumstances, the controlling limitations law may be federal law. *E.g., West v. Conrail, Inc.*, 481 U.S. 35 (1987). *Cf. Burlington Northern R. Co. v. Woods*, 480 U.S. 1 (1987); *Stewart Organization v. Ricoh*, 487 U.S. 22 (1988). Whatever may be the controlling body of limitations law, if that law affords a more forgiving principle of relation back than the one provided in this rule, it should be available to save the claim. *Accord, Marshall v. Mulrenin*, 508 F.2d 39 (1st Cir. 1974). If *Schiavone v. Fortune*, 477 U.S. 21 (1986) implies the contrary, this paragraph is intended to make a material change in the rule.

Paragraph (c)(3). This paragraph has been revised to change the result in *Schiavone v. Fortune, supra*, with respect to the problem of a misnamed defendant. An intended defendant who is notified of an action within the period allowed by Rule 4(m) for service of a summons and complaint may not under the revised rule defeat the action on account of a defect in the pleading with respect to the defendant's name, provided that the requirements of clauses (A) and (B) have been met. If the notice requirement is met within the Rule 4(m) period, a complaint may be amended at any time to correct a formal defect such as a misnomer or misidentification. On the basis of the text of the former rule, the Court reached a result in *Schiavone v. Fortune* that was inconsistent with the liberal pleading practices secured by Rule 8. *See* Bauer, *Schiavone: An Un-Fortune-ate Illustration of the Supreme Court's Role as Interpreter of the Federal Rules of Civil Procedure*, 63 Notre Dame L. Rev. 720 (1988); Brussack, *Outrageous Fortune: The Case for Amending Rule 15(c) Again*, 61 S. Cal. L. Rev. 671 (1988); Lewis, *The Excessive History of Federal Rule 15(c) and Its Lessons for Civil Rules Revision*, 86 Mich. L. Rev. 1507 (1987).

In allowing a name-correcting amendment within the time allowed by Rule 4(m), this rule allows not only the 120 days specified in that rule, but also any additional time resulting from any extension ordered by the court pursuant to that rule, as may be granted, for example, if the defendant is a fugitive from service of the summons.

RULE 35

The revision authorizes the court to require physical or mental examinations conducted by any person who is suitably licensed or certified.

The rule was revised in 1988 by Congressional enactment to authorize mental examinations by licensed clinical psychologists. This revision extends that amendment to include other certified or licensed professionals, such as dentists or occupational therapists, who are not physicians or clinical psychologists, but who may be well-qualified to give valuable testimony about the physical or mental condition that is the subject of dispute.

The requirement that the examiner be suitably licensed or certified is a new requirement. The court is thus expressly authorized to assess the credentials of the examiner to assure that no person is subjected to a court-ordered examination by an examiner whose testimony would be of such limited value that it would be unjust to require the person to undergo the invasion of privacy associated with the examination.

This authority is not wholly new, for under the former rule, the court retained discretion to refuse to order an examination, or to restrict an examination. The revision is intended to encourage the exercise of this discretion, especially with respect to examinations by persons having narrow qualifications.

The court's responsibility to determine the suitability of the examiner's qualifications applies even to a proposed examination by a physician. If the proposed examination and testimony calls for an expertise that the proposed examiner does not have, it should not be ordered, even if the proposed examiner is a physician. The rule does not, however, require that the license or certificate be conferred by the jurisdiction in which the examination is conducted.

RULE 45

The purposes of this revision are (1) to clarify and enlarge the protections afforded persons who are required to assist the court by giving information or evidence; (2) to facilitate access outside the deposition procedure provided by Rule 30 to documents and other information in the possession of persons who are not parties; (3) to facilitate service of subpoenas for depositions or productions of evidence at places distant from the district in which an action is proceeding; (4) to enable the court to compel a witness found within the state in which the court sits to attend trial; (5) to clarify the organization of the text of the rule.

Subdivision (a). This subdivision is amended in seven significant respects.

First, Paragraph (a)(3) modifies the requirement that a subpoena be issued by the clerk of court. Provision is made for the issuance of subpoenas by attorneys as officers of the court. This revision perhaps culminates an evolution. Subpoenas were long issued by specific order of the court. As this became a burden to the court, general orders were made authorizing clerks to issue subpoenas on request. Since 1948, they have been issued in blank by the clerk of any federal court to any lawyer, the clerk serving as stationer to the bar. In allowing counsel to issue the subpoena, the rule is merely a recognition of present reality.

Although the subpoena is in a sense the command of the attorney who completes the form, defiance of a subpoena is nevertheless an act in defiance of a court order and exposes the defiant witness to contempt sanctions. In *ICC v. Brimson*, 154 U.S. 447 (1894), the Court upheld a statute directing federal courts to issue subpoenas to compel testimony before the ICC. In *CAB v. Hermann*, 353 U.S. 322 (1957), the Court approved as established practice the issuance of administrative subpoenas as a matter of absolute agency right. And in *NLRB v. Warren Co.*, 350 U.S. 107 (1955), the Court held that the lower court had no discretion to withhold sanctions against a contemnor who violated such subpoenas. The 1948 revision of Rule 45 put the attorney in a position similar to that of the administrative agency, as a public officer entitled to use the court's contempt power to investigate facts in dispute. Two courts of appeals have touched on the issue and have described lawyer-issued subpoenas as mandates of the court. *Waste Conversion, Inc. v. Rollins Environmental Services (NJ), Inc.*, 893 F.2d 605 (3d Cir. 1990); *Fisher v. Marubent Cotton Corp.*, 526 F.2d 1338, 1340 (8th Cir. 1975). *Cf. Young v. United States ex rel Vuitton et Fils S.A.*, 481 U.S. 787, 821 (1987) (Scalia, J., concurring). This revision makes the rule explicit that the attorney acts as an officer of the court in issuing and signing subpoenas.

Necessarily accompanying the evolution of this power of the lawyer as officer of the court is the development of increased responsibility and liability for the misuse of this power. The latter development is reflected in the provisions of subdivision (c) of this rule, and also in the requirement imposed by paragraph (3) of this subdivision that the attorney issuing a subpoena must sign it.

Second, Paragraph (a)(3) authorizes attorneys in distant districts to serve as officers authorized to issue commands in the name of the court. Any attorney permitted to represent a client in a federal court, even one admitted pro haec vice, has the same authority as a clerk to issue a subpoena from any federal court for the district in which the subpoena is served and enforced. In authorizing attorneys to issue subpoenas from distant courts, the amended rule effectively authorizes service of a subpoena anywhere in the United States by an attorney representing any party. This change is intended to ease the administrative burdens of inter-district law practice. The former rule resulted in delay and expense caused by the need to secure forms from clerks' offices some distance from the place at which the action proceeds. This change does not enlarge the burden on the witness.

Pursuant to Paragraph (a)(2), a subpoena for a deposition must still issue from the court in which the deposition or production would be compelled. Accordingly, a motion to quash such a subpoena if it overbears the limits of the subpoena power must, as under the previous rule, be presented to the court for the district in which the deposition would occur. Likewise, the court in whose name the subpoena is issued is responsible for its enforcement.

Third, in order to relieve attorneys of the need to secure an appropriate seal to affix to a subpoena issued as an officer of a distant court, the requirement that a subpoena be under seal is abolished by the provisions of Paragraph (a)(1).

Fourth, Paragraph (a)(1) authorizes the issuance of a subpoena to compel a non-party to produce evidence independent of any deposition. This revision spares the necessity of a deposition of the custodian of evidentiary material required to be produced. A party seeking additional production from a person subject to such a subpoena may serve an additional subpoena requiring additional production at the same time and place.

Fifth, Paragraph (a)(2) makes clear that the person subject to the subpoena is required to produce materials in that person's control whether or not the materials are located within the district or within the territory within which the subpoena can be served. The non-party witness is subject to the same scope of discovery under this rule as that person would be as a party to whom a request is addressed pursuant to Rule 34.

Sixth, Paragraph (a)(1) requires that the subpoena include a statement of the rights and duties of witnesses by setting forth in full the text of the new subdivisions (c) and (d).

Seventh, the revised rule authorizes the issuance of a subpoena to compel the inspection of premises in the possession of a non-party. Rule 34 has authorized such inspections of premises in the possession of a party as discovery compelled under Rule 37, but prior practice required an independent proceeding to secure such relief ancillary to the federal proceeding when the premises were not in the possession of a party. Practice in some states has long authorized such use of a subpoena for this purpose without apparent adverse consequence.

Subdivision (b). ... The reference to the United States marshal and deputy marshal is deleted because of the infrequency of the use of these officers for this purpose. Inasmuch as these officers meet the age requirement, they may still be used if available.

A provision requiring service of prior notice pursuant to Rule 5 of compulsory pretrial production or inspection has been added to paragraph (b)(1). The purpose of such notice is to afford other parties an opportunity to object to the production or inspection, or to serve a demand for additional documents or things. Such additional notice is not needed with respect to a deposition because of the requirement of notice imposed by Rule 30 or 31. But when production or inspection is sought independently of a deposition, other parties may need notice in order to monitor the discovery and in order to pursue access to any information that may or should be produced....

Subdivision (c). ... Paragraph (c)(1) gives specific application to the principle stated in Rule 26(g) and specifies liability for earnings lost by a non-party witness as a result of a misuse of the subpoena. No change in existing law is thereby effected. Abuse of a subpoena is an actionable tort, ... and the duty of the attorney to the non-party is also embodied in Model Rule of Professional Conduct 4.4. The liability of the attorney is correlative to the expanded power of the attorney to issue subpoenas. The liability may include the cost of fees to collect attorneys' fees owed as a result of a breach of this duty.

Paragraph (c)(2) retains language from the former subdivision (b) and paragraph (d)(1). The 10-day period for response to a subpoena is extended to 14 days to avoid the complex calculations associated with short time periods under Rule 6 and to allow a bit more time for such objections to be made.

A non-party required to produce documents or materials is protected against significant expense resulting from involuntary assistance to the court. This provision applies, for example, to a non-party required to provide a list of class members. The court is not required to fix the costs in advance of production, although this will often be the most satisfactory accommodation to protect the party seeking discovery from excessive costs. In some instances, it may be preferable to leave uncertain costs to be determined after the materials have been produced, provided that the risk of uncertainty is fully disclosed to the discovering party. *See, e.g., United States v. Columbia Broadcasting Systems, Inc.,* 666 F.2d 364 (9th Cir. 1982).

Paragraph (c)(3) explicitly authorizes the quashing of a subpoena as a means of protecting a witness from misuse of the subpoena power. It replaces and enlarges on the former subdivision (b) of this rule and tracks the provisions of Rule 26(c). While largely repetitious, this rule is addressed to the witness who may read it on the subpoena, where it is required to be printed by the revised paragraph (a)(1) of this rule.

Subparagraph (c)(3)(A) identifies those circumstances in which a subpoena must be quashed or modified. It restates the former provisions with respect to the limits of mandatory travel that are set forth in the former paragraphs (d)(2) and (e)(1), with one important change. Under the revised rule, a federal court can compel a witness to come from any place in the state to attend trial, whether or not the local state law so provides.

This extension is subject to the qualification provided in the next paragraph, which authorizes the court to condition enforcement of a subpoena compelling a non-party witness to bear substantial expense to attend trial. The traveling non-party witness may be entitled to reasonable compensation for the time and effort entailed.

Clause (c)(3)(A)(iv) requires the court to protect all persons from undue burden imposed by the use of the subpoena power. Illustratively, it might be unduly burdensome to compel an adversary to attend trial as a witness if the adversary is known to have no personal knowledge of matters in dispute, especially so if the adversary would be required to incur substantial travel burdens.

Subparagraph (c)(3)(B) identifies circumstances in which a subpoena should be quashed unless the party serving the subpoena shows a substantial need and the court can devise an appropriate accommodation to protect the interests of the witness. An additional circumstance in which such action is required is a request for costly production of documents; that situation is expressly governed by subparagraph (b)(2)(B).

Clause (c)(3)(B)(i) authorizes the court to quash, modify, or condition a subpoena to protect the person subject to or affected by the subpoena from unnecessary or unduly harmful disclosures of confidential information. It corresponds to Rule 26(c)(7).

Clause (c)(3)(B)(ii) provides appropriate protection for the intellectual property of the non-party witness; it does not apply to the expert retained by a party, whose information is subject to the provisions of Rule 26(b)(4). A growing problem has been the use of subpoenas to compel the giving of evidence and information by unretained experts. Experts are not exempt from the duty to give evidence, even if they cannot be compelled to prepare themselves to give effective testimony, but compulsion to give evidence may threaten the intellectual property of experts denied the opportunity to bargain for the value of their services. *See generally* Maurer, *Compelling the Expert Witness: Fairness and Utility Under the Federal Rules of Civil Procedure*, 19 Ga. L. Rev. 71 (1984); Note, *Discovery and Testimony of Unretained Experts*, 1987 Duke L.J. 140. Arguably the compulsion to testify can be regarded as a "taking" of intellectual property. The rule establishes the right of such persons to withhold their expertise, at least unless the party seeking it makes the kind of showing required for a conditional denial of a motion to quash as provided in the final sentence of subparagraph (c)(3)(B); that requirement is the same as that necessary to secure work product under Rule 26(b)(3) and gives assurance of reasonable compensation. The Rule thus approves the accommodation of competing interests exemplified in *United States v. Columbia Broadcasting Systems Inc.*, 666 F.2d 364 (9th Cir. 1982)....

As stated in *Kaufman v. Edelstein*, 539 F.2d 811, 822 (2d Cir. 1976), the district court's discretion in these matters should be informed by "the degree to which the expert is being called because of his knowledge of facts relevant to the case rather than in order to give opinion testimony; the difference between testifying to a previously formed or expressed opinion and forming a new one; the possibility that, for other reasons, the witness is a unique expert; the extent to which the calling party is able to show the unlikelihood that any comparable witness will willingly testify; and the degree to which the witness is able to show that he has been oppressed by having continually to testify...."

Clause (c)(3)(B)(iii) protects non-party witnesses who may be burdened to perform the duty to travel in order to provide testimony at trial. The provision requires the court to condition a subpoena requiring travel of more than 100 miles on reasonable compensation.

Subdivision (d). This provision is new. Paragraph (d)(1) extends to non-parties the duty imposed on parties by the last paragraph of Rule 34(b), which was added in 1980.

Paragraph (d)(2) is new and corresponds to the new Rule 26(b)(5). Its purpose is to provide a party whose discovery is constrained by a claim of privilege or work product protection with information sufficient to evaluate such a claim and to resist if it seems unjustified. The person claiming a privilege or protection cannot decide the limits of that party's own entitlement.

A party receiving a discovery request who asserts a privilege or protection but fails to disclose that claim is at risk of waiving the privilege or protection. A person claiming a privilege or protection who fails to provide adequate information about the privilege or protection claim to the party seeking the information is subject to an order to show cause why the person should not be held in contempt under subdivision (e). Motions for such orders and responses to motions are subject to the sanctions provisions of Rules 7 and 11.

A person served a subpoena that is too broad may be faced with a burdensome task to provide full information regarding all that person's claims to privilege or work product protection. Such a person is entitled to protection that may be secured through an objection made pursuant to paragraph (c)(2).

Subdivision (e). ... "Adequate cause" for a failure to obey a subpoena remains undefined. In at least some circumstances, a non-party might be guilty of contempt for refusing to obey a subpoena even though the subpoena manifestly overreaches the appropriate limits of the subpoena power. *E.g., Walker v. City of Birmingham*, 388 U.S. 307 (1967). But, because the command of the subpoena is not in fact one uttered by a judicial officer, contempt should be very sparingly applied when the non-party witness has been overborne by a party or attorney. The language added to subdivision (f) is intended to assure that result where a non-party has been commanded, on the signature of an attorney, to travel greater distances than can be compelled pursuant to this rule.

RULE 47

Subdivision (b). The former provision for alternate jurors is stricken and the institution of the alternate juror abolished....

The use of alternate jurors has been a source of dissatisfaction with the jury system because of the burden it places on alternates who are required to listen to the evidence but denied the satisfaction of participating in its evaluation.

Subdivision (c). This provision makes it clear that the court may in appropriate circumstances excuse a juror during the jury deliberations without causing a mistrial. Sickness, family emergency or juror misconduct that might occasion a mistrial are examples of appropriate grounds for excusing a juror. It is not grounds for the dismissal of a juror that the juror refuses to join with fellow jurors in reaching a unanimous verdict.

RULE 48

The former rule was rendered obsolete by the adoption in many districts of local rules establishing six as the standard size for a civil jury.

It appears that the minimum size of a jury consistent with the Seventh Amendment is six. *Cf. Ballew v. Georgia*, 435 U.S. 223 (1978) (holding that a conviction based on a jury of less than six is a denial of due process of law). If the parties agree to trial before a smaller jury, a verdict can be taken, but the parties should not other than in exceptional circumstances be encouraged to waive the right to a jury of six, not only because of the constitutional stature of the right, but also because smaller juries are more erratic and less effective in serving to distribute responsibility for the exercise of judicial power.

Because the institution of the alternate juror has been abolished by the proposed revision of Rule 47, it will ordinarily be prudent and necessary, in order to provide for sickness or disability among jurors, to seat more than six jurors. The use of jurors in excess of six increases the representativeness of the jury and harms no interest of a party. *Ray v. Parkside Surgery Center*, 13 F.R. Serv. 585 (6th Cir. 1989).

If the court takes the precaution of seating a jury larger than six, an illness occurring during the deliberation period will not result in a mistrial, as it did formerly, because all seated jurors will participate in the verdict and a sufficient number will remain to render a unanimous verdict of six or more.

In exceptional circumstances, as where a jury suffers depletions during trial and deliberation that are greater than can reasonably be expected, the parties may agree to be bound by a verdict rendered by fewer than six jurors. The court should not, however, rely upon the availability of such an agreement, for the use of juries smaller than six is problematic for reasons fully explained in *Ballew v. Georgia, supra*.

RULE 50

Subdivision (a). The revision of this subdivision aims to facilitate the exercise by the court of its responsibility to assure the fidelity of its judgment to the controlling law, a responsibility imposed by the Due Process Clause of the Fifth Amendment. *Cf. Galloway v. United States*, 319 U.S. 372 (1943).

The revision abandons the familiar terminology of direction of verdict for several reasons. The term is misleading as a description of the relationship between judge and jury. It is also freighted with anachronisms some of which are the subject of the text of former subdivision (a) of this rule that is deleted in this revision. Thus, it should not be necessary to state in the text of this rule that a motion made pursuant to it is not a waiver of the right to jury trial, and only the antiquities of directed verdict practice suggest that it might have been. The term "judgment as a matter of law" is an almost equally familiar term and appears in the text of Rule 56; its use in Rule 50 calls attention to the relationship between the two rules. Finally, the change enables the rule to refer to preverdict and post-verdict motions with a terminology that does not conceal the common identity of two motions made at different times in the proceeding.

If a motion is denominated a motion for directed verdict or for judgment notwithstanding the verdict, the party's error is merely formal. Such a motion should be treated as a motion for judgment as a matter of law in accordance with this rule.

Paragraph (a)(1) articulates the standard for the granting of a motion for judgment as a matter of law. It effects no change in the existing standard. That existing standard was not expressed in the former rule, but was articulated in long-standing case law. *See generally* Cooper, *Directions for Directed Verdicts: A Compass for Federal Courts*, 55 Minn. L. Rev. 903 (1971). The expressed standard makes clear that action taken under the rule is a performance of the court's duty to assure enforcement of the controlling law and is not an intrusion on any responsibility for factual determinations conferred on the jury by the Seventh Amendment or any other provision of federal law. Because this standard is also used as a reference point for entry of summary judgment under 56(a), it serves to link the two related provisions.

The revision authorizes the court to perform its duty to enter judgment as a matter of law at any time during the trial, as soon as it is apparent that either party is unable to carry a burden of proof that is essential to that party's case. Thus, the second sentence of paragraph (a)(1) authorizes the court to consider a motion for judgment as a matter of law as soon as a party has completed a presentation on a fact essential to that party's case. Such early action is appropriate when economy and expedition will be served. In no event, however, should the court enter judgment against a party who has not been apprised of the materiality of the dispositive fact and been afforded an opportunity to present any available evidence bearing on that fact. In order further to facilitate the exercise of the authority provided by this rule, Rule 16 is also revised to encourage the court to schedule an order of trial that proceeds first with a presentation on an issue that is likely to be dispositive, if such an issue is identified in the course of pretrial. Such scheduling can be appropriate where the court is uncertain whether favorable action should be taken under Rule 56. Thus, the revision affords the court the alternative of denying a motion for summary judgment while scheduling a separate trial of the issue under Rule 42(b) or scheduling the trial to begin with a presentation on that essential fact which the opposing party seems unlikely to be able to maintain.

Paragraph (a)(2) retains the requirement that a motion for judgment be made prior to the close of the trial, subject to renewal after a jury verdict has been rendered. The purpose of this requirement is to assure the responding party an opportunity to cure any deficiency in that party's proof that may have been overlooked until called to the party's attention by a late motion for judgment. *Cf. Farley Transp. Co. v. Santa Fe Trail Transp. Co.*, 786 F.2d 1342 (9th Cir. 1986) ("If the moving party is then permitted to make a later attack on the evidence through a motion for judgment notwithstanding the verdict or an appeal, the opposing party may be prejudiced by having lost the opportunity to present additional evidence before the case was submitted to the jury"); *Benson v. Allphin*, 786 F.2d 268 (7th Cir. 1986) ("the motion for directed verdict at the close of all the evidence provides the nonmovant an opportunity to do what he can to remedy the deficiencies in his case . . .); *McLaughlin v. The Fellows Gear Shaper Co.*, 4 F.R. Serv. 3d 607 (3d Cir. 1986) (per Adams, J., dissenting: "This Rule serves important practical purposes in ensuring that neither party is precluded from presenting the most persuasive case possible and in preventing unfair surprise after a matter has been submitted to the jury"). At one time, this requirement was held to be of constitutional stature, being compelled by the Seventh Amendment. *Cf. Slocum v. New York Insurance Co.*, 228 U.S. 364 (1913). *But cf. Baltimore & Carolina Line v. Redman*, 295 U.S. 654 (1935).

The second sentence of paragraph (a)(2) does impose a requirement that the moving party articulate the basis on which a judgment as a matter of law might be rendered. The articulation is necessary to achieve the purpose of the requirement that the motion be made before the case is submitted to the jury, so that the responding party may seek to correct any overlooked deficiencies in the proof. The revision thus alters the result in cases in which courts have used various techniques to avoid the requirement that a motion for a directed verdict be made as a predicate to a motion for judgment notwithstanding the verdict. *E.g., Benson v. Allphin*, 788 F.2d. 268 (7th Cir. 1986) ("this circuit has allowed something less than a formal motion for directed verdict to preserve a party's right to move for judgment notwithstanding the verdict").… The information required with the motion may be supplied by explicit reference to materials and argument previously supplied to the court.

This subdivision deals only with the entry of judgment and not with the resolution of particular factual issues as a matter of law. The court may, as before, properly refuse to instruct a jury to decide an issue if a reasonable jury could on the evidence presented decide that issue in only one way.

Subdivision (b). This provision retains the concept of the former rule that the post-verdict motion is a renewal of an earlier motion made at the close of the evidence. One purpose of this concept was to avoid any question arising under the Seventh Amendment. *Montgomery Ward & Co. v. Duncan*, 311 U.S. 243 (1940). It remains useful as a means of defining the appropriate issue posed by the post-verdict motion. A post-trial motion for judgment can be granted only on grounds advanced in the pre-verdict motion. *E.g., Kutner Buick, Inc. v. American Motors Corp.*, 848 F.2d 614 (3d Cir. 1989).

Often it appears to the court or to the moving party that a motion for judgment as a matter of law made at the close of the evidence should be reserved for a post-verdict decision. This is so because a jury verdict for the moving party moots the issue and because a preverdict ruling gambles that a reversal may result in a new trial that might have been avoided. For these reasons, the court may often wisely decline to rule on a motion for judgment as a matter of law made at the close of the evidence, and it is not inappropriate for the moving party to suggest such a postponement of the ruling until after the verdict has been rendered.

In ruling on such a motion, the court should disregard any jury determination for which there is no legally sufficient evidentiary basis enabling a reasonable jury to make it. The court may then decide such issues as a matter of law and enter judgment if all other material issues have been decided by the jury on the basis of legally sufficient evidence, or by the court as a matter of law.

The revised rule is intended for use in this manner with Rule 49. Thus, the court may combine facts established as a matter of law either before trial under Rule 56 or at trial on the basis of the evidence presented with other facts determined by the jury under instructions provided under Rule 49 to support a proper judgment under this rule.

RULE 52

Subdivision (c) is added. It parallels the revised Rule 50(a), but is applicable to non-jury trials. It authorizes the court to enter judgment at any time that it can appropriately make a dispositive finding of fact on the evidence….

Judgment entered under this rule differs from a summary judgment under Rule 56 in the nature of the evaluation made by the court. A judgment on partial findings is made after the court has heard all the evidence bearing on the crucial issue of fact, and the finding is reversible only if the appellate court finds it to be "clearly erroneous." A summary judgment, in contrast, is made on the basis of facts established on account of the absence of contrary evidence or presumptions; such establishments of fact are rulings on questions of law as provided in Rule 56(a) and are not shielded by the "clear error" standard of review.

RULE 77

This revision is a companion to the concurrent amendment to Rule 4 of the Federal Rules of Appellate Procedure. The purpose of the revisions is to permit district courts to ease strict sanctions now imposed on appellants whose notices of appeal are filed late because of their failure to receive notice of entry of a judgment....

Failure to receive notice may have increased in frequency with the growth in the caseload in the clerks' offices. The present strict rule imposes a duty on counsel to maintain contact with the court while a case is under submission. Such contact is more difficult to maintain if counsel is outside the district, as is increasingly common, and can be a burden to the court as well as counsel.

The effect of the revisions is to place a burden on prevailing parties who desire certainty that the time for appeal is running. Such parties can take the initiative to assure that their adversaries receive effective notice. An appropriate procedure for such notice is provided in Rule 5.

The revised rule lightens the responsibility but not the workload of the clerk's offices, for the duty of that office to give notice of entry of judgment must be maintained.

ADVISORY COMMITTEE NOTES TO 1993 AMENDMENTS

RULE 1

The purpose of this revision, adding the words "and administered" to the second sentence, is to recognize the affirmative duty of the court to exercise the authority conferred by these rules to ensure that civil litigation is resolved not only fairly, but also without undue cost or delay. As officers of the court, attorneys share this responsibility with the judge to whom the case is assigned.

RULE 4

SPECIAL NOTE: Mindful of the constraints of the Rules Enabling Act, the Committee calls the attention of the Supreme Court and Congress to new subdivision (k)(2). Should this limited extension of service be disapproved, the Committee nevertheless recommends adoption of the balance of the rule, with subdivision (k)(1) becoming simply subdivision (k). The Committee Notes would be revised to eliminate references to subdivision (k)(2).

The general purpose of this revision is to facilitate the service of the summons and complaint. The revised rule explicitly authorizes a means for service of the summons and complaint on any defendant. While the methods of service so authorized always provide appropriate notice to persons against whom claims are made, effective service under this rule does not assure that personal jurisdiction has been established over the defendant served.

First, the revised rule authorizes the use of any means of service provided by the law not only of the forum state, but also of the state in which a defendant is served, unless the defendant is a minor or incompetent.

Second, the revised rule clarifies and enhances the cost-saving practice of securing the assent of the defendant to dispense with actual service of the summons and complaint. This practice was introduced to the rule in 1983 by an act of Congress authorizing "service-by-mail," a procedure that effects economic service with cooperation of the defendant. Defendants that magnify costs of service by requiring expensive service not necessary to achieve full notice of an action brought against them are required to bear the wasteful costs. This provision is made available in actions against defendants who cannot be served in the districts in which the actions are brought.

Third, the revision reduces the hazard of commencing an action against the United States or its officers, agencies, and corporations. A party failing to effect service on all the offices of the United States as required by the rule is assured adequate time to cure defects in service.

Fourth, the revision calls attention to the important effect of the Hague Convention and other treaties bearing on service of documents in foreign countries and favors the use of internationally agreed means of service. In some respects, these treaties have facilitated service in foreign countries but are not fully known to the bar.

Finally, the revised rule extends the reach of federal courts to impose jurisdiction over the person of all defendants against whom federal law claims are made and who can be constitutionally subjected to the jurisdiction of the courts of the United States. The present territorial limits on the effectiveness of service to subject a defendant to the jurisdiction of the court over the defendant's person are retained for all actions in which there is a state in which personal jurisdiction can be asserted consistently with state law and the Fourteenth Amendment. A new provision enables district courts to exercise jurisdiction, if permissible under the Constitution and not precluded by statute, when a federal claim is made against a defendant not subject to the jurisdiction of any single state.

The revised rule is reorganized to make its provisions more accessible to those not familiar with all of them. Additional subdivisions in this rule allow for more captions; several overlaps among subdivisions are eliminated; and several disconnected provisions are removed, to be relocated in a new Rule 4.1....
Prior to this revision, Rule 4 was entitled "Process" and applied to the service of not only the summons but also other process as well, although these are not covered by the revised rule. Service of process in eminent domain proceedings is governed by Rule 71A. Service of a subpoena is governed by Rule 45, and service of papers such as orders, motions, notices, pleadings, and other documents is governed by Rule 5.

The revised rule is entitled "Summons" and applies only to that form of legal process. Unless service of the summons is waived, a summons must be served whenever a person is joined as a party against whom a claim is made. Those few provisions of the former rule which relate specifically to service of process other than a summons are relocated in Rule 4.1 in order to simplify the test of this rule.

Subdivision (a). Revised subdivision (a) contains most of the language of the former subdivision (b). The second sentence of the former subdivision (b) has been stricken, so that the federal court summons will be the same in all cases. Few states now employ distinctive requirements of form for a summons and the applicability of such a requirement in federal court can only serve as a trap for an unwary party or attorney. A sentence is added to this subdivision authorizing an amendment of a summons....

Subdivision (b). Revised subdivision (b) replaces the former subdivision (a). The revised text makes clear that the responsibility for filling in the summons falls on the plaintiff, not the clerk of the court. If there are multiple defendants, the plaintiff may secure issuance of a summons for each defendant, or may serve copies of a single original bearing the names of multiple defendants if the addressee of the summons is effectively identified.

Subdivision (c). Paragraph (1) of revised subdivision (c) retains language from the former subdivision (d)(1). Paragraph (2) retains language from the former subdivision (a), and adds an appropriate caution regarding the time limit for service set forth in subdivision (m).

The 1983 revision of Rule 4 relieved the marshals' offices of much of the burden of serving the summons. Subdivision (c) eliminates the requirement for service by the marshal's office in actions in which the party seeking service is the United States. The United States, like other civil litigants, is now permitted to designate any person who is 18 years of age and not a party to serve its summons.

The court remains obligated to appoint a marshal, a deputy, or some other person to effect service of a summons in two classes of cases specified by statute: actions brought in forma pauperis or by a seaman. 28 U.S.C. §§ 1915, 1916. The court also retains discretion to appoint a process server on motion of a party. If a law enforcement presence appears to be necessary or advisable to keep the peace, the court should appoint a marshal or deputy or other official person to make the service. The Department of Justice may also call upon the Marshals Service to perform services in actions brought by the United States. 28 U.S.C. § 651.

Subdivision (d). This text is new, but is substantially derived from the former subdivision (c)(2)(C) and (D), added to the rule by Congress in 1983. The aims of the provision are to eliminate the costs of service of a summons on many parties and to foster cooperation among adversaries and counsel. The rule operates to impose upon the defendant those costs that could have been avoided if the defendant had cooperated reasonably in the manner prescribed. This device is useful in dealing with defendants who are furtive, who reside in places not easily reached by process servers, or who are outside the United States and can be served only at substantial and unnecessary expense. Illustratively, there is no useful purpose achieved by requiring a plaintiff to comply with all the formalities of service in a foreign country, including costs of translation, when suing a defendant manufacturer, fluent in English, whose products are widely distributed in the United States. *See Bankston v. Toyota Motor Corp.*, 889 F.2d 172 (8th Cir. 1989).

The former text described this process as service-by-mail. This language misled some plaintiffs into thinking that service could be effected by mail without the affirmative cooperation of the defendant. *E.g., Gulley v. Mayo Foundation*, 886 F.2d 161 (8th Cir. 1989). It is more accurate to describe the communication sent to the defendant as a request for a waiver of formal service.

The request for waiver of service may be sent only to defendants subject to service under subdivision (e), (f), or (h). The United States is not expected to waive service for the reason that its mail receiving facilities are inadequate to assure that the notice is actually received by the correct person in the Department of Justice. The same principle is applied to agencies, corporations, and officers of the United States and to other governments and entities subject to service under subdivision (j). Moreover, there are policy reasons why governmental entities should not be confronted with the potential for hearing costs of service in cases in which they ultimately prevail. Infants or incompetent persons likewise are not called upon to waive service because, due to their presumed inability to understand the request and its consequences, they must generally be served through fiduciaries.

It was unclear whether the former rule authorized mailing of a request for "acknowledgment of service" to defendants outside the forum state. *See* 1 R. Casad, *Jurisdiction in Civil Actions* (2d Ed.) 5-29, 30 (1991) and cases cited. But, as Professor Casad observed, there was no reason not to employ this device in an effort to obtain service outside the state, and there are many instances in which it was in fact so used, with respect both to defendants within the United States and to defendants in other countries.

The opportunity for waiver has distinct advantages to a foreign defendant. By waiving service, the defendant can reduce the costs that may ultimately be taxed against it if unsuccessful in the lawsuit, including the sometimes substantial expense of translation that may be wholly unnecessary for defendants fluent in English. Moreover, a defendant that waives service is afforded substantially more time to defend against the action than if it had been formally served: under Rule 12, a defendant ordinarily has only 20 days after service in which to file its answer or raise objections by motion, but by signing a waiver it is allowed 90 days after the date the request for waiver was mailed in which to submit its defenses. Because of the additional time needed for mailing and the unreliability of some foreign mail services, a period of 60 days (rather than the 30 days required for domestic transmissions) is provided for a return of a waiver sent to a foreign country.

It is hoped that, since transmission of the notice and waiver forms is a private nonjudicial act, does not purport to effect service, and is not accompanied by any summons or directive from a court, use of the procedure will not offend foreign sovereignties, even those that have withheld their assent to formal service by mail or have objected to the "service-by-mail" provisions of the former rule. Unless the addressee consents, receipt of the request under the revised rule does not give rise to any obligation to answer the lawsuit, does not provide a basis for default judgment, and does not suspend the statute of limitations in those states where the period continues to run until service. Nor are there any adverse consequences to a foreign defendant, since the provisions for shifting the expense of service to a defendant that declines to waive service apply only if the plaintiff and defendant are both located in the United States.

With respect to a defendant located in a foreign country like the United Kingdom, which accepts documents in English, whose Central Authority acts promptly in effecting service, and whose policies discourage it residents from waiving formal service, there will be little reasons for a plaintiff to send the notice and request under subdivision (d) rather than use convention methods. On the other hand, the procedure offers significant potential benefits to a plaintiff when suing a defendant that, though fluent in English, is located in country where, as a condition to formal service under a convention, documents must be translated into another language or where formal service will be otherwise costly or time-consuming.

Paragraph (1) is explicit that a timely waiver of service of a summons does not prejudice the right of a defendant to object by means of a motion authorized by Rule 12(b)(2) to the absence of jurisdiction over the defendant's person, or to assert other defenses that may be available. The only issues eliminated are those involving the sufficiency of the summons or the sufficiency of the method by which it is served.

Paragraph (2) states what the present rule implies: the defendant has a duty to avoid costs associated with the service of a summons not needed to inform the defendant regarding the commencement of an action. The text of the rule also sets forth the requirements for a Notice and Request for Waiver sufficient to put the cost-shifting provision in place. These requirements are illustrated in Forms 1A and 1B, which replace the former Form 18-A.

Paragraph (2)(A) is explicit that a request for waiver of service by a corporate defendant must be addressed to a person qualified to receive service. The general mail rooms of large organizations cannot be required to identify the appropriate individual recipient for an institutional summons.

Paragraph (2)(B) permits the use of alternatives to the United States mails in sending the Notice and Request. While private messenger services or electronic communications may be more expensive than the mail, they may be equally reliable and on occasion more convenient to the parties. Especially with respect to transmissions to foreign countries, alternative means may be desirable, for in some countries facsimile transmission is the most efficient and economical means of communication. If electronic means such as facsimile transmission are employed, the sender should maintain a record of the transmission to assure proof of transmission if receipt is denied, but a party receiving such a transmission has a duty to cooperate and cannot avoid liability for the resulting cost of formal service if the transmission is prevented at the point of receipt.

A defendant failing to comply with a request for waiver shall be given an opportunity to show good cause for the failure, but sufficient cause should be rare. It is not a good cause for failure to waive service that the claim is unjust or that the court lacks jurisdiction. Sufficient cause not to shift the cost of service would exist, however, if the defendant did not receive the request; or was insufficiently literate in English to understand it. It should be noted that the provisions for shifting the cost of service apply only if the plaintiff and the defendant are both located in the United States, and accordingly a foreign defendant need not show "good cause" for its failure to waive service.

Paragraph (3) extends the time for answer if, before being served with process, the defendant waives formal service. The extension is intended to serve as an inducement to waive service and to assure that a defendant will not gain any delay by declining to waive service and thereby causing the additional time needed to effect service. By waiving service, a defendant is not called upon to respond to the complaint until 60 days from the date the notice was sent to it — 90 days if the notice was sent to a foreign country — rather than within the 20 day period from date of service specified in Rule 12.

Paragraph (4) clarifies the effective date of service when service is waived; the provision is needed to resolve an issue arising when applicable law requires service of process to toll the statute of limitations. *E.g., Morse v. Elmira Country Club*, 752 F.2d 35 (2d Cir. 1984). *Cf. Walker v. Armco Steel Corp.*, 446 U.S. 740 (1980).

The provisions in former subdivision (c)(2)(C)(ii) of this rule may have been misleading to some parties. Some plaintiffs, not reading the rule carefully, supposed that receipt by the defendant of the mailed complaint had the effect both of establishing the jurisdiction of the court over the defendant's person and of tolling the statute of limitations in actions in which service of the summons is required to toll the limitations period. The revised rule is clear that, if the waiver is not returned and filed, the limitations period under such a law is not tolled and the action will not otherwise proceed until formal service of process is effected.

Some state limitations laws may toll an otherwise applicable statute at the time when the defendant receives notice of the action. Nevertheless, the device of requested waiver of service is not suitable if a limitations period which is about to expire is not tolled by filing the action. Unless there is ample time, the plaintiff should proceed directly to the formal methods for service identified in subdivisions (e), (f), or (h).

The procedure of requesting waiver of service should also not be used if the time for service under subdivision (m) will expire before the date on which the waiver must be returned. While a plaintiff has been allowed additional time for service in that situation, *e.g., Prather v. Raymond Constr. Co.*, 570 F. Supp. 278 (N.D. Ga. 1983), the court could refuse a request for additional time unless the defendant appears to have evaded service pursuant to subdivision (e) or (h). It may be noted that the presumptive time limit for service under subdivision (m) does not apply to service in a foreign country.

Paragraph (5) is a cost-shifting provision retained from the former rule. The costs that may be imposed on the defendant could include, for example, costs of unneeded translation or the cost of the time of a process server required to make contact with a defendant residing in guarded apartment houses or residential developments. The paragraph is explicit that the costs of enforcing the cost-shifting provision are themselves recoverable from a defendant who fails to return the waiver. In the absence of such a provision, the purpose of the rule would be frustrated by the cost of its enforcement, which is likely to be high in relation to the small benefit secured by the plaintiff.

Some plaintiffs may send a notice and request for waiver and, without waiting for return of the waiver, also proceed with efforts to effect formal service on the defendant. To discourage this practice, the cost-shifting provisions in paragraphs (2) and (5) are limited to costs of effecting service incurred after the time expires for the defendant to return the waiver. Moreover, by returning the waiver within the time allowed and before being served with process, a defendant receives the benefit of the longer period for responding to the complaint afforded for waivers under paragraph (3).

Subdivision (e). This subdivision replaces former subdivisions (c)(2)(C)(i) and (d)(1). It provides a means for service of summons on individuals within a judicial district of the United States. Together with subdivision (f), it provides for service on persons anywhere, subject to constitutional and statutory constraints.

Service of the summons under this subdivision does not conclusively establish the jurisdiction of the court over the person of the defendant. A defendant may assert the territorial limits of the court's reach set forth in subdivision (k), including the constitutional limitations that may be imposed by the Due Process Clause of the Fifth Amendment.

Paragraph (1) authorizes service in any judicial district in conformity with state law. This paragraph sets forth the language of former subdivision (c)(2)(C)(i), which authorized the use of the law of the state in which the district court sits, but adds as an alternative the use of the law of the state in which the service is effected.

Paragraph (2) retains the text of the former subdivision (d)(1) and authorizes the use of the familiar methods of personal or abode service or service on an authorized agent in any judicial district.

To conform to these provisions, the former subdivision (e) bearing on proceedings against parties not found within the state is stricken. Likewise stricken is the first sentence of the former subdivision (f), which had restricted the authority of the federal process server to the state in which the district court sits.

Subdivision (f). This subdivision provides for service on individuals who are in a foreign country, replacing the former subdivision (i) that was added to Rule 4 in 1963. Reflecting the pattern of Rule 4 in incorporating state law limitations on the exercise of jurisdiction over persons, the former subdivision (i) limited service outside the United States to cases in which extraterritorial service was authorized by state or federal law. The new rule eliminates the requirement of explicit authorization. On occasion, service in a foreign country was held to be improper for lack of statutory authority. *E.g., Martens v. Winde*, 341 F.2d 197 (9th Cir.), *cert. denied*, 382 U.S. 937 (1965). This authority, however, was found to exist by implication. *E.Q., SEC v. VTR. Inc.*, 39 F.R.D. 19 (S.D.N.Y. 1966). Given the substantial increase in the number of international transactions and events that are the subject of litigation in federal courts, it is appropriate to infer a general legislative authority to effect service on defendants in a foreign country.

A secondary effect of this provision for foreign service of a federal summons is to facilitate the use of federal long-arm law in actions brought to enforce the federal law against defendants who cannot be served under any state law but who can be constitutionally subjected to the jurisdiction of the federal court. Such a provision is set forth in paragraph (2) of subdivision (k) of this rule, applicable only to persons not subject to the territorial jurisdiction of any particular state.

Paragraph (1) gives effect to the Hague Convention on the Service Abroad of Judicial and Extrajudicial Documents, which entered into force for the United States on February 10, 1969. See 28 U.S.C.A., Fed. R. Civ. P. 4 (Supp. 1986). This Convention is an important means of dealing with problems of service in a foreign country. *See generally* 1 B. Ristau, *International Judicial Assistance* §§ 4-1-1 to 4-5-2 (1990). Use of the Convention procedures, when available, is mandatory if documents must be transmitted abroad to effect service. *See Volkswagenwerk Aktiengesellschaft v. Schlunk*, 486 U.S. 694 (1988) (noting that voluntary use of these procedures may be desirable even when service could constitutionally be effected in another manner); J. Weis, *The Federal Rules and the Hague Conventions: Concerns of Conformity and Comity*, 50 U. Pitt. L. Rev. 903 (1989). Therefore, this paragraph provides that, when service is to be effected outside a judicial district of the United States, the methods of service appropriate under an applicable treaty shall be employed if available and if the treaty so requires.

The Hague Convention furnishes safeguards against the abridgment of rights of parties through inadequate notice. Article 15 provides for verification of actual notice or a demonstration that process was served by a method prescribed by the internal laws of the foreign state before a default judgment may be entered. Article 16 of the Convention also enables the judge to extend the time for appeal after judgment if the defendant shows a lack of adequate notice either to defend or to appeal the judgment, or has disclosed a prima facie case on the merits.

The Hague Convention does not specify a time within which a foreign country's Central Authority must effect service, but Article 15 does provide that alternate methods may be used if a Central Authority does not respond within six months. Generally, a Central Authority can be expected to respond much more quickly than that limit might permit, but there have been occasions when the signatory state was dilatory or refused to cooperate for substantive reasons. In such cases, resort may be had to the provisions set forth in subdivision (f)(3).

Two minor changes in the text reflect the Hague Convention. First, the term "letter of request" has been added. Although these words are synonymous with "letter rogatory," "letter of request" is preferred in modern usage. The provision should not be interpreted to authorize use of a letter of request when there is in fact no treaty obligation on the receiving country to honor such a request from this country or when the United States does not extend diplomatic recognition to the foreign nation. Second, the passage formerly found in subdivision (i)(1)(B), "when service in either case is reasonably calculated to give actual notice," has been relocated.

Paragraph (2) provides alternative methods for use when internationally agreed methods are not intended to be exclusive, or where there is no international agreement applicable. It contains most of the language formerly set forth in subdivision (i) of the rule. Service by methods that would violate foreign law is not generally authorized. Subparagraphs (A) and (B) prescribe the more appropriate methods for conforming to local practice or using a local authority. Subparagraph (C) prescribes other methods authorized by the former rule.

Paragraph (3) authorizes the court to approve other methods of service not prohibited by international agreements. The Hague Convention, for example, authorizes special forms of service in cases of urgency if convention methods will not permit service within the time required by the circumstances. Other circumstances that might justify the use of additional methods include the failure of the foreign country's Central Authority to effect service within the six-month period provided by the Convention, or the refusal of the Central Authority to serve a complaint seeking punitive damages or to enforce the antitrust laws of the United States. In such cases, the court may direct a special method of service not explicitly authorized by international agreement if not prohibited by the agreement. Inasmuch as our Constitution requires that reasonable notice be given, an earnest effort should be made to devise a method of communication that is consistent with due process and minimizes offense to foreign law. A court may in some instances specially authorize use of ordinary mail. *Cf. Levin v. Ruby Trading Corp.*, 248 F. Supp. 537 (S.D.N.Y. 1965)....

Subdivision (h). ... Frequent use should be made of the Notice and Request procedure set forth in subdivision (d) in actions against corporations. Care must be taken, however, to address the request to an individual officer or authorized agent of the corporation. It is not effective use of the Notice and Request procedure if the mail is sent undirected to the mail room of the organization....

Subdivision (k). This subdivision replaces the former subdivision (f), with no change in the title. Paragraph (1) retains the substance of the former rule in explicitly authorizing the exercise of personal jurisdiction over persons who can be reached under state long-arm law, the "100-mile bulge" provision added in 1963, or the federal interpleader act. Paragraph (1)(D) is new, but merely calls attention to federal legislation that may provide for nationwide or even world-wide service of process in cases arising under particular federal laws. Congress has provided for nationwide service of process and full exercise of territorial jurisdiction by all district courts with respect to specified federal actions....

Paragraph (2) is new. It authorizes the exercise of territorial jurisdiction over the person of any defendant against whom is made a claim arising under any federal law if that person is subject to personal jurisdiction in no state. This addition is a companion to the amendments made in revised subdivisions (e) and (f).

This paragraph corrects a gap in the enforcement of federal law. Under the former rule, a problem was presented when the defendant was a non-resident of the United States having contacts with the United States sufficient to justify the application of United States law and to satisfy federal standards of forum selection, but having insufficient contact with any single state to support jurisdiction under state long-arm legislation or meet the requirements of the Fourteenth Amendment limitation on state court territorial jurisdiction. In such cases, the defendant was shielded from the enforcement of federal law by the fortuity of a favorable limitation on the power of state courts, which was incorporated into the federal practice by the former rule. In this respect, the revision responds to the suggestion of the Supreme Court made in *Omni Capital Int'l v. Rudolf Wolff & Co., Ltd.*, 484 U.S. 97, 111 (1987).

There remain constitutional limitations on the exercise of territorial jurisdiction by federal courts over persons outside the United States. These restrictions arise from the Fifth Amendment rather than from the Fourteenth Amendment, which limits state-court reach and which was incorporated into federal practice by the reference to state law in the text of the former subdivision (e) that is deleted by this revision. The Fifth Amendment requires that any defendant have affiliating contacts with the United States sufficient to justify the exercise of personal jurisdiction over that party. *Cf. Wells Fargo & Co. v. Wells Fargo Express Co.*, 556 F.2d 406, 418 (9th Cir. 1977). There also may be a further Fifth Amendment constraint in that a plaintiff's forum selection might be so inconvenient to a defendant that it would be a denial of "fair play and substantial justice" required by the due process clause, even though the defendant had significant affiliating contacts with the United States. *See DeJames v. Magnificent Carriers*, 654 F.2d 280, 286 n.3 (3d Cir.), *cert. denied*, 454 U.S 1085 (1981). *Compare World-Wide Volkswagen Corp. v. Woodson*, 444 U.S. 286, 293-94 (1980); *Insurance Corp. of Ireland v. Compagnie des Bauxites de Guinee*, 456 U.S. 694, 702-03 (1982); *Burger King Corp. v. Rudzewicz*, 471 U.S. 462, 476-78 (1985); *Asahi Metal Indus. v. Superior Court of Cal., Solano County*, 480 U.S. 102, 108-13 (1987). *See generally* R. Lusardi, *Nationwide Service of Process: Due Process Limitations on the Power of the Sovereign*, 33 Vill. L. Rev. 1 (1988).

This provision does not affect the operation of federal venue legislation. *See generally* 28 U.S.C. § 1391. Nor does it affect the operation of federal law providing for the change of venue. 28 U.S.C. §§ 1404, 1406. The availability of transfer for fairness and convenience under § 1404 should preclude most conflicts between the full exercise of territorial jurisdiction permitted by this rule and the Fifth Amendment requirement of "fair play and substantial justice."

The district court should be especially scrupulous to protect aliens who reside in a foreign country from forum selection so onerous that injustice could result. "[G]reat care and reserve should be exercised when extending our notions of personal jurisdiction into the international field." *Asahi Metal Indus. v. Superior Court of Cal., Solano County*, 480 U.S. 102, 115 (1987), *quoting United States v. First Nat'l City Bank*, 379 U.S. 378, 404 (1965) (Harlan, J., dissenting).

This narrow extension of the federal reach applies only if a claim is made against the defendant under federal law. It does not establish personal jurisdiction if the only claims are those arising under state law or the law of another country, even though there might be diversity or alienage subject matter jurisdiction as to such claims. If, however, personal jurisdiction is established under this paragraph with respect to federal claim, then 28 U.S.C. § 1367(a) provides supplemental jurisdiction over related claims against that defendant, subject to the court's discretion to decline exercise of that jurisdiction under 28 U.S.C. § 1367(c)....

Subdivision (m). ...The new subdivision explicitly provides that the court shall allow additional time if there is good cause for the plaintiff's failure to effect service in the prescribed 120 days, and authorizes the court to relieve a plaintiff of the consequences of an application of this subdivision even if there is no good cause shown. Such relief formerly was afforded in some cases, partly in reliance on Rule 6(b). Relief may be justified, for example, if the applicable statute of limitations would bar the refiled action, or if the defendant is evading service or conceals a defect in attempted service. *E.g., Ditkof v. Owens-Illinois, Inc.*, 114 F.R.D. 104 (E.D. Mich. 1987). A specific instance of good cause is set forth in paragraph (3) of this Rule, which provides for extensions if necessary to correct oversights in compliance with the requirements of multiple service in actions against the United States or its officers, agencies, and corporations. The district court should also take care to protect pro se plaintiffs from consequences of confusion or delay attending the resolution of an informa pauperis petition. *Robinson v. America's Best Contacts & Eyeglasses*, 876 F.2d 596 (7th Cir. 1989).

The 1983 revision of this subdivision referred to the "party on whose behalf such service was required," rather than to the "plaintiff," a term used generically elsewhere in this rule to refer to any party initiating a claim against a person who is not a party to the action. To simplify the text, the revision returns to the usual practice in the rule of referring simply to the plaintiff even though its principles apply with equal force to defendants who may assert claims against non-parties under Rules 13(h), 14, 19, 20, or 21.

Subdivision (n). This subdivision provides for in rem and quasi-in-rem jurisdiction. Paragraph (1) incorporates any requirements of 28 U.S.C. § 1655 or similar provisions bearing on seizures or liens.

Paragraph (2) provides for other uses of quasi-in-rem jurisdiction but limits its use to exigent circumstance. Provisional remedies may be employed as a means to secure jurisdiction over the property of a defendant whose person is not within reach of the court, but occasions for the use of this provision should be rare, as where the defendant is a fugitive or assets are in imminent danger of disappearing. Until 1963, it was not possible under Rule 4 to assert jurisdiction in a federal court over the property of a defendant not personally served. The 1963 amendment to subdivision (e) authorized the use of state law procedures authorizing seizures of assets as a basis for jurisdiction. Given the liberal availability of long-arm jurisdiction, the exercise of power quasi-in-rem has become almost an anachronism. Circumstances too spare to affiliate the defendant to the forum state sufficiently to support long-arm jurisdiction over the defendant's person are also inadequate to support seizure of the defendant's assets fortuitously found within the state. *Shaffer v. Heitner*, 433 U.S. 186 (1977).

RULE 4.1

This is a new rule. Its purpose is to separate those few provisions of the former Rule 4 bearing on matters other than service of a summons to allow greater textual clarity in Rule 4. Subdivision (a) contains no new language.

Subdivision (b) replaces the final clause of the penultimate sentence of the former subdivision 4(f), a clause added to the rule in 1963. The new rule provides for nationwide service of orders of civil commitment enforcing decrees of injunctions issued to compel compliance with federal law. The rule makes no change in the practice with respect to the enforcement of injunctions or decrees not involving the enforcement of federally-created rights.

Service of process is not required to notify a party of a decree or injunction, or of an order that the party show cause why that party should not be held in contempt of such an order. With respect to a party who has once been served with a summons, the service of the decree or injunction itself or of an order to show cause can be made pursuant to Rule 5. Thus, for example, an injunction may be served on a party through that person's attorney. *Chagas v. United*, 369 F.2d 643 (5th Cir. 1966). The same is true for service of an order to show cause. *Waffenschmidt v. Mackay*, 763 F.2d 711 (5th Cir. 1985).

The new rule does not affect the reach of the court to impose criminal contempt sanctions. Nationwide enforcement of federal decrees and injunctions is already available with respect to criminal contempt: a federal court may effect the arrest of a criminal contemnor anywhere in the United States, 28 U.S.C. § 3041, and a contemnor when arrested may be subject to removal to the district in which punishment may be imposed. Fed. R. Crim. P. 40. Thus, the present law permits criminal contempt enforcement against a contemnor wherever that person may be found.

The effect of the revision is to provide a choice of civil or criminal contempt sanctions in those situations to which it applies. Contempt proceedings, whether civil or criminal, must be brought in the court that was allegedly defied by a contumacious act. *Ex parte Bradley*, 74 U.S. 366 (1869). This is so even if the offensive conduct or inaction occurred outside the district of the court in which the enforcement proceeding must be conducted. *E.g., McCourtney v. United States*, 291 Fed. 497 (8th Cir.), *cert. denied*, 263 U.S. 714 (1923). For this purpose, the rule as before does not distinguish between parties and other persons subject to contempt sanctions by reason of their relation or connection to parties.

RULE 11

This revision is intended to remedy problems that have arisen in the interpretation and application of the 1983 revision of the rule. For empirical examination of experience under the 1983 rule, *see, e.g.,* New York State Bar Committee on Federal Courts, *Sanctions and Attorneys' Fees* (1987); T. Willging, *The Rule 11 Sanctioning Process* (1989); American Judicature Society, *Report of the Third Circuit Task Force on Federal Rule of Civil Procedure 11* (S. Burbank ed., 1989); E. Wiggins, T. Willging, and D. Stienstra, *Report on Rule 11* (Federal Judicial Center 1991). For book-length analyses of the case law, *see* G. Joseph, *Sanctions: The Federal Law of Litigation Abuse* (1989); G. Solovy, *The Federal Law of Sanctions* (1991); G. Vairo, *Rule 11 Sanctions: Case Law Perspectives and Preventative Measures* (1991).

The rule retains the principle that attorneys and pro se litigants have an obligation to the court to refrain from conduct that frustrates the aims of Rule 1. The revision broadens the scope of this obligation, but places greater constraints on the imposition of sanctions and should reduce the number of motions for sanctions presented to the court. New subdivision (d) removes from the ambit of this rule all discovery requests, responses, objections, and motions subject to the provisions of Rule 26 through 37.

Subdivision (a). Retained in this subdivision are the provisions requiring signatures on pleadings, written motions, and other papers. Unsigned papers are to be received by the Clerk, but then are to be stricken if the omission of the signature is not corrected promptly after being called to the attention of the attorney or pro se litigant. Correction can be made by signing the paper on file or by submitting a duplicate that contains the signature. A court may require by local rule that papers contain additional identifying information regarding the parties or attorneys, such as telephone numbers to facilitate facsimile transmissions, though, as for omission of a signature, the paper should not be rejected for failure to provide such information.

The sentence in the former rule relating to the effect of answers under oath is no longer needed and has been eliminated. The provision in the former rule that signing a paper constitutes a certificate that it has been read by the signer also has been eliminated as unnecessary. The obligations imposed under subdivision (b) obviously require that a pleading, written motion, or other paper be read before it is filed or submitted to the court.

Subdivisions (b) and (c). The subdivisions restate the provisions requiring attorneys and pro se litigants to conduct a reasonable inquiry into the law and facts before signing pleadings, written motions, and other documents, and mandating sanctions for violation of these obligations. The revision in part expands the responsibilities of litigants to the court, while providing greater constraints and flexibility in dealing with infractions of the rule. The rule continues to require litigants to "stop-and-think" before initially making legal or factual contentions. It also, however, emphasizes the duty of candor by subjecting litigants to potential sanctions for insisting upon a position after it is no longer tenable and by generally providing protection against sanctions if they withdraw or correct contentions after a potential violation is called to their attention.

The rule applies only to assertions contained in papers filed with or submitted to the court. It does not cover matters arising for the first time during oral presentations to the court, when counsel may make statements that would not have been made if there had been more time for study and reflection. However, a litigant's obligations with respect to the contents of these papers are not measured solely as of the time they are filed with or submitted to the court, but include reaffirming to the court and advocating positions contained in those pleadings and motions after learning that they cease to have any merit. For example, an attorney who during a pretrial conference insists on a claim or defense should be viewed as "presenting to the court" that contention and would be subject to the obligations of subdivision (b) measured as of that time. Similarly, if after a notice of removal is filed, a party urges in federal court the allegations of a pleading filed in state court (whether as claims, defenses, or in disputes regarding removal or remand), it would be viewed as "presenting"—and hence certifying to the district court under Rule 11—those allegations.

The certification with respect to allegations and other factual contentions is revised in recognition that sometimes a litigant may have good reason to believe that a fact is true or false but may need discovery, formal or informal, from opposing parties or third persons to gather and confirm the evidentiary basis for the allegation. Tolerance of factual contentions in initial pleadings by plaintiffs or defendants when specifically identified as made on information and belief does not relieve litigants from the obligation to conduct an appropriate investigation into the facts that is reasonable under the circumstances; it is not a license to join parties, make claims, or present defenses without any factual basis or justification. Moreover, if evidentiary support is not obtained after a reasonable opportunity for further investigation or discovery, the party has a duty under the rule not to persist with that contention. Subdivision (b) does not require a formal amendment to pleadings for which evidentiary support is not obtained, but rather calls upon a litigant not thereafter to advocate such claims or defenses.

The certification is that there is (or likely will be) "evidentiary support" for the allegation, not that the party will prevail with respect to its contention regarding the fact. That summary judgment is rendered against a party does not necessarily mean, for purposes of this certification, that it had no evidentiary support for its position. On the other hand, if a party has evidence with respect to a contention that would suffice to defeat a motion for summary judgment based thereon, it would have sufficient "evidentiary support" for purposes of Rule 11.

Denials of factual contentions involve somewhat different considerations. Often, of course, a denial is premised upon the existence of evidence contradicting the alleged fact. At other times a denial is permissible because, after an appropriate investigation, a party has no information concerning the matter or, indeed, has a reasonable basis for doubting the credibility of the only evidence relevant to the matter. A party should not deny an allegation it knows to be true; but it is not required, simply because it lacks contradictory evidence, to admit an allegation that it believes is not true.

The changes in subdivisions (b)(3) and (b)(4) will serve to equalize the burden of the rule upon plaintiffs and defendants, who under Rule 8(b) are in effect allowed to deny allegations by stating that from their initial investigation they lack sufficient information to form a belief as to the truth of the allegation. If, after further investigation or discovery, a denial is no longer warranted, the defendant should not continue to insist on that denial. While sometimes helpful, formal amendment of the pleadings to withdraw an allegation or denial is not required by subdivision (b).

Arguments for extensions, modifications, or reversals of existing law or for creation of new law do not violate subdivision (b)(2) provided they are "nonfrivolous." This establishes an objective standard, intended to eliminate any "empty-head pure-heart" justification for patently frivolous arguments. However, the extent to which a litigant has researched the issues and found some support for its theories even in minority opinions, in law review articles, or through consultation with other attorneys should certainly be taken into account in determining whether paragraph (2) has been violated. Although arguments for a change of law are not required to be specifically so identified, a contention that is so identified should be viewed with greater tolerance under the rule.

The court has available a variety of possible sanctions to impose for violations, such as striking the offending paper; issuing an admonition, reprimand, or censure; requiring participation in seminars or other educational programs; ordering a fine payable to the court; referring the matter to disciplinary authorities (or, in the case of government attorneys, to the Attorney General, Inspector General, or agency head), etc. *See Manual for Complex Litigation, Second,* § 42.3. The rule does not attempt to enumerate the factors a court should consider in deciding whether to impose a sanction or what sanctions would be appropriate in the circumstances; but, for emphasis, it does specifically note that a sanction may be nonmonetary as well as monetary. Whether the improper conduct was willful, or negligent; whether it was part of a pattern of activity, or an isolated event; whether it infected the entire pleading, or only one particular count or defense; whether the person has engaged in similar conduct in other litigation; whether it was intended to injure; what effect it had on the litigation process in time or expense; whether the responsible person is trained in the law; what amount, given the financial resources of the responsible person, is needed to deter that person from repetition in the same case; what amount is needed to deter similar activity by other litigants: all of these may in a particular case be proper considerations. The court has significant discretion in determining what sanctions, if any, should be imposed for a violation, subject to the principle that the sanctions should not be more severe than reasonably necessary to deter repetition of the conduct by the offending person or comparable conduct by similarly situated persons.

Since the purpose of Rule 11 sanctions is to deter rather than to compensate, the rule provides that, if a monetary sanction is imposed, it should ordinarily be paid into court as a penalty. However, under unusual circumstances, particularly for (b)(1) violations, deterrence may be ineffective unless the sanction not only requires the person violating the rule to make a monetary payment, but also directs that some or all of this payment be made to those injured by the violation. Accordingly, the rule authorizes the court, if requested in a motion and if so warranted, to award attorney's fees to another party. Any such award to another party, however, should not exceed the expenses and attorneys' fees for the services directly and unavoidably caused by the violation of the certification requirement. If, for example, a wholly unsupportable count were included in a multi-count complaint or counterclaim for the purpose of needlessly increasing the cost of litigation to an impecunious adversary, any award of expenses should be limited to those directly caused by inclusion of the improper count, and not those resulting from the filing of the complaint or answer itself. The award should not provide compensation for services that could have been avoided by an earlier disclosure of evidence or an earlier challenge to the groundless claims or defenses. Moreover, partial reimbursement of fees may constitute a sufficient deterrent with respect to violations by persons having modest financial resources. In cases brought under statutes providing for fees to be awarded to prevailing parties, the court should not employ cost-shifting under this rule in a manner that would be inconsistent with the standards that govern the statutory award of fees, such as stated in *Christiansburg Garment Co. v. EEOC*, 434 U.S. 412 (1978).

The sanction should be imposed on the persons—whether attorneys, law firms, or parties—who have violated the rule or who may be determined to be responsible for the violation. The person signing, filing, submitting, or advocating a document has a nondelegable responsibility to the court, and in most situations should be sanctioned for a violation. Absent exceptional circumstances, a law firm is to be held also responsible when, as a result of a motion under subdivision (c)(1)(A), one of its partners, associates, or employees is determined to have violated the rule. Since such a motion may be filed only if the offending paper is not withdrawn or corrected within 21 days after service of the motion, it is appropriate that the law firm ordinarily be viewed as jointly responsible under established principles of agency. This provision is designed to remove the restrictions of the former rule. *Cf. Pavelic & LeFlore v. Marvel Entertainment Group*, 493 U.S. 120 (1989) (1983 version of Rule 11 does not permit sanctions against law firm of attorney signing groundless complaint).

The revision permits the court to consider whether other attorneys in the firm, co-counsel, other law firms, or the party itself should be held accountable for their part in causing a violation. When appropriate, the court can make an additional inquiry in order to determine whether the sanctions should be imposed on such persons, firms, or parties either in addition to or, in unusual circumstances, instead of the person actually making the presentation to the court. For example, such an inquiry may be appropriate in cases involving governmental agencies or other institutional parties that frequently impose substantial restrictions on the discretion of individual attorneys employed by it.

Sanctions that involve monetary awards (such as a fine or an award of attorney's fees) may not be imposed on a represented party for violations of subdivision (b)(2), involving frivolous contentions of law. Monetary responsibility for such violations is more properly placed solely on the party's attorneys. With this limitation, the rule should not be subject to attack under the Rules Enabling Act. *See Willy v. Coastal Corp.*, __ U.S. __ (1992); *Business Guides, Inc. v. Chromatic Communications Enter. Inc.*, __ U.S. __ (1991). This restriction does not limit the court's power to impose sanctions or remedial orders [that] may have collateral financial consequences upon a party, such as dismissal of a claim, preclusion of a defense, or preparation of amended pleadings.

Explicit provision is made for litigants to be provided notice of the alleged violation and an opportunity to respond before sanctions are imposed. Whether the matter should be decided solely on the basis of written submissions or should be scheduled for oral argument (or, indeed, for evidentiary presentation) will depend on the circumstances. If the court imposes a sanction, it must, unless waived, indicate its reasons in a written order or on the record; the court should not ordinarily have to explain its denial of a motion for sanctions. Whether a violation has occurred and what sanctions, if any, to impose for a violation are matters committed to the discretion of the trial court; accordingly, as under current law, the standard for appellate review of these decisions will be for abuse of discretion. *See Cooter & Gell v. Hartmarx Corp.*, 496 U.S. 384 (1990) (noting, however, that an abuse would be established if the court based its ruling on an erroneous view of the law or on a clearly erroneous assessment of the evidence).

The revision leaves for resolution on a case-by-case basis, considering the particular circumstances involved, the question as to when a motion for violation of Rule 11 should be served and when, if filed, it should be decided. Ordinarily the motion should be served promptly after the inappropriate paper is filed, and, if delayed too long, may be viewed as untimely. In other circumstances, it should not be served until the other party has had a reasonable opportunity for discovery. Given the "safe harbor" provisions discussed below, a party cannot delay serving its Rule 11 motion until conclusion of the case (or judicial rejection of the offending contention). Rule 11 motions should not be made or threatened for minor, inconsequential violations of the standards prescribed by subdivision (b). They should not be employed as a discovery device or to test the legal sufficiency or efficacy of allegations in the pleadings; other motions are available for those purposes. Nor should Rule 11 motions be prepared to emphasize the merits of a party's position, to exact an unjust settlement, to intimidate an adversary into withdrawing contentions that are fairly debatable, to increase the costs of litigation, to create a conflict of interest between attorney and client, or to seek disclosure of matters otherwise protected by the attorney-client privilege or the work-product doctrine. As under the prior rule, the court may defer its ruling (or its decision as to the identity of the persons to be sanctioned) until final resolution of the case in order to avoid immediate conflicts of interest and to reduce the disruption created if a disclosure of attorney-client communications is needed to determine whether a violation occurred or to identify the person responsible for the violation.

The rule provides that requests for sanctions must be made as a separate motion, i.e., not simply included as an additional prayer for relief contained in another motion. The motion for sanctions is not, however, to be filed until at least 21 days (or such other period as the court may set) after being served. If, during this period, the alleged violation is corrected, as by withdrawing (whether formally or informally) some allegations or contention, the motion should not be filed with the court. These provisions are intended to provide a type of "safe harbor" against motions under Rule 11 in that a party will not be subject to sanctions on the basis of another party's motion unless, after receiving the motion, it refuses to withdraw that position or to acknowledge candidly that it does not currently have evidence to support a specified allegation. Under the former rule, parties were sometimes reluctant to abandon a questionable contention lest that be viewed as evidence of a violation of Rule 11; under the revision, the timely withdrawal of a contention will protect a party against a motion for sanctions.

To stress the seriousness of a motion for sanctions and to define precisely the conduct claimed to violate the rule, the revision provides that the "safe harbor" period begins to run only upon service of the motion. In most cases, however, counsel should be expected to give informal notice to the other party, whether in person or by a telephone call or letter, of a potential violation before proceeding to prepare and serve a Rule 11 motion.

As under former Rule 11, the filing of a motion for sanctions is itself subject to the requirements of the rule and can lead to sanctions. However, service of a cross motion under Rule 11 should rarely be needed since under the revision the court may award to the person who prevails on a motion under Rule 11 — whether the movant or the target of the motion — reasonable expenses, including attorney's fees, incurred in presenting or opposing the motion.

The power of the court to act on its own initiative is retained, but with the condition that this be done through a show cause order. This procedure provides the person with notice and an opportunity to respond. The revision provides that a monetary sanction imposed after a court-initiated show cause order be limited to a penalty payable to the court and that it be imposed only if the show cause order is issued before any voluntary dismissal or an agreement of the parties to settle the claims made by or against the litigant. Parties settling a case should not be subsequently faced with an unexpected order from the court leading the monetary sanctions that might have affected their willingness to settle or voluntarily dismiss a case. Since show cause orders will ordinarily be issued only in situations that are akin to a contempt of court, the rule does not provide a "safe harbor" to a litigant for withdrawing a claim, defense, etc., after a show cause order has been issued on the court's own initiative. Such corrective action, however, should be taken into account in deciding what sanction to impose if, after consideration of the litigant's response, the court concludes that a violation has occurred.

Subdivision (d). Rules 26(g) and 37 establish certification standards and sanctions that apply to discovery disclosures, requests, responses, objections, and motions. It is appropriate that Rules 26 through 37, which are specially designed for the discovery process, govern such documents and conduct rather than the more general provisions of Rule 11. Subdivision (d) has been added to accomplish this result. Rule 11 is not the exclusive source for control of improper presentations of claims, defenses, or contentions. It does not supplant statutes permitting awards of attorney's fees to prevailing parties or alter the principles governing such awards. It does not inhibit the court in punishing for contempt, in exercising its inherent powers, or in imposing sanctions, awarding expenses, or directing remedial action authorized under other rules or under 28 U.S.C. § 1927. *See Chambers v. NASCO*, 501 U.S. 32 (1991). *Chambers* cautions, however, against reliance upon inherent powers if appropriate sanctions can be imposed under provisions such as Rule 11, and the procedures specified in Rule 11 — notice, opportunity to respond, and findings — should ordinarily be employed when imposing a sanction under the court's inherent powers. Finally, it should be noted that Rule 11 does not preclude a party from initiating an independent action for malicious prosecution or abuse of process.

RULE 12

Subdivision (a) is divided into paragraphs for greater clarity, and paragraph (1)(B) is added to reflect amendments to Rule 4. Consistent with Rule 4(d)(3), a defendant that timely waives service is allowed 60 days from the date the request was mailed in which to respond to the complaint, with an additional 30 days afforded if the request was sent out of the country. Service is timely waived if the waiver is returned within the time specified in the request (30 days after the request was mailed, or 60 days if mailed out of the country) and before being formally served with process. Sometimes a plaintiff may attempt to serve a defendant with process while also sending the defendant a request for waiver of service; if the defendant executes the waiver of service within the time specified and before being served with process, it should have the longer time to respond afforded by waiving service.

The date of sending the request is to be inserted by the plaintiff on the face of the request for waiver and on the waiver itself. This date is used to measure the return day for the waiver form, so that the plaintiff can know on a day certain whether formal service of process will be necessary; it is also a useful date to measure the time for answer when service is waived. The defendant who returns the waiver is given additional time for answer in order to assure that it loses nothing by waiving service of process.

RULE 16

Subdivision (b). One purpose of this amendment is to provide a more appropriate deadline for the initial scheduling order required by the rule. The former rule directed that the order be entered within 120 days from the filing of the complaint. This requirement has created problems because Rule 4(m) allows 120 days for service and ordinarily at least one defendant should be available to participate in the process of formulating the scheduling order. The revision provides that the order is to be entered within 90 days after the date a defendant first appears (whether by answer or by a motion under Rule 12 or, if earlier (as may occur in some actions against the United States or if service is waived under Rule 4), within 120 days after service of the complaint on a defendant. The longer time provided by the revision is not intended to encourage unnecessary delays in entering the scheduling order. Indeed, in most cases the order can and should be entered at a much earlier date. Rather, the additional time is intended to alleviate problems in multi-defendant cases and should ordinarily be adequate to enable participation by all defendants initially named in the action.

In many cases the scheduling order can and should be entered before this deadline. However, when setting a scheduling conference, the court should take into account the effect this setting will have in establishing deadlines for the parties to meet under revised Rule 26(f) and to exchange information under revised Rule 26(a)(1). While the parties are expected to stipulate to additional time for making their disclosures when warranted by the circumstances, a scheduling conference held before defendants have had time to learn much about the case may result in diminishing the value of the Rule 26(f) meeting, the parties' proposed discovery plan, and indeed the conference itself.

New paragraph (4) has been added to highlight that it will frequently be desirable for the scheduling order to include provisions relating to the timing of disclosures under Rule 26(a). While the initial disclosures required by Rule 26(a)(1) will ordinarily have been made before entry of the scheduling order, the timing and sequence for disclosure of expert testimony and of the witnesses and exhibits to be used at trial should be tailored to the circumstances of the case and is a matter that should be considered at the initial scheduling conference. Similarly, the scheduling order might contain provisions modifying the extent of discovery (e.g., number and length of depositions) otherwise permitted under these rules or by a local rule.

The report from the attorneys concerning their meeting and proposed discovery plan, as required by revised Rule 26(f), should be submitted to the court before the scheduling order is entered. Their proposals, particularly regarding matters on which they agree, should be of substantial value to the court in setting the timing and limitations on discovery and should reduce the time of the court needed to conduct a meaningful conference under Rule 16(b). As under the prior rule, while a scheduling order is mandated, a scheduling conference is not. However, in view of the benefits to be derived from the litigants and a judicial officer meeting in person, a Rule 16(b) conference should, to the extent practicable, be held in all cases that will involve discovery.

This subdivision, as well as subdivision (c)(8), also is revised to reflect the new title of United States Magistrate Judges pursuant to the Judicial Improvements Act of 1990.

Subdivision (c). The primary purposes of the changes in subdivision (c) are to call attention to the opportunities for structuring of trial under Rules 42, 50, and 52 and to eliminate questions that have occasionally been raised regarding the authority of the court to make appropriate orders designed either to facilitate settlement or to provide for an efficient and economical trial. The prefatory language of this subdivision is revised to clarify the court's power to enter appropriate orders at a conference notwithstanding the objection of a party. Of course settlement is dependent upon agreement by the parties and, indeed, a conference is most effective and productive when the parties participate in a spirit of cooperation and mindful of their responsibilities under Rule 1.

Paragraph (4) is revised to clarify that in advance of trial the court may address the need for, and possible limitations on, the use of expert testimony under Rule 702 of the Federal Rules of Evidence. Even when proposed expert testimony might be admissible under the standards of Rules 403 and 702 of the evidence rules, the court may preclude or limit such testimony if the cost to the litigants—which may include the cost to adversaries of securing testimony on the same subjects by other experts—would be unduly expensive given the needs of the case and the other evidence available at trial.

Paragraph (5) is added (and the remaining paragraphs renumbered) in recognition that use of Rule 56 to avoid or reduce the scope of trial is a topic that can, and often should, be considered at a pretrial conference. Renumbered paragraph (11) enables the court to rule on pending motions for summary adjudication that are ripe for decision at the time of the conference. Often, however, the potential use of Rule 56 is a matter that arises from discussions during a conference. The court may then call for motions to be filed or, under revised Rule 56(g)(3), enter a show cause order that initiates the process.

Paragraph (6) is added to emphasize that a major objective of pretrial conferences should be to consider appropriate controls on the extent and timing of discovery. In many cases the court should also specify the times and sequence for disclosure of written reports from experts under revised Rule 26(a)(2)(B) and perhaps direct changes in the types of experts from whom written reports are required. Consideration should also be given to possible changes in the timing or form of the disclosure of trial witnesses and documents under Rule 26(a)(3).

Paragraph (9) is revised to describe more accurately the various procedures that, in addition to traditional settlement conferences, may be helpful in settling litigation. Even if a case cannot immediately be settled, the judge and attorneys can explore possible use of alternative procedures such as mini-trials, summary jury trials, mediation, neutral evaluation, and nonbinding arbitration that can lead to consensual resolution of the dispute without a full trial on the merits. The rule acknowledges the presence of statutes and local rules or plans that may authorize use of some of these procedures even when not agreed to by the parties. *See* 28 U.S.C. §§ 473(a)(6), 473(b)(4), 651-68; Section 104(b)(2), Pub. L. 101-650. The rule does not attempt to resolve questions as to the extent a court would be authorized to require such proceedings as an exercise of its inherent powers.

The amendment of paragraph (9) should be read in conjunction with the sentence added to the end of subdivision (c), authorizing the court to direct that, in appropriate cases, a responsible representative of the parties be present or available by telephone during a conference in order to discuss possible settlement of the case. The sentence refers to participation by a party or its representative. Whether this would be the individual party, an officer of a corporate party, a representative from an insurance carrier, or someone else would depend on the circumstances. Particularly in litigation in which governmental agencies or large amounts of money are involved, there may be no one with on-the-spot settlement authority, and the most that should be expected is access to a person who would have a major role in submitting a recommendation to the body or board with ultimate decision-making responsibility. The selection of the appropriate representative should ordinarily be left to the party and its counsel. Finally, it should be noted that the unwillingness of a party to be available, even by telephone, for a settlement conference may be a clear signal that the time and expense involved in pursuing settlement is likely to be unproductive and that personal participation by the parties should not be required.

The explicit authorization in the rule to require personal participation in the manner stated is not intended to limit the reasonable exercise of the court's inherent powers, *e.g.*, *G. Heileman Brewing Co. v. Joseph Oat Corp.*, 871 F.2d 648 (7th Cir. 1989), or its power to require party participation under the Civil Justice Reform Act of 1990. *See* 28 U.S.C. § 473(b)(5) (civil justice expense and delay reduction plans adopted by district courts may include requirement that representatives "with authority to bind [parties] in settlement discussions" be available during settlement conferences).

New paragraphs (13) and (14) are added to call attention to the opportunities for structuring of trial under Rule 42 and under revised Rules 50 and 52.

Paragraph (15) is also new. It supplements the power of the court to limit the extent of evidence under rules 403 and 611(a) of the Federal Rules of Evidence, which typically would be invoked as a result of developments during trial. Limits on the length of trial established at a conference in advance of trial can provide the parties with a better opportunity to determine priorities and exercise selectivity in presenting evidence than when limits are imposed during trial. Any such limits must be reasonable under the circumstances, and ordinarily the court should impose them only after receiving appropriate submissions from the parties outlining the nature of the testimony expected to be presented through various witnesses, and the expected duration of direct and cross-examination.

RULE 26

[Text of amended Rule, indicating changes]

Rule 26. General Provisions Governing Discovery; Duty of Disclosure

(a) Required Disclosures; ~~Discovery~~ Methods to Discover Additional Matter.

(1) Initial Disclosures. Except to the extent otherwise stipulated or directed by order or local rule, a party shall, without awaiting a discovery request, provide to other parties:

(A) the name and, if known, the address and telephone number of each individual likely to have discoverable information relevant to disputed facts alleged with particularity in the pleadings, identifying the subjects of the information;

(B) a copy of, or a description by category and location of, all documents, data compilations, and tangible things in the possession, custody, or control of the party that are relevant to disputed facts alleged with particularity in the pleadings;

(C) a computation of any category of damages claimed by the disclosing party, making available for inspection and copying as under Rule 34 the documents or other evidentiary material, not privileged or protected from disclosure, on which such computation is based, including materials bearing on the nature and extent of injuries suffered; and

(D) for inspection and copying as under Rule 34 any insurance agreement under which any person carrying on an insurance business may be liable to satisfy part or all of a judgment which may be entered in the action or to indemnify or reimburse for payments made to satisfy the judgment.

Unless otherwise stipulated or directed by the court, these disclosures shall be made at or within 10 days after the meeting of the parties under subdivision (f). A party shall make its initial disclosures based on the information then reasonably available to it and is not excused from making its disclosures because it has not fully completed its investigation of the case or because it challenges the sufficiency of another party's disclosures or because another party has not made its disclosures.

(2) Disclosure of Expert Testimony.

(A) In addition to the disclosures required by paragraph (1), a party shall disclose to other parties the identity of any person who may be used at trial to present evidence under Rules 702, 703, or 705 of the Federal Rules of Evidence.

(B) Except as otherwise stipulated or directed by the court, this disclosure shall, with respect to a witness who is retained or specially employed to provide expert testimony in the case or whose duties as an employee of the party regularly involve giving expert testimony, be accompanied by a written report prepared and signed by the witness. The report shall contain a complete statement of all opinions to be expressed and the basis and reasons therefor; the data or other information considered by the witness in forming the opinions; any exhibits to be used as a summary of or support for the opinions; the qualifications of the witness, including a list of all publications authored by the witness within the preceding ten years; the compensation to be paid for the study and testimony; and a listing of any other cases in which the witness has testified as an expert at trial or by deposition within the preceding four years.

(C) These disclosures shall be made at the times and in the sequence directed by the court. In the absence of other directions from the court or stipulation by the parties, the disclosures shall be made at least 90 days before the trial date or the date the case is to be ready for trial or, if the evidence is intended solely to contradict or rebut evidence on the same subject matter identified by another party under paragraph (2)(B), within 30 days after the disclosure made by the other party. The parties shall supplement these disclosures when required under subdivision (e)(1).

(3) Pretrial Disclosures. In addition to the disclosures required in the preceding paragraphs, a party shall provide to other parties the following information regarding the evidence that it may present at trial other than solely for impeachment purposes:

(A) the name and, if not previously provided, the address and telephone number of each witness, separately identifying those whom the party expects to present and those whom the party may call if the need arises;

(B) the designation of those witnesses whose testimony is expected to be presented by means of a deposition and, if not taken stenographically, a transcript of the pertinent portions of the deposition testimony; and

(C) an appropriate identification of each document or other exhibit, including summaries of other evidence, separately identifying htose which the party expects to offer and those which the party may offer if the need arises.

Unless otherwise directed by the court, these disclosures shall be made at least 30 days before trial. Within 14 days thereafter, unless a different time is specified by the court, a party may serve and file a list disclosing (i) any objections to the use under Rule 32(a) of a deposition designated by another party under subparagraph (B) and (ii) any objection, together with the grounds therefor, that may be made to the admissibility of materials identified under subparagraph (c). Objections not so disclosed, other than objections under Rules 402 and 403 of the Federal Rules of Evidence, shall be deemed waived unless excused by the court for good cause shown.

(4) Form of Disclosures; Filing. Unless otherwise directed by order or local rule, all disclosures under paragraphs (1) through 3) shall be made in writing, signed, served, and promptly filed with the court.

(5) Methods to Discover Additional Matter. Parties may obtain discovery by one or more of the following methods: depositions upon oral examination or written questions; written interrogatories; production of documents or things or permission to enter upon land or other property under Rule 34

171

or 45 (a)(1)(C), for inspection and other purposes; physical and mental examinations; and requests for admission.

(b) Discovery Scope and Limits. Unless otherwise limited by order of the court in accordance with these rules, the scope of discovery is as follows:

(1) In general. Parties may obtain discovery regarding any matter, not privileged, which is relevant to the subject matter involved in the pending action, whether it relates to the claim or defense of the party seeking discovery or to the claim or defense of any other party, including the existence, description, nature, custody, condition, and location of any books, documents, or other tangible things and the identity and location of persons having knowledge of any discoverable matter. It is not ground for objection that tThe information sought need not be will be inadmissible at the trial if the information sought appears reasonably calculated to lead to the discovery of admissible evidence.

(2) Limitations. By order or by local rule, the court may alter the limits in these rules on the number of depositions and interrogatories and may also limit the length of depositions under Rule 30 and the number of requests under Rule 36. The frequency or extent of use of the discovery methods set forth in subdivision (a) otherwise permitted under these rules and by any local rule shall be limited by the court if it determines that: (i) the discovery sought is unreasonably cumulative or duplicative, or is obtainable from some other source that is more convenient, less burdensome, or less expensive; (ii) the party seeking discovery has had ample opportunity by discovery in the action to obtain the information sought; or (iii) the discovery is unduly burdensome or expensive the burden or expense of the proposed discovery outweighs its likely benefit, taking into account the needs of the case, the amount in controversy, limitations on the parties' resources, and the importance of the issues at stake in the litigation, and the importance of the proposed discovery in resolving the issues. The court may act upon its own initiave after reasonable notice or pursuant to a motion under subdivision (c).

(2) Insurance agreements. A party may obtain discovery of the existence and contents of any insurance agreement under which any person carrying on an insurance business may be liable to satisfy part or all of a judgment which may be entered in the action or to indemnify or reimburse for payments made to satisfy the judgment. Information concerning the insurance agreement is not by reason of disclosure admissible in evidence at trial. For purposes of this paragraph, an application for insurance shall not be treated as part of an insurance agreement.

(3) Trial preparation: Materials. Subject to the provisions of subdivision (b)(4) of this rule, a party may obtain discovery of documents and tangible things otherwise discoverable under subdivision (b)(1) of this rule and prepared in anticipation of litigation or for trial by or for another party or by or for that other party's representative (including the other party's attorney, consultant, surety, indemnitor, insurer, or agent) only upon a showing that the party seeking discovery has substantial need of the materials in the preparation of the party's case and that the party is unable without undue hardship to obtain the substantial equivalent of the materials by other means. In ordering discovery of such materials when the required showing has been made, the court shall protect against disclosure of the mental impressions, conclusions, opinions, or legal theories of an attorney or other representative of a party concerning the litigation.

A party may obtain without the required showing a statement concerning the action or its subject matter previously made by that party. Upon request, a person not a party may obtain without the required showing a statement concerning the action or its subject matter previously made by that person. If the request is refused, the person may move for a court order. The provisions of Rule 37(a)(4) apply to the award of expenses incurred in relation to the motion. For purposes of this paragraph, a statement previously made is (A) a written statement signed or otherwise adopted or approved by the person making it, or (B) a stenographic, mechanical, electrical, or other recording, or a transcription thereof, which is a substantially verbatim recital of an oral statement by the person making it and contemporaneously recorded.

(4) Trial preparation: Experts. Discovery of facts known and opinions held by experts, otherwise discoverable under th eprovisions of subdivision (b)(1) of this rule and acquired or developed in anticipation of litigation or for trial, may be obtained only as follows:

(A) (i) A party may through interrogatories require any other party to identify each person whom the other party expects to call as an expert witness at trial, to state the subject matter on which the expert is expected to testify, and to state the substance of the facts and opinions to which the expert is expected to testify and a summary of the grounds for each opinion. (ii) Upon motion, the court may order further discovery by other means, subject to such restrictions as to scope and such provisions, pursuant to subdivision (b)(4)(C) of this rule, concerning fees and expenses as the court may deem appropriate. depose any person who has been identified as an expert whose opinions may be presented at trial. If a report is required under subdivision (a)(2)(B), the deposition shall not be conducted until after the report is provided.

(B) A party may, through interrogatories or by deposition, discover facts known or opinions held by an expert who has been retained or specially employed by another party in anticipation of litigation or preparation for trial and who is not expected to be called as a witness at trial, only as provided in Rule 35(b) or upon a showing of exceptional circumstances under which it is impracticable for the party seeking discovery to obtain facts or opinions on the same subject by other means.

(C) Unless manifest injustice would result, (i) the court shall require that the party seeking discovery pay the expert a reasonable fee for time spent in responding to discovery under this subdivisions (b)(4)(A)(ii) and (b)(4)(B) of this rule; and (ii) with respect to discovery obtained under subdivision (b)(4)(A)(ii) of this rule the court may require, and with respect to discovery obtained under subdivision (b)(4)(B) of this rule the court shall require, the party seeking discovery to pay the other party a fair portion of the fees and expenses reasonably incurred by the latter party in obtaining facts and opinions from the expert.

(5) Claims of Privilege or Protection of Trial Preparation Materials. When a party withholds information otherwise discoverable under these rules by claiming that it is privileged or subject to protection as trial preparation material, the party shall make the claim expressly and shall describe the nature of the documents, communications, or things not produced or disclosed in a manner that, without revealing information itself privileged or protected, will enable other parties to assess the applicability of the privilege or protection.

(c) Protective orders.

Upon motion by a party or by the person from whom discovery is sought, accompanied by a certification that the movant has in good faith conferred or attempted to confer with other affected parties in an effort to resolve the dispute without court action, and for good cause shown, the court in which the action is pending or alternatively, on matters relating to a deposition, the court in the district where the deposition is to be taken may make any order which justice requires to protect a party or person from annoyance, embarrassment, oppression, or undue burden or expense, including one or more of the following:

(1) that the disclosure or discovery not be had;

(2) that the disclosure or discovery may be had only on specified terms and conditions, including a designation of the time or place;

(3) that the discovery may be had only by a method of discovery other than that selected by the party seeking discovery;

(4) that certain matters not be inquired into, or that the scope of the disclosure or discovery be limited to certain matters;

(5) that discovery be conducted with no one present except persons designated by the court;

(6) that a deposition, after being sealed, be opened only by order of the court;

(7) that a trade secret or other confidential research, development, or commercial information not be disclosed revealed or be disclosed revealed only in a designated way; and

(8) that the parties simultaneously file specified documents or information enclosed in sealed envelopes to be opened as directed by the court.

If the motion for a protective order is denied in whole or in part, the court may, on such terms and conditions as are just, order that any party or other person provide or permit discovery. The provisions of Rule 37(a)(4) apply to the award of expenses incurred in relation to the motion.

(d) Sequence and Timing and Sequence of Discovery. Except when authorized under these rules or by local rule, order, or agreement of the parties, a party may not seek discovery from any source before the parties have met and conferred as required by subdivision (f). Unless the court upon motion, for the convenience of parties and witnesses and in the interests of justice, orders otherwise, methods of discovery may be used in any sequence, and the fact that a party is conducting discovery, whether by deposition or otherwise, shall not operate to delay any other party's discovery.

(e) Supplementation of Disclosures and Responses.

A party who has made a disclosure under subdivision (a) or responded to a request for discovery with a disclosure or response that was complete when made is under no a duty to supplement or correct the disclosure or response to include information thereafter acquired, except as follows if ordered by the court or in the following circumstances:

(1) A party is under a duty seasonably to supplement the response with respect to any question directly addressed to (A) the identity and location of persons having knowledge of discoverable matters, and (B) the identity of each person expected to be called as an expert witness at trial, the subject matter on which the person is expected to testify, and the substance of the person's testimony. at appropriate intervals its disclosures under subdivision (a) if the party learns that in some material respect the

information disclosed is incomplete or incorrect and if the additional or corrective information has not otherwise been made known to the other parties during the discovery process or in writing. With respect to testimony of an expert from whom a report is required under subdivision (a)(2)(B) the duty extends both to information contained in the report and to information provided through a deposition of the expert, and any additions or other changes to this information shall be disclosed by the time the party's disclosures under Rule 269a)(3) are due.

(2) A party is under a duty seasonably to amend a prior response to an interrogatory, request for production, or request for admission if the party learns ~~obtains information upon the basis of which (A) the party knows~~ that the response ~~was incorrect when made, or (B) the party knows that the response though correct when made is no longer true and the circumstances are such that a failure to amend the response is in substance a knowing concealment.~~ is in some material respect incomplete or incorrect and if the additional or corrective information has not otherwise been made known to the other parties during the discovery process or in writing.

~~(3) A duty to supplement responses may be imposed by order of the court, agreement of the parties, or at any time prior to trial through new requests for supplementation of prior responses.~~

(f) Meeting of Parties; Planning for Discovery ~~Conference~~.

~~At any time after commencement of an action the court may direct the attorneys for the parties to appear before it for a conference on the subject of discovery. The court shall do so upon motion by the attorney for any party if the motion includes~~ Except in actions exempted by local rule or when otherwise ordered, the parties shall, as soon as practicable and in any event at least 14 days before a scheduling conference is held or a scheduling order is due under Rule 16(b), meet to discuss the nature and basis of their claims and defenses and the possibilities for a prompt settlement or resolution of the case, to make or arrange for the disclosures required by subdivision (a)(1), and to develop a proposed discovery plan. The plan shall indicate the parties' views and proposals concerning:

(1) ~~A statement of the issues as they then appear~~ what changes should be made in the timing, form, or requirement for disclosures under subdivision (a) or local rule, including a statement as to when disclosures under subdivision (a)(1) were made or will be made;

(2) ~~A proposed plan and schedule of discovery~~ the subjects on which discovery may be needed, when discovery should be completed, and whether discovery should be conducted in phases or be limited to or focused upon particular issues;

(3) ~~Any limitations proposed to be placed on discovery~~ what changes should be made in the limitations on discovery imposed under these rules or by local rule, and what other limitations should be imposed; and

(4) ~~A~~any other ~~proposed~~ orders ~~with respect to discovery~~ that should be entered by the court under subdivision (c) or under Rule 16(b) and (c).~~; and~~

~~(5) A statement showing that the attorney making the motion has made a reasonable effort to reach agreement with opposing attorneys on the matters set forth in the motion. Each party and each party's attorney are under a duty to participate in good faith in the framing of a discovery plan if a plan is proposed by the attorney for any party. Notice of the motion shall be served on all parties. Objections or additions to matters set forth in the motion shall be served not later than 10 days after service of the motion.~~

The attorneys of record and all unrepresented parties that have appeared in the case are jointly responsible for arranging and being present or represented at the meeting, for attempting in good faith to agree on the proposed discovery plan, and for submitting to the court within 10 days after the meeting a written report outlining the plan. ~~Following the discovery conference, the court shall enter an order tentatively identifying the issues for discovery purposes, establishing a plan and schedule for discovery, setting limitations on discovery, if any; and determining such other matters, including the allocation of expenses, as are necessary for the proper management of discovery in the action. An order may be altered or amended whenever justice so requires.~~

~~Subject to the right of a party who properly moves for a discovery conference to prompt convening of the conference, the court may combine the discovery conference with a pretrial conference authorized by Rule 16.~~

(g) Signing of Disclosures, Discovery Requests, Responses, and Objections.

(1) Every disclosure made pursuant to subdivision (a)(1) or subdivision (a)(3) shall be signed by at least one attorney of record in the attorney's individual name, whose address shall be stated. An unrepresented party shall sign the disclosure and state the party's address. The signature of the attorney or party constitutes a certification that to the best of the signer's knowledge, information, and belief, formed after a reasonable inquiry, the disclosure is complete and correct as of the time it is made.

(2) Every discovery request, for discovery or response, or objection thereto made by a party represented by an attorney shall be signed by at least one attorney of record in the attorney's individual name, whose address shall be stated. An unrepresented party who is not represented by an attorney shall sign the request, response, or objection and state the party's address. The signature of the attorney or party constitutes a certification that the signer has read the request, response, or objection, and that to the best of the signer's knowledge, information, and belief, formed after a reasonable inquiry, it the request, response or objection is:

(1A) consistent with these rules and warranted by existing law or a good faith argument for the extension, modification, or reversal of existing law;

(2B) not interposed for any improper purpose, such as to harass or to cause unnecessary delay or needless increase in the cost of litigation; and

(3C) not unreasonable or unduly burdensome or expensive, given the needs of the case, the discovery already had in the case, the amount in controversy, and the importance of the issues at stake in the litigation.

If a request, response or objection is not signed, it shall be stricken unless it is signed promptly after the omission is called to the attention of the party making the request, response, or objection, and a party shall not be obligated to take any action with respect to it until it is signed.

(3) If without substantial justification a certification is made in violation of the rule, the court, upon motion or upon its own initiative, shall impose upon the person who made the certification, the party on whose behalf the disclosure, request, response, or objection is made, or both, an appropriate sanction, which may include an order to pay the amount of the reasonable expenses incurred because of the violation, including a reasonable attorney's fee.

* * *

Subdivision (a). Through the addition of paragraphs (1)-(4), this subdivision imposes on parties a duty to disclose, without awaiting formal discovery requests, certain basic information that is needed in most cases to prepare for trial or make an informed decision about settlement. The rule requires all parties (1) early in the case to exchange information regarding potential witnesses, documentary evidence, damages, and insurance, (2) at an appropriate time during the discovery period to identify expert witnesses and provide a detailed written statement of the testimony that may be offered at trial through specially retained experts, and (3), as the trial date approaches, to identify the particular evidence that may be offered at trial. The enumeration in Rule 26(a) of items to be disclosed does not prevent a court from requiring by order or local rule that the parties disclose additional information without a discovery request. Nor are parties precluded from using traditional discovery methods to obtain further information regarding these matters, as for example asking an expert during a deposition about testimony given in other litigation beyond the four-year period specified in Rule 26(a)(2)(B).

A major purpose of the revision is to accelerate the exchange of basic information about the case and to eliminate the paper work involved in requesting such information, and the rule should be applied in a manner to achieve those objectives. The concepts of imposing a duty of disclosure were set forth in Brazil, *The Adversary Character of Civil Discovery: A Critique and Proposals for Change*, 31 Vand. L. Rev. 1348 (1978), and Schwarzer, *The Federal Rules, the Adversary Process, and Discovery Reform*, 50 U. Pitt. L. Rev. 703, 721-23 (1989).

The rule is based upon the experience of district courts that have required disclosure of some of this information through local rules, court-approved standard interrogatories, and standing orders. Most have required pretrial disclosure of the kind of information described in Rule 26(a)(3). Many have required written reports from experts containing information like that specified in Rule 26(a)(2)(B). While far more limited, the experience of the few state and federal courts that have required pre-discovery exchange of core information such as is contemplated in Rule 26(a)(1) indicates that savings in time and expense can be achieved, particularly if the litigants meet and discuss the issues in the case as a predicate for this exchange and if a judge supports the process, as by using the results to guide further proceedings in the case. Courts in Canada and the United Kingdom have for many years required disclosure of certain information without awaiting a request from an adversary.

Paragraph (1). As the functional equivalent of court-ordered interrogatories, this paragraph requires early disclosure, without need for any request, of four types of information that have been customarily secured early in litigation through formal discovery. The introductory clause permits the court, by local rule, to exempt all or particular types of cases from these disclosure requirement or to modify the nature of the information to be disclosed. It is expected that courts would, for example, exempt cases like Social Security reviews and government collection cases in which discovery would not be appropriate or would be unlikely. By order the court may eliminate or modify the disclosure requirements in a particular case, and similarly the parties, unless precluded by order or local rule, can stipulate to elimination or modification of the requirements for that case. The disclosure obligations specified in paragraph (1) will not be appropriate for all cases, and it is expected that changes in these obligations will be made by the court or parties when the circumstances warrant.

Authorization of these local variations is, in large measure, included in order to accommodate to the Civil Justice Reform Act of 1990, which implicitly directs districts to experiment during the study period with differing procedures to reduce the time and expense of civil litigation. The civil justice delay and expense reduction plans adopted by the courts under the Act differ as to the type, form, and timing of disclosures required. Section 105(c)(1) of the Act calls for a report by the Judicial Conference to Congress by December 31, 1995, comparing experience in twenty of these courts; and section 105(c)(2)(B) contemplates that some changes in the Rules may then be needed. While these studies may indicate the desirability of further changes in Rule 26(a)(1), these changes probably could not become effective before December 1998 at the earliest. In the meantime, the present revision puts in place a series of disclosure obligations that, unless a court acts affirmatively to impose other requirements or indeed to reject all such requirements for the present, are designed to eliminate certain discovery, help focus the discovery that is needed, and facilitate preparation for trial or settlement.

Subparagraph (A) requires identification of all persons who, based on the investigation conducted thus far, are likely to have discoverable information relevant to the factual disputes between the parties. All persons with such information should be disclosed, whether or not their testimony will be supportive of the position of the disclosing party. As officers of the court, counsel are expected to disclose the identity of those persons who may be used by them as witnesses or who, if their potential testimony were known, might reasonably be expected to be deposed or called as a witness by any of the other parties. Indicating briefly the general topics on which such persons have information should not be burdensome, and will assist other parties in deciding which depositions will actually be needed.

Subparagraph (B) is included as a substitute for the inquiries routinely made about the existence and location of documents and other tangible things in the possession, custody, or control of the disclosing party. Although, unlike subdivision (a)(3)(C), an itemized listing of each exhibit is not required, the disclosure should describe and categorize, to the extent identified during the initial investigation, the nature and location of potentially relevant documents and records, including computerized data and other electronically-recorded information, sufficiently to enable opposing parties (1) to make an informed decision concerning which documents might need to be examined, at least initially, and (2) to frame their document requests in a manner likely to avoid squabbles resulting from the wording of the requests. As with potential witnesses, the requirement for disclosure of documents applies to all potentially relevant items then known to the party, whether or not supportive of its contentions in the case.

Unlike subparagraphs (C) and (D), subparagraph (B) does not require production of any documents. Of course, in cases involving few documents a disclosing party may prefer to provide copies of the documents rather than prescribe them, and the rule is written to afford this option to the disclosing party. If, as will be more typical, only the description is provided, the other parties are expected to obtain the documents desired by proceeding under Rule 34 or through informal requests. The disclosing party does not, by describing documents under subparagraph (B), waive its right to object to production on the basis of privilege or work product protection, or to assert that the documents are not sufficiently relevant to justify the burden or expense of production.

The initial disclosure requirements of subparagraphs (A) and (B) are limited to identification of potential evidence "relevant to disputed facts alleged with particularity in the pleadings." There is no need for a party to identify potential evidence with respect to allegations that are admitted. Broad, vague, and conclusory allegations sometimes tolerated in notice pleading—for example, the assertion that a product with many component parts is defective in some unspecified manner—should not impose upon responding parties the obligation at that point to search for and identify all persons possibly involved in, or all documents affecting, the design, manufacture, and assembly of the product. The greater the specificity and clarity of the allegations in the pleadings, the more complete should be the listing of potential witnesses and types of documentary evidence. Although paragraphs (1)(A) and (1)(B) by their terms refer to the factual disputes defined in the pleadings, the rule contemplates that these issues would be informally refined and clarified during the meeting of the parties under subdivision (f) and that the disclosure obligations would be adjusted in the light of these discussions. The disclosure requirements should, in short, be applied with common sense in light of the principles of Rule 1, keeping in mind the salutary purposes that the rule is intended to accomplish. The litigants should not indulge in gamesmanship with respect to the disclosure obligations.

Subparagraph (C) imposes a burden of disclosure that includes the functional equivalent of a standing Request for Production under Rule 34. A party claiming damages or other monetary relief must, in addition to disclosing the calculation of such damages, make available the supporting documents for inspection and copying as if a request for such materials had been made under Rule 34. This obligation applies only with respect to documents then reasonably available to it and not privileged or protected as work product. Likewise, a party would not be expected to provide a calculation of damages which, as in many patent infringement actions, depends on information in the possession of another party or person.

Subparagraph (D) replaces subdivision (b)(2) of Rule 26, and provides that liability insurance policies be made available for inspection and copying. The last two sentences of that subdivision have been omitted as unnecessary, not to signify any change of law. The disclosure of insurance information does not thereby render such information admissible in evidence. *See* Rule 411, Federal Rules of Evidence. Nor does subparagraph (D) require disclosure of applications for insurance, though in particular cases such information may be discoverable in accordance with revised subdivision (a)(5).

Unless the court directs a different time, the disclosures required by subdivision (a)(1) are to be made at or within 10 days after the meeting of the parties under subdivision (f). One of the purposes of this meeting is to refine the factual disputes with respect to which disclosures should be made under paragraphs (1)(A) and (1)(B), particularly if an answer has not been filed by a defendant, or, indeed, to afford the parties an opportunity to modify by stipulation the timing or scope of these obligations. The time of this meeting is generally left to the parties provided it is held at least 14 days before a scheduling conference is held or before a scheduling order is due under Rule 16(b). In cases in which no scheduling conference is held, this will mean that the meeting must ordinarily be held within 75 days after a defendant has first appeared in the case and hence that the initial disclosures would be due no later than 85 days after the first appearance of a defendant.

Before making its disclosures, a party has the obligation under subdivision (g)(1) to make a reasonable inquiry into the facts of the case. The rule does not demand an exhaustive investigation at this stage of the case, but one that is reasonable under the circumstances, focusing on the facts that are alleged with particularity in the pleadings. The type of investigation that can be expected at this point will vary based upon such factors as the number and complexity of the issues; the location, nature, number, and availability of potentially relevant witnesses and documents; the extent of past working relationships between the attorney and the client, particularly in handling related or similar litigation; and of course how long the party has to conduct an investigation, either before or after filing of the case. As provided in the last sentence of subdivision (a)(1), a party is not excused from the duty of disclosure merely because its investigation is incomplete. The party should make its initial disclosures based on the pleadings and the information then reasonably available to it. As its investigation continues and as the issues in the pleadings are clarified, it should supplement its disclosures as required by subdivision (e)(1). A party is not relieved from its obligation of disclosure merely because another party has not made its disclosures or has made an inadequate disclosure.

It will often be desirable, particularly if the claims made in the complaint are broadly stated, for the parties to have their Rule 26(f) meeting early in the case, perhaps before a defendant has answered the complaint or had time to conduct other than a cursory investigation. In such circumstances, in order to facilitate more meaningful and useful initial disclosures, they can and should stipulate to a period of more than 10 days after the meeting in which to make these disclosures, at least for defendants who had no advance notice of the potential litigation. A stipulation at an early meeting affording such a defendant at least 60 days after receiving the complaint in which to make its disclosures under subdivision (a)(1) — a period that is two weeks longer than the time formerly specified for responding to interrogatories served with a complaint — should be adequate and appropriate in most cases.

Paragraph (2). This paragraph imposes an additional duty to disclose information regarding expert testimony sufficiently in advance of trial that opposing parties have a reasonable opportunity to prepare for effective cross examination and perhaps arrange for expert testimony from other witnesses. Normally the court should prescribe a time for these disclosures in a scheduling order under Rule 16(b), and in most cases the party with the burden of proof on an issue should disclose its expert testimony on that issue before other parties are required to make their disclosures with respect to that issue. In the absence of such a direction, the disclosures are to be made by all parties at least 90 days before the trial date or the date by which the case is to be ready for trial, except that an additional 30 days is allowed (unless the court specifies another time) for disclosure of expert testimony to be used solely to contradict or rebut the testimony that may be presented by another party's expert. For a discussion of procedures that have been used to enhance the reliability of expert testimony, *see* M. Graham, *Expert Witness Testimony and the Federal Rules of Evidence: Insuring Adequate Assurance of Trustworthiness*, 1986 U. Ill. L. Rev. 90.

Paragraph (2)(B) requires that persons retained or specially employed to provide expert testimony, or whose duties as an employee of the party regularly involve the giving of expert testimony, must prepare a detailed and complete written report, stating the testimony the witness is expected to present during direct examination, together with the reasons therefor. The information disclosed under the former rule in answering interrogatories about the "substance" of expert testimony was frequently so sketchy and vague that it rarely dispensed with the need to depose the expert and often was even of little help in preparing for a deposition of the witness. Revised Rule 37(c)(1) and revised Rule 702 of the Federal Rules of Evidence provide an incentive for full disclosure; namely, that a party will not ordinarily be permitted to use on direct examination any expert testimony not so disclosed. Rule 26(a)(2)(B) does not preclude counsel from providing assistance to experts in preparing the reports, and indeed, with experts such as automobile mechanics, this assistance may be needed. Nevertheless, the report, which is intended to set forth the substance of the direct examination, should be written in a manner that reflects the testimony to be given by the witness and it must be signed by the witness.

The report is to disclose the data and other information considered by the expert and any exhibits or charts and summarize or support the expert's opinions. Given this obligation of disclosure, litigants should no longer be able to argue that materials furnished to their experts to be used in forming their opinions—whether or not ultimately relied upon by the expert—are privileged or otherwise protected from disclosure when such persons are testifying or being deposed.

Revised subdivision (b)(3)(A) authorizes the deposition of expert witnesses. Since depositions of experts required to prepare a written report may be taken only after the report has been served, the length of the deposition of such experts should be reduced, and in many cases the report may eliminate the need for a deposition. Revised subdivision (e)(1) requires disclosure of any material changes made in the opinions of an expert from whom a report is required, whether the changes are in the written report or in testimony given at a deposition.

For convenience, this rule and revised Rule 30 continue to use the term "expert" to refer to those persons who will testify under Rule 702 of the Federal Rules of Evidence with respect to scientific, technical, and other specialized matters. The requirement of a written report in paragraph (2)(B), however, applies only to those experts who are retained or specially employed to provide such testimony in the case or whose duties as an employee of a party regularly involve the giving of such testimony. A treating physician, for example, can be deposed or called to testify at trial without any requirement for a written report. By local rule, order, or written stipulation, the requirement of a written report may be waived for particular experts or imposed upon additional persons who will provide opinions under Rule 702.

Paragraph (3). This paragraph imposes an additional duty to disclose, without any request, information customarily needed in final preparation for trial. These disclosures are to be made in accordance with schedules adopted by the court under Rule 16(b) or by special order. If no such schedule is directed by the court, the disclosures are to be made at least 30 days before commencement of the trial. By its terms, Rule 26(a)(3) does not require disclosure of evidence to be used solely for impeachment purposes; however, disclosure of such evidence—as well as other items relating to conduct of trial—may be required by local rule or a pretrial order.

Subparagraph (A) requires the parties to designate the persons whose testimony they may present as substantive evidence at trial, whether in person or by deposition. Those who will probably be called as witnesses should be listed separately from those who are not likely to be called but who are being listed in order to preserve the right to do so if needed because of developments during trial. Revised Rule 37(c)(1) provides that only persons so listed may be used at trial to present substantive evidence. This restriction does not apply unless the omission was "without substantial justification" and hence would not bar an unlisted witness if the need for such testimony is based upon developments during trial that could not reasonably have been anticipated—e.g., a change of testimony.

Listing a witness does not obligate the party to secure the attendance of the person at trial, but should preclude the party from objecting if the person is called to testify by another party who did not list the person as a witness.

Subparagraph (B) requires the party to indicate which of these potential witnesses will be presented by deposition at trial. A party expecting to use at trial a deposition not recorded by stenographic means is required by revised Rule 32 to provide the court with a transcript of the pertinent portions of such depositions. This rule requires that copies of the transcript of a nonstenographic deposition be provided to other parties in advance of trial for verification, an obvious concern since counsel often utilize their own personnel to prepare transcripts from audio or video tapes. By order or local rule, the court may require that parties designate the particular portions of stenographic depositions to be used at trial.

Subparagraph (C) requires disclosure of exhibits, including summaries (whether to be offered in lieu of other documentary evidence or to be used as an aid in understanding such evidence), that may be offered as substantive evidence. The rule requires a separate listing of each such exhibit, though it should permit voluminous items of a similar or standardized character to be described by meaningful categories. For example, unless the court has otherwise directed, a series of vouchers might be shown collectively as a single exhibit with their starting and ending dates. As with witnesses, the exhibits that will probably be offered are to be listed separately from those which are unlikely to be offered but which are listed in order to preserve the right to do so if needed because of developments during trial. Under revised Rule 37(c)(1) the court can permit use of unlisted documents the need for which could not reasonably have been anticipated in advance of trial.

Upon receipt of these final pretrial disclosures, other parties have 14 days (unless a different time is specified by the court) to disclose any objections they wish to preserve to the usability of the deposition testimony or to the admissibility of the documentary evidence (other than under Rules 402 and 403 of the Federal Rules of Evidence). Similar provisions have become commonplace either in pretrial orders or by local rules, and significantly expedite the presentation of evidence at trial, as well as eliminate the need to have available witnesses to provide "foundation" testimony for most items of documentary evidence. The listing of a potential objection does not constitute the making of that objection or require the court to rule on the objection; rather, it preserves the right of the party to make the objection when and as appropriate during trial. The court may, however, elect to treat the listing as a motion "in limine" and rule upon the objections in advance of trial to the extent appropriate.

The time specified in the rule for the final pretrial disclosures is relatively close to the trial date. The objective is to eliminate the time and expense in making these disclosures of evidence and objections in those cases that settle shortly before trial, while affording a reasonable time for final preparation for trial in those cases that do not settle. In many cases, it will be desirable for the court in a scheduling or pretrial order to set an earlier time for disclosures of evidence and provide more time for disclosing potential objections.

Paragraph (4). This paragraph prescribes the form of disclosures. A signed written statement is required, reminding the parties and counsel of the solemnity of the obligations imposed; and the signature on the initial or pretrial disclosure is a certification under subdivision (g)(1) that it is complete and correct as of the time when made. Consistent with Rule 5(d), these disclosures are to be filed with the court unless otherwise directed. It is anticipated that many courts will direct that expert reports required under paragraph (2)(B) not be filed until needed in connection with a motion or for trial.

Paragraph (5). This paragraph is revised to take note of the availability of revised Rule 45 for inspection for non-parties of documents and premises without the need for a deposition.

Subdivision (b). This subdivision is revised in several respects. First, former paragraph (1) is subdivided into two paragraphs for ease of reference and to avoid renumbering of paragraphs (3) and (4). Textual changes are then made in new paragraph (2) to enable the court to keep tighter rein on the extent of discovery. The information explosion of recent decades has greatly increased both the potential cost of wide-ranging discovery and the potential for discovery to be used as an instrument for delay or oppression. Amendments to Rules 30, 31, and 33 place presumptive limits on the number of depositions and interrogatories, subject to leave of court to pursue additional discovery. The revisions in Rule 26(b)(2) are intended to provide the court with broader discretion to impose additional restrictions on the scope and extent of discovery and to authorize courts that develop case tracking systems based on the complexity of cases to increase or decrease by local rule the presumptive number of depositions and interrogatories allowed in particular types or classifications of cases. The revision also dispels any doubt as to the power of the court to impose limitations on the length of depositions under Rule 30 or on the number of requests for admission under Rule 36.

Second, former paragraph (2), relating to insurance, has been relocated as part of the required initial disclosures under subdivision (a)(1)(D), and revised to provide for disclosure of the policy itself.

Third, paragraph (4)(A) is revised to provide that experts who are expected to be witnesses will be subject to deposition prior to trial, conforming the norm stated in the rule to the actual practice followed in most courts, in which depositions of experts have become standard. Concerns regarding the expense of such depositions should be mitigated by the fact that the expert's fees for the deposition will ordinarily be borne by the party taking the deposition. The requirement under subdivision (a)(2)(B) of a complete and detailed report of the expected testimony of certain forensic experts may, moreover, eliminate the need for some such depositions or at least reduce the length of the depositions. Accordingly, the deposition of an expert required by subdivision (a)(2)(B) to provide a written report may be taken only after the report has been served....

Paragraph (5) is a new provision. A party must notify other parties if it is withholding materials otherwise subject to disclosure under the rule or pursuant to a discovery request because it is asserting a claim of privilege or work product production. To withhold materials without such notice is contrary to the rule, subjects the party to sanctions under Rule 37(b)(2), and may be viewed as a waiver of the privilege or protection.

The party must also provide sufficient information to enable other parties to evaluate the applicability of the claimed privilege or protection. Although the person from whom the discovery is sought decides whether to claim a privilege or protection, the court ultimately decides whether, if this claim is challenged, the privilege or protection applies. Providing information pertinent to the applicability of the privilege or protection should reduce the need for in camera examination of the documents.

The rule does not attempt to define for each case what information must be provided when a party asserts a claim of privilege or work product protection. Details concerning time, persons, general subject matter, etc., may be appropriate if only a few items are withheld, but may be unduly burdensome when voluminous documents are claimed to be privileged or protected, particularly if the items can be described by categories. A party can seek relief through a protective order under subdivision (c) if compliance with the requirement for providing this information would be an unreasonable burden. In rare circumstances some of the pertinent information affecting applicability of the claim, such as the identity of the client, may itself be privileged; the rule provides that such information need not be disclosed.

The obligation to provide pertinent information concerning withheld privileged materials applies only to items "otherwise discoverable." If a broad discovery request is made—for example, for all documents of a particular type during a twenty year period—and the responding party believes in good faith that production of documents for more than the past three years would be unduly burdensome, it should make its objection to the breadth of the request and, with respect to the documents generated in that three year period, produce the unprivileged documents and describe those withheld under the claim of privilege. If the court later rules that documents for a seven year period are properly discoverable, the documents for the additional four years should then be either produced (if not privileged) or described (if claimed to be privileged).

Subdivision (c). The revision requires that before filing a motion for a protective order the movant must confer—either in person or by telephone—with the other affected parties in a good faith effort to resolve the discovery dispute without the need for court intervention. If the movant is unable to get opposing parties even to discuss the matter, the efforts in attempting to arrange such a conference should be indicated in the certificate.

Subdivision (d). This subdivision is revised to provide that formal discovery—as distinguished from interviews of potential witnesses and other informal discovery—not commence until the parties have met and conferred as required by subdivision (f). Discovery can begin earlier if authorized under Rule 30(a)(2)(C) (deposition of person about to leave the country) or by local rule, order, or stipulation. This will be appropriate in some cases, such as those involving requests for a preliminary injunction or motions challenging personal jurisdiction. If a local rule exempts any types of cases in which discovery may be needed from the requirement of a meeting under Rule 26(f), it should specify when discovery may commence in those cases.

The meeting of counsel is to take place as soon as practicable and in any event at least 14 days before the date of the scheduling conference under Rule 16(b) or the date a scheduling order is due under Rule 16(b). The court can assure that discovery is not unduly delayed either by entering a special order or by setting the case for a scheduling conference.

Subdivision (e). This subdivision is revised to provide that the requirement for supplementation applies to all disclosures required by subdivisions (a)(1)-(3). Like the former rule, the duty, while imposed on a "party," applies whether the corrective information is learned by the client or by the attorney. Supplementations need not be made as each new item of information is learned but should be made at appropriate intervals during the discovery period, and with special promptness as the trial date approaches. It may be useful for the scheduling order to specify the time or times when supplementations should be made.

The revision also clarifies that the obligation to supplement responses to formal discovery requests applies to interrogatories, requests for production, and requests for admissions, but not ordinarily to deposition testimony. However, with respect to experts from whom a written report is required under subdivision (a)(2)(B), changes in the opinions expressed by the expert whether in the report or at a subsequent deposition are subject to a duty of supplemental disclosure under subdivision (e)(1).

The obligation to supplement disclosures and discovery responses applies whenever a party learns that its prior disclosures or responses are in some material respect incomplete or incorrect. There is, however, no obligation to provide supplemental or corrective information that has been otherwise made known to the parties in writing or during the discovery process, as when a witness not previously disclosed is identified during the taking of a deposition or when an expert during a deposition corrects information contained in an earlier report.

Subdivision (f). This subdivision was added in 1980 to provide a party threatened with abusive discovery with a special means for obtaining judicial intervention other than through discrete motions under Rules 26(c) and 37(a). The amendment envisioned a two-step process: first, the parties would attempt to frame a mutually agreeable plan; second, the court would hold a "discovery conference" and then enter an order establishing a schedule and limitations for the conduct of discovery. It was contemplated that the procedure, an elective one triggered on request of a party, would be used in special cases rather than as a routine matter. As expected, the device has been used only sparingly in most courts, and judicial controls over the discovery process have ordinarily been imposed through scheduling orders under Rule 16(b) or through rulings on discovery motions.

The provisions relating to a conference with the court are removed from subdivision (f). This change does not signal any lessening of the importance of judicial supervision. Indeed, there is a greater need for early judicial involvement to consider the scope and timing of the disclosure requirements of Rule 26(a) and the presumptive limits on discovery imposed under these rules or by local rules. Rather, the change is made because the provisions addressing the use of conferences with the court to control discovery are more properly included in Rule 16, which is being revised to highlight the court's powers regarding the discovery process.

The desirability of some judicial control of discovery can hardly be doubted. Rule 16, as revised, requires that the court set a time for completion of discovery and authorizes various other orders affecting the scope, timing, and extent of discovery and disclosures. Before entering such orders, the court should consider the views of the parties, preferably by means of a conference, but at the least through written submissions. Moreover, it is desirable that the parties' proposals regarding discovery be developed through a process where they meet in person, informally explore the nature and basis of the issues, and discuss how discovery can be conducted most efficiently and economically.

As noted above, former subdivision (f) envisioned the development of proposed discovery plans as an optional procedure to be used in relatively few cases. The revised rule directs that in all cases not exempted by local rule or special order the litigants must meet in person and plan for discovery. Following this meeting, the parties submit to the court their proposals for a discovery plan and can begin formal discovery. Their report will assist the court in seeing that the timing and scope of disclosures under revised Rule 26(a) and the limitations on the extent of discovery under these rules and local rules are tailored to the circumstances of the particular case.

To assure that the court has the litigants' proposals before deciding on a scheduling order and that the commencement of discovery is not delayed unduly, the rule provides that the meeting of the parties take place as soon as practicable and in any event at least 14 days before a scheduling conference is held or before a scheduling order is due under Rule 16(b). (Rule 16(b) requires that a scheduling order be entered within 90 days after the first appearance of a defendant or, if earlier, within 120 days after the complaint has been served on any defendant.) The obligation to participate in the planning process is imposed on all parties that have appeared in the case, including defendants who, because of a pending Rule 12 motion, may not have yet filed an answer in the case. Each such party should attend the meeting, either through one of its attorneys or in person if unrepresented. If more parties are joined or appear after the initial meeting, an additional meeting may be desirable.

Subdivision (f) describes certain matters that should be accomplished at the meeting and included in the proposed discovery plan. This listing does not exclude consideration of other subjects, such as the time when any dispositive motions should be filed and when the case should be ready for trial.

The parties are directed under subdivision (a)(1) to make the disclosures required by that subdivision at or within 10 days after this meeting. In many cases the parties should use the meeting to exchange, discuss, and clarify their respective disclosures. In other cases, it may be more useful if the disclosures are delayed until after the parties have discussed at the meeting the claims and defenses in order to define the issues with respect to which the initial disclosures should be made. As discussed in the Notes to subdivision (a)(1), the parties may also need to consider whether a stipulation extending this 10-day period would be appropriate, as when a defendant would otherwise have less than 60 days after being served in which to make its initial disclosure. The parties should also discuss at the meeting what additional information, although not subject to the disclosure requirements, can be made available informally without the necessity for formal discovery requests.

The report is to be submitted to the court within 10 days after the meeting and should not be difficult to prepare. In most cases counsel should be able to agree that one of them will be responsible for its preparation and submission to the court. Form 35 has been added in the Appendix to the Rules, both to illustrate the type of report that is contemplated and to serve as a checklist for the meeting.

The litigants are expected to attempt in good faith to agree on the contents of the proposed discovery plan. If they cannot agree on all aspects of the plan, their report to the court should indicate the competing proposals of the parties on those items, as well as the matters on which they agree. Unfortunately, there may be cases in which, because of disagreements about time or place or for other reasons, the meeting is not attended by all parties or, indeed, no meeting takes place. In such situations, the report — or reports — should describe the circumstances and the court may need to consider sanctions under Rule 37(g).

By local rule or special order, the court can exempt particular cases or types of cases from the meet-and-confer requirement of subdivision (f). In general this should include any types of cases which are exempted by local rule from the requirement for a scheduling order under Rule 16(b), such as cases in which there will be no discovery (e.g., bankruptcy appeals and reviews of social security determinations). In addition, the court may want to exempt cases in which discovery is rarely needed (e.g., government collection cases and proceedings to enforce administrative summonses) or in which a meeting of the parties might be impracticable (e.g,. actions by unrepresented prisoners). Note that if a court exempts from the requirements for a meeting any types of cases in which discovery may be needed, it should indicate when discovery may commence in those cases.

RULE 28

This revision is intended to make effective use of the Hague Convention on the Taking of Evidence Abroad in Civil or Commercial Matters, and of any similar treaties that the United States may enter into in the future which provide procedures for taking depositions abroad. The party taking the deposition is ordinarily obliged to conform to an applicable treaty or convention if an effective deposition can be taken by such internationally approved means, even though a verbatim transcript is not available or testimony cannot be taken under oath. For a discussion of the impact of such treaties upon the discovery process, and of the application of principles of comity upon discovery in countries not signatories to a convention, *see* *Societe Nationale Industrielle Aerospatiale v. United States District Court*, 482 U.S. 522 (1987).

The term "letter of request" has been substituted in the rule for the term "letter rogatory" because it is the primary method provided by the Hague Convention. A letter rogatory is essentially a form of letter of request. There are several other minor changes that are designed merely to carry out the intent of the other alterations.

RULE 29

This rule is revised to give greater opportunity for litigants to agree upon modifications to the procedures governing discovery or to limitations upon discovery. Counsel are encouraged to agree on less expensive and time-consuming methods to obtain information, as through voluntary exchange of documents, use of interviews in lieu of depositions, etc. Likewise, when more depositions or interrogatories are needed than allowed under these rules or when more time is needed to complete a deposition than allowed under a local rule, they can, by agreeing to the additional discovery, eliminate the need for a special motion addressed to the court.

Under the revised rule, the litigants ordinarily are not required to obtain the court's approval of these stipulations. By order or local rule, the court can, however, direct that its approval be obtained for particular types of stipulations; and, in any event, approval must be obtained if a stipulation to extend the 30-day period for responding to interrogatories, requests for production, or requests for admissions would interfere with dates set by the court for completing discovery, for hearing of a motion, or for trial.

RULE 30

Subdivision (a). ...Paragraph (2) collects all provisions bearing on requirements of leave of court to take a deposition.

Paragraph (2)(A) is new. It provides a limit on the number of depositions the parties may take, absent leave of court or stipulation with the other parties. One aim of this revision is to assure judicial review under the standards stated in Rule 26(b)(2) before any side will be allowed to take more than ten depositions in a case without agreement of the other parties. A second objective is to emphasize that counsel have a professional obligation to develop a mutual cost-effective plan for discovery in the case. Leave to take additional depositions should be granted when consistent with the principles of Rule 26(b)(2), and in some cases the ten-per-side limit should be reduced in accordance with those same principles. Consideration should ordinarily be given at the planning meeting of the parties under Rule 26(f) and at the time of a scheduling conference under Rule 16(b) as to enlargements or reductions in the number of depositions, eliminating the need for special motions.

A deposition under Rule 30(b)(6) should, for purposes of this limit, be treated as a single deposition even though more than one person may be designated to testify.

In multi-party cases, the parties on any side are expected to confer and agree as to which depositions are most needed, given the presumptive limit on the number of depositions they can take without leave of court. If these disputes cannot be amicably resolved, the court can be requested to resolve the dispute or permit additional depositions.

Paragraph (2)(B) is new. It requires leave of court if any witness is to be deposed in the action more than once. This requirement does not apply when a deposition is temporarily recessed for convenience of counsel or the deponent or to enable additional materials to be gathered before resuming the deposition. If significant travel costs would be incurred to resume the deposition, the parties should consider the feasibility of conducting the balance of the examination by telephonic means.

Paragraph (2)(C) revises the second sentence of the former subdivision (a) as to when depositions may be taken. Consistent with the changes made in Rule 26(d), providing that formal discovery ordinarily not commence until after the litigants have met and conferred as directed in revised Rule 26(f), the rule requires leave of court or agreement of the parties if a deposition is to be taken before that time (except when a witness is about to leave the country).

Subdivision (b). The primary change in subdivision (b) is that parties will be authorized to record deposition testimony by nonstenographic means without first having to obtain permission of the court or agreement from other counsel....

New paragraph (2) confers on the party taking the deposition the choice of the method of recording, without the need to obtain prior court approval for one taken other than stenographically. A party choosing to record a deposition only by videotape or audiotape should understand that a transcript will be required by Rule 26(a)(3)(B) and Rule 32(c) if the deposition is later to be offered as evidence at trial or on a dispositive motion under Rule 56. Objections to the nonstenographic recording of a deposition, when warranted by the circumstances, can be presented to the court under Rule 26(c).

Paragraph (3) provides that other parties may arrange, at their own expense, for the recording of a deposition by a means (stenographic, visual, or sound) in addition to the method designated by the person noticing the deposition. The former provisions of this paragraph, relating to the court's power to change the date of a deposition, have been eliminated as redundant in view of Rule 26(c)(2).

Revised paragraph (4) requires that all depositions be recorded by an officer designated or appointed under Rule 28 and contains special provisions designed to provide basic safeguards to assure the utility and integrity of recordings taken other than stenographically.

Paragraph (7) is revised to authorize the taking of a deposition not only by telephone but also by other remote electronic means, such as satellite television, when agreed to by the parties or authorized by the court.

Subdivision (c). ...[T]he revision addresses a recurring problem as to whether other potential deponents can attend a deposition. Courts have disagreed, some holding that witnesses should be excluded through invocation of Rule 61 of the evidence rules, and others holding that witnesses may attend unless excluded by an order under Rule 26(c)(5). The revision provides that other witnesses are not automatically excluded from a deposition simply by the request of a party. Exclusion, however, can be ordered under Rule 26(c)(5) when appropriate; and, if exclusion is ordered, consideration should be given as to whether the excluded witnesses likewise should be precluded from reading, or being otherwise informed about, the testimony given in the earlier depositions. The revision addresses only the matter of attendance by potential deponents, and does not attempt to resolve issues concerning attendance by others, such as members of the public or press.

Subdivision (d). The first sentence of new paragraph (1) provides that any objections during a deposition must be made concisely and in a non-argumentative and non-suggestive manner. Depositions frequently have been unduly prolonged, if not unfairly frustrated, by lengthy objections and colloquy, often suggesting how the deponent should respond. While objections may, under the revised rule, be made during a deposition, they ordinarily should be limited to those that under Rule 32(d)(3) might be waived if not made at that time, i.e., objections on grounds that might be immediately obviated, removed, or cured, such as to the form of a question or the responsiveness of an answer. Under Rule 32(b), other objections can, even without the so-called "usual stipulation" preserving objections, be raised for the first time at trial and therefore should be kept to a minimum during a deposition.

Directions to a deponent not to answer a question can be even more disruptive than objections. The second sentence of new paragraph (1) prohibits such directions except in the three circumstances indicated: to claim a privilege or protection against disclosure (e.g., as work product), to enforce a court directive limiting the scope or length of permissible discovery, or to suspend a deposition to enable presentation of a motion under paragraph (3).

Paragraph (2) is added to this subdivision to dispel any doubts regarding the power of the court by order or local rule to establish limits on the length of depositions. The rule also explicitly authorizes the court to impose the cost resulting from obstructive tactics that unreasonably prolong a deposition on the person engaged in such obstruction. This sanction may be imposed on a non-party witness as well as a party or attorney, but is otherwise congruent with Rule 26(g).

It is anticipated that limits on the length of depositions prescribed by local rules would be presumptive only, subject to modification by the court or by agreement of the parties. Such modifications typically should be discussed by the parties in their meeting under Rule 26(f) and included in the scheduling order required by Rule 16(b). Additional time, moreover, should be allowed under the revised rule when justified under the principles stated in Rule 26(b)(2). To reduce the number of special motions, local rules should ordinarily permit—and indeed encourage—the parties to agree to additional time, as when, during the taking of a deposition, it becomes clear that some additional examination is needed.

Paragraph (3) authorizes appropriate sanctions not only when a deposition is unreasonably prolonged, but also when an attorney engages in other practices that improperly frustrate the fair examination of the deponent, such as making improper objections or giving directions not to answer prohibited by paragraph (1). In general, counsel should not engage in any conduct during a deposition that would not be allowed in the presence of a judicial officer. The making of an excessive number of unnecessary objections may itself constitute sanctionable conduct, as may the refusal of an attorney to agree with other counsel on a fair apportionment of the time allowed for examination of a deponent or a refusal to agree to a reasonable request for some additional time to complete a deposition, when that is permitted by the local rule or order.

Subdivision (e). Various changes are made in this subdivision to reduce problems sometimes encountered when depositions are taken stenographically. Reporters frequently have difficulties obtaining signatures—and the return of depositions—from deponents. Under the revision pre-filing review by the deponent is required only if requested before the deposition is completed. If review is requested, the deponent will be allowed 30 days to review the transcript or recording and to indicate any changes in form or substance. Signature of the deponent will be required only if review is requested and changes are made.

Subdivision (f). Minor changes are made in this subdivision to reflect those made in subdivision (b). In courts which direct that depositions not be automatically filed, the reporter can transmit the transcript or recording to the attorney taking the deposition (or ordering the transcript or record), who then becomes custodian for the court of the original record of the deposition. Pursuant to subdivision (f)(2), as under the prior rule, any other party is entitled to secure a copy of the deposition from the officer designated to take the deposition; accordingly, unless ordered or agreed, the officer must retain a copy of the recording or the stenographic notes.

RULE 33

The purpose of this revision is to reduce the frequency and increase the efficiency of interrogatory practice. The revision is based on experience with local rules. For ease of reference, subdivision (a) is divided into two subdivisions and the remaining subdivisions renumbered.

Subdivision (a). Revision of this subdivision limits interrogatory practice. Because Rule 26(a)(1)-(3) requires disclosure of much of the information previously obtained by this form of discovery, there should be less occasion to use it. Experience in over half of the district courts has confirmed that limitations on the number of interrogatories are useful and manageable. Moreover, because the device can be costly and may be used as a means of harassment, it is desirable to subject its use to the control of the court consistent with the principles stated in Rule 26(b)(2), particularly in multi-party cases where it has not been unusual for the same interrogatory to be propounded to a party by more than one of its adversaries.

Each party is allowed to serve 25 interrogatories upon any other party, but must secure leave of court (or a stipulation from the opposing party) to serve a larger number. Parties cannot evade this presumptive limitation through the device of joining as "subparts" questions that seek information about discrete separate subjects. However, a question asking about communications of a particular type should be treated as a single interrogatory even though it requests that the time, place, persons present, and contents be stated separately for each such communication.

As with the number of depositions authorized by Rule 30, leave to serve additional interrogatories is to be allowed when consistent with Rule 26(b)(2). The aim is not to prevent needed discovery, but to provide judicial scrutiny before parties make potentially excessive use of this discovery device. In many cases it will be appropriate for the court to permit a larger number of interrogatories in the scheduling order entered under Rule 16(b)....

When a case with outstanding interrogatories exceeding the number permitted by this rule is removed to federal court, the interrogating party must seek leave allowing the additional interrogatories, specify which twenty-five are to be answered, or resubmit interrogatories that comply with the rule. Moreover, under Rule 26(d), the time for response would be measured from the date of the parties' meeting under Rule 26(f). *See* Rule 81(c), providing that these rules govern procedures after removal.

Subdivision (b). A separate subdivision is made of the former second paragraph of subdivision (a). Language is added to paragraph (1) of this subdivision to emphasize the duty of the responding party to provide full answers to the extent not objectionable. If, for example, an interrogatory seeking information about numerous facilities or products is deemed objectionable, but an interrogatory seeking information about a lesser number of facilities or products would not have been objectionable, the interrogatory should be answered with respect to the latter even though an objection is raised as to the balance of the facilities or products. Similarly, the fact that additional time may be needed to respond to some questions (or to some aspects of questions) should not justify a delay in responding to those questions (or other aspects of questions) that can be answered within the prescribed time.

Paragraph (4) is added to make clear that objections must be specifically justified, and that unstated or untimely grounds for objection ordinarily are waived. Note also the provisions of revised Rule 26(b)(5), which require a responding party to indicate when it is withholding information under a claim of privilege or as trial preparation materials.

These provisions should be read in light of Rule 26(g), authorizing the court to impose sanctions on a party and attorney making an unfounded objection to an interrogatory.

RULE 37

Subdivision (a). ... Pursuant to new subdivision (a)(2)(A), a party dissatisfied with the disclosure made by an opposing party may under this rule move for an order to compel disclosure. In providing for such a motion, the revised rule parallels the provisions of the former rule dealing with failures to answer particular interrogatories. Such a motion may be needed when the information to be disclosed might be helpful to the party seeking the disclosure but not to the party required to make the disclosure. If the party required to make the disclosure would need the material to support its own contentions, the more effective enforcement of the disclosure requirement will be to exclude the evidence not disclosed, as provided in subdivision (c)(1) of this revised rule.

Language is included in the new paragraph and added to the subparagraph (B) that requires litigants to seek to resolve discovery disputes by informal means before filing a motion with the court. This requirement is based on successful experience with similar local rules of court promulgated pursuant to Rule 83....

Under revised paragraph (3), evasive or incomplete disclosures and responses to interrogatories and production requests are treated as failures to disclose or respond. Interrogatories and requests for production should not be read or interpreted in an artificially restrictive or hypertechnical manner to avoid disclosure of information fairly covered by the discovery request, and to do so is subject to appropriate sanctions under subdivision (a).

Revised paragraph (4) is divided into three subparagraphs for ease of reference, and in each the phrase "after opportunity for hearing" is changed to "after affording an opportunity to be heard" to make clear that the court can consider such questions on written submissions as well as on oral hearings.

Subparagraph (A) is revised to cover the situation where information that should have been produced without a motion to compel is produced after the motion is filed but before it is brought on for hearing.

The rule also is revised to provide that a party should not be awarded its expenses for filing a motion that could have been avoided by conferring with opposing counsel.

Subparagraph (C) is revised to include the provision that formerly was contained in subdivision (a)(2) and to include the same requirement of an opportunity to be heard that is specified in subparagraphs (A) and (B).

Subdivision (c). The revision provides a self-executing sanction for failure to make a disclosure required by Rule 26(a), without need for a motion under subdivision (a)(2)(A).

Paragraph (1) prevents a party from using as evidence any witnesses or information that, without substantial justification, has not been disclosed as required by Rules 26(a) and 26(e)(1). This automatic sanction provides a strong inducement for disclosure of material that the disclosing party would expect to use as evidence, whether at a trial, at a hearing, or on a motion, such as one under Rule 56. As disclosure of evidence offered solely for impeachment purposes is not required under those rules, this preclusion sanction likewise does not apply to that evidence.

Limiting the automatic sanction to violations "without substantial justification," coupled with the exception for violations that are "harmless," is needed to avoid unduly harsh penalties in a variety of situations: e.g., the inadvertent omission from a Rule 26(a)(1)(A) disclosure of the name of a potential witness known to all parties; the failure to list as a trial witness a person so listed by another party; or the lack of knowledge of a pro se litigant of the requirement to make disclosures. In the latter situation, however, exclusion would be proper if the requirement for disclosure had been called to the litigant's attention by either the court or another party.

Preclusion of evidence is not an effective incentive to compel disclosure of information that, being supportive of the position of the opposing party, might advantageously be concealed by the disclosing party. However, the rule provides the court with a wide range of other sanctions—such as declaring specified facts to be established, preventing contradictory evidence, or, like spoliation of evidence, allowing the jury to be informed of the fact of nondisclosure—that, though not self-executing, can be imposed when found to be warranted after a hearing. The failure to identify a witness or document in a disclosure statement would be admissible under the Federal Rules of Evidence under the same principles that allow a party's interrogatory answers to be offered against it.

Subdivision (d). This subdivision is revised to require that, where a party fails to file any response to interrogatories or a Rule 34 request, the discovering party should informally seek to obtain such responses before filing a motion for sanctions.

The last sentence of this subdivision is revised to clarify that it is the pendency of a motion for protective order that may be urged as an excuse for a violation of subdivision (d). If a party's motion has been denied, the party cannot argue that its subsequent failure to comply would be justified. In this connection, it should be noted that the filing of a motion under Rule 26(c) is not self-executing—the relief authorized under that rule depends on obtaining the court's order to that effect.

ADVISORY COMMITTEE NOTES TO 1995 AMENDMENTS

RULE 83

Subdivision (a). This rule is amended to reflect the requirement that local rules be consistent not only with the national rules but also with Acts of Congress. The amendment also states that local rules should not repeat Acts of Congress or local rules.

The amendment also requires that the numbering of local rules conform with any uniform numbering system that may be prescribed by the Judicial Conference. Lack of uniform numbering might create unnecessary traps for counsel and litigants. A uniform numbering system would make it easier for an increasingly national bar and for litigants to locate a local rule that applies to a particular procedural issue.

Paragraph (2) is new. Its aim is to protect against loss of rights in the enforcement of local rules relating to matters of form. For example, a party should not be deprived of a right to a jury trial because its attorney, unaware of—or forgetting—a local rule directing that jury demands be noted in the caption of the case, includes a jury demand only in the body of the pleading. The proscription of paragraph (2) is narrowly drawn—covering only violations attributable to nonwillful failure to comply and only those involving local rules directed to matters of form. It does not limit the court's power to impose substantive penalties upon a party if it or its attorney contumaciously or willfully violates a local rule, even one involving merely a matter of form. Nor does it affect the court's power to enforce local rules that involve more than mere matters of form—for example, a local rule requiring parties to identify evidentiary matters relied upon to support or oppose motions for summary judgments.

Subdivision (b). This rule provides flexibility to the court in regulating practice when there is no controlling law. Specifically, it permits the court to regulate practice in any manner consistent with Acts of Congress, with rules adopted under 28 U.S.C. §§ 2072 and 2075, and with the district local rules.

This rule recognizes that courts rely on multiple directives to control practice. Some courts regulate practice through the published Federal Rules and the local rules of the court. Some courts also have used internal operating procedures, standing orders, and other internal directives. Although such directives continue to be authorized, they can lead to problems. Counsel or litigants may be unaware of various directives. In addition, the sheer volume of directives may impose an unreasonable barrier. For example, it may be difficult to obtain copies of the directives. Finally, counsel or litigants may be unfairly sanctioned for failing to comply with a directive. For these reasons, the amendment to this rule disapproves imposing any sanction or other disadvantage on a person for noncompliance with such an internal directive, unless the alleged violator has been furnished actual notice of the requirement in a particular case.

There should be no adverse consequence to a party or attorney for violating special requirements relating to practice before a particular court unless the party or attorney has actual notice of those requirements. Furnishing litigants with a copy outlining the judge's practices—or attaching instructions to a notice setting a case for conference or trial—would suffice to give actual notice, as would an order in a case specifically adopting by reference a judge's standing order and indicating how copies can be obtained.

ADVISORY COMMITTEE NOTES TO 2000 AMENDMENTS

RULE 5

Subdivision (d). Rule 5(d) is amended to provide that disclosures under Rule 26(a)(1) and (2), and discovery requests and responses under Rules 30, 31, 33, 34, and 36 must not be filed until they are used in the action. "Discovery requests" includes deposition notices and "discovery responses" includes objections. The rule supersedes and invalidates local rules that forbid, permit, or require filing of these materials before they are used in the action. The former Rule 26(a)(4) requirement that disclosures under Rule 26(a)(1) and (2) be filed has been removed. Disclosures under Rule 26(a)(3), however, must be promptly filed as provided in Rule 26(a)(3). Filings in connection with Rule 35 examinations, which involve a motion proceeding when the parties do not agree, are unaffected by these amendments.

Recognizing the costs imposed on parties and courts by required filing of discovery materials that are never used in an action, Rule 5(d) was amended in 1980 to authorize court orders that excuse filing. Since then, many districts have adopted local rules that excuse or forbid filing. In 1989 the Judicial Conference Local Rules Project concluded that these local rules were inconsistent with Rule 5(d), but urged the Advisory Committee to consider amending the rule. Local Rules Project at 92 (1989). The Judicial Conference of the Ninth Circuit gave the Committee similar advice in 1997. The reality of nonfiling reflected in these local rules has even been assumed in drafting the national rules. In 1993, Rule 30(f)(1) was amended to direct that the officer presiding at a deposition file it with the court or send it to the attorney who arranged for the transcript or recording. The Committee Note explained that this alternative to filing was designed for "courts which direct that depositions not be automatically filed." Rule 30(f)(1) has been amended to conform to this change in Rule 5(d).

Although this amendment is based on widespread experience with local rules, and confirms the results directed by these local rules, it is designed to supersede and invalidate local rules. There is no apparent reason to have different filing rules in different districts. Even if districts vary in present capacities to store filed materials that are not used in an action, there is little reason to continue expending court resources for this purpose. These costs and burdens would likely change as parties make increased use of audio- and videotaped depositions. Equipment to facilitate review and reproduction of such discovery materials may prove costly to acquire, maintain, and operate.

The amended rule provides that discovery materials and disclosures under Rule 26(a)(1) and (a)(2) must not be filed until they are "used in the proceeding." This phrase is meant to refer to proceedings in court. This filing requirement is not triggered by "use" of discovery materials in other discovery activities, such as depositions. In connection with proceedings in court, however, the rule is to be interpreted broadly; any use of discovery materials in court in connection with a motion, a pretrial conference under Rule 16, or otherwise, should be interpreted as use in the proceeding.

Once discovery or disclosure materials are used in the proceeding, the filing requirements of Rule 5(d) should apply to them. But because the filing requirement applies only with regard to materials that are used, only those parts of voluminous materials that are actually used need be filed. Any party would be free to file other pertinent portions of materials that are so used. See Fed. R. Evid. 106; cf. Rule 32(a)(4). If the parties are unduly sparing in their submissions, the court may order further filings. By local rule, a court could provide appropriate direction regarding the filing of discovery materials, such as depositions, that are used in proceedings.

RULE 26

The Rule 26(a)(1) initial disclosure provisions are amended to establish a nationally uniform practice. The scope of the disclosure obligation is narrowed to cover only information that the disclosing party may use to support its position. In addition, the rule exempts specified categories of proceedings from initial disclosure, and permits a party who contends that disclosure is not appropriate in the circumstances of the case to present its objections to the court, which must then determine whether disclosure should be made. Related changes are made in Rules 26(d) and (f).

The initial disclosure requirements added by the 1993 amendments permitted local rules directing that disclosure would not be required or altering its operation. The inclusion of the "opt out" provision reflected the strong opposition to initial disclosure felt in some districts, and permitted experimentation with differing disclosure rules in those districts that were favorable to disclosure. The local option also recognized that—partly in response to the first publication in 1991 of a proposed disclosure rule—many districts had adopted a variety of disclosure programs under the aegis of the Civil Justice Reform Act. It was hoped that developing experience under a variety of disclosure systems would support eventual refinement of a uniform national disclosure practice. In addition, there was hope that local experience could identify categories of actions in which disclosure is not useful.

A striking array of local regimes in fact emerged for disclosure and related features introduced in 1993. *See* D. Stienstra, *Implementation of Disclosure in United States District Courts, With Specific Attention to Courts' Responses to Selected Amendments to Federal Rule of Civil Procedure* 26 (Federal Judicial Center, March 30, 1998) (describing and categorizing local regimes). In its final report to Congress on the CJRA experience, the Judicial Conference recommended reexamination of the need for national uniformity, particularly in regard to initial disclosure. Judicial Conference, *Alternative Proposals for Reduction of Cost and Delay: Assessment of Principles, Guidelines and Techniques,* 175 F.R.D. 62, 98 (1997).

At the Committee's request, the Federal Judicial Center undertook a survey in 1997 to develop information on current disclosure and discovery practices. *See* T. Willging, J. Shapard, D. Stienstra & D. Miletich, *Discovery and Disclosure Practice, Problems, and Proposals for Change* (Federal Judicial Center, 1997). In addition, the Committee convened two conferences on discovery involving lawyers from around the country and received reports and recommendations on possible discovery amendments from a number of bar groups. Papers and other proceedings from the second conference are published in 39 B. C. L. Rev. 517-840 (1998).

The Committee has discerned widespread support for national uniformity. Many lawyers have experienced difficulty in coping with divergent disclosure and other practices as they move from one district to another. Lawyers surveyed by the Federal Judicial Center ranked adoption of a uniform national disclosure rule second among proposed rule changes (behind increased availability of judges to resolve discovery disputes) as a means to reduce litigation expenses without interfering with fair outcomes. *Discovery and Disclosure Practice, supra,* at 44-45. National uniformity is also a central purpose of the Rules Enabling Act of 1934, as amended, 28 U.S.C. §§ 2072-2077.

These amendments restore national uniformity to disclosure practice. Uniformity is also restored to other aspects of discovery by deleting most of the provisions authorizing local rules that vary the number of permitted discovery events or the length of depositions. Local rule options are also deleted from Rules 26(d) and (f).

Subdivision (a)(1). The amendments remove the authority to alter or opt out of the national disclosure requirements by local rule, invalidating not only formal local rules but also informal "standing" orders of an individual judge or court that purport to create exemptions from—or limit or expand—the disclosure provided under the national rule. *See* Rule 83. Case-specific orders remain proper, however, and are expressly required if a party objects that initial disclosure is not appropriate in the circumstances of the action. Specified categories of proceedings are excluded from initial disclosure under subdivision (a)(1)(E). In addition, the parties can stipulate to forgo disclosure, as was true before. But even in a case excluded by subdivision (a)(1)(E) or in which the parties stipulate to bypass disclosure, the court can order exchange of similar information in managing the action under Rule 16.

The initial disclosure obligation of subdivisions (a)(1)(A) and (B) has been narrowed to identification of witnesses and documents that the disclosing party may use to support its claims or defenses. "Use" includes any use at a pretrial conference, to support a motion, or at trial. The disclosure obligation is also triggered by intended use in discovery, apart from use to respond to a discovery request; use of a document to question a witness during a deposition is a common example. The disclosure obligation attaches both to witnesses and documents a party intends to use and also to witnesses and to documents the party intends to use if—in the language of Rule 26(a)(3)—"the need arises."

A party is no longer obligated to disclose witnesses or documents, whether favorable or unfavorable, that it does not intend to use. The obligation to disclose information the party may use connects directly to the exclusion sanction of Rule 37(c)(1). Because the disclosure obligation is limited to material that the party may use, it is no longer tied to particularized allegations in the pleadings. Subdivision (e)(1), which is unchanged, requires supplementation if information later acquired would have been subject to the disclosure requirement. As case preparation continues, a party must supplement its disclosures when it determines that it may use a witness or document that it did not previously intend to use.

The disclosure obligation applies to "claims and defenses," and therefore requires a party to disclose information it may use to support its denial or rebuttal of the allegations, claim, or defense of another party. It thereby bolsters the requirements of Rule 11(b)(4), which authorizes denials "warranted on the evidence," and disclosure should include the identity of any witness or document that the disclosing party may use to support such denials.

Subdivision (a)(3) presently excuses pretrial disclosure of information solely for impeachment. Impeachment information is similarly excluded from the initial disclosure requirement.

Subdivisions (a)(1)(C) and (D) are not changed. Should a case be exempted from initial disclosure by Rule 26(a)(1)(E) or by agreement or order, the insurance information described by subparagraph (D) should be subject to discovery, as it would have been under the principles of former Rule 26(b)(2), which was added in 1970 and deleted in 1993 as redundant in light of the new initial disclosure obligation.

New subdivision (a)(1)(E) excludes eight specified categories of proceedings from initial disclosure. The objective of this listing is to identify cases in which there is likely to be little or no discovery, or in which initial disclosure appears unlikely to contribute to the effective development of the case. The list was developed after a review of the categories excluded by local rules in various districts from the operation of Rule 16(b) and the conference requirements of subdivision (f). Subdivision (a)(1)(E) refers to categories of "proceedings" rather than categories of "actions" because some might not properly be labeled " actions." Case designations made by the parties or the clerk's office at the time of filing do not control application of the exemptions. The descriptions in the rule are generic and are intended to be administered by the parties—and, when needed, the courts—with the flexibility needed to adapt to gradual evolution in the types of proceedings that fall within these general categories. The exclusion of an action for review on an administrative record, for example, is intended to reach a proceeding that is framed as an "appeal" based solely on an administrative record. The exclusion should not apply to a proceeding in a form that commonly permits admission of new evidence to supplement the record. Item (vii), excluding a proceeding ancillary to proceedings in other courts, does not refer to bankruptcy proceedings; application of the Civil Rules to bankruptcy proceedings is determined by the Bankruptcy Rules.

Subdivision (a)(1)(E) is likely to exempt a substantial proportion of the cases in most districts from the initial disclosure requirement. Based on 1996 and 1997 case filing statistics, Federal Judicial Center staff estimate that, nationwide, these categories total approximately one-third of all civil filings.

The categories of proceedings listed in subdivision (a)(1)(E) are also exempted from the subdivision (f) conference requirement and from the subdivision (d) moratorium on discovery. Although there is no restriction on commencement of discovery in these cases, it is not expected that this opportunity will often lead to abuse since there is likely to be little or no discovery in most such cases. Should a defendant need more time to respond to discovery requests filed at the beginning of an exempted action, it can seek relief by motion under Rule 26(c) if the plaintiff is unwilling to defer the due date by agreement.

Subdivision (a)(1)(E)'s enumeration of exempt categories is exclusive. Although a case-specific order can alter or excuse initial disclosure, local rules or "standing" orders that purport to create general exemptions are invalid. *See* Rule 83.

The time for initial disclosure is extended to 14 days after the subdivision (f) conference unless the court orders otherwise. This change is integrated with corresponding changes requiring that the subdivision (f) conference be held 21 days before the Rule 16(b) scheduling conference or scheduling order, and that the report on the subdivision (f) conference be submitted to the court 14 days after the meeting. These changes provide a more orderly opportunity for the parties to review the disclosures, and for the court to consider the report. In many instances, the subdivision (f) conference and the effective preparation of the case would benefit from disclosure before the conference, and earlier disclosure is encouraged.

The presumptive disclosure date does not apply if a party objects to initial disclosure during the subdivision (f) conference and states its objection in the subdivision (f) discovery plan. The right to object to initial disclosure is not intended to afford parties an opportunity to "opt out" of disclosure unilaterally. It does provide an opportunity for an objecting party to present to the court its position that disclosure would be "inappropriate in the circumstances of the action." Making the objection permits the objecting party to present the question to the judge before any party is required to make disclosure. The court must then rule on the objection and determine what disclosures—if any—should be made. Ordinarily, this determination would be included in the Rule 16(b) scheduling order, but the court could handle the matter in a different fashion. Even when circumstances warrant suspending some disclosure obligations, others—such as the damages and insurance information called for by subdivisions (a)(1)(C) and (D)—may continue to be appropriate.

The presumptive disclosure date is also inapplicable to a party who is "first served or otherwise joined" after the subdivision (f) conference. This phrase refers to the date of service of a claim on a party in a defensive posture (such as a defendant or third-party defendant), and the date of joinder of a party added as a claimant or an intervenor. Absent court order or stipulation, a new party has 30 days in which to make its initial disclosures. But it is expected that later-added parties will ordinarily be treated the same as the original parties when the original parties have stipulated to forgo initial disclosure, or the court has ordered disclosure in a modified form.

Subdivision (a)(3). The amendment to Rule 5(d) forbids filing disclosures under subdivisions (a)(1) and (a)(2) until they are used in the proceeding, and this change is reflected in an amendment to subdivision (a)(4). Disclosures under subdivision (a)(3), however, may be important to the court in connection with the final pretrial conference or otherwise in preparing for trial. The requirement that objections to certain matters be filed points up the court's need to be provided with these materials. Accordingly, the requirement that subdivision (a)(3) materials be filed has been moved from subdivision (a)(4) to subdivision (a)(3), and it has also been made clear that they—and any objections—should be filed "promptly."

Subdivision (a)(4). The filing requirement has been removed from this subdivision. Rule 5(d) has been amended to provide that disclosures under subdivisions (a)(1) and (a)(2) must not be filed until used in the proceeding. Subdivision (a)(3) has been amended to require that the disclosures it directs, and objections to them, be filed promptly. Subdivision (a)(4) continues to require that all disclosures under subdivisions (a)(1), (a)(2), and (a)(3) be in writing, signed, and served.

RULE 30

Subdivision (d). Paragraph (1) has been amended to clarify the terms regarding behavior during depositions. The references to objections "to evidence" and limitations "on evidence" have been removed to avoid disputes about what is "evidence" and whether an objection is to, or a limitation is on, discovery instead. It is intended that the rule apply to any objection to a question or other issue arising during a deposition, and to any limitation imposed by the court in connection with a deposition, which might relate to duration or other matters.

The current rule places limitations on instructions that a witness not answer only when the instruction is made by a "party." Similar limitations should apply with regard to anyone who might purport to instruct a witness not to answer a question. Accordingly, the rule is amended to apply the limitation to instructions by any person. The amendment is not intended to confer new authority on nonparties to instruct witnesses to refuse to answer deposition questions. The amendment makes it clear that, whatever the legitimacy of giving such instructions, the nonparty is subject to the same limitations as parties.

Paragraph (2) imposes a presumptive durational limitation of one day of seven hours for any deposition. The Committee has been informed that overlong depositions can result in undue costs and delays in some circumstances. This limitation contemplates that there will be reasonable breaks during the day for lunch and other reasons, and that the only time to be counted is the time occupied by the actual deposition. For purposes of this durational limit, the deposition of each person designated under Rule 30(b)(6) should be considered a separate deposition. The presumptive duration may be extended, or otherwise altered, by agreement. Absent agreement, a court order is needed. The party seeking a court order to extend the examination, or otherwise alter the limitations, is expected to show good cause to justify such an order.

Parties considering extending the time for a deposition—and courts asked to order an extension— might consider a variety of factors. For example, if the witness needs an interpreter, that may prolong the examination. If the examination will cover events occurring over a long period of time, that may justify allowing additional time. In cases in which the witness will be questioned about numerous or lengthy documents, it is often desirable for the interrogating party to send copies of the documents to the witness sufficiently in advance of the deposition so that the witness can become familiar with them. Should the witness nevertheless not read the documents in advance, thereby prolonging the deposition, a court could consider that a reason for extending the time limit. If the examination reveals that documents have been requested but not produced, that may justify further examination once production has occurred. In multi-party cases, the need for each party to examine the witness may warrant additional time, although duplicative questioning should be avoided and parties with similar interests should strive to designate one lawyer to question about areas of common interest. Similarly, should the lawyer for the witness want to examine the witness, that may require additional time. Finally, with regard to expert witnesses, there may more often be a need for additional time—even after the submission of the report required by Rule 26(a)(2)—for full exploration of the theories upon which the witness relies.

It is expected that in most instances the parties and the witness will make reasonable accommodations to avoid the need for resort to the court. The limitation is phrased in terms of a single day on the assumption that ordinarily a single day would be preferable to a deposition extending over multiple days; if alternative arrangements would better suit the parties, they may agree to them. It is also assumed that there will be reasonable breaks during the day. Preoccupation with timing is to be avoided.

The rule directs the court to allow additional time where consistent with Rule 26(b)(2) if needed for a fair examination of the deponent. In addition, if the deponent or another person impedes or delays the examination, the court must authorize extra time. The amendment makes clear that additional time should also be allowed where the examination is impeded by an "other circumstance," which might include a power outage, a health emergency, or other event.

In keeping with the amendment to Rule 26(b)(2), the provision added in 1993 granting authority to adopt a local rule limiting the time permitted for depositions has been removed. The court may enter a case-specific order directing shorter depositions for all depositions in a case or with regard to a specific witness. The court may also order that a deposition be taken for limited periods on several days.

Paragraph (3) includes sanctions provisions formerly included in paragraph (2). It authorizes the court to impose an appropriate sanction on any person responsible for an impediment that frustrated the fair examination of the deponent. This could include the deponent, any party, or any other person involved in the deposition. If the impediment or delay results from an "other circumstance" under paragraph (2), ordinarily no sanction would be appropriate....

Subdivision (f)(1): This subdivision is amended because Rule 5(d) has been amended to direct that discovery materials, including depositions, ordinarily should not be filed. The rule already has provisions directing that the lawyer who arranged for the transcript or recording preserve the deposition. Rule 5(d) provides that, once the deposition is used in the proceeding, the attorney must file it with the court.

RULE 37

Subdivision (c)(1). When this subdivision was added in 1993 to direct exclusion of materials not disclosed as required, the duty to supplement discovery responses pursuant to Rule 26(e)(2) was omitted. In the face of this omission, courts may rely on inherent power to sanction for failure to supplement as required by Rule 26(e)(2), *see* 8 Federal Practice & Procedure § 2050 at 607-09, but that is an uncertain and unregulated ground for imposing sanctions. There is no obvious occasion for a Rule 37(a) motion in connection with failure to supplement, and ordinarily only Rule 37(c)(1) exists as rule-based authority for sanctions if this supplementation obligation is violated.

The amendment explicitly adds failure to comply with Rule 26(e)(2) as a ground for sanctions under Rule 37(c)(1), including exclusion of withheld materials. The rule provides that this sanction power only applies when the failure to supplement was "without substantial justification." Even if the failure was not substantially justified, a party should be allowed to use the material that was not disclosed if the lack of earlier notice was harmless....

ADVISORY COMMITTEE NOTES TO 2001 AMENDMENTS

RULE 6

The additional three days provided by Rule 6(e) is extended to the means of service authorized by the new paragraph (D) added to Rule 5(b), including—with the consent of the person served—service by electronic or other means. The three-day addition is provided as well for service on a person with no known address by leaving a copy with the clerk of the court.

ADVISORY COMMITTEE NOTES TO 2002 AMENDMENTS

RULE 58

Rule 58 has provided that a judgment is effective only when set forth on a separate document and entered as provided in Rule 79(a). This simple separate document requirement has been ignored in many cases. The result of failure to enter judgment on a separate document is that the time for making motions under Rules 50, 52, 54(d)(2)(B), 59, or 60 motions, but there have been many and horridly confused problems under Appellate Rule 4(a). These amendments are designed to work in conjunction with Appellate Rule 4(a) to ensure that appeal time does not linger on indefinitely, and to maintain the integration of the time periods set for Rules 50, 52, 54(d)(2)(B), 59, and 60 with Appellate Rule 4(a).

Rule 58(a) preserves the core of the present separate document requirement, both for the initial judgment and for any amended judgment. No attempt is made to sort through the confusion that some courts have found in addressing the elements of a separate document. It is easy to prepare a separate document that recites the terms of the judgment without offering additional explanation or citation of authority. Forms 31 and 32 provide examples.

Rule 58 is amended, however, to address a problem that arises under Appellate Rule 4(a). Some courts treat such orders as those that deny a motion for new trial as a "judgment," so that appeal time does not start to run until the order is entered on a separate document. Without attempting to address the question whether such orders are appealable, and thus judgments as defined by Rule 54(a), the amendment provides that entry on a separate document is not required for an order disposing of the motions listed in Appellate Rule 4(a). The enumeration of motions drawn from the Appellate Rule 4(a) list is generalized by omitting details that are important for appeal time purposes but that would unnecessarily complicate the separate document requirement. As one example, it is not required that any of the enumerated motions be timely. Many of the enumerated motions are frequently made before judgment is entered. The exemption of the order disposing of the motion does not excuse the obligation to set forth the judgment itself on a separate document. And if disposition of the motion results in an amended judgment, the amended judgment must be set forth on a separate document.

Rule 58(d) discards the attempt to define the time when a judgment becomes "effective." Taken in conjunction with the Rule 54(a) definition of a judgment to include "any order form which an appeal lies," the former Rule 58 definition of effectiveness could cause strange difficulties in implementing pretrial orders that are appealable under interlocutory appeal provisions or under expansive theories of finality. Rule 58(b) replaces the definition of effectiveness with a new provision that defines the time when judgment is entered. If judgment is promptly set forth on a separate document, as should be done when required by Rule 58(a)(1), the new provision will not change the effect of Rule 58. But in the cases in which court and clerk fail to comply with this simple requirement, the motion time periods set by Rules 50, 52, 54, 59, and 60 begin to run after expiration of 150 days from entry of the judgment in the civil docket as required by Rule 79(a)....

The new all-purpose definition of the entry of judgment must be applied with common sense to other questions that may turn on the time when judgment is entered. If the 150-day provision in Rule 58(b)(2)(B) — designed to integrate the time for post-judgment motions with appeal time — serves no purpose, or would defeat the purpose of another rule, it should be disregarded. In theory, for example, the separate document requirement continues to apply to an interlocutory order that is appealable as a final decision under collateral-order doctrine. Appealability under collateral-order doctrine should not be complicated by failure to enter the order as a judgment on a separate document — there is little reason to force trial judges to speculate about the potential appealability of every order, and there is no means to ensure that the trial judge will always reach the same conclusion as the court of appeals. Appeal time should start to run when the collateral order is entered without regard to creation of a separate document and without awaiting expiration of the 150 days provided by Rule 58(b)(2). Drastic surgery on Rules 54(a) and 58 would be required to address this and related issues, however, and it is better to leave this conundrum to the pragmatic disregard that seems its present fate. The present amendments do not seem to make matters worse, apart from one false appearance. If a pretrial order is set forth on a separate document that meets the requirements of Rule 58(b), the time to move for reconsideration seems to begin 150 days after entry in the civil docket. This apparent problem is resolved by Rule 54(b), which expressly permits revision of all orders not made final under Rule 54(b) "at any time before the entry of judgment adjudicating all the claims and the rights and liabilities of all the parties."

New Rule 58(d) replaces the provision that attorneys shall not submit forms of judgment except on direction of the court. This provision was added to Rule 58 to avoid the delays that were frequently encountered by the former practice of directing the attorneys for the prevailing party to prepare a form of judgment, and also to avoid the occasionally inept drafting that resulted from attorney-prepared judgments. *See* 11 Wright, Miller & Kane, *Federal Practice & Procedure: Civil 2d*, § 2786. The express direction in Rule 58(a)(2) for prompt action by the clerk, and by the court if court action is required, addresses this concern. The new provision allowing any party to move for entry of judgment on a separate document will protect all needs for prompt commencement of the periods for motions, appeals, and execution or other enforcement

ADVISORY COMMITTEE NOTES TO 2003 AMENDMENTS

RULE 23

Subdivision (c). Subdivision (c) is amended in several respects. The requirement that the court determine whether to certify a class "as soon as practicable after commencement of an action" is replaced by requiring determination "at an early practicable time." The notice provisions are substantially revised.

Paragraph (1). Subdivision (c)(1)(A) is changed to require that the determination whether to certify a class be made "at an early practicable time." The "as soon as practicable" exaction neither reflects prevailing practice nor captures the many valid reasons that may justify deferring the initial certification decision. *See* Willging, Hooper & Niemic, *Empirical Study of Class Actions in Four Federal District Courts: Final Report to the Advisory Committee on Civil Rules* 26-36 (Federal Judicial Center 1996).

Time may be needed to gather information necessary to make the certification decision. Although an evaluation of the probable outcome on the merits is not properly part of the certification decision, discovery in aid of the certification decision often includes information required to identify the nature of the issues that actually will be presented at trial. In this sense it is appropriate to conduct controlled discovery into the "merits," limited to those aspects relevant to making the certification decision on an informed basis. Active judicial supervision may be required to achieve the most effective balance that expedites an informed certification determination without forcing an artificial and ultimately wasteful division between "certification discovery" and "merits discovery." A critical need is to determine how the case will be tried. An increasing number of courts require a party requesting class certification to present a "trial plan" that describes the issues likely to be presented at trial and tests whether they are susceptible of class-wide proof. *See Manual For Complex Litigation Third*, § 21.213, p. 44; § 30.11, p. 214; § 30.12, p. 215.

Other considerations may affect the timing of the certification decision. The party opposing the class may prefer to win dismissal or summary judgment as to the individual plaintiffs without certification and without binding the class that might have been certified. Time may be needed to explore designation of class counsel under Rule 23(g), recognizing that in many cases the need to progress toward the certification determination may require designation of interim counsel under Rule 23(g)(2)(A).

Although many circumstances may justify deferring the certification decision, active management may be necessary to ensure that the certification decision is not unjustifiably delayed.

Subdivision (c)(1)(C) reflects two amendments. The provision that a class certification "may be conditional" is deleted. A court that is not satisfied that the requirements of Rule 23 have been met should refuse certification until they have been met. The provision that permits alteration or amendment of an order granting or denying class certification is amended to set the cut-off point at final judgment rather than "the decision on the merits." This change avoids the possible ambiguity in referring to "the decision on the merits." Following a determination of liability, for example, proceedings to define the remedy may demonstrate the need to amend the class definition or subdivide the class. In this setting the final judgment concept is pragmatic. It is not the same as the concept used for appeal purposes, but it should be flexible, particularly in protracted litigation.

The authority to amend an order under Rule 23(c)(1) before final judgment does not restore the practice of "one-way intervention" that was rejected by the 1966 revision of Rule 23. A determination of liability after certification, however, may show a need to amend the class definition. Decertification may be warranted after further proceedings.

If the definition of a class certified under Rule 23(b)(3) is altered to include members who have not been afforded notice and an opportunity to request exclusion, notice—including an opportunity to request exclusion—must be directed to the new class members under Rule 23(c)(2)(B).

Paragraph (2). The first change made in Rule 23(c)(2) is to call attention to the court's authority— already established in part by Rule 23(d)(2)—to direct notice of certification to a Rule 23(b)(1) or (b)(2) class. The present rule expressly requires notice only in actions certified under Rule 23(b)(3). Members of classes certified under Rules 23(b)(1) or (b)(2) have interests that may deserve protection by notice.

The authority to direct notice to class members in a (b)(1) or (b)(2) class action should be exercised with care. For several reasons, there may be less need for notice than in a (b)(3) class action. There is no right to request exclusion from a (b)(1) or (b)(2) class. The characteristics of the class may reduce the need for formal notice. The cost of providing notice, moreover, could easily cripple actions that do not seek damages. The court may decide not to direct notice after balancing the risk that notice costs may deter the pursuit of class relief against the benefits of notice.

When the court does direct certification notice in a (b)(1) or (b)(2) class action, the discretion and flexibility established by subdivision (c)(2)(A) extend to the method of giving notice. Notice facilitates the opportunity to participate. Notice calculated to reach a significant number of class members often will protect the interests of all. Informal methods may prove effective. A simple posting in a place visited by many class members, directing attention to a source of more detailed information, may suffice. The court should consider the costs of notice in relation to the probable reach of inexpensive methods.

If a Rule 23(b)(3) class is certified in conjunction with a (b)(2) class, the (c)(2)(B) notice requirements must be satisfied as to the (b)(3) class.

The direction that class-certification notice be couched in plain, easily understood language is a reminder of the need to work unremittingly at the difficult task of communicating with class members. It is difficult to provide information about most class actions that is both accurate and easily understood by class members who are not themselves lawyers. Factual uncertainty, legal complexity, and the complication of class-action procedure raise the barriers high. The Federal Judicial Center has created illustrative clear-notice forms that provide a helpful starting point for actions similar to those described in the forms.

Subdivision (e). Subdivision (e) is amended to strengthen the process of reviewing proposed class-action settlements. Settlement may be a desirable means of resolving a class action. But court review and approval are essential to assure adequate representation of class members who have not participated in shaping the settlement.

Paragraph (1). Subdivision (e)(1)(A) expressly recognizes the power of a class representative to settle class claims, issues, or defenses.

Rule 23(e)(1)(A) resolves the ambiguity in former Rule 23(e)'s reference to dismissal or compromise of "a class action." That language could be—and at times was—read to require court approval of settlements with putative class representatives that resolved only individual claims. See Manual for Complex Litigation Third, § 30.41. The new rule requires approval only if the claims, issues, or defenses of a certified class are resolved by a settlement, voluntary dismissal, or compromise.

Subdivision (e)(1)(B) carries forward the notice requirement of present Rule 23(e) when the settlement binds the class through claim or issue preclusion; notice is not required when the settlement binds only the individual class representatives. Notice of a settlement binding on the class is required either when the settlement follows class certification or when the decisions on certification and settlement proceed simultaneously.

Reasonable settlement notice may require individual notice in the manner required by Rule 23(c)(2)(B) for certification notice to a Rule 23(b)(3) class. Individual notice is appropriate, for example, if class members are required to take action—such as filing claims—to participate in the judgment, or if the court orders a settlement opt-out opportunity under Rule 23(e)(3).

Subdivision (e)(1)(C) confirms and mandates the already common practice of holding hearings as part of the process of approving settlement, voluntary dismissal, or compromise that would bind members of a class.

Subdivision (e)(1)(C) states the standard for approving a proposed settlement that would bind class members. The settlement must be fair, reasonable, and adequate. A helpful review of many factors that may deserve consideration is provided by In re: Prudential Ins. Co. America Sales Practice Litigation

Agent Actions, 148 F.3d 283, 316-24 (3d Cir. 1998). Further guidance can be found in the Manual for Complex Litigation.

The court must make findings that support the conclusion that the settlement is fair, reasonable, and adequate. The findings must be set out in sufficient detail to explain to class members and the appellate court the factors that bear on applying the standard.

Settlement review also may provide an occasion to review the cogency of the initial class definition. The terms of the settlement themselves, or objections, may reveal divergent interests of class members and demonstrate the need to redefine the class or to designate subclasses. Redefinition of a class certified under Rule 23(b)(3) may require notice to new class members under Rule 23(c)(2)(B). *See* Rule 23(c)(1)(C).

Paragraph (2). Subdivision (e)(2) requires parties seeking approval of a settlement, voluntary dismissal, or compromise under Rule 23(e)(1) to file a statement identifying any agreement made in connection with the settlement. This provision does not change the basic requirement that the parties disclose all terms of the settlement or compromise that the court must approve under Rule 23(e)(1). It aims instead at related undertakings that, although seemingly separate, may have influenced the terms of the settlement by trading away possible advantages for the class in return for advantages for others. Doubts should be resolved in favor of identification.

Further inquiry into the agreements identified by the parties should not become the occasion for discovery by the parties or objectors. The court may direct the parties to provide to the court or other parties a summary or copy of the full terms of any agreement identified by the parties. The court also may direct the parties to provide a summary or copy of any agreement not identified by the parties that the court considers relevant to its review of a proposed settlement. In exercising discretion under this rule, the court may act in steps, calling first for a summary of any agreement that may have affected the settlement and then for a complete version if the summary does not provide an adequate basis for review. A direction to disclose a summary or copy of an agreement may raise concerns of confidentiality. Some agreements may include information that merits protection against general disclosure. And the court must provide an opportunity to claim work-product or other protections.

Paragraph (3). Subdivision (e)(3) authorizes the court to refuse to approve a settlement unless the settlement affords class members a new opportunity to request exclusion from a class certified under Rule 23(b)(3) after settlement terms are known. An agreement by the parties themselves to permit class members to elect exclusion at this point by the settlement agreement may be one factor supporting approval of the settlement. Often there is an opportunity to opt out at this point because the class is certified and settlement is reached in circumstances that lead to simultaneous notice of certification and notice of settlement. In these cases, the basic opportunity to elect exclusion applies without further complication. In some cases, particularly if settlement appears imminent at the time of certification, it may be possible to achieve equivalent protection by deferring notice and the opportunity to elect exclusion until actual settlement terms are known. This approach avoids the cost and potential confusion of providing two notices and makes the single notice more meaningful. But notice should not be delayed unduly after certification in the hope of settlement.

Rule 23(e)(3) authorizes the court to refuse to approve a settlement unless the settlement affords a new opportunity to elect exclusion in a case that settles after a certification decision if the earlier opportunity to elect exclusion provided with the certification notice has expired by the time of the settlement notice. A decision to remain in the class is likely to be more carefully considered and is better informed when settlement terms are known.

The opportunity to request exclusion from a proposed settlement is limited to members of a (b)(3) class. Exclusion may be requested only by individual class members; no class member may purport to opt out other class members by way of another class action.

The decision whether to approve a settlement that does not allow a new opportunity to elect exclusion is confided to the court's discretion. The court may make this decision before directing notice to the class under Rule 23(e)(1)(B) or after the Rule 23(e)(1)(C) hearing. Many factors may influence the court's decision. Among these are changes in the information available to class members since expiration of the first opportunity to request exclusion, and the nature of the individual class members' claims.

The terms set for permitting a new opportunity to elect exclusion from the proposed settlement of a Rule 23(b)(3) class action may address concerns of potential misuse. The court might direct, for example, that class members who elect exclusion are bound by rulings on the merits made before the settlement was proposed for approval. Still other terms or conditions may be appropriate.

Paragraph (4). Subdivision (e)(4) confirms the right of class members to object to a proposed settlement, voluntary dismissal, or compromise. The right is defined in relation to a disposition that, because it would bind the class, requires court approval under subdivision (e)(1)(C).

Subdivision (e)(4)(B) requires court approval for withdrawal of objections made under subdivision (e)(4)(A). Review follows automatically if the objections are withdrawn on terms that lead to modification of the settlement with the class. Review also is required if the objector formally withdraws the objections. If the objector simply abandons pursuit of the objection, the court may inquire into the circumstances.

Approval under paragraph (4)(B) may be given or denied with little need for further inquiry if the objection and the disposition go only to a protest that the individual treatment afforded the objector under the proposed settlement is unfair because of factors that distinguish the objector from other class members. Different considerations may apply if the objector has protested that the proposed settlement is not fair, reasonable, or adequate on grounds that apply generally to a class or subclass. Such objections, which purport to represent class-wide interests, may augment the opportunity for obstruction or delay. If such objections are surrendered on terms that do not affect the class settlement or the objector's participation in the class settlement, the court often can approve withdrawal of the objections without elaborate inquiry.

Once an objector appeals, control of the proceeding lies in the court of appeals. The court of appeals may undertake review and approval of a settlement with the objector, perhaps as part of appeal settlement procedures, or may remand to the district court to take advantage of the district court's familiarity with the action and settlement.

Subdivision (g). Subdivision (g) is new. It responds to the reality that the selection and activity of class counsel are often critically important to the successful handling of a class action. Until now, courts have scrutinized proposed class counsel as well as the class representative under Rule 23(a)(4). This experience has recognized the importance of judicial evaluation of the proposed lawyer for the class, and this new subdivision builds on that experience rather than introducing an entirely new element into the class certification process. Rule 23(a)(4) will continue to call for scrutiny of the proposed class representative, while this subdivision will guide the court in assessing proposed class counsel as part of the certification decision. This subdivision recognizes the importance of class counsel, states the obligation to represent the interests of the class, and provides a framework for selection of class counsel. The procedure and standards for appointment vary depending on whether there are multiple applicants to be class counsel. The new subdivision also provides a method by which the court may make directions from the outset about the potential fee award to class counsel in the event the action is successful.

Paragraph (1) sets out the basic requirement that class counsel be appointed if a class is certified and articulates the obligation of class counsel to represent the interests of the class, as opposed to the potentially conflicting interests of individual class members. It also sets out the factors the court should consider in assessing proposed class counsel.

Paragraph (1)(A) requires that the court appoint class counsel to represent the class. Class counsel must be appointed for all classes, including each subclass that the court certifies to represent divergent interests.

Paragraph (1)(A) does not apply if "a statute provides otherwise." This recognizes that provisions of the Private Securities Litigation Reform Act of 1995, Pub. L. No. 104-67, 109 Stat. 737 (1995) (codified in various sections of 15 U.S.C.), contain directives that bear on selection of a lead plaintiff and the retention of counsel. This subdivision does not purport to supersede or to affect the interpretation of those provisions, or any similar provisions of other legislation.

Paragraph 1(B) recognizes that the primary responsibility of class counsel, resulting from appointment as class counsel, is to represent the best interests of the class. The rule thus establishes the obligation of class counsel, an obligation that may be different from the customary obligations of counsel to individual clients. Appointment as class counsel means that the primary obligation of counsel is to the class rather than to any individual members of it. The class representatives do not have an unfettered right to "fire" class counsel. In the same vein, the class representatives cannot command class counsel to accept or reject a settlement proposal. To the contrary, class counsel must determine whether seeking the court's approval of a settlement would be in the best interests of the class as a whole.

Paragraph (1)(C) articulates the basic responsibility of the court to appoint class counsel who will provide the adequate representation called for by paragraph (1)(B). It identifies criteria that must be considered and invites the court to consider any other pertinent matters. Although couched in terms of the court's duty, the listing also informs counsel seeking appointment about the topics that should be addressed in an application for appointment or in the motion for class certification.

The court may direct potential class counsel to provide additional information about the topics mentioned in paragraph (1)(C) or about any other relevant topic. For example, the court may direct applicants to inform the court concerning any agreements about a prospective award of attorney fees or nontaxable costs, as such agreements may sometimes be significant in the selection of class counsel. The court might also direct that potential class counsel indicate how parallel litigation might be coordinated or consolidated with the action before the court.

The court may also direct counsel to propose terms for a potential award of attorney fees and nontaxable costs. Attorney fee awards are an important feature of class action practice, and attention to this subject from the outset may often be a productive technique. Paragraph (2)(C) therefore authorizes the court to provide directions about attorney fees and costs when appointing class counsel. Because there will be numerous class actions in which this information is not likely to be useful, the court need not consider it in all class actions.

Some information relevant to class counsel appointment may involve matters that include adversary preparation in a way that should be shielded from disclosure to other parties. An appropriate protective order may be necessary to preserve confidentiality.

In evaluating prospective class counsel, the court should weigh all pertinent factors. No single factor should necessarily be determinative in a given case. For example, the resources counsel will commit to the case must be appropriate to its needs, but the court should be careful not to limit consideration to lawyers with the greatest resources.

If, after review of all applicants, the court concludes that none would be satisfactory class counsel, it may deny class certification, reject all applications, recommend that an application be modified, invite new applications, or make any other appropriate order regarding selection and appointment of class counsel.

Paragraph (2). This paragraph sets out the procedure that should be followed in appointing class counsel. Although it affords substantial flexibility, it provides the framework for appointment of class counsel in all class actions. For counsel who filed the action, the materials submitted in support of the motion for class certification may suffice to justify appointment so long as the information described in paragraph (g)(1)(C) is included. If there are other applicants, they ordinarily would file a formal application detailing their suitability for the position.

In a plaintiff class action the court usually would appoint as class counsel only an attorney or attorneys who have sought appointment. Different considerations may apply in defendant class actions.

The rule states that the court should appoint "class counsel." In many instances, the applicant will be an individual attorney. In other cases, however, an entire firm, or perhaps numerous attorneys who are not otherwise affiliated but are collaborating on the action will apply. No rule of thumb exists to determine when such arrangements are appropriate; the court should be alert to the need for adequate staffing of the case, but also to the risk of overstaffing or an ungainly counsel structure.

Paragraph (2)(A) authorizes the court to designate interim counsel during the pre-certification period if necessary to protect the interests of the putative class. Rule 23(c)(1)(B) directs that the order certifying the class include appointment of class counsel. Before class certification, however, it will usually be important for an attorney to take action to prepare for the certification decision. The amendment to Rule 23(c)(1) recognizes that some discovery is often necessary for that determination. It also may be important to make or respond to motions before certification. Settlement may be discussed before certification. Ordinarily, such work is handled by the lawyer who filed the action. In some cases, however, there may be rivalry or uncertainty that makes formal designation of interim counsel appropriate. Rule 23(g)(2)(A) authorizes the court to designate interim counsel to act on behalf of the putative class before the certification decision is made. Failure to make the formal designation does not prevent the attorney who filed the action from proceeding in it. Whether or not formally designated interim counsel, an attorney who acts on behalf of the class before certification must act in the best interests of the class as a whole. For example, an attorney who negotiates a pre-certification settlement must seek a settlement that is fair, reasonable, and adequate for the class.

Rule 23(c)(1) provides that the court should decide whether to certify the class "at an early practicable time," and directs that class counsel should be appointed in the order certifying the class. In some cases, it may be appropriate for the court to allow a reasonable period after commencement of the action for filing applications to serve as class counsel. The primary ground for deferring appointment would be that there is reason to anticipate competing applications to serve as class counsel. Examples might include instances in which more than one class action has been filed, or in which other attorneys have filed individual actions on behalf of putative class members. The purpose of facilitating competing applications in such a case is to afford the best possible representation for the class. Another possible reason for deferring appointment would be that the initial applicant was found inadequate, but it seems appropriate to permit additional applications rather than deny class certification.

Paragraph (2)(B) states the basic standard the court should use in deciding whether to certify the class and appoint class counsel in the single applicant situation—that the applicant be able to provide the representation called for by paragraph (1)(B) in light of the factors identified in paragraph (1)(C).

If there are multiple adequate applicants, paragraph (2)(B) directs the court to select the class counsel best able to represent the interests of the class. This decision should also be made using the factors outlined in paragraph (1)(C), but in the multiple applicant situation the court is to go beyond scrutinizing the adequacy of counsel and make a comparison of the strengths of the various applicants. As with the decision whether to appoint the sole applicant for the position, no single factor should be dispositive in selecting class counsel in cases in which there are multiple applicants. The fact that a given attorney filed the instant action, for example, might not weigh heavily in the decision if that lawyer had not done significant work identifying or investigating claims. Depending on the nature of the case, one important consideration might be the applicant's existing attorney-client relationship with the proposed class representative.

Paragraph (2)(C) builds on the appointment process by authorizing the court to include provisions regarding attorney fees in the order appointing class counsel. Courts may find it desirable to adopt guidelines for fees or nontaxable costs, or to direct class counsel to report to the court at regular intervals on the efforts undertaken in the action, to facilitate the court's later determination of a reasonable attorney fee.

Subdivision (h). Subdivision (h) is new. Fee awards are a powerful influence on the way attorneys initiate, develop, and conclude class actions. Class action attorney fee awards have heretofore been handled, along with all other attorney fee awards, under Rule 54(d)(2), but that rule is not addressed to the particular concerns of class actions. This subdivision is designed to work in tandem with new subdivision (g) on appointment of class counsel, which may afford an opportunity for the court to provide an early framework for an eventual fee award, or for monitoring the work of class counsel during the pendency of the action.

Subdivision (h) applies to "an action certified as a class action." This includes cases in which there is a simultaneous proposal for class certification and settlement even though technically the class may not be certified unless the court approves the settlement pursuant to review under Rule 23(e). When a settlement is proposed for Rule 23(e) approval, either after certification or with a request for certification, notice to class members about class counsel's fee motion would ordinarily accompany the notice to the class about the settlement proposal itself.

This subdivision does not undertake to create new grounds for an award of attorney fees or nontaxable costs. Instead, it applies when such awards are authorized by law or by agreement of the parties. Against that background, it provides a format for all awards of attorney fees and nontaxable costs in connection with a class action, not only the award to class counsel. In some situations, there may be a basis for making an award to other counsel whose work produced a beneficial result for the class, such as attorneys who acted for the class before certification but were not appointed class counsel, or attorneys who represented objectors to a proposed settlement under Rule 23(e) or to the fee motion of class counsel. Other situations in which fee awards are authorized by law or by agreement of the parties may exist.

This subdivision authorizes an award of "reasonable" attorney fees and nontaxable costs. This is the customary term for measurement of fee awards in cases in which counsel may obtain an award of fees under the "common fund" theory that applies in many class actions, and is used in many fee-shifting statutes. Depending on the circumstances, courts have approached the determination of what is reasonable in different ways. In particular, there is some variation among courts about whether in "common fund" cases the court should use the lodestar or a percentage method of determining what fee is reasonable. The rule does not attempt to resolve the question whether the lodestar or percentage approach should be viewed as preferable.

Active judicial involvement in measuring fee awards is singularly important to the proper operation of the class-action process. Continued reliance on caselaw development of fee-award measures does not diminish the court's responsibility. In a class action, the district court must ensure that the amount and mode of payment of attorney fees are fair and proper whether the fees come from a common fund or are otherwise paid. Even in the absence of objections, the court bears this responsibility.

Courts discharging this responsibility have looked to a variety of factors. One fundamental focus is the result actually achieved for class members, a basic consideration in any case in which fees are sought on the basis of a benefit achieved for class members. The Private Securities Litigation Reform Act of 1995 explicitly makes this factor a cap for a fee award in actions to which it applies. *See* 15 U.S.C. §§ 77z-1(a)(6); 78u-4(a)(6) (fee award should not exceed a "reasonable percentage of the amount of any damages and prejudgment interest actually paid to the class"). For a percentage approach to fee measurement, results achieved is the basic starting point.

In many instances, the court may need to proceed with care in assessing the value conferred on class members. Settlement regimes that provide for future payments, for example, may not result in significant actual payments to class members. In this connection, the court may need to scrutinize the manner and operation of any applicable claims procedure. In some cases, it may be appropriate to defer some portion of the fee award until actual payouts to class members are known. Settlements involving nonmonetary provisions for class members also deserve careful scrutiny to ensure that these provisions have actual value to the class. On occasion the court's Rule 23(e) review will provide a solid basis for this sort of evaluation, but in any event it is also important to assessing the fee award for the class.

At the same time, it is important to recognize that in some class actions the monetary relief obtained is not the sole determinant of an appropriate attorney fees award. *Cf. Blanchard v. Bergeron*, 489 U.S. 87, 95 (1989) (cautioning in an individual case against an "undesirable emphasis" on "the importance of the recovery of damages in civil rights litigation" that might "shortchange efforts to seek effective injunctive or declaratory relief").

Any directions or orders made by the court in connection with appointing class counsel under Rule 23(g) should weigh heavily in making a fee award under this subdivision.

Courts have also given weight to agreements among the parties regarding the fee motion, and to agreements between class counsel and others about the fees claimed by the motion. Rule 54(d)(2)(B) provides: "If directed by the court, the motion shall also disclose the terms of any agreement with respect to fees to be paid for the services for which claim is made." The agreement by a settling party not to oppose a fee application up to a certain amount, for example, is worthy of consideration, but the court remains responsible to determine a reasonable fee. "Side agreements" regarding fees provide at least perspective pertinent to an appropriate fee award.

In addition, courts may take account of the fees charged by class counsel or other attorneys for representing individual claimants or objectors in the case. In determining a fee for class counsel, the court's objective is to ensure an overall fee that is fair for counsel and equitable within the class. In some circumstances individual fee agreements between class counsel and class members might have provisions inconsistent with those goals, and the court might determine that adjustments in the class fee award were necessary as a result.

Finally, it is important to scrutinize separately the application for an award covering nontaxable costs. If costs were addressed in the order appointing class counsel, those directives should be a presumptive starting point in determining what is an appropriate award.

Paragraph (1). Any claim for an award of attorney fees must be sought by motion under Rule 54(d)(2), which invokes the provisions for timing of appeal in Rule 58 and Appellate Rule 4. Owing to the distinctive features of class action fee motions, however, the provisions of t his subdivision control disposition of fee motions in class actions, while Rule 54(d)(2) applies to matters not addressed in this subdivision.

The court should direct when the fee motion must be filed. For motions by class counsel in cases subject to court review of a proposed settlement under Rule 23(e), it would be important to require the filing of at least the initial motion in time for inclusion of information about the motion in the notice to the class about the proposed settlement that is required by Rule 23(e). In cases litigated to judgment, the court might also order class counsel's motion to be filed promptly so that notice to the class under this subdivision (h) can be given.

Besides service of the motion on all parties, notice of class counsel's motion for attorney fees must be "directed to the class in a reasonable manner." Because members of the class have an interest in the arrangements for payment of class counsel whether that payment comes from the class fund or is made directly by another party, notice is required in all instances. In cases in which settlement approval is contemplated under Rule 23(e), notice of class counsel's fee motion should be combined with notice of the proposed settlement, and the provision regarding notice to the class is parallel to the requirements for notice under Rule 23(e). In adjudicated class actions, the court may calibrate the notice to avoid undue expense.

Paragraph (2). A class member and any party from whom payment is sought may object to the fee motion. Other parties — for example, nonsettling defendants — may not object because they lack a sufficient interest in the amount the court awards. The rule does not specify a time limit for making an objection. In setting the date objections are due, the court should provide sufficient time after the full fee motion is on file to enable potential objectors to examine the motion.

The court may allow an objector discovery relevant to the objections. In determining whether to allow discovery, the court should weigh the need for the information against the cost and delay that would attend discovery. *See* Rule 26(b)(2). One factor in determining whether to authorize discovery is the completeness of the material submitted in support of the fee motion, which depends in part on the fee measurement standard applicable to the case. If the motion provides thorough information, the burden should be on the objector to justify discovery to obtain further information.

Paragraph (3). Whether or not there are formal objections, the court must determine whether a fee award is justified and, if so, set a reasonable fee. The rule does not require a formal hearing in all cases. The form and extent of a hearing depend on the circumstances of the case. The rule does require findings and conclusions under Rule 52(a).

Paragraph (4). By incorporating Rule 54(d)(2), this provision gives the court broad authority to obtain assistance in determining the appropriate amount to award. In deciding whether to direct submission of such questions to a special master or magistrate judge, the court should give appropriate consideration to the cost and delay that such a process might entail.

RULE 51

Rule 51 is revised to capture many of the interpretations that have emerged in practice. The revisions in text will make uniform the conclusions reached by a majority of decisions on each point. Additions also are made to cover some practices that cannot now be anchored in the text of Rule 51.

Scope. Rule 51 governs instructions to the trial jury on the law that governs the verdict. A variety of other instructions cannot practicably be brought within Rule 51. Among these instructions are preliminary instructions to a venire, and cautionary or limiting instructions delivered in immediate response to events at trial.

Requests. Subdivision (a) governs requests. Apart from the plain error doctrine recognized in subdivision (d)(2), a court is not obliged to instruct the jury on issues raised by the evidence unless a party requests an instruction. The revised rule recognizes the court's authority to direct that requests be submitted before trial.

The close-of-the-evidence deadline may come before trial is completed on all potential issues. Trial may be formally bifurcated or may be sequenced in some less formal manner. The close of the evidence is measured by the occurrence of two events: completion of all intended evidence on an identified phase of the trial and impending submission to the jury with instructions.

The risk in directing a pretrial request deadline is that trial evidence may raise new issues or reshape issues the parties thought they had understood. Courts need not insist on pretrial requests in all cases. Even if the request time is set before trial or early in the trial, subdivision (a)(2)(A) permits requests after the close of the evidence to address issues that could not reasonably have been anticipated at the earlier time for requests set by the court.

Subdivision (a)(2)(B) expressly recognizes the court's discretion to act on an untimely request. The most important consideration in exercising the discretion confirmed by subdivision (a)(2)(B) is the importance of the issue to the case—the closer the issue lies to the "plain error" that would be recognized under subdivision (d)(2), the better the reason to give an instruction. The cogency of the reason for failing to make a timely request also should be considered. To be considered under subdivision (a)(2)(B) a request should be made before final instructions and before final jury arguments. What is a "final" instruction and argument depends on the sequence of submitting the case to the jury. If separate portions of the case are submitted to the jury in sequence, the final arguments and final instructions are those made on submitting to the jury the portion of the case addressed by the arguments and instructions.

Instructions. Subdivision (b)(1) requires the court to inform the parties, before instructing the jury and before final jury arguments related to the instruction, of the proposed instructions as well as the proposed action on instruction requests. The time limit is addressed to final jury arguments to reflect the practice that allows interim arguments during trial in complex cases; it may not be feasible to develop final instructions before such interim arguments. It is enough that counsel know of the intended instructions before making final arguments addressed to the issue. If the trial is sequenced or bifurcated, the final arguments addressed to an issue may occur before the close of the entire trial.

Subdivision (b)(2) complements subdivision (b)(1) by carrying forward the opportunity to object established by present Rule 51. It makes explicit the opportunity to object on the record, ensuring a clear memorial of the objection.

Subdivision (b)(3) reflects common practice by authorizing instructions at any time after trial begins and before the jury is discharged.

Objections. Subdivision (c) states the right to object to an instruction or the failure to give an instruction. It carries forward the formula of present Rule 51 requiring that the objection state distinctly the matter objected to and the grounds of the objection, and makes explicit the requirement that the objection be made on the record. The provisions on the time to object make clear that it is timely to object promptly after learning of an instruction or action on a request when the court has not provided advance information as required by subdivision (b)(1). The need to repeat a request by way of objection is continued by new subdivision (d)(1)(B) except where the court made a definitive ruling on the record.

Preserving a claim of error and plain error. Many cases hold that a proper request for a jury instruction is not alone enough to preserve the right to appeal failure to give the instruction. The request must be renewed by objection. This doctrine is appropriate when the court may not have sufficiently focused on the request, or may believe that the request has been granted in substance although in different words. But this doctrine may also prove a trap for the unwary who fail to add an objection after the court has made it clear that the request has been considered and rejected on the merits. Subdivision (d)(1)(B) establishes authority to review the failure to grant a timely request, despite a failure to add an objection, when the court has made a definitive ruling on the record rejecting the request.

Many circuits have recognized that an error not preserved under Rule 51 may be reviewed in exceptional circumstances. The language adopted to capture these decisions in subdivision (d)(2) is borrowed from Criminal Rule 52. Although the language is the same, the context of civil litigation often differs from the context of criminal prosecution; actual application of the plain-error standard takes account of the differences. The Supreme Court has summarized application of Criminal Rule 52 as involving four elements: (1) there must be an error; (2) the error must be plain; (3) the error must affect substantial rights; and (4) the error must seriously affect the fairness, integrity, or public reputation of judicial proceedings. *Johnson v. U.S.*, 520 U.S. 461, 466-67, 469-70 (1997). (The *Johnson* case quoted the fourth element from its decision in a civil action, *U.S. v. Atkinson*, 297 U.S. 157, 160 (1936): "In exceptional circumstances, especially in criminal cases, appellate courts, in the public interest, may, of their own motion, notice errors to which no exception has been taken, if the errors are obvious, or if they otherwise substantially affect the fairness, integrity, or public reputation of judicial proceedings.")

The court's duty to give correct jury instructions in a civil action is shaped by at least four factors.

The factor most directly implied by a "plain" error rule is the obviousness of the mistake. The importance of the error is a second major factor. The costs of correcting an error reflect a third factor that is affected by a variety of circumstances. In a case that seems close to the fundamental error line, account also may be taken of the impact a verdict may have on nonparties.

RULE 53

Rule 53 is revised extensively to reflect changing practices in using masters. From the beginning in 1938, Rule 53 focused primarily on special masters who perform trial functions. Since then, however, courts have gained experience with masters appointed to perform a variety of pretrial and post-trial functions. *See* Willging, Hooper, Leary, Miletich, Reagan, & Shapard, *Special Masters' Incidence and Activity* (Federal Judicial Center 2000). This revised Rule 53 recognizes that in appropriate circumstances masters may properly be appointed to perform these functions and regulates such appointments. Rule 53 continues to address trial masters as well, but permits appointment of a trial master in an action to be tried to a jury only if the parties consent. The new rule clarifies the provisions that govern the appointment and function of masters for all purposes. Rule 53(g) also changes the standard of review for findings of fact made or recommended by a master. The core of the original Rule 53 remains, including its prescription that appointment of a master must be the exception and not the rule.

Special masters are appointed in many circumstances outside the Civil Rules. Rule 53 applies only to proceedings that Rule 1 brings within its reach.

Subdivision (a)(1)

District judges bear primary responsibility for the work of their courts. A master should be appointed only in limited circumstances. Subdivision (a)(1) describes three different standards, relating to appointments by consent of the parties, appointments for trial duties, and appointments for pretrial or post-trial duties.

Consent Masters. Subparagraph (a)(1)(A) authorizes appointment of a master with the parties' consent. Party consent does not require that the court make the appointment; the court retains unfettered discretion to refuse appointment.

Trial Masters. Use of masters for the core functions of trial has been progressively limited. These limits are reflected in the provisions of subparagraph (a)(1)(B) that restrict appointments to exercise trial functions. The Supreme Court gave clear direction to this trend in *La Buy v. Howes Leather Co.*, 352 U.S. 249 (1957); earlier roots are sketched in *Los Angeles Brush Mfg. Corp. v. James*, 272 U.S. 701 (1927). As to nonjury trials, this trend has developed through elaboration of the "exceptional condition" requirement in present Rule 53(b). This phrase is retained, and will continue to have the same force as it has developed. Although the provision that a reference "shall be the exception and not the rule" is deleted, its meaning is embraced for this setting by the exceptional condition requirement.

Subparagraph (a)(1)(B)(ii) carries forward the approach of present Rule 53(b), which exempts from the "exceptional condition" requirement "matters of account and of difficult computation of damages." This approach is justified only as to essentially ministerial determinations that require mastery of much detailed information but that do not require extensive determinations of credibility. Evaluations of witness credibility should only be assigned to a trial master when justified by an exceptional condition.

The use of a trial master without party consent is abolished as to matters to be decided by a jury unless a statute provides for this practice.

Abolition of the direct power to appoint a trial master as to issues to be decided by a jury leaves the way free to appoint a trial master with the consent of all parties. A trial master should be appointed in a jury case, with consent of the parties and concurrence of the court, only if the parties waive jury trial with respect to the issues submitted to the master or if the master's findings are to be submitted to the jury as evidence in the manner provided by former Rule 53(e)(3). In no circumstance may a master be appointed to preside at a jury trial.

The central function of a trial master is to preside over an evidentiary hearing on the merits of the claims or defenses in the action. This function distinguishes the trial master from most functions of pretrial and post-trial masters. If any master is to be used for such matters as a preliminary injunction hearing or a determination of complex damages issues, for example, the master should be a trial master. The line, however, is not distinct. A pretrial master might well conduct an evidentiary hearing on a discovery dispute, and a post-trial master might conduct evidentiary hearings on questions of compliance.

Rule 53 has long provided authority to report the evidence without recommendations in nonjury trials. This authority is omitted from Rule 53(a)(1)(B). In some circumstances a master may be appointed under Rule 53(a)(1)(A) or (C) to take evidence and report without recommendations.

For nonjury cases, a master also may be appointed to assist the court in discharging trial duties other than conducting an evidentiary hearing.

Pretrial and Post-Trial Masters. Subparagraph (a)(1)(C) authorizes appointment of a master to address pretrial or post-trial matters. Appointment is limited to matters that cannot be addressed effectively and in a timely fashion by an available district judge or magistrate judge of the district. A master's pretrial or post-trial duties may include matters that could be addressed by a judge, such as reviewing discovery documents for privilege, or duties that might not be suitable for a judge. Some forms of settlement negotiations, investigations, or administration of an organization are familiar examples of duties that a judge might not feel free to undertake.

Magistrate Judges. Particular attention should be paid to the prospect that a magistrate judge may be available for special assignments. United States magistrate judges are authorized by statute to perform many pretrial functions in civil actions. 28 U.S.C. § 636(b)(1). Ordinarily a district judge who delegates these functions should refer them to a magistrate judge acting as magistrate judge.

There is statutory authority to appoint a magistrate judge as special master. 28 U.S.C. § 636(b)(2). In special circumstances, or when expressly authorized by a statute other than § 636(b)(2), it may be appropriate to appoint a magistrate judge as a master when needed to perform functions outside those listed in § 636(b)(1). There is no apparent reason to appoint a magistrate judge to perform as master duties that could be performed in the role of magistrate judge. Party consent is required for trial before a magistrate judge, moreover, and this requirement should not be undercut by resort to Rule 53 unless specifically authorized by statute; see 42 U.S.C. § 2000e-5(f)(5).

Pretrial Masters. The appointment of masters to participate in pretrial proceedings has developed extensively over the last two decades as some district courts have felt the need for additional help in managing complex litigation. This practice is not well regulated by present Rule 53, which focuses on masters as trial participants. Rule 53 is amended to confirm the authority to appoint—and to regulate the use of—pretrial masters.

A pretrial master should be appointed only when the need is clear. Direct judicial performance of judicial functions may be particularly important in cases that involve important public issues or many parties. At the extreme, a broad delegation of pretrial responsibility as well as a delegation of trial responsibilities can run afoul of Article III.

A master also may be appointed to address matters that blur the divide between pretrial and trial functions. The court's responsibility to interpret patent claims as a matter of law, for example, may be greatly assisted by appointing a master who has expert knowledge of the field in which the patent operates. Review of the master's findings will be de novo under Rule 53(g)(4), but the advantages of initial determination by a master may make the process more effective and timely than disposition by the judge acting alone. Determination of foreign law may present comparable difficulties. The decision whether to appoint a master to address such matters is governed by subdivision (a)(1)(C), not the trial-master provisions of subdivision (a)(1)(B).

Post-Trial Masters. Courts have come to rely on masters to assist in framing and enforcing complex decrees. Present Rule 53 does not directly address this practice. Amended Rule 53 authorizes appointment of post-trial masters for these and similar purposes. The constraint of subdivision (a)(1)(C) limits this practice to cases in which the master's duties cannot be performed effectively and in a timely fashion by an available district judge or magistrate judge of the district.

Reliance on a master is appropriate when a complex decree requires complex policing, particularly when a party has proved resistant or intransigent. This practice has been recognized by the Supreme Court, see Local 28, Sheet Metal Workers' Internat. Assn. v. EEOC, 478 U.S. 421, 481-82 (1986). The master's role in enforcement may extend to investigation in ways that are quite unlike the traditional role of judicial officers in an adversary system.

Expert Witness Overlap. This rule does not address the difficulties that arise when a single person is appointed to perform overlapping roles as master and as court-appointed expert witness under Evidence Rule 706. Whatever combination of functions is involved, the Rule 53(a)(1)(B) limit that confines trial masters to issues to be decided by the court does not apply to a person who also is appointed as an expert witness under Evidence Rule 706.

Subdivision (a)(2) and (3). Masters are subject to the Code of Conduct for United States Judges, with exceptions spelled out in the Code. Special care must be taken to ensure that there is no actual or apparent conflict of interest involving a master. The standard of disqualification is established by 28 U.S.C. § 455. The affidavit required by Rule 53(b)(3) provides an important source of information about possible grounds for disqualification, but careful inquiry should be made at the time of making the initial appointment. The disqualification standards established by § 455 are strict. Because a master is not a public judicial officer, it may be appropriate to permit the parties to consent to appointment of a particular person as master in circumstances that would require disqualification of a judge. The judge must be careful to ensure that no party feels any pressure to consent, but with such assurances—and with the judge's own determination that there is no troubling conflict of interests or disquieting appearance of impropriety—consent may justify an otherwise barred appointment.

One potential disqualification issue is peculiar to the master's role. It may happen that a master who is an attorney represents a client whose litigation is assigned to the judge who appointed the attorney as master. Other parties to the litigation may fear that the attorney-master will gain special respect from the judge. A flat prohibition on appearance before the appointing judge during the time of service as master, however, might in some circumstances unduly limit the opportunity to make a desirable appointment. These matters may be regulated to some extent by state rules of professional responsibility. The question of present conflicts, and the possibility of future conflicts, can be considered at the time of appointment.

Depending on the circumstances, the judge may consider it appropriate to impose a non-appearance condition on the lawyer-master, and perhaps on the master's firm as well.

Subdivision (b). The order appointing a pretrial master is vitally important in informing the master and the parties about the nature and extent of the master's duties and authority. Care must be taken to make the order as precise as possible. The parties must be given notice and opportunity to be heard on the question whether a master should be appointed and on the terms of the appointment. To the extent possible, the notice should describe the master's proposed duties, time to complete the duties, standards of review, and compensation. Often it will be useful to engage the parties in the process of identifying the master, inviting nominations, and reviewing potential candidates. Party involvement may be particularly useful if a pretrial master is expected to promote settlement.

The hearing requirement of Rule 53(b)(1) can be satisfied by an opportunity to make written submissions unless the circumstances require live testimony.

Rule 53(b)(2) requires precise designation of the master's duties and authority. Clear identification of any investigating or enforcement duties is particularly important. Clear delineation of topics for any reports or recommendations is also an important part of this process. And it is important to protect against delay by establishing a time schedule for performing the assigned duties. Early designation of the procedure for fixing the master's compensation also may provide useful guidance to the parties.

Ex parte communications between a master and the court present troubling questions. Ordinarily the order should prohibit such communications, assuring that the parties know where authority is lodged at each step of the proceedings. Prohibiting ex parte communications between master and court also can enhance the role of a settlement master by assuring the parties that settlement can be fostered by confidential revelations that will not be shared with the court. Yet there may be circumstances in which the master's role is enhanced by the opportunity for ex parte communications with the court. A master assigned to help coordinate multiple proceedings, for example, may benefit from off-the-record exchanges with the court about logistical matters. The rule does not directly regulate these matters. It requires only that the court exercise its discretion and address the topic in the order of appointment.

Similarly difficult questions surround ex parte communications between a master and the parties. Ex parte communications may be essential in seeking to advance settlement. Ex parte communications also may prove useful in other settings, as with in camera review of documents to resolve privilege questions. In most settings, however, ex parte communications with the parties should be discouraged or prohibited. The rule requires that the court address the topic in the order of appointment.

Subdivision (b)(2)(C) provides that the appointment order must state the nature of the materials to be preserved and filed as the record of the master's activities, and (b)(2)(D) requires that the order state the method of filing the record. It is not feasible to prescribe the nature of the record without regard to the nature of the master's duties. The records appropriate to discovery duties may be different from those appropriate to encouraging settlement, investigating possible violations of a complex decree, or making recommendations for trial findings. A basic requirement, however, is that the master must make and file a complete record of the evidence considered in making or recommending findings of fact on the basis of evidence. The order of appointment should routinely include this requirement unless the nature of the appointment precludes any prospect that the master will make or recommend evidence-based findings of fact. In some circumstances it may be appropriate for a party to file materials directly with the court as provided by Rule 5(e), but in many circumstances filing with the court may be inappropriate. Confidentiality is important with respect to many materials that may properly be considered by a master. Materials in the record can be transmitted to the court, and filed, in connection with review of a master's order, report, or recommendations under subdivisions (f) and (g). Independently of review proceedings, the court may direct filing of any materials that it wishes to make part of the public record.

The provision in subdivision (b)(2)(D) that the order must state the standards for reviewing the master's orders, findings, or recommendations is a reminder of the provisions of subdivision (g)(3) that recognize stipulations for review less searching than the presumptive requirement of de novo decision by the court. Subdivision (b)(2)(D) does not authorize the court to supersede the limits of subdivision (g)(3).

In setting the procedure for fixing the master's compensation, it is useful at the outset to establish specific guidelines to control total expense. The court has power under subdivision (h) to change the basis and terms for determining compensation after notice to the parties.

Subdivision (b)(3) permits entry of the order appointing a master only after the master has filed an affidavit disclosing whether there is any ground for disqualification under 28 U.S.C. § 455. If the affidavit discloses a possible ground for disqualification, the order can enter only if the court determines that there is no ground for disqualification or if the parties, knowing of the ground for disqualification, consent with the court's approval to waive the disqualification.

The provision in Rule 53(b)(4) for amending the order of appointment is as important as the provisions for the initial order. Anything that could be done in the initial order can be done by amendment. The hearing requirement can be satisfied by an opportunity to make written submissions unless the circumstances require live testimony.

Subdivision (c). Subdivision (c) is a simplification of the provisions scattered throughout present Rule 53. It is intended to provide the broad and flexible authority necessary to discharge the master's responsibilities. The most important delineation of a master's authority and duties is provided by the Rule 53(b) appointing order.

Subdivision (d). The subdivision (d) provisions for evidentiary hearings are reduced from the extensive provisions in current Rule 53. This simplification of the rule is not intended to diminish the authority that may be delegated to a master. Reliance is placed on the broad and general terms of subdivision (c).

Subdivision (e). Subdivision (e) provides that a master's order must be filed and entered on the docket. It must be promptly served on the parties, a task ordinarily accomplished by mailing or other means as permitted by Rule 5(b). In some circumstances it may be appropriate to have the clerk's office assist the master in mailing the order to the parties.

Subdivision (f). Subdivision (f) restates some of the provisions of present Rule 53(e)(1). The report is the master's primary means of communication with the court. The materials to be provided to support review of the report will depend on the nature of the report. The master should provide all portions of the record preserved under Rule 53(b)(2)(C) that the master deems relevant to the report. The parties may designate additional materials from the record, and may seek permission to supplement the record with evidence. The court may direct that additional materials from the record be provided and filed. Given the wide array of tasks that may be assigned to a pretrial master, there may be circumstances that justify sealing a report or review record against public access—a report on continuing or failed settlement efforts is the most likely example. A post-trial master may be assigned duties in formulating a decree that deserve similar protection. Such circumstances may even justify denying access to the report or review materials by the parties, although this step should be taken only for the most compelling reasons. Sealing is much less likely to be appropriate with respect to a trial master's report.

Before formally making an order, report, or recommendations, a master may find it helpful to circulate a draft to the parties for review and comment. The usefulness of this practice depends on the nature of the master's proposed action.

Subdivision (g). The provisions of subdivision (g)(1), describing the court's powers to afford a hearing, take evidence, and act on a master's order, report, or recommendations are drawn from present Rule 53(e)(2), but are not limited, as present Rule 53(e)(2) is limited, to the report of a trial master in a nonjury action. The requirement that the court must afford an opportunity to be heard can be satisfied by taking written submissions when the court acts on the report without taking live testimony.

The subdivision (g)(2) time limits for objecting to—or seeking adoption or modification of—a master's order, report, or recommendations, are important. They are not jurisdictional. Although a court may properly refuse to entertain untimely review proceedings, the court may excuse the failure to seek timely review. The basic time period is lengthened to 20 days because the present 10-day period may be too short to permit thorough study and response to a complex report dealing with complex litigation. If no party asks the court to act on a master's report, the court is free to adopt the master's action or to disregard it at any relevant point in the proceedings.

Subdivision (g)(3) establishes the standards of review for a master's findings of fact or recommended findings of fact. The court must decide de novo all objections to findings of fact made or recommended by the master unless the parties stipulate, with the court's consent, that the findings will be reviewed for clear error or—with respect to a master appointed on the parties' consent or appointed to address pretrial or post-trial matters—that the findings will be final. Clear-error review is more likely to be appropriate with respect to findings that do not go to the merits of the underlying claims or defenses, such as findings of fact bearing on a privilege objection to a discovery request. Even if no objection is made, the court is free to decide the facts de novo; to review for clear error if an earlier approved stipulation provided clear-error review; or to withdraw its consent to a stipulation for clear-error review or finality, and then to decide de novo. If the court withdraws its consent to a stipulation for finality or clear-error review, it may reopen the opportunity to object.

Under Rule 53(g)(4), the court must decide de novo all objections to conclusions of law made or recommended by a master. As with findings of fact, the court also may decide conclusions of law de novo when no objection is made.

Apart from factual and legal questions, masters often make determinations that, when made by a trial court, would be treated as matters of procedural discretion. The court may set a standard for review of such matters in the order of appointment, and may amend the order to establish the standard. If no standard is set by the original or amended order appointing the master, review of procedural matters is for abuse of discretion. The subordinate role of the master means that the trial court's review for abuse of discretion may be more searching than the review that an appellate court makes of a trial court.

If a master makes a recommendation on any matter that does not fall within Rule 53(g)(3), (4), or (5), the court may act on the recommendation under Rule 53(g)(1).

Subdivision (h). The need to pay compensation is a substantial reason for care in appointing private persons as masters.

Payment of the master's fees must be allocated among the parties and any property or subject-matter within the court's control. The amount in controversy and the means of the parties may provide some guidance in making the allocation. The nature of the dispute also may be important—parties pursuing matters of public interest, for example, may deserve special protection. A party whose unreasonable behavior has occasioned the need to appoint a master, on the other hand, may properly be charged all or a major portion of the master's fees. It may be proper to revise an interim allocation after decision on the merits. The revision need not await a decision that is final for purposes of appeal, but may be made to reflect disposition of a substantial portion of the case.

The basis and terms for fixing compensation should be stated in the order of appointment. The court retains power to alter the initial basis and terms, after notice and an opportunity to be heard, but should protect the parties against unfair surprise.

The provision of former Rule 53(a) that the "provision for compensation shall not apply when a United States Magistrate Judge is designated to serve as a master" is deleted as unnecessary. Other provisions of law preclude compensation.

2006 ADVISORY COMMITTEE NOTES

RULE 26

Subdivision (a). Rule 26(a)(1)(B) is amended to parallel Rule 34(a) by recognizing that a party must disclose electronically stored information as well as documents that it may use to support its claims or defenses. The term "electronically stored information" has the same broad meaning in Rule 26(a)(1) as in Rule 34(a). This amendment is consistent with the 1993 addition of Rule 26(a)(1)(B). The term "data compilations" is deleted as unnecessary because it is a subset of both documents and electronically stored information.

Subdivision (a)(1)(E). Civil forfeiture actions are added to the list of exemptions from Rule 26(a)(1) disclosure requirements. These actions are governed by new Supplemental Rule G. Disclosure is not likely to be useful.

Subdivision (b)(2). The amendment to Rule 26(b)(2) is designed to address issues raised by difficulties in locating, retrieving, and providing discovery of some electronically stored information. Electronic storage systems often make it easier to locate and retrieve information. These advantages are properly taken into account in determining the reasonable scope of discovery in a particular case. But some sources of electronically stored information can be accessed only with substantial burden and cost. In a particular case, these burdens and costs may make the information on such sources not reasonably accessible.

It is not possible to define in a rule the different types of technological features that may affect the burdens and costs of accessing electronically stored information. Information systems are designed to provide ready access to information used in regular ongoing activities. They also may be designed so as to provide ready access to information that is not regularly used. But a system may retain information on sources that are accessible only by incurring substantial burdens or costs. Subparagraph (B) is added to regulate discovery from such sources.

Under this rule, a responding party should produce electronically stored information that is relevant, not privileged, and reasonably accessible, subject to the (b)(2)(C) limitations that apply to all discovery. The responding party must also identify, by category or type, the sources containing potentially responsive information that it is neither searching nor producing. The identification should, to the extent possible, provide enough detail to enable the requesting party to evaluate the burdens and costs of providing the discovery and the likelihood of finding responsive information on the identified sources.

A party's identification of sources of electronically stored information as not reasonably accessible does not relieve the party of its common-law or statutory duties to preserve evidence. Whether a responding party is required to preserve unsearched sources of potentially responsive information that it believes are not reasonably accessible depends on the circumstances of each case. It is often useful for the parties to discuss this issue early in litigation.

The volume of − and the ability to search—much electronically stored information means that in many cases the responding party will be able to produce information from reasonably accessible sources that will fully satisfy the parties' discovery needs. In many circumstances the requesting party should obtain and evaluate the information from such sources before insisting that the responding party search and produce information contained on sources that are not reasonably accessible. If the requesting party continues to seek discovery of information from sources identified as not reasonably accessible, the parties should discuss the burdens and costs of accessing and retrieving the information, the needs that may establish good cause for requiring all or part of the requested discovery even if the information sought is not reasonably accessible, and conditions on obtaining and producing the information that may be appropriate.

If the parties cannot agree whether, or on what terms, sources identified as not reasonably accessible should be searched and discoverable information produced, the issue may be raised either by a motion to compel discovery or by a motion for a protective order. The parties must confer before bringing either motion. If the parties do not resolve the issue and the court must decide, the responding party must show that the identified sources of information are not reasonably accessible because of undue burden or cost. The requesting party may need discovery to test this assertion. Such discovery might take the form of requiring the responding party to conduct a sampling of information contained on the sources identified as not reasonably accessible; allowing some form of inspection of such sources; or taking depositions of witnesses knowledgeable about the responding party's information systems.

Once it is shown that a source of electronically stored information is not reasonably accessible, the requesting party may still obtain discovery by showing good cause, considering the limitations of Rule 26(b)(2)(C) that balance the costs and potential benefits of discovery. The decision whether to require a responding party to search for and produce information that is not reasonably accessible depends not only on the burdens and costs of doing so, but also on whether those burdens and costs can be justified in the circumstances of the case. Appropriate considerations may include: (1) the specificity of the discovery request; (2) the quantity of information available from other and more easily accessed sources; (3) the failure to produce relevant information that seems likely to have existed but is no longer available on more easily accessed sources; (4) the likelihood of finding relevant, responsive information that cannot be obtained from other, more easily accessed sources; (5) predictions as to the importance and usefulness of the further information; (6) the importance of the issues at stake in the litigation; and (7) the parties' resources.

The responding party has the burden as to one aspect of the inquiry -- whether the identified sources are not reasonably accessible in light of the burdens and costs required to search for, retrieve, and produce whatever responsive information may be found. The requesting party has the burden of showing that its need for the discovery outweighs the burdens and costs of locating, retrieving, and producing the information. In some cases, the court will be able to determine whether the identified sources are not reasonably accessible and whether the requesting party has shown good cause for some or all of the discovery, consistent with the limitations of Rule 26(b)(2)(C), through a single proceeding or presentation. The good-cause determination, however, may be complicated because the court and parties may know little about what information the sources identified as not reasonably accessible might contain, whether it is relevant, or how valuable it may be to the litigation. In such cases, the parties may need some focused discovery, which may include sampling of the sources, to learn more about what burdens and costs are involved in accessing the information, what the information consists of, and how valuable it is for the litigation in light of information that can be obtained by exhausting other opportunities for discovery.

The good-cause inquiry and consideration of the Rule 26(b)(2)(C) limitations are coupled with the authority to set conditions for discovery. The conditions may take the form of limits on the amount, type, or sources of information required to be accessed and produced. The conditions may also include payment by the requesting party of part or all of the reasonable costs of obtaining information from sources that are not reasonably accessible. A requesting party's willingness to share or bear the access costs may be weighed by the court in determining whether there is good cause. But the producing party's burdens in reviewing the information for relevance and privilege may weigh against permitting the requested discovery.

The limitations of Rule 26(b)(2)(C) continue to apply to all discovery of electronically stored information, including that stored on reasonably accessible electronic sources.

Subdivision (b)(5). The Committee has repeatedly been advised that the risk of privilege waiver, and the work necessary to avoid it, add to the costs and delay of discovery. When the review is of electronically stored information, the risk of waiver, and the time and effort required to avoid it, can increase substantially because of the volume of electronically stored information and the difficulty in ensuring that all information to be produced has in fact been reviewed. Rule 26(b)(5)(A) provides a procedure for a party that has withheld information on the basis of privilege or protection as trial-preparation material to make the claim so that the requesting party can decide whether to contest the claim and the court can resolve the dispute. Rule 26(b)(5)(B) is added to provide a procedure for a party to assert a claim of privilege or trial-preparation material protection after information is produced in discovery in the action and, if the claim is contested, permit any party that received the information to present the matter to the court for resolution.

Rule 26(b)(5)(B) does not address whether the privilege or protection that is asserted after production was waived by the production. The courts have developed principles to determine whether, and under what circumstances, waiver results from inadvertent production of privileged or protected information. Rule 26(b)(5)(B) provides a procedure for presenting and addressing these issues. Rule 26(b)(5)(B) works in tandem with Rule 26(f), which is amended to direct the parties to discuss privilege issues in preparing their discovery plan, and which, with amended Rule 16(b), allows the parties to ask the court to include in an order any agreements the parties reach regarding issues of privilege or trial-preparation material protection. Agreements reached under Rule 26(f)(4) and orders including such agreements entered under Rule 16(b)(6) may be considered when a court determines whether a waiver has occurred. Such agreements and orders ordinarily control if they adopt procedures different from those in Rule 26(b)(5)(B).

A party asserting a claim of privilege or protection after production must give notice to the receiving party. That notice should be in writing unless the circumstances preclude it. Such circumstances could include the assertion of the claim during a deposition. The notice should be as specific as possible in identifying the information and stating the basis for the claim. Because the receiving party must decide whether to challenge the claim and may sequester the information and submit it to the court for a ruling on whether the claimed privilege or protection applies and whether it has been waived, the notice should be sufficiently detailed so as to enable the receiving party and the court to understand the basis for the claim and to determine whether waiver has occurred. Courts will continue to examine whether a claim of privilege or protection was made at a reasonable time when delay is part of the waiver determination under the governing law.

After receiving notice, each party that received the information must promptly return, sequester, or destroy the information and any copies it has. The option of sequestering or destroying the information is included in part because the receiving party may have incorporated the information in protected trial-preparation materials. No receiving party may use or disclose the information pending resolution of the privilege claim. The receiving party may present to the court the questions whether the information is privileged or protected as trial-preparation material, and whether the privilege or protection has been waived. If it does so, it must provide the court with the grounds for the privilege or protection specified in the producing party's notice, and serve all parties. In presenting the question, the party may use the content of the information only to the extent permitted by the applicable law of privilege, protection for trial-preparation material, and professional responsibility.

If a party disclosed the information to nonparties before receiving notice of a claim of privilege or protection as trial-preparation material, it must take reasonable steps to retrieve the information and to return it, sequester it until the claim is resolved, or destroy it.

Whether the information is returned or not, the producing party must preserve the information pending the court's ruling on whether the claim of privilege or of protection is properly asserted and whether it was waived. As with claims made under Rule 26(b)(5)(A), there may be no ruling if the other parties do not contest the claim.

Subdivision (f). Rule 26(f) is amended to direct the parties to discuss discovery of electronically stored information during their discovery-planning conference. The rule focuses on "issues relating to disclosure or discovery of electronically stored information"; the discussion is not required in cases not involving electronic discovery, and the amendment imposes no additional requirements in those cases. When the parties do anticipate disclosure or discovery of electronically stored information, discussion at the outset may avoid later difficulties or ease their resolution.

When a case involves discovery of electronically stored information, the issues to be addressed during the Rule 26(f) conference depend on the nature and extent of the contemplated discovery and of the parties' information systems. It may be important for the parties to discuss those systems, and accordingly important for counsel to become familiar with those systems before the conference. With that information, the parties can develop a discovery plan that takes into account the capabilities of their computer systems. In appropriate cases identification of, and early discovery from, individuals with special knowledge of a party's computer systems may be helpful.

The particular issues regarding electronically stored information that deserve attention during the discovery planning stage depend on the specifics of the given case. See Manual for Complex Litigation (4th) § 40.25(2) (listing topics for discussion in a proposed order regarding meet-and-confer sessions). For example, the parties may specify the topics for such discovery and the time period for which discovery will be sought. They may identify the various sources of such information within a party's control that should be searched for electronically stored information. They may discuss whether the information is reasonably accessible to the party that has it, including the burden or cost of retrieving and reviewing the information. See Rule 26(b)(2)(B). Rule 26(f)(3) explicitly directs the parties to discuss the form or forms in which electronically stored information might be produced. The parties may be able to reach agreement on the forms of production, making discovery more efficient. Rule 34(b) is amended to permit a requesting party to specify the form or forms in which it wants electronically stored information produced. If the requesting party does not specify a form, Rule 34(b) directs the responding party to state the forms it intends to use in the production. Early discussion of the forms of production may facilitate the application of Rule 34(b) by allowing the parties to determine what forms of production will meet both parties' needs. Early identification of disputes over the forms of production may help avoid the expense and delay of searches or productions using inappropriate forms.

Rule 26(f) is also amended to direct the parties to discuss any issues regarding preservation of discoverable information during their conference as they develop a discovery plan. This provision applies to all sorts of discoverable information, but can be particularly important with regard to electronically stored information. The volume and dynamic nature of electronically stored information may complicate preservation obligations. The ordinary operation of computers involves both the automatic creation and the automatic deletion or overwriting of certain information. Failure to address preservation issues early in the litigation increases uncertainty and raises a risk of disputes.

The parties' discussion should pay particular attention to the balance between the competing needs to preserve relevant evidence and to continue routine operations critical to ongoing activities. Complete or broad cessation of a party's routine computer operations could paralyze the party's activities. Cf. Manual for Complex Litigation (4th) § 11.422 ("A blanket preservation order may be prohibitively expensive and unduly burdensome for parties dependent on computer systems for their day-to-day operations.") The parties should take account of these considerations in their discussions, with the goal of agreeing on reasonable preservation steps.

The requirement that the parties discuss preservation does not imply that courts should routinely enter preservation orders. A preservation order entered over objections should be narrowly tailored. Ex parte preservation orders should issue only in exceptional circumstances.

Rule 26(f) is also amended to provide that the parties should discuss any issues relating to assertions of privilege or of protection as trial-preparation materials, including whether the parties can facilitate discovery by agreeing on procedures for asserting claims of privilege or protection after production and whether to ask the court to enter an order that includes any agreement the parties reach. The Committee has repeatedly been advised about the discovery difficulties that can result from efforts to guard against waiver of privilege and work-product protection. Frequently parties find it necessary to spend large amounts of time reviewing materials requested through discovery to avoid waiving privilege. These efforts are necessary because materials subject to a claim of privilege or protection are often difficult to identify. A failure to withhold even one such item may result in an argument that there has been a waiver of privilege as to all other privileged materials on that subject matter. Efforts to avoid the risk of waiver can impose substantial costs on the party producing the material and the time required for the privilege review can substantially delay access for the party seeking discovery.

These problems often become more acute when discovery of electronically stored information is sought. The volume of such data, and the informality that attends use of e-mail and some other types of electronically stored information, may make privilege determinations more difficult, and privilege review correspondingly more expensive and time consuming. Other aspects of electronically stored information pose particular difficulties for privilege review. For example, production may be sought of information automatically included in electronic files but not apparent to the creator or to readers. Computer programs may retain draft language, editorial comments, and other deleted matter (sometimes referred to as "embedded data" or "embedded edits") in an electronic file but not make them apparent to the reader. Information describing the history, tracking, or management of an electronic file (sometimes called "metadata") is usually not apparent to the reader viewing a hard copy or a screen image. Whether this information should be produced may be among the topics discussed in the Rule 26(f) conference. If it is, it may need to be reviewed to ensure that no privileged information is included, further complicating the task of privilege review.

Parties may attempt to minimize these costs and delays by agreeing to protocols that minimize the risk of waiver. They may agree that the responding party will provide certain requested materials for initial examination without waiving any privilege or protection -- sometimes known as a "quick peek." The requesting party then designates the documents it wishes to have actually produced. This designation is the Rule 34 request. The responding party then responds in the usual course, screening only those documents actually requested for formal production and asserting privilege claims as provided in Rule 26(b)(5)(A). On other occasions, parties enter agreements -- sometimes called "clawback agreements"-- that production without intent to waive privilege or protection should not be a waiver so long as the responding party identifies the documents mistakenly produced, and that the documents should be returned under those circumstances. Other voluntary arrangements may be appropriate depending on the circumstances of each litigation. In most circumstances, a party who receives information under such an arrangement cannot assert that production of the information waived a claim of privilege or of protection as trial-preparation material.

Although these agreements may not be appropriate for all cases, in certain cases they can facilitate prompt and economical discovery by reducing delay before the discovering party obtains access to documents, and by reducing the cost and burden of review by the producing party. A case-management or other order including such agreements may further facilitate the discovery process. Form 35 is amended to include a report to the court about any agreement regarding protections against inadvertent forfeiture or waiver of privilege or protection that the parties have reached, and Rule 16(b) is amended to recognize that the court may include such an agreement in a case-management or other order. If the parties agree to entry of such an order, their proposal should be included in the report to the court.

Rule 26(b)(5)(B) is added to establish a parallel procedure to assert privilege or protection as trial-preparation material after production, leaving the question of waiver to later determination by the court.

RULE 34

Subdivision (a). As originally adopted, Rule 34 focused on discovery of "documents" and "things." In 1970, Rule 34(a) was amended to include discovery of data compilations, anticipating that the use of computerized information would increase. Since then, the growth in electronically stored information and in the variety of systems for creating and storing such information has been dramatic. Lawyers and judges interpreted the term "documents" to include electronically stored information because it was obviously improper to allow a party to evade discovery obligations on the basis that the label had not kept pace with changes in information technology. But it has become increasingly difficult to say that all forms of electronically stored information, many dynamic in nature, fit within the traditional concept of a "document." Electronically stored information may exist in dynamic databases and other forms far different from fixed expression on paper. Rule 34(a) is amended to confirm that discovery of electronically stored information stands on equal footing with discovery of paper documents. The change clarifies that Rule 34 applies to information that is fixed in a tangible form and to information that is stored in a medium from which it can be retrieved and examined. At the same time, a Rule 34 request for production of "documents" should be understood to encompass, and the response should include, electronically stored information unless discovery in the action has clearly distinguished between electronically stored information and "documents."

Discoverable information often exists in both paper and electronic form, and the same or similar information might exist in both. The items listed in Rule 34(a) show different ways in which information may be recorded or stored. Images, for example, might be hard-copy documents or electronically stored information. The wide variety of computer systems currently in use, and the rapidity of technological change, counsel against a limiting or precise definition of electronically stored information. Rule 34(a)(1) is expansive and includes any type of information that is stored electronically. A common example often sought in discovery is electronic communications, such as e-mail. The rule covers -- either as documents or as electronically stored information -- information "stored in any medium," to encompass future developments in computer technology. Rule 34(a)(1) is intended to be broad enough to cover all current types of computer-based information, and flexible enough to encompass future changes and developments.

References elsewhere in the rules to "electronically stored information" should be understood to invoke this expansive approach. A companion change is made to Rule 33(d), making it explicit that parties choosing to respond to an interrogatory by permitting access to responsive records may do so by providing access to electronically stored information. More generally, the term used in Rule 34(a)(1) appears in a number of other amendments, such as those to Rules 26(a)(1), 26(b)(2), 26(b)(5)(B), 26(f), 34(b), 37(f), and 45. In each of these rules, electronically stored information has the same broad meaning it has under Rule 34(a)(1). References to "documents" appear in discovery rules that are not amended, including Rules 30(f), 36(a), and 37(c)(2). These references should be interpreted to include electronically stored information as circumstances warrant.

The term "electronically stored information" is broad, but whether material that falls within this term should be produced, and in what form, are separate questions that must be addressed under Rules 26(b), 26(c), and 34(b).

The Rule 34(a) requirement that, if necessary, a party producing electronically stored information translate it into reasonably usable form does not address the issue of translating from one human language to another. See In re Puerto Rico Elect. Power Auth., 687 F.2d 501, 504-510 (1st Cir. 1989).

Rule 34(a)(1) is also amended to make clear that parties may request an opportunity to test or sample materials sought under the rule in addition to inspecting and copying them. That opportunity may be important for both electronically stored information and hard-copy materials. The current rule is not clear that such testing or sampling is authorized; the amendment expressly permits it. As with any other form of discovery, issues of burden and intrusiveness raised by requests to test or sample can be addressed under Rules 26(b)(2) and 26(c). Inspection or testing of certain types of electronically stored information or of a responding party's electronic information system may raise issues of confidentiality or privacy. The addition of testing and sampling to Rule 34(a) with regard to documents and electronically stored information is not meant to create a routine right of direct access to a party's electronic information system, although such access might be justified in some circumstances. Courts should guard against undue intrusiveness resulting from inspecting or testing such systems.

Rule 34(a)(1) is further amended to make clear that tangible things must -- like documents and land sought to be examined -- be designated in the request.

Subdivision (b). Rule 34(b) provides that a party must produce documents as they are kept in the usual course of business or must organize and label them to correspond with the categories in the discovery request. The production of electronically stored information should be subject to comparable requirements to protect against deliberate or inadvertent production in ways that raise unnecessary obstacles for the requesting party. Rule 34(b) is amended to ensure similar protection for electronically stored information.

The amendment to Rule 34(b) permits the requesting party to designate the form or forms in which it wants electronically stored information produced. The form of production is more important to the exchange of electronically stored information than of hard-copy materials, although a party might specify hard copy as the requested form. Specification of the desired form or forms may facilitate the orderly, efficient, and cost-effective discovery of electronically stored information. The rule recognizes that different forms of production may be appropriate for different types of electronically stored information. Using current technology, for example, a party might be called upon to produce word processing documents, e-mail messages, electronic spreadsheets, different image or sound files, and material from databases. Requiring that such diverse types of electronically stored information all be produced in the same form could prove impossible, and even if possible could increase the cost and burdens of producing and using the information. The rule therefore provides that the requesting party may ask for different forms of production for different types of electronically stored information.

The rule does not require that the requesting party choose a form or forms of production. The requesting party may not have a preference. In some cases, the requesting party may not know what form the producing party uses to maintain its electronically stored information, although Rule 26(f)(3) is amended to call for discussion of the form of production in the parties' prediscovery conference.

The responding party also is involved in determining the form of production. In the written response to the production request that Rule 34 requires, the responding party must state the form it intends to use for producing electronically stored information if the requesting party does not specify a form or if the responding party objects to a form that the requesting party specifies. Stating the intended form before the production occurs may permit the parties to identify and seek to resolve disputes before the expense and work of the production occurs. A party that responds to a discovery request by simply producing electronically stored information in a form of its choice, without identifying that form in advance of the production in the response required by Rule 34(b), runs a risk that the requesting party can show that the produced form is not reasonably usable and that it is entitled to production of some or all of the information in an additional form. Additional time might be required to permit a responding party to assess the appropriate form or forms of production.

If the requesting party is not satisfied with the form stated by the responding party, or if the responding party has objected to the form specified by the requesting party, the parties must meet and confer under Rule 37(a)(2)(B) in an effort to resolve the matter before the requesting party can file a motion to compel. If they cannot agree and the court resolves the dispute, the court is not limited to the forms initially chosen by the requesting party, stated by the responding party, or specified in this rule for situations in which there is no court order or party agreement.

If the form of production is not specified by party agreement or court order, the responding party must produce electronically stored information either in a form or forms in which it is ordinarily maintained or in a form or forms that are reasonably usable. Rule 34(a) requires that, if necessary, a responding party "translate" information it produces into a "reasonably usable" form. Under some circumstances, the responding party may need to provide some reasonable amount of technical support, information on application software, or other reasonable assistance to enable the requesting party to use the information. The rule does not require a party to produce electronically stored information in the form it which it is ordinarily maintained, as long as it is produced in a reasonably usable form. But the option to produce in a reasonably usable form does not mean that a responding party is free to convert electronically stored information from the form in which it is ordinarily maintained to a different form that makes it more difficult or burdensome for the requesting party to use the information efficiently in the litigation. If the responding party ordinarily maintains the information it is producing in a way that makes it searchable by electronic means, the information should not be produced in a form that removes or significantly degrades this feature.

Some electronically stored information may be ordinarily maintained in a form that is not reasonably usable by any party. One example is "legacy" data that can be used only by superseded systems. The questions whether a producing party should be required to convert such information to a more usable form, or should be required to produce it at all, should be addressed under Rule 26(b)(2)(B).

Whether or not the requesting party specified the form of production, Rule 34(b) provides that the same electronically stored information ordinarily need be produced in only one form.

RULE 37
Subdivision (f). Subdivision (f) is new. It focuses on a distinctive feature of computer operations, the routine alteration and deletion of information that attends ordinary use. Many steps essential to computer operation may alter or destroy information, for reasons that have nothing to do with how that information might relate to litigation. As a result, the ordinary operation of computer systems creates a risk that a party may lose potentially discoverable information without culpable conduct on its part. Under Rule 37(f), absent exceptional circumstances, sanctions cannot be imposed for loss of electronically stored information resulting from the routine, good-faith operation of an electronic information system.

Rule 37(f) applies only to information lost due to the "routine operation of an electronic information system" -- the ways in which such systems are generally designed, programmed, and implemented to meet the party's technical and business needs. The "routine operation" of computer systems includes the alteration and overwriting of information, often without the operator's specific direction or awareness, a feature with no direct counterpart in hard-copy documents. Such features are essential to the operation of electronic information systems.

Rule 37(f) applies to information lost due to the routine operation of an information system only if the operation was in good faith. Good faith in the routine operation of an information system may involve a party's intervention to modify or suspend certain features of that routine operation to prevent the loss of information, if that information is subject to a preservation obligation. A preservation obligation may arise from many sources, including common law, statutes, regulations, or a court order in the case. The good faith requirement of Rule 37(f) means that a party is not permitted to exploit the routine operation of an information system to thwart discovery obligations by allowing that operation to continue in order to destroy specific stored information that it is required to preserve. When a party is under a duty to preserve information because of pending or reasonably anticipated litigation, intervention in the routine operation of an information system is one aspect of what is often called a "litigation hold." Among the factors that bear on a party's good faith in the routine operation of an information system are the steps the party took to comply with a court order in the case or party agreement requiring preservation of specific electronically stored information.

Whether good faith would call for steps to prevent the loss of information on sources that the party believes are not reasonably accessible under Rule 26(b)(2) depends on the circumstances of each case. One factor is whether the party reasonably believes that the information on such sources is likely to be discoverable and not available from reasonably accessible sources.

The protection provided by Rule 37(f) applies only to sanctions "under these rules." It does not affect other sources of authority to impose sanctions or rules of professional responsibility.

This rule restricts the imposition of "sanctions." It does not prevent a court from making the kinds of adjustments frequently used in managing discovery if a party is unable to provide relevant responsive information. For example, a court could order the responding party to produce an additional witness for deposition, respond to additional interrogatories, or make similar attempts to provide substitutes or alternatives for some or all of the lost information.

RULE 50

The language of Rule 50(a) has been amended as part of the general restyling of the Civil Rules to make them more easily understood and to make style and terminology consistent throughout the rules. These changes are intended to be stylistic only.

Rule 50(b) is amended to permit renewal of any Rule 50(a) motion for judgment as a matter of law, deleting the requirement that a motion be made at the close of all the evidence. Because the Rule 50(b) motion is only a renewal of the preverdict motion, it can be granted only on grounds advanced in the preverdict motion. The earlier motion informs the opposing party of the challenge to the sufficiency of the evidence and affords a clear opportunity to provide additional evidence that may be available. The earlier motion also alerts the court to the opportunity to simplify the trial by resolving some issues, or even all issues, without submission to the jury. This fulfillment of the functional needs that underlie present Rule 50(b) also satisfies the Seventh Amendment. Automatic reservation of the legal questions raised by the motion conforms to the decision in Baltimore & Carolina Line v. Redman, 297 U.S. 654 (1935).

This change responds to many decisions that have begun to move away from requiring a motion for judgment as a matter of law at the literal close of all the evidence. Although the requirement has been clearly established for several decades, lawyers continue to overlook it. The courts are slowly working away from the formal requirement. The amendment establishes the functional approach that courts have been unable to reach under the present rule and makes practice more consistent and predictable.

Many judges expressly invite motions at the close of all the evidence. The amendment is not intended to discourage this useful practice.

Finally, an explicit time limit is added for making a posttrial motion when the trial ends without a verdict or with a verdict that does not dispose of all issues suitable for resolution by verdict. The motion must be made no later than 10 days after the jury was discharged.

2007 ADVISORY COMMITTEE NOTES

RULE 8

[Text of Rule prior to amendment:]

Rule 8. General Rules of Pleading

(a) Claims for Relief

A pleading which sets forth a claim for relief, whether an original claim, counterclaim, cross-claim, or third-party claim, shall contain (1) a short and plain statement of the grounds upon which the court's jurisdiction depends, unless the court already has jurisdiction and the claim needs no new grounds of jurisdiction to support it, (2) a short and plain statement of the claim showing that the pleader is entitled to relief, and (3) a demand for judgment for the relief the pleader seeks. Relief in the alternative or of several different types may be demanded.

(b) Defenses; Form of Denials

A party shall state in short and plain terms the party's defenses to each claim asserted and shall admit or deny the averments upon which the adverse party relies. If a party is without knowledge or information sufficient to form a belief as to the truth of an averment, the party shall so state and this has the effect of a denial. Denials shall fairly meet the substance of the averments denied. When a pleader intends in good faith to deny only a part or a qualification of an averment, the pleader shall specify so much of it as is true and material and shall deny only the remainder. Unless the pleader intends in good faith to controvert all the averments of the preceding pleading, the pleader may make denials as specific denials of designated averments or paragraphs, or may generally deny all the averments except such designated averments or paragraphs as the pleader expressly admits; but, when the pleader does so intend to controvert all its averments, including averments of the grounds upon which the court's jurisdiction depends, the pleader may do so by general denial subject to the obligations set forth in Rule 11.

(c) Affirmative Defenses

In pleading to a preceding pleading, a party shall set forth affirmatively accord and satisfaction, arbitration and award, assumption of risk, contributory negligence, discharge in bankruptcy, duress, estoppel, failure of consideration, fraud, illegality, injury by fellow servant, laches, license, payment, release, res judicata, statute of frauds, statute of limitations, waiver, and any other matter constituting an avoidance or affirmative defense. When a party has mistakenly designated a defense as a counterclaim or a counterclaim as a defense, the court on terms, if justice so requires, shall treat the pleading as if there had been a proper designation.

(d) Effect of Failure to Deny

Averments in a pleading to which a responsive pleading is required, other than those as to the amount of damage, are admitted when not denied in the responsive pleading. Averments in a pleading to which no responsive pleading is required or permitted shall be taken as denied or avoided.

(e) Pleading to be Concise and Direct; Consistency

(1) Each averment of a pleading shall be simple, concise, and direct. No technical forms of pleading or motions are required.

(2) A party may set forth two or more statements of a claim or defense alternately or hypothetically, either in one count or defense or in separate counts or defenses. When two or more statements are made in the alternative and one of them if made independently would be sufficient, the pleading is not made insufficient by the insufficiency of one or more of the alternative statements. A party may also state as many separate claims or defenses as the party has regardless of consistency and whether based on legal, equitable, or maritime grounds. All statements shall be made subject to the obligations set forth in Rule 11.

(f) Construction of Pleadings

All pleadings shall be so construed as to do substantial justice.

RULE 11

[Text of Rule prior to amendment:]

Rule 11. Signing of Pleadings, Motions, and Other Papers; Representations to Court; Sanctions

(a) Signature

Every pleading, written motion, and other paper shall be signed by at least one attorney of record in the attorney's individual name, or, if the party is not represented by an attorney, shall be signed by the party. Each paper shall state the signer's address and telephone number, if any. Except when otherwise specifically provided by rule or statute, pleadings need not be verified or accompanied by affidavit. An unsigned paper shall be stricken unless omission of the signature is corrected promptly after being called to the attention of the attorney or party.

(b) Representations to Court

By presenting to the court (whether by signing, filing, submitting, or later advocating) a pleading, written motion, or other paper, an attorney or unrepresented party is certifying that to the best of the person's knowledge, information, and belief, formed after an inquiry reasonable under the circumstances,—

(1) it is not being presented for any improper purpose, such as to harass or to cause unnecessary delay or needless increase in the cost of litigation;

(2) the claims, defenses, and other legal contentions therein are warranted by existing law or by a nonfrivolous argument for the extension, modification, or reversal of existing law or the establishment of new law;

(3) the allegations and other factual contentions have evidentiary support or, if specifically so identified, are likely to have evidentiary support after a reasonable opportunity for further investigation or discovery; and

(4) the denials of factual contentions are warranted on the evidence or, if specifically so identified, are reasonably based on a lack of information or belief.

(c) Sanctions

If, after notice and a reasonable opportunity to respond, the court determines that subdivision (b) has been violated, the court may, subject to the conditions stated below, impose an appropriate sanction upon the attorneys, law firms, or parties that have violated subdivision (b) or are responsible for the violation.

(1) How Initiated

(A) By Motion. A motion for sanctions under this rule shall be made separately from other motions or requests and shall describe the specific conduct alleged to violate subdivision (b). It shall be served as provided in Rule 5, but shall not be filed with or presented to the court unless, within 21 days after service of the motion (or such other period as the court may prescribe), the challenged paper, claim, defense, contention, allegation, or denial is not withdrawn or appropriately corrected. If warranted, the court may award to the party prevailing on the motion the reasonable expenses and attorney's fees incurred in presenting or opposing the motion. Absent exceptional circumstances, a law firm shall be held jointly responsible for violations committed by its partners, associates, and employees.

(B) On Court's Initiative. On its own initiative, the court may enter an order describing the specific conduct that appears to violate subdivision (b) and directing an attorney, law firm, or party to show cause why it has not violated subdivision (b) with respect thereto.

(2) Nature of Sanction; Limitations

A sanction imposed for violation of this rule shall be limited to what is sufficient to deter repetition of such conduct or comparable conduct by others similarly situated. Subject to the limitations in subparagraphs (A) and (B), the sanction may consist of, or include, directives of a nonmonetary nature, an order to pay a penalty into court, or, if imposed on motion and warranted for effective deterrence, an order directing payment to the movant of some or all of the reasonable attorneys' fees and other expenses incurred as a direct result of the violation.

(A) Monetary sanctions may not be awarded against a represented party for a violation of subdivision (b)(2).

(B) Monetary sanctions may not be awarded on the court's initiative unless the court issues its order to show cause before a voluntary dismissal or settlement of the claims made by or against the party which is, or whose attorneys are, to be sanctioned.

(3) Order

When imposing sanctions, the court shall describe the conduct determined to constitute a violation of this rule and explain the basis for the sanction imposed.

(d) Inapplicability to Discovery

Subdivisions (a) through (c) of this rule do not apply to disclosures and discovery requests, responses, objections, and motions that are subject to the provisions of Rules 26 through 37.

RULE 15

[Text of Rule prior to amendment:]

Rule 15. Amended and Supplemental Pleadings

(a) Amendments

A party may amend the party's pleading once as a matter of course at any time before a responsive pleading is served or, if the pleading is one to which no responsive pleading is permitted and the action has not been placed upon the trial calendar, the party may so amend it at any time within 20 days after it is served. Otherwise a party may amend the party's pleading only by leave of court or by written consent of the adverse party; and leave shall be freely given when justice so requires. A party shall plead in response to an amended pleading within the time remaining for response to the original pleading or within 10 days after service of the amended pleading, whichever period may be the longer, unless the court otherwise orders.

(b) Amendments to Conform to the Evidence

When issues not raised by the pleadings are tried by express or implied consent of the parties, they shall be treated in all respects as if they had been raised in the pleadings. Such amendment of the pleadings as may be necessary to cause them to conform to the evidence and to raise these issues may be made upon motion of any party at any time, even after judgment; but failure so to amend does not affect the result of the trial of these issues. If evidence is objected to at the trial on the ground that it is not within the issues made by the pleadings, the court may allow the pleadings to be amended and shall do so freely when the presentation of the merits of the action will be subserved thereby and the objecting party fails to satisfy the court that the admission of such evidence would prejudice the party in maintaining the party's action or defense upon the merits. The court may grant a continuance to enable the objecting party to meet such evidence.

(c) Relation Back of Amendments

An amendment of a pleading relates back to the date of the original pleading when

(1) relation back is permitted by the law that provides the statute of limitations applicable to the action, or

(2) the claim or defense asserted in the amended pleading arose out of the conduct, transaction, or occurrence set forth or attempted to be set forth in the original pleading, or

(3) the amendment changes the party or the naming of the party against whom a claim is asserted if the foregoing provision (2) is satisfied and, within the period provided by Rule 4(m) for service of the summons and complaint, the party to be brought in by amendment (A) has received such notice of the institution of the action that the party will not be prejudiced in maintaining a defense on the merits, and (B) knew or should have known that, but for a mistake concerning the identity of the proper party, the action would have been brought against the party.

The delivery or mailing of process to the United States Attorney, or United States Attorney's designee, or the Attorney General of the United States, or an agency or officer who would have been a proper defendant if named, satisfies the requirement of subparagraphs (A) and (B) of this paragraph (3) with respect to the United States or any agency or officer thereof to be brought into the action as a defendant.

(d) Supplemental Pleadings

Upon motion of a party the court may, upon reasonable notice and upon such terms as are just, permit the party to serve a supplemental pleading setting forth transactions or occurrences or events which have happened since the date of the pleading sought to be supplemented. Permission may be granted even though the original pleading is defective in its statement of a claim for relief or defense. If the court deems it advisable that the adverse party plead to the supplemental pleading, it shall so order, specifying the time therefor.

RULE 19

[Text of Rule prior to amendment:]

Rule 19. Joinder of Persons Needed for Just Adjudication

(a) Persons to be Joined if Feasible

A person who is subject to service of process and whose joinder will not deprive the court of jurisdiction over the subject matter of the action shall be joined as a party in the action if (1) in the person's absence complete relief cannot be accorded among those already parties, or (2) the person claims an interest relating to the subject of the action and is so situated that the disposition of the action in the person's absence may (i) as a practical matter impair or impede the person's ability to protect that interest or (ii) leave any of the persons already parties subject to a substantial risk of incurring double, multiple, or otherwise inconsistent obligations by reason of the claimed interest. If the person has not been so joined, the court shall order that the person be made a party. If the person should join as a plaintiff but refuses to do so, the person may be made a defendant, or, in a proper case, an involuntary plaintiff. If the joined party objects to venue and joinder of that party would render the venue of the action improper, that party shall be dismissed from the action.

(b) Determination by Court Whenever Joinder Not Feasible

If a person as described in subdivision (a)(1)-(2) hereof cannot be made a party, the court shall determine whether in equity and good conscience the action should proceed among the parties before it, or should be dismissed, the absent person being thus regarded as indispensable. The factors to be considered by the court include: first, to what extent a judgment rendered in the person's absence might be prejudicial to the person or those already parties; second, the extent to which, by protective provisions in the judgment, by the shaping of relief, or other measures, the prejudice can be lessened or avoided; third, whether a judgment rendered in the person's absence will be adequate; fourth, whether the plaintiff will have an adequate remedy if the action is dismissed for nonjoinder.

(c) Pleading Reasons for Nonjoinder

A pleading asserting a claim for relief shall state the names, if known to the pleader, of any persons as described in subdivision (a)(1)-(2) hereof who are not joined, and the reasons why they are not joined.

(d) Exception of Class Actions

This rule is subject to the provisions of Rule 23.

RULE 37

[Text of Rule prior to amendment:]

Rule 37. Failure to Make Disclosure or Cooperate in Discovery; Sanctions

(a) Motion for Order Compelling Disclosure or Discovery

A party, upon reasonable notice to other parties and all persons affected thereby, may apply for an order compelling disclosure or discovery as follows:

(1) Appropriate Court. An application for an order to a party shall be made to the court in which the action is pending. An application for an order to a person who is not a party shall be made to the court in the district where the discovery is being, or is to be, taken.

(2) Motion

(A) If a party fails to make a disclosure required by Rule 26(a), any other party may move to compel disclosure and for appropriate sanctions. The motion must include a certification that the movant has in good faith conferred or attempted to confer with the party not making the disclosure in an effort to secure the disclosure without court action.

(B) If a deponent fails to answer a question propounded or submitted under Rules 30 or 31, or a corporation or other entity fails to make a designation under Rule 30(b)(6) or 31(a), or a party fails to answer an interrogatory submitted under Rule 33, or if a party, in response to a request for inspection submitted under Rule 34, fails to respond that inspection will be permitted as requested or fails to permit inspection as requested, the discovering party may move for an order compelling answer, or a designation, or an order compelling inspection in accordance with the request. The motion must include a certification that the movant has in good faith conferred or attempted to confer with the person or party failing to make the discovery in an effort to secure the information or material without court action. When taking a deposition on oral examination, the proponent of the question may complete or adjourn the examination before applying for an order.

(3) Evasive or Incomplete Disclosure, Answer, or Response. For purposes of this subdivision an evasive or incomplete disclosure, answer, or response is to be treated as a failure to disclose, answer, or respond.

(4) Expenses and Sanctions

(A) If the motion is granted or if the disclosure or requested discovery is provided after the motion was filed, the court shall, after affording an opportunity to be heard, require the party or deponent whose conduct necessitated the motion or the party or attorney advising such conduct or both of them to pay to the moving party the reasonable expenses incurred in making the motion, including attorney's fees, unless the court finds that the motion was filed without the movant's first making a good faith effort to obtain the disclosure or discovery without court action, or that the opposing party's nondisclosure, response, or objection was substantially justified, or that other circumstances make an award of expenses unjust.

(B) If the motion is denied, the court may enter any protective order authorized under Rule 26(c) and shall, after affording an opportunity to be heard, require the moving party or the attorney filing the motion or both of them to pay to the party or deponent who opposed the motion the reasonable expenses incurred in opposing the motion, including attorney's fees, unless the court finds that the making of the motion was substantially justified or that other circumstances make an award of expenses unjust.

(C) If the motion is granted in part and denied in part, the court may enter any protective order authorized under Rule 26(c) and may, after affording an opportunity to be heard, apportion the reasonable expenses incurred in relation to the motion among the parties and persons in a just manner.

(b) Failure to Comply with Order

(1) Sanctions by Court in District Where Deposition is Taken. If a deponent fails to be sworn or to answer a question after being directed to do so by the court in the district in which the deposition is being taken, the failure may be considered a contempt of that court.

(2) Sanctions by Court in Which Action is Pending. If a party or an officer, director, or managing agent of a party or a person designated under Rule 30(b)(6) or 31(a) to testify on behalf of a party fails to obey an order to provide or permit discovery, including an order made under subdivision (a) of this rule or Rule 35, or if a party fails to obey an order entered under Rule 26(f), the court in which the action is pending may make such orders in regard to the failure as are just, and among others the following:

(A) An order that the matters regarding which the order was made or any other designated facts shall be taken to be established for the purposes of the action in accordance with the claim of the party obtaining the order;

(B) An order refusing to allow the disobedient party to support or oppose designated claims or defenses, or prohibiting that party from introducing designated matters in evidence;

(C) An order striking out pleadings or parts thereof, or staying further proceedings until the order is obeyed, or dismissing the action or proceeding or any part thereof, or rendering a judgment by default against the disobedient party;

(D) In lieu of any of the foregoing orders or in addition thereto, an order treating as a contempt of court the failure to obey any orders except an order to submit to a physical or mental examination;

(E) Where a party has failed to comply with an order under Rule 35(a) requiring that party to produce another for examination, such orders as are listed in paragraphs (A), (B), and (C) of this subdivision, unless the party failing to comply shows that that party is unable to produce such person for examination.

In lieu of any of the foregoing orders or in addition thereto, the court shall require the party failing to obey the order or the attorney advising that party or both to pay the reasonable expenses, including attorney's fees, caused by the failure, unless the court finds that the failure was substantially justified or that other circumstances make an award of expenses unjust.

(c) Failure to Disclose; False or Misleading Disclosure; Refusal to Admit

(1) A party that without substantial justification fails to disclose information required by Rule 26(a) or 26(e)(1), or to amend a prior response to discovery as required by Rule 26(e)(2), is not, unless such failure is harmless, permitted to use as evidence at a trial, at a hearing, or on a motion any witness or information not so disclosed. In addition to or in lieu of this sanction, the court, on motion and after affording an opportunity to be heard, may impose other appropriate sanctions. In addition to requiring payment of reasonable expenses, including attorney's fees, caused by the failure, these sanctions may include any of the actions authorized under Rule 37(b)(2)(A), (B), and (C) and may include informing the jury of the failure to make the disclosure.

(2) If a party fails to admit the genuineness of any document or the truth of any matter as requested under Rule 36, and if the party requesting the admissions thereafter proves the genuineness of the document or the truth of the matter, the requesting party may apply to the court for an order requiring the other party to pay the reasonable expenses incurred in making that proof, including reasonable attorney's fees. The court shall make the order unless it finds that (A) the request was held objectionable pursuant to Rule 36(a), or (B) the admission sought was of no substantial importance, or (C) the party failing to admit had reasonable ground to believe that the party might prevail on the matter, or (D) there was other good reason for the failure to admit.

(d) Failure of Party to Attend at Own Deposition or Serve Answers to Interrogatories or Respond to Request for Inspection

If a party or an officer, director, or managing agent of a party or a person designated under Rule 30(b)(6) or 31(a) to testify on behalf of a party fails (1) to appear before the officer who is to take the deposition, after being served with a proper notice, or (2) to serve answers or objections to interrogatories submitted under Rule 33, after proper service of the interrogatories, or (3) to serve a written response to a request for inspection submitted under Rule 34, after proper service of the request, the court in which the action is pending on motion may make such orders in regard to the failure as are just, and among others it may take any action authorized under subparagraphs (A), (B), and (C) of subdivision (b)(2) of this rule. Any motion specifying a failure under clause (2) or (3) of this subdivision shall include a certification that the movant has in good faith conferred or attempted to confer with the party failing to answer or respond in an effort to obtain such answer or response without court action. In lieu of any order or in addition thereto, the court shall require the party failing to act or the attorney advising that party or both to pay the reasonable expenses, including attorney's fees, caused by the failure unless the court finds that the failure was substantially justified or that other circumstances make an award of expenses unjust.

The failure to act described in this subdivision may not be excused on the ground that the discovery sought is objectionable unless the party failing to act has a pending motion for a protective order as provided by Rule 26(c).

(e) Abrogated

(f) Electronically Stored Information

Absent exceptional circumstances, a court may not impose sanctions under these rules on a party for failing to provide electronically stored information lost as a result of the routine, good-faith operation of an electronic information system.

(g) Failure to Participate in the Framing of a Discovery Plan

If a party or a party's attorney fails to participate in good faith in the development and submission of a proposed discovery plan as required by Rule 26(f) the court may, after opportunity for hearing, require such party or attorney to pay to any other party the reasonable expenses, including attorney's fees, caused by the failure.

RULE 50

The language of Rule 50 has been amended as part of the general restyling of the Civil Rules to make them more easily understood and to make style and terminology consistent throughout the rules. These changes are intended to be stylistic only.

Former Rule 50(b) stated that the court reserves ruling on a motion for judgment as a matter of law made at the close of all the evidence "[i]f, for any reason, the court does not grant" the motion. The words "for any reason" reflected the proposition that the reservation is automatic and inescapable. The ruling is reserved even if the court explicitly denies the motion. The same result follows under the amended rule. If the motion is not granted, the ruling is reserved.

Amended Rule 50(e) identifies the appellate court's authority to direct the entry of judgment. This authority was not described in former Rule 50(d), but was recognized in Weisgram v. Marley Co., 528 U.S. 440 (2000), and in Neely v. Martin K. Eby Construction Company, 386 U.S. 317 (1967). When Rule 50(d) was drafted in 1963, the Committee Note stated that "[s]ubdivision (d) does not attempt a regulation of all aspects of the procedure where the motion for judgment n.o.v. and any accompanying motion for a new trial are denied * * *." Express recognition of the authority to direct entry of judgment does not otherwise supersede this caution.

[Text of Rule prior to amendment:]

Rule 50. Judgment as a Matter of Law in Jury Trials; Alternative Motion for New Trial; Conditional Rulings

(a) Judgment as a Matter of Law

(1) In General. If a party has been fully heard on an issue during a jury trial and the court finds that a reasonable jury would not have a legally sufficient evidentiary basis to find for the party on that issue, the court may:

(A) resolve the issue against the party; and

(B) grant a motion for judgment as a matter of law against the party on a claim or defense that, under the controlling law, can be maintained or defeated only with a favorable finding on that issue.

(2) Motion. A motion for judgment as a matter of law may be made at any time before the case is submitted to the jury. The motion must specify the judgment sought and the law and facts that entitle the movant to the judgment.

(b) Renewing a Motion for Judgment After Trial; Alternative Motion for New Trial; Conditional Rulings

If the court does not grant a motion for judgment as a matter of law made under subdivision (a), the court is considered to have submitted the action to the jury subject to the court's later deciding the legal questions raised by the motion. The movant may renew its request for judgment as a matter of law by filing a motion no later than 10 days after the entry of judgment or—if the motion addresses a jury issue not decided by a verdict—no later than 10 days after the jury was discharged. The movant may alternatively request a new trial or join a motion for a new trial under Rule 59. In ruling on a renewed motion, the court may:

(1) if a verdict was returned:

(A) allow the judgment to stand,

(B) order a new trial, or

(C) direct entry of judgment as a matter of law; or

(2) if no verdict was returned:

(A) order a new trial, or

(B) direct entry of judgment as a matter of law.

(c) Granting Renewed Motion for Judgment as a Matter of Law; Conditional Rulings; New Trial Motion

(1) If the renewed motion for judgment as a matter of law is granted, the court shall also rule on the motion for a new trial, if any, by determining whether it should be granted if the judgment is thereafter vacated or reversed, and shall specify the grounds for granting or denying the motion for the new trial. If the motion for a new trial is thus conditionally granted, the order thereon does not affect the finality of the judgment. In case the motion for a new trial has been conditionally granted and the judgment is reversed on appeal, the new trial shall proceed unless the appellate court has otherwise ordered. In case the motion for a new trial has been conditionally denied, the appellee on appeal may assert error in that denial; and if the judgment is reversed on appeal, subsequent proceedings shall be in accordance with the order of the appellate court.

(2) Any motion for a new trial under Rule 59 by a party against whom judgment as a matter of law is rendered shall be filed no later than 10 days after entry of the judgment.

(d) Same: Denial of Motion for Judgment as a Matter of Law

If the motion for judgment as a matter of law is denied, the party who prevailed on that motion may, as appellee, assert grounds entitling the party to a new trial in the event the appellate court concludes that the trial court erred in denying the motion for judgment. If the appellate court reverses the judgment, nothing in this rule precludes it from determining that the appellee is entitled to a new trial, or from directing the trial court to determine whether a new trial shall be granted.

TOPIC 1. GENERAL RULES APPLICABLE TO JUDGMENTS

§ 13. Requirement of Finality

The rules of res judicata are applicable only when a final judgment is rendered. However, for purposes of issue preclusion (as distinguished from merger and bar), "final judgment" includes any prior adjudication of an issue in another action that is determined to be sufficiently firm to be accorded conclusive effect.

Comment:

a. Rationale. The rules of res judicata state when a judgment in one action is to be carried over to a second action and given a conclusive effect there, whether by way of bar, merger, or issue preclusion. This Section makes the general common-sense point that such conclusive carry-over effect should not be accorded a judgment which is considered merely tentative in the very action in which it was rendered. On the contrary, the judgment must ordinarily be a firm and stable one, the "last word" of the rendering court—a "final" judgment.

b. Comparison with finality for purposes of appellate review. The question whether a judgment is "final" also arises in the context of statutes providing for appellate review of "final decisions" (as in 28 U.S.C. § 1291, "Final decisions of district courts"), or "final judgments or decrees" (as in 28 U.S.C. § 1257, "State courts; appeal, certiorari"). It has often been suggested that finality for appellate review is the same as finality for purposes of res judicata, but that has probably never been quite true, and it is surely not true at present when considerable liberties are being taken with finality in the context of appeal in order to take care of various exigent situations in which prompt review by the higher courts is thought necessary. The fact that a trial court order may be reviewable by interlocutory appeal, for example under 28 U.S.C. § 1292(b), does not necessarily mean that the matter resolved in the order should be treated as final for purposes of res judicata. A general working description of finality in the field of former adjudication will, however, resemble the older, traditional, strict formulation of the concept of finality for appellate review. Thus when res judicata is in question a judgment will ordinarily be considered final in respect to a claim (or a separable part of a claim, see Comment e below) if it is not tentative, provisional, or contingent and represents the completion of all steps in the adjudication of the claim by the court, short of any steps by way of execution or enforcement that may be consequent upon the particular kind of adjudication. Finality will be lacking if an issue of law or fact essential to the adjudication of the claim has been reserved for future determination, or if the court has decided that the plaintiff should have relief against the defendant of the claim but the amount of the damages, or the form or scope of other relief, remains to be determined.

The fact that a judgment is treated as final for purposes of res judicata does not necessarily mean that it is final for other purposes, for example, priority among lienors on property.

As to the more pliant view of finality that is appropriate with respect to issue preclusion, see the second sentence of the text of this Section and Comment g below.

c. Judgments granting or denying continuing relief. A judgment concluding an action is not deprived of finality for purposes of res judicata by reason of the fact that it grants or denies continuing relief, that is, requires the defendant, or holds that the defendant may not be required, to perform acts over a period of time. Judgments of these types are rendered typically in actions for injunctions, specific performance, alimony, separate maintenance, and child support and custody.

The res judicata consequences of such judgments follow normal lines while circumstances remain constant, but those consequences may be affected when a material change of the circumstances occurs after the judgment. Thus if the judgment denied on the merits the continuing relief sought, but there has been a later material change of conditions, a new claim may arise upon the later facts (to be considered sometimes in combination with the old), and that claim will be held not barred by the previous judgment. See § 24, Comment f. If the judgment was one granting continuing relief, and a change of circumstances makes the judgment too burdensome or otherwise inapposite as a regulation of ongoing conduct, it is ordinarily possible for the party concerned to apply to the rendering court for a modification of the terms of the judgment. See § 73. And in deciding whether a judgment granting or denying continuing relief should be given any preclusive effect in a later action on a different claim, the question arises whether the issues in the two actions are materially different because of events which occurred in the interim, in which case preclusion is to that extent to be denied. See § 27, Comment c.

As to the special problem that arises in determining whether or to what extent a judgment granting continuing relief is entitled to full faith and credit, see § 18, Comment d; Restatement, Second, Conflict of Laws § 109.

d. Judgment final but not a bar. A judgment may be final for purposes of res judicata although it embodies an adjudication that does not bar the plaintiff from maintaining another action against the defendant on the same claim. In such a case, there may be issue preclusion in another action between the parties on the same or a different claim as to issues that were decided as a basis for the judgment. See § 17(3) and Comments c and d; § 20 and Comment b. Examples of judgments that do not bar another action on the same claim are those resulting from a decision that the court lacks jurisdiction over the subject matter of the action or over the defendant, or from certain voluntary or involuntary dismissals of an action. See § 20. A judgment denying an application for intervention does not preclude assertion after intervenor's claim in a subsequent action unless the denial was on grounds having a preclusive effect, for example, that the intervenor's application failed to state a claim upon which relief might be granted.

e. Judgment final as to a part of an action or claim. A judgment may be final in a res judicata sense as to a part of an action although the litigation continues as to the rest. Thus in a bankruptcy or receivership proceeding the claim of a particular creditor may be finally adjudicated although the proceeding is not closed. So also in an action in which the plaintiff has joined a number of claims against the defendant, the rules of practice—for example, Rule 54(b) of the Federal Rules of Civil Procedure—may permit entry of judgment on particular claims as they are adjudicated, with the action continuing as to the remaining claims.

A judgment may be final as to part of a claim. Thus in an action upon a running account which is ordinarily taken to comprise but a single claim (see § 24, Comment d), the parties may agree or the court may direct that particular items be separately litigated and there may then be final judgments with respect to those items.

f. Proceedings to set aside or reverse judgment. A judgment otherwise final for purposes of the law of res judicata is not deprived of such finality by the fact that time still permits commencement of proceedings in the trial court to set aside the judgment and grant a new trial or the like; nor does the fact that a party has made such a motion render the judgment nonfinal. This is the case even when a statute or rule of court provides that the judgment cannot be executed upon or otherwise enforced during the period allowed for making such a motion and the further period until the motion if made is decided. The judgment ceases to be final if it is in fact set aside by the trial court, as it would be upon the granting of a motion for a new trial.

There have been differences of opinion about whether, or in what circumstances, a judgment can be considered final for purposes of res judicata when proceedings have been taken to reverse or modify it by appeal. The better view is that a judgment otherwise final remains so despite the taking of an appeal unless what is called an appeal actually consists of a trial de novo; finality is not affected by the fact that the taking of the appeal operates automatically as a stay or supersedeas of the judgment appealed from that prevents its execution or enforcement, or by the fact that the appellant has actually obtained a stay or supersedeas pending appeal.

The pendency of a motion for new trial or to set aside a judgment, or of an appeal from a judgment, is relevant in deciding whether the question of preclusion should be presently decided in the second action. It may be appropriate to postpone decision of that question until the proceedings addressed to the judgment are concluded.

Application of this Comment may give rise to a problem of inconsistent judgments when a judgment under appeal, relied on as a basis for a second judgment, is later reversed. This problem is considered at § 16.

g. Criteria for determining finality in the application of issue preclusion. The requirement of finality of judgment is interpreted strictly, as indicated in Comment a, when bar or merger is at stake. This is natural when it is considered that the effect of a judgment as bar or merger is to "extinguish" a claim, and, when there is merger, to create a new claim based on the judgment itself. See § 17(1),(2). Usually there is no occasion to interpret finality less strictly when the question is one of issue preclusion, that is, when the question is whether decision of a given issue in an action may be carried over to a second action in which it is again being litigated. (If the second action is on the same claim, preclusion is an instance of direct estoppel; if it is on a different claim, preclusion is an instance of collateral estoppel. See § 17, Comment c.) But to hold invariably that that kind of carry-over is not to be permitted until a final judgment in the strict sense has been reached in the first action can involve hardship—either needless duplication of effort and expense in the second action to decide the same issue, or, alternatively, postponement of decision of the issue in the second action for a possibly lengthy period of time until the first action has gone to a complete finish. In particular circumstances the wisest course is to regard the prior decision of the issue as final for the purpose of issue preclusion without awaiting the end judgment. See Illustrations 1-3. Before doing so, the court should determine that the decision to be carried over was adequately deliberated and firm, even if not final in the sense of forming a basis for a judgment already entered. Thus preclusion should be refused if the decision was avowedly tentative. On the other hand, that the parties were fully heard, that the court supported its decision with a reasoned opinion, that the decision was subject to appeal or was in fact reviewed on appeal, are factors supporting the conclusion that the decision is final for the purpose of preclusion. The test of finality, however, is whether the conclusion in question is procedurally definite and not whether the court might have had doubts in reaching the decision.

Application of the present Comment, like application of Comment f, may result in inconsistent judgments; see § 16.

ILLUSTRATIONS:

1. A, owner, brings an action against B, builder, for fraudulently inducing A to enter a construction contract. A moves in that action to stay arbitration of B's claim against A for payments due under the contract, contending that the arbitration clause is ineffective because it was induced by fraud. After a thorough hearing, the court grants A a preliminary injunction against arbitration. B appeals under a statute permitting review of such an interlocutory order. The appellate court reverses on the facts, finding that A failed to show that there was even a substantial issue as to fraud. If the court in a separate action by B against A to compel arbitration determines that the negative finding as to fraud in the first action was adequately deliberated and firm, that finding should be accepted as conclusive even though the first action has not reached final judgment in the strict sense.

2. In the course of an interpleader action to determine the security interests of a number of claimants in property of a debtor, claimant A applies for a determination as to the validity of notes made by claimant B and endorsed to A, evidently secured by part of the interpleaded property. The interpleader court makes various findings upholding the validity of the notes, but an appeal is dismissed on the ground that a determination of liability without more is not an appealable final decision. If the court in a separate action by A against B to recover the amount of the notes determines that the findings as to the validity of the notes were adequately deliberated and firm, it should hold those findings conclusive in the separate action. The court as a discretionary matter may hold the issues as to the validity of the notes to be conclusively settled.

3. In a jurisdiction that permits "split" trials (a trial of liability followed, if liability is found, by a separate trial to ascertain the damages), the jury in a negligence case finds for the plaintiff A as to liability, the defendant B having denied his own negligence and pleaded contributory negligence on the part of A. Under the law of the jurisdiction, B cannot appeal at this point as there is no judgment that qualifies as final for that purpose; an appealable judgment would be reached later, when, in the second phase of trial, another jury assessed the damages. But prior to the second phase, the jury's verdict as to liability may be held conclusive as to the issues of A's and B's negligence in any other action between them in which the same issues appear.

§ 14. Effective Date Of Final Judgment

For purposes of res judicata, the effective date of a final judgment is the date of its rendition, without regard to the date of commencement of the action in which it is rendered or the action in which it is to be given effect.

Comment:

a. **General**. In order that a final judgment shall be given res judicata effect in a pending action, it is not required that the judgment shall have been rendered before that action was commenced. Nor is a judgment, otherwise entitled to res judicata effect in a pending action, to be deprived of such effect by the fact that the action in which it was rendered was commenced later than the pending action. It is merely required that rendition of the final judgment shall antedate its application as res judicata in the pending action. Thus when two actions are pending which are based on the same claim, or which involve the same issue, it is the final judgment first rendered in one of the actions which becomes conclusive in the other action (assuming any further prerequisites are met), regardless of which action was first brought.

b. **Cross-reference**. As to the question of which of two inconsistent judgments is entitled to conclusive effect in a third pending action, see § 15.

§ 15. Inconsistent Judgments

When in two actions inconsistent final judgments are rendered, it is the later, not the earlier, judgment that is accorded conclusive effect in a third action under the rules of res judicata.

Comment:

a. **Cross-reference**. As to what constitutes the "later" judgment, see § 14.

b. **Rationale**. The considerations of policy which support the doctrine of res judicata are not so strong as to require that the court apply them of its own motion when the party himself has failed to claim such benefits as may flow from them. Accordingly, when a prior judgment is not relied upon in a pending action in which it would have had conclusive effect as res judicata, the judgment in that action is valid even though it is inconsistent with the prior judgment. It follows that it is this later judgment, rather than the earlier, that may be successfully urged as res judicata in a third action, assuming that other prerequisites are satisfied. Indeed, the later of the two inconsistent judgments is ordinarily held conclusive in a third action even when the earlier judgment was relied on in the second action and the court erroneously held that it was not conclusive. See Comment e below.

c. **Application to merger, bar, and issue preclusion**. The rule stated in this Section governs the effect of a judgment by way of merger, bar, or issue preclusion. See Illustrations 1-3.

ILLUSTRATIONS:

1. A sues B on a promissory note. B denies that he executed the note. There is a trial resulting in a verdict for B, and judgment is rendered in B's favor. A brings a second action against B on the note, and B defaults, and judgment is given for A for the amount of the note and interest thereon. Thereafter A brings an action against B on the second judgment. The judgment for B in the first action is no defense.

2. A sues B on a promissory note. Judgment is given for A against B by default. A brings an action against B on the judgment. B defends on the ground that the court had no jurisdiction over him in the original action, and the defense is upheld and judgment given for B. Thereafter A brings an action against B on the first judgment. The judgment in the second action is a defense, even though the court is of the opinion that the court in the first action had jurisdiction over B.

3. In an action between the taxing authority and a taxpayer a question as to the value of property on January 1, 1970, to be used as the basis for a deduction for depreciation, is litigated and determined. In a second action between the same parties involving a tax for the following year the same issue is raised but the prior judgment is not shown, and the court makes a different determination as to the value of the property on January 1, 1970. In a third action between the same parties involving a tax for a third year, the judgment in the second action, if shown, is conclusive as to the value of the property on January 1, 1970.

d. **Application to actions involving title**. The rule of this Section is applicable where a question of title to property is raised in the three actions. If the first judgment adjudges that one of the parties has title, and in a second action the prior judgment is not alleged, or is alleged but erroneously held to be not conclusive, and title is adjudged to be in the other party, then in a third action the later judgment and not the earlier is conclusive under the rules of res judicata.

e. **Cross-reference to Restatement, Second, of Conflicts**. Although the later judgment is ordinarily held conclusive even though it erroneously denied res judicata effect to the earlier judgment, the rule may be different if the error consisted of a denial of full faith and credit to the judgment of a sister state and the losing party was denied review in the Supreme Court of the United States. "In such a situation, it might be thought inappropriate to require that conclusive effect be given under full faith and credit to the later inconsistent judgment." Restatement, Second, Conflict of Laws § 114, Comment b.

§ 16. Judgment Based Upon A Judgment That Is Subsequently Reversed

A judgment based on an earlier judgment is not nullified automatically by reason of the setting aside, or reversal on appeal, or other nullification of that earlier judgment; but the later judgment may be set aside, in appropriate proceedings, with provision for any suitable restitution of benefits received under it.

Note: For rules concerning relief from judgments, see Chapter 5.

Comment:

a. **How the problem arises**. Under § 13, Comments f and g, a judgment in an action may be regarded as final for purposes of res judicata, and be entitled to conclusive effect in a second action, notwithstanding the fact that it is still liable to be nullified, for example, by a post-judgment motion such as a motion for a new trial, or by reversal on appeal. If judgment is rendered in the second action on the basis of the judgment in the first, and the judgment in the first is then nullified, the problem arises what is to happen to the second, dependent judgment.

b. **How the problem may be avoided**. This Section states a solution to the problem just put, but it is an inconvenient solution at best. It may be feasible for the court in the second action to avoid the problem. When the second action is being maintained in the same jurisdiction as the first, and is simply repetitious of the first, that is, involves the same claim between the same parties, the second action may be subject from the outset to dismissal ("abatement") on the basis of the defense of "other action pending," leaving only the first action and obviating the problem altogether. When that step has not been taken, or the actions are being maintained in different jurisdictions, or there is not an identity of claims but rather an identity of issues, it may still be advisable for the court that is being asked to apply the judgment as res judicata to stay its own proceedings to await the ultimate disposition of the judgment in the trial court or on appeal. This course commends itself if the disposition will not be long delayed and especially if there is substantial doubt whether the judgment will be upheld.

c. Solution of the problem. As stated in Comment a above, the problem when met head-on is that of a judgment based and dependent upon an earlier judgment which subsequently is nullified. It has been contended that the later judgment should then be automatically nullified. The current doctrine, however, is that the later judgment remains valid, but a party, upon a showing that the earlier judgment has been nullified and that relief from the later judgment is warranted, may by appropriate proceedings secure such relief.

If, when the earlier judgment is set aside or reversed, the later judgment is still subject to a post-judgment motion for a new trial or the like, or is still open to appeal, or such a motion has actually been made and is pending or an appeal has been taken and remains undecided, a party may inform the trial or appellate court of the nullification of the earlier judgment and the consequent elimination of the basis for the later judgment. The court should then normally set aside the later judgment. When the later judgment is no longer open to a motion for a new trial or the like at the trial court level, nor subject to appeal, the fact of the nullification of the earlier judgment may be made the ground for appropriate proceedings for relief from the later judgment with any suitable provision for restitution of benefits that may have been obtained under that judgment. See Chapter 5.

TOPIC 2. PERSONAL JUDGMENTS

TITLE A. IN GENERAL

§ 17. Effects of Former Adjudication—General Rules

A valid and final personal judgment is conclusive between the parties, except on appeal or other direct review, to the following extent:

(1) If the judgment is in favor of the plaintiff, the claim is extinguished and merged in the judgment and a new claim may arise on the judgment (see § 18);

(2) If the judgment is in favor of the defendant, the claim is extinguished and the judgment bars a subsequent action on that claim (see § 19);

(3) A judgment in favor of either the plaintiff or the defendant is conclusive, in a subsequent action between them on the same or a different claim, with respect to any issue actually litigated and determined if its determination was essential to that judgment (see § 27).

These general rules are subject to exceptions: as to Subsections (1) and (2), see §§ 20 and 26; as to Subsection (3), see § 28.

Cross-reference to Restatement, Second, of Conflicts. This Section, like the whole of the present Restatement, is concerned mainly with the res judicata effects of a judgment upon later actions in the courts of the same state. Effects in the courts of a sister state are dealt with in Restatement, Second, Conflict of Laws §§ 93-121. Attention is invited particularly to the discussion of the problem of merger in interstate situations, summarized herein at § 18, Comment d.

Comment:

a. Merger (Subsection (1)). When a valid and final personal judgment is rendered in favor of the plaintiff, the claim is generally merged in the judgment. This means that the claim, whether it was valid or not, is extinguished, and the judgment with new rights of enforcement thereof is substituted for the claim. Merger is dealt with in greater detail in § 18. Compare the exceptions to the general rule against splitting of claims in § 26.

b. Bar (Subsection (2)). When a valid and final personal judgment is rendered in favor of the defendant, the judgment is generally a bar to a subsequent action on the claim. It is sometimes said that there is an "estoppel by judgment," but that term is not used in the Restatement of this subject. If the original claim was valid, it is extinguished by the judgment; if it was not valid, the effect of the judgment is conclusively to establish its invalidity. The general rule as to bar is dealt with in greater detail in § 19, and the exceptions to the general rule in § 20.

c. Issue preclusion (Subsection (3)). A valid and final personal judgment, whether in favor of the plaintiff or of the defendant, has a further effect—that of issue preclusion. In a subsequent action between the parties, the judgment generally is conclusive as to the issues raised in the subsequent action if those issues were actually litigated and determined in the prior action and if their determination was essential to the judgment. When the subsequent action is on a different claim, this effect of the judgment is sometimes designated a collateral estoppel. It is also sometimes called an "estoppel by verdict," but that phrase is not used in this Restatement; it is misleading, since it is not a verdict but the judgment that is conclusive upon the parties.

When an issue is actually litigated and determined in an action, the determination is also generally conclusive in any subsequent action between the parties on the same claim. This effect of the judgment is sometimes designated a direct estoppel. Ordinarily, after a judgment is rendered in an action, the claim is extinguished by the judgment's bar or merger effect, and therefore it is impossible to maintain a subsequent action on the claim. But there are exceptions. For example, when a judgment for the defendant is based on lack of jurisdiction, improper venue, or nonjoinder or misjoinder of parties, the plaintiff is not precluded from maintaining another action on the claim (see § 20 (1)). Also, when the defendant interposes a counterclaim on which an affirmative judgment in his favor is not permitted to be rendered, and he obtains judgment on the counterclaim, he is not precluded from subsequently maintaining an action on his claim to secure further relief (see § 21(2)). See also the exceptional interstate situations referred to in § 18, Comment d below, where after judgment upon a claim there may be a subsequent action upon that claim in a sister state.

d. **Erroneous judgment**. The general rules stated in this Section are applicable to a valid (see §§ 1-12) and final (see § 13) judgment, even if it is erroneous and subject to reversal. If the judgment is erroneous, the unsuccessful party's remedy is to have it set aside or reversed in the original proceedings. Such a remedy may be sought by a motion for a new trial or other relief in the court that rendered the judgment, or by an appeal or other proceedings for review of the judgment in an appellate court.

e. **Relief from judgment**. Questions as to the right to relief from a judgment obtained by fraud or the like are dealt with in Chapter 5.

f. **Effect of judgment on persons who were not parties**. Questions as to the effect of a judgment upon persons who were not parties to the action in which the judgment was rendered are dealt with in Chapter 4.

TITLE B. EFFECTS ON THE ORIGINAL CLAIM

§ 18. Judgment For Plaintiff—The General Rule Of Merger

When a valid and final personal judgment is rendered in favor of the plaintiff:

(1) The plaintiff cannot thereafter maintain an action on the original claim or any part thereof, although he may be able to maintain an action upon the judgment; and

(2) In an action upon the judgment, the defendant cannot avail himself of defenses he might have interposed, or did interpose, in the first action.

This general rule is subject to the exception stated in § 26.

Cross-reference to exceptions. The question of the dimensions of a claim for purposes of merger (as well as bar) is considered in §§ 24-26. Attention is invited particularly to § 26; in the cases there described, maintenance of an action on all or part of an original claim is permitted even though, by the ordinary application of the present Section, the claim would be wholly merged in a judgment previously obtained upon it.

Comment:

a. **The doctrine of merger**. When the plaintiff recovers a valid and final personal judgment, his original claim is extinguished and rights upon the judgment are substituted for it. The plaintiff's original claim is said to be "merged" in the judgment. It is immaterial whether the defendant had a defense to the original action if he did not rely on it, or if he did rely on it and judgment was nevertheless given against him. It is immaterial whether the judgment was rendered upon a verdict or upon a motion to dismiss or other objection to the pleadings or upon consent, confession, or default.

b. **Action not maintainable on the original claim in the same state**. After merger of the original claim in a judgment for the plaintiff, the plaintiff may not maintain an action on the original claim in the state that rendered the judgment. If he attempts to do so, the defendant can set up the prior judgment as a defense.

This rule has practical effects because it might be advantageous to the plaintiff, despite his judgment, to bring a new action on the original claim. It is true that if the judgment was obtained on a liquidated claim, it would not be of any advantage to bring another action; but if the claim was unliquidated, the plaintiff might hope to recover a larger sum than that awarded to him by the judgment. Thus, if he brought an action against the defendant for negligently causing him personal injury, and after a trial the jury awarded him a certain sum and judgment was given for that sum, he might later be able to prove that the injury was more serious than had appeared at the trial. Even though he had no further evidence to offer, he might hope that new jury would award a greater sum. Since, however, his claim has been merged in the judgment, he cannot maintain an action on the original claim. See Illustrations 1-2, and § 25, Comment c, where certain exceptional situations are noted.

The same principle holds where the judgment obtained in the original action required the defendant to perform acts other than the payment of money or to refrain from such acts. The judgment precludes an action on the original claim seeking, perhaps, alternative or additional relief. See Illustration 3, and compare § 25, Comment j.

The fact that the judgment was based on error does not preclude the defendant from setting the judgment up as a defense to an action on the original claim. If it was erroneous, the plaintiff might have taken steps to have it set aside or reversed in the original proceeding.

ILLUSTRATIONS:

1. A brings an action against B for negligently causing injury to A. At the trial A is unable to prove any serious injury to his person. Verdict is given for A for $100 and judgment is entered thereon. Thereafter it appears that A's injuries are more serious than proved at the trial. A is precluded by the judgment from maintaining a second action against B for the collision.

2. The facts are the same as stated in Illustration 1, except that at the trial of the first action A offers evidence of nervous shock, and the court erroneously excludes such evidence. A is precluded by the judgment from maintaining a second action against B for the collision.

3. A and B enter into a contract for the sale of land located in State X. B refuses to convey the land. A brings an action for specific performance in State X, and a judgment is entered in his favor ordering B to convey the land. A is precluded by the judgment from maintaining a second action in State X to secure money damages in lieu of specific performance, or to obtain damages for delay in conveying the land in addition to the specific performance already adjudged.

c. **Enforcement of a judgment in the same state**. A judgment for the plaintiff awarding him a sum of money creates a debt in that amount in his favor. He may maintain proceedings by way of execution for enforcement of the judgment. He may also be able to maintain an action upon the judgment. Ordinarily no useful purpose is served by bringing an action in the same state upon the judgment instead of executing upon it, but if the period for executing upon a judgment has run or the period of the statute of limitations applicable to the judgment has almost run, the plaintiff can by appropriate proceedings revive the executability of the judgment or bring an action upon the judgment and obtain a new judgment upon which the limitations period will run again.

Similarly, when a plaintiff has obtained a judgment other than one for the payment of money — such as a judgment ordering the defendant to engage or refrain from engaging in certain conduct — the plaintiff may seek enforcement of the judgment by proceedings in the nature of execution or by application for contempt or other sanctions, and with the passage of time, revivor or suit upon the judgment may become necessary to effectuate or preserve the plaintiff's rights.

When the plaintiff brings an action upon the judgment, the defendant cannot avail himself of defenses which he might have interposed in the original action. See Illustration 4. It is immaterial whether he interposed the defense or failed to do so or even defaulted in the original action. Nor does the fact that the judgment was erroneous preclude the plaintiff from maintaining an action upon it. See Illustrations 5 and 6.

In an action on the judgment the defendant may interpose matters which have arisen since the rendition of the judgment and constitute defenses to its enforcement such as payment, release, accord and satisfaction, or the statute of limitations. He may also interpose a counterclaim. It is immaterial that he might have interposed that counterclaim in the original action but did not do so, see § 22, unless the counterclaim was required to be interposed in the original action for the reasons set forth in § 22(2).

When the judgment calls for performance, positive or negative, over a period of time, the question may arise whether circumstances have so changed as to make enforcement inequitable.

A special problem arises when a plaintiff obtains judgment in an action based on a prior judgment and that prior judgment is then reversed on appeal. This question is considered in § 16.

ILLUSTRATIONS:

4. A brings an action against B on a promissory note. B defaults. Judgment is given for A. A brings an action against B on the judgment. In this action B is precluded from denying that he executed the note and from setting up an affirmative defense such as fraud or illegality.

5. A brings an action against B for breach of contract. B defends on the ground that his promise was without consideration. The court erroneously rules that the promise, although without consideration, is enforceable. Verdict and judgment are given for A. A brings an action against B on the judgment. B is precluded from setting up the lack of consideration as a defense to the action.

6. A brings an action against B for negligently injuring him. Verdict is given for A for $10,000. B moves for a new trial on the ground that the damages awarded by the jury are excessive. The court erroneously denies the motion and judgment is given for A on the verdict. A brings an action against B on the judgment. B is precluded from defending on the ground that the damages awarded in the first action were excessive.

d. **Effect of judgment in another state — full faith and credit**. This subject is dealt with in Restatement, Second, Conflict of Laws §§ 93-121, but a summary statement in this and the following Comments may be found useful.

Under the Full Faith and Credit Clause of the Constitution, a large category of judgments must be given the same res judicata effects by sister states as they are accorded in the respective states of rendition. Thus, valid, final, nonmodifiable judgments for the payments of money are entitled to such full respect in sister states. See id. §§ 100-01, and Illustrations 7 and 8 below.

Certain judgments, although valid and final, may constitutionally be denied all res judicata effects in the courts of sister states, but sister states may choose to give these judgments res judicata effects including that of merger. Thus, under current constitutional interpretation, a sister state may deny all effect to a judgment for support or the like insofar as it remains subject to modification in the state of rendition either as to sums that have accrued and are unpaid or as to sums that will accrue in the future; on the other hand, the sister state may elect to accord to such judgments the res judicata consequences that would attach in the respective states where rendered. See id. § 109. So also a judgment which involves an improper interference with important interests of a sister state may be denied res judicata effects by that sister state. See id. § 103. A judgment denying equitable relief is entitled to effect in a sister state under the rules of bar. And a judgment ordering the doing of an act other than payment of money or enjoining the doing of the act is entitled to effect in a sister state by way of issue preclusion; arguably the Constitution does not require that such a judgment be given effect in a sister state by way of merger, but the current tendency is to accord that effect also. See id. § 102, and Illustration 9 below.

ILLUSTRATIONS:

7. A brings an action in State X against B for battery. B denies the battery. Verdict and judgment are given for A for $100. A sues B in State Y for the same battery. B sets up the prior judgment as a defense. The court in State Y is bound to give full faith and credit to the judgment and thus may not entertain the action.

8. A brings an action for divorce against B, her husband, in State X, in which A and B are domiciled. The court grants the divorce and directs B to pay A the sum of $10,000 as alimony, the amount being based upon the resources of the defendant including land in State Y. After receiving payment of the $10,000, A sues in State Y to obtain further alimony out of the land of B in that state. The court in State Y is bound to give full faith and credit to the judgment by dismissing the action.

9. A and B enter into a contract for sale of land located in State Y. B refuses to convey the land. A brings an action for specific performance in State X and judgment is entered in his favor ordering B to convey the land. State Y may perhaps be within its constitutional rights in refusing to entertain an action by A against B to enforce the State X judgment. On the other hand, it is constitutionally permissible for State Y to entertain such an action and respect the State X judgment fully, and correspondingly to refuse to entertain an action on A's original claim. See also Illustration 10.

e. Action on original claim in another state. When State Y is not required by the Constitution to regard a State X judgment as merging the claim, and State Y accordingly, in exercising its discretion, refuses to allow enforcement of the judgment as such, the plaintiff is not precluded from maintaining in State Y an action on the original claim. As indicated in Comment d, in certain cases State Y is then at liberty to deny all carry-over effects from the State X judgment; in other cases, as where the State X judgment ordered or prohibited acts other than the payment of money, State Y is required to accept the judgment as conclusive upon the issues actually litigated and determined in the State X action. See Restatement, Second, Conflict of Laws §§ 95, 102, and Illustration 10 below. In the latter class of cases, therefore, State Y will be entitled to deviate from the State X adjudication only in respect to the form of relief it is prepared to provide; the practical distinction between, on the one hand, allowing an action on the original claim but with issues concluded by direct estoppel based on the State X judgment, and, on the other hand, granting enforcement of the State X judgment, may be quite narrow. See Comment f below.

ILLUSTRATION:

10. On the facts of Illustration 9, if State Y chooses to entertain an action on the original claim, it is nevertheless required to give direct estoppel effect to issues determined by State X.

f. Enforcement of judgment in another state. State Y may be required by the Constitution or, when not so required, may as a matter of comity choose to regard a State X judgment as merging the underlying claim and accordingly to enforce the State X judgment. When the State X judgment is for payment of money, the customary way to secure enforcement of the judgment in State Y is to bring an action there upon the judgment. But a more direct method of enforcement may be available in State Y; for example, the Uniform Enforcement of Foreign Judgments Act provides for the registration of the State X judgment in State Y and facilitates its enforcement there. See also Title 28, U.S. Code, § 1963; Restatement, Second, Conflict of Laws § 99. When the State X judgment orders or forbids acts other than the payment of money, enforcement of the judgment in State Y is obtained in some situations by bringing an action on the judgment but in other cases by less direct procedures as prescribed by State Y. See Restatement, Second, Conflict of Laws § 99; § 102 and Comment e thereon.

g. Incidents of claim preserved. When by reason of the plaintiff's obtaining judgment upon a claim the original claim is extinguished and rights arise upon the judgment, advantages to which the plaintiff was entitled with respect to the original claim may still be preserved despite the judgment. Thus if a creditor has a lien upon property of the debtor and obtains a judgment against him, the creditor does not thereby lose the benefit of the lien. Similarly, where by statute an employee is given priority as to a claim for personal injuries in the reorganization of a railroad, such priority is not lost when the employee has obtained a judgment against the railroad.

h. Effect on claim based on federal law. When a judgment has been rendered on a claim based on state law, there are circumstances in which a claim based on federal law may still be asserted. See § 86.

i. Counterclaim. This Section is applicable not only when the plaintiff brings a subsequent action against the defendant, but also when he attempts to interpose a counterclaim in a subsequent action brought by the defendant against him. When the plaintiff has obtained a judgment against the defendant which has the effect under this Section of merging the original claim, he cannot avail himself of the original claim by interposing it as a counterclaim in a subsequent action brought by the defendant against him. See Illustration 11. On the other hand he may interpose the judgment by way of counterclaim. See Illustration 12.

ILLUSTRATIONS:

11. A brings an action against B on a promissory note. B denies that he executed the note. Verdict and judgment are given for A in the amount of the note, with interest and costs. Thereafter B brings an action against A for the breach of contract. Since A's right of action on the note is merged in the judgment, A is precluded from relying on the note by way of counterclaim.

12. The facts are as stated in Illustration 11. A can set up the judgment by way of counterclaim.

j. Merger in a judgment on a judgment. When the plaintiff has obtained a judgment against the defendant and brings an action upon the judgment, and obtains a judgment in that action, the first judgment is not merged in the second judgment, whether the second action is brought in the same State in which the first judgment was rendered or is brought in another State. The plaintiff can enforce either judgment by execution or otherwise, but satisfaction of one of the judgments operates also as satisfaction of the other.

k. Judgment of a federal court. When the judgment is that of a federal court, federal law in general governs its effects. See § 87.

§ 19. Judgment For Defendant — The General Rule Of Bar

A valid and final personal judgment rendered in favor of the defendant bars another action by the plaintiff on the same claim.

This general rule is subject to the exceptions stated in §§ 20 and 26.

Comment:

a. Rationale. It is frequently said that a valid and final personal judgment for the defendant will bar another action on the same claim only if the judgment is rendered "on the merits." The prototype case continues to be one in which the merits of the claim are in fact adjudicated against the plaintiff after trial of the substantive issues. Increasingly, however, by statute, rule, or court decision, judgments not passing directly on the substance of the claim have come to operate as a bar. Although such judgments are often described as "on the merits" or as "operating as an adjudication on the merits," that terminology is not used here in the statement of the general rule because of its possibly misleading connotations.

The rule that a defendant's judgment acts as a bar to a second action on the same claim is based largely on the ground that fairness to the defendant, and sound judicial administration, require that at some point litigation over the particular controversy come to an end. These considerations may impose such a requirement even though the substantive issues have not been tried, especially if the plaintiff has failed to avail himself of opportunities to pursue his remedies in the first proceeding, or has deliberately flouted orders of the court.

The general rule stated in this Section requires that errors underlying a judgment be corrected on appeal or other available proceedings to modify the judgment or to set it aside, and not made the basis for a second action on the same claim.

The rule stated in this Section is subject to the exceptions set forth in § 20 as well as to the exceptions to the rule against the splitting of a claim set forth in § 26.

b. Statutes and rules of court. In determining the scope of the general rule (and the exceptions to it) in a particular jurisdiction, it is essential to consult the relevant statutes and rules of court in that jurisdiction. Among the most significant of these provisions is Rule 41 of the Federal Rules of Civil Procedure, which has served as a model for similar provisions in many states...:

c. Counterclaim. The rule stated in this Section is applicable not only to a case in which the plaintiff brings another action against the defendant on the same claim, but also to one in which the plaintiff seeks to avail himself of the original claim by interposing it as a counterclaim in a subsequent action brought by the defendant against him.

d. Judgment for defendant on insufficiency of the complaint. The rule stated in this Section is applicable to a judgment for the defendant on demurrer or motion to dismiss for failure to state a claim. Such a result is warranted by the ease with which pleadings may be amended, normally at least once as a matter of course, and by the unfairness of requiring the defendant to submit to a second action (often initiated long after the first has come to an end) when no such amendment is sought, or when no appeal has been taken from an erroneous denial of leave to amend.

ILLUSTRATION:

1. A brings an action against B to obtain a one-half interest in land and to establish a trust on the land. A demurrer to the complaint is sustained on the grounds that it fails to allege a writing sufficient to satisfy the applicable statute of frauds. Judgment is rendered for B and A does not seek leave to amend; one year later A brings a second action on the same claim in which he alleges a writing sufficient to satisfy the statute of frauds. The second action is barred by the first judgment.

e. Judgment for defendant based on the plaintiff's failure to prosecute, to obey an order of the court, or to appear. The rule stated in this Section is applicable to a judgment for defendant based on the failure of the plaintiff to prosecute his claim with diligence, to obey an order of the court, or to appear at the appointed time. This result is explicitly provided for in Rule 41 of the Federal Rules of Civil Procedure, quoted in Comment b, above. In those jurisdictions where statutes or rules provide that such dismissals shall not operate as an adjudication "on the merits" (i.e., shall not operate as a bar), or shall not so operate unless otherwise specified, the effect of the dismissal would be governed by § 20.

f. Judgment for defendant on grounds that may not preclude an action in another jurisdiction. This Restatement is concerned primarily with the effect of a judgment in the state in which it is rendered. Generally, a judgment that operates to bar another action on the same claim in one state will, under the Full Faith and Credit Clause of the United States Constitution, bar an action on the same claim in another state. See Restatement, Second, Conflict of Laws § 95, Comment c. This may not necessarily be the case, however, if the action is barred by the statute of limitations of the first state but not of the second, or if a contract valid where made is unenforceable under the public policy of the first state but is enforceable under the public policy of the second. See Restatement, Second, Conflict of Laws § 110. With respect to the rendering state, a judgment for the defendant on such grounds falls within the rule of this Section.

g. Summary judgment for defendant. The rule stated in this Section is applicable to a case in which it is determined before trial that there is no genuine dispute with respect to any material fact and that, as a matter of law, the defendant is entitled to judgment. See, for example, Rule 56 of the Federal Rules of Civil Procedure.

h. Judgment for defendant during or after trial. The rule stated in this Section is applicable to a judgment for defendant based on a direct verdict, on a jury verdict, on a judgment notwithstanding the verdict, or on any other determination during or after trial. Under the modern systems of procedure prevailing in most jurisdictions, issues not raised by the pleadings that are tried by express or implied consent are treated as if they had been raised in the pleadings. In such jurisdictions, the claim or claims barred by a judgment for defendant must be determined on the basis of the whole record, including the pleadings and the evidence. It is generally possible in such jurisdictions for any party to obtain an amendment of the pleadings, even after judgment, in order that the pleadings will conform to the evidence, and such an amendment may be of assistance in resolving any future controversy over the res judicata effect of the judgment.

i. Cross-references. Exceptions to the rule of this Section are dealt with in §§ 20 and 26.

For the requisites of a "valid" judgment, see § 1, and for the requisites of a "final" judgment, see § 13.

For the definition of a "counterclaim," see the Introductory Note to Title C of this Chapter.

The circumstances in which relief against a judgment is given are dealt with in Chapter 5.

§ 20. Judgment For Defendant — Exceptions to the General Rule of Bar

(1) A personal judgment for the defendant, although valid and final, does not bar another action by the plaintiff on the same claim:

(a) When the judgment is one of dismissal for lack of jurisdiction, for improper venue, or for nonjoinder or misjoinder of parties; or

(b) When the plaintiff agrees to or elects a nonsuit (or voluntary dismissal) without prejudice or the court directs that the plaintiff be nonsuited (or that the action be otherwise dismissed) without prejudice; or

(c)   When by statute or rule of court the judgment does not operate as a bar to another action on the same claim, or does not so operate unless the court specifies, and no such specification is made.

(2) A valid and final personal judgment for the defendant, which rests on the prematurity of the action or on the plaintiff's failure to satisfy a precondition to suit, does not bar another action by the plaintiff instituted after the claim has matured, or the precondition has been satisfied, unless a second action is precluded by operation of the substantive law.

Comment:

a. General. This Section enumerates the situations in which a valid and final personal judgment for the defendant does not bar the plaintiff from bringing another action on the same claim. It takes special note of the substantial impact of statutes and rules of court.

There is, perhaps inevitably, some degree of overlap between the matters dealt with in this Section and the exceptions, set forth in § 26, to the general rule against splitting of a "claim." There are, however, two important lines of distinction. First, the present Section deals with instances in which the general rule of bar does not apply—i.e., instances in which the plaintiff remains entirely free to prosecute all or any part of his claim (except as limited by the direct estoppel effect of the first judgment); Section 26, on the other hand, deals in large part with instances in which after the first judgment the plaintiff no longer retains the full freedom he once had—with instances of what might be described as "partial merger or bar." Compare, for example, Illustration 2 to the present Section with Illustration 1 to § 26. Second, the present Section does not deal with instances in which policy reasons favoring the maintenance of the second action come to light only after the first action is completed; such instances are included within the scope of § 26. See, for example, Illustrations 4 and 6 to § 26.

b. Effect of judgment as to issues decided. The rules of issue preclusion (see §§ 27, 28) apply to a valid and final personal judgment for the defendant even though the judgment is one which, under this Section, does not bar another action on the same claim.

ILLUSTRATION:

1. A brings an action against B for personal injuries, and the action is dismissed for improper venue on the ground that the judicial district in which suit was brought was not the district of defendant's residence as required by law. Although A is not barred from maintaining an action on the claim in another district, the rules of issue preclusion are applicable to the determination that venue was improper in the initial action.

c. Rationale of Subsection (1)(a). The grounds stated in this Clause for the granting of judgments of dismissal that do not operate as a bar to a second action are among the most frequent and widely recognized grounds for such dismissals. The reason for this result may be found in the threshold character of the determination on which the judgment is based.

Dismissals on the grounds specified in this Clause are explicitly referred to as not operating as an adjudication "on the merits" in Rule 41(b) of the Federal Rules of Civil Procedure and in many of the state rules patterned on that provision.

ILLUSTRATION:

2. A brings an action against B for personal injuries in a federal court, basing jurisdiction on diversity of citizenship. The action is dismissed on the ground that the alleged diversity does not in fact exist. A is not barred from bringing another action on the same claim in a court of competent jurisdiction.

d. Specification that dismissal on any of the grounds in Subsection (1)(a) is "with prejudice" or "on the merits". A court in dismissing on any of these grounds may specify that its decision is "with prejudice" or "on the merits", or words to that effect. While there are instances in which a court may have discretion to determine that a judgment of dismissal shall operate as a bar (see Comment n to this Section), a judgment may not have an effect contrary to that prescribed by the statutes, rules of court, or other rules of law operative in the jurisdiction in which the judgment is rendered. Thus in a jurisdiction having a rule patterned on Rule 41(b) of the Federal Rules of Civil Procedure, a dismissal for lack of jurisdiction, for improper venue, or for nonjoinder may not be a bar regardless of the specification made. And even in the absence of such a rule, a dismissal on any of these grounds is so plainly based on a threshold determination that a specification that the dismissal will be a bar should ordinarily be of no effect.

e. Alternative determinations. A dismissal may be based on two or more determinations, each of which, standing alone, would render the judgment a bar to another action on the same claim. In such a case the judgment operates as a bar. See Illustration 3.

A dismissal may be based on two or more determinations, at least one of which, standing alone, would not render the judgment a bar to another action on the same claim. In such a case, if the judgment is one rendered by a court of first instance, it should not operate as a bar. See Illustration 4. Even if another of the determinations, standing alone, would render the judgment a bar, that determination may not have been as carefully or rigorously considered as it would have if it had been necessary to the result, and in

227

that sense it has some of the characteristics of dicta. And, of critical importance, the losing party, although entitled to appeal from both determination, may be dissuaded from doing so as to the determination going to the "merits" because the alternative determinations, which in itself does not preclude a second action, is clearly correct. The rules of res judicata should not encourage or foster appeals in such instances.

If the judgment resting on alternative determinations discussed in the preceding paragraph is that of an appellate court, the question whether it bars another action on the same claim is a difficult one. See the discussion of an analogous question on the context of issue preclusion, § 27, Comments i and o. But in any event, the judgment should not operate as a bar if one of the determinations is that the court in which the action was brought lacked subject matter or personal jurisdiction to adjudicate the claim.

ILLUSTRATIONS:

3. A brings an action against B for breach of contract and after trial without a jury, the court holds for B on the basis that (a) the contract is unenforceable because not in writing and (b) in any event B was induced to enter the agreement by A's fraud. A is barred from bringing a second action on the same claim.

4. The facts are the same as in Illustration 3, but the trial court also holds that the action is premature because the time for B's performance has not yet arrived. A is not barred from bringing suit on the claim after that time has arrived.

f. Voluntary nonsuit or dismissal without prejudice (Subsection (1)(b)). At common law the plaintiff is permitted to submit to a nonsuit, which does not operate as a bar to another action on the same claim, at any time before the jury has rendered its verdict or before the court, sitting without a jury, has announced its judgment. By statute or rule of court in most states, an earlier stage is fixed after which the plaintiff cannot insist on such a nonsuit. This stage is sometimes the close of the evidence, sometimes the opening of trial or some specified period prior to trial, sometimes (as in Rule 41(a) of the Federal Rules of Civil Procedure) the filing of an answer or a motion for summary judgment. When these modifications of the common law rule so permit, it is generally held that the parties may agree to a voluntary nonsuit or dismissal without prejudice at a later stage or the court may allow such a dismissal on such terms and conditions as it deems proper.

g. Compulsory nonsuit or dismissal without prejudice. Formerly the plaintiff could not be compelled to submit to a nonsuit or involuntary dismissal without prejudice because of the insufficiency of evidence. By statute, rule of court, or rule of decision in most jurisdictions, however, the court has authority to order a dismissal without prejudice in such circumstances in order to afford the plaintiff another opportunity to make out his case. In a few jurisdictions—and their number is diminishing—it is the practice at the close of the plaintiff's evidence to grant a nonsuit, on defendant's motion, if the evidence is insufficient to justify a verdict in plaintiff's favor, but not to direct a verdict in favor of the defendant unless the defendant has put in his own evidence or has rested without putting in such evidence.

Whether a nonsuit or involuntary dismissal should be granted or a verdict directed is a matter of local practice not within the scope of this Restatement.

h. Effect of statute or rule providing that dismissal shall operate as a bar. In order for Subsection (1)(b) to be applicable, the specification that a dismissal is without prejudice must not be inconsistent with a governing statute or rule in the jurisdiction. For example, by statute or rule of court in many jurisdictions, a voluntary dismissal operates as a bar to another action on the same claim when filed by a plaintiff who has once dismissed in any court of the United States or any state an action based on or including that claim. In such circumstances, a notation in the record that a nonsuit or dismissal is "without prejudice," or words to that effect, is not effective because the judgment operates as a bar as a matter of law.

i. Form of direction by the court. It is not necessary that the court employ the words "without prejudice" in order for a nonsuit or dismissal to come within the scope of Subsection (1)(b). What is essential is that the court manifest an intention on the record that the judgment shall not bar another action on the same claim. Thus, for example, if dismissal of an action is based on the pendency of another action between the parties on the same claim, the dismissal plainly contemplates that the other action shall be allowed to proceed.

j. Dismissals which, by statute or rule of court, do not operate as a bar to another action on the same claim (Subsection (1)(c)). Subsection (1)(c) recognizes the growing importance in this area of statutes and rules of court, which reflect a wide variety of views as to the circumstances in which fairness to the defendant and avoidance of undue burdens on the courts require that a dismissal operate as a bar. Thus even among those states that have statutes or rules closely patterned on Rule 41 of the Federal Rules of Civil Procedure, there are variations, for example as to the time periods when there is a right to a voluntary dismissal, and as to whether certain dismissals (e.g., for failure to prosecute) operate as a bar in the absence of a specification by the court. Among the states whose statutes or rules are not closely patterned on Rule 41, variations are even wider. A few have left the matter largely to the common law, while others have made specific provision as to the availability of nonsuits, or as to the effect of other dismissals before or during trial. Reference to these local materials is essential in determining whether a given judgment operates as a bar.

k. Rationale for Subsection (2). A determination by the court that the plaintiff has no enforceable claim because the action is premature, or because he has failed to satisfy a precondition to suit, is not a determination that he may not have an enforceable claim thereafter, and does not normally preclude him from maintaining an action when the claim has become enforceable. The rule of this Subsection and the rationale behind it shade over into the rule that subsequent events may give rise to a new claim that is not barred by a prior judgment (see § 24, Comment f).

The rule stated in this Subsection is applicable whether the fact that the action is premature, or that a precondition has not been satisfied, appears on the face of the pleadings, as a result of pretrial discovery, or from the evidence at trial.

l. Where time for performance has not arrived. The rule stated in this Subsection is applicable to a case in which the time for performance had not arrived when the plaintiff brought the action.

ILLUSTRATION:

5. On January 1, 1972, A sues B alleging that in consideration of the payment of $100 by A, B agreed to deliver certain goods to A, and that B has failed to deliver the goods. At the trial it appears that the goods were to be delivered on June 1, 1972. The court directs a verdict for B and judgment is given on the verdict for B. A is not precluded from maintaining an action for breach of the contract after June 1, 1972, if B has failed to deliver the goods on or before that day.

m. Where a condition precedent has not been performed. The rule stated in this Subsection is applicable where the liability of the defendant is conditional upon the happening of some event (see Illustration 6). As a matter of substantive law, however, the failure of the plaintiff to establish the existence of the condition precedent in the original action may fix the relationship of the parties so that it is no longer open to him to satisfy that condition. For example, failure of one party to render substantial performance under a contract at the time of suit against the other party for nonpayment may free the other party of any obligation on the contract (see Illustration 7). In addition, the failure of a party to satisfy a condition precedent within a reasonable time may defeat a second action even though the first dismissal does not itself operate as a bar.

ILLUSTRATIONS:

6. A suffers personal injuries when hit by a car driven by B, and brings an action against B's insurer to recover for those injuries. The action is dismissed on the ground that, in the absence of a judgment against B, no action can be brought by A against B's insurer. A is not precluded from suing the insurer after a judgment against B has been obtained.

7. A sues B for failure to pay the contract price for certain services. Judgment is given for B on the ground that A has not rendered substantial performance. If, as a matter of substantive contract law, the effect of the judgment is to discharge B from any duty under the contract, A is barred from bringing a second action for breach of the same contract whether or not he renders, or offers to render, the remaining services due under the contract. See Restatement, Second, Contracts § 237.

n. Unfair to subject defendant to a second action. The rule of this Subsection is not an inflexible one. In some instances, the doctrines of estoppel or laches could require the conclusion that it would be plainly unfair to subject the defendant to a second action.

TITLE C. COUNTERCLAIMS

§ 21. Judgment For Defendant On His Counterclaim

(1) Where the defendant interposes a counterclaim on which judgment is rendered in his favor, the rules of merger are applicable to the claim stated in the counterclaim, except as stated in Subsection (2).

(2) Where judgment on a counterclaim is rendered in favor of the defendant, but he is unable to obtain full recovery in the action because of the inability of the court to render such a judgment and the unavailability of such devices as removal to another court or consolidation with another action in the same court, the defendant is not precluded from subsequently maintaining an action for the balance due on the claim stated in the counterclaim.

For statement of the general rule of merger and its exceptions, see §§ 18, 26.

Comment:

a. Effect of judgment for defendant on the counterclaim. A defendant who interposes a counterclaim is, in substance, a plaintiff as far as the counterclaim is concerned. The general rule of merger stated in § 18, and its exceptions in § 26, are therefore applicable: the claim asserted in the counterclaim will normally be merged in the judgment if the defendant obtains judgment in his favor on the counterclaim.

The rule stated in this Subsection is applicable whether or not the claim stated in the counterclaim is liquidated, whether or not the plaintiff has obtained judgment in his favor on his claim against the defendant, and whether or not there is an affirmative award to the plaintiff because the plaintiff proved his claim and his judgment exceeded in amount the judgment on the defendant's counterclaim. See Illustrations 1 and 2.

ILLUSTRATIONS:

1. A brings an action against B for breach of a contract. B denies that he broke the contract, and sets up by way of counterclaim a claim against A for breach of another contract. At the trial there is a verdict for A on the first contract for $200, and a verdict for B on the second contract for $300, and judgment is given for B for $100. B can maintain an action against A on the judgment, but cannot maintain an action on the contract which was the subject of the counterclaim, even though he may now be able to prove greater damages than the jury awarded him.

2. The facts are as stated in Illustration 1, except that the verdict for A is for $300 and the verdict for B is for $200, and the judgment is for A for $100. B cannot maintain an action on the contract which was the subject of the counterclaim.

b. Rationale for Subsection (2). In most jurisdictions, it is provided by statute or rule that an affirmative judgment may be rendered in favor of the defendant on his counterclaim. Even where no such judgment may be rendered, it may be possible for the defendant to bring a separate action in the same court and to have it consolidated with the original action against him. And if the original action is brought in a court of limited jurisdiction, it is frequently provided that a defendant having a counterclaim exceeding that limit may have the entire case transferred to a competent court. Nevertheless there may be instances when a defendant is unable to obtain full recovery on a counterclaim because the law imposes a limitation on the authority of the court to render such a judgment and devices such as removal or consolidation are unavailable (see Illustration 3), or because the plaintiff is suing as an assignee and is not personally liable on the counterclaim (see Illustration 4).

It is true that in these instances the defendant, under the rule in Subsection (2), is allowed to split his claim by employing it partially as a defense to the plaintiff's claim and partially as a basis for a subsequent action. But since the plaintiff has selected the time and place of suit, it would be unfair to the defendant to put him to the choice on the one hand of permitting the plaintiff to recover against him and bringing a separate action, or on the other hand of preventing the plaintiff's recovery only by the entire extinguishment of his claim.

ILLUSTRATIONS:

3. In a court that has jurisdiction to give judgments for not more than $100, A brings an action against B on a promissory note for $60. B denies that he executed the note and pleads by way of counterclaim a claim against A for damages for breach of another contract. (The law of the state where the action is brought does not allow removal of the entire case to a court of general jurisdiction under such circumstances, nor does it provide any other device for recovery of more than $100 in the original action.) At the trial it is determined that B did not execute the note and that A is liable for breach of contract in the amount of $500. Judgment is given that B recover from A $100. B is not precluded from subsequently maintaining an action against A for breach of the same contract. (The application of the doctrine of issue preclusion in a subsequent action is governed by §§ 27, 28.)

4. A (B's assignee) sues C on a claim for $300 which B had against C for money lent. C sets up a defense to this claim and pleads by way of counterclaim a claim for $500 against B which arose before the assignment and of which A had notice at the time of the assignment. At the trial there is a verdict for A on his claim and a verdict for C on the counterclaim, and judgment is given that A recover nothing. C is not precluded by the judgment from subsequently maintaining an action against B to recover on the same claim as that interposed as a counterclaim.

c. Effect of judgment on subsequent actions. Whenever a subsequent action is permitted to be brought on the same claim as that stated in a prior counterclaim, the principle of direct estoppel applies to issues actually litigated and determined in the prior action. See § 17 and Comment (d) thereon; § 27. If the prior action was litigated in a court of limited jurisdiction, the preclusive effect of any determinations in that court should be governed by the criteria set forth in § 28 and Comment d thereon.

d. Where ruling denying judgment of full recovery for defendant is erroneous. The rule of this Subsection is applicable where a judgment awarding full recovery for the defendant on his counterclaim is denied on the ground of the court's inability or lack of authority to render such a judgment, although the ruling is erroneous. See § 26 and Comment d thereon.

§ 22. Effect Of Failure To Interpose Counterclaim

(1) Where the defendant may interpose a claim as a counterclaim but he fails to do so, he is not thereby precluded from subsequently maintaining an action on that claim, except as stated in Subsection (2).

(2) A defendant who may interpose a claim as a counterclaim in an action but fails to do so is precluded, after the rendition of judgment in that action, from maintaining an action on the claim if:

(a) The counterclaim is required to be interposed by a compulsory counterclaim statute or rule of court, or

(b) The relationship between the counterclaim and the plaintiff's claim is such that successful prosecution of the second action would nullify the initial judgment or would impair rights established in the initial action.

Comment:

a. **Rationale for Subsection (1)**. In the absence of a statute or rule of court otherwise providing (see Subsection (2)(a) and Comment e), the defendant normally has the option of interposing a claim as a counterclaim or of bringing a separate action against the plaintiff. The justification for the existence of such an option is that the defendant should not be required to assert his claim in the forum or the proceeding chosen by the plaintiff but should be allowed to bring suit at a time and place of his own selection.

Even in jurisdictions having a statute or rule making certain counterclaims compulsory, such provisions may not apply when no answer or other responsive pleading is filed, and generally do not apply when the counterclaim does not arise out of the same transaction or occurrence as the plaintiff's claim. See Rule 13(a) of the Federal Rules of Civil Procedure, quoted in Comment e, below.

b. **Where facts constituting defense are ground for counterclaims**. In the absence of a statute or rule of court otherwise providing, the defendant's failure to allege certain facts either as a defense or as a counterclaim does not normally preclude him from relying on those facts in an action subsequently brought by him against the plaintiff. See Subsection (2)(b) and Comment f thereon for discussion of the exception to this rule. The failure to interpose a defense to the plaintiff's claim precludes the defendant from thereafter asserting the defense as a basis for attacking the judgment (see § 18). But the defendant's claim against the plaintiff is not normally merged in the judgment given in that action, and issue preclusion does not apply to issues not actually litigated (see § 27). The defendant, in short, is entitled to his day in court on his own claim.

ILLUSTRATIONS:

1. A brings an action against B for the negligent driving of an automobile by B resulting in a collision with an automobile driven by A. B fails to plead and judgment by default is given against him. B is not precluded from subsequently maintaining an action against A for his own injuries on the ground that those injuries were the result of A's negligence.

2. A, a physician, brings an action against B for the price of medical services rendered to B. B fails to plead and judgment by default is given against him. B is not precluded from subsequently maintaining an action against A for malpractice relating to the services sued upon in the prior action. (B is precluded, however, from seeking restitution of any amount paid pursuant to the judgment. See Comment f.)

3. A brings an action against B for the purchase price of a boiler sold by A to B. B defends on the sole ground that the price has been paid, and judgment is given for A. B is not precluded from subsequently maintaining an action against A, in which he alleges that A was guilty of breach of warranty and that the boiler was defective and exploded, causing damage to B. (B is precluded, however, from seeking restitution of any amount paid pursuant to the judgment. See Comment f.)

c. **Defense and counterclaim—Judgment for plaintiff; issue preclusion**. Where the same facts constitute a ground of defense to the plaintiff's claim and also a ground for a counterclaim, the defendant alleges those facts as a defense but not as a counterclaim, and after litigation of the defense judgment is given for the plaintiff, the rules of issue preclusion apply. See §§ 27, 28. Those rules will normally preclude relitigation, in a second proceeding between the parties, of issues determined in the first proceeding.

ILLUSTRATION:

4. A, a physician, brings an action against B for the price of medical services rendered to B. B in his answer alleges that A was negligent and that the services were of no value. It is determined that A was not negligent, and judgment is given for A. B is precluded from thereafter relitigating the issue of A's negligence in an action against A for injuries caused by A's alleged malpractice relating to the services sued upon in the prior action.

d. **Defense and counterclaim—Judgment for defendant; splitting claims**. Where the same facts constitute a defense to the plaintiff's claim and a ground for counterclaim, and the defendant sets up these facts as a defense but not as a counterclaim, and after litigation of the defense judgment is given for the defendant, the defendant is not precluded by the rule of merger from maintaining a subsequent action against the plaintiff based upon these facts. See Illustration 5. In the subsequent action, the rules of issue preclusion (see §§ 27, 28) will apply to issues litigated and determined in the first action.

In the early law a defendant in an action at law having some equitable ground for resisting the action could not interpose it as a defense but had to assert it, if at all, in an independent suit in equity which would serve as a check upon the law action. (A common example was a claim of fraud, mistake, or duress as a ground for rescission of a contract that was the subject of an action at law.) Later it became possible for the defendant in such a situation to interpose the equitable matter as a defense to the action at law, and such a course is now generally open. For most purposes, it is of no consequence whether such equitable matter is categorized as a defense or a counterclaim, but it is significant for purposes of applying the rule against splitting. Because of the difficulty of determining whether or not a particular defense should be considered "equitable" in such cases, application of the rule against splitting should turn on whether the defendant's grounds for resisting the claim are cast as a defense or as a counterclaim; if the latter, the rule will preclude a later action on the same claim. Though formalistic, such an approach facilitates predictability and obviates the need for historical inquiry into the scope of equity jurisdiction. See Illustration 6.

ILLUSTRATIONS:

5. A brings an action against B for the negligent driving of an automobile by B resulting in a collision with an automobile driven by A. B in his answer denies that he was negligent and alleges that the collision was due to A's negligence. After trial of these issues judgment is given for B. B is not precluded by the doctrine of merger from thereafter maintaining an action against A for the damage done to him by the collision.

6. A brings an action against B for breach of contract. Judgment is rendered for B on the ground that the contract was obtained by fraud. B is not precluded from thereafter bringing an action against A for damages resulting from the fraud if the ground was asserted as a defense, but is precluded if it was asserted as a counterclaim for rescission.

e. **Compulsory counterclaim statutes and rules of court.** Rule 13(a) of the Federal Rules of Civil Procedure provides that, with certain exceptions, "A pleading shall state as a counterclaim any claim which at the time of serving the pleading the pleader has against the opposing party, if it arises out of the transaction or occurrence that is the subject matter of the opposing party's claim and does not require for its adjudication the presence of third parties of whom the court cannot acquire jurisdiction." Failure to interpose such a counterclaim by a defendant who has appeared precludes its assertion in a subsequent action.

Many states have adopted compulsory counterclaim statutes or rules of court similar or identical to Federal Rule 13(a). The relevant provisions of governing statutes and rules must therefore be consulted to determine the result of the failure to interpose a counterclaim in a particular jurisdiction. (Such provisions may require dismissal of a second action even while the initial action, in which the counterclaim could have been asserted, is still pending.)

ILLUSTRATIONS:

7. The facts are the same as in Illustration 3 but the action by A against B is brought in a jurisdiction having a rule identical to Rule 13 of the Federal Rules of Civil Procedure. B is precluded from thereafter bringing an action against A for breach of warranty.

8. The facts are the same as in Illustration 7 but B files only a motion to dismiss for failure to state a claim, and the motion is granted. If such a motion is not "a pleading" within the meaning of the compulsory counterclaim rule, B is not precluded from thereafter bringing an action against A for damage done to him by the collision.

f. **Special circumstances under which failure to interpose a counterclaim will operate as a bar.** Normally, in the absence of a compulsory counterclaim statute or rule of court, the defendant has a choice as to whether or not he will pursue his counterclaim in the action brought against him by the plaintiff. There are occasions, however, when allowance of a subsequent action would so plainly operate to undermine the initial judgment that the principle of finality requires preclusion of such an action. This need is recognized in Subsection (2)(b).

For such an occasion to arise, it is not sufficient that the counterclaim grow out of the same transaction or occurrence as the plaintiff's claim, nor is it sufficient that the facts constituting a defense also form the basis of the counterclaim. The counterclaim must be such that its successful prosecution in a subsequent action would nullify the judgment, for example, by allowing the defendant to enjoin enforcement of the judgment, or to recover on a restitution theory the amount paid pursuant to the judgment (see Illustration 9), or by depriving the plaintiff in the first action of property rights vested in him under the first judgment (see Illustration 10). Ordinarily the conclusion that the subsequent action could not be maintained under

Subsection (2)(b) would not be reached unless the prior action had eventuated in a judgment for plaintiff since only in such a case would there be the threat of nullification of the judgment or of impairment of rights to which the Subsection is addressed.

The instances in which this Subsection applies are to be distinguished from instances in which the defendant has grounds for relief from the judgment that were not available to him in the form of a counterclaim in the original action. See Chapter 5. In addition, in some jurisdictions, continued separation of law and equity may necessitate a separate equitable action by the defendant in order to assert matters which, under most procedural systems, may be asserted as a defense or counterclaim in the original action. Cf. § 26(c) and Comment c thereon.

ILLUSTRATIONS:

9. A brings an action against B for failure to pay the contract price for goods sold and delivered and recovers judgment by default. After entry of final judgment and payment of the price, B brings an action against A to rescind the contract for mutual mistake, seeking restitution of the contract price and offering to return the goods. The action is precluded.

10. A brings an action against B to quiet title to certain real estate and obtains judgment by default. B then brings an action against A to quiet title to the same property, alleging that at the time of the first action, B had acquired title to the property by adverse possession. The action is precluded.

§ 23. Judgment For Plaintiff On Defendant's Counterclaim

Where the defendant interposes a claim as a counterclaim and a valid and final judgment is rendered against him on the counterclaim, the rules of bar are applicable to the judgment.

For statement of the general rule of bar and its exceptions, see §§ 19, 20, and 26.

Comment:

a. **Rationale.** A defendant who interposes a counterclaim is, in substance, a plaintiff, as far as the counterclaim is concerned, and the plaintiff is, in substance, a defendant. Thus under the general rule of bar stated in § 19, if a judgment is rendered against the defendant on his counterclaim, he cannot thereafter maintain an action on the claim stated in the counterclaim unless the judgment does not operate as a bar under the exceptions stated in §§ 20 and 26.

TITLE D. THE SCOPE OF "CLAIM"

§ 24. Dimensions Of "Claim" For Purposes Of Merger Or Bar—General Rule Concerning "Splitting"

(1) When a valid and final judgment rendered in an action extinguishes the plaintiff's claim pursuant to the rules of merger or bar (see §§ 18, 19), the claim extinguished includes all rights of the plaintiff to remedies against the defendant with respect to all or any part of the transaction, or series of connected transactions, out of which the action arose.

(2) What factual grouping constitutes a "transaction", and what groupings constitute a "series", are to be determined pragmatically, giving weight to such considerations as whether the facts are related in time, space, origin, or motivation, whether they form a convenient trial unit, and whether their treatment as a unit conforms to the parties' expectations or business understanding or usage.

The general rule of this Section is exemplified in § 25, and is subject to the exceptions stated in § 26.

Comment:

a. **Rationale of a transactional view of claim.** In defining claim to embrace all the remedial rights of the plaintiff against the defendant growing out of the relevant transaction (or series of connected transactions), this Section responds to modern procedural ideas which have found expression in the Federal Rules of Civil Procedure and other procedural systems.

"Claim," in the context of res judicata, has never been broader than the transaction to which it related. But in the days when civil procedure still bore the imprint of the forms of action and the division between law and equity, the courts were prone to associate claim with a single theory of recovery, so that, with respect to one transaction, a plaintiff might have as many claims as there were theories of the substantive law upon which he could seek relief against the defendant. Thus, defeated in an action based on one theory, the plaintiff might be able to maintain another action based on a different theory, even though both actions were grounded upon the defendant's identical act or connected acts forming a single life-situation. In those earlier days there was also some adherence to a view that associated claim with the assertion of a single primary right as accorded by the substantive law, so that, if it appeared that the defendant had invaded a number of primary rights conceived to be held by the plaintiff, the plaintiff had the same number of claims, even though they all sprang from a unitary occurrence. There was difficulty in knowing which rights were primary and what was their extent, but a primary right and the corresponding claim might turn out to be narrow. Thus it was held by some courts that a judgment for or against the plaintiff in an action for personal injuries did not preclude an action by him for property damage occasioned by the same negligent conduct on the part of the defendant— this deriving from the idea that the right to be free of bodily injury was distinct from the property right. Still another view of claim looked to sameness of evidence; a second action was precluded where the evidence to support it was the same as that needed to support the first. Sometimes this was made the sole test of identity of claim; sometimes it figured as a positive but not as a negative test; that is, in certain situations a second action might be precluded although the evidence material to it varied from that in the first action. Even so, claim was not coterminous with the transaction itself.

The present trend is to see claim in factual terms and to make it coterminous with the transaction regardless of the number of substantive theories, or variant forms of relief flowing from those theories, that may be available to the plaintiff; regardless of the number of primary rights that may have been invaded; and regardless of the variations in the evidence needed to support the theories or rights. The transaction is the basis of the litigative unit or entity which may not be split.

This definition of claim to engross the relevant transaction, as envisioned in this Topic, simplifies the application of the rules of merger and bar (see, for example, § 25, Comment a); it enhances the benefits deriving from those rules without causing undue hardship. Equating claim with transaction, however, is justified only when the parties have ample procedural means for fully developing the entire transaction in the one action going to the merits to which the plaintiff is ordinarily confined. A modern procedural system does furnish such means. It permits the presentation in the action of all material relevant to the transaction without artificial confinement to any single substantive theory or kind of relief and without regard to historical forms of action or distinctions between law and equity. A modern system allows allegations to be made in general form and reads them indulgently; it allows allegations to be mutually inconsistent subject to the pleader's duty to be truthful. It permits considerable freedom of amendment and is willing to tolerate changes of direction in the course of litigation. Parties can resort to compulsory processes besides private investigations to ascertain the facts surrounding the transaction, thereby measurably avoiding surprise at the trial. The pretrial conference contributes to the same end of developing the whole case. The law of res judicata now reflects the expectation that parties who are given the capacity to present their "entire controversies" shall in fact do so.

The developments here described should be seen in relation to modern liberal provisions as to counterclaims and joinder of claims and parties as well as the liberal attitude taken by federal courts toward "ancillary" and "pendent" jurisdiction. It should be noted, however, that if more than one party has a right to relief arising out of a single transaction, each such party has a separate claim for purposes of merger and bar.

Because the transactional view set forth in this Section assumes as the present standard a modern system of procedure with the general characteristics described in this Comment, there is a need to allow exceptions to the general rule where the judgment is rendered in a jurisdiction whose procedural system has not been modernized, especially one where unification of law and equity has not been achieved. These exceptions are set forth in § 26(c).

b. **Transaction: application of a pragmatic standard.** The expression "transaction, or series of connected transactions," is not capable of a mathematically precise definition; it invokes a pragmatic standard to be applied with attention to the facts of the cases. And underlying the standard is the need to strike a delicate balance between, on the one hand, the interests of the defendant and of the courts in bringing litigation to a close and, on the other, the interest of the plaintiff in the vindication of a just claim.

It should be emphasized that the concept of a transaction is here used in the broad sense it has come to acquire in the interpretation of statutes and rules governing pleading and other aspects of civil procedure. Thus the overtones of voluntary interchange often associated with the term in normal speech do not obtain.

In general, the expression connotes a natural grouping or common nucleus of operative facts. Among the factors relevant to a determination whether the facts are so woven together as to constitute a single claim are their relatedness in time, space, origin, or motivation, and whether, taken together, they form a convenient unit for trial purposes. Though no single factor is determinative, the relevance of trial convenience makes it appropriate to ask how far the witnesses or proofs in the second action would tend to overlap the witnesses or proofs relevant to the first. If there is a substantial overlap, the second action should ordinarily be held precluded. But the opposite does not hold true; even when there is not a substantial overlap, the second action may be precluded if it stems from the same transaction or series.

c. **Transaction may be single despite different harms, substantive theories, measures or kinds of relief.** A single transaction ordinarily gives rise to but one claim by one person against another. When a person by one act takes a number of chattels belonging to another, the transaction is single, and judgment for the value of some of the goods exhausts the claim and precludes the injured party from maintaining one action for the remainder. In the more complicated case where one act causes a number of harms to, or invades a number of different interests of the same person, there is still but one transaction; a judgment based on the act usually prevents the person from maintaining another action for any of the harms not sued for in the first action. See Illustrations 1 and 2.

That a number of different legal theories casting liability on an actor may apply to a given episode does not create multiple transactions and hence multiple claims. This remains true although the several legal theories depend on different shadings of the facts, or would emphasize different elements of the facts, or would call for different measures of liability or different kinds of relief. See Illustrations 3 and 4.

ILLUSTRATIONS:

1. A and B, driving their respective cars, have a collision injuring A and damaging his car. The occurrence is single, and so is A's claim. If A obtains a judgment against B on the ground of negligence for the damage to the car, he is prevented by the doctrine of merger from subsequently maintaining an action for the harm to his person.

2. The facts are the same as in Illustration 1, except that B obtains a judgment on the ground that A has failed to prove B's negligence. The preclusion is the same, but explained by the doctrine of bar. (Note: Illustrations 1 and 2 assume that A is the sole owner of the right to recover for harm to his person and to his car. Questions of the effect of subrogation, and partial subrogation, are dealt with in § 37.)

3. A lends goods to B on the understanding that B will return them in good condition. Upon B's failure to return A's goods to him, A might conceivably have rights against B upon alternative theories of negligent loss of the goods, breach of a contractual duty to return the goods, or wrongful conversion of the goods, depending upon the precise facts proved or varying emphasis put upon the facts, and A's relief might be for the return of the goods or for money damages (possibly calculated in varying ways). The transaction is single and it follows that if A sues upon it and a judgment is rendered which extinguishes the claim under the rules of merger or bar, A is precluded from suing B a second time, even on a view of the facts or a theory not presented, or a form or measure of relief not sought, in the first action.

4. A and B both mistakenly believe that A is indebted to B. A delivers a chattel to B in payment of the supposed debt. Upon discovery of the mutual mistake, A under the old law might have alternative recourses as follows: to notify B that he rescinded and to demand return of the chattel and, upon refusal, to sue at law in replevin for return of the chattel (assuming the jurisdiction did not require a trespassory taking to maintain replevin) or in trover for the value of the chattel; to sue at law in general assumpsit for goods sold and delivered; to bring a bill in equity for specific restitution. Under modern law A could still proceed on alternative theories to recover the chattel or its value (possibly calculated in varying ways). The transaction, however, is single and if a judgment is rendered which extinguishes the claim, A is precluded from suing B a second time, even on a theory not presented in the first action.

d. Successive acts or events as transaction or connected series; considerations of business practice. When a defendant is accused of successive but nearly simultaneous acts, or acts which though occurring over a period of time were substantially of the same sort and similarly motivated, fairness to the defendant as well as the public convenience may require that they be dealt with in the same action. The events constitute but one transaction or a connected series. See Illustration 5 and 6, and compare Illustrations 7 and 8 in which the events are not so related as to constitute one transaction or a connected series.

When a person trespasses daily upon the land of another for a week, although the owner of the land might have maintained an action each day, such a series of trespasses is considered a unit up to the time when action is brought. Thus if in the case stated the landowner were to bring suit on January 15, including in his action only the trespass on January 10, and obtain a judgment, he could not later maintain an action for the trespasses on January 11 through January 15.

When a number of items are overdue on a running account between two persons, and the creditor, bringing an action on the account, fails to include one among several past due items, judgment for or against the creditor precludes a further action by him to recover the omitted item. This conforms to ordinary commercial understanding and convenience. On the other hand, when there is an undertaking, for which the whole consideration has been previously given, to make a series of payments of money — perhaps represented by a series of promissory notes, whether or not negotiable — the obligation to make each payment is considered separate from the others and judgment can be obtained on any one or a number of them without affecting the right to maintain an action on the others. The same applies to the obligations represented by coupons attached to bonds or other evidences of indebtedness which are similarly considered separate. See also Illustration 9.

ILLUSTRATIONS:

5. A brings an action against B Co., a street railway company, alleging that the motorman was negligent in starting the car while A was alighting and that as a result A broke his arm. After a verdict and judgment for A, A brings a new action against B Co. alleging that after alighting from the car he fell into a

trench negligently left by B Co. beside the road and broke his leg. The action is precluded.

6. On the false accusation that A was engaging in disorderly conduct at a racetrack, B Co., the owner of the track, caused A in successive acts to be assaulted, slandered, physically detained, and prosecuted criminally. A sues B Co. for the assault and slander. If a judgment is rendered that extinguishes the claim, A may not maintain a second action for the detention or for malicious prosecution.

7. B owes A $500 on an obligation that matured on February 1. A visits B on June 1 and requests payment, whereupon B commits an unprovoked assault upon A. A sues B on the debt and recovers. A may maintain a second action against B based on the assault.

8. A, under a contract of employment with B, is discharged from the job on the alleged ground of his technical incompetence. A year later B, in response to an inquiry from C, a prospective employer of A, states that A is an habitual drunkard. A may sue B and recover against him for wrongful discharge without thereby forfeiting his right to sue B on the basis of his report to C.

9. A pays state income taxes for the years 1973 and 1974 and state property tax for the year 1973. Each of these annual taxes is considered separate so that actions for refund of these tax payments respectively could be maintained without fear of splitting.

e. **Multiple parties**. The rule against splitting as stated in this Section takes as its model a claim and action by a single plaintiff against a single defendant. A transaction may, however, involve more than two persons, and an adjudication between two parties may have legal effects upon third persons who may or may not have been involved in the transaction. As to situations of these types, see §§ 36, 37, 41-61.

The problem of splitting as it may affect a person not a party to an action is dealt with at §§ 37, 45-58. Splitting in relation to assignment of, or subrogation to a claim is dealt with at §§ 37 and 55.

f. **Change of circumstances**. Material operative facts occurring after the decision of an action with respect to the same subject matter may in themselves, or taken in conjunction with the antecedent facts, comprise a transaction which may be made the basis of a second action not precluded by the first. See Illustrations 10-12. Where important human values—such as the lawfulness of a continuing personal disability or restraint—are at stake, even a slight change of circumstances may afford a sufficient basis for concluding that a second action may be brought.

Compare § 13, Comment c (judgments granting or denying continuing relief); § 20(2) (judgment for defendant when action is premature); § 25, Comment c (attempts to recover increased damages); § 26(f) (extraordinary situations where merger or bar is inapposite).

ILLUSTRATIONS:

10. A brings an action against B to set aside a transfer of land on the ground that it was procured by fraud. A fails to prove the fraud and judgment is given for the defendant. A is not precluded from maintaining an action to recover the land on the ground that since judgment was rendered B has forfeited the land to the plaintiff for breach of a condition in the conveyance.

11. A judgment of divorce awards custody of a minor child of the marriage to the wife after a contest over her suitability as a mother. Upon a later demonstration by the husband, on the basis of subsequent experience, that the wife is in fact unsuitable, custody may be awarded to the husband.

12. The government fails in an action against a defendant under an antitrust statute for lack of adequate proof that the defendant participated in a conspiracy to restrain trade. The government is not precluded from a second action against the same defendant in which it relies on conspiratorial acts post-dating the judgment in the first action, and may rely also on acts preceding the judgment insofar as these lend significance to the later acts.

g. **When the jurisdiction of the court is limited**. The rule stated in this Section as to splitting a claim is applicable although the first action is brought in a court which has no jurisdiction to give a judgment for more than a designated amount. When the plaintiff brings an action in such a court and recovers judgment for the maximum amount which the court can award, he is precluded from thereafter maintaining an action for the balance of his claim. See Illustrations 13 and 15. It is assumed here that a court was available to the plaintiff in the same system of courts—say a court of general jurisdiction in the same state—where he could have sued for the entire amount. Compare § 26, Comment c. The same considerations apply when the first action is brought in a court which has jurisdiction to redress an invasion of a certain interest of the plaintiff, but not another, and the action goes to judgment on the merits. See Illustration 14. The plaintiff, having voluntarily brought his action in a court which can grant him only limited relief, cannot insist upon maintaining another action on the claim.

Compare § 25, Comment e, and § 26, Comment d(1), on special problems of state and federal competencies.

ILLUSTRATIONS:

13. A brings an action against B for negligently causing him personal injury. Instead of suing in a court of general jurisdiction of the state, A brings his action in a court which has no jurisdiction to give a

judgment for more than $500. At the trial A's damages are assessed at $1,000. Judgment is given for A for $500. A cannot maintain an action against B to recover further damages.

14. In an automobile collision, A is injured and his car damaged as a result of the negligence of B. Instead of suing in a court of general jurisdiction of the state, A brings his action for the damage to his car in a justice's court, which has jurisdiction in actions for damage to property but has no jurisdiction in actions for injury to the person. Judgment is rendered for A for the damage to the car. A cannot thereafter maintain an action against B to recover for the injury to his person arising out of the same collision.

15. A person suing upon certain claims against the United States has a choice of courts: he may sue in a United States District Court, but in that event he may not recover in excess of $10,000; alternatively he may sue in the United States Court of Claims, and recovery is then unlimited. A sues the United States in the District Court; his claim is assessed at $25,000; he recovers judgment for $10,000. A cannot maintain an action in the Court of Claims to recover further damages.

h. Joinder of multiple claims. As provided in this Section, a plaintiff who brings an action upon part of a claim and succeeds or loses on the merits may not sue to recover upon the rest of the claim. Thus the plaintiff is under some compulsion not to split a claim. There is no like compulsion on a plaintiff who has a number of claims against a defendant to join them in a single action; he may join them if he wishes, but he is not obliged to do so out of fear that he will lose any claims that he omits to join. Joinder of multiple claims is permissive, not compulsory. Rule 18(a) of the Federal Rules of Civil Procedure is typical. It provides: "Joinder of claims. A party asserting a claim to relief as an original claim, counterclaim, cross-claim, or third-party claim, may join, either as independent or as alternate claims, as many claims, legal, equitable, or maritime, as he has against an opposing party."

This still leaves the possibility that a plaintiff, actually having a single claim but mistakenly believing that he has a number of them, may commence a limited lawsuit and then run afoul of the rule against splitting. A plaintiff must take this risk into account in framing his action.

As to counterclaims, permissive or compulsory, see §§ 21-23.

§ 25. Exemplifications Of General Rule Concerning Splitting

The rule of § 24 applies to extinguish a claim by the plaintiff against the defendant even though the plaintiff is prepared in the second action

(1) To present evidence or grounds or theories of the case not presented in the first action, or

(2) To seek remedies or forms of relief not demanded in the first action.

Comment:

a. Evidence, grounds, theories of recovery, remedies, forms of relief. It is difficult to draw clear lines among these terms. Fortunately, the sense of §§ 24 and 25 is such that sharp delineations are not required.

The rule of § 24 puts some pressure on the plaintiff to present all his material relevant to the claim in the first action; this is similar to the coercion on the defendant to produce all his defenses (see § 18). The material to be brought forward comprises, roughly, "evidence" – connoting facts; "grounds" – facts grouped under a legal characterization; "theories of the case" – premises drawn from the substantive law; "remedies or forms of relief" – measures or kinds of recovery.

The purpose of the present Section is to show how the rule of § 24 applies to various situations, some of which have given trouble under earlier formulations of the concept of claim (see § 24, Comment a).

b. Successive actions based on different evidence supporting the same ground. A mere shift in the evidence offered to support a ground held unproved in a prior action will not suffice to make a new claim avoiding the preclusive effect of the judgment. It is immaterial that the plaintiff in the first action sought to prove the acts relied on in the second action and was not permitted to do so because they were not alleged in the complaint and an application to amend the complaint came too late. See Illustrations 1-3.

ILLUSTRATIONS:

1. A brings an action against B, alleging that A was employed by B, that B did not furnish A a safe place to work, and that as a result A suffered personal injuries. After a verdict and judgment for B, A brings a new action for the same injuries alleging other acts of negligence on the part of B, for example, improper instruction by B's foreman. The second action is precluded.

2. A sues B for breach of a contract calling for delivery of certain appliances, alleging as the breach that the appliances did not meet the agreed specifications. After judgment for B, A commences a second action, this time alleging late delivery of the appliances as the breach. The second action is precluded.

3. A brings an action to recover damages for his expulsion from the B society, alleging that his expulsion was wrongful because of want of notice. After judgment for B, A commences a second action to recover damages for the same expulsion, this time alleging that the expulsion was wrongful because he was not given a proper hearing. The second action is precluded.

c. Attempts to recover increased damages. Typically, even when the injury caused by an actionable wrong extends into the future and will be felt beyond the date of judgment, the damages awarded by the judgment are nevertheless supposed to embody the money equivalent of the entire injury. Accordingly, if a plaintiff who has recovered a judgment against a defendant in a certain amount becomes dissatisfied with his recovery and commences a second action to obtain increased damages, the court will hold him precluded; his claim has been merged in the judgment and may not be split. See Illustrations 4-5. It is immaterial that in trying the first action he was not in possession of enough information about the damages, past or prospective, or that the damages turned out in fact to be unexpectedly large and in excess of the judgment. Similarly, when judgment has gone against the defendant in a certain amount, he may not maintain an action against the former plaintiff to reclaim part of the judgment when it appears from subsequent events that the judgment was excessive.

In cases in which a second action is precluded as stated above, it may be open to a party to make a direct attack on the judgment by appeal for any errors in assessing the damages. In exceptional cases relief from the judgment can possibly be secured by motion for a new trial on newly discovered evidence or by other procedures for post-judgment relief. See § 71. Also in some instances the substantive law of the jurisdiction may provide for periodic payments, subject to reconsideration on the basis of changed circumstances, or may allow express reservation in the judgment of a party's right, upon the future happening of described events, to claim additional damages (or, possibly, remission of some of the damages awarded in the judgment) (see Illustration 6). Compare § 26(b) (express reservation of plaintiff's right to split a claim); § 13, Comment c (modification of continuing judgment upon proof of changed circumstances).

ILLUSTRATIONS:

4. A brings an action against B for conversion of a derrick, and obtains judgment for the value of the derrick. Thereafter he brings a new action to recover the loss of profits from a valuable contract which he was unable to perform because of the conversion of the derrick. The prior judgment merges the claim and precludes the action.

5. A brings an action against B for conversion of goods, claiming $50 as damages. B pays this amount into court and judgment for the amount is given for A. A then brings another action for the same conversion, alleging that the goods were worth $100, and giving credit for the amount he has already received, stating that he had underestimated the value of the goods. The action is precluded.

6. A's farm is injured by the continuous discharge of sulphur dioxide gas by B Co.'s manufacturing plant on adjacent land. In A's nuisance action against B Co., the court finding that the pollution "has continued for several years and will continue for an indefinite period into the future," awards A a certain amount of damages for the "permanent loss of market value" of A's farm. The judgment may provide, if the substantive law permits, that A has a right to seek additional damages if the level of pollution caused by defendant's continuing conduct should increase.

d. Successive actions changing the theory or ground. Having been defeated on the merits in one action, a plaintiff sometimes attempts another action seeking the same or approximately the same relief but adducing a different substantive law premise or ground. This does not constitute the presentation of a new claim when the new premise or ground is related to the same transaction or series of transactions, and accordingly the second action should be held barred. See Illustrations 7-9.

ILLUSTRATIONS:

7. A brings an action against B for the cancellation of a contract made with B, alleging that the contract was procured by the undue influence and fraud of B. After verdict and judgment for B, A brings a new action for the cancellation of the contract, alleging mental incompetency of A. The prior judgment is a bar.

8. A sues B alleging that while A was riding in an automobile owned and driven by B, a collision occurred which resulted from wilful and wanton misconduct by B, and that A suffered personal injuries. After verdict and judgment for B, A brings a new action for the same injury alleging that A was a passenger for hire and that the injury resulted from B's negligence. The prior judgment bars the action.

9. The trustee in bankruptcy of A Co. commences an action against B Co. charging that B Co., in order to destroy A Co. as a competitor, acquired the controlling stock interest in A Co. and manipulated its affairs so that it was forced into bankruptcy. This action is brought in a federal court under section 7 of the Clayton Act, and judgment is rendered for the defendant because the trustee fails to establish the necessary elements of a violation of that statute. The trustee is precluded from a second action against B Co. charging substantially the same acts but as part of a conspiracy under sections 1 and 2 of the Sherman Act.

e. State and federal theories or grounds. A given claim may find support in theories or grounds arising from both state and federal law. When the plaintiff brings an action on the claim in a court, either state or federal, in which there is no jurisdictional obstacle to his advancing both theories or grounds, but he presents only one of them, and judgment is entered with respect to it, he may not maintain a second action in which he tenders the other theory or ground. If however, the court in the first action would clearly not have had jurisdiction to entertain the omitted theory or ground (or, having jurisdiction, would clearly have declined to exercise it as a matter of discretion), then a second action in a competent court presenting the omitted theory or ground should be held not precluded. See Illustrations 10-11.

Compare § 26(1)(c), Comment c(1), dealing with the case where the plaintiff is unable for jurisdictional reasons to present both the state and federal theories or grounds in the first action. See also § 86.

ILLUSTRATIONS:

10. A commences an action against B in a federal court for treble damages under the federal antitrust laws. After trial, judgment is entered for the defendant. A then seeks to commence an action for damages against B in a state court under the state antitrust law grounded upon substantially the same business dealings as had been alleged in the federal action. Even if diversity of citizenship between the parties did not exist, the federal court would have had "pendent" jurisdiction to entertain the state theory. Therefore unless it is clear that the federal court would have declined as a matter of discretion to exercise that jurisdiction (for example, because the federal claim, though substantial, was dismissed in advance of trial), the state action is barred.

11. A sues B on a common law basis in a state court for unfair competition. After trial judgment is entered for the defendant. A then attempts to bring an action against B in a federal court upon the same behavior, now claiming infringement of A's federally protected trademark. The action is barred. The claimed violation of federal right could have been urged as a ground of liability in the state court action, as state courts have concurrent jurisdiction with the federal courts to enforce that right.

f. Successive actions for different remedies. As the result of a single transaction or a connected series of transactions giving rise to a unitary claim, the plaintiff may be entitled to a number of alternative or cumulative remedies or forms of relief against the defendant. In a modern system of procedure it is ordinarily open to the plaintiff to pursue in one action all the possible remedies whether or not consistent, whether alternative or cumulative, and whether of the types historically called legal or equitable.

Therefore it is fair to hold that after judgment for or against the plaintiff, the claim is ordinarily exhausted so that the plaintiff is precluded from seeking any other remedies deriving from the same grouping of facts.

Preclusion is narrower when a procedural system in fact does not permit the plaintiff to claim all possible remedies in one action; see § 26(c) and Comment c(2) thereon.

g. Alternative remedies for tort. When a person has alternative remedies in tort or for restitution, he may in the same action apply for the two remedies alternatively and try them both out. On the other hand he may content himself from the outset with seeking only one remedy. In either case, judgment for the plaintiff for one of the remedies or against him with respect to the relief sought ordinarily extinguishes the entire claim. See Restatement of Restitution §§ 145-46.

Thus where the defendant converts and sells the plaintiff's chattel, the plaintiff is entitled to maintain an action in tort for conversion, or for money had and received to recover the amount of the proceeds of the sale of the chattel. Judgment granting or denying one of the remedies precludes the plaintiff from another action on the claim under the rules of merger or bar even if he did not seek the other alternative remedy.

In an action for conversion of a chattel a judgment for the plaintiff for the value of the chattel precludes him from maintaining a subsequent action of replevin. Since, however, the judgment until it is satisfied does not transfer to the defendant the title to the chattel, the plaintiff is not deprived of the privilege of self-help and may seize the chattel. In that case, however, he loses his right to enforce the judgment. See Restatement of Restitution § 145, Comment b.

h. Action for breach of contract or for restitution. When an enforceable contract has existed between plaintiff and defendant, and the plaintiff asserts that he has performed in accordance with the terms of the contract, but that the defendant has failed to perform his corresponding duties, the remedies or forms of relief that can typically be claimed by the plaintiff are recovery of the value of the defendant's promised performance less the value of any as yet unperformed part of the plaintiff's promised performance (called an action for breach of contract), or recovery of the value of what the plaintiff has given in performance of the contract (called an action for restitution). The plaintiff may pursue both remedies alternatively in one action, but whether he chooses to do so or sues for only one of the two remedies, a judgment in the action which extinguishes the claim under the rules of merger or bar precludes the plaintiff from another action on the same transaction. See Illustrations 12-14.

There are situations where it is found that no enforceable contract has existed, and the defendant is accordingly not liable for breach of contract, but the plaintiff would nevertheless be entitled to the remedy of restitution consisting of the value of the benefit received by the defendant from the plaintiff. Here, too, the plaintiff is free to litigate the entire transaction in one lawsuit, is expected to do so, and is not permitted simply to try out one theory after the other in separate actions.

Ordinarily the plaintiff avoids any question of being precluded from a remedy through merger or bar by seeking all plausible remedies at the outset of the action, proving his full case, and securing the recovery to which he is entitled on the facts. If the plaintiff fears that he may suffer in a strategic sense from mingling his case for breach of contract with his alternative case for restitution, he may apply to the court for the clear separation of the issues for trial.

If the plaintiff was initially confident of what he could prove and confined his suit to breach of contract, only to find that that remedy was doubtful, he would ordinarily react by amending promptly to extend the suit to the restitutionary remedy (having obtained leave of court, if needed, for the amendment) and the action would proceed on the changed basis. In many procedural systems, it is provided by statute or rule that "leave to amend shall be freely given when justice so requires." See, for example, Rule 15(a) of the Federal Rules of Civil Procedure. And even in the absence of such a provision, it is clear that the scope of a trial court's discretion to refuse an amendment is considerably narrower when the effect of the refusal is wholly to preclude presentation of a theory of recovery than it is when the question is simply one of the time and place of presentation.

In exceptional situations, despite diligent preparations on either side, it may be unfair to expect the plaintiff to support a sudden shift of position or the defendant to meet it. In such an event the court, in entering judgment for the defendant (the charge of breach of contract having failed of proof), may declare that the judgment is without prejudice to a new trial or a further action in which the plaintiff may seek the restitutionary remedy. Thereby any unjust retention of benefits may be prevented; see § 26(b) and Comment b thereon. See Illustrations 15-16.

ILLUSTRATIONS:

12. A and B enter into a contract by which A agrees to deliver a horse to B and B agrees to deliver a cow to A. A delivers the horse to B but B refuses to deliver the cow to A. A sues B for the recovery of the value of the cow. The jury finds a verdict for A for $100 and judgment is given for A for that amount. A is precluded from maintaining an action against B for the value of the horse.

13. A and B enter into a contract by which A agrees to deliver a horse and a mare to B and B agrees to deliver a cow to A. A delivers the horse to B and B then refuses to go on with the contract. A sues B for the recovery of the value of the cow less the value of the mare. Upon a jury verdict for A for $50, judgment is given for A for that amount. A is precluded from maintaining an action against B for the value of the horse.

14. A brings an action against B alleging that A and B entered into a contract by which A agreed to pay B $100 and B agreed to deliver a horse to A, and that A paid B the $100 but B refused to deliver the horse. A demands repayment of the $100. B denies the payment and after trial, A's evidence being inadequate, judgment is entered for B. An action by A for the value of the horse is barred.

15. A brings an action against B for damages on a theory of breach of contract. At trial, A is unable to establish the claimed agreement with sufficient clarity, and judgment goes for B. A is precluded from maintaining an action for restitution of the benefits he conferred upon B through his performance under the agreement until B wrongfully discharged him. When it appeared at the trial that adequate proof of the terms of the agreement might be lacking, A could have applied to amend as far as might be necessary to try the case on a restitutionary theory. If the amendment was refused, A could apply for a declaration in the ensuing judgment for B that the judgment was without prejudice to a new trial or a fresh action on the restitutionary remedy. (The correctness of a refusal of leave to amend or to make the requested declaration in the judgment could be made the subject of review on appeal.)

16. The situation is the same as in Illustration 15, except that A's action for breach of contract fails (a) because there is no contract owing to mutual mistake, or (b) because the statute of limitations has run, or (c) because the contract is unenforceable under the statute of frauds. Judgment for B in each instance has the ordinary preclusive effect of a judgment for the defendant given for such a reason. A could have requested leave to amend to a restitution theory, attempting thereby to obviate the respective defenses to his action, and ultimately A could have sought a declaration in the judgment to prevent preclusion of the restitutionary theory.

i. "Legal" and "equitable" phases of a claim. When "law" and "equity" with their distinctive remedies were separately administered, a plaintiff had to choose between the two "sides" when he brought his action, and the choice could be difficult, as the dividing line was not exact. Also, it was sometimes impossible to dispose completely in a single action of an entire transaction or controversy, since it might require a combination of legal and equitable remedies. The difficult remedial situation created by the law-equity division naturally had important restrictive effects on the operation of the doctrines of merger and bar. These are overcome when law and equity are "merged" or unified into the "one form of action" so that a pleader may and is expected to demand in a single action any and all remedies suited to the case. The point is emphasized by the customary provision in modern rules or codes of procedure that, except where judgment is by default, "every final judgment shall grant the relief to which the party in whose favor it is rendered is entitled, even if the party has not demanded such relief in his pleadings." See Rule 54(c) of the Federal Rules of Civil Procedure.

(1) Remission from "law" to "equity" or "equity" to "law" unnecessary and improper. Formerly, if the plaintiff brought an action at law in which judgment was given for the defendant because the plaintiff's remedy was solely by a suit in equity, the plaintiff was not precluded from maintaining a suit in equity. Conversely, if the plaintiff brought a suit in equity that was dismissed because his remedy was solely by an action at law, the plaintiff was not precluded from maintaining an action at law; this was true, for example, where the suit in equity was dismissed because the plaintiff had an adequate remedy at law, or on the ground of such delay or hardship or impropriety of the plaintiff's conduct as barred a suit in equity but not an action at law.

In a unified system of procedure, the plaintiff in the situations mentioned would ordinarily be entitled to be awarded in the first action any remedy called for by the facts, whether the remedy would formerly have been denominated legal or equitable; hence one action should suffice. See Illustrations 17-18.

(2) "Legal" and "equitable" relief possible in single action. Formerly, a plaintiff who brought a suit in equity to enjoin the continuance of wrongful conduct might not be permitted to demand in the same suit the prior damages resulting from the wrong, or, where the system was somewhat less strict, might be permitted, but would not be obliged to make the demand in the same suit (a demand for "cleanup" damages). Accordingly, judgment in the equity suit either would not preclude an action by the plaintiff at law to recover the damages, or, in the laxer systems, would preclude the action only if the plaintiff had in fact sought the damage remedy in the equity suit. Today, after unification, the damage remedy would be considered part of the unitary claim for purposes of merger and bar. See Illustration 19. So also a judgment granting or denying specific performance of a contract should preclude an action for money damages for breach.

(3) Alternative relief in a single action on a contract as written or as reformed. Formerly, when the plaintiff brought an action at law for breach of a written contract and failed to prove a breach, and judgment was accordingly given for the defendant, the plaintiff was not precluded from a suit in equity to reform the contract on the ground of mistake or fraud or some other ground, and to enforce the contract as reformed. Today, in a unified system, he would ordinarily be precluded from a second action, assuming, as would very likely be the case, that the facts basing the proposed second action were part of the same transaction as those grounding the first. See Illustration 20.

(4) "Equitable" ground for a claim withheld from an action cannot be used as a defense in a later action. Where an action is brought for cancellation of a contract, and the plaintiff in his complaint alleges certain grounds for cancellation, and at the trial he is unable to prove these grounds and judgment is given against him, and thereafter an action is brought against him for breach of the contract, he cannot defeat the action by setting up as a defense any ground for cancellation that existed at the time of the original action. See Illustration 21. Compare § 22(2)(b) and Comment f thereon.

(5) Cross-reference. This Comment i, like the general rule of § 24 which it exemplifies, assumes as the present standard situation a modern system of procedure with the general characteristics described in § 24, Comment a. For exceptions to the general rule of § 24 where the judgment was rendered in a jurisdiction whose procedural system has not been modernized—especially one where unification of law and equity has not been substantially achieved—see § 26(c).

ILLUSTRATIONS:

17. A sues B seeking specific restitution of grain belonging to A and converted by B. Formerly, if the action was brought in equity it would be dismissed because the plaintiff had an adequate remedy at law, and A would not be precluded from an action at law. In a modern system there would be no reason for dismissal or remission to a second action.

18. A, a manufacturer, contracts with B for the manufacture and delivery by B to A of certain subassemblies in which B is expert. B commits a material breach of contract. It is doubtful whether B's performance is so special as to entitle A to a judgment of specific performance. Formerly, if A brought an action in equity and the court held that specific enforcement was not available, it might dismiss the action, remitting A to an action at law. In a modern system, A in a single action could demand specific performance or, if that were held unavailable, money damages, and relief would be given as found appropriate. Indeed, appropriate relief could be given without regard to the demands.

19. A student at a state university commences an action against the state authorities seeking to enjoin them from exacting from him tuition charges which, he claims, discriminate unconstitutionally against him, a nonresident of the State, as compared with resident students paying lower tuition charges. Judgment

goes for the defendants, the court finding no constitutional deprivation. The student then commences a second action, on Constitutional and other grounds, to secure a refund of a portion of the tuition charges paid. When law and equity were separate, the second action might not be precluded. In a unified system it would be. (If in the first action the student had succeeded in obtaining an injunction and he then sought to bring a second action for a refund, he would likewise be precluded.)

20. A sues B for breach of a written contract claiming money damages. There is no breach unless the contract is interpreted in a certain way. At trial A fails because the court does not accept A's interpretation and rejects parol evidence offered by A as to the meaning of the contract. Formerly the action—an action at law—would have been dismissed but A would be free to commence a suit in equity to reform the contract to accord with what A claims to have been the true intention of the parties. In a modern system A could seek any needed remedy in a single action. Hence if in the first action judgment went for B for failure to prove a breach of the contract as written, and A did not seek reformation in that action, A would be barred from a second action for reformation.

21. A policy insuring against liability from the operation of an automobile is issued by A Insurance Co. to B, the owner of a truck. In operating the truck B injures a third person and the third person recovers against B. A Co. brings a suit in equity to cancel the policy, alleging that it was secured by B by fraud. A Co. fails to prove fraud, and a judgment is given for B. B sues on the policy. A Co. interposes two defenses, alleging that the policy was procured by fraud and that it was issued by an employee of A Co. who was not authorized to issue it. A Co. is precluded by the prior judgment from relying upon either of these defenses.

j. **Cumulative remedies.** Where the plaintiff may in one action claim two or more remedies cumulatively rather than alternatively, all arising from the same transaction, but seeks fewer than all of these remedies, and a judgment is entered that extinguishes the claim under the rules of merger or bar, he is precluded from maintaining another action for the other remedies. Thus if the plaintiff in an action against another in wrongful possession of his land may claim judgment not only for repossession but for damages for the wrongful detention, but seeks and recovers a judgment for repossession only, he may not maintain another action for damages for the detention. In the older law, when the several cumulative remedies might have to be sued for in successive separate actions (in the case supposed, an action of ejectment followed by an action for trespass for mesne profits), judgment in an action for one remedy would not preclude a second action for another remedy, but today a plaintiff may generally cumulate his remedies in a single action, with the preclusionary results mentioned.

k. **Mutually exclusive remedies.** A plaintiff is said to have mutually exclusive remedies where, in consequence of a single transaction, he has one remedy if, but only if, a certain proposition is found, and another remedy if, but only if, a contrary proposition is found. Where the plaintiff commences his action in a tribunal or jurisdiction which allows him to demand the two remedies in the alternative upon allegations of the two contrary propositions, the situation is similar to that discussed in Comment g (alternative remedies for tort). The case is otherwise where the plaintiff is obliged for jurisdictional or other reasons to sue in one court or tribunal if he means to base his action on one proposition, and to sue in a different court or tribunal if he means to rely on the contrary proposition. In that situation, if the plaintiff obtains a judgment for one of the remedies, he is precluded from maintaining a second action for the other remedy, but if he fails in one action because the foundational proposition is held not to exist, he may maintain the second action. See Illustration 22.

Compare § 26(c) and Comment c(1) thereon.

ILLUSTRATION:

22. A suffers personal injuries in consequence of negligence for which B is responsible. Under the law of the State, if A was an employee of B at the time, his sole remedy is under the workmen's compensation law; if A was not an employee, then he has an ordinary common law action. A applies to the workmen's compensation tribunal but fails because he is found not to have been B's employee. A is not precluded from maintaining a court action against B on the common law basis.

l. **Forms of action.** At common law under the formulary system the plaintiff had to cast his action in one appropriate form, or two or more appropriate alternative forms regarded as mutually compatible. He could not join alternative forms that were regarded as mutually repugnant. Thus trover could be joined with trespass upon the case, but trespass and trespass upon the case were repugnant and could not be joined as alternatives even where each was independently appropriate to the facts. If the plaintiff recovered judgment, he was precluded from another action; if judgment went against him for failure to prove the necessary facts, he was likewise precluded; but if judgment went against him because he had selected an inappropriate form, he was not precluded from maintaining another action in the proper remedial form.

Some jurisdictions even after the abolition of the forms of action reached rather similar results under a doctrine called "theory of pleadings." When the plaintiff in his complaint relied upon one theory, he was not entitled to recover on a different theory, even though he had alleged facts sufficient to entitle him to recover on that other theory and had proved those facts at the trial. If judgment was given for the defendant because of such a discrepancy, the plaintiff was held not precluded from maintaining an action on the other theory. So if the plaintiff alleged that he had been induced to enter a described contract by the defendant's fraud, and that he had performed under the contract, but the defendant had failed to give the promised counter-performance, judgment would go for the defendant if the plaintiff failed to prove the fraud, even though he proved his other allegations which made out a case for breach of contract. The plaintiff could then commence a fresh action for breach of contract if the limitations period had not run.

The possibilities of repetitive litigation fostered by the formulary system or the "theory of pleadings" philosophy should be eliminated in a modern system of procedure where, in general, the remedy is to accord with the facts proved and the applicable substantive law without artificial constriction by forms of action or the like.

m. Election of remedies. This subject cannot be fully treated in this Restatement, but the bearing it should have upon res judicata can be briefly sketched.

There are some situations in which a plaintiff who originally had two alternative remedies has by his conduct before bringing an action—followed, perhaps, by justified reliance on the part of the defendant—disentitled himself to one of the remedies. For example, if a buyer, after learning that he has been defrauded, uses and thereby materially alters the condition of the thing bought, he may lose the remedy of rescission for the fraud, involving a tender of return of the thing and recovery of the purchase price, and be confined to an action for deceit, that is, a money recovery of the difference between the value of the thing as falsely represented, and its actual value. The commencement of an action looking to a particular remedy accompanied by prejudicial reliance by the defendant may conceivably have a similar effect by way of estoppel.

Sometimes it is held that the mere beginning of an action for one remedy is itself an election preventing recourse to another remedy deemed in some sense "inconsistent". In a mature procedural system the mere commencement of an action for a given remedy should not of itself prevent the granting of a different remedy when warranted by the facts proved (perhaps after amendment in the course of trial). Ordinarily a plaintiff may pursue alternative remedies, however "inconsistent," with final "election" postponed to a late stage of the action—after the proof is in or even after the fact-finder, court or jury, has made its findings on both alternatives. See Illustration 23. In such circumstances, if the plaintiff seeks but one remedy, and judgment is entered for or against him, he should be precluded from a second action by the rules of merger or bar. This is properly explained on res judicata principles rather than on any notions of election of remedies. See Illustrations 24-25. Courts have not always analyzed the situation carefully. Thus, in the case where a plaintiff could have sued for alternative remedies, but has sued for only one, and after denial of the relief sought has commenced a second action for the other remedy, the second court sometimes says that the result in the first action proves that the plaintiff did not in fact have alternative remedies and that therefore he could not have made a true election; whence, says the court, it follows that he may maintain the second action for the remedy he did not pursue in the first action. Sometimes a court reaches the same conclusion by asserting that the two remedies were not "inconsistent" and so no election was involved. As already indicated, in a modern procedural system in which the plaintiff had ample opportunity to develop his whole case in the first action, he should be held precluded from a second action.

ILLUSTRATIONS:

23. A bought certain shares of stock on the strength of alleged false representations made by the seller B. A commences an action for the alternative remedies associated with rescission and deceit. If he succeeds in establishing the facts, the judgment may appropriately provide that he may elect within a certain period either to recover back the purchase price upon tendering the shares, or to receive damages in the amount determined by the evidence.

24. On the facts stated in Illustration 23, A brings an action for deceit, demanding the difference between the value of the shares had they been as represented and their actual value. Judgment is entered for the defendant after trial, upon a finding that he did not make the alleged representations. A second action for rescission, in which A offers to return the shares and demands his money back, is precluded by the rule of bar.

25. If, on the facts stated in Illustration 23, A had first commenced an action for rescission and failed because of laches, he would be barred from commencing a second action for damages for deceit.

§ 26. Exceptions To The General Rule Concerning Splitting

(1) When any of the following circumstances exists, the general rule of § 24 does not apply to extinguish the claim, and part or all of the claim subsists as a possible basis for a second action by the plaintiff against the defendant:

(a) The parties have agreed in terms or in effect that the plaintiff may split his claim, or the defendant has acquiesced therein; or

(b) The court in the first action has expressly reserved the plaintiff's right to maintain the second action; or

(c) The plaintiff was unable to rely on a certain theory of the case or to seek a certain remedy or form of relief in the first action because of the limitations on the subject matter jurisdiction of the courts or restrictions on their authority to entertain multiple theories or demands for multiple remedies or forms of relief in a single action, and the plaintiff desires in the second action to rely on that theory or to seek that remedy or form of relief; or

(d) The judgment in the first action was plainly inconsistent with the fair and equitable implementation of a statutory or constitutional scheme, or it is the sense of the scheme that the plaintiff should be permitted to split his claim; or

(e) For reasons of substantive policy in a case involving a continuing or recurrent wrong, the plaintiff is given an option to sue once for the total harm, both past and prospective, or to sue from time to time for the damages incurred to the date of suit, and chooses the latter course; or

(f) It is clearly and convincingly shown that the policies favoring preclusion of a second action are overcome for an extraordinary reason, such as the apparent invalidity of a continuing restraint or condition having a vital relation to personal liberty or the failure of the prior litigation to yield a coherent disposition of the controversy.

(2) In any case described in (f) of Subsection (1), the plaintiff is required to follow the procedure set forth in §§ 78-82.

Cross-reference. This Section presents a set of exceptional cases in which, after judgment that would otherwise extinguish the claim under the rules of merger or bar (see §§ 18, 19), the plaintiff is nevertheless free to maintain a second action on the same claim or part of it. There is a kinship between this Section and § 20, which describes the exceptions to the general rule of bar. Lines of distinction between the two Sections are suggested at § 20, Comment a.

Comment:
a. **Consent to or acquiescence in splitting (Subsection (1) (a)).** A main purpose of the general rule stated in § 24 is to protect the defendant from being harassed by repetitive actions based on the same claim. The rule is thus not applicable where the defendant consents, in express words or otherwise, to the splitting of the claim.

The parties to a pending action may agree that some part of the claim shall be withdrawn from the action with the understanding that the plaintiff shall not be precluded from subsequently maintaining an action based upon it. The agreement will normally be given effect. Or there may be an effective agreement, before an action is commenced, to litigate a part of a claim in that action but to reserve the rest of the claim for another action. So also the parties may enter into an agreement, not directed to a particular contemplated action, which may have the effect of preserving a claim that might otherwise be superseded by a judgment, for example, a clause included routinely in separation agreements between husband and wife providing that the terms of the separation agreement shall not be invalidated or otherwise affected by a judgment of divorce and that those terms shall survive such a judgment.

Where the plaintiff is simultaneously maintaining separate actions based upon parts of the same claim, and in neither action does the defendant make the objection that another action is pending based on the same claim, judgment in one of the actions does not preclude the plaintiff from proceeding and obtaining judgment in the other action. The failure of the defendant to object to the splitting of the plaintiff's claim is effective as an acquiescence in the splitting of the claim. See Illustration 1.

ILLUSTRATION:
1. After a collision in which A suffers personal injuries and property damage, A commences in the same jurisdiction one action for his personal injuries and another for the property damage against B. B does not make known in either action his objection (usually called "other action pending") to A's maintaining two actions on parts of the same claim. After judgment for A for the personal injuries, B requests dismissal of the action for property damage on the ground of merger. Dismissal should be refused as B consented in effect to the splitting of the claim.

b. **Express reservation by the court (Subsection (1)(b)).** It may appear in the course of an action that the plaintiff is splitting a claim, but that there are special reasons that justify his doing so, and accordingly that the judgment in the action ought not to have the usual consequences of extinguishing the entire claim; rather the plaintiff should be left with an opportunity to litigate in a second action that part of the claim which he justifiably omitted from the first action. A determination by the court that its judgment is "without prejudice" (or words to that effect) to a second action on the omitted part of the claim, expressed in the judgment itself, or in the findings of fact, conclusions of law, opinion, or similar record, unless reversed or set aside, should ordinarily be given effect in the second action. Cf. § 20(1)(b), and Comments f-i thereto.

For an instance where such special treatment of the plaintiff may be called for, see § 25, Comment h (possible reservation of action for restitution relief after plaintiff fails in action for breach of contract).

It is emphasized that the mere refusal of the court in the first action to allow an amendment of the complaint to permit the plaintiff to introduce additional material with respect to a claim, even where the refusal of the amendment was urged by the defendant, is not a reservation by the court within the meaning of Clause (b). The plaintiff's ordinary recourse against an incorrect refusal of an amendment is direct attack by means of appeal from an adverse judgment. See § 25(a), Comment b.

c. Where formal barriers existed against full presentation of claim in first action (Subsection (1)(c)). The general rule of § 24 is largely predicated on the assumption that the jurisdiction in which the first judgment was rendered was one which put no formal barriers in the way of a litigant's presenting to a court in one action the entire claim including any theories of recovery or demands for relief that might have been available to him under applicable law. When such formal barriers in fact existed and were operative against a plaintiff in the first action, it is unfair to preclude him from a second action in which he can present those phases of the claim which he was disabled from presenting in the first.

The formal barriers referred to may stem from limitations on the competency of the system of courts in which the first action was instituted, or from the persistence in the system of courts of older modes of procedure—the forms of action or the separation of law from equity or vestigial procedural doctrines associated with either.

(1) Limitations on the jurisdiction of a system of courts. A given transaction may result in possible liability under the law of a state and alternatively under a federal statute enforceable exclusively in a federal court. When the plaintiff brings an action in the state court, and judgment is rendered for the defendant, the plaintiff is not barred from an action in the federal court in which he may press his claim against the same defendant under the federal statute. See Illustration 2. Compare § 25(1), Comment e.

Similarly, a given transaction may result in possible liability under several theories of the law of a state, but the state's provisions for "long-arm" service of process may, on the facts presented, limit judicial jurisdiction over the defendant to the adjudication of only one of those theories. For example, an out-of-state defendant may be subject to a state's jurisdiction for the commission of a tort but not, on the particular facts, for a breach of contract. In such a case, the plaintiff, having lost his action in tort, should not be precluded from pursuing a contract remedy in a state in which jurisdiction over the defendant can be obtained.

ILLUSTRATION:

2. A Co. brings an action against B Co. in a state court under a state antitrust law and loses on the merits. It then commences an action in a federal court upon the same facts, charging violations of the federal antitrust laws, of which the federal courts have exclusive jurisdiction. The second action is not barred.

(2) Effect of the persistence of older modes of procedure. Section 25, Comments i and l, describe a series of situations in which a plaintiff in earlier times was disabled from presenting his full claim in a single action because of formal inhibitions imposed by the historical division between "law" and "equity," or the forms of action, or related procedural modes. The rules of merger and bar reflected those disabilities and in various situations permitted a plaintiff to present in a second action what he was disabled from presenting in the first. In a modern system of procedure such disabilities should no longer exist, and the law as to merger and bar adjusts itself correspondingly. Where, however, a jurisdiction has not yet modernized its procedure, then, to the extent that the disabilities continue, the older law of merger and bar, as sketched in the cited Section and Comments, would apply to judgments rendered by those courts.

d. Erroneous decision that formal barrier exists. Where the court determines that the plaintiff cannot enforce a given claim or a part of it in that action but must enforce it, if at all, in another action, the judgment does not preclude the plaintiff from maintaining the other action even though it appears that the determination made in the first action was erroneous. The determination is binding between the parties under the principle of direct estoppel. See § 17, Comment c. It is immaterial that no appeal was taken from the ruling of the court in the first action. See Illustration 3.

Although the erroneous decision in the first action does not preclude the plaintiff from maintaining a second action, it does not necessarily follow that the second court will entertain the action; for example, the action may be based on a subject matter which is beyond the subject matter jurisdiction of the second court.

ILLUSTRATION:

3. A brings suit against B upon a contract by which A agreed to buy from B, and B to sell and deliver to A, certain shares of stock. A prays specific performance of the contract, or if that remedy be not available,

for money damages. The court finds that the contract is not of a type subject to specific performance, and thereupon dismisses the action stating that the plaintiff must start a fresh action "at law." A is entitled to maintain an action seeking to recover money damages, although the court in the second action is persuaded that under the controlling precedents the dismissal of the first action was erroneous and that that action should have gone forward on the demand for money damages.

e. Implementation of a statutory or constitutional scheme (Subsection (1)(d)). The adjudication of a particular action may in retrospect appear to create such inequities in the context of a statutory scheme as a whole that a second action to correct the inequity may be called for even though it would normally be precluded as arising upon the same claim. See Illustration 4. Again, it may appear from a consideration of the entire statutory scheme that litigation, which on ordinary analysis might be considered objectionable as repetitive, is here intended to be permitted. See Illustration 5.

Similar inequities in the implementation of a constitutional scheme may result from inflexible application of the rules of merger and bar, especially when there is a change of law after the initial decision. When such inequities involve important ongoing social or political relationships, a second action should be allowed even if the claim set forth is not viewed as different from that presented in the initial proceeding. See Illustration 6.

ILLUSTRATIONS:

4. At the time a bank is closed for insolvency, 326 shares of bank stock stand in the name of shareholder A; 325 shares have been previously presented to the bank for transfer but have not in fact been transferred. B, the superintendent of banks, sues for the statutory assessment on the one share not presented for transfer and recovers judgment. After it is decided in separate litigation against other shareholders that there is statutory liability on shares not actually transferred prior to closing, B sues A on the 325 shares. The action may be maintained. Ordinarily the action would be precluded as B would be held to have split his claim, but here the interest in uniform treatment of shareholders of the bank, the policy that none should benefit by mistake or even misconduct of the public official, predominates.

5. For nonpayment of rent, landlord A brings a summary action to dispossess tenant B from leased premises. A succeeds in the action. A then brings an action for payment of the past due rent. The action is not precluded if, for example, the statutory system discloses a purpose to give the landlord a choice between, on the one hand, an action with expedited procedure to reclaim possession which does not preclude and may be followed by a regular action for rent, and, on the other hand, a regular action combining the two demands.

6. A et al., black pupils and parents, bring suit against the B board of education to invalidate and enjoin the operation of a state school "tuition grant" law on the ground that it fosters racial discrimination and is therefore unconstitutional. The court holds the law constitutional as applied and enters judgment for the defendant. Appeal is not taken, and is not warranted by the state of the law at the time of the judgment. Thereafter the United States Supreme Court in another action between different parties strikes down as unconstitutional a similar tuition grant law of another state. A et al. then commence a new action against the B board seeking the relief that was denied in the previous action. Whether or not the claims in the two actions by A et al. are regarded as the same, the second action is not barred by the first judgment. In a matter of such public importance the policy of nationwide adherence to the authoritative constitutional interpretation overcomes the policies supporting the law of res judicata.

See also §§ 83, 86.

f. Substantive policy: rationale for Subsection (1)(e). Just as the allowance of several actions with respect to the same transaction may be required by a statutory scheme of regulation, so the courts, unaided by statute, may conclude that strong substantive policies favor such allowance with respect to cases involving anticipated continuing or recurrent wrongs. Illustrations from the fields of contracts and torts are discussed in Comments g and h.

g. Contracts—plaintiff's option in case of material breach. A judgment in an action for breach of contract does not normally preclude the plaintiff from thereafter maintaining an action for breaches of the same contract that consist of failure to render performance due after commencement of the first action. Compare § 24, Comment d. But if the initial breach is accompanied or followed by a "repudiation" (see Restatement, Second, Contracts § 250), and the plaintiff thereafter commences an action for damages, he is obliged in order to avoid "splitting," to claim all his damages with respect to the contract, prospective as well as past, and judgment in the action precludes any further action by the plaintiff for damages arising from the contract.

In the event of a "material" breach (see Restatement, Second, Contracts § 241) that is not accompanied or followed by a repudiation, the plaintiff is entitled to treat the contract as at an end and to recover damages for performances not yet due as well as those already due on the theory that there has been a total breach of contract. If the plaintiff does this, a judgment extinguishing the claim under the rules of merger or bar precludes another action by him for further recovery on the contract. On the other hand, although the breach is material, the plaintiff may elect to treat it as being merely a partial breach. If he so elects, he is entitled to maintain an action for damages sustained from breaches up to the time of the institution of the action, and the judgment does not preclude a further action by him for a breach occurring after that date. See Illustration 7, and Restatement, Second, Contracts § 236, Comment b.

ILLUSTRATION:

7. A and B make a contract under which A employs B. B commits a material breach of the contract, but requests A to allow the employment to continue. A says that he will do so, but that he must have damages for the breach already committed. A accordingly brings an action against B for the breach. Judgment is given for A. A is not precluded from thereafter maintaining an action against B for a breach of the contract committed after the first action was commenced.

h. Nuisance — plaintiff's option to treat as "temporary" or "permanent." When the defendant is maintaining a structure or operating a business on his own land which causes continuing or recurrent harm to the plaintiff in the use of his land, it is clear that in suing for damages the plaintiff, to avoid splitting, must claim all damages suffered to the time of suit. This follows from the same principle that applies to an action for repeated trespasses. See § 24, Comment d.

A number of jurisdictions distinguish "temporary" from "permanent" nuisances, the plaintiff being confined to successive actions for damages when the nuisance is temporary, but allowed only a single action for total damages when the nuisance is "permanent". However, the criteria for deciding whether a nuisance is temporary or permanent are often unclear. The plaintiff is then at risk if he mistakenly believes that the nuisance is temporary rather than permanent. He is in danger of splitting his claim if he seeks and recovers only past damages; and if he delays his suit, believing that on the footing of a temporary nuisance he can at least recover the damages sustained during the period of limitations preceding the institution of suit, he may lose his claim for damages altogether, for with respect to a permanent nuisance, limitations may be held to run as a single period from the time when the nuisance arose, and that period may have expired.

To avoid the traps just described, the Restatement, Second, Torts § 930(1) and Comment b thereon, supported by some authority, would allow the plaintiff an option in cases of "continuing or recurrent tortious invasions." The plaintiff may elect, at least in doubtful cases, to treat a nuisance as temporary and sue from time to time for damages sustained in the period next preceding the institution of suit without fear of splitting. On the other hand the plaintiff may elect to sue for total damages alleging that the nuisance will probably continue for the indefinite future. If the defendant disputes the allegation, the issue is tried, and if held for the plaintiff, he recovers in full; otherwise he is remitted to successive actions. (In some instances, where the public interest precludes injunctive relief against a nuisance, an award of damages for the past and future is said to rest on a theory of "inverse condemnation.")

i. Extraordinary situations where merger or bar is inapposite (Subsection (1)(f)). In addition to cases falling within Subsections (a)-(e), there remains a small category of cases in which the policies supporting merger or bar may be overcome by other significant policies. Such an exception to the rules of merger and bar is not lightly to be found but must be based on a clear and convincing showing of need. And although it may not be feasible to compile an exhaustive description of cases in this category, it is both feasible and desirable to describe illustrative instances in an effort to give content to the concept of "extraordinary circumstances." Confined within proper limits, this concept is central to the fair administration of the doctrine of res judicata.

One instance is a case in which the question at issue is the validity of a continuing restraint or condition having a vital relation to personal liberty. Although civil actions attacking penal custody resulting from criminal convictions are beyond the scope of this Restatement, such actions do illustrate the need to moderate conventional notions of finality when personal liberty is at stake. A similar need may be found in cases involving civil commitment of the mentally ill, or the custody of a child. And substantive policy may militate in favor of allowing one spouse to sue the other for divorce even though the grounds sued upon could fairly have been comprehended within the transaction, or nucleus of facts, underlying a previous action between the same parties. See Illustration 8.

It is not suggested that the concept of finality has no place in such cases, or that the court in every such case must allow splitting or relitigation without limit. What is indicated is the need for greater flexibility and, in some matters of this type, the need for special legislative treatment.

See also the discussion in § 24, Comment f, of situations in which changed circumstances afford a basis for concluding that the second action constitutes a different claim from the first.

Another instance is a case in which the prior litigation has failed to yield a coherent disposition of the controversy. Such cases are extremely rare, but may occur, for example, when the disposition of a claim and counterclaim in a prior action has left the parties with inconsistent interests in disputed property. See Illustration 9.

ILLUSTRATIONS:

8. A wife, A, sues her husband, B, for separate maintenance on the basis of desertion, and secures a judgment. A later commences another action for divorce against B on grounds which existed when she sued for maintenance. A should not be precluded, for it is unwise to compel her to demand the most drastic remedy against B in the first action, and also unwise to deprive her of a divorce if she is now prepared to make the case for it.

9. Husband A contracts to sell a farm by warranty deed to be signed also by his wife to release her dower; the purchaser B makes a down payment and enters into possession. The wife then refuses to join in the deed. B sues A for a form of specific performance unprecedented in the jurisdiction, namely, a deed from A alone but with some allowance or arrangement to provide for the outstanding inchoate dower. A answers and counterclaims for rescission. Judgment goes against B on the main claim as the requested relief is held to be unavailable; judgment is against A on the counterclaim as no basis for rescission on his part is shown. Subsequently A commences an action for ejectment against B because of B's refusal to complete payment except on the impossible condition of the tender of a deed in which the wife joins. B in his answer relies on the dismissal of the counterclaim in the first action as res judicata, and he counterclaims, tendering the balance of the purchase price and seeking specific performance in the form of a deed by A alone. A's reply to the counterclaim relies on the dismissal of B's claim in the first action as res judicata. By the usual rules both claim and counterclaim might well be precluded. But here the previous action has left the parties not in a state of repose but in an unstable and intolerable condition. A cannot complain of harassment as he himself has commenced the second action. B's position is the more equitable. B is entitled to judgment on his counterclaim.

j. **Mistake or fraud, concealment, or misrepresentation by the defendant.** A defendant cannot justly object to being sued on a part or phase of a claim that the plaintiff failed to include in an earlier action because of the defendant's own fraud. Thus, when the defendant takes several articles at one time and on being asked by the plaintiff fraudulently denies taking some of them and suit is brought for the remainder, a judgment in that action does not bar the plaintiff from subsequently maintaining an action for those articles not included in the first action. So when there have been several breaches of contract some of which are concealed by the defendant, a judgment for the other breaches does not prevent an action for those concealed although prior in occurrence to the others. So also when the plaintiff brings an action against the defendant for cancellation of a contract made between them, alleging that the plaintiff was mentally incompetent at the time of the making of the contract, and a verdict and judgment are given for the defendant, the plaintiff is not precluded from maintaining a second action for the cancellation of the contract on the ground of a misrepresentation the defendant concealed from the plaintiff at the time when the first action was brought. See §§ 71, 72.

The result is the same when the defendant was not fraudulent, but by an innocent misrepresentation prevented the plaintiff from including the entire claim in the original action.

The result is different, however, where the failure of the plaintiff to include the entire claim in the original action was due to a mistake, not caused by the defendant's fraud or innocent misrepresentation.

k. **Procedural condition upon certain Subsection (1) cases.** The reference in Subsection (2) to the procedure set forth in Chapter 5 points to a possible requirement that the plaintiff in the specified cases must apply to the court that rendered the first judgment for a decision as to whether a second action is maintainable. See § 78.

TITLE E. ISSUE PRECLUSION

§ 27. Issue Preclusion—General Rule

When an issue of fact or law is actually litigated and determined by a valid and final judgment, and the determination is essential to the judgment, the determination is conclusive in a subsequent action between the parties, whether on the same or a different claim.

Exceptions to this general rule are stated in § 28.

Comment:

a. **Subsequent action between the same parties**. The rule of issue preclusion is operative where the second action is between the same persons who were parties to the prior action, and who were adversaries (see § 38) with respect to the particular issue, whether the second action is brought by the plaintiff or by the defendant in the original action. It is operative whether the judgment in the first action is in favor of the plaintiff or of the defendant. The effect of a judgment for the defendant in the first action may be to require a judgment for the defendant in the second action. See Illustration 1. A judgment for the plaintiff in the first action may have the effect of enabling him to recover in the second action without proving his claim, provided that the controlling issues were litigated and determined in the prior action, but the defendant is not precluded from defending the second action on the basis of an issue not litigated and determined in the first action. See Illustration 2.

ILLUSTRATIONS:

1. A brings an action against B to recover interest due on a promissory note which A alleges was executed by B and was payable to A. B denies that he executed the note. After a trial on this issue there is a verdict and judgment for B. Thereafter A sues B for a second installment of interest. The determination that B did not execute the note is conclusive in the second action.

2. A brings an action against B for failure to deliver goods on January 1, 1972, in accordance with the terms of an installment contract. B defends on the basis that the contract should be rescinded because of A's fraud in obtaining it. After a trial on this issue, there is a verdict and judgment for A. Thereafter, A sues B for failure to deliver goods on June 1, 1972, in accordance with the same contract. B is precluded by the prior judgment from seeking rescission on the basis of fraud. B is not precluded, however, from setting up other defenses, for example, that he was discharged of the duty to deliver on June 1 because of occurrences beyond his control.

b. Direct and collateral estoppel. In some cases, a judgment does not preclude relitigation of all or part of the claim on which the action is brought. See §§ 20, 26. In such cases, the rule of this Section precludes relitigation of issues actually litigated and determined in the first action when a second action is brought on the same claim. See Illustration 3. Issue preclusion in a second action on the same claim is sometimes designated as direct estoppel. If, as more frequently happens, the second action is brought on a different claim, the rule of this Section also applies; in such cases, preclusion is sometimes designated as collateral estoppel.

ILLUSTRATION:

3. A brings an action against B for personal injuries arising out of an automobile accident. Jurisdiction is asserted over B, a nonresident, on the basis that the automobile involved in the accident was being operated in the state by or on his behalf. After trial of this issue, the action is dismissed for lack of jurisdiction. In a subsequent action by A against B for the same injuries, brought in the state of B's residence, the prior determination that the automobile was not being operated by or on behalf of B is conclusive.

c. Dimensions of an issue. One of the most difficult problems in the application of the rule of this Section is to delineate the issue on which litigation is, or is not, foreclosed by the prior judgment. The problem involves a balancing of important interests: on the one hand, a desire not to deprive a litigant of an adequate day in court; on the other hand, a desire to prevent repetitious litigation of what is essentially the same dispute. When there is a lack of total identity between the particular matter presented in the second action and that presented in the first, there are several factors that should be considered in deciding whether for purposes of the rule of this Section the "issue" in the two proceedings is the same, for example: Is there a substantial overlap between the evidence or argument to be advanced in the second proceeding and that advanced in the first? Does the new evidence or argument involve application of the same rule of law as that involved in the prior proceeding? Could pretrial preparation and discovery relating to the matter presented in the first action reasonably be expected to have embraced the matter sought to be presented in the second? How closely related are the claims involved in the two proceedings? For examples of cases in which such factors are relevant, see Illustrations 4, 5, and 6.

Sometimes, there is a lack of total identity between the matters involved in the two proceedings because the events in suit took place at different times. In some such instances, the overlap is so substantial that preclusion is plainly appropriate. See Illustration 8. Preclusion ordinarily is proper if the question is one of the legal effect of a document identical in all relevant respects to another document whose effect was adjudicated in a prior action. And, in the absence of a showing of changed circumstances, a determination that, for example, a person was disabled, or a nonresident of the state, in one year will be conclusive with respect to the next as well. In other instances the burden of showing changed or different circumstances should be placed on the party against whom the prior judgment is asserted. See Illustration 7. In still other instances, the bearing of the first determination is so marginal because of the separation in time and other factors negating any similarity that the first judgment may properly be given no effect. See Illustration 9.

An issue on which relitigation is foreclosed may be one of evidentiary fact, of "ultimate fact" (i.e., the application of law to fact), or of law. See also Comment j below. Thus, for example, if the party against whom preclusion is sought did in fact litigate an issue of ultimate fact and suffered an adverse determination, new evidentiary facts may not be brought forward to obtain a different determination of that ultimate fact. See Illustration 4. And similarly if the issue was one of law, new arguments may not be presented to obtain a different determination of that issue. See Illustration 6.

ILLUSTRATIONS:

4. A brings an action against B to recover for personal injuries in an automobile accident. A seeks to establish that B was negligent in driving at an excessive rate of speed. After trial, verdict and judgment are given for B. In a subsequent action by B against A for injuries in the same accident, A is precluded from setting up B's negligence as a defense, whether or not the alleged negligence is based on an assertion

of excessive speed. It is reasonable to require A to bring forward all evidence in support of the alleged negligence in the initial proceeding. (It is assumed in this Illustration that the forum has no applicable compulsory counterclaim rule. See § 22.)

5. A brings an action against B to recover royalties due under an oil lease for oil produced from certain wells. After trial, judgment is given for A, the court finding that all the wells in question are covered by the lease. In a second action by A against B for later royalties under the lease with respect to the same wells, B seeks to assert for the first time that one of the wells was not covered by the lease because it was diagonally drilled into state-owned underwater land adjacent to the leased land. Whether B is precluded with respect to this assertion under the rule of this Section should turn on application of the factors described in this Comment, particularly the relation between the evidentiary presentation, the applicable rule of law, and the claim involved in each of the two proceedings.

6. A brings an action against B to recover an installment payment due under a contract. B's sole defense is that the contract is unenforceable under the statute of frauds. After trial, judgment is given for A, the court ruling that an oral contract of the kind sued upon is enforceable. In a subsequent action by A against B to recover a second installment falling due after the first action was brought, B is precluded from raising the statute of frauds as a defense, whether or not on the basis of arguments made in the prior action, but is not precluded from asserting as a defense that the installment is not owing as a matter of law on any other ground.

7. A brings an action against B to set aside a conveyance of Blackacre by C to B on the ground that at the time of the conveyance C was mentally incompetent. After trial, verdict and judgment are given for A. A second action is brought by A against B to set aside a conveyance of Whiteacre by C to B which took place one week after the conveyance of Blackacre. Unless B can establish changed circumstances occurring in the time between the two conveyances, the prior judgment is conclusive that C was incompetent when Whiteacre was conveyed. (The result would be the same if the Whiteacre conveyance had occurred one week before the Blackacre conveyance.)

8. The facts are as stated in Illustration 7, except that the Whiteacre conveyance occurred immediately after the Blackacre conveyance. If the two actions are held to involve different claims, the prior judgment is conclusive that B was incompetent when Whiteacre was conveyed.

9. In an action brought by the A corporation against the taxing authorities with respect to taxes for the year 1940, judgment is based on a determination that A should have been taxed as a nonresident corporation because it had no office or place of business in the state. A similar action is brought by A with respect to taxes for the year 1970. If it is concluded that the separation in time between the two proceedings is so great that the first determination has little if any bearing on the question whether A had an office or place of business in the state in 1970, then the first judgment should be given no effect on that question and A should have the same burden of proof as that imposed on any other taxpayer.

d. When an issue is actually litigated. When an issue is properly raised, by the pleadings or otherwise, and is submitted for determination, and is determined, the issue is actually litigated within the meaning of this Section. An issue may be submitted and determined on a motion to dismiss for failure to state a claim, a motion for judgment on the pleadings, a motion for summary judgment (see Illustration 10), a motion for directed verdict, or their equivalents, as well as on a judgment entered on a verdict. A determination may be based on a failure of pleading or of proof as well as on the sustaining of the burden of proof.

The determination of an issue by a judge in a proceeding conducted without a jury is conclusive in a subsequent action whether or not there would have been a right to a jury in that subsequent action if collateral estoppel did not apply. See Illustrations 10 and 11.

ILLUSTRATIONS:

10. In January, B agrees to buy a horse from A, and in February B agrees to buy Blackacre from A. A brings a suit for specific performance of the February agreement; B alleges with supporting proof that he was an infant when the agreement was made, and the court enters summary judgment for B on that ground. Thereafter A brings an action against B for damages for breach of the January agreement and demands a jury. The judgment in the prior suit is conclusive that B was an infant when the contract was made.

11. The facts are as stated in Illustration 10, except that in the first proceeding the issue of infancy is decided for B after trial without a jury on the basis of conflicting evidence of B's age. The judgment in the prior suit is conclusive that B was an infant when the contract was made.

e. Issues not actually litigated. A judgment is not conclusive in a subsequent action as to issues which might have been but were not litigated and determined in the prior action. There are many reasons why a party may choose not to raise an issue, or to contest an assertion, in a particular action. The action may involve so small an amount that litigation of the issue may cost more than the value of the lawsuit.

Or the forum may be an inconvenient one in which to produce the necessary evidence or in which to litigate at all. The interests of conserving judicial resources, of maintaining consistency, and of avoiding oppression or harassment of the adverse party are less compelling when the issue on which preclusion is sought has not actually been litigated before. And if preclusive effect were given to issues not litigated, the result might serve to discourage compromise, to decrease the likelihood that the issues in an action would be narrowed by stipulation, and thus to intensify litigation.

It is true that it is sometimes difficult to determine whether an issue was actually litigated; even if it was not litigated, the party's reasons for not litigating in the prior action may be such that preclusion would be appropriate. But the policy considerations outlined above weigh strongly in favor of nonpreclusion, and it is in the interest of predictability and simplicity for such a result to obtain uniformly.

Sometimes the party against whom preclusion is asserted is covered by an insurance policy and represented by insurance company counsel in the prior action but not in the subsequent action. In such instances, preclusion with respect to unlitigated issues seems particularly unfair.

An issue is not actually litigated if the defendant might have interposed it as an affirmative defense but failed to do so; nor is it actually litigated if it is raised by a material allegation of a party's pleading but is admitted (explicitly or by virtue of a failure to deny) in a responsive pleading; nor is it actually litigated if it is raised in an allegation by one party and is admitted by the other before evidence on the issue is adduced at trial; nor is it actually litigated if it is the subject of a stipulation between the parties. A stipulation may, however, be binding in a subsequent action between the parties if the parties have manifested an intention to that effect. Furthermore under the rules of evidence applicable in the jurisdiction, an admission by a party may be treated as conclusive or be admissible in evidence against that party in a subsequent action.

In the case of a judgment entered by confession, consent, or default, none of the issues is actually litigated. Therefore, the rule of this Section does not apply with respect to any issue in a subsequent action. The judgment may be conclusive, however, with respect to one or more issues, if the parties have entered an agreement manifesting such an intention.

It should be noted that, although issue preclusion does not apply to issues not actually litigated, there is a concept of estoppel in pais, not dealt with in this Restatement, which may be applicable in appropriate cases. Under this concept, a person who makes a representation may be estopped to deny its truth if the person to whom it was made has changed his position in reliance.

f. Extrinsic evidence to determine what issues were litigated. If it cannot be determined from the pleadings and other materials of record in the prior action what issues, if any, were litigated and determined by the verdict and judgment, extrinsic evidence is admissible to aid in such a determination. Extrinsic evidence may also be admitted to show that the record in the prior action does not accurately indicate what issues, if any, were litigated and determined.

The party contending that an issue has been conclusively litigated and determined in a prior action has the burden of proving that contention.

g. If several issues litigated. If several issues are litigated in an action, and in a subsequent action between the parties, one of the parties relies on the judgment as conclusive of one of the issues, that party must show that the issue was determined by the judgment in the prior action.

If several issues are litigated in an action, and a judgment cannot properly be rendered in favor of one party unless all of the issues are decided in his favor, and judgment is given for him, the judgment is conclusive with respect to all the issues.

ILLUSTRATION:

12. A brings an action against B to recover interest on a promissory note payable to A, the principal not yet being due. B alleges that he was induced by the fraud of A to execute the note, and further alleges that A gave him a release under seal of the obligation to pay interest. After a trial of these issues, verdict and judgment are given for A. After the note matures, A brings an action against B for the principal. The judgment in the prior suit is conclusive that B was not induced by the fraud of A to execute the note.

h. Determinations not essential to the judgment. If issues are determined but the judgment is not dependent upon the determinations, relitigation of those issues in a subsequent action between the parties is not precluded. Such determinations have the characteristics of dicta, and may not ordinarily be the subject of an appeal by the party against whom they were made. In these circumstances, the interest in providing an opportunity for a considered determination, which if adverse may be the subject of an appeal, outweighs the interest in avoiding the burden of relitigation.

ILLUSTRATIONS:

13. A brings an action against B to recover interest on a promissory note payable to A, the principal not yet being due. B alleges that he was induced by the fraud of A to execute the note, and further alleges that A gave him a release under seal of the obligation to pay interest. The court, sitting without a jury,

finds that A had given such a release but that B was not induced by A's fraud to execute the note, and gives verdict for B on which judgment is entered. After the note matures A brings an action against B for the principal of the note. B is not precluded from defending this action on the ground that B was induced by A's fraud to execute the note.

14. A, as owner of a trademark, brings an action against B for infringement. B denies the validity of the trademark and denies infringement. The court finds that the trademark is valid, but that B had not infringed it, and gives judgment for B. Thereafter A brings an action against B alleging that since the rendition of the judgment B infringed the trademark. B is not precluded from defending this action on the ground that the trademark is invalid.

i. Alternative determinations by court of first instance. If a judgment of a court of first instance is based on determinations of two issues, either of which standing independently would be sufficient to support the result, the judgment is not conclusive with respect to either issue standing alone. See Illustration 14. Cf. § 20, Comment e.

It might be argued that the judgment should be conclusive with respect to both issues. The matter has presumably been fully litigated and fairly decided; the determination does support, and is in itself sufficient to support, the judgment for the prevailing party; and the losing party is in a position to seek reversal of the determination from an appellate court. Moreover, a party who would otherwise urge several matters in support of a particular result may be deterred from doing so if a judgment resting on alternative determinations does not effectively preclude relitigation of particular issues.

There are, however, persuasive reasons for analogizing the case to that of the nonessential determination discussed in Comment h. First, a determination in the alternative may not have been as carefully or rigorously considered as it would have if it had been necessary to the result, and in that sense it has some of the characteristics of dicta. Second, and of critical importance, the losing party, although entitled to appeal from both determinations, might be dissuaded from doing so because of the likelihood that at least one of them would be upheld and the other not even reached. If he were to appeal solely for the purpose of avoiding the application of the rule of issue preclusion, then the rule might be responsible for increasing the burdens of litigation on the parties and the courts rather than lightening those burdens. Compare Comment o, dealing with the effect of an appellate decision based on alternative determinations.

There may be causes where, despite these considerations, the balance tips in favor of preclusion because of the fullness with which the issue was litigated and decided in the first action. But since the question of preclusion will almost always be a close one if each case is to rest on its own particular facts, it is in the interest of predictability and simplicity for the result of nonpreclusion to be uniform.

The case discussed, and exemplified by Illustration 15, is to be distinguished from a case in which there are alternative bases for a determination that is essential to the judgment. In such a case, failure to appeal from that determination cannot be attributed to the losing party's anticipation that the judgment will be affirmed on other grounds. Thus relitigation of the issue so determined is properly precluded under the rule of this Section. See Illustration 16.

ILLUSTRATIONS:

15. A brings an action against B to recover interest on a promissory note payable to A, the principal not yet being due. B alleges that he was induced by the fraud of A to execute the note, and further alleges that A gave him a binding release of the obligation to pay interest. The court, sitting without a jury, finds that B was induced by A's fraud to execute the note and also finds that A had given him a binding release of the obligation to pay interest. Judgment for B is not appealed. After the note matures, A brings an action against B for the principal of the note. The prior judgment is not a defense to the action, and the issue of fraud must be relitigated if B chooses to raise it.

16. The facts of the first action are as stated in Illustration 15, but in the second action A sues for another installment of interest before the principal becomes due. The determination that B is not liable for interest on the note is conclusive, even though there were alternative bases for that determination.

The distinction between Illustrations 15 and 16 is that the first action, even though decided on alternative grounds, necessarily adjudicated the issue as to liability for interest, but did not necessarily adjudicate the issue — fraud — relevant to recovery of the principal.

j. Determinations essential to the judgment. It is sometimes stated that even when a determination is a necessary step in the formulation of a decision and judgment, the determination will not be conclusive between the parties if it relates only to a "mediate datum" or "evidentiary fact" rather than to an "ultimate fact" or issue of law. It has also been stated than even a determination of "ultimate fact" will not be conclusive in a later action if it constitutes only an "evidentiary fact" or "mediate datum" in that action. Such a formulation is occasionally used to support a refusal to apply the rule of issue preclusion when the refusal could more appropriately be based on the lack of similarity between the issues in the two proceedings. If applied more broadly, the formulation causes great difficulty, and is at odds with the rationale on which the rule of issue preclusion is based. The line between ultimate and evidentiary facts is often impossible to draw. Moreover, even if a fact is categorized as evidentiary, great effort may have been expended by both parties in seeking to persuade the adjudicator of its existence or nonexistence and it may well have been regarded as the key issue in the dispute. In these circumstances the determination of the issue should be conclusive whether or not other links in the chain had to be forged before the question of liability could be determined in the first or second action.

The appropriate question, then, is whether the issue was actually recognized by the parties as important and by the trier as necessary to the first judgment. If so, the determination is conclusive between the parties in a subsequent action, unless there is a basis for an exception under § 28 — for example, that the significance of the issue for purposes of the subsequent action was not sufficiently foreseeable at the time of the first action.

ILLUSTRATIONS:

17. A brings an action against C to recover for personal injuries caused in an automobile accident involving a car driven by B and owned by C. A alleges that C is liable for B's negligence because B was driving with C's express or implied permission within the meaning of applicable state law making an owner liable in such circumstances. The action is defended by C's insurer; at the trial, the evidence is in conflict as to whether B was employed by C at the time of the accident and whether he was driving the car on C's business or on a frolic of his own. After trial, verdict and judgment are given for A, with explicit findings that B was C's employee and was driving the car within the scope of his employment at the time of the accident. When C fails to satisfy the judgment, A brings an action against C's insurer to collect the proceeds of the policy. C's insurer is precluded from defending on the basis of a clause in the policy limiting coverage to accidents caused by the owner or by persons acting within the scope of their employment by the owner. Although the "ultimate" question in the first action was one of express or implied permission to use the car, the finding as to scope of employment precludes relitigation of that issue in the second action. (Note: C's insurer, having defended the first action, is bound to the same extent as C. See § 57.)

18. A, an attorney, brings an action against B, an attorney, for a declaratory judgment as to the rights and interests of the parties in certain attorneys' fees collected by B. At trial, there is a conflict in the evidence with respect to the terms of an oral agreement between A and B, and in particular with respect to the date after which all fees received would be shared. After trial, judgment is given for B on the basis that A had no right or interest in the fees in question. There is an explicit finding that the fee-sharing agreement between A and B did not apply to sums collected before January 1971, and that the fees in question were collected before that date. In a subsequent action by A against B for a share of fees collected by B after the first action was instituted but before January 1971, A is precluded from showing that his agreement with B extended to these fees.

k. **Requirement of a valid, final judgment**. The requisites of a valid judgment are set forth in § 1, and the definition of a final judgment may be found in § 13. Particular reference is made to the distinction in § 13 between finality for purposes of merger and bar and finality for purposes of issue preclusion. Pursuant to this distinction, a litigation may have reached a stage at which issue preclusion is appropriate even though claim preclusion — application of the rules of merger and bar — is not.

l. **Effect on pending action**. If two actions which involve the same issue are pending between the same parties, it is the first final judgment rendered in one of the actions which becomes conclusive in the other action, regardless of which action was brought first. See § 14.

m. **Inconsistent judgments**. If in two successive actions between the same parties the same issue is actually litigated and determined, and that issue arises in a third action between the parties, the rules for determining which judgment is conclusive with respect to that issue are those set forth in § 15.

n. **Judgment not precluding another action on the same claim**. A judgment that does not preclude another action on the same claim — one that is not a bar — may have collateral as well as direct estoppel effects. See § 20, Comment b. If, however, a judgment of dismissal is wholly without prejudice, then it has no conclusive effect between the parties in a subsequent action on the same or a different claim.

o. **Effect of an appeal**. If a judgment rendered by a court of first instance is reversed by the appellate court and a final judgment is entered by the appellate court (or by the court of first instance in pursuance of the mandate of the appellate court), this latter judgment is conclusive between the parties.

If the judgment of the court of first instance was based on a determination of two issues, either of which standing independently would be sufficient to support the result, and the appellate court upholds both of these determinations as sufficient, and accordingly affirms the judgment, the judgment is conclusive as to both determinations. In contrast to the case discussed in Comment i, the losing party has here obtained an appellate decision on the issue, and thus the balance weighs in favor of preclusion.

If the appellate court upholds one of these determinations as sufficient but not the other, and accordingly affirms the judgment, the judgment is conclusive as to the first determination.

If the appellate court upholds one of these determinations as sufficient and refuses to consider whether or not the other is sufficient and accordingly affirms the judgment, the judgment is conclusive as to the first determination.

§ 28. Exceptions To The General Rule Of Issue Preclusion

Although an issue is actually litigated and determined by a valid and final judgment, and the determination is essential to the judgment, relitigation of the issue in a subsequent action between the parties is not precluded in the following circumstances:

(1) The party against whom preclusion is sought could not, as a matter of law, have obtained review of the judgment in the initial action; or

(2) The issue is one of law and (a) the two actions involve claims that are substantially unrelated, or (b) a new determination is warranted in order to take account of an intervening change in the applicable legal context or otherwise to avoid inequitable administration of the laws; or

(3) A new determination of the issue is warranted by differences in the quality or extensiveness of the procedures followed in the two courts or by factors relating to the allocation of jurisdiction between them; or

(4) The party against whom preclusion is sought had a significantly heavier burden of persuasion with respect to the issue in the initial action than in the subsequent action; the burden has shifted to his adversary; or the adversary has a significantly heavier burden than he had in the first action; or

(5) There is a clear and convincing need for a new determination of the issue (a) because of the potential adverse impact of the determination on the public interest or the interests of persons not themselves parties in the initial action, (b) because it was not sufficiently foreseeable at the time of the initial action that the issue would arise in the context of a subsequent action, or (c) because the party sought to be precluded, as a result of the conduct of his adversary or other special circumstances, did not have an adequate opportunity or incentive to obtain a full and fair adjudication in the initial action.

Comment:

a. Inability to obtain review (Subsection (1)). As noted in § 27, Comments h and i, the availability of review for the correction of errors has become critical to the application of preclusion doctrine. If review is unavailable because the party who lost on the issue obtained a judgment in his favor, the general rule of § 27 is inapplicable by its own terms. Similarly, if there was an alternative determination adequate to support the judgment, the rule of § 27 does not apply.

There is a need for an analogous exception to the rule of preclusion when the determination of an issue is plainly essential to the judgment but the party who lost on that issue is, for some other reason, disabled as a matter of law from obtaining review by appeal or, where appeal does not lie, by injunction, extraordinary writ, or statutory review procedure. Such cases can arise, for example, because the controversy has become moot, or because the law does not allow review of the particular category of judgments.

The exception in Subsection (1) applies only when review is precluded as a matter of law. It does not apply in cases where review is available but is not sought. Nor does it apply when there is discretion in the reviewing court to grant or deny review and review is denied; such denials by a first tier appellate court are generally tantamount to a conclusion that the questions raised are without merit.

Note: With respect to controversies that have become moot, it is a procedural requirement in some jurisdictions, in order to avoid the impact of issue preclusion, that the appellate court reverse or vacate the judgment below and remand with directions to dismiss.

Cross-reference. An acquittal in a criminal case in certain limited contexts can have preclusive effect in a subsequent civil proceeding, even though the prosecution is unable to obtain review. See § 85. One reason why such effect is generally not accorded is the difference in the burden of proof in the two proceedings. Cf. Comment f, below.

b. Issues of law (Subsection (2)). The distinction between issues of fact and issues of law is often an elusive one. In an action tried to a jury, a party may be entitled to a directed verdict "as a matter of law," or a question like that of the meaning of a written contract may be a question of "law" in the sense that it is decided by the judge rather than the jury. In addition, courts and Commentators frequently refer to "mixed question of fact and law," suggesting that the journey from a pure question of fact to a pure question of law is one of subtle gradations rather than one marked by a rigid divide. Thus the question whether A negligently caused injury to B, for example, may involve the application of a recognized legal standard to a set of undisputed historical facts, may involve a dispute over the allocation and extent of the burden of persuasion, or over the legal standard of due care, or may involve a dispute over what actually happened.

When the claims in two separate actions between the same parties are the same or are closely related — for example, when they involve asserted obligations arising out of the same subject matter — it is not ordinarily necessary to characterize an issue as one of fact or of law for purposes of issue preclusion. If the issue has been actually litigated and determined and the determination was essential to the judgment, preclusion will apply. See § 27, and Comment c and Illustration 6 thereto. See also Illustration 1, below. In such a case, it is unfair to the winning party and an unnecessary burden on the courts to allow repeated litigation of the same issue in what is essentially the same controversy, even if the issue is regarded as one of "law." Thus if a corporation issues a series of notes for the repayment of a loan, and the holder of the notes brings an action on one of them, and the corporation's defense that issuance of the notes was ultra vires is rejected by the court, the judgment is conclusive on that issue in a subsequent action on another of the notes.

On the other hand, if the issue is one of the formulation or scope of the applicable legal rule, and if the claims in the two actions are substantially unrelated, the more flexible principle of stare decisis is sufficient to protect the parties and the court from unnecessary burdens. A rule of law declared in an action between two parties should not be binding on them for all time, especially as to claims arising after the first proceeding has been concluded, when other litigants are free to urge that the rule should be rejected. Such preclusion might unduly delay needed changes in the law and might deprive a litigant of a right that the court was prepared to recognize for other litigants in the same position. See Illustration 2.

ILLUSTRATIONS:

1. A brings an action against B to recover for infringement of the trademark "Florasynth" by use of the trade name "Flora Essential Oils." The court grants judgment for B on B's motion to dismiss for failure to state a claim, holding that the name "Flora" is a descriptive word of extensive and common use and is not subject to appropriation as a trademark. In a second action by A against B for infringement of the same trademark, in which the allegations of the complaint are the same except that the asserted infringement is limited to the period after the first judgment, the judgment in the first action is conclusive on the issue whether the name "Flora" is subject to appropriation as a trademark.

2. A brings an action against the municipality of B for tortious injury. The court sustains B's defense of sovereign immunity and dismisses the action. Several years later A brings a second action against B for an unrelated tortious injury occurring after the dismissal. The judgment in the first action is not conclusive on the question whether the defense of sovereign immunity is available to B. Note: The doctrine of stare decisis may lead the court to refuse to reconsider the question of sovereign immunity. See § 29, Comment i.

c. **Change in applicable legal context; avoidance of inequitable administration of the laws**. Even when claims in two actions are closely related, an intervening change in the relevant legal climate may warrant reexamination of the rule of law applicable as between the parties. Such reexamination is particularly appropriate when the application of the rule of issue preclusion would impose on one of the parties a significant disadvantage, or confer on him a significant benefit, with respect to his competitors. See Illustration 3. But even when such competition is lacking, reexamination is appropriate if the change in the law, or other circumstances, are such that preclusion would result in a manifestly inequitable administration of the laws. See Illustration 4.

In determining whether the applicable legal context has changed, or that applying preclusion would result in inequitable administration of the law, it is important to recognize that two concepts of equality are in competition with each other. One is the concept that the outcomes of similar legal disputes between the same parties at different points in time should not be disparate. The other is that the outcomes of similar legal disputes being contemporaneously determined between different parties should be resolved according to the same legal standards. Applying issue preclusion invokes the first of these concepts, treating temporally separated controversies the same way at the expense of applying different legal standards to persons similarly situated at the time of the second litigation. The problem is illustrated by the situation where a taxpayer's liability for tax in a certain transaction in one tax year is determined according to a particular interpretation of the tax law, and that interpretation is thereafter abandoned in favor of another interpretation. If issue preclusion is applied in a subsequent tax year, the taxpayer will receive treatment different from that accorded to other taxpayers similarly situated at that time. On the other hand, refusing to apply issue preclusion invokes the second concept of equality. Thus, in the situation posed, if the taxpayer's liability in subsequent years is determined according to the new interpretation of the law, the taxpayer will be treated in those years in the same way as other taxpayers but in a way inconsistent with the determination previously made with respect to him. Comparable problems can arise in other types of transactions in which the same fact pattern presents itself in adjudications occurring over the course of time.

In deciding whether to apply issue preclusion, or instead to apply a subsequent emerging legal standard, the choice is between two forms of disparity in resolution of legal controversy. In making the choice, the courts sometime pose the question as whether the "rights" involved in the two successive actions are the same. This only poses the problem in different terminology. The same is true of attempting a distinction between an issue of "mixed law and fact" and an issue of the "governing legal rule" because the essential problem is that there has been change in the law but not the facts. Rather, the choice must be made in terms of the importance of stability in the legal relationships between the immediate parties, the actual likelihood that there are similarly situated persons who are subject to application of the rule in question, and the consequences to the latter if they are subject to different legal treatment. In this connection it can be particularly significant that one of the parties is a government agency responsible for continuing administration of a body of law that affects members of the public generally, as in the case of tax law. Refusal of preclusion is ordinarily justified if the effect of applying preclusion is to give one person a favored position in current administration of a law.

ILLUSTRATIONS:

3. A, a state agency, brings an action against B to revoke B's wholesale liquor license on the ground that B has violated the law governing the license by selling only to himself as a retailer. The court grants B's motion to dismiss for failure to state a claim, holding that the conduct charged does not violate the law. In a subsequent action by A against C, a higher court holds that identical conduct by C is ground for the revocation of C's wholesale liquor license. In a second action against B for revocation of B's license, A is not precluded from asserting that since the first dismissal, B has continued, as before, to sell only to himself as a retailer.

4. A, a non-profit organization, brings an action against B, the tax commissioner, for a refund of property taxes on the ground that it is exempt as a charity. The court gives judgment for B, adopting a narrow definition of the charitable exemption. Shortly after, a higher court of the same jurisdiction grants a property tax refund to C, an organization quite similar to A, and in doing so formulates a much broader definition of the exemption. In a subsequent action by A against B for a refund of property taxes paid for the following year, A is not precluded from asserting that it is entitled to the charitable exemption. It does not matter that the nature of A's activities has not changed since the first action.

5. A, an employer, brings an action against B, a labor union, to enjoin a strike in breach of a collective bargaining agreement. The action is dismissed on the ground that a statute deprives the court of jurisdiction to issue such injunctions. In a subsequent case involving two different parties, the decision in A v. B is overruled and jurisdiction to enjoin such a strike is sustained. A is not precluded from asserting jurisdiction in an action to enjoin B from continuing the same strike, from engaging in another strike in breach of the same contract, or from engaging in a strike in breach of a subsequent contract.

d. Courts of the same state (Subsection (3)). Not infrequently, issue preclusion will be asserted in an action over which the court rendering the prior judgment would not have had subject matter jurisdiction. In many such cases, there is no reason why preclusion should not apply; the procedures followed in the two courts are comparable in quality and extensiveness, and the first court was fully competent to render a determination of the issue on which preclusion is sought. In other cases, however, there may be compelling reasons why preclusion should not apply. For example, the procedures available in the first court may have been tailored to the prompt, inexpensive determination of small claims and thus may be wholly inappropriate to the determination of the same issues when presented in the context of a much larger claim. The scope of review in the first action may have been very narrow. Or the legislative allocation of jurisdiction among the courts of the state may have been designed to insure that when an action is brought to determine a particular issue directly, it may only be maintained in a court having special competence to deal with it. In such instances, after a court has incidently determined an issue that it lacks jurisdiction to determine directly, the determination should not be binding when a second action is brought in a court having such jurisdiction. The question in each case should be resolved in the light of the nature of litigation in the courts involved and the legislative purposes in allocating jurisdiction among the courts of the state.

ILLUSTRATIONS:

6. A brings an action against B to recover for property damage in a court whose jurisdiction is limited to claims not exceeding $2,000. The rules governing the conduct of litigation applicable in the court are substantially the same as those in courts of general jurisdiction. After trial, verdict and judgment are rendered for A on the basis of a finding of B's negligence. In a subsequent action by B against A for $10,000 for personal injuries arising out of the same occurrence, the finding of B's negligence in the first action is conclusive.

7. The facts are the same as in Illustration 6, except that the first action is brought in a small claims

court which has a jurisdictional ceiling of $500, and which operates informally without pleadings, counsel, or rules of evidence. The finding of B's negligence is not conclusive in the second action.

8. In a probate court proceeding involving the estate of A, in which B and C are active and adverse participants, it is determined that C is A's legitimate son. A subsequent action by B against C is brought in a court of general jurisdiction for a declaratory judgment that C is not entitled to share in the proceeds of a certain inter vivos trust because he is not A's legitimate son. The procedures followed in the probate court are of comparable quality to those in the court of general jurisdiction. The determination of legitimacy in the prior action is conclusive.

9. H brings an action for forcible entry and detainer against W before a justice of the peace. W defends on the ground that the parties are legally married and that under the law of the State such an action cannot be maintained between spouses. The justice of the peace rejects the defense, ruling that the parties are not legally married. A subsequent action for divorce is brought between W and H in the domestic relations court, which has exclusive jurisdiction over divorce actions. The determination in the prior action that the parties are not legally married is not conclusive.

e. Courts of different states; state and federal courts. This Restatement deals primarily with the effect of a judgment in the courts of the state in which it was rendered. The problem covered in Subsection (3), however, frequently arises when the second action is brought in the courts of another state, or in the federal courts. The problem also arises when the first action [is] brought in a federal court and the second action in a state court. In many such cases, the Full Faith and Credit Clause or the Supremacy Clause of the United States Constitution, or federal statutes or rules of decision, may require that preclusive effect be given to the first judgment. For example, in a state court action on a patent license agreement, a determination may be made that the agreement terminated on a particular date; such a determination would be conclusive in a subsequent federal court action between the same parties for patent infringement. See 28 U.S.C. § 1738. And in a federal court action for patent infringement, a determination that the patent is invalid would be conclusive on that issue in a subsequent state court action on a license agreement. See Article VI, Clause 2, of the U.S. Constitution (the Supremacy Clause). On the other hand, a determination in a state court action on a patent license agreement upholding the defense that the patent was invalid for want of invention would not be held binding in a subsequent federal court action for patent infringement if the Congressional grant of exclusive jurisdiction in patent infringement cases to the federal district courts is construed to require otherwise. The question in each such case would be resolved in the light of the legislative purpose in vesting exclusive jurisdiction in a particular court. See § 86. See also the related discussion in Comment d to this Section.

As a further example, a court in State A may determine an issue involving title to land in State B, even though the A court would not have had jurisdiction over the land itself. In such a case, the determination is conclusive as between the parties to the proceeding in State A and should be given preclusive effect in State B and other states. See Restatement, Second, Conflict of Laws § 95. The different question of the extraterritorial effect of a decree ordering the conveyance of land in another state, or of other equity decrees, is dealt with in Restatement, Second, Conflict of Laws § 102, and discussed in § 18, Comment d.

f. Differences in the burden of persuasion (Subsection (4)). To apply issue preclusion in the cases described in Subsection (4) would be to hold, in effect, that the losing party in the first action would also have lost had a significantly different burden being imposed. While there may be many occasions when such a holding would be correct, there are many others in which the allocation and weight of the burden of persuasion (or burden of proof, as it is called in many jurisdictions) are critical in determining who should prevail. Since the process by which the issue was adjudicated cannot be reconstructed on the basis of a new and different burden, preclusive effect is properly denied. This is a major reason for the general rule that, even when the parties are the same, an acquittal in a criminal proceeding is not conclusive in a subsequent civil action arising out of the same event. See § 85.

ILLUSTRATIONS:

10. A brings an action against B for injuries incurred in an automobile accident involving cars driven by A and B. Under the governing law, A has the burden of proving his freedom from contributory negligence. Verdict and judgment are given for B on the basis that A has not sustained that burden. In a subsequent action by B against A for injuries incurred in the same accident, the issue of A's negligence (on which B now has the burden of persuasion) is not concluded by the first judgment.

11. A brings an action against B to recover on a promissory note. B defends on the ground that he was induced by A's fraud to give this and other notes in the series, but fails to establish fraud by clear and convincing evidence as required by law. After judgment for A, the law is changed to provide that in such cases fraud need be proved only by a preponderance of the evidence. In an action by A on another note in the series, B is not precluded from asserting the defense of fraud.

g. Rationale for Subsection (5). As stated in the introduction to Title E, the policy supporting issue preclusion is not so unyielding that it must invariably be applied, even in the face of strong competing considerations. There are instances in which the interests supporting a new determination of an issue already determined outweigh the resulting burden on the other party and on the courts. But such instances must be the rare exception, and litigation to establish an exception in a particular case should not be encouraged. Thus it is important to admit an exception only when the need for a redetermination of the issue is a compelling one.

h. Potential adverse impact on persons not parties. There are many instances in which the nature of an action is such that the judgment will have a direct impact on those who are not themselves parties. For example, an agency of government may bring an action for the protection or relief of particular persons or of a broad segment of the public, or an individual may sue as representative of a class. In such cases, when a second action is brought, due consideration of the interests of persons not themselves before the court in the prior action may justify relitigation of an issue actually litigated and determined in that action. For example, in a class action, see § 41, members of the class may be content to have a particular person represent them in connection with one claim, not knowing or having reason to know that an issue may be litigated in the action that is crucial to the determination of another, unrelated claim in which they have an interest.

i. Unforeseeability that issue would arise in the context of the second action. As noted in § 27, Comment j, it is not necessary to the application of the rule of preclusion that the issue be one of "ultimate fact" in either the first or the second action. But at the same time, preclusion should not operate to foreclose redetermination of an issue if it was unforeseeable when the first action was litigated that the issue would arise in the context of the second action, and if that lack of foreseeability may have contributed to the losing party's failure to litigate the issue fully. Such instances are rare, but they may arise, for example, between institutional litigants as a result of a change in the governing law. Thus, a determination in an action between the taxing authorities and a corporate taxpayer that a transfer of property has not occurred may become relevant to a wholly different question of tax liability under an amendment to the tax law passed after the initial judgment was rendered. Another example of a case in which a determination may have unforeseeable consequences is one in which that determination is relevant to a claim involving property acquired after the first judgment has become final.

j. Lack of fair opportunity to litigate in the initial action. In an action in which an issue is litigated and determined, one party may conceal from the other information that would materially affect the outcome of the case. Such concealment may be of particular concern if there is a fiduciary relationship between the parties. Or one of the parties may have been laboring under a mental or physical disability that impeded effective litigation and that has since been removed. Or it may be evident from the jury's verdict that the verdict was the result of compromise. Or the amount in controversy in the first action may have been so small in relation to the amount in controversy in the second that preclusion would be plainly unfair.

In some of these instances, relief from the first judgment may be available, at least within specified time limits, see §§ 70-73; in others such relief is unavailable. But whether or not relief from the first judgment may be obtained, the court in the second proceeding may conclude that issue preclusion should not apply because the party sought to be bound did not have an adequate opportunity or incentive to obtain a full and fair adjudication in the first proceeding. Such a refusal to give the first judgment preclusive effect should not occur without a compelling showing of unfairness, nor should it be based simply on a conclusion that the first determination was patently erroneous. But confined within proper limits, discretion to deny preclusive effect to a determination under the circumstances stated is central to the fair administration of preclusion doctrine.

§ 29. Issue Preclusion In Subsequent Litigation With Others

A party precluded from relitigating an issue with an opposing party, in accordance with §§ 27 and 28, is also precluded from doing so with another person unless the fact that he lacked full and fair opportunity to litigate the issue in the first action or other circumstances justify affording him an opportunity to relitigate the issue. The circumstances to which considerations should be given include those enumerated in § 28 and also whether:

(1) Treating the issue as conclusively determined would be incompatible with an applicable scheme of administering the remedies in the actions involved;

(2) The forum in the second action affords the party against whom preclusion is asserted procedural opportunities in the presentation and determination of the issue that were not available in the first action and could likely result in the issue being differently determined;

(3) The person seeking to invoke favorable preclusion, or to avoid unfavorable preclusion, could have effected joinder in the first action between himself and his present adversary;

(4) The determination relied on as preclusive was itself inconsistent with another determination of the same issue;

(5) The prior determination may have been affected by relationships among the parties to the first action that are not present in the subsequent action, or apparently was based on a compromise verdict or finding;

(6) Treating the issue as conclusively determined may complicate determination of issues in the subsequent action or prejudice the interests of another party thereto;

(7) The issue is one of law and treating it as conclusively determined would inappropriately foreclose opportunity for obtaining reconsideration of the legal rule upon which it was based;

(8) Other compelling circumstances make it appropriate that the party be permitted to relitigate the issue.

Comment:

a. **Issues affected**. The rule of this Section applies only to preclude relitigation of issues that the party would have been precluded from relitigating with his original adversary. Accordingly, preclusion may be imposed only if, as stated in § 27, the issue was the same as that involved in the present action and was actually litigated and essential to a prior judgment that is valid and final.

b. **Rationale**. A party who has had a full and fair opportunity to litigate an issue has been accorded the elements of due process. In the absence of circumstances suggesting the appropriateness of allowing him to relitigate the issue, there is no good reason for refusing to treat the issue as settled so far as he is concerned other than that of making the burden of litigation risk and expense symmetrical between him and his adversaries. Equivalence of litigating risk, while a proper element in determining whether preclusion should be imposed, is only one of several considerations relevant in determining the fairness of estopping a party from retrying an issue he has already contested. The relevant considerations include all of those pertinent in determining whether issue preclusion should be applicable between the party sought to be bound and the adversary with whom he originally litigated the issue. If issue preclusion is inappropriate as between the original parties, it is likewise ordinarily inappropriate when invoked by a non-party. Accordingly, the qualifications stated in § 28 apply to issue preclusion when it is invoked by a non-party. Illustrations 3, 4, 5, 7, 9, 10, and 11 to that Section exemplify circumstances in which a party should not be precluded from relitigating an issue against one who was not a party to the prior action.

When a non-party invokes issue preclusion, however, greater weight may be given to the factors stated in § 28 and additional considerations may indicate the inappropriateness of imposing preclusion. These circumstances are enumerated in this Section. What combination of circumstances justifies withholding preclusion is a matter of sound descretion, guided by the general principle that a party should not be precluded unless his previous opportunity was at least the equivalent of that otherwise awaiting him in the present litigation.

c. **Incompatibility with remedial scheme**. Where a scheme of remedies limits the effect to be given the prior determination of an issue, the determination should not be given preclusive effect if doing so would be incompatible with that scheme. Thus, if a statute provides that a determination is limited to the action in which it is made, or that it is to be treated in subsequent actions as only prima facie evidence of the facts involved, the determination should not be given preclusive effect. Whether the scheme of remedies is properly construed as requiring such a limitation is beyond the scope of this Section. See §§ 83, 86.

d. **Fuller procedural opportunities in second action**. Preclusion may be withheld when the party against whom it is invoked can avail himself of procedures in the second action that were not available to him in the first action and that may have been significantly influential in determination of the issue. Differences in this regard include such procedures as discovery devices and plenary as distinct from summary hearing. It may also be relevant that the party against whom preclusion is invoked had no choice, or restricted choice, as to the forum in which the issue was litigated. The latter consideration is most often pertinent when preclusion is invoked in connection with establishing liability of the defendant in the second action ("offensive" use of preclusion), but is neither decisive in that situation nor irrelevant when preclusion is invoked to resist recovery by the plaintiff in the second action ("defensive" use of preclusion).

ILLUSTRATIONS:

1. A is the payee of a note executed by B and cosigned by C. In a summary proceeding involving B, A's claim on the note is defended on the ground of part payment and determined adversely to A. In A's subsequent action against C, the fact that A was compelled to litigate in the summary proceeding may be considered in determining whether A should be precluded on the issue of part payment.

2. A, the driver of a car involved in a collision with a car driven by C, brings an action for substantial personal injuries against C in the state where the collision occurred. Judgment is for A. In a subsequent

action by B, a passenger in A's car, against C, in the absence of other considerations the issues determined in the first action are conclusive against C notwithstanding that C was a defendant in the first action.

e. Failure to effectuate party joinder. A person in such a position that he might ordinarily have been expected to join as plaintiff in the first action, but who did not do so, may be refused the benefits of "offensive" issue preclusion where the circumstances suggest that he wished to avail himself of the benefits of a favorable outcome without incurring the risk of an unfavorable one. Such a refusal may be appropriate where the person could reasonably have been expected to intervene in the prior action, and ordinarily is appropriate where he withdrew from an action to which he had been a party. See also § 42, Comment d, on opting out by a member of a class. Due recognition should be given, however, to the normally available option of a plaintiff to prosecute his claim without the encumbrance of joining with others whose situation does not substantially coincide with his own. On the other hand, where a plaintiff brings a subsequent action involving the same issues against a person whom he could appropriately have joined as a co-defendant in the first action, only strongly compelling circumstances justify withholding preclusion. See also § 51.

ILLUSTRATIONS:

3. A stores goods in B's warehouse. The warehouse is destroyed as the result of C's alleged negligence. A brings an action against C for the loss of his property and recovers judgment. The fact that B could have joined in A's action may be considered in deciding whether, in a subsequent action by B against C, to give preclusive effect to determinations made in the first action.

4. A, injured while a passenger in a car owned by B and driven by C during the course of C's employment by D, brings an action against D for damages. D defends on the ground that C was not negligent; judgment is for D. In a subsequent action by A against B, the first action is preclusive against A on the issue of C's negligence.

f. Inconsistent prior determination. Giving a prior determination of an issue conclusive effect in subsequent litigation is justified not merely as avoiding further costs of litigation but also by underlying confidence that the result reached is substantially correct. Where a determination relied on as preclusive is itself inconsistent with some other adjudication of the same issue, that confidence is generally unwarranted. The inference, rather, is that the outcomes may have been based on equally reasonable resolutions of doubt as to the probative strength of the evidence or the appropriate application of a legal rule to the evidence. That such a doubtful determination has been given effect in the action in which it was reached does not require that it be given effect against the party in litigation against another adversary.

g. Ambivalence of prior determination. The circumstances attending the determination of an issue in the first action may indicate that it could reasonably have been resolved otherwise if those circumstances were absent. Resolution of the issue in question may have entailed reference to such matters as the intention, knowledge, or comparative responsibility of the parties in relation to each other. Particularly where the issues have been tried to a jury, the circumstances may suggest that the issue was resolved by compromise or with more or less conscious reference to such matters as insurance coverage or the litigants' relative financial position. In these and similar situations, taking the prior determination at face value for purposes of the second action would extend the effects of imperfections in the adjudicative process beyond the limits of the first adjudication, within which they are accepted only because of the practical necessity of achieving finality.

ILLUSTRATIONS:

5. A, a real estate developer, advertises vacation lots for sale. B, a real estate broker, and C, a retired schoolteacher, each contract to buy a lot but subsequently refuse to complete their contracts. In A's action for breach against C, C successfully defends on the ground that he reasonably relied on the advertising. The determination in the action between A and C that the statements were ones on which reliance might reasonably be placed is not preclusive in an action for breach by A against B.

6. A, a passenger asleep while traveling in C's car, is injured in a collision between C and a car driven by D. A recovers judgment against C on allegations that C was willfully negligent. B, a passenger who was awake and seated beside C, brings an action for his injuries to which C pleads contributory negligence and assumption of risk. C is not precluded as to the issue of his willful negligence.

7. In the crash of C's plane, A and B are killed. In a wrongful death action by A's representative, a judgment is awarded of $35,000 despite evidence establishing damages recoverable by A's representative substantially exceeding that amount. In a subsequent action for the wrongful death of B, C is not precluded as to the issue of his liability.

h. Complication or prejudice in second action. Treating a previously litigated issue as conclusively determined may in some circumstances complicate the trial of the subsequent action or prejudice the interests of a party thereto who has a legal relationship to the party sought to be precluded. Where this is the case, little is gained by way of economy in foreclosing retrial of the issue, because substantial recanvassing of the evidence will in any event be necessary. At the same time, since the primary consideration in administering the rule of preclusion is fairness rather than consistency, it is inappropriate to invoke preclusion where it will embarrass or hinder a party who has not yet had his day in court.

ILLUSTRATION:

8. A, while on premises owned by C, engages in an altercation with B, C's employee, as a result of which A is injured. B is thereafter tried and convicted of assaulting A, his plea of self-defense being rejected. In A's action for damages against B and C, the issue of B's liability may be litigated by both B and C if it appears that invoking preclusion against B may prejudice defense of the action by C.

i. Fresh determination of law. When the issue involved is one of law, stability of decision can be regulated by the rule of issue preclusion or by the more flexible rule of stare decisis. See § 28, Comment b. If the rule of issue preclusion is applied, the party against whom it is applied is foreclosed from advancing the contention that stare decisis should not bind the court in determining the issue. Correlatively, the court is foreclosed from an opportunity to reconsider the applicable rule, and thus to perform its function of developing the law. This consideration is especially pertinent when there is a difference in the forums in which the two actions are to be determined, as when the issue was determined in the first action by a trial court and in the second action will probably be taken to an appellate court; when the issue was determined in an appellate court whose jurisdiction is coordinate with or subordinate to that of an appellate court to which the second action can be taken; or when the issue is of general interest and has not been resolved by the highest appellate court that can resolve it. As indicated in § 28, Comment c, it is also pertinent that the party against whom the rule of preclusion is to be applied is a government agency responsible for continuing administration of a body of law applicable to many similarly situated persons. When any of these factors is present, the rule of preclusion should ordinarily be superseded by the less limiting principle of stare decisis.

j. Other circumstances. The circumstances specified in this Section are illustrative rather than definitive of those that may be considered in determining application of issue preclusion. Important among such other circumstances is the disclosure that the prior determination was plainly wrong or that new evidence has become available that could likely lead to a different result. It is unnecessary that the party seeking to avoid preclusion show, as he must in seeking to set aside a judgment, that the evidence could not have been discovered with due diligence; the question is not whether a prior determination should be set aside but whether it should be treated as conclusive for further purposes.

ILLUSTRATION:

9. C engages in conduct resulting in damage to the property of A and B that is stored in the same location. In A's action against C for damages, a key witness for C on the issue of C's negligence is unavailable. Judgment is for A. In B's subsequent action for his damage, C may be permitted to relitigate the issue of negligence upon a showing that the witness can be available at trial of the action.

CHAPTER 5. RELIEF FROM A JUDGMENT

TOPIC 1. RELIEF SOUGHT BY A PARTY

TITLE A. DEFAULT JUDGMENT

§ 65. Invalid Default Judgment: Lack Of Subject Matter Or Territorial Jurisdiction Or Adequate Notice

Except as stated in § 66, a judgment by default may be avoided if it was rendered without compliance with the requirements stated in § 1.

Section 1 provides:

A court has authority to render judgment in an action when the court has jurisdiction of the subject matter of the action, as stated in § 11, and

(1) The party against whom judgment is to be rendered has submitted to the jurisdiction of the court, or

(2) Adequate notice has been afforded the party, as stated in § 5, and the court has territorial jurisdiction of the action, as stated in §§ 4 to 9.

Comment:

a. Scope. As used in this Section, "jurisdiction of the subject matter" means authority to adjudicate the type of controversy involved in the action, see § 11, and "territorial jurisdiction" means the relationship of the state to the person, property, or status, referred to in §§ 4-9. "Adequate notice" means the notice defined in §§ 2-3. "Default judgment" means a judgment rendered without any appearance. See Introduction to Topic 1 of this Chapter.

The rule stated in this Section applies when it is the case both that the judgment was rendered by default and that the proceeding in which the judgment was rendered lacked one or more of the requisites of validity stated in § 1. The situations referred to are to be distinguished from those in which the judgment was rendered after an appearance or where, although there was no appearance, the conditions existed under which the court could properly exercise jurisdiction, see §§ 67-68.

b. Rationale. Relief sought on the ground of the invalidity of the judgment may be obtained without regard to time limits, except when a statute of limitations applies to the claim for relief from the judgment itself. See Comment c. The justification for permitting such a delayed challenge to judicial authority varies according to the ground of invalidity that is availed of by the applicant. When the person against whom judgment was rendered did not have adequate notice, then the judgment is unjust because there was a denial of a fair opportunity to defend the action. See § 2. When the person knew about the action but perceived that the court lacked territorial or subject matter jurisdiction, he is given a right to ignore the proceeding at his own risk but to suffer no detriment if his assessment proves correct. The right to challenge jurisdiction makes him an instrument for confining judicial authority to its prescribed limits. The fact that the challenge may be asserted after judgment gives it additional weight and effect. In any case, no public purpose is served by protecting the judgment. By hypothesis the proceeding was infected by fundamental error, usually attributable to the plaintiff's own acts or omissions. Since the judgment was by default no significant investment of judicial effort was made. Thus, the judgment is supported by none of the considerations supporting preclusion and properly may be treated as wholly abortive.

ILLUSTRATIONS:

1. P brings an action against B for $5,000 in a court whose subject matter jurisdiction is limited to controversies in which the amount in controversy does not exceed $1,000. B receives notice complying with § 5 but makes no appearance in the action. Judgment by default for $5,000 is rendered against B. By appropriate procedure B may avoid the judgment, except in the circumstances stated in § 66.

2. P brings an action against various persons including B for determination of their respective interests in a certain fund. A procedure of notice is used with regard to B that does not comply with the requirements of § 5. Judgment by default is rendered against B. By appropriate procedure B may avoid the judgment, except in the circumstances stated in § 66.

3. P is injured in an accident occurring in State X as a result of acts of B occurring wholly in State X. P brings an action against B in State Y, with which B has no contacts. Judgment by default is rendered against B. By appropriate procedure B may avoid the judgment, except in the circumstances stated in § 66.

c. Effect of delay. The right to avoid a judgment subject to the infirmities referred to in this Section is not lost by reason of delay on the part of the moving party. In traditional theory this was attributed to the proposition that a "void" judgment is necessarily void ab initio and hence can never have the effect of securing rights. It appears more accurate to say that lapse of time alone does not create reliance interests in a judgment, for when lapse of time is accompanied by change of circumstance there may be grounds for refusing to treat the judgment as a nullity. See § 66. Related to this is the fact that when the judgment is for money, it may not affect the parties' future conduct—and hence create interests of reliance on the judgment—until an attempt is made to execute on the judgment. Many of the cases asserting that delay does not affect the right to attack a void judgment involve attacks made in resistance to execution of money judgments. In contrast, when a judgment has prominent future effects, such as a judgment determining marital or filial status, reliance interests are very likely to arise.

d. Procedural error or invalid judgment. A critical distinction in the application of the rule of this Section is that between a procedural error and a defect going to the validity of the judgment. The practical importance of this distinction is greater in situations involving judgments after contested actions, because in a default judgment there is only a limited number of procedural events that could be called "jurisdictional," beyond the issues of adequate notice, territorial jurisdiction, and subject matter jurisdiction. Nevertheless, the cases show some inclination to characterize certain types of defects as "jurisdictional," thereby giving a defaulting party a broader opportunity to obtain relief from his default. One group of cases includes those in which a deviation from the prescribed procedure of notice giving is treated as the equivalent of inadequate notice. See § 2(1)(c). A second includes cases in which the complaint fails to state a cause of action and that failure is held to disable the court from entering a valid default judgment. The latter situation seems better analyzed as a mistake on the part of the court. See § 68, Comment c and Illustration 5 thereto.

§ 66. Denial Of Relief From Invalid Default Judgment

Relief from a default judgment on the ground that the judgment is invalid will be denied if:

(1) The party seeking relief, after having had actual notice of the judgment, manifested an intention to treat the judgment as valid; and

(2) Granting the relief would impair another person's substantial interest of reliance on the judgment.

Comment:

    a. Rationale. Although the parties to an action may not endow an invalid judgment with validity as such, it has long been recognized that under certain circumstances relief may be denied against a judgment that was rendered without the requisites of validity. The apparent anomaly of thus according a "void" judgment the dispositive effect of a valid judgment has had various explanations. In an earlier era, when law and equity were separately administered, it was possible to say that the judgment remained "void" but that relief would be denied as a matter of the independent jurisprudence of equity. However, this only replaced the anomaly of a "void" judgment's being valid with the peculiarity that one part of the remedial system granted relief that another part of the system would deny. In some decisions, when considerations of fairness suggested the propriety of denying relief from a "void" judgment, it was explained that estoppel precluded the party from seeking relief, even though other decisions held that invalidity of a judgment cannot be repaired by estoppel.

    On closer analysis of the circumstances under which relief has been denied, these anomalies can be coherently resolved. The essential point is that parties to a dispute may resolve it not only by adjudication but by contract or concord, express or implied by conduct giving rise to an estoppel. Such a concord may be reached not only by direct communication with that purpose in view, but also by manifestation of intention concerning the matter in dispute. A judgment purporting to determine the rights of the parties, though lacking effect of its own force because of invalidity, can thus be adopted as a consensual resolution of the parties' rights. The party who obtained the judgment expresses his assent to the terms by obtaining the judgment; the other party expresses adherence by some act following the judgment in which the judgment is recognized as determinative.

    b. Manifestation of intent. There are various forms by which acceptance of the terms of an invalid judgment may be manifested. Occasionally a situation is found in which an express intention is forthcoming. More commonly encountered is that form of conduct often referred to as "acceptance of benefits," wherein the defaulting party conducts his own affairs on the basis of rights accorded him by the terms of the judgment. In some instances, the party against whom the judgment was rendered may in subsequent events be placed in a position where he would be expected to deny the effect of the judgment but does not do so. His failure to protest the judgment in such a situation can be taken as an affirmation of the judgment because the circumstances invited an expression of a contrary position. However, in the absence of such circumstances, silence is not a manifestation of assent. It is not enough that the person against whom the judgment was rendered simply failed to take action to attack the judgment or to protest the fact that it had been rendered. In this connection, it may be noted that under Federal Rule 60(b), passage of time does not preclude a party from seeking relief from a judgment that is "void" as defined in Rule 60(b)(4), a definition that corresponds to that in § 65.

ILLUSTRATIONS:

    1. A brings an action against B for settlement of accounts and division of property jointly owned by them. Inadequate notice is given to B. Judgment by default is entered, of which B becomes aware. In a subsequent negotiation with C, B describes his interest in the property by reference to the terms of the judgment. This may be regarded as a sufficient manifestation by B of an intention to treat the division of property by the judgment as binding on him.

    2. Same judgment as in Illustration 1. After the judgment, B pays taxes on only that portion of the property that was apportioned to him under the judgment. Under applicable law B would be liable for taxes on the whole of the property if he were still its joint owner. This may be regarded as sufficient manifestation by B of an intention to treat the division of property by the judgment as binding on him.

    c. Interests of reliance. The interests of reliance protected by denying relief may include property interests, interests in status, or interest in repose from legal controversy. Whether an interest of reliance is sufficient to justify denying relief is determined not only by the extent of reliance but also by the relative equities between the parties, as appraised according to the tradition that the court exercises discretion in determining whether to grant relief.

ILLUSTRATION:

    3. W brings an action against H for divorce and determination of their property interests. H is not served with process. Judgment is entered awarding certain property to W. Thereafter H fails to pay taxes on the property in circumstances like those stated in Illustration 2 and the property is then sold by W to C. As against C, H should be denied relief from the judgment.

    d. Qualified relief. The court has discretion to require as a condition of relief that the moving party redress any unjust inconvenience suffered by the party obtaining judgment and to limit the scope of relief to the extent necessary to protect interests of reliance. See § 74.

§ 67. Valid Default Judgment: Excuse From Default

Subject to the limitations in § 74, a judgment by default may be avoided if:

(1) The failure to appear was the result of excusable neglect;

(2) The applicant for relief acted with due diligence in ascertaining that the judgment had been rendered and with reasonable promptness in seeking relief, and the application was made within the time limitation of an applicable statute or rule of court; and

(3) The application for relief shows there is a genuine issue upon which the judgment depends and which should be adjudicated.

Comment:

a. Rationale. Rules of procedure prescribe a fixed time within which a person notified of an action must appear and defend. Observance of these time limits is enforced by authorizing entry of judgment for the relief claimed if the notified person does not appear on time. Furthermore, the fact that no appearance is made within the prescribed period may be taken as an acknowledgement that the claim is just and the relief appropriate. However, if after the time for appearance has expired the notified person manifests an intention to contest the claim, the inference no longer may be drawn that he acknowledges the justness of this claim. The question posed by his belated appearance is whether to withhold the sanction of judgment for noncompliance with the rule governing the time for appearance.

The terms of answering this question are derived from an estimate of the needed strength of the sanction against tardy appearance compared with the injustice involved in denying an opportunity to litigate on the merits. If relief from default were freely given, the effectiveness of the deadline for appearance would be substantially nullified. On the other hand, if relief were given only when the applicant was entirely blameless, many litigants would be compelled to suffer judgment without a hearing. The problem thus is to strike a balance between these considerations so that the sanction remains reasonably effective but is not imposed too readily or too widely.

The formulation in this section is substantially recognized in all jurisdictions. However, there are significant differences among various jurisdictions in the liberality with which the formula is applied, and there have been like differences over time in a single jurisdiction. The predominant tendency is to insist that the conditions stated in this Section be met, except when the applicant is shown to have limited capacity to cope with the eventuality of being sued. Assuming that the conditions are met, however, relief is granted of course; the court has no discretion to deny relief for punitive or exemplary purposes. This policy is sometimes expressed as the "presumption" that cases should be tried on their merits if relief from the default is promptly sought.

b. Excusable neglect. The first requirement is that the initial failure to respond to notice of the action be plausibly explained. This requirement is commonly referred to as "excusable neglect," although that seems a misnomer because excusing the neglect depends not only on the circumstances of the initial failure to respond but also on the other conditions stated in this Section. At any rate, what must be shown is that the failure to respond was attributable to mishap and not indifference or deliberate disregard of the notice. In the case of ordinary individuals, the test is in essence one of good faith. In the case of persons or organizations that ought to expect to be sued from time to time, the question is whether their procedure for responding, particularly the procedure for putting the case in the hands of counsel, could be expected to function within the time allowed.

ILLUSTRATIONS:

1. A sues D, a subsidiary corporation of C, a corporation insured by I through the services of B, an insurance broker. Upon receiving the summons, D forwards it to C, which forwards it to B, which forwards it to I, which forwards it to counsel, who receives it twenty days after the time for responding has expired. The failure to respond on time may be held not to be excusable neglect.

2. Same facts as Illustration 1, except that the summons is lost in the mail in transit between D and C, a fact of which D does not become aware for 30 days. D's failure to respond on time is excusable.

c. Neglect of attorney or insurer. A subsidiary issue in determining excusable neglect is whether inexcusable neglect by the party's attorney or insurer is to be attributed to the party. The effect of attributing such neglect to the party himself is to impose judgment liability on him despite his effort to place responsibility for defending the suit in proper hands. The effect of not attributing the neglect to the party is to excuse the attorney of what amounts to professional negligence or to excuse the insurer of neglect in its duty to defend the insured. If the party obtaining the judgment was on notice of facts indicating the neglect by the attorney or insurer, that is a factor weighing in favor of relief. In the absence of such indication, however, the consequences of the neglect ordinarily should be charged to the defaulting party — who contracted with the attorney or insurer and who then may have an action for negligence against one of them — rather than the party who obtained the judgment.

d. Diligence and timeliness in seeking relief. The defaulting party must show that he exercised due diligence in discovering the judgment. Essentially this requires him to undertake reasonable inquiry in the light of information coming to his attention about the proceeding. Once having discovered that he is in default, the applicant for relief must act with reasonable promptness and within the time limits of an applicable statute or rule of court. The concept of reasonable promptness is necessarily flexible, but it would seem that the outer time limit after discovery of the default ordinarily ought not to exceed the interval regularly allowed in which to appear after receipt of notice.

Independent of the requirement of promptness, there may be a fixed period beyond which default for tardy appearance cannot be remedied. Under Federal Rule 60(b), for example, there is a one year limit that applies unless the default is attributable to extraordinary circumstances. The one year period runs from the date of the judgment, not the date on which the defaulting party discovers the judgment. As a result, if the party discovers the default near to or beyond the expiration of the one year period, he may be unable to obtain relief even if he acts with all possible speed from that point. The only escape from this constraint is to classify the application as based not on excusable neglect but upon a ground to which the one year limitation does not apply, such as that the judgment is "void" or that the circumstances are extraordinary. This manipulation is sometimes encountered in the decisions.

e. Genuine issue on the merits. The applicant must satisfy the court that granting him relief will serve a useful purpose. Hence, he must show that there is an issue, or several issues, whose resolution is required before judgment may justly be entered against him. This is sometimes expressed as a requirement that the applicant have a "meritorious defense." That term may imply that the applicant has the burden of proving such a defense in order to have the judgment set aside. The cases usually do not require such a strong showing. The test employed appears to be essentially the same as used in considering summary judgment, i.e., whether there is enough evidence to present an issue for submission to the trier of fact, or a showing that on the undisputed facts it is not clear that the judgment is warranted as a matter of law.

f. Interests of reliance. Granting relief from a default is a matter of equitable discretion, not absolute right. The court is required to consider the effect that setting aside the judgment may have on interests of reliance on the judgment. Given the requirement that the applicant have acted promptly, in the usual case it is unlikely that interests of reliance would have had time to arise. However, if they are present they are to be given place in determining whether and to what extent to award relief. Compare § 74.

§ 68. Fraud, Mistake, And Other Grounds Of Relief From Default Judgment

Subject to the limitations stated in § 74, a judgment by default may be avoided if the judgment:

(1) Resulted from the defaulting party's being induced by fraud or duress to submit to the jurisdiction of the court or to refrain from contesting the action;

(2) Was based on a claim that the party obtaining the judgment knew to be fraudulent;

(3) Resulted from the defaulting party's failure to contest the action by reason of justifiable mistake or from a substantial mistake by the court;

(4) Was against a minor, a person adjudicated as incompetent, or a person known by the party obtaining the judgment to be incapable of adequately defending the action, and no representative was appointed to act for the defaulting party; or

(5) Ought to be set aside on account of changed circumstances, as stated in § 73.

Comment:

a. Scope and Rationale. The grounds stated in §§ 70-73 include fraud or duress, mistake, incapacity, and changed circumstances. A judgment may be avoided on these grounds whether the judgment is by default or has been entered after a contest. Formally, therefore, a single rule is applied when these grounds of relief are involved. However, in the default cases the fraud, mistake, or other ground usually relates to some preliminary matter in the action, such as notice, appearance, or the obligation of the defendant to interpose a defense. Many of the cases involve defaults by persons not represented by counsel. In contrast, where fraud, mistake, etc., is asserted after a contested action, the case usually involves a contention concerning the merits, for example that the decision rested on perjured testimony or that evidence was newly discovered after the judgment. Most of these cases also involved litigants who were represented by counsel.

It can be observed that this pattern in the cases roughly corresponds to the distinction formerly drawn between "extrinsic" and "intrinsic" fraud. That is, the default judgment cases typically involve situations in which the aggrieved party was "prevented" from contesting the action (to use the classic term), while the contested action cases involve situations where the grievance concerns the contest itself. Furthermore, the default cases involving fraud, mistake, etc., almost invariably involve situations in which the applicant for relief has a substantial defense on the merits. The allegation of fraud or other special circumstance indeed may be asserted either to make the application more compelling or to avoid a time bar that applies in "excusable neglect" situations. Thus, some decisions state that the requirement of due diligence, see § 67(2), does not apply when the judgment in question was procured by fraud. Through a similar line of reasoning, it is sometimes concluded that a judgment procured by fraud, or some kinds of mistake, is "void," a conclusion that circumvents a time limit such as that in Federal Rule 60(b). Compare § 67, Comment d.

In this perspective, when the judgment from which relief is sought on the ground of fraud, mistake, etc., is a default judgment, the question presented is much the same as in the "excusable neglect" cases, i.e., is there good enough reason to allow the defaulting party an opportunity to contest the action notwithstanding his delay in seeking to do so? The reasons offered under the rubric of fraud or mistake often amount to especially strong excuse that explains unusually long neglect.

b. Fraud. Relief from a default judgment is granted when the failure to appear is attributable to a fraudulent act of the party procuring the judgment. The fraud may inhere in the process of establishing jurisdiction or giving notice or in inducing the defendant not to appear after he was given notice. Most of the cases of this kind could equally well be characterized as involving mistake, and often are so characterized when the plaintiff's scienter is not fully apparent.

ILLUSTRATIONS:

1. P brings suit against D, alleging in connection with the summons that P has no knowledge of D's present address and seeking permission to give notice by publication. In fact, P knows D's whereabouts. Notice is published but does not come to D's attention. A default judgment in favor of P may be set aside on D's application.

2. P brings suit against D. P and D agree that D may have an indefinite extension of time to make an appearance. Without further notice to D, P obtains a default judgment for D's failure to appear. The judgment may be set aside on D's application.

Relief may also be granted from a judgment based on knowingly false allegations if some explanation can be given for the defendant's failure to appear and contest the action, or for fraud in the proofs offered in substantiating the basis of complaint before the court. These situations present difficulty. They resemble judgments procured in contested actions on the basis of perjured testimony, for the defendant has not been prevented from making a defense and the matter offered to justify relief could as well have been offered as a defense to the action. Hence, the rule might be applied that relief will not be granted to remedy the effects of perjury. See § 70. Relief is usually granted, however, sometimes on the proposition that "fraud on the court" was involved. A better explanation seems to be that when the applicant for relief makes out a plain case of fraud on the merits, it weighs decisively in an assessment of comparative equities where the applicant was dilatory in responding to the suit. Indeed, the difference between the cases giving relief for fraud going to the merits and those denying relief in such circumstances may well be the particularity and substantiality with which the charge of fraud is supported in the application for relief.

ILLUSTRATION:

3. P brings an action against D on an account. D fails to appear. At a hearing to substantiate the claim, P testifies that no part of the amount due has been paid. Judgment is rendered for P. Within a short time thereafter, D applies for relief, attaching to his application copies of a receipt signed by P expressly acknowledging payment of a substantial part of the account. Relief may be granted to D.

c. Mistake. Relief may be granted for mistake in connection with the defendant's failure to appear, particularly when the plaintiff had some reason to suppose that the defendant did not acquiesce in the justness of the claim. These cases are essentially similar to those involving "excusable neglect" except that the neglect may be explained by some positive misunderstanding on the part of the defendant. Within the limits of § 74, substantial liberality is shown in granting relief on the basis of mistaken failure to defend an action. Those limits confine relief to situations where there has been no undue delay in seeking relief and no interest of reliance on the judgment, and there has been compliance with applicable time limits, such as those imposed by Federal Rule 60(b). Assuming those conditions are met, the value of protecting the integrity of a default judgment ordinarily is strongly outweighed by the value of allowing a person acting in good faith to have a day in court. This posture toward relief from a default judgment is quite different from that when the mistake concerns a contested judgment. See § 71.

ILLUSTRATION:

4. P brings an action against D for damage to goods allegedly damaged while in D's possession. D does not obtain counsel or make an appearance in the action but writes P directly, stating that he has no obligation for the damage because the goods did not come into his possession until after the damage occurred. P obtains a default judgment. D may obtain relief upon a showing that he thought his letter was a sufficient "answer" to the complaint.

If the mistake is induced by the plaintiff, the case for relief is stronger, and so also if the mistake is by the court itself.

ILLUSTRATION:

5. P brings an action in contract against D alleging facts showing damages of $10,000 but with a prayer for $20,000. D defaults. The court enters judgment for $20,000 despite the absence of any factual basis for that amount of damages. D seeks to set aside the judgment on a showing that he supposed the judgment would be limited to $10,000. Relief should be granted to reduce the judgment to $10,000.

d. Incapacity. Procedural statutes or rules of court generally provide that a default may not be entered against a minor or an incompetent unless he is represented by a general guardian or guardian ad litem. See Federal Rules of Civil Procedure 55(b). Furthermore, according to rule or practice in most jurisdictions, a consent judgment may not be entered with respect to a minor or incompetent without approval of the court. Hence, if a default judgment is entered against a minor or incompetent, it may be inferred that there was no representative or that the representative failed adequately to protect the defaulting party's interests. Compare §§ 35 and 42. As a result, a default judgment against a minor or an adjudicated incompetent can be set aside virtually as a matter of course. Once the minor has come of age or the incompetent restored to capacity, however, their right to set aside the judgment can be lost by failure to act promptly.

When the defaulting party is an adult who is in fact incapable of managing his affairs but has not been adjudicated an incompetent, it is relevant whether the party obtaining the judgment knew of the disability. If he did know, the situation can be assimilated to failure to give notice to someone who can act in behalf of the disabled person. See § 2(2). If he did not know, the defaulting party's disability can be assimilated to a unilateral mistake on his part. In either event, relief will be granted unless doing so will significantly prejudice interests of reliance on the judgment.

e. Changed circumstances. A judgment by default is subject to relief on the basis of change of circumstances no less than a judgment after contest. By hypothesis the occasion for relief on account of changed circumstances relates neither to the opportunity to defend nor the merits of the outcome but to some subsequent event external to the proceeding. Hence the same rule applies to default judgments and those rendered after contest. See § 73.

f. Interests of reliance. The intervention of interests of reliance may preclude relief that is otherwise warranted. The classic interest of reliance is that of a purchaser in good faith without notice, but reliance interests of other kinds also arise, particularly with respect to judgments determining status.

g. Delay after learning of grounds. Once the defaulting party has become aware of the facts indicating a basis for relief, he is required to act with reasonable promptness in seeking relief. See § 73.

TITLE B. RELIEF FROM A JUDGMENT IN A CONTESTED ACTION

§ 69. Lack Of Subject Matter Jurisdiction

A judgment rendered in a contested action may be avoided in the circumstances stated in § 12, except when relief should be denied in order to protect a justifiable interest of reliance on the judgment.

Comment:

a. Scope. This Section incorporates § 12, which deals with lack of subject matter jurisdiction as affecting the right to avoid a judgment. It does not refer to other grounds of invalidity of a judgment, i.e., lack of adequate notice and lack of territorial jurisdiction. See § 1. Lack of adequate notice or lack of territorial jurisdiction, as well as lack of subject matter jurisdiction, may be invoked as grounds for avoiding a default judgment. See § 65; § 12, Comment f. When the judgment has been rendered after contest, however, the questions of adequacy of notice and territorial jurisdiction must necessarily have been foreclosed from further consideration. If the party summoned to or otherwise notified of the proceeding omitted to raise objections on those grounds upon appearing in the action, the appearance constitutes a submission to the court and an abandonment of the objections. See Introductory Note to Chapter 2. If the party raised one or the other of those objections and it was sustained, the action would have been dismissed and there would be no judgment against him. If one or the other objection was raised but overruled, the court's decision precludes later assertion of either objection in subsequent litigation. See § 10. Thus, when the action leading to the judgment was a contested one, under all contingencies the questions of adequacy of notice and of territorial jurisdiction will have been resolved when the judgment was rendered. Accordingly, this Section applies only to relief from a judgment challenged as invalid for lack of subject matter jurisdiction.

In very limited circumstances a judgment in a contested action may be subsequently attacked for lack of subject matter jurisdiction. As stated in § 12, it must appear that:

(1) The subject matter of the action was so plainly beyond the court's jurisdiction that its entertaining the action was a manifest abuse of authority; or

(2) Allowing the judgment to stand would substantially infringe the authority of another tribunal or other agency of government; or

(3) The judgment was rendered by a court lacking capability to make an adequately informed determination of a question concerning its own jurisdiction and as a matter of procedural fairness the party seeking to avoid the judgment should have opportunity belatedly to attack the court's subject matter jurisdiction.

   b. **Procedural error or jurisdictional defect**. The distinction between procedural error and jurisdictional defect, see § 65, Comment d, is perhaps more significant in contested actions than in those where judgment is by default. In a contested action, a departure from the rules governing the court's procedures may be challenged contemporaneously with the commission of the error or, if the error is serious, by a motion for a new trial or through an appeal, or, in some instances such as fraud, a post-trial motion under a procedure such as Federal Rule 60(b). If such a remedy is not timely pursued, however, the error becomes irretrievable. These remedies may be used as well to challenge the lack of subject matter jurisdiction in a contested action. But it has often been said that a "jurisdictional" defect may also be remedied by a motion made at any time or, in some circumstances, by a separate action to set aside the judgment. See § 79.

   The practical difference between a "procedural error" and a "jurisdictional defect" can thus be very significant. The former is submerged in the judgment and ordinarily beyond remedy after the judgment has become final and the time to appeal expired; the latter in some situations can be a basis for future avoidance of the judgment.

   This difference in consequences generates heavy pressure to characterize a miscarriage as "jurisdictional" when the asserted defect is serious but has been tardily raised. The miscarriage may be remedied if it is called "jurisdictional" when it would be too late to do so if it is characterized as "procedural." In a similar fashion, to characterize an erroneous interlocutory order as "jurisdictional" can open the way for its being reviewed immediately by extraordinary writ instead of relegating its review to appeal from final judgment. In response to these pressures, there are decisions holding all kinds of serious procedural errors to be "jurisdictional."

   Many if not all of these decisions can be explained as mechanisms to give relief to an applicant who has sought relief tardily but in good faith. The modern decisions, moreover, generally display realism if not complete candor in their manipulation of the term "jurisdiction." Hence, many defects that are characterized as "jurisdictional" for purposes of interlocutory review by extraordinary writ, or relief from a default judgment in favor of a dilatory party, are not treated as "jurisdictional" for purposes of relief after judgment in a contested action. The better considered decisions recognize that a judgment in the latter category may be attacked only when the court's want of authority is of the clear and serious kind defined in § 12.

   c. **Denial of relief**. Assuming that the conditions stated in § 12 are met, relief from the judgment ought to be granted under almost all circumstances. The conditions stated in § 12 are defined in terms of conduct that usually is clearly manifested, i.e., plain excess of authority or substantial infringement of the authority of another tribunal or agency. Such violations of authority ordinarily import warning, or at least circumstances that reasonably require inquiry, as to the possibility that the judgment may lack validity. Such a warning in turn militates against there being justifiable interests of reliance on the judgment. Only the protection of such an interest of reliance, and not delay in seeking relief of itself, would justify refusing to set aside a judgment where the rendering tribunal's authority was so clearly lacking.

§ 70. Judgment Procured By Corruption, Duress, Or Fraud

   (1) Subject to the limitations stated in § 74, a judgment in a contested action may be avoided if the judgment:

   (a) Resulted from corruption of or duress upon the court or the attorney for the party against whom the judgment was rendered, or duress upon that party, or

   (b) Was based on a claim that the party obtaining the judgment knew to be fraudulent.

   (2) A party seeking relief under Subsection (1) must:

   (a) Have acted with due diligence in discovering the facts constituting the basis for relief;

   (b) Assert his claim for relief from the judgment with such particularity as to indicate it is well founded and prove the allegations by clear and convincing evidence; and

   (c) When his claim is based on falsity of the evidence on which the judgment was based, show that he had made a reasonable effort in the original action to ascertain the truth of the matter.

Comment:

   a. **Rationale**. Judgments are taken as finally determining claims because of confidence that the procedure leading to judgment is reasonably effective to ascertain the merits of the controversy. It is recognized that no system of procedure is infallible and that mistakes and miscarriages of justice may occur despite such protective devices as the right to be heard, the assistance of counsel, and the availability of appellate review. But it is assumed that modern systems of procedure generally yield results that are as just as may be expected, given the uncertainties of proof in contested cases and elements of individual judgment inherent in application of legal rules and principles to specific instances. Indeed, if this confidence did not exist, the concept of finality itself would be rationally insupportable.

It is for this reason that attacks are not permitted on a judgment simply on the ground that the losing party neglected to take best advantage of his day in court or that additional evidence or argument would produce a different outcome. See §§ 24, 27. Furthermore, inasmuch as losing parties have strong inducement to contrive attractive reasons why a controversy should be reopened, the rules concerning relief from a judgment are properly cast in narrow terms. On the other hand, it is equally inappropriate that all judgments be treated as absolutely inviolable. Particularly is this true when a judgment has been procured by the fraud of the successful party. To immunize such a judgment from attack is to compound the injustice of its result on the merits with the injustice of the means by which it was reached. Equally important, if judgments were wholly immune it would give powerful incentive to use of fraudulent tactics in obtaining a judgment. A litigant would know that if he could sustain duress or deception through the moment of finality, the benefit of the judgment would be his forever.

b. Bribery or duress. When a judgment is shown to have been procured by the prevailing party through corruption of the tribunal, or of the attorney for the party against whom the judgment was rendered, no worthwhile interest is served in protecting the judgment. The only serious question concerns the showing that must be made by the applicant for relief to substantiate his claim. To discourage ill-considered assertion of claims of corruption or duress, it is required that such a claim be alleged with particularity and that it be proven by clear and convincing evidence. See also Comment d.

c. Fraud: Extrinsic and intrinsic, and similar distinctions. Defining the circumstances under which the conclusiveness of a judgment can be overcome on account of fraud is especially difficult. The question presented by a charge of fraud is whether a judgment that is fair on its face should be examined in its underpinnings concerning the very matters it purports to resolve. Reexamination of those matters typically involves testimonial conflicts, often the same that were presented in the original action. Such conflicts are easy to propound and difficult to resolve with confidence. The definitional task is therefore to state criteria that cannot so easily be met as to create open opportunity for relitigation, but which are not so demanding that plain cases of fraud cannot be remedied.

From an early date some decisions permitted a judgment to be attacked on the ground that it was based on perjured or fabricated evidence. The only qualification was that the application for relief show clearly and persuasively that the evidence had indeed been perjured or fabricated. Since in the early days the procedure of seeking relief was a separate suit in equity, the complaint was permitted and required to go into detail concerning the evidence of the fraud and the reason it had not been discovered at the time of trial. Later decisions, however, attempted to draw distinctions in terms other than the positiveness with which the fraud could be shown, and these have led to much confusion.

The most widely recognized distinction was between "extrinsic" and "intrinsic" fraud. In its core meaning, "extrinsic" fraud meant fraud that induced a party to default or to consent to judgment against him. See § 68. "Intrinsic" fraud meant knowing use of perjured testimony or otherwise fabricated evidence. But this distinction was obliterated by decisions in which it was reasoned that offering fabricated evidence "prevented" the other party from contesting the proposition for which the fabricated evidence was offered as proof. Hence, in many jurisdictions the distinction between "extrinsic" and "intrinsic" fraud was accepted nominally but not in substance. Moreover, it was never satisfactorily explained why a litigant misled into defaulting should be more fully protected than one who suffered judgment by reason of deception committed in open court.

Three other distinctions arose, each as an exception to the proposition that "intrinsic" fraud is not a basis for relief. One is that if the fraud was practiced by a party having a fiduciary capacity, then relief was obtainable even though the fraud concerned the proofs at trial. In some of the decisions making this distinction, the fiduciary was representing a non-party beneficiary and the fiduciary's fraud consisted of connivance with the opposing party. This situation can be convincingly analogized to that of a fraudulently procured default judgment against the beneficiary, because both situations involved fraudulent deprivation of a day in court for the beneficiary. Compare §§ 67, 42. However, the exception concerning fiduciaries was extended to actions between the fiduciary and the beneficiary.

Another distinction involves the concept of "fraud on the court." It is not entirely clear what this concept entails. Some decisions indicate it means corruption of the judge or other court officials. Other decisions indicate it means fabrication of evidence by the attorney as distinct from fabrication by the party who preferred it, on the theory that the attorney is an officer of the court and that his corruption is equivalent to judicial corruption. This distinction, too, seems unsatisfactory, although it is suggestive of a more coherent analysis. The fact that the fabrication of evidence was procured by or with the aid of the party's attorney may result in it being easier clearly to prove the fabrication, because the potential sources of such proof include both the party and the attorney. Hence, the point would seem to be that the cases where the attorney is involved also involve strong proof of deliberate fabrication of evidence.

Still a third distinction, found in a few cases, is made when the judgment amounts to a fraud against the government or the public welfare. Such a judgment is said to be open to relief even though procured by "intrinsic" fraud. Assuming that a clear case of fraud is made out, however, it is difficult to see why it should make a difference that the victim is a private person.

Aside from not being very persuasive, these various distinctions are not consistently applied. Specifically, when the evidence of fraud is weak, or when it appears that the victim should have anticipated the possibility of fabrication or concealment, the decisions often invoke the proposition that relief may not be granted on the basis of "intrinsic" fraud. It is also clear that there is discord in the underlying judicial attitudes toward relief on the basis of fraud, some courts being more responsive than others. Allowing for all these factors, if the cases are read with close attention to their facts, the critical considerations usually are whether the claim of fraud is well substantiated and not merely asserted at large and whether in the original action the victim had pursued reasonable precautions against deception.

d. Elements required for relief from fraud. Four elements must be established to obtain relief. First, it must be shown that the fabrication or concealment was a material basis for the judgment and was not merely cumulative or relevant only to a peripheral issue. Second, the party seeking relief must show that he adequately pursued means for discovering the truth available to him in the original action. Under modern procedure in trial courts of general jurisdiction in cases involving substantial stakes, abundant devices exist for discovering an opposing party's proof and subjecting it to investigation prior to trial and adequate incentive usually exists to use such devices. Hence, in such circumstances, only a well concealed or unforeseeable fraud is likely to survive a reasonably diligent effort to ascertain the truth. On the other hand, in cases involving limited stakes, it may be unreasonably costly to pursue intensive discovery or investigation when there is no indication that the other side may offer fabricated evidence. Furthermore, in some situations a litigant is entitled to be passive and unquestioning with respect to the proofs of another party. Thus, the cases allowing relief from fraud practiced by a trustee often advert to the fact that a beneficiary should not have to anticipate a trustee's deliberate falsification of the accounts he presents to the court.

Third, the applicant must show due diligence after judgment, in that he discovered the fraud as soon as might reasonably have been expected. This is an application of the general principle of due diligence, see § 74.

Finally, the party seeking relief must demonstrate, before being allowed to present his case, that he has a substantial case to present, and must offer clear and convincing proof to establish that the evidence underlying the judgment was indeed fabricated or concealed. This heavy burden of proof is an important measure of protection against attacks on honestly procured judgments. It also transforms the issue from a retrial of a question previously litigated to a search for something approaching incontestable proof as to truth of the underlying matter in issue.

ILLUSTRATIONS:

1. P brings an action against D for dissolution of a partnership of which they are members. P fails to take D's deposition or otherwise to obtain evidence from him prior to trial concerning the extent of D's dealings with partnership property, a fact that is relevant in determining the division of the partnership assets. After a judgment is rendered dissolving the partnership and dividing its assets, P discovers that D made withdrawals from the partnership to an extent far greater than that to which he testified at trial. P's failure to use discovery on the issue could be found to be a lack of due diligence, depending on the circumstances, and hence a ground for denying P relief from the judgment.

2. P obtains a judgment against D for professional services rendered, P testifying that he was a duly licensed professional. The names of licensees in P's profession is a matter of public record. A year later, D seeks to set aside the judgment on the ground that P was not licensed and therefore that under applicable law P could not properly have maintained the action for his fees. D's delay in discovering the facts is a ground for denying D relief.

3. P brings an action against D for injuries sustained in a collision with a car allegedly driven by D. At deposition and trial D denies having been the driver at the time of the accident, and judgment is for D. Later C, who knows D but was not present at the accident, tells P that D admits having been the driver. P seeks relief from the judgment, stating in his application that D knowingly testified falsely that he was not driving at the time of the accident. In the absence of greater substantiation, such as an affidavit from C concerning D's admission, the application is insufficient for relief from the judgment.

4. T performs work for C, a corporation, and then dies. A, T's administrator, brings suit against C for the reasonable value of T's services. C's officers testify on deposition and at trial that there was no agreement to pay for T's services. In response to A's pretrial demand for production of documents, C states that there are no relevant documents in its files. Judgment is for C. Shortly after trial A obtains a

copy of a document containing C's commitment to pay T for his services. An application for relief from the judgment stating the foregoing facts and attaching a copy of the document is sufficient to entitle A to a hearing for relief.

§ 71. Judgment Based On Mistake

Subject to the limitations stated in § 74, a judgment rendered in a contested action may be avoided if the judgment resulted from a mistake of law or fact and:

(1) During the course of the action the party seeking relief had made a reasonable effort to ascertain the matter with respect to which the mistake was made, and

(2) The mistake:

(a) Consisted of a failure to express the judgment of the court; or

(b) Was such that allowing its correction by relief from the judgment will obviate an appeal in which the mistake is certain to result in reversal, or will similarly expedite ultimate decision in the action; or

(c) Involved the denial of a fair hearing because of the plainly insufficient representation of a party or denial by the court of the opportunity to present a claim or a defense.

Comment:

a. Scope and rationale. This Section applies to judgments rendered in contested actions as distinct from default judgments. The fact that the judgment is contested materially affects the nature of mistakes that might be complained of and the considerations involved in determining whether relief is warranted. When a default judgment is in question, the mistakes complained of usually relate to the defendant's failure to appear or the failure of his attorney to organize a defense or response. Compare §§ 67 and 68. Furthermore, relief from default rarely involves questions going to the merits or a reconsideration of issues deliberately ruled upon by the court. In contrast, when the judgment has been entered after contest, the claim of mistake usually concerns an issue of the merits actually litigated by the parties and resolved by the court. An application for relief after a contested proceeding therefore partakes of a petition for reconsideration, and all the reasons for finality of judgment are arrayed against such an application.

Moreover, such an application is by definition an unusually delayed petition for reconsideration. Procedural rules provide means of seeking reconsideration that may be invoked immediately after judgment, such as a motion for new trial or for revision of the judgment. See Federal Rules of Civil Procedure Rule 59. Relief on the basis of mistake under Rule 60(b) and similar procedures becomes an appropriate device only when the time has expired for such an ordinary post-trial motion. Yet application for 60(b) relief on the basis of mistake comes too late unless the applicant can show that he had used reasonable effort to ascertain the matter during the course of the proceedings and that he acted with due diligence in discovering the mistake. See Subsection (1) of this Section. Thus, a quest for relief on the ground of mistake is narrowly confined by the policy of finality not only in scope but also in time.

The problem of relief from a contested judgment on the ground of mistake may be contrasted with that of relief on the ground of fraud. When fabrication or concealment of evidence is involved, the parties have disparate moral positions with regard to the judgment, one being guilty of wrongdoing and the other its victim. When mistake is involved there is no such disparity; both parties were exposed alike to the inadequacies of information and mishaps in procedure that attend litigation. Moreover, the matter in question was, in most cases, open to discovery by means of investigation that would occur to an attentive mind. The applicant for relief on the ground of mistake therefore often has to overcome an element of fault, at least the fault of not having used a sufficiently high standard of care in preparing the case. When the party seeking relief had appeared pro se, for example in a small claims court, the burden of justification for relief may be less than when the party was represented by competent counsel. Compare Comment g.

Given these considerations against disturbing the judgment in an action that has been fairly contested, the circumstances are very limited in which such a judgment may be set aside on the ground of mistake.

b. Mistakes and errors of judgment at trial. Many miscarriages in a contested action represent tactical mistakes or choices in the face of uncertainty that turn out unfortunately. Although these are "mistakes" in some sense, they are not mistakes upon which relief from a judgment may be granted. It is recognized that all kinds of such decisions must be made in litigation and that their outcome is a measure of the attorney's professional skill but not of the propriety of setting aside a judgment. In extreme cases, where counsel is so derelict as in effect to present no case for his client, the situation can be analogized to a default, for it results in the party's not having a day in court. See Comment g. Short of this, however, the party's remedy is through redress against his attorney and not against the opposing party.

c. Materiality of matter. Relief may be granted only if the judgment depended on the matter with respect to which the mistake was made. A mistake concerning cumulative evidence or sources of law, or a peripheral issue, will not justify setting aside a judgment.

d. Due diligence (Subsection (1)). The requirements concerning due diligence with regard to relief based on mistake are essentially similar to those applicable to relief on the ground of fraud. See § 70, Comment c. The requirement that reasonable effort to ascertain the matter in question have been used during the course of the action is, in modern procedure, an insuperable barrier to relief except in very unusual cases. Modern discovery procedure affords virtually unlimited means of ascertaining facts that are not deliberately concealed. Failure to have ascertained matter that could have been uncovered by discovery procedure should preclude relief except when the failure is itself excusable. If the action is in a tribunal whose procedure does not provide for discovery, then the question is whether the opportunity for unofficial pretrial discovery and for discovery at trial had been exploited with reasonable vigor.

e. Mistake in expressing decision. Relief should be granted if the judgment incorrectly formalizes the decision that was reached in deliberation. This kind of mistake is often referred to as "clerical" mistake as distinct from "judicial error," but it is not limited to mistakes of transcription or other clerical functions. Rather, the question is whether the deliberative process led to a decision but the decision is not correctly expressed in the award embodied in the judgment. These mistakes arise most often when the decision involves several components that have to be integrated, such as distinct claims for damages, or damages and interest, or claim and counterclaim. Their correction does not undercut the decisional process but seeks to give its outcome accurate expression. This category of mistake does not include errors by the court in reaching decision, for example in misinterpreting the legal rule that should be applied in determining liability or damages. That sort of error should be corrected by ordinary post-trial motion or by appeal.

ILLUSTRATION:

1. P is injured by the concurrent acts of B and C. P obtains $5,000 in settlement with B and brings an action against C for $50,000 as the whole value of his injuries. The fact of the $5,000 settlement is of record in the action but is withheld from the jury. The jury returns a verdict for $15,000 and judgment for P is entered in that amount. Under applicable law P's recovery against C should be diminished by any amount received from a concurrent tortfeasor. On timely application by C, the judgment may be set aside and judgment for $10,000 entered instead.

f. Obviating an appeal. As often remarked, relief on the basis of mistake is not a substitute for an appeal. Affording such relief instead of relegating the aggrieved party to an appeal has the effect of extending the time when a judgment's finality is uncertain, for the time within which such a relief may be sought is longer than the time permitted to take an appeal. Providing such relief would also confuse the role of the trial court with that of an appellate court. Nevertheless, in a narrowly defined situation relief by motion on the basis of mistake is an appropriate substitute for an appeal. This is the situation where supervening change in the law applicable to the case occurs after the time has expired for an ordinary post-trial motion but before the time to appeal has expired. Since the time for ordinary post-trial motions has expired, the trial court cannot give relief by that means; since the time to appeal has not expired, the aggrieved party is in a position to overturn the judgment, given the change in the law that has occurred. But it is less burdensome for the trial court to set aside its own judgment than for it to await the appellate court's direction to do so.

There might be other situations in which such practical considerations would dictate the propriety of circumventing the normal post-judgment procedural channels.

g. Failure to accord fair hearing. Although errors and mistakes of a party or his counsel ordinarily are not a basis for relief from a judgment, there can be a point at which the effect is that the party's case was not presented at all. If the party attempted to represent himself when it was evident that he should have had counsel, the circumstances may indicate he lacks capacity to represent himself. Compare § 72. If the party sought but was denied assistance of counsel in circumstances where such assistance was plainly necessary, the denial of counsel could be appealable error. However, when a party who is not manifestly incapacitated undertakes to represent himself, he may properly be burdened with the consequence even if it is apparently unjust. Otherwise, the effect would be to shift to the opposing party an additional burden of uncertainty as to whether the judgment was final.

More serious questions arise when representation of the losing party was plainly insufficient or where it is manifest that the court deprived the party of fair opportunity to present his claim or defense. Insufficiency of representation justifying relief from a civil judgment must be clearer in its manifestation and effect than the "inadequacy" of representation that might justify relief from a criminal judgment. For civil cases generally differ significantly in their consequences and in the duty of the judge to assure a fair trial. Ordinarily, the remedies of new trial are sufficient to remedy such complete failures of justice, but there can be circumstances where such a remedy would have been unavailing.

§ 72. Judgment Against Incapacitated Party

Subject to the limitations stated in § 74, a judgment rendered in a contested action may be avoided if:

(1) The party was a minor, a person adjudicated as incompetent, or a person known by the party obtaining the judgment to be incapable of adequately maintaining or defending the action; and

(2) The person was:

(a) Represented by an appointed representative but the representative failed to prosecute or defend the action with due diligence and reasonable prudence, and the opposing party was on notice of facts making that failure apparent; or

(b) Not represented by an appointed representative and the representation on behalf of the person was inadequate.

Comment:

a. **Scope and rationale**. This Section applies to judgments in contested actions against minors, who are deemed incapable of conducting litigation; persons found to be incapable of handling their own affairs; and persons known by the opposing party to suffer that disability. Although such a party's disability indicates that his interests will be inadequately represented, the circumstances may suggest that they have been protected. The fact that the action was contested itself may be indicative, for if the person participated in the action it implies that his incapacity was not total. Furthermore, except when the incapacitated person has attempted to appear in propria persona, a contest indicates the assistance of counsel, which as a practical matter is usually more significant as protection of the incapacitated person's interests than his having had a guardian.

The essential question is whether the incapacitated person's interests were represented with reasonable adequacy. There is some authority that the lack of a guardian, whether previously appointed or appointed ad litem, results in representation that is inadequate by definition. This is now a minority view and its application in any event has been chiefly in cases involving default judgments. See § 35, Comment e, and § 68, Comment d. As applied to contested actions that approach is an excess of formalism. A contested action involves a presentation to the court of the factual and legal basis of the incapacitated person's claim. Yet that is essentially what is involved in the procedure for appointment of a guardian ad litem, or in obtaining judicial approval of the settlement of an incapacitated person's claim. Hence, the contest can be considered as simultaneously a demonstration for the court that the incapacitated person has a claim to be protected, and submission of the claim for determination.

b. **Proof of inadequate representation**. Whether the incapacitated person was adequately represented is often seriously debatable. In resolving the question, consideration should be given to the inherent strength of the claim or defense, the apparent skill and diligence with which it was presented, and surrounding circumstances such as the genuineness of the adversarial relation and the possibility of collusion. When the incapacitated person had an appointed representative, the appointment and the attendant court supervision of the representative's conduct constitute substantial assurance, amounting to a presumption, that the representation will be adequate. The opposing party can rely on that presumption and can be deprived of the benefit of the judgment only on the exacting showing prescribed in Subsection (2)(a). See § 42(e). Where no representative has been appointed, the question is considered without reference to such a presumption. In the case of an adult who has not been adjudicated an incompetent, however, the party seeking relief from the judgment must first show that the party obtaining the judgment knew his opponent was suffering from the disability.

ILLUSTRATION:

1. H brings suit for divorce against W on the ground of infliction of mental suffering. W is at the time under psychiatric care and periodically behaves in bizarre ways. W retains counsel, counterclaims for divorce in her favor, and gives her testimony at a contested hearing. Presentation of the case in W's behalf appears to have been adequate. Judgment of divorce is awarded H. W later seeks relief from the judgment on the ground that she was in fact incapable of protecting her interests. Relief should be denied.

See also Illustration 1 to § 35.

c. **Limitation on relief**. The requirement that an applicant for relief act promptly has special significance in the case of a person under an incapacity. So long as the incapacity continues to exist and he has no legal representative, time does not run on the opportunity to seek relief from the judgment. Once the disability has ceased, however, relief must be sought promptly. By the same token, it may be unjust to recognize interests of reliance that accrue during the continuation of the disability independent of conduct of the disabled person. On the other hand, when the disability has ceased, an express or implied ratification of the judgment, such as accepting its benefits, is itself a justifiable basis for reliance on the judgment.

TITLE C. RELIEF BASED ON EVENTS SUBSEQUENT TO JUDGMENT

§ 73. Changed Conditions

Subject to the limitations stated in § 74, a judgment may be set aside or modified if:

(1) The judgment was subject to modification by its own terms or by applicable law, and events have occurred subsequent to the judgment that warrant modification of the contemplated kind; or

(2) There has been such a substantial change in the circumstances that giving continued effect to the judgment is unjust.

Comment:

a. Judgment expressly modifiable. By its own terms or by provisions of law governing certain kinds of judgments, a judgment may be expressly subject to future modification in the light of post-judgment change of conditions whose possibility is anticipated. Judgments awarding custody and support of children in connection with divorce or separation are a prime example but there are other kinds as well, such as decrees involving management of public schools and other institutions. The power to modify may be expressly reserved in the judgment or it may flow from a statute making particular classes of judgments, such as support awards, subject to modification. It is also true in general that an injunction regulating a future course of continuing conduct is inherently subject to modification if future conditions change. In some instances, a judgment may avowedly be experimental, to be modified if implementation of its original terms proves impractical.

A judgment governing future events ordinarily is subject to modification even though it is a consent judgment. However, such a judgment may be deemed to embody a contract between the parties and its modification accordingly permitted only in accordance with the more confining rules under which a contract may be modified; provisions for spousal support and division of property in divorce decrees are often of this character. Furthermore, when the conduct enjoined was not only a private wrong but a public offense, for example an antitrust violation, modification may require particularly strong showing that the original terms of the injunction are no longer appropriate.

A judgment that is expressly modifiable is not subject to modification simply upon the lapse of time, nor may the original adjudication be retracted in the guise of modification. The purpose and proper scope of modification is to change the obligation created by the judgment in response to post-judgment events that substantially alter the intended balance of benefit and burden resulting from the judgment.

ILLUSTRATION:

1. A divorce judgment between H and W provides that W is to pay support for their two children and to have their custody for the summer months of each year, upon a finding that both W and H are suitable to have custody of the children. H later seeks as increase in support to reflect changes in the cost of living and a reduction in the period of W's custody to one month a year. If the general cost of living has increased, increase in the support award may be justified. In the absence of evidence that W's suitability as a parent has deteriorated or that there has been change in the needs of the children, a modification of the provision for custody is not justified.

b. Judgments governing future events. Judgments that govern continuing or recurring courses of conduct may be subject to modification even though the power of doing so is not expressly provided. Whether a judgment whose modification was not expressly anticipated ought to be open to modification depends on the nature of the controversy resolved by the judgment and the remedy awarded. If the controversy concerned a transaction that was complete when the judgment was rendered and the remedy was that of damages, the judgment is designed to close the matter. So also if the controversy concerned ownership claims to specific property and the judgment determined the parties' interests in the property, a modification would amount to an improper redetermination of those interests. On the other hand, an injunction against particular use of property, for example the control of a nuisance, is within the tradition that an injunction remains open for modification as long as it remains in effect. And in very unusual circumstances a judgment for damages may be subject to relief by reason of subsequent events. See Comment c. It is therefore impossible to say categorically that a judgment for damages is never subject to relief on account of changed conditions, or that a judgment regulating a course of future conduct may always be modified if circumstances prove to be different from those anticipated when the judgment was entered. See Illustration 3.

Nevertheless, the principal factor in whether a judgment is subject to modification is whether it contemplates an interaction between the activity of the judgment obligor and some other conditions over which the judgment does not exercise control. When an unforeseen or uncontrollable interaction occurs between the judgment obligor and the surrounding circumstances, the balance between burden and benefit can be disturbed. If the disturbance assumes substantial proportion, redress by modification may be appropriate.

ILLUSTRATIONS:

2. In a suit by adjoining residential landowners, D is enjoined from operating a chemical plant on his property. Fifteen years later the residential area has become predominantly commercial in use and the processes employed by D have been changed so as materially to reduce emissions. Either or both changes of circumstance may justify modifications of the judgment.

3. P brings an action against D for specific performance of a contract for sale of land, the contract stating that it is in contemplation of D's building a chemical plant on the property. Simultaneously, adjoining landowners sue both P and D to enjoin construction of the plant on the ground that the plant would be a nuisance. Judgment is entered for the landowners in their action and specific performance is denied to P in his action. Five years later the area becomes predominantly commercial and the chemical processes usable by D have been improved so as materially to reduce emissions. Neither change justifies modification of the judgment denying specific performance.

c. Reversal of judgment on which judgment was based. If a judgment is based upon a prior judgment, and the prior judgment is reversed or vacated, the reversal or vacating may be a change of circumstance justifying relief from the second judgment.

ILLUSTRATION:

4. P brings an action against D for damages on a claim with respect to which D has a right of indemnity against T. D separately sues T to enforce the claim for indemnity. Judgment is given for P against D in the first action and for D against T in the second action. The judgment for P against D is later reversed on appeal. T may have the judgment against him set aside.

In some jurisdictions, the foregoing proposition is embodied in statute or rule of court. See Federal Rule 60(b)(5). The rule has been construed as also applying to a situation where a subsequent judicial decision changes the law that was applied in reaching an earlier judgment, but this seems a misinterpretation of the rule and a very unsound policy. If it were adopted it is not clear why all judgments rendered on the basis of a particular interpretation of law should not be reopened when the interpretation is substantially changed. On the other hand, when a change of law occurs following a judgment regulating future conduct, that may be a circumstance justifying relief from the judgment.

ILLUSTRATION:

5. A is the adopted child of P, who is the child of T. T dies leaving a testamentary trust the income from which is to be paid to T's "heirs," the principal to be distributed to T's "heirs" on P's death. In an action to determine income interests in the trust, judgment is rendered against A under a decisional rule that adopted children are not "heirs" of the parents of their adopted parents. The rule is subsequently overruled. A may be granted relief from the judgment with regard to future payments of income and distribution of the principal. The same result would be proper if the decisional rule concerning "heirs" had been overruled by statute.

See also § 26(d) and (f), Illustration 6 to § 26, and § 29, Comment e.

d. Delay in seeking relief. The requirement of promptness in § 74 can have special application to relief on the basis of changed circumstances, particularly where other parties may develop interests of reliance upon the basis of the changed circumstances.

TITLE D. EQUITABLE CONSIDERATIONS IN DETERMINING RELIEF

§ 74. Denial Or Limitation Of Relief

Except with regard to judgments referred to in §§ 65-66 and 69, relief from a judgment will be denied if:

(1) The person seeking relief failed to exercise reasonable diligence in discovering the ground for relief, or after such discovery was unreasonably dilatory in seeking relief; or

(2) The application for relief is barred by lapse of time; or

(3) Granting the relief will inequitably disturb an interest of reliance on the judgment. When such an interest can be adequately protected by giving the applicant limited or conditional relief, the relief will be shaped accordingly.

Comment:

a. Scope. The rule of this Section is limited to relief from judgments other than those that are invalid as defined in §§ 65 and 69. Compare § 66. It presupposes that an appropriate mode of relief has been sought in an appropriate forum by a person with standing to obtain relief who has shown, in his application or submission, that there is ground for relief. The question addressed is whether there are circumstances that nevertheless warrant denial of relief.

This Section applies whether the judgment from which relief is sought is "void" or "merely voidable." It is often said that a judgment that is "void" may be expunged at any time, so that the factors of due diligence and intervention of reliance interests are irrelevant. An examination of the cases in which this formula is repeated, however, indicates that practically all of them involve either invalid default judgments, governed by the rule stated in § 66, or situations in which the factors stated in this Section would have resulted in granting of relief in any event. On the other hand, when a substantial reliance interest is involved or when the delay in seeking relief is unreasonably long, courts often deny relief by characterizing the judgment under attack as being "merely voidable."

In modern context, the distinction between "void" and "voidable" judgments, particularly in connection with relief based on fraud in procurement of the judgment, is unlikely to arise except in a suit on a sister state judgment, and hence governed by the rules of §§ 81 and 82. When it does arise, in modern procedure the equitable principles stated in this Section should apply regardless of the form of proceeding in which the question might present itself.

b. Relation to § 67. The matters referred to in this Section are usually treated as ones of affirmative defense against an application for relief. As such, they must be pleaded and proved by the party resisting the application for relief. In contrast, the requirements stated in § 67, concerning relief from a valid default judgment, are elements of the claim for relief and as such usually must be alleged and proved by the applicant.

c. Rationale. The relevant factors in denying relief to which an applicant is prima facie entitled include undue delay, possible prejudice to the winner of the judgment, and protection of interests of innocent third persons. Undue delay and prejudice to the judgment winner merge into each other. While delay in assertion of a claim does not as such produce adverse consequences, it can induce a sense of repose that itself may become a protectible interest. Correlatively, the likelihood and extent of reliance on a judgment, or of change in conditions, increases as time passes after the judgment's rendition. Protection of third party interests involves chiefly the question whether the third party reliance was innocent and justified, the classic instance being the bona fide purchaser for value.

In the articulation of rules for dealing with this problem, no success has been achieved in attempts to state definitively the equities sufficient to overcome a prima facie case for equitable relief. For example, the proposition that certain defects in a judgment render it "void" implies that in no set of circumstances would relief from such a judgment be denied. But there is solid authority for the proposition that relief should be denied from a judgment that is "void" if the equities are compelling enough. Similarly, many decisions say that delay alone, without a showing of prejudice to others, is never a ground for denying relief, while others dealing with similar situations "presume" prejudicial effects if the delay is long and no explanation for it has been offered. The more reflective decisions recognize that the considerations stated in this Section have to be considered in aggregate.

d. Discovering ground for relief. The requirement that the person seeking relief have exercised reasonable diligence applies to his conduct both before and after the judgment. He is required to have investigated possible sources of evidence before bringing the action, to have availed himself of available discovery devices in pretrial procedure, and at trial to have marshalled his own proofs and challenged those of the opposing party. Following the judgment he is required to have promptly and vigorously pursued available information concerning the ground upon which relief is sought. When the ground is change of circumstances, he is required to have ascertained the change promptly after it occurred.

e. Acting promptly. In addition to acting diligently to discover the grounds of relief, the applicant must act promptly in seeking relief. This requirement is cumulative with the requirement that application be made within the time permitted by applicable statute of rule of court, such as the one year limit applicable to Federal Rule 60(b)(1)-(3). Thus, an application made within such a fixed time limit should nevertheless be denied if it was not made promptly after discovery of the circumstances on which it is based.

f. Protection of interests of reliance. In its very nature a judgment creates reliance on the fact that the dispute involved has been legally terminated. This interest is protected by the requirement that the applicant act diligently and by the definition of the grounds of relief themselves, i.e., that the matter be material to the judgment and of substantial dimension as distinct from the usual mishaps of litigation. But beyond resolving legal dispute over events of the past, a judgment also creates relationships for the future. A judgment for money usually in effect affirms the relationship of creditor and debtor, which leaves the parties free to act subject to financial accounting. A judgment determining interests in property or status or establishing rights and obligations concerning future conduct, however, is usually a base of reference for specific future plans and acts by the parties. In proportion as the plans and acts in reliance on the judgment are substantial in moment and prolonged in duration, they become considerations that ought to give stability to the judgment. Hence it is that relief should be denied, or granted only in part, when the effect of granting relief would be unjustly to disturb that stability.

g. Discretion of the court. It is said that the granting of relief is in the "discretion" of the court. This does not mean it is a matter of idiosyncratic choice whether relief is to be granted, for what is required is the exercise of "sound discretion." What is meant is that the decision involves taking account of several incommensurable factors, some relating to the particular case and others to the larger system of administered justice. The factors relating to the particular case include the magnitude and consequences of the judgment, the relative clarity with which it appears that the judgment was unjust, the relative fault of the parties (fraud being different from mistake or change of circumstances), the requirements of diligence referred to in Subsection (1) of this Section, and the equities in the interests of reliance. Factors relating to the system of justice are the degree of diligence and competence expected of counsel (since many of the cases involve lapses on their part), the extent to which the court should rely on the adversary presentations in contrast with seeking a just result on its own initiative, the balance to be struck between finality and correctness of judgments, and the distribution of responsibility for deciding upon relief between the trial court and the appellate court. Given this variety of relevant factors, the criteria for granting relief cannot be stated in categorical terms. What can be said is that in modern context, given the abundant means of acquiring information through self-help, the power of usually available discovery techniques, and the rapidity with which events evolve in the out-of-court world, proper exercise of discretion entails granting relief only in a very strong case.

ALI/UNIDROIT
Rules of Transnational Civil Procedure
Cambridge University Press (2006)

INTERPRETATION AND SCOPE

2. Disputes to Which These Rules Apply

2.1.   Subject to domestic constitutional provisions, and statutory provisions not superseded by these Rules, these Rules apply to disputes arising from transnational commercial transactions, if the dispute:

2.1.1. Is between parties from different states, determined by the habitual residence of an individual and by the principal place of business of a jural entity;

2.1.2. Concerns property located in the forum state (including movable property and intangible property), to which a party from a different state claims an interest, whether of ownership, lien, security, or otherwise; or

2.1.3. Is governed by an arbitration agreement providing that these Rules apply.

2.2. In a proceeding involving multiple claims or multiple parties, some of which are not within the scope of this Rule, the court must determine which are the principal matters in dispute.

2.2.1. If the principal matters in dispute are within the scope of these Rules, the Rules apply to all parties and all claims. Otherwise, the rules of the forum apply.

2.2.2. The court may separate the proceeding and then apply Rule 2.2.1.

2.3. The forum state may exclude categories of matters from application of these Rules and may extend application of these Rules to other civil and commercial matters.

JURISDICTION, JOINDER, AND VENUE

3. Forum and Territorial Competence

3.1   Proceedings under these Rules should be conducted in a court of specialized jurisdiction for commercial disputes or in the forum state's first-instance courts of general jurisdiction.

3.2   Appellate jurisdiction of a proceeding under these Rules must be in the court having jurisdiction over the first-instance court.

3.3   Whenever possible, territorial competence should be established, either originally or by transfer of the proceeding, at a place in the forum state that is reasonably convenient to a defendant.

Comment:

R-3A Territorial competence is the equivalent of "venue" in some common-law systems.

R-3B Typically it would be convenient that a specialized court or division of court be established in a principal commercial city, such as Milan in Italy or London in the United Kingdom. Committing disputes under these rules to specialized courts would facilitate development of a more uniform procedural jurisprudence.

4. Jurisdiction over Parties

4.1   Jurisdiction is established over a plaintiff by the plaintiff's commencement of a proceeding or over a person who intervenes by the act of intervention.

4.2   Jurisdiction may be established over another person as follows:

4.2.1   By consent of that person to the jurisdiction of the court;

4.2.2   Over an individual who is a habitual resident of the forum;

4.2.3   Over a jural entity that has received its charter of organization from the forum state or maintains its principal place of business or administrative headquarters in the state; or

4.2.4   Over a person who has:

4.2.4.1   Provided goods or services in the forum state, or agreed to do so, when the proceeding concerns such goods or services; or

4.2.4.2   Committed tortious conduct in the forum state, or conduct having direct effect in the forum state, when the proceeding concerns such conduct.

4.3   Jurisdiction may be exercised over a person who claims an interest (of ownership, lien, security, or otherwise) in property located in the forum state with respect to that interest.

4.4   Jurisdiction may be exercised, when no other forum is reasonably available, on the basis of:

4.4.1   Presence or nationality of the defendant in the forum state; or

4.4.2   Presence in the forum state of the defendant's property, whether or not the dispute relates to the property, but the court's authority is limited to the property or its value.

4.5   A court may grant provisional measures with respect to a person or to property in the territory of the forum state, even if the court does not have jurisdiction over the controversy.

4.6   The forum should decline to exercise jurisdiction or suspend the proceeding, if:

4.6.1   Another forum was validly designated by the parties as exclusive;

4.6.2   The forum is manifestly inappropriate relative to another forum that could exercise jurisdiction; or

4.6.3   The dispute is previously pending in another court.

4.7   The forum may nevertheless exercise its jurisdiction or reinstate the proceeding when it appears that the dispute cannot otherwise be effectively and expeditiously resolved or there are other compelling reasons for doing so.

Comment:

R-4A   The standard of "substantial connection" has been generally accepted for international legal disputes. That standard excludes mere physical presence, which within the United States is colloquially called "tag jurisdiction." Mere physical presence as a basis of jurisdiction within the American federation has historical justification but is inappropriate in international disputes. But see Rule 4.4.1.

R-4B   The concept of "jural entity" includes a corporation, société anonyme, unincorporated association, partnership, or other organization recognized as a jural entity by forum law.

R-4C   Rule 4.4.2 recognizes that when no other forum is reasonably available a state may exercise jurisdiction by sequestration or attachment of locally situated property, even though the property is not the object or subject of the dispute. The procedure is called "quasi in rem jurisdiction" in some legal systems.

R-4D   The concept recognized in Rule 4.6.2 corresponds in common-law systems to the rule of forum non conveniens.

5. Multiple Claims and Parties; Intervention

5.1   A party may assert any claim substantially connected to the subject matter of the proceeding against another party or against a third person subject to the jurisdiction of the court.

5.2   A third person made a party as provided in Rule 5.1 should be summoned as provided in Rule 7.

5.3   A person having an interest substantially connected with the subject matter of the proceeding may apply to intervene. The court itself or on motion of a party may require notice to a party having such an interest, inviting intervention. Intervention may be permitted unless it will unduly delay, introduce confusion into the proceeding, or otherwise unfairly prejudice a party.

5.4   A party added to the proceeding ordinarily has the same rights and obligations of participation and cooperation as the original parties. The extent of these rights and obligations should be adjusted according to the basis, timing, and circumstances of the joinder or intervention.

5.5   When appropriate the court should grant permission for a person to be substituted for or to be admitted in succession to a party.

5.6   The court may order separation of claims, issues, or parties, or consolidation with other proceedings, for a fair or more efficient management and determination or in the interest of justice. That authority should extend to parties or claims that are not within the scope of these Rules.

7. Due Notice

7.1   A party must be given formal notice of the proceeding commenced against that party, provided in accordance with forum law by means reasonably likely to be effective.

7.2   The notice must:

7.2.1   Contain a copy of the statement of claim;

7.2.2   Advise that plaintiff invokes these Rules;

7.2.3   Specify the time within which response is required and state that a default judgment may be entered against a party who does not respond within that time; and

7.2.4   Be in a language of the forum and also in a language of the state of an individual's habitual residence or of a jural entity's principal place of business, or in the language of the principal documents in the transaction.

7.3   All parties must have prompt notice of claims, defenses, motions, and applications of other parties, and of determinations and suggestions by the court. Parties must have a fair opportunity and reasonably adequate time to respond.

Comment:

R-7A   Responsibility for giving notice in most civil-law systems and some common-law systems is assigned to the court. In other common-law systems it is assigned to the parties. In most systems the notice (called a summons in common-law terminology) must be accompanied by a copy of the complaint, which itself contains detailed notice about the dispute. Many systems require a recital of advice as to how to respond. The warning about default is especially important. See Comment R-11B.

R-7B   Concerning the language of the notice, the court ordinarily will assume that its own language is appropriate. The parties therefore may have responsibility to inform the court when that assumption is inaccurate. The requirement that notice could be in a language of the state of the person to whom it is addressed establishes an objective standard for specification of language.

R-7C   In all systems, after the complaint has been transmitted and the defendant has responded, communications among the court and the parties ordinarily are conducted through the parties' lawyers.

PLEADING STAGE

11. Commencement of the Proceeding and Notice

11.1   The plaintiff shall submit to the court a statement of claim, as provided in Rule 12. The court shall thereupon give notice of the proceeding, as provided in Rule 7.

11.2   The time of lodging of the complaint with the court determines compliance with statutes of limitations, lis pendens, and other requirements of timeliness, subject to compliance with requirements of timely notice to the party affected thereby.

Comment:

R-11A   Rule 11 specifies the rule for commencement of suit for purposes of determining the competence of the court, lis pendens, interruption of statutes of limitations, and other purposes as provided by the forum law.

R-11B   Rule 11 also provides for giving notice of the proceeding to the defendant, or "service of process" as it is called in common-law procedure. The Hague Service Convention specifies rules of notice that govern proceedings in countries signatory to that Convention. When judicial assistance from the courts of another country is required in order to effect notice, the procedure for obtaining such assistance should be followed. In any event, the notice must include a copy of the statement of claim, a statement that the proceeding is conducted under these Rules, and a warning that default judgment may be taken against a defendant that does not respond. See Rule 7.2. Beyond these requirements, the rules of the forum govern the mechanisms and formalities for giving notice of the proceeding. In some states it is sufficient to mail the notice; some states require that notice, such as a summons, be delivered by an officer of the court.

12. Statement of Claim (Complaint)

12.1   The plaintiff must state the facts on which the claim is based, describe the evidence to support those statements, and refer to the legal grounds that support the claim, including foreign law, if applicable.

12.2   The reference to legal grounds must be sufficient to permit the court to determine the legal validity of the claim.

12.3   The statement of facts must, so far as reasonably practicable, set forth detail as to time, place, participants, and events.

12.4   A party who is justifiably uncertain of a fact or legal grounds may make statements about them in the alternative. In connection with an objection that a pleading lacks sufficient detail, the court should give due regard to the possibility that necessary facts and evidence will develop in the course of the proceeding.

12.5   If plaintiff is required to have first resorted to arbitration or conciliation procedure, or to have made a demand concerning the claim, or to have complied with another condition precedent, the complaint must allege compliance therewith.

12.6   The complaint must state the remedy requested, including the monetary amount demanded and the terms of any other remedy sought.

Comment:

R-12A Rule 12.1 requires the plaintiff to state the facts upon which the claim is based. Rule 12.3 calls for particularity of statement, such as that required in most civil-law and most common-law jurisdictions. In contrast, some American systems, notably those employing "notice pleading" as under the Federal Rules of Civil Procedure, permit very general allegations. In these Rules, the facts pleaded in the statements of claim and defense establish the standard of relevance for exchange of evidence, which is limited to matters relevant to the facts of the case as stated in the pleadings. See Rule 25.2.

R-12B Under Rules 12.1 and 12.2, the complaint must refer to the legal grounds on which the plaintiff relies to support the claim. Reference to such grounds is a common requirement in many legal systems and is especially appropriate when the transaction may involve the law of more than one legal system and present problems of choice of law. Rules of procedure in many national systems require a party's pleading to set forth foreign law when the party intends to rely on that law. However, according to Principle 22.1, the court has responsibility for determining the correct legal basis for its decisions.

R-12C According to Rule 7.2.2, the notice must advise that plaintiff invokes these Rules. The court or a defendant or other party may challenge that application, or demand it if plaintiff has not done so.

R-12D Some systems require that a claim or demand be made against a prospective defendant before commencing litigation, for example, claims against public agencies or insurance companies.

R-12E Rule 12.6 requires a statement of the amount of money demanded and, if injunctive or declaratory relief is sought, the nature and terms of the requested remedy. If the defendant defaults, the court may not award a judgment in an amount greater or in terms more severe than that demanded in the complaint, so that the defendant can calculate on an informed basis whether to dispute the claim. See Rule 15.4. It is an important requirement that a default judgment may be entered only when the plaintiff has offered sufficient proof of the claims for which judgment is awarded. See Rule 15.3.3.

13. Statement of Defense and Counterclaims

13.1   A defendant must, within [60] consecutive days from the date of service of notice, answer the complaint. The time for answer may be extended for a reasonable time by agreement of the parties or by court order.

13.2   A defendant in the answer must admit, admit with explanations, or allege an alternative statement of facts, and deny allegations defendant wishes to controvert. Failure explicitly to deny an allegation is considered an admission for purposes of the proceeding and obviates proof thereof, except as provided in Rule 15 concerning default judgment.

13.3   The defendant may state a counterclaim seeking relief from a plaintiff, or a claim against a co-defendant or a third person. Such a claim must be answered by the party to whom it is addressed as provided in this Rule.

13.4   The requirements of Rule 12 concerning the detail of statements of claims apply to the answer, affirmative defenses, counterclaims, and third-party claims.

13.5   Objections referred to in Rule 19.1.1 and 19.1.2 may be presented in a motion before the answer but such a motion does not extend the time in which to answer unless the court so orders or the parties agree.

Comment:

R-13A Forum law should specify the time within which a defendant's response is required. The specification should take into account the transnational character of the dispute.

R-13B Rule 13.2 requires that the defendant's statement of defense address the allegations of the complaint, denying or admitting with explanation those allegations that are to be controverted. Allegations not so controverted are admitted for purposes of the litigation. The defendant may assert an "alternative statement of facts," which is simply a different narrative of the circumstances that the defendant presents in order to clarify the dispute. Whether an admission in a proceeding under these Rules has effect in other proceedings is determined by the law governing such other proceedings. An "affirmative defense" is the allegation of additional facts or contentions that avoids the legal effect of the facts and contentions raised by the plaintiff, rather than contradict them directly. An example is the defense that an alleged debt has previously been discharged in bankruptcy. A "negative defense" is the denial.

R-13C These Rules generally do not specify the number of days within which a specific procedural act should be performed. A transnational proceeding must be expeditious, but international transactions often involve severe problems of communications. It is generally understood that the time should be such as to impose an obligation of prompt action, but should not be so short as to create unfair risk of prejudice. Therefore, a period of 60 days in which to respond generally should be sufficient. However, if the defendant is at a remote location, additional time may be necessary and should be granted as of course. In any event, the forum state should prescribe time limits, and the basis on which they are calculated, in its adoption of the Rules....

14. Amendments

14.1   A party, upon showing good reason to the court and notice to other parties, has a right to amend its claims or defenses when doing so does not unreasonably delay the proceeding or otherwise result in injustice. In particular, amendments may be justified to take account of events occurring after those alleged in earlier pleadings, newly discovered facts or evidence that could not previously have been obtained through reasonable diligence, or evidence obtained through exchange of evidence.

14.2   Leave to amend must be granted on such terms as are just, including, when necessary, adjournment or continuance, or compensation by an award of costs to another party.

14.3   The amendment must be served on the opposing party, who has [30] consecutive days in which to respond, or such other time as the court may order.

14.4   If the complaint has been amended, default judgment may be obtained on the basis of an amended pleading only if the amended pleading has been served on the party against whom default judgment is to be entered and the party has not timely responded.

14.5   Any party may request that the court order another party to provide by amendment a more specific statement of that party's pleading on the ground that the challenged statement does not comply with the requirements of these Rules. This request temporarily suspends the duty to answer.

Comment:

R-14A The scope of permissible amendment differs among various legal systems, the rule in the United States, for example, being very liberal and that in many civil-law systems being less so. In many civil-law systems amendment of the legal basis of a claim is permitted, as distinct from the factual basis, but amendment of factual allegations is permitted only upon a showing that there is newly discovered probative evidence and that the amendment is within the scope of the dispute. See Comment R-2C for reference to the civil-law concept of "dispute."

R-14B The appropriateness of permitting amendment also depends on the basis of the request. For example, an amendment to address material evidence newly discovered should be more readily granted than an amendment to add a new party whose participation could have been anticipated. An amendment sometimes could have some adverse effect on an opposing party. On the other hand, compensation for costs reasonably incurred by the party, or rescheduling of the final hearing, could eliminate some unfair prejudicial effects. Accordingly, exercise of judicial judgment may be required in considering an amendment. The court may postpone the award of costs until the final disposition of the case. See Rule 14.2....

15. Dismissal and Default Judgment

15.1   Dismissal of the proceeding must be entered against a plaintiff who without justification fails to prosecute the proceeding with reasonable efficiency. Before entering such a dismissal, the court must give plaintiff a reasonable warning thereof.

15.2   Default judgment must be entered against a defendant or other party who, without justification, fails to appear or respond within the prescribed time.

15.3   In entering a default judgment for failure to appear or respond within the prescribed time, the court must determine that:

15.3.1   There is no jurisdiction over the party against whom judgment is to be entered;

15.3.2   There has been compliance with notice provisions and that the party has had sufficient time to respond;

15.3.3   The claim is reasonably supported by evidence and is legally sufficient, including the amount of damages and any claim for costs.

15.4   A default judgment may be no greater in monetary amount or in severity of other remedy than was demanded in the complaint.

15.5   A party who appears or responds after the time prescribed, but before judgment, may be permitted to enter a defense upon offering reasonable excuse, but the court may order compensation for costs resulting to the opposing party.

15.6   The court may enter default judgment as a sanction against a party who without justification fails to offer a substantial answer or otherwise fails to continue participation after responding.

15.7   Dismissal or default judgment is subject to appeal or request to set aside the judgment according to the law of the forum.

Comment:

R-15A Default judgment permits termination of a dispute. It is a mechanism for compelling a defendant to acknowledge the court's authority. If the court lacked authority to enter a default judgment, a defendant could avoid liability simply by ignoring the proceeding and later dispute the validity of the judgment.

It is important to consider the reason why the party did not answer or did not proceed after having answered. For example, a party may have failed to answer because that party was obliged by his or her national law not to appear by reason of hostility between the countries.

Reasonable care should be exercised before entering a default judgment because notice may not have been given to a defendant, or the defendant may have been confused about the need to respond. Forum procedure in many systems requires that, after a defendant has failed to respond, an additional notice be given to the defendant of intention to enter default judgment.

R-15B A plaintiff's abandonment of prosecution of the proceeding is usually referred to as "failure to prosecute" and results in "involuntary dismissal." It is the equivalent of a default.

R-15C The absence of a substantial answer may be treated as no answer at all.

R-15D A decision that the claim is reasonably supported by evidence and legally justified under Rule 15.3.3 does not require a full inquiry on the merits of the case. The judge need only determine whether the default judgment is consistent with the available evidence and is legally justified. For that decision, the judge must analyze critically the evidence supporting the statement of claims. See Rule 21.1. The judge may request production of more evidence or schedule an evidentiary hearing....

R-15H Every system has a procedure for invalidating a default judgment obtained without compliance with the rules governing default. In some systems, including most common-law systems, the procedure is pursued in the first-instance court, and in other systems, including many civil-law systems, it is through an appeal. This Rule defers to forum law.

16. Settlement Offer

16.1   After commencement of a proceeding under these Rules, a party may deliver to another party a written offer to settle one or more claims and the related costs and expenses. The offer must be designated "Settlement Offer" and must refer to the penalties imposed under this Rule. The offer must remain open for [60] days, unless rejected or withdrawn by a writing delivered to the offeree before delivery of an acceptance.

16.2   The offeree may counter with its own offer, which must remain open for at least [30] days. If the counteroffer is not accepted, the offeree may accept the original offer, if still open.

16.3   An offer neither withdrawn nor accepted before its expiration is rejected.

16.4   Except by consent of both parties, an offer must not be made public or revealed to the court before acceptance or entry of judgment, under penalty of sanctions, including adverse determination of the merits.

16.5   Not later than [30] days after notice of entry of judgment, a party who made an offer may file with the court a declaration that an offer was made but rejected. If the offeree has failed to obtain a judgment that is more advantageous than the offer, the court may impose an appropriate sanction, considering all the relevant circumstances of the case.

16.6   Unless the court finds that special circumstances justify a different sanction, the sanction must be the loss of the right to be reimbursed for the costs as provided in Rule 32, plus reimbursement of a reasonable amount of the offeror's costs taking into account the date of delivery of the offer. This sanction must be in addition to the costs determined in accordance with Rule 32.

16.7   If an accepted offer is not complied with in the time specified in the offer, or in a reasonable time, the offeree may either enforce it or continue with the proceeding.

16.8   This procedure is not exclusive of the court's authority and duty to conduct informal discussion of settlement and does not preclude parties from conducting settlement negotiations outside this Rule and that are not subject to sanctions.

Comment:

R-16A This Rule aims at encouraging compromises and settlements and also deters parties from pursuing or defending a case that does not deserve a full and complete proceeding.

This Rule departs from traditions in some countries in which the parties generally do not have an obligation to negotiate or otherwise consider settlement proposals from the opposing party. It allocates risk of unfavorable outcome and is not based on bad faith or misconduct. It protects a party from the expense of litigation in a dispute that the party has reasonably sought to settle. However, it imposes severe cost consequences on a party who fails to achieve a judgment more favorable than a formal offer that has been rejected. For this reason, the procedure may be regarded as impairing access to justice.

R-16B Rule 16 is based on a similar provision under the Ontario (Canada) civil-procedure rules and Part 36 of the new English Procedural Rules. The detailed protocol is designed to permit submission and consideration of serious offers of settlement, from either a plaintiff or a defendant. At the same time, the protocol prohibits use of such offers or responses to influence the court and thereby to prejudice the parties. Experience indicates that a precisely defined procedure, to which conformity is strictly required, can facilitate settlement. The law of the forum may permit or require the deposit of the offer into court.

This procedure is a mechanism whereby a party can demand from an opposing party serious consideration of a settlement offer at any time during the litigation. It is not exclusive of the court's authority and duty to conduct informal discussions and does not preclude parties from conducting settlement negotiations by procedures that are not subject to the Rule 16.5 sanction. See Rule 16.8.

R-16C The offer must remain open for a determinate amount of time, but it can be withdrawn prior to acceptance. According to general principles of contract law, in general the withdrawal of an offer can be accomplished only before the offer reaches the offeree. See, e.g., UNIDROIT's Principles of International Commercial Contracts article 2.3. However, the context of litigation requires a different protocol designed to facilitate settlement: facts or evidence may develop, or expenses may be incurred, that justify the withdrawal, reduction, or increase of the offer. When the offer is withdrawn, there will be no cost sanctions.

The offeree may deliver a counter-offer. According to the principle of equality of the parties, a counteroffer is regulated by the same rules as the offer. See Principle 3. For example, it can be withdrawn under the same conditions as an offer can be withdrawn. In addition, the counteroffer may lead to the same sanctions as an offer.

According to general principles of private contract law, the delivery of a counteroffer means rejection of the offer. See, e.g., UNIDROIT's Principles of International Commercial Contracts article 2.11. However, the rule specified here is more effective in the context of settlement offers in litigation, in which a rejection of an offer may lead to serious consequences.

R-16D Rule 16.4 prohibits public disclosure of the offer or disclosure to the court before acceptance or entry of judgment. Parties might be reluctant to make a settlement offer if doing so could be interpreted as an admission of liability or of weakness of one's position.

R-16E Rule 16.5, permitting notice to the court of an offer that was not accepted, is linked to Rule 31.3, which provides that the court must promptly give the parties notice of judgment. When such notice has been received, the party whose offer was not accepted may inform the court, in order to obtain the cost sanctions prescribed in this Rule.

R-16F If the offeree fails to obtain a judgment that is more advantageous than the offer of settlement under this Rule, that party loses the right to be reimbursed for the costs and expenses incurred after the offer, including attorneys' fees. Instead, the offeree (even if it is the winning party) must pay the costs and expenses thereafter incurred by the offeror (even if it is the loser.) The court will award an appropriate proportion of the costs and expenses taking into account the date of delivery of the offer.

According to Rule 16.6, the cost sanction in this Rule is independent from and in addition to the costs awarded according to Rule 32. If the person who has to pay the cost sanction was also the loser of the action, that person may have to pay both the opponent's fees and the cost sanctions.

When the offer is partial, or the offeree fails only in part to obtain a more advantageous judgment, the sanction should be proportional. The rejection of the offer may have been reasonable under the specific circumstances of the case, and under Rule 16.6 the judge may determine the sanction accordingly.

GENERAL AUTHORITY OF THE COURT

17. Provisional and Protective Measures

17.1 The court may grant provisional relief to restrain or require conduct of a party or other person when necessary to preserve the ability to grant effective relief by final judgment or to maintain or otherwise regulate the status quo. The grant or extent of the remedy is governed by the principle of proportionality. Disclosure of assets wherever located may be ordered.

17.2 The provisional relief may be issued before the opposing party has an opportunity to respond only upon proof of urgent necessity and preponderance of considerations of fairness. The applicant must fully disclose facts and legal issues of which the court properly should be aware.

17.3 A person against whom an ex parte order is directed must have an opportunity at the earliest practicable time to respond concerning the appropriateness of the order.

17.4 The court may, after hearing those interested, issue, dissolve, renew, or modify an order.

17.5 An applicant for provisional relief is liable for compensation of a person against whom an order is issued if the court thereafter determines that the relief should not have been granted.

17.5.1 The court may require the applicant for provisional relief to post a bond or formally to assume a duty of compensation.

17.6 The granting or denial of a provisional relief is subject to immediate appellate review.

Comment:

R-17A Provisional relief consists of an order requiring or prohibiting the performance of a specified act, for example, preserving property in its present condition. Rule 17.1 authorizes the court to issue an order that is either affirmative, in that it requires performance of an act, or negative in that it prohibits a specific act or course of action. The term is used here in a generic sense to include attachment, sequestration, and other directives. The concept of regulation of the status quo may include measures to ameliorate the underlying dispute, for example, supervision of management of a partnership during litigation among the partners. Availability of provisional remedies or interim measures, such as attachment or sequestration, should be determined by forum law, including applicable principles of international law. A court may also order disclosure of assets wherever located, or grant provisional relief to facilitate arbitration or to enforce arbitration provisional measures.

R-17B If allowed by forum law, the court may, upon reasonable notice to the person to whom an order is directed, require persons who are not parties to the proceeding to comply with an order issued in accordance with Rule 17.1 or to retain a fund or other property the right to which is in dispute in the proceeding, and to deal with it only in accordance with an order of the court. See Comment R-20A.

R-17C Rule 17.2 authorizes the court to issue an order without notice to the person against whom it is directed where doing so is justified by urgent necessity. "Urgent necessity," required as a basis for an ex parte order, is a practical concept, as is the concept of preponderance of considerations of fairness. The latter term corresponds to the common-law concept of "balance of equities." Considerations of fairness include the strength of the merits of the applicant's claim, the urgency of the need for a provisional remedy, and the practical burdens that may result from granting the remedy. Such an injunction is usually known as an ex parte injunction. In common-law procedure such an order is usually referred to as a "temporary restraining order." See Rule 10.4.

The question for the court, in considering an application for an ex parte order, is whether the applicant has made a reasonable and specific demonstration that such an order is required to prevent an irreparable deterioration in the situation to be addressed in the litigation and that it would be imprudent to postpone the order until the opposing party has opportunity to be heard. The burden is on the party requesting an ex parte order to justify its issuance. However, opportunity for the opposing party or person to whom the order is addressed to be heard should be afforded at the earliest practicable time. The party or person must have the opportunity of a de novo consideration of the decision, including opportunity to present new evidence. See Rule 17.3.

R-17D Rules of procedure generally require that a party requesting an ex parte order make full disclosure to the court of all aspects of the situation, including those favorable to the opposing party. Failure to make such disclosure is grounds to vacate an order and may be a basis of liability for damages against the requesting party.

R-17E As indicated in Rule 17.4, if the court had declined to issue an order ex parte, it may nevertheless issue an order upon a hearing. If the court previously issued an order ex parte, it may revoke, renew, or modify its order in light of the matters developed at the hearing. The burden is on the party seeking the order to show that the order is justified.

R-17F Rule 17.5.1 authorizes the court to require a bond or other compensation as protection against the disturbance and injury that may result from an order. The particulars should be determined by reference to the law of the forum.

R-17G Review of an order granting or denying provisional relief is provided under Rule 33.2 and should be afforded according to the procedure of the forum.

18. Case Management

18.1   The court should assume active management of the proceeding in all stages of the litigation. Consideration should be given to the transnational character of the dispute.

18.2   The court should order a planning conference early in the proceeding and may schedule other conferences thereafter. A lawyer for each of the parties and an unrepresented party must attend such conferences and other persons may be ordered to do so.

18.3   In giving direction to the proceeding, the court, after discussion with the parties, may:

18.3.1   Suggest amendment of the pleadings for the addition, elimination, or revision of claims, defenses, and issues in light of the parties' contentions at that stage;

18.3.2   Order the separation for a preliminary or separate hearing and decision of one or more issues in the case and enter an interlocutory judgment addressing such issues and their relation to the remainder of the case;

18.3.3   Order the separation or consolidation of cases pending before itself, whether those cases proceed under these Rules or those of the forum, when doing so may facilitate the proceeding and decision;

18.3.4   Make decisions concerning admissibility and exclusion of evidence; the sequence, dates, and times of hearing evidence; and other matters to simplify or expedite the proceeding; and

18.3.5   Order any person subject to the court's authority to produce documents or other evidence, or to submit to deposition as provided in Rule 23.

18.4   To facilitate efficient determination of a dispute, the first-instance court may take evidence at another location or delegate taking of evidence to another court of the forum state or of another state or to a judicial officer specially appointed for the purpose.

18.5   The court may at any time suggest that the parties consider settlement, mediation, or arbitration or any other form of alternative dispute resolution. If requested by all parties, the court must stay the proceeding while the parties explore those alternatives.

18.6   In conducting the proceeding the court may use any means of communication, including telecommunication devices such as video or audio transmission.

18.7   Time limits for complying with procedural obligations should begin to run from the date of notice to the party having the obligation.

Comment:

R-18A This Rule determines the role of the court in organizing the case and preparing for the final hearing. The court has wide discretion in deciding how to conclude the interim phase, and in determining how to provide for the following final phase of the proceedings.

R-18B The court should order a planning conference early in the proceeding and may decide that, in order to clarify the issues and to specify the terms of the dispute at the final hearing, one or more further conferences may be useful. The court may conduct a conference by any means of communication available such as telephone, videoconference, or the like.

R-18C The court fixes the date or dates for such conferences. The parties' lawyers are required to attend. Participation of lawyers for the parties is essential to facilitate orderly progression to resolution of the dispute. Lawyers in many systems have some authority to make agreements concerning conduct of the litigation. Parties may have additional authority in some systems. If matters to be discussed are outside of the scope of the lawyers' authority, the court has authority to require the parties themselves to attend in order to discuss and resolve matters concerning progression to resolution, including discussion of settlement. The rule does not exclude the possibility of pro se litigants.

R-18D In conferences after the initial planning conference, the court should discuss the issues of the case; which facts, claims, or defenses are not disputed; whether new disputed facts have emerged from disclosure or exchange of evidence; whether new claims or defenses have been presented; and what evidence will be admitted at the final hearing. The principal aim of the conference is to exclude issues that are no longer disputed and to identify precisely the facts, claims, defenses, and evidence concerning those issues that will be addressed at the final hearing. However, exceptionally, the court may decide that a conference is unnecessary, and that the final hearing may proceed simply on the basis of the parties' pleadings and stipulations if any.

R-18E After consultation with the parties, the court may give directives for the final hearing as provided in Rule 18.3. The court may summarize the terms of claims and defenses, rule on issues concerning admissibility of evidence, specify the items of admissible evidence, and determine the order of their examination. The court may also resolve disputed claims of privilege. The court should fix the date for final hearing and enter other orders to ensure that it will be carried on in a fair and expedited manner.

Rule 18 authorizes various measures by the court to facilitate an efficient hearing. It is often useful to isolate one or more issues for hearing upon one occasion, with other issues reserved for consideration later if necessary. So also, it is often useful that a hearing be consolidated with another case when the same or substantially similar issues are to be considered. As recognized in Rule 18.3.4, it is often convenient for the court to rule on admissibility of evidence before its presentation, especially evidence that is complicated, such as voluminous documents.

R-18F The court may consider the possibility that the parties may settle the dispute or refer it to a mediator. In such a case the court, before entering the rulings described in Rule 18.3, may fix a hearing to explore the possibility of a settlement, if necessary with the mediation of the court itself, or a referral of the dispute to mediation or any other form of alternative dispute resolution. This Rule authorizes the court to encourage discussion between the parties, but not to exercise coercion. If a settlement is reached, the proceedings ordinarily are terminated and judgment entered or the case dismissed with prejudice. If the parties agree about a deferral to mediation or arbitration, that agreement should be put into the record of the case and the proceeding suspended....

19. Early Court Determinations

19.1   On its own motion or motion of a party, the court at any stage before the final hearing may:

19.1.1   Determine that the dispute is not governed by these Rules or that the court lacks competence to adjudicate the dispute;

19.1.2   Upon a party's motion, determine that the court lacks jurisdiction over that party;

19.1.3   Render a complete or partial judgment by deciding only questions of law;

19.1.4   Render a complete or partial judgment on the basis of evidence immediately available, in which case the court must have regard for the opportunity under these Rules for offering contradictory evidence or obtaining evidence before making such a determination.

19.2 Before rendering a decision under this Rule, the court must allow the party against whom the determination is made reasonable opportunity to amend its statement of claims or defense when it appears that the deficiency can be remedied by amendment and that affording such opportunity will not unreasonably postpone the proceeding or otherwise result in injustice.

Comment:

R-19A It is a universal procedural principle that the court may make determinations of the sufficiency of the pleadings and other contentions, concerning either substantive law or procedure, that materially affect the rights of a party or the ability of the court to render substantial justice. In civil-law systems, the court has an obligation to scrutinize the procedural regularity of the proceeding. In common-law systems, authority to make such determinations ordinarily is exercised only upon initiative of a party made through a motion. However, the court in common-law systems may exercise that authority on its own initiative and in civil-law systems the court may do so in response to a suggestion or motion of a party.

According to Rule 13.5, the objections referred to in Rules 19.1.1 and 19.1.2 can be made by defendant either by a motion or by answer to the complaint.

R-19B Rules 19.1.1 and 19.1.2 express a universal principle that the court's competence over the dispute and its jurisdiction over the parties may be questioned. A valid objection of this kind usually requires termination of the proceeding. A similar objection may be made that the dispute is not within the scope prescribed in Rule 2 and hence is not governed by these Rules. Among factors that may be considered under Rule 19.1.1 is dismissal for forum non conveniens. See Rule 4.6.2. Procedural law varies as to whether there are time limitations or other restrictions on delay in making any of these objections, and whether participation in the proceeding without making such an objection results in its waiver or forfeiture.

R-19C Rules 19.1.3 and 19.1.4 empower the court to adjudicate the merits of a claim or defense at the preliminary stage. Such an adjudication may be based on matters of law or matters of fact, or both. Judgment is appropriate when the claim or defense in question is legally insufficient as stated. Evidence may be in the form of written testimony as provided in Rule 23.4. Judgment is also appropriate when it is demonstrated that evidence to support or refute the claim or defense is incontrovertible. When it is contended that the evidence is incontrovertible, the court should consider whether exchange of evidence might disclose sufficient proof to support the claim or defense at issue....

In civil-law systems, the foregoing powers are exercised by the court as a matter of course. In common-law systems, the power to determine that a claim or defense is substantively insufficient derives from the old common-law demurrer and the modern motions for dismissal for failure to state a claim and for summary judgment and is usually exercised on the basis of a motion by a party. Examples of claims that typically may be so adjudicated are claims based on a written contract calling for payment of money, or to ownership of specific property, when no valid defense or denial is offered. Examples of defenses that typically may be so adjudicated are the defense of elapse of time (statute of limitations or prescription), release, and res judicata.

20. Orders Directed to a Third Person

20.1 The court may order persons who are not parties to the proceeding:

    20.1.1 To give testimony as provided in Rules 23 and 29; and

    20.1.2 To produce information, documents, electronically stored information or other things as evidence or for inspection by the court or a party.

20.2 The court shall require a party seeking an order directed to a third person to provide compensation for the costs of compliance.

20.3 An order directed to a third person may be enforced by means authorized against such person by forum law, including imposition of cost sanctions, a monetary penalty, astreintes, contempt of court, or seizure of documents or other things. If the third party is not subject to the court's jurisdiction, any party may seek assistance of a court that has such jurisdiction to enforce the order.

EVIDENCE

21. Disclosure

21.1   In accordance with the court's scheduling order, a party must identify to the court and other parties the evidence on which the party intends to rely, in addition to that provided in the pleading including:

21.1.1   Copies of documents or other records, such as contracts and correspondence; and

21.1.2   Summaries of expected testimony of witnesses, including parties, witnesses, and experts, then known to the party. Witnesses must be identified, so far as practicable, by name, address, and telephone number.

21.1.3   In lieu of a summary of expected testimony, a party may present a written statement of testimony.

21.2   A party must amend the specification required in Rule 21.1 to include documents or witnesses not known when the list was originally prepared. Any change in the list of documents or witnesses must be immediately communicated in writing to the court and to all other parties, together with a justification for the amendment.

21.3   To facilitate compliance with this Rule, a lawyer for a party may have a voluntary interview with a potential nonparty witness. The interview may be on reasonable notice to other parties, who may be permitted to attend the interview.

Comment:

R-21A Rule 21.1 requires that a party disclose documents on which that party relies in support of the party's position. A party must also list the witnesses upon whom it intends to rely and include a summary of expected testimony. The summary of expected testimony should address all propositions to which the witness will give testimony and should be reasonably specific in detail.... If a party later ascertains that there are additional documents or witnesses, it must submit an amended list.... In accordance with Rules 12.1 and 13.4, the parties must state with reasonable detail the facts and the legal grounds supporting their position.

R-21B Under the concept of professional ethics in some civil-law systems, a lawyer should not discuss the matters in dispute with prospective witnesses (other than the lawyer's own client). That norm is designed to protect testimony from improper manipulation, but it also has the effect of limiting the effectiveness of a lawyer in investigating and organizing evidence for consideration by the court. In discussion with a prospective witness, the lawyer should not suggest what the testimony should be nor offer improper inducement. Although there is some risk of abuse in allowing lawyers to confer with a prospective witness, that risk is less injurious to fair adjudication than is the risk that relevant and important evidence may remain undisclosed....

22. Exchange of Evidence

22.1   A party who has complied with disclosure duties prescribed in Rule 21, on notice to the other parties, may request the court to order production by any person of any evidentiary matter, not protected by confidentiality or privilege, that is relevant to the case and that may be admissible, including:

22.1.1   Documents and other records of information that are specifically identified or identified within specifically defined categories;

22.1.2   Identifying information, such as name and address, about specified persons having knowledge of a matter in issue; and

22.1.3   A copy of the report of any expert that another party intends to present.

22.2   The court must determine the request and order production accordingly. The court may order production of other evidence as necessary in the interest of justice. Such evidence must be produced within a reasonable time prior to the final hearing....

22.5   A party who did not have possession of requested evidence when the court's order was made, but who thereafter comes into possession of it, must thereupon comply with the order.

22.6   The fact that the demanded information is adverse to the interest of the party to which the demand is directed is not a valid objection to its production.

22.7   The court should recognize evidentiary privileges when exercising authority to compel disclosure of evidence or other information. The court should consider whether a privilege may justify a party's failure to disclose evidence or other information when deciding whether to draw adverse inferences or to impose other indirect sanctions.

Comment:

R-22A These Rules adopt, as a model of litigation, a system consisting of preliminary hearings followed by a concentrated form of final hearing. The essential core of the first stage is preliminary disclosure and clarification of the evidence. The principal consideration in favor of a unitary final hearing is that of expeditious justice. To achieve this objective, a concentrated final hearing should be used, so that arguments and the taking of evidence are completed in a single hearing or in a few hearings on consecutive judicial days. A concentrated final hearing requires a preliminary phase (called pretrial in common-law systems) in which evidence is exchanged and the case is prepared for concentrated presentation.

R-22B Rules 21 and 22 define the roles and the rights of the parties, the duty of voluntary disclosure, the procedure for exchange of evidence, the role of the court, and the devices to ensure that the parties comply with demands for evidence. Proper compliance with these obligations is not only a matter of law for the parties, but also a matter of professional honor and obligation on the part of the lawyers involved in the litigation.

R-22C The philosophy expressed in Rules 21 and 22 is essentially that of the common-law countries other than the United States. In those countries, the scope of discovery or disclosure is specified and limited, as in Rules 21 and 22. However, within those specifications disclosure is generally a matter of right....

R-22D Discovery under prevailing U.S. procedure, exemplified in the Federal Rules of Civil Procedure, is much broader, including the broad right to seek information that "appears reasonably calculated to lead to the discovery of admissible evidence." This broad discovery is often criticized as responsible for the increasing costs of the administration of justice. However, reasonable disclosure and exchange of evidence facilitates discovery of truth.

R-22E Disclosure and exchange of evidence under the civil-law systems are generally more restricted, or nonexistent. In particular, a broader immunity is conferred against disclosure of trade and business secrets. This Rule should be interpreted as striking a balance between the restrictive civil-law systems and the broader systems in common-law jurisdictions....

R-22G Rule 22.1 provides that every party is entitled to obtain from any person the disclosure of any unprivileged relevant evidence in possession of that person. Formal requests for evidence should be made to the court, and the court should direct the opposing party to comply with an order to produce evidence or information. This procedure can be unnecessarily burdensome on the parties and on the courts, especially in straightforward requests. Ideally, full disclosure of relevant evidence should result through dialogue among the parties, whereby the parties voluntarily satisfy each other's demands without intervention of the court. A party therefore may present the request directly to the opposing party, who should comply with an adequate request within a reasonable time....

R-22H According to Rule 22.1, compulsory exchange of evidence is limited to matters directly relevant to the issues in the case as they have been stated in the pleadings.... A party is not entitled to disclosure of information merely that "appears reasonably calculated to lead to the discovery of admissible evidence," which is permitted under Rule 26 of the Fed. R. Civ. P. in the United States. "Relevant" evidence is that which supports or contravenes the allegations of one of the parties. This Rule is aimed at preventing overdiscovery or unjustified "fishing expeditions."...

R-22L In cases involving voluminous documents or remotely situated witnesses, or in similar circumstances of practical necessity, the court may appoint someone as a special officer to supervise exchange of evidence....

R-22M If a party fails to comply with a demand for exchange of evidence, the court may impose sanctions to make disclosure effective. The determination of sanctions is within the discretion of the court, taking into account relevant features of the parties' behavior in accordance with Principle 17. The sanctions are: (1) Adverse inferences against the noncomplying party including conclusive determination of the facts. (2) A monetary penalty, fixed by the court in its discretion, or other means of legal compulsion permitted by forum law, including contempt of court. The court should graduate the penalty or contempt sanction according to the circumstances of the case. (3) The most severe sanction against noncompliance with disclosure demands or orders is entry of adverse judgment with respect to one or more of the claims.... Unless the court finds that special circumstances justify a different sanction, the preferred sanction is to draw adverse inferences....

23. Deposition and Testimony by Affidavit

23.1   A deposition of a party or other person may be taken by order of the court. Unless the court orders otherwise, a deposition may be presented as evidence in the record....

23.4   With written permission of the court, a party may present a written statement of sworn testimony of any person, containing statements in their own words about relevant facts....

APPELLATE AND SUBSEQUENT PROCEEDINGS

34. Rescission of Judgment

34.1   A final judgment may be rescinded only through a new proceeding and only upon a showing that the applicant acted with due diligence and that:

34.1.1   The judgment was procured without notice to or jurisdiction over the party seeking relief;

34.1.2   The judgment was procured through fraud;

34.1.3   There is evidence available that would lead to a different outcome and that was not previously available or could not have been known through exercise of due diligence, or by reason of fraud in disclosure, exchange, or presentation of evidence; or

34.1.4   The judgment constitutes a manifest miscarriage of justice.

34.2   An application for rescission of judgment must be made within [90] days from the date of discovery of the circumstances justifying rescission.

35. Enforcement of Judgment

35.1   A final judgment, as well as a judgment for a provisional remedy, is immediately enforceable, unless it has been stayed as provided in Rule 35.3.

35.2   If a person against whom a judgment has been entered does not comply within the time specified, or, if no time is specified, within 30 days after the judgment becomes final, enforcement measures may be imposed on the obligor. These measures may include compulsory revelation of assets wherever they are located and a monetary penalty on the obligor, payable to the judgment obligee, to the court, or to whomever the court may direct....

35.3   The trial court of first instance or the appellate court, on motion of the party against whom the judgment was rendered, may grant a stay of enforcement of the judgment pending appeal when necessary in the interest of justice.

35.4   The court may require a suitable bond or other security from the appellant as a condition of granting a stay or from the respondents as a condition of denying a stay.

Comment:

R-35A Rule 35.1 provides that a final judgment is immediately enforceable. If the judgment will be enforced in the country of the court in which the judgment was entered, the enforcement will be based on the forum's law governing the enforcement of final judgments. Otherwise, the international rules such as the "Brussels I Regulation" and the Brussels and Lugano Conventions on Jurisdiction and Enforcement of Judgments will apply. When a monetary judgment is to be enforced, attachment of property owned by the judgment obligor, or obligations owed to the obligor, may be ordered. Monetary penalties may be imposed by the court for delay in compliance, with discretion concerning the amount of the penalty.

R-35B Rule 35.2 authorizes the court, upon request of the judgment holder, to impose monetary penalties upon the judgment obligor that take effect if the obligor does not pay the obligation within the time specified, or within 30 days after the judgment has become final if no time is specified. The monetary penalties are to be imposed according to the following standards:

1) Application for the enforcement costs and penalties may be made by any party entitled to enforce the judgment.

2) Enforcement costs include the fees required for the enforcement, including the attorneys' fees, and an additional penalty in case of defiance of the court. An additional penalty may not exceed twice the amount of the judgment. The court may require the penalty to be paid to the person obtaining the judgment or to the court or otherwise.

3) Additional penalties may be added against an obligor who persists in refusal to pay, considering the amount of the judgment and the economic situation of the parties. Here, too, the court may require the penalty to be paid to the person obtaining the judgment or to the court, or otherwise.

4) No penalty will be imposed on a person who satisfactorily demonstrates to the court an inability to comply with the judgment.

5) "Nonparties" includes any institution that holds an account of the debtor.

R-35C Rule 35.3 permits either the first-instance court or the appellate court to grant a stay of enforcement when necessary in the interest of justice, as it is, for example, when a meritorious appeal is pending. Rule 35.4 authorizes the court to require a bond or other security as a condition either to permit or to stay the immediate enforcement.

36. Recognition and Judicial Assistance

36.1   A final judgment in a proceeding conducted in another forum in substantial compliance with these Rules must be recognized and enforced unless substantive public policy requires otherwise. A provisional measure must be recognized in the same terms.

36.2   Courts of states that have adopted these Rules must provide reasonable judicial assistance in aid of proceedings conducted under these Rules in another state, including provisional remedies, assistance in the identification or production of evidence, and enforcement of a judgment.

Comment:

R-36A It is a general principle of private international law that judgments of one state will be recognized and enforced in the courts of other states. The extent of such assistance and the procedures by which it may be provided are governed in many respects by the "Brussels I Regulation" and Brussels and Lugano Conventions.

R-36B Rule 36 provides that, as a matter of the domestic law of the forum, assistance to the courts of another state is to be provided to such extent as may be appropriate, including provisional measures. The general governing standard is the measure of assistance that one court within the state would provide to another court in the same state.

UNITED STATES CONSTITUTION

ARTICLE I

Section 1. All legislative Powers herein granted shall be vested in a Congress of the United States, which shall consist of a Senate and House of Representatives.

Section 2. The House of Representatives shall be composed of Members chosen every second Year by the People of the several States, and the Electors in each State shall have the Qualifications requisite for Electors of the most numerous Branch of the State Legislature.

No Person shall be a Representative who shall not have attained to the Age of twenty five Years, and been seven Years a Citizen of the United States, and who shall not, when elected, be an Inhabitant of that State in which he shall be chosen.

Representatives and direct Taxes shall be apportioned among the several States which may be included within this Union, according to their respective Numbers, which shall be determined by adding to the whole Number of free Persons, including those bound to Service for a Term of Years, and excluding Indians not taxed, three fifths of all other Persons.

The actual Enumeration shall be made within three Years after the first Meeting of the Congress of the United States, and within every subsequent Term of ten Years, in such Manner as they shall by Law direct. The Number of Representatives shall not exceed one for every thirty Thousand, but each State shall have at Least one Representative; and until such enumeration shall be made, the State of New Hampshire shall be entitled to chuse three, Massachusetts eight, Rhode Island and Providence Plantations one, Connecticut five, New York six, New Jersey four, Pennsylvania eight, Delaware one, Maryland six, Virginia ten, North Carolina five, South Carolina five and Georgia three.

When vacancies happen in the Representation from any State, the Executive Authority thereof shall issue Writs of Election to fill such Vacancies.

The House of Representatives shall chuse their Speaker and other Officers; and shall have the sole Power of Impeachment.

Section 3. The Senate of the United States shall be composed of two Senators from each State, chosen by the Legislature thereof, for six Years; and each Senator shall have one Vote.

Immediately after they shall be assembled in Consequence of the first Election, they shall be divided as equally as may be into three Classes. The Seats of the Senators of the first Class shall be vacated at the Expiration of the second Year, of the second Class at the Expiration of the fourth Year, and of the third Class at the Expiration of the sixth Year, so that one third may be chosen every second Year; and if Vacancies happen by Resignation, or otherwise, during the Recess of the Legislature of any State, the Executive thereof may make temporary Appointments until the next Meeting of the Legislature, which shall then fill such Vacancies.

No person shall be a Senator who shall not have attained to the Age of thirty Years, and been nine Years a Citizen of the United States, and who shall not, when elected, be an Inhabitant of that State for which he shall be chosen.

The Vice President of the United States shall be President of the Senate, but shall have no Vote, unless they be equally divided.

The Senate shall chuse their other Officers, and also a President pro tempore, in the absence of the Vice President, or when he shall exercise the Office of President of the United States.

The Senate shall have the sole Power to try all Impeachments. When sitting for that Purpose, they shall be on Oath or Affirmation. When the President of the United States is tried, the Chief Justice shall preside: And no Person shall be convicted without the Concurrence of two thirds of the Members present.

Judgment in Cases of Impeachment shall not extend further than to removal from Office, and disqualification to hold and enjoy any Office of honor, Trust or Profit under the United States: but the Party convicted shall nevertheless be liable and subject to Indictment, Trial, Judgment and Punishment, according to Law.

Section 4. The Times, Places and Manner of holding Elections for Senators and Representatives, shall be prescribed in each State by the Legislature thereof; but the Congress may at any time by Law make or alter such Regulations, except as to the Place of Chusing Senators.

The Congress shall assemble at least once in every Year, and such Meeting shall be on the first Monday in December, unless they shall by Law appoint a different Day.

Section 5. Each House shall be the Judge of the Elections, Returns and Qualifications of its own Members, and a Majority of each shall constitute a Quorum to do Business; but a smaller number may adjourn from day to day, and may be authorized to compel the Attendance of absent Members, in such Manner, and under such Penalties as each House may provide.

Each House may determine the Rules of its Proceedings, punish its Members for disorderly Behavior, and, with the Concurrence of two-thirds, expel a Member.

Each House shall keep a Journal of its Proceedings, and from time to time publish the same, excepting such Parts as may in their Judgment require Secrecy; and the Yeas and Nays of the Members of either House on any question shall, at the Desire of one fifth of those Present, be entered on the Journal.

Neither House, during the Session of Congress, shall, without the Consent of the other, adjourn for more than three days, nor to any other Place than that in which the two Houses shall be sitting.

Section 6. The Senators and Representatives shall receive a Compensation for their Services, to be ascertained by Law, and paid out of the Treasury of the United States. They shall in all Cases, except Treason, Felony and Breach of the Peace, be privileged from Arrest during their Attendance at the Session of their respective Houses, and in going to and returning from the same; and for any Speech or Debate in either House, they shall not be questioned in any other Place.

No Senator or Representative shall, during the Time for which he was elected, be appointed to any civil Office under the Authority of the United States which shall have been created, or the Emoluments whereof shall have been increased during such time; and no Person holding any Office under the United States, shall be a Member of either House during his Continuance in Office.

Section 7. All bills for raising Revenue shall originate in the House of Representatives; but the Senate may propose or concur with Amendments as on other Bills.

Every Bill which shall have passed the House of Representatives and the Senate, shall, before it become a Law, be presented to the President of the United States; If he approve he shall sign it, but if not he shall return it, with his Objections to that House in which it shall have originated, who shall enter the Objections at large on their Journal, and proceed to reconsider it. If after such Reconsideration two thirds of that House shall agree to pass the Bill, it shall be sent, together with the Objections, to the other House, by which it shall likewise be reconsidered, and if approved by two thirds of that House, it shall become a Law. But in all such Cases the Votes of both Houses shall be determined by Yeas and Nays, and the Names of the Persons voting for and against the Bill shall be entered on the Journal of each House respectively. If any Bill shall not be returned by the President within ten Days (Sundays excepted) after it shall have been presented to him, the Same shall be a Law, in like Manner as if he had signed it, unless the Congress by their Adjournment prevent its Return, in which Case it shall not be a Law.

Every Order, Resolution, or Vote to which the Concurrence of the Senate and House of Representatives may be necessary (except on a question of Adjournment) shall be presented to the President of the United States; and before the Same shall take Effect, shall be approved by him, or being disapproved by him, shall be repassed by two thirds of the Senate and House of Representatives, according to the Rules and Limitations prescribed in the Case of a Bill.

Section 8. The Congress shall have Power To lay and collect Taxes, Duties, Imposts and Excises, to pay the Debts and provide for the common Defence and general Welfare of the United States; but all Duties, Imposts and Excises shall be uniform throughout the United States;

To borrow money on the credit of the United States;

To regulate Commerce with foreign Nations, and among the several States, and with the Indian Tribes;

To establish an uniform Rule of Naturalization, and uniform Laws on the subject of Bankruptcies throughout the United States;

To coin Money, regulate the Value thereof, and of foreign Coin, and fix the Standard of Weights and Measures;

To provide for the Punishment of counterfeiting the Securities and current Coin of the United States;

To establish Post Offices and Post Roads;

To promote the Progress of Science and useful Arts, by securing for limited Times to Authors and Inventors the exclusive Right to their respective Writings and Discoveries;

To constitute Tribunals inferior to the supreme Court;

To define and punish Piracies and Felonies committed on the high Seas, and Offenses against the Law of Nations;

To declare War, grant Letters of Marque and Reprisal, and make Rules concerning Captures on Land and Water;

To raise and support Armies, but no Appropriation of Money to that Use shall be for a longer Term than two Years;

To provide and maintain a Navy;

To make Rules for the Government and Regulation of the land and naval Forces;

To provide for calling forth the Militia to execute the Laws of the Union, suppress Insurrections and repel Invasions;

To provide for organizing, arming, and disciplining the Militia, and for governing such Part of them as may be employed in the Service of the United States, reserving to the States respectively, the Appointment of the Officers, and the Authority of training the Militia according to the discipline prescribed by Congress;

To exercise exclusive Legislation in all Cases whatsoever, over such District (not exceeding ten Miles square) as may, by Cession of particular States, and the acceptance of Congress, become the Seat of the Government of the United States, and to exercise like Authority over all Places purchased by the Consent of the Legislature of the State in which the Same shall be, for the Erection of Forts, Magazines, Arsenals, dock-Yards, and other needful Buildings; And

To make all Laws which shall be necessary and proper for carrying into Execution the foregoing Powers, and all other Powers vested by this Constitution in the Government of the United States, or in any Department or Officer thereof.

Section 9. The Migration or Importation of such Persons as any of the States now existing shall think proper to admit, shall not be prohibited by the Congress prior to the Year one thousand eight hundred and eight, but a tax or duty may be imposed on such Importation, not exceeding ten dollars for each Person.

The privilege of the Writ of Habeas Corpus shall not be suspended, unless when in Cases of Rebellion or Invasion the public Safety may require it.

No Bill of Attainder or ex post facto Law shall be passed.

No capitation, or other direct, Tax shall be laid, unless in Proportion to the Census or Enumeration herein before directed to be taken.

No Tax or Duty shall be laid on Articles exported from any State.

No Preference shall be given by any Regulation of Commerce or Revenue to the Ports of one State over those of another: nor shall Vessels bound to, or from, one State, be obliged to enter, clear, or pay Duties in another.

No Money shall be drawn from the Treasury, but in Consequence of Appropriations made by Law; and a regular Statement and Account of the Receipts and Expenditures of all public Money shall be published from time to time.

No Title of Nobility shall be granted by the United States: And no Person holding any Office of Profit or Trust under them, shall, without the Consent of the Congress, accept of any present, Emolument, Office, or Title, of any kind whatever, from any King, Prince or foreign State.

Section 10. No State shall enter into any Treaty, Alliance, or Confederation; grant Letters of Marque and Reprisal; coin Money; emit Bills of Credit; make any Thing but gold and silver Coin a Tender in Payment of Debts; pass any Bill of Attainder, ex post facto Law, or Law impairing the Obligation of Contracts, or grant any Title of Nobility.

No State shall, without the Consent of the Congress, lay any Imposts or Duties on Imports or Exports, except what may be absolutely necessary for executing it's inspection Laws: and the net Produce of all Duties and Imposts, laid by any State on Imports or Exports, shall be for the Use of the Treasury of the United States; and all such Laws shall be subject to the Revision and Controul of the Congress.

No State shall, without the Consent of Congress, lay any duty of Tonnage, keep Troops, or Ships of War in time of Peace, enter into any Agreement or Compact with another State, or with a foreign Power, or engage in War, unless actually invaded, or in such imminent Danger as will not admit of delay.

ARTICLE II

Section 1. The executive Power shall be vested in a President of the United States of America. He shall hold his Office during the Term of four Years, and, together with the Vice-President chosen for the same Term, be elected, as follows:

Each State shall appoint, in such Manner as the Legislature thereof may direct, a Number of Electors, equal to the whole Number of Senators and Representatives to which the State may be entitled in the Congress: but no Senator or Representative, or Person holding an Office of Trust or Profit under the United States, shall be appointed an Elector.

The Electors shall meet in their respective States, and vote by Ballot for two persons, of whom one at least shall not lie an Inhabitant of the same State with themselves. And they shall make a List of all the Persons voted for, and of the Number of Votes for each; which List they shall sign and certify, and transmit sealed to the Seat of the Government of the United States, directed to the President of the Senate. The President of the Senate shall, in the Presence of the Senate and House of Representatives, open all the Certificates, and the Votes shall then be counted. The Person having the greatest Number of Votes shall be the President, if such Number be a Majority of the whole Number of Electors appointed; and if there be more than one who have such Majority, and have an equal Number of Votes, then the House of Representatives shall immediately chuse by Ballot one of them for President; and if no Person have a Majority, then from the five highest on the List the said House shall in like Manner chuse the President. But in chusing the President, the Votes shall be taken by States, the Representation from each State having one Vote; a quorum for this Purpose shall consist of a Member or Members from two-thirds of the States, and a Majority of all the States shall be necessary to a Choice. In every Case, after the Choice of the President, the Person having the greatest Number of Votes of the Electors shall be the Vice President. But if there should remain two or more who have equal Votes, the Senate shall chuse from them by Ballot the Vice-President.

The Congress may determine the Time of chusing the Electors, and the Day on which they shall give their Votes; which Day shall be the same throughout the United States.

No person except a natural born Citizen, or a Citizen of the United States, at the time of the Adoption of this Constitution, shall be eligible to the Office of President; neither shall any Person be eligible to that Office who shall not have attained to the Age of thirty-five Years, and been fourteen Years a Resident within the United States.

In Case of the Removal of the President from Office, or of his Death, Resignation, or Inability to discharge the Powers and Duties of the said Office, the same shall devolve on the Vice President, and the Congress may by Law provide for the Case of Removal, Death, Resignation or Inability, both of the President and Vice President, declaring what Officer shall then act as President, and such Officer shall act accordingly, until the Disability be removed, or a President shall be elected.

The President shall, at stated Times, receive for his Services, a Compensation, which shall neither be increased nor diminished during the Period for which he shall have been elected, and he shall not receive within that Period any other Emolument from the United States, or any of them.

Before he enter on the Execution of his Office, he shall take the following Oath or Affirmation:

"I do solemnly swear (or affirm) that I will faithfully execute the Office of President of the United States, and will to the best of my Ability, preserve, protect and defend the Constitution of the United States."

Section 2. The President shall be Commander in Chief of the Army and Navy of the United States, and of the Militia of the several States, when called into the actual Service of the United States; he may require the Opinion, in writing, of the principal Officer in each of the executive Departments, upon any subject relating to the Duties of their respective Offices, and he shall have Power to Grant Reprieves and Pardons for Offenses against the United States, except in Cases of Impeachment.

He shall have Power, by and with the Advice and Consent of the Senate, to make Treaties, provided two thirds of the Senators present concur; and he shall nominate, and by and with the Advice and Consent of the Senate, shall appoint Ambassadors, other public Ministers and Consuls, Judges of the supreme Court, and all other Officers of the United States, whose Appointments are not herein otherwise provided for, and which shall be established by Law: but the Congress may by Law vest the Appointment of such inferior Officers, as they think proper, in the President alone, in the Courts of Law, or in the Heads of Departments.

The President shall have Power to fill up all Vacancies that may happen during the Recess of the Senate, by granting Commissions which shall expire at the End of their next Session.

Section 3. He shall from time to time give to the Congress Information of the State of the Union, and recommend to their Consideration such Measures as he shall judge necessary and expedient; he may, on extraordinary Occasions, convene both Houses, or either of them, and in Case of Disagreement between them, with Respect to the Time of Adjournment, he may adjourn them to such Time as he shall think proper; he shall receive Ambassadors and other public Ministers; he shall take Care that the Laws be faithfully executed, and shall Commission all the Officers of the United States.

Section 4. The President, Vice President and all civil Officers of the United States, shall be removed from Office on Impeachment for, and Conviction of, Treason, Bribery, or other high Crimes and Misdemeanors.

ARTICLE III

Section 1. The judicial Power of the United States, shall be vested in one supreme Court, and in such inferior Courts as the Congress may from time to time ordain and establish. The Judges, both of the supreme and inferior Courts, shall hold their Offices during good Behavior, and shall, at stated Times, receive for their Services a Compensation which shall not be diminished during their Continuance in Office.

Section 2. The judicial Power shall extend to all Cases, in Law and Equity, arising under this Constitution, the Laws of the United States, and Treaties made, or which shall be made, under their Authority; to all Cases affecting Ambassadors, other public Ministers and Consuls; to all Cases of admiralty and maritime Jurisdiction; to Controversies to which the United States shall be a Party; to Controversies between two or more States; between a State and Citizens of another State; between Citizens of different States; between Citizens of the same State claiming Lands under Grants of different States, and between a State, or the Citizens thereof, and foreign States, Citizens or Subjects.

In all Cases affecting Ambassadors, other public Ministers and Consuls, and those in which a State shall be Party, the supreme Court shall have original Jurisdiction. In all the other Cases before mentioned, the supreme Court shall have appellate Jurisdiction, both as to Law and Fact, with such Exceptions, and under such Regulations as the Congress shall make.

The Trial of all Crimes, except in Cases of Impeachment, shall be by Jury; and such Trial shall be held in the State where the said Crimes shall have been committed; but when not committed within any State, the Trial shall be at such Place or Places as the Congress may by Law have directed.

Section 3. Treason against the United States, shall consist only in levying War against them, or in adhering to their Enemies, giving them Aid and Comfort. No Person shall be convicted of Treason unless on the Testimony of two Witnesses to the same overt Act, or on Confession in open Court.

The Congress shall have power to declare the Punishment of Treason, but no Attainder of Treason shall work Corruption of Blood, or Forfeiture except during the Life of the Person attainted.

ARTICLE IV

Section 1. Full Faith and Credit shall be given in each State to the public Acts, Records, and judicial Proceedings of every other State. And the Congress may by general Laws prescribe the Manner in which such Acts, Records and Proceedings shall be proved, and the Effect thereof.

Section 2. The Citizens of each State shall be entitled to all Privileges and Immunities of Citizens in the several States.

A Person charged in any State with Treason, Felony, or other Crime, who shall flee from Justice, and be found in another State, shall on demand of the executive Authority of the State from which he fled, be delivered up, to be removed to the State having Jurisdiction of the Crime.

No Person held to Service or Labour in one State, under the Laws thereof, escaping into another, shall, in Consequence of any Law or Regulation therein, be discharged from such Service or Labour, But shall be delivered up on Claim of the Party to whom such Service or Labour may be due.

Section 3. New States may be admitted by the Congress into this Union; but no new States shall be formed or erected within the Jurisdiction of any other State; nor any State be formed by the Junction of two or more States, or parts of States, without the Consent of the Legislatures of the States concerned as well as of the Congress.

The Congress shall have Power to dispose of and make all needful Rules and Regulations respecting the Territory or other Property belonging to the United States; and nothing in this Constitution shall be so construed as to Prejudice any Claims of the United States, or of any particular State.

Section 4. The United States shall guarantee to every State in this Union a Republican Form of Government, and shall protect each of them against Invasion; and on Application of the Legislature, or of the Executive (when the Legislature cannot be convened) against domestic Violence.

ARTICLE V

The Congress, whenever two thirds of both Houses shall deem it necessary, shall propose Amendments to this Constitution, or, on the Application of the Legislatures of two thirds of the several States, shall call a Convention for proposing Amendments, which, in either Case, shall be valid to all Intents and Purposes, as part of this Constitution, when ratified by the Legislatures of three fourths of the several States, or by Conventions in three fourths thereof, as the one or the other Mode of Ratification may be proposed by the Congress; Provided that no Amendment which may be made prior to the Year One thousand eight hundred and eight shall in any Manner affect the first and fourth Clauses in the Ninth Section of the first Article; and that no State, without its Consent, shall be deprived of its equal Suffrage in the Senate.

ARTICLE VI

All Debts contracted and Engagements entered into, before the Adoption of this Constitution, shall be as valid against the United States under this Constitution, as under the Confederation.

This Constitution, and the Laws of the United States which shall be made in Pursuance thereof; and all Treaties made, or which shall be made, under the Authority of the United States, shall be the supreme Law of the Land; and the Judges in every State shall be bound thereby, any Thing in the Constitution or Laws of any State to the Contrary notwithstanding.

The Senators and Representatives before mentioned, and the Members of the several State Legislatures, and all executive and judicial Officers, both of the United States and of the several States, shall be bound by Oath or Affirmation, to support this Constitution; but no religious Test shall ever be required as a Qualification to any Office or public Trust under the United States.

ARTICLE VII

The Ratification of the Conventions of nine States, shall be sufficient for the Establishment of this Constitution between the States so ratifying the Same.

Done in Convention by the Unanimous Consent of the States present the Seventeenth Day of September in the Year of our Lord one thousand seven hundred and Eighty seven and of the Independence of the United States of America the Twelfth. In Witness whereof We have hereunto subscribed our Names.

AMENDMENT I

Congress shall make no law respecting an establishment of religion, or prohibiting the free exercise thereof; or abridging the freedom of speech, or of the press; or the right of the people peaceably to assemble, and to petition the Government for a redress of grievances.

AMENDMENT II

A well regulated Militia, being necessary to the security of a free State, the right of the people to keep and bear Arms, shall not be infringed.

AMENDMENT III

No Soldier shall, in time of peace be quartered in any house, without the consent of the Owner, nor in time of war, but in a manner to be prescribed by law.

AMENDMENT IV

The right of the people to be secure in their persons, houses, papers, and effects, against unreasonable searches and seizures, shall not be violated, and no Warrants shall issue, but upon probable cause, supported by Oath or affirmation, and particularly describing the place to be searched, and the persons or things to be seized.

AMENDMENT V

No person shall be held to answer for a capital, or otherwise infamous crime, unless on a presentment or indictment of a Grand Jury, except in cases arising in the land or naval forces, or in the Militia, when in actual service in time of War or public danger; nor shall any person be subject for the same offense to be twice put in jeopardy of life or limb; nor shall be compelled in any criminal case to be a witness against himself, nor be deprived of life, liberty, or property, without due process of law; nor shall private property be taken for public use, without just compensation.

AMENDMENT VI

In all criminal prosecutions, the accused shall enjoy the right to a speedy and public trial, by an impartial jury of the State and district wherein the crime shall have been committed, which district shall have been previously ascertained by law, and to be informed of the nature and cause of the accusation; to be confronted with the witnesses against him; to have compulsory process for obtaining witnesses in his favor, and to have the Assistance of Counsel for his defence.

AMENDMENT VII

In Suits at common law, where the value in controversy shall exceed twenty dollars, the right of trial by jury shall be preserved, and no fact tried by a jury, shall be otherwise re-examined in any Court of the United States, than according to the rules of the common law.

AMENDMENT VIII

Excessive bail shall not be required, nor excessive fines imposed, nor cruel and unusual punishments inflicted.

AMENDMENT IX

The enumeration in the Constitution, of certain rights, shall not be construed to deny or disparage others retained by the people.

AMENDMENT X

The powers not delegated to the United States by the Constitution, nor prohibited by it to the States, are reserved to the States respectively, or to the people.

AMENDMENT XI

The Judicial power of the United States shall not be construed to extend to any suit in law or equity, commenced or prosecuted against one of the United States by Citizens of another State, or by Citizens or Subjects of any Foreign State.

AMENDMENT XII

The Electors shall meet in their respective states, and vote by ballot for President and Vice-President, one of whom, at least, shall not be an inhabitant of the same state with themselves; they shall name in their ballots the person voted for as President, and in distinct ballots the person voted for as Vice-President, and they shall make distinct lists of all persons voted for as President, and of all persons voted for as Vice-President and of the number of votes for each, which lists they shall sign and certify, and transmit sealed to the seat of the government of the United States, directed to the President of the Senate;

The President of the Senate shall, in the presence of the Senate and House of Representatives, open all the certificates and the votes shall then be counted;

The person having the greatest Number of votes for President, shall be the President, if such number be a majority of the whole number of Electors appointed; and if no person have such majority, then from the persons having the highest numbers not exceeding three on the list of those voted for as President, the House of Representatives shall choose immediately, by ballot, the President. But in choosing the President, the votes shall be taken by states, the representation from each state having one vote; a quorum for this purpose shall consist of a member or members from two-thirds of the states, and a majority of all the states shall be necessary to a choice. And if the House of Representatives shall not choose a President whenever the right of choice shall devolve upon them, before the fourth day of March next following, then the Vice-President shall act as President, as in the case of the death or other constitutional disability of the President.

The person having the greatest number of votes as Vice-President, shall be the Vice-President, if such number be a majority of the whole number of Electors appointed, and if no person have a majority, then from the two highest numbers on the list, the Senate shall choose the Vice-President; a quorum for the purpose shall consist of two-thirds of the whole number of Senators, and a majority of the whole number shall be necessary to a choice. But no person constitutionally ineligible to the office of President shall be eligible to that of Vice-President of the United States.

AMENDMENT XIII

1. Neither slavery nor involuntary servitude, except as a punishment for crime whereof the party shall have been duly convicted, shall exist within the United States, or any place subject to their jurisdiction.

2. Congress shall have power to enforce this article by appropriate legislation.

AMENDMENT XIV

1. All persons born or naturalized in the United States, and subject to the jurisdiction thereof, are citizens of the United States and of the State wherein they reside. No State shall make or enforce any law which shall abridge the privileges or immunities of citizens of the United States; nor shall any State deprive any person of life, liberty, or property, without due process of law; nor deny to any person within its jurisdiction the equal protection of the laws.

2. Representatives shall be apportioned among the several States according to their respective numbers, counting the whole number of persons in each State, excluding Indians not taxed. But when the right to vote at any election for the choice of electors for President and Vice-President of the United States, Representatives in Congress, the Executive and Judicial officers of a State, or the members of the Legislature thereof, is denied to any of the male inhabitants of such State, being twenty-one years of age, and citizens of the United States, or in any way abridged, except for participation in rebellion, or other crime, the basis of representation therein shall be reduced in the proportion which the number of such male citizens shall bear to the whole number of male citizens twenty-one years of age in such State.

3. No person shall be a Senator or Representative in Congress, or elector of President and Vice-President, or hold any office, civil or military, under the United States, or under any State, who, having previously taken an oath, as a member of Congress, or as an officer of the United States, or as a member of any State legislature, or as an executive or judicial officer of any State, to support the Constitution of the United States, shall have engaged in insurrection or rebellion against the same, or given aid or comfort to the enemies thereof. But Congress may by a vote of two-thirds of each House, remove such disability.

4. The validity of the public debt of the United States, authorized by law, including debts incurred for payment of pensions and bounties for services in suppressing insurrection or rebellion, shall not be questioned. But neither the United States nor any State shall assume or pay any debt or obligation incurred in aid of insurrection or rebellion against the United States, or any claim for the loss or emancipation of any slave; but all such debts, obligations and claims shall be held illegal and void.

5. The Congress shall have power to enforce, by appropriate legislation, the provisions of this article.

AMENDMENT XV

1. The right of citizens of the United States to vote shall not be denied or abridged by the United States or by any State on account of race, color, or previous condition of servitude.

2. The Congress shall have power to enforce this article by appropriate legislation.

AMENDMENT XVI

The Congress shall have power to lay and collect taxes on incomes, from whatever source derived, without apportionment among the several States, and without regard to any census or enumeration.

AMENDMENT XVII

The Senate of the United States shall be composed of two Senators from each State, elected by the people thereof, for six years; and each Senator shall have one vote. The electors in each State shall have the qualifications requisite for electors of the most numerous branch of the State legislatures.

When vacancies happen in the representation of any State in the Senate, the executive authority of such State shall issue writs of election to fill such vacancies: Provided, That the legislature of any State may empower the executive thereof to make temporary appointments until the people fill the vacancies by election as the legislature may direct.

This amendment shall not be so construed as to affect the election or term of any Senator chosen before it becomes valid as part of the Constitution.

AMENDMENT XVIII

1. After one year from the ratification of this article the manufacture, sale, or transportation of intoxicating liquors within, the importation thereof into, or the exportation thereof from the United States and all territory subject to the jurisdiction thereof for beverage purposes is hereby prohibited.

2. The Congress and the several States shall have concurrent power to enforce this article by appropriate legislation.

3. This article shall be inoperative unless it shall have been ratified as an amendment to the Constitution by the legislatures of the several States, as provided in the Constitution, within seven years from the date of the submission hereof to the States by the Congress.

AMENDMENT XIX

The right of citizens of the United States to vote shall not be denied or abridged by the United States or by any State on account of sex.

Congress shall have power to enforce this article by appropriate legislation.

AMENDMENT XX

1. The terms of the President and Vice President shall end at noon on the 20th day of January, and the terms of Senators and Representatives at noon on the 3d day of January, of the years in which such terms would have ended if this article had not been ratified; and the terms of their successors shall then begin.

2. The Congress shall assemble at least once in every year, and such meeting shall begin at noon on the 3d day of January, unless they shall by law appoint a different day.

3. If, at the time fixed for the beginning of the term of the President, the President elect shall have died, the Vice President elect shall become President. If a President shall not have been chosen before the time fixed for the beginning of his term, or if the President elect shall have failed to qualify, then the Vice President elect shall act as President until a President shall have qualified; and the Congress may by law provide for the case wherein neither a President elect nor a Vice President elect shall have qualified, declaring who shall then act as President, or the manner in which one who is to act shall be selected, and such person shall act accordingly until a President or Vice President shall have qualified.

4. The Congress may by law provide for the case of the death of any of the persons from whom the House of Representatives may choose a President whenever the right of choice shall have devolved

upon them, and for the case of the death of any of the persons from whom the Senate may choose a Vice President whenever the right of choice shall have devolved upon them.

5. Sections 1 and 2 shall take effect on the 15th day of October following the ratification of this article.

6. This article shall be inoperative unless it shall have been ratified as an amendment to the Constitution by the legislatures of three-fourths of the several States within seven years from the date of its submission.

AMENDMENT XXI

1. The eighteenth article of amendment to the Constitution of the United States is hereby repealed.

2. The transportation or importation into any State, Territory, or possession of the United States for delivery or use therein of intoxicating liquors, in violation of the laws thereof, is hereby prohibited.

3. The article shall be inoperative unless it shall have been ratified as an amendment to the Constitution by conventions in the several States, as provided in the Constitution, within seven years from the date of the submission hereof to the States by the Congress.

AMENDMENT XXII

1. No person shall be elected to the office of the President more than twice, and no person who has held the office of President, or acted as President, for more than two years of a term to which some other person was elected President shall be elected to the office of the President more than once. But this Article shall not apply to any person holding the office of President, when this Article was proposed by the Congress, and shall not prevent any person who may be holding the office of President, or acting as President, during the term within which this Article becomes operative from holding the office of President or acting as President during the remainder of such term.

2. This article shall be inoperative unless it shall have been ratified as an amendment to the Constitution by the legislatures of three-fourths of the several States within seven years from the date of its submission to the States by the Congress.

AMENDMENT XXIII

1. The District constituting the seat of Government of the United States shall appoint in such manner as the Congress may direct: A number of electors of President and Vice President equal to the whole number of Senators and Representatives in Congress to which the District would be entitled if it were a State, but in no event more than the least populous State; they shall be in addition to those appointed by the States, but they shall be considered, for the purposes of the election of President and Vice President, to be electors appointed by a State; and they shall meet in the District and perform such duties as provided by the twelfth article of amendment.

2. The Congress shall have power to enforce this article by appropriate legislation.

AMENDMENT XXIV

1. The right of citizens of the United States to vote in any primary or other election for President or Vice President, for electors for President or Vice President, or for Senator or Representative in Congress, shall not be denied or abridged by the United States or any State by reason of failure to pay any poll tax or other tax.

2. The Congress shall have power to enforce this article by appropriate legislation.

AMENDMENT XXV

1. In case of the removal of the President from office or of his death or resignation, the Vice President shall become President.

2. Whenever there is a vacancy in the office of the Vice President, the President shall nominate a Vice President who shall take office upon confirmation by a majority vote of both Houses of Congress.

3. Whenever the President transmits to the President pro tempore of the Senate and the Speaker of the House of Representatives his written declaration that he is unable to discharge the powers and duties of his office, and until he transmits to them a written declaration to the contrary, such powers and duties shall be discharged by the Vice President as Acting President.

4. Whenever the Vice President and a majority of either the principal officers of the executive departments or of such other body as Congress may by law provide, transmit to the President pro tempore of the Senate and the Speaker of the House of Representatives their written declaration that the President is unable to discharge the powers and duties of his office, the Vice President shall immediately assume the powers and duties of the office as Acting President.

Thereafter, when the President transmits to the President pro tempore of the Senate and the Speaker of the House of Representatives his written declaration that no inability exists, he shall resume the powers and duties of his office unless the Vice President and a majority of either the principal officers of the executive department or of such other body as Congress may by law provide, transmit within four days to the President pro tempore of the Senate and the Speaker of the House of Representatives their written declaration that the President is unable to discharge the powers and duties of his office. Thereupon Congress shall decide the issue, assembling within forty eight hours for that purpose if not in session. If the Congress, within twenty one days after receipt of the latter written declaration, or, if Congress is not in session, within twenty one days after Congress is required to assemble, determines by two thirds vote of both Houses that the President is unable to discharge the powers and duties of his office, the Vice President shall continue to discharge the same as Acting President; otherwise, the President shall resume the powers and duties of his office.

AMENDMENT XXVI

1. The right of citizens of the United States, who are eighteen years of age or older, to vote shall not be denied or abridged by the United States or by any State on account of age.

2. The Congress shall have power to enforce this article by appropriate legislation.

AMENDMENT XXVII

No law, varying the compensation for the services of the Senators and Representatives, shall take effect, until an election of Representatives shall have intervened.

CHAPTER 1. GENERAL PROVISIONS

§ 1. "MARITIME TRANSACTIONS" AND "COMMERCE" DEFINED; EXCEPTIONS TO OPERATION OF TITLE

"Maritime transactions", as herein defined, means charter parties, bills of lading of water carriers, agreements relating to wharfage, supplies furnished vessels or repairs to vessels, collisions, or any other matters in foreign commerce which, if the subject of controversy, would be embraced within admiralty jurisdiction; "commerce", as herein defined, means commerce among the several States or with foreign nations, or in any Territory of the United States or in the District of Columbia, or between any such Territory and another, or between any such Territory and any State or foreign nation, or between the District of Columbia and any State or Territory or foreign nation, but nothing herein contained shall apply to contracts of employment of seamen, railroad employees, or any other class of workers engaged in foreign or interstate commerce.

§ 2. VALIDITY, IRREVOCABILITY, AND ENFORCEMENT OF AGREEMENTS TO ARBITRATE

A written provision in any maritime transaction or a contract evidencing a transaction involving commerce to settle by arbitration a controversy thereafter arising out of such contract or transaction, or the refusal to perform the whole or any part thereof, or an agreement in writing to submit to arbitration an existing controversy arising out of such a contract, transaction, or refusal, shall be valid, irrevocable, and enforceable, save upon such grounds as exist at law or in equity for the revocation of any contract.

§ 3. STAY OF PROCEEDINGS WHERE ISSUE THEREIN REFERABLE TO ARBITRATION

If any suit or proceeding be brought in any of the courts of the United States upon any issue referable to arbitration under an agreement in writing for such arbitration, the court in which such suit is pending, upon being satisfied that the issue involved in such suit or proceeding is referable to arbitration under such an agreement, shall on application of one of the parties stay the trial of the action until such arbitration has been had in accordance with the terms of the agreement, providing the applicant for the stay is not in default in proceeding with such arbitration.

§ 4. FAILURE TO ARBITRATION UNDER AGREEMENT; PETITION TO UNITED STATES COURT HAVING JURISDICTION FOR ORDER TO COMPEL ARBITRATION; NOTICE AND SERVICE THEREOF; HEARING AND DETERMINATION

A party aggrieved by the alleged failure, neglect, or refusal of another to arbitrate under a written agreement for arbitration may petition any United States district court which, save for such agreement, would have jurisdiction under Title 28, in a civil action or in admiralty of the subject matter of a suit arising out of the controversy between the parties, for an order directing that such arbitration proceed in the manner provided for in such agreement. Five days' notice in writing of such application shall be served upon the party in default. Service thereof shall be made in the manner provided by the Federal Rules of Civil Procedure. The court shall hear the parties, and upon being satisfied that the making of the agreement for arbitration or the failure to comply therewith is not in issue, the court shall make an order directing the parties to proceed to arbitration in accordance with the terms of the agreement. The hearing and proceedings, under such agreement, shall be within the district in which the petition for an order directing such arbitration is filed. If the making of the arbitration agreement or the failure, neglect, or refusal to perform the same be in issue, the court shall proceed summarily to the trial thereof. If no jury trial be demanded by the party alleged to be in default, or if the matter in dispute is within admiralty jurisdiction, the court shall hear and determine such issue. Where such an issue is raised, the party alleged to be in default may, except in cases of admiralty, on or before the return day of the notice of application, demand a jury trial of such issue, and upon such demand the court shall make an order referring the issue or issues to a jury in the manner provided by the Federal Rules of Civil Procedure, or may specially call a jury for that purpose. If the jury find that no agreement in writing for arbitration was made or that there is no default in proceeding thereunder, the proceeding shall be dismissed. If the jury find that an agreement for arbitration was made in writing and that there is a default in proceeding thereunder, the court shall make an order summarily directing the parties to proceed with the arbitration in accordance with the terms thereof.

§ 5. APPOINTMENT OF ARBITRATORS OR UMPIRE

If in the agreement provision be made for a method of naming or appointing an arbitrator or arbitrators or an umpire, such method shall be followed; but if no method be provided therein, or if a method be provided and any party thereto shall fail to avail himself of such method, or if for any other reason there shall be a lapse in the naming of an arbitrator or arbitrators or umpire, or in filling a vacancy, then upon the application of either party to the controversy the court shall designate and appoint an arbitrator or arbitrators or umpire, as the case may require, who shall act under the said agreement with the same force and effect as if he or they had been specifically named therein; and unless otherwise provided in the agreement the arbitration shall be by a single arbitrator.

§ 6. APPLICATION HEARD AS MOTION
Any application to the court hereunder shall be made and heard in the manner provided by law for the making and hearing of motions, except as otherwise herein expressly provided.

§ 7. WITNESSES BEFORE ARBITRATORS; FEES; COMPELLING ATTENDANCE
The arbitrators selected either as prescribed in this title or otherwise, or a majority of them, may summon in writing any person to attend before them or any of them as a witness and in a proper case to bring with him or them any book, record, document, or paper which may be deemed material as evidence in the case. The fees for such attendance shall be the same as the fees of witnesses before masters of the United States courts. Said summons shall issue in the name of the arbitrator or arbitrators, or a majority of them, and shall be signed by the arbitrators, or a majority of them, and shall be directed to the said person and shall be served in the same manner as subpoenas to appear and testify before the court; if any person or persons so summoned to testify shall refuse or neglect to obey said summons, upon petition the United States district court for the district in which such arbitrators, or a majority of them, are sitting may compel the attendance of such person or persons before said arbitrator or arbitrators, or punish said person or persons for contempt in the same manner provided by law for securing the attendance of witnesses or their punishment for neglect or refusal to attend in the courts of the United States.

§ 8. PROCEEDINGS BEGUN BY LIBEL IN ADMIRALTY AND SEIZURE OF VESSEL OR PROPERTY
If the basis of jurisdiction be a cause of action otherwise justiciable in admiralty, then, notwithstanding anything herein to the contrary, the party claiming to be aggrieved may begin his proceeding hereunder by libel and seizure of the vessel or other property of the other party according to the usual course of admiralty proceedings, and the court shall then have jurisdiction to direct the parties to proceed with the arbitration and shall retain jurisdiction to enter its decree upon the award.

§ 9. AWARD OF ARBITRATORS; CONFIRMATION; JURISDICTION; PROCEDURE
If the parties in their agreement have agreed that a judgment of the court shall be entered upon the award made pursuant to the arbitration, and shall specify the court, then at any time within one year after the award is made any party to the arbitration may apply to the court so specified for an order confirming the award, and thereupon the court must grant such an order unless the award is vacated, modified, or corrected as prescribed in sections 10 and 11 of this title. If no court is specified in the agreement of the parties, then such application may be made to the United States court in and for the district within which such award was made. Notice of the application shall be served upon the adverse party, and thereupon the court shall have jurisdiction of such party as though he had appeared generally in the proceeding. If the adverse party is a resident of the district within which the award was made, such service shall be made upon the adverse party or his attorney as prescribed by law for service of notice of motion in an action in the same court. If the adverse party shall be a nonresident, then the notice of the application shall be served by the marshal of any district within which the adverse party may be found in like manner as other process of the court.

§ 10. SAME; VACATION; GROUNDS; REHEARING
(a) In any of the following cases the United States court in and for the district wherein the award was made may make an order vacating the award upon the application of any party to the arbitration —

(1) where the award was procured by corruption, fraud, or undue means;

(2) where there was evident partiality or corruption in the arbitrators, or either of them;

(3) where the arbitrators were guilty of misconduct in refusing to postpone the hearing, upon sufficient cause shown, or in refusing to hear evidence pertinent and material to the controversy; or of any other misbehavior by which the rights of any party have been prejudiced; or

(4) where the arbitrators exceeded their powers, or so imperfectly executed them that a mutual, final, and definite award upon the subject matter submitted was not made.

(b) If an award is vacated and the time within which the agreement required the award to be made has not expired, the court may, in its discretion, direct a rehearing by the arbitrators.

(c) The United States district court for the district wherein an award was made that was issued pursuant to section 580 of title 5 may make an order vacating the award upon the application of a person, other than a party to the arbitration, who is adversely affected or aggrieved by the award, if the use of arbitration or the award is clearly inconsistent with the factors set forth in section 572 of title 5.

§ 11. SAME; MODIFICATION OR CORRECTION; GROUNDS; ORDER
In either of the following cases the United States court in and for the district wherein the award was made may make an order modifying or correcting the award upon the application of any party to the arbitration —

(a) Where there was an evident material miscalculation of figures or an evident material mistake in the description of any person, thing, or property referred to in the award.

(b) Where the arbitrators have awarded upon a matter not submitted to them, unless it is a matter not affecting the merits of the decision upon the matter submitted.

(c) Where the award is imperfect in matter of form not affecting the merits of the controversy.

The order may modify and correct the award, so as to effect the intent thereof and promote justice between the parties.

§ 12. NOTICE OF MOTIONS TO VACATE OR MODIFY; SERVICE; STAY OF PROCEEDINGS

Notice of a motion to vacate, modify, or correct an award must be served upon the adverse party or his attorney within three months after the award is filed or delivered. If the adverse party is a resident of the district within which the award was made, such service shall be made upon the adverse party or his attorney as prescribed by law for service of notice of motion in an action in the same court. If the adverse party shall be a nonresident then the notice of the application shall be served by the marshal of any district within which the adverse party may be found in like manner as other process of the court. For the purposes of the motion any judge who might make an order to stay the proceedings in an action brought in the same court may make an order, to be served with the notice of motion, staying the proceedings of the adverse party to enforce the award.

§ 13. PAPERS FILED WITH ORDER ON MOTIONS; JUDGMENT; DOCKETING; FORCE AND EFFECT; ENFORCEMENT

The party moving for an order confirming, modifying, or correcting an award shall, at the time such order is filed with the clerk for the entry of judgment thereon, also file the following papers with the clerk:

(a) The agreement; the selection or appointment, if any, of an additional arbitrator or umpire; and each written extension of the time, if any, within which to make the award.

(b) The award.

(c) Each notice, affidavit, or other paper used upon an application to confirm, modify, or correct the award, and a copy of each order of the court upon such an application.

The judgment shall be docketed as if it was rendered in an action. The judgment so entered shall have the same force and effect, in all respects, as, and be subject to all the provisions of law relating to, a judgment in an action; and it may be enforced as if it had been rendered in an action in the court in which it is entered.

§ 14. CONTRACTS NOT AFFECTED

This title shall not apply to contracts made prior to January 1, 1926.

§ 15. INAPPLICABILITY OF THE ACT OF STATE DOCTRINE

Enforcement of arbitral agreements, confirmation of arbitral awards, and execution upon judgments based on orders confirming such awards shall not be refused on the basis of the Act of State doctrine.

§ 16. APPEALS

(a) An appeal may be taken from—

(1) an order—

(A) refusing a stay of any action under section 3 of this title,

(B) denying a petition under section 4 of this title to order arbitration to proceed,

(C) denying an application under section 206 of this title to compel arbitration,

(D) confirming or denying confirmation of an award or partial award, or

(E) modifying, correcting, or vacating an award;

(2) an interlocutory order granting, continuing, or modifying an injunction against an arbitration that is subject to this title; or

(3) a final decision with respect to an arbitration that is subject to this title.

(b) Except as otherwise provided in section 1292(b) of title 28, an appeal may not be taken from an interlocutory order—

(1) granting a stay of any action under section 3 of this title;

(2) directing arbitration to proceed under section 4 of this title;

(3) compelling arbitration under section 206 of this title; or

(4) refusing to enjoin an arbitration that is subject to this title.

CHAPTER 2. CONVENTION ON THE RECOGNITION AND ENFORCEMENT OF FOREIGN ARBITRAL AWARDS

§ 201. ENFORCEMENT OF CONVENTION

The Convention on the Recognition and Enforcement of Foreign Arbitral Awards of June 10, 1958, shall be enforced in United States courts in accordance with this chapter.

§ 202. AGREEMENT OR AWARD FALLING UNDER THE CONVENTION

An arbitration agreement or arbitral award arising out of a legal relationship, whether contractual or not, which is considered as commercial, including a transaction, contract, or agreement described in section 2 of this title, falls under the Convention. An agreement or award arising out of such a relationship which is entirely between citizens of the United States shall be deemed not to fall under the Convention unless that relationship involves property located abroad, envisages performance or enforcement abroad, or has some other reasonable relation with one or more foreign states. For the purpose of this section a corporation is a citizen of the United States if it is incorporated or has its principal place of business in the United States.

§ 203. JURISDICTION; AMOUNT IN CONTROVERSY

An action or proceeding falling under the Convention shall be deemed to arise under the laws and treaties of the United States. The district courts of the United States (including the courts enumerated in section 460 of title 28) shall have original jurisdiction over such an action or proceeding, regardless of the amount in controversy.

§ 204. VENUE

An action or proceeding over which the district courts have jurisdiction pursuant to section 203 of this title may be brought in any such court in which save for the arbitration agreement an action or proceeding with respect to the controversy between the parties could be brought, or in such court for the district and division which embraces the place designated in the agreement as the place of arbitration if such place is within the United States.

§ 205. REMOVAL OF CASES FROM STATE COURTS

Where the subject matter of an action or proceeding pending in a State court relates to an arbitration agreement or award falling under the Convention, the defendant or the defendants may, at any time before the trial thereof, remove such action or proceeding to the district court of the United States for the district and division embracing the place where the action or proceeding is pending. The procedure for removal of causes otherwise provided by law shall apply, except that the ground for removal provided in this section need not appear on the face of the complaint but may be shown in the petition for removal. For the purposes of Chapter 1 of this title any action or proceeding removed under this section shall be deemed to have been brought in the district court to which it is removed.

§ 206. ORDER TO COMPEL ARBITRATION; APPOINTMENT OF ARBITRATORS

A court having jurisdiction under this chapter may direct that arbitration be held in accordance with the agreement at any place therein provided for, whether that place is within or without the United States. Such court may also appoint arbitrators in accordance with the provisions of the agreement.

§ 207. AWARD OF ARBITRATORS; CONFIRMATION; JURISDICTION; PROCEEDING

Within three years after an arbitral award falling under the Convention is made, any party to the arbitration may apply to any court having jurisdiction under this chapter for an order confirming the award as against any other party to the arbitration. The court shall confirm the award unless it finds one of the grounds for refusal or deferral of recognition or enforcement of the award specified in the said Convention.

§ 208. CHAPTER 1; RESIDUAL APPLICATION

Chapter 1 applies to actions and proceedings brought under this chapter to the extent that chapter is not in conflict with this chapter or the Convention as ratified by the United States.

CHAPTER 3. INTER-AMERICAN CONVENTION ON INTERNATIONAL COMMERCIAL ARBITRATION

§ 301. ENFORCEMENT OF CONVENTION

The Inter-American Convention on International Commercial Arbitration of January 30, 1975, shall be enforced in United States courts in accordance with this chapter.

§ 302. INCORPORATION BY REFERENCE

Sections 202, 203, 204, 205 and 207 of this title shall apply to this chapter as if specifically set forth herein, except that for the purposes of this chapter "the Convention" shall mean the Inter-American Convention.

§ 303. ORDER TO COMPEL ARBITRATION; APPOINTMENT OF ARBITRATORS; LOCALE

(a) A court having jurisdiction under this chapter may direct that arbitration be held in accordance with the agreement at any place therein provided for, whether that place is within or without the United States. The court may also appoint arbitrators in accordance with the provisions of the agreement.

(b) In the event the agreement does not make provision for the place of arbitration or the appointment of arbitrators, the court shall direct that the arbitration shall be held and the arbitrators be appointed in accordance with Article 3 of the Inter-American Convention.

§ 304. RECOGNITION AND ENFORCEMENT OF FOREIGN ARBITRAL DECISIONS AND AWARDS; RECIPROCITY

Arbitral decisions or awards made in the territory of a foreign State shall, on the basis of reciprocity, be recognized and enforced under this chapter only if that State has ratified or acceded to the Inter-American Convention.

§ 305. RELATIONSHIP BETWEEN THE INTER-AMERICAN CONVENTION AND THE CONVENTION ON THE RECOGNITION AND ENFORCEMENT OF FOREIGN ARBITRAL AWARDS OF JUNE 10, 1958

When the requirements for application of both the Inter-American Convention and the Convention on the Recognition and Enforcement of Foreign Arbitral Awards of June 10, 1958, are met, determination as to which Convention applies shall, unless otherwise expressly agreed, be made as follows:

(1) If a majority of the parties to the arbitration agreement are citizens of a State or States that have ratified or acceded to the Inter-American Convention and are member States of the Organization of American States, the Inter-American Convention shall apply.

(2) In all other cases the Convention on the Recognition and Enforcement of Foreign Arbitral Awards of June 10, 1958, shall apply.

§ 306. APPLICABLE RULES OF INTER-AMERICAN COMMERCIAL ARBITRATION COMMISSION

(a) For the purposes of this chapter the rules of procedure of the Inter- American Commercial Arbitration Commission referred to in Article 3 of the Inter-American Convention shall, subject to subsection (b) of this section, be those rules as promulgated by the Commission on July 1, 1988.

(b) In the event the rules of procedure of the Inter-American Commercial Arbitration Commission are modified or amended in accordance with the procedures for amendment of the rules of that Commission, the Secretary of State, by regulation in accordance with section 553 of title 5, consistent with the aims and purposes of this Convention, may prescribe that such modifications or amendments shall be effective for purposes of this chapter.

§ 307. CHAPTER 1; RESIDUAL APPLICATION

Chapter 1 applies to actions and proceedings brought under this chapter to the extent chapter 1 is not in conflict with this chapter or the Inter-American Convention as ratified by the United States.

TITLE 28, JUDICIARY AND JUDICIAL PROCEDURE

PART I. ORGANIZATION OF COURTS

CHAPTER 1. SUPREME COURT

§ 1. NUMBER OF JUSTICES; QUORUM

The Supreme Court of the United States shall consist of a Chief Justice of the United States and eight associate justices, any six of whom shall constitute a quorum.

§ 2. TERMS OF COURT

The Supreme Court shall hold at the seat of government a term of court commencing on the first Monday in October of each year and may hold such adjourned or special terms as may be necessary.

§ 3. VACANCY IN OFFICE OF CHIEF JUSTICE; DISABILITY

Whenever the Chief Justice is unable to perform the duties of his office or the office is vacant, his powers and duties shall devolve upon the associate justice next in precedence who is able to act, until such disability is removed or another Chief Justice is appointed and duly qualified.

§ 4. PRECEDENCE OF ASSOCIATE JUSTICES

Associate justices shall have precedence according to the seniority of their commissions. Justices whose commissions bear the same date shall have precedence according to seniority in age.

CHAPTER 3 COURTS OF APPEALS

§ 41. NUMBER AND COMPOSITION OF CIRCUITS

The thirteen judicial circuits of the United States are constituted as follows:

Circuits	Composition
District of Columbia	District of Columbia
First	Maine, Massachusetts, New Hampshire, Puerto Rico, Rhode Island
Second	Connecticut, New York, Vermont
Third	Delaware, New Jersey, Pennsylvania, Virgin Islands
Fourth	Maryland, North Carolina, South Carolina, Virginia, West Virginia
Fifth	District of the Canal Zone, Louisiana, Mississippi, Texas
Sixth	Kentucky, Michigan, Ohio, Tennessee
Seventh	Illinois, Indiana, Wisconsin

Eighth	Arkansas, Iowa, Minnesota, Missouri, Nebraska, North Dakota, South Dakota
Ninth	Alaska, Arizona, California, Idaho, Montana, Nevada, Oregon, Washington, Guam, Hawaii
Tenth	Colorado, Kansas, New Mexico, Oklahoma, Utah, Wyoming
Eleventh	Alabama, Florida, Georgia
Federal	All Federal judicial districts

§ 43. CREATION AND COMPOSITION OF COURTS

(a) There shall be in each circuit a court of appeals, which shall be a court of record, known as the United States Court of Appeals for the circuit.

(b) Each court of appeals shall consist of the circuit judges of the circuit in regular active service. The circuit justice and justices or judges designated or assigned shall be competent to sit as judges of the court.

CHAPTER 5. DISTRICT COURTS

§ 132. CREATION AND COMPOSITION OF DISTRICT COURTS

(a) There shall be in each judicial district a district court which shall be a court of record known as the United States District Court for the district.

(b) Each district court shall consist of the district judge or judges for the district in regular active service. Justices or judges designated or assigned shall be competent to sit as judges of the court.

(c) Except as otherwise provided by law, or rule or order of court, the judicial power of a district court with respect to any action, suit or proceeding may be exercised by a single judge, who may preside alone and hold a regular or special session of court at the same time other sessions are held by other judges.

CHAPTER 15. CONFERENCES AND COUNCILS OF JUDGES

§ 331. JUDICIAL CONFERENCE OF THE UNITED STATES

The Chief Justice of the United States shall summon annually the chief judge of each judicial circuit, the chief judge of the Court of International Trade, and a district judge from each judicial circuit to a conference at such time and place in the United States as he may designate. He shall preside at such conference which shall be known as the Judicial Conference of the United States. Special sessions of the Conference may be called by the Chief Justice at such times and places as he may designate.

The district judge to be summoned from each judicial circuit shall be chosen by the circuit and district judges of the circuit and shall serve as a member of the Judicial Conference of the United States for a term of not less than 3 successive years nor more than 5 successive years, as established by majority vote of all circuit and district judges of the circuit. A district judge serving as a member of the Judicial Conference may be either a judge in regular active service or a judge retired from regular active service under section 371(b) of this title.

If the chief judge of any circuit, the chief judge of the Court of International Trade, or the district judge chosen by the judges of the circuit is unable to attend, the Chief Justice may summon any other circuit or district judge from such circuit or any other judge of the Court of International Trade, as the case may be. Every judge summoned shall attend and, unless excused by the Chief Justice, shall remain throughout the sessions of the conference and advise as to the needs of his circuit or court and as to any matters in respect of which the administration of justice in the courts of the United States may be improved.

The Conference shall make a comprehensive survey of the condition of business in the courts of the United States and prepare plans for assignment of judges to or from circuits or districts where necessary. It shall also submit suggestions and recommendations to the various courts to promote uniformity of management procedures and the expeditious conduct of court business. The Conference is authorized to exercise the authority provided in chapter 16 of this title as the Conference, or through a standing committee. If the Conference elects to establish a standing committee, it shall be appointed by the Chief Justice and all petitions for review shall be reviewed by that committee. The Conference or the standing committee may hold hearings, take sworn testimony, issue subpoenas and subpoenas duces tecum, and make necessary and appropriate orders in the exercise of its authority. Subpoenas and subpoenas duces tecum shall be issued by the clerk of the Supreme Court or by the clerk of any court of appeals, at the direction of the Chief Justice or his designee and under the seal of the court, and shall be served in the manner provided in rule 45(c) of the Federal Rules of Civil Procedure for subpoenas and subpoenas duces tecum issued on behalf of the United States or an officer or any agency thereof. The Conference may also prescribe and modify rules for the exercise of the authority provided in chapter 16 of this title. All judicial officers and employees of the United States shall promptly carry into effect all orders of the Judicial Conference or the standing committee established pursuant to this section.

The Conference shall also carry on a continuous study of the operation and effect of the general rules of practice and procedure now or hereafter in use as prescribed by the Supreme Court for the other courts of the United States pursuant to law. Such changes in and additions to those rules as the Conference may deem desirable to promote simplicity in procedure, fairness in administration, the just determination of litigation, and the elimination of unjustifiable expense and delay shall be recommended by the Conference from time to time to the Supreme Court for its consideration and adoption, modification or rejection, in accordance with law.

The Judicial Conference shall review rules prescribed under section 2071 of this title by the courts, other than the Supreme Court and the district courts, for consistency with Federal law. The Judicial Conference may modify or abrogate any such rule so reviewed found inconsistent in the course of such a review.

The Attorney General shall, upon request of the Chief Justice, report to such Conference on matters relating to the business of the several courts of the United States, with particular reference to cases to which the United States is a party.

The Chief Justice shall submit to Congress an annual report of the proceedings of the Judicial Conference and its recommendations for legislation.

The Judicial Conference shall consult with the Director of United States Marshals Service on a continuing basis regarding the security requirements for the judicial branch of the United States Government, to ensure that the views of the Judicial Conference regarding the security requirements for the judicial branch of the Federal Government are taken into account when determining staffing levels, setting priorities for programs regarding judicial security, and allocating judicial security resources. In this paragraph, the term "judicial security" includes the security of buildings housing the judiciary, the personal security of judicial officers, the assessment of threats made to judicial officers, and the protection of all other judicial personnel. The United States Marshals Service retains final authority regarding security requirements for the judicial branch of the Federal Government.

CHAPTER 23. CIVIL JUSTICE EXPENSE AND DELAY REDUCTION PLANS

§ 471. REQUIREMENT FOR A DISTRICT COURT CIVIL JUSTICE EXPENSE AND DELAY REDUCTION PLAN

There shall be implemented by each United States district court, in accordance with this chapter, a civil justice expense and delay reduction plan. The plan may be a plan developed by such district court or a model plan developed by the Judicial Conference of the United States. The purposes of each plan are to facilitate deliberate adjudication of civil cases on the merits, monitor discovery, improve litigation management, and ensure just, speedy, and inexpensive resolutions of civil disputes.

PART III. COURT OFFICERS AND EMPLOYEES

CHAPTER 43. UNITED STATES MAGISTRATE JUDGES

§ 631. APPOINTMENT AND TENURE

(a) The judges of each United States district court and the district courts of the Virgin Islands, Guam, and the Northern Mariana Islands (including any judge in regular active service and any judge who has retired from regular active service under section 371(b) of this title, when designated and assigned to the court to which such judge was appointed) shall appoint United States magistrate judges in such numbers and to serve at such locations within the judicial districts as the Judicial Conference may determine under this chapter. In the case of a magistrate judge appointed by the district court of the Virgin Islands, Guam, or the Northern Mariana Islands, this chapter shall apply as though the court appointing such a magistrate judge were a United States district court. Where there is more than one judge of a district court, the appointment, whether an original appointment or a reappointment, shall be by the concurrence of a majority of all the judges of such district court, and when there is no such concurrence, then by the chief judge. Where the conference deems it desirable, a magistrate judge may be designated to serve in one or more districts adjoining the district for which he is appointed. Such a designation shall be made by the concurrence of a majority of the judges of each of the district courts involved and shall specify the duties to be performed by the magistrate judge in the adjoining district or districts.

(b) No individual may be appointed or reappointed to serve as a magistrate judge under this chapter unless:

(1) He has been for at least five years a member in good standing of the bar of the highest court of a State, the District of Columbia, the Commonwealth of Puerto Rico, the Territory of Guam, the Commonwealth of the Northern Mariana Islands, or the Virgin Islands of the United States, except that an individual who does not meet the bar membership requirements of this paragraph may be appointed and serve as a part-time magistrate judge if the appointing court or courts and the conference find that no qualified individual who is a member of the bar is available to serve at a specific location;

(2) He is determined by the appointing district court or courts to be competent to perform the duties of the office;

(3) In the case of an individual appointed to serve in a national park, he resides within the exterior boundaries of that park, or at some place reasonably adjacent thereto;

(4) He is not related by blood or marriage to a judge of the appointing court or courts at the time of

his initial appointment; and

(5) He is selected pursuant to standards and procedures promulgated by the Judicial Conference of the United States. Such standards and procedures shall contain provision for public notice of all vacancies in magistrate judge positions and for the establishment by the district courts of merit selection panels, composed of residents of the individual judicial districts, to assist the courts in identifying and recommending persons who are best qualified to fill such positions.

(c) A magistrate judge may hold no other civil or military office or employment under the United States: Provided, however, That, with the approval of the conference, a part-time referee in bankruptcy or a clerk or deputy clerk of a court of the United States may be appointed and serve as a part-time United States magistrate judge, but the conference shall fix the aggregate amount of compensation to be received for performing the duties of part-time magistrate judge and part-time referee in bankruptcy, clerk or deputy clerk: And provided further, That retired officers and retired enlisted personnel of the Regular and Reserve components of the Army, Navy, Air Force, Marine Corps, and Coast Guard, members of the Reserve components of the Army, Navy, Air Force, Marine Corps, and Coast Guard, and members of the Army National Guard of the United States, the Air National Guard of the United States, and the Naval Militia and of the National Guard of a State, territory, or the District of Columbia, except the National Guard disbursing officers who are on a full-time salary basis, may be appointed and serve as United States magistrate judges.

(d) Except as otherwise provided in section 375 and 636(h) of this title, no individual may serve under this chapter after having attained the age of seventy years: Provided, however, That upon a majority vote of all the judges of the appointing court or courts, which is taken upon the magistrate judge's attaining age seventy and upon each subsequent anniversary thereof, a magistrate judge who has attained the age of seventy years may continue to serve and may be reappointed under this chapter.

(e) The appointment of any individual as a full-time magistrate judge shall be for a term of eight years, and the appointment of any individuals as a part- time magistrate judge shall be for a term of four years, except that the term of a full-time or part-time magistrate judge appointed under subsection (k) shall expire upon—

(1) the expiration of the absent magistrate judge's term,

(2) the reinstatement of the absent magistrate judge in regular service in office as a magistrate judge,

(3) the failure of the absent magistrate judge to make timely application under subsection (j) of this section for reinstatement in regular service in office as a magistrate judge after discharge or release from military service,

(4) the death or resignation of the absent magistrate judge, or

(5) the removal from office of the absent magistrate judge pursuant to subsection (i) of this section, whichever may first occur.

(f) Upon the expiration of his term, a magistrate judge may, by a majority vote of the judges of the appointing district court or courts and with the approval of the judicial council of the circuit, continue to perform the duties of his office until his successor is appointed, or for 180 days after the date of the expiration of the magistrate judge's term, whichever is earlier.

(g) Each individual appointed as a magistrate judge under this section shall take the oath or affirmation prescribed by section 453 of this title before performing the duties of his office.

(h) Each appointment made by a judge or judges of a district court shall be entered of record in such court, and notice of such appointment shall be given at once by the clerk of that court to the Director.

(i) Removal of a magistrate judge during the term for which he is appointed shall be only for incompetency, misconduct, neglect of duty, or physical or mental disability, but a magistrate judge's office shall be terminated if the conference determines that the services performed by his office are no longer needed. Removal shall be by the judges of the district court for the judicial district in which the magistrate judge serves; where there is more than one judge of a district court, removal shall not occur unless a majority of all the judges of such court concur in the order of removal; and when there is a tie vote of the judges of the district court on the question of the removal or retention in office of a magistrate judge, then removal shall be only by a concurrence of a majority of all the judges of the council. In the case of a magistrate judge appointed under the third sentence of subsection (a) of this section, removal shall not occur unless a majority of all the judges of the appointing district courts concur in the order of removal; and where there is a tie vote on the question of the removal or retention in office of a magistrate judge, then removal shall be only by a concurrence of a majority of all the judges of the council or councils. Before any order or removal shall be entered, a full specification of the charges shall be furnished to the magistrate judge, and he shall be accorded by the judge or judges of the removing court, courts, council, or councils an opportunity to be heard on the charges.

(j) Upon the grant by the appropriate district court or courts of a leave of absence to a magistrate judge entitled to such relief under chapter 43 of title 38, such court or courts may proceed to appoint, in the manner specified in subsection (a) of this section, another magistrate judge, qualified for appointment and service under subsections (b), (c), and (d) of this section, who shall serve for the period specified in subsection (e) of this section.

(k) A United States magistrate judge appointed under this chapter shall be exempt from the provisions of subchapter I of chapter 63 of title 5.

§ 632. CHARACTER OF SERVICE

(a) Full-time United States magistrate judges may not engage in the practice of law, and may not engage in any other business, occupation, or employment inconsistent with the expeditious, proper, and impartial performance of their duties as judicial officers.

(b) Part-time United States magistrate judges shall render such service as judicial officers as is required by law. While so serving they may engage in the practice of law, but may not serve as counsel in any criminal action in any court of the United States, nor act in any capacity that is, under such regulations as the conference may establish, inconsistent with the proper discharge of their office. Within such restrictions, they may engage in any other business, occupation, or employment which is not inconsistent with the expeditious, proper, and impartial performance of their duties as judicial officers.

§ 636. JURISDICTION, POWERS, AND TEMPORARY ASSIGNMENT

(a) Each United States magistrate judge serving under this chapter shall have within the district court in which sessions are held by the court that appointed the magistrate judge, at other places where that court may function, and elsewhere as authorized by law —

(1) all powers and duties conferred or imposed upon United States commissioners by law or by the Rules of Criminal Procedure for the United States District Courts;

(2) the power to administer oaths and affirmations, issue orders pursuant to section 3142 of title 18 concerning release or detention of persons pending trial, and take acknowledgements, affidavits, and depositions;

(3) the power to conduct trials under section 3401, title 18, United States Code, in conformity with and subject to the limitations of that section;

(4) the power to enter a sentence for a petty offense; and

(5) the power to enter a sentence for a class A misdemeanor in a case in which the parties have consented.

(b) (1) Notwithstanding any provision of law to the contrary:

(A) a judge may designate a magistrate judge to hear and determine any pretrial matter pending before the court, except a motion for injunctive relief, for judgment on the pleadings, for summary judgment, to dismiss or quash an indictment or information made by the defendant, to suppress evidence in a criminal case, to dismiss or to permit maintenance of a class action, to dismiss for failure to state a claim upon which relief can be granted, and to involuntarily dismiss an action. A judge of the court may reconsider any pretrial matter under this subparagraph (A) where it has been shown that the magistrate judge's order is clearly erroneous or contrary to law.

(B) a judge may also designate a magistrate judge to conduct hearings, including evidentiary hearings, and to submit to a judge of the court proposed findings of fact and recommendations for the disposition, by a judge of the court, of any motion excepted in subparagraph (A), of applications for posttrial relief made by individuals convicted of criminal offenses and of prisoner petitions challenging conditions of confinement.

(C) the magistrate judge shall file his proposed findings and recommendations under subparagraph (B) with the court and a copy shall forthwith be mailed to all parties.

Within ten days after being served with a copy, any party may serve and file written objections to such proposed findings and recommendations as provided by rules of court. A judge of the court shall make a de novo determination of those portions of the report or specified proposed findings or recommendations to which objection is made. A judge of the court may accept, reject, or modify, in whole or in part, the findings or recommendations made by the magistrate judge. The judge may also receive further evidence or recommit the matter to the magistrate judge with instructions.

(2) A judge may designate a magistrate judge to serve as a special master pursuant to the applicable provisions of this title and the Federal Rules of Civil Procedure for the United States district courts. A judge may designate a magistrate judge to serve as a special master in any civil case, upon consent of the parties, without regard to the provisions of rule 53(b) of the Federal Rules of Civil Procedure for the United States district courts.

(3) A magistrate judge may be assigned such additional duties as are not inconsistent with the Constitution and laws of the United States.

(4) Each district court shall establish rules pursuant to which the magistrate judges shall discharge their duties.

(c) Notwithstanding any provision of law to the contrary:

(1) Upon the consent of the parties, a full-time United States magistrate judge or a part-time United States magistrate judge who serves as a full-time judicial officer may conduct any or all proceedings in a jury or nonjury civil matter and order the entry of judgment in the case, when specially designated to exercise such jurisdiction by the district court or courts he serves. Upon the consent of the parties, pursuant to their specific written request, any other part-time magistrate judge may exercise such jurisdiction, if such magistrate judge meets the bar membership requirements set forth in section 631(b)(1) and the chief judge of the district court certifies that a full-time magistrate judge is not reasonably available in accordance with guidelines established by the judicial council of the circuit. When there is more than one judge of a district court, designation under this paragraph shall be by the concurrence of a majority of all the judges of such district court, and when there is no such concurrence, then by the chief judge.

(2) If a magistrate judge is designated to exercise civil jurisdiction under paragraph (1) of this subsection, the clerk of court shall, at the time the action is filed, notify the parties of the availability of a magistrate judge to exercise such jurisdiction. The decision of the parties shall be communicated to the clerk of court. Thereafter, either the district court judge or the magistrate judge may again advise the parties of the availability of the magistrate judge, but in so doing, shall also advise the parties that they are free to withhold consent without adverse substantive consequences. Rules of court for the reference of civil matters to magistrate judges shall include procedures to protect the voluntariness of the parties' consent.

(3) Upon entry of judgment in any case referred under paragraph (1) of this subsection, an aggrieved party may appeal directly to the appropriate United States court of appeals from the judgment of the magistrate judge in the same manner as an appeal from any other judgment of a district court. The consent of the parties allows a magistrate judge designated to exercise civil jurisdiction under paragraph (1) of this subsection to direct the entry of a judgment of the district court in accordance with the Federal Rules of Civil Procedure. Nothing in this paragraph shall be construed as a limitation of any party's right to seek review by the Supreme Court of the United States.

(4) The court may, for good cause shown on its own motion, or under extraordinary circumstances shown by any party, vacate a reference of a civil matter to a magistrate judge under this subsection.

(5) The magistrate judge shall, subject to guidelines of the Judicial Conference, determine whether the record taken pursuant to this section shall be taken by electronic sound recording, by a court reporter, or by other means.

(d) The practice and procedure for the trial of cases before officers serving under this chapter shall conform to rules promulgated by the Supreme Court pursuant to section 2072 of this title.

(e) Contempt authority:

(1) In general. A United States magistrate judge serving under this chapter shall have within the territorial jurisdiction prescribed by the appointment of such magistrate judge the power to exercise contempt authority as set forth in this subsection.

(2) Summary criminal contempt authority. A magistrate judge shall have the power to punish summarily by fine or imprisonment, or both, such contempt of the authority of such magistrate judge constituting misbehavior of any person in the magistrate judge's presence so as to obstruct the administration of justice. The order of contempt shall be issued under the Federal Rules of Criminal Procedure.

(3) Additional criminal contempt authority in civil consent and misdemeanor cases. In any case in which a United States magistrate judge presides with the consent of the parties under subsection (c) of this section, and in any misdemeanor case proceeding before a magistrate judge under section 3401 of title 18, the magistrate judge shall have the power to punish, by fine or imprisonment, or both, criminal contempt constituting disobedience or resistance to the magistrate judge's lawful writ, process, order, rule, decree, or command. Disposition of such contempt shall be conducted upon notice and hearing under the Federal Rules of Criminal Procedure.

(4) Civil contempt authority in civil consent and misdemeanor cases. In any case in which a United States magistrate judge presides with the consent of the parties under subsection (c) of this section, and in any misdemeanor case proceeding before a magistrate judge under section 3401 of title 18, the magistrate judge may exercise the civil contempt authority of the district court. This paragraph shall not be construed to limit the authority of a magistrate judge to order sanctions under any other statute, the Federal Rules of Civil Procedure, or the Federal Rules of Criminal Procedure.

(5) Criminal contempt penalties. The sentence imposed by a magistrate judge for any criminal contempt provided for in paragraphs (2) and (3) shall not exceed the penalties for a Class C misdemeanor as set forth in sections 3581(b)(8) and 3571(b)(6) of title 18.

(6) Certification of other contempts to the district court. Upon the commission of any such act:

(A) in any case in which a United States magistrate judge presides with the consent of the parties under subsection (c) of this section, or in any misdemeanor case proceeding before a magistrate judge under section 3401 of title 18, that may, in the opinion of the magistrate judge, constitute a serious criminal contempt punishable by penalties exceeding those set forth in paragraph (5) of this subsection, or

(B) in any other case or proceeding under subsection (a) or (b) of this section, or any other statute, where:

(i) the act committed in the magistrate judge's presence may, in the opinion of the magistrate judge, constitute a serious criminal contempt punishable by penalties exceeding those set forth in paragraph (5) of this subsection,

(ii) the act that constitutes a criminal contempt occurs outside the presence of the magistrate judge, or

(iii) the act constitutes a civil contempt,

the magistrate judge shall forthwith certify the facts to a district judge and may serve or cause to be served, upon any person whose behavior is brought into question under this paragraph, an order requiring such person to appear before a district judge upon a day certain to show cause why that person should not be adjudged in contempt by reason of the facts so certified. The district judge shall thereupon hear the evidence as to the act or conduct complained of and, if it is such as to warrant punishment, punish such person in the same manner and to the same extent as for a contempt committed before a district judge.

(7) Appeals of magistrate judge contempt orders. The appeal of an order of contempt under this subsection shall be made to the court of appeals in cases proceeding under subsection (c) of this section. The appeal of any other order of contempt issued under this section shall be made to the district court.

(f) In an emergency and upon the concurrence of the chief judges of the districts involved, a United States magistrate judge may be temporarily assigned to perform any of the duties specified in subsection (a), (b), or (c) of this section in a judicial district other than the judicial district for which he has been appointed. No magistrate judge shall perform any of such duties in a district to which he has been temporarily assigned until an order has been issued by the chief judge of such district specifying (1) the emergency by reason of which he has been transferred, (2) the duration of his assignment, and (3) the duties which he is authorized to perform. A magistrate judge so assigned shall not be entitled to additional compensation but shall be reimbursed for actual and necessary expenses incurred in the performance of his duties in accordance with section 635.

(g) A United States magistrate judge may perform the verification function required by section 4107 of title 18, United States Code. A magistrate judge may be assigned by a judge of any United States district court to perform the verification required by section 4108 and the appointment of counsel authorized by section 4109 of title 18, United States Code, and may perform such functions beyond the territorial limits of the United States. A magistrate judge assigned such functions shall have no authority to perform any other function within the territory of a foreign country.

(h) A United States magistrate judge who has retired may, upon the consent of the chief judge of the district involved, be recalled to serve as a magistrate judge in any judicial district by the judicial council of the circuit within which such district is located. Upon recall, a magistrate judge may receive a salary for such service in accordance with regulations promulgated by the Judicial Conference, subject to the restrictions on the payment of an annuity set forth in section 377 of this title or in subchapter III of chapter 83, and chapter 84, of title 5 which are applicable to such magistrate judge. The requirements set forth in subsections (a), (b)(3), and (d) of section 631, and paragraph (1) of subsection (b) of such section to the extent such paragraph requires membership of the bar of the location in which an individual is to serve as a magistrate judge, shall not apply to the recall of a retired magistrate judge under this subsection or section 375 of this title. Any other requirement set forth in section 631(b) shall apply to the recall of a retired magistrate judge under this subsection or section 375 of this title unless such retired magistrate judge met such requirement upon appointment or reappointment as a magistrate judge under section 361.

CHAPTER 44. ALTERNATIVE DISPUTE RESOLUTION

§ 651. AUTHORIZATION OF ALTERNATIVE DISPUTE RESOLUTION

(a) Definition. For purposes of this chapter, an alternative dispute resolution process includes any process or procedure, other than an adjudication by a presiding judge, in which a neutral third party participates to assist in the resolution of issues in controversy, through processes such as early neutral evaluation, mediation, minitrial, and arbitration as provided in sections 654 through 658.

(b) Authority. Each United States district court shall authorize, by local rule adopted under section 2071(a), the use of alternative dispute resolution processes in all civil actions, including adversary proceedings in bankruptcy, in accordance with this chapter, except that the use of arbitration may be authorized only as provided in section 654. Each United States district court shall devise and implement its own alternative dispute resolution program, by local rule adopted under section 2071(a), to encourage and promote the use of alternative dispute resolution in its district.

(c) Existing alternative dispute resolution programs. In those courts where an alternative dispute resolution program is in place on the date of the enactment of the Alternative Dispute Resolution Act of 1998, the court shall examine the effectiveness of that program and adopt such improvements to the program as are consistent with the provisions and purposes of this chapter [28 U.S.C.A. § 651 et seq.].

(d) Administration of alternative dispute resolution programs. Each United States district court shall designate an employee, or a judicial officer, who is knowledgeable in alternative dispute resolution practices and processes to implement, administer, oversee, and evaluate the court's alternative dispute resolution program. Such person may also be responsible for recruiting, screening, and training attorneys to serve as neutrals and arbitrators in the court's alternative dispute resolution program.

(e) Title 9 not affected. This chapter [28 U.S.C.A. § 651 et seq.] shall not affect title 9, United States Code.

(f) Program support. The Federal Judicial Center and the Administrative Office of the United States Courts are authorized to assist the district courts in the establishment and improvement of alternative dispute resolution programs by identifying particular practices employed in successful programs and providing additional assistance as needed and appropriate.

§ 652. JURISDICTION

(a) Consideration of alternative dispute resolution in appropriate cases. Notwithstanding any provision of law to the contrary and except as provided in subsections (b) and (c), each district court shall, by local rule adopted under section 2071(a), require that litigants in all civil cases consider the use of an alternative dispute resolution process at an appropriate stage in the litigation. Each district court shall provide litigants in all civil cases with at least one alternative dispute resolution process, including, but not limited to, mediation, early neutral evaluation, minitrial, and arbitration as authorized in sections 654 through 658. Any district court that elects to require the use of alternative dispute resolution in certain cases may do so only with respect to mediation, early neutral evaluation, and, if the parties consent, arbitration.

(b) Actions exempted from consideration of alternative dispute resolution. Each district court may exempt from the requirements of this section specific cases or categories of cases in which use of alternative dispute resolution would not be appropriate. In defining these exemptions, each district court shall consult with members of the bar, including the United States Attorney for that district.

(c) Authority of the Attorney General. Nothing in this section shall alter or conflict with the authority of the Attorney General to conduct litigation on behalf of the United States, with the authority of any Federal agency authorized to conduct litigation in the United States courts, or with any delegation of litigation authority by the Attorney General.

(d) Confidentiality provisions. Until such time as rules are adopted under chapter 131 of this title [28 U.S.C.A. § 2071 et seq.] providing for the confidentiality of alternative dispute resolution processes under this chapter [28 U.S.C.A. § 651 et seq.], each district court shall, by local rule adopted under section 2071(a), provide for the confidentiality of the alternative dispute resolution processes and to prohibit disclosure of confidential dispute resolution communications.

§ 653. NEUTRALS

(a) Panel of neutrals. Each district court that authorizes the use of alternative dispute resolution processes shall adopt appropriate processes for making neutrals available for use by the parties for each category of process offered. Each district court shall promulgate its own procedures and criteria for the selection of neutrals on its panels.

(b) Qualifications and training. Each person serving as a neutral in an alternative dispute resolution process should be qualified and trained to serve as a neutral in the appropriate alternative dispute resolution process. For this purpose, the district court may use, among others, magistrate judges who have been trained to serve as neutrals in alternative dispute resolution processes, professional neutrals from the private sector, and persons who have been trained to serve as neutrals in alternative dispute resolution processes. Until such time as rules are adopted under chapter 131 of this title [28 U.S.C.A. § 2071 et seq.] relating to the disqualification of neutrals, each district court shall issue rules under section 2071(a) relating to the disqualification of neutrals (including, where appropriate, disqualification under section 455 of this title, other applicable law, and professional responsibility standards).

§ 654. ARBITRATION

(a) Referral of actions to arbitration. Notwithstanding any provision of law to the contrary and except as provided in subsections (a), (b), and (c) of section 652 and subsection (d) of this section, a district court may allow the referral to arbitration of any civil action (including any adversary proceeding in bankruptcy) pending before it when the parties consent, except that referral to arbitration may not be made where:

    (1) the action is based on an alleged violation of a right secured by the Constitution of the United States;

    (2) jurisdiction is based in whole or in part on section 1343 of this title; or

    (3) the relief sought consists of money damages in an amount greater than $150,000.

(b) Safeguards in consent cases. Until such time as rules are adopted under chapter 131 of this title relating to procedures described in this subsection, the district court shall, by local rule adopted under section 2071(a), establish procedures to ensure that any civil action in which arbitration by consent is allowed under subsection (a):

(1) consent to arbitration is freely and knowingly obtained; and

(2) no party or attorney is prejudiced for refusing to participate in arbitration.

(c) Presumptions. For purposes of subsection (a)(3), a district court may presume damages are not in excess of $150,000 unless counsel certifies that damages exceed such amount.

(d) Existing programs. Nothing in this chapter is deemed to affect any program in which arbitration is conducted pursuant to section [sic] title IX of the Judicial Improvements and Access to Justice Act (Public Law 100-702), as amended by section 1 of Public Law 105-53.

§ 655. ARBITRATORS

(a) Powers of arbitrators. An arbitrator to whom an action is referred under section 654 shall have the power, within the judicial district of the district court which referred the action to arbitration:

(1) to conduct arbitration hearings;

(2) to administer oaths and affirmations; and

(3) to make awards.

(b) Standards for certification. Each district court that authorizes arbitration shall establish standards for the certification of arbitrators and shall certify arbitrators to perform services in accordance with such standards and this chapter. The standards shall include provisions requiring that any arbitrator:

(1) shall take the oath or affirmation described in section 453; and

(2) shall be subject to the disqualification rules under section 455.

(c) Immunity. All individuals serving as arbitrators in an alternative dispute resolution program under this chapter are performing quasi-judicial functions and are entitled to the immunities and protections that the law accords to persons serving in such capacity.

§ 656. SUBPOENAS

Rule 45 of the Federal Rules of Civil Procedure (relating to subpoenas) applies to subpoenas for the attendance of witnesses and the production of documentary evidence at an arbitration hearing under this chapter.

§ 657. ARBITRATION AWARD AND JUDGMENT

(a) Filing and effect of arbitration award. An arbitration award made by an arbitrator under this chapter, along with proof of service of such award on the other party by the prevailing party or by the plaintiff, shall be filed promptly after the arbitration hearing is concluded with the clerk of the district court that referred the case to arbitration. Such award shall be entered as the judgment of the court after the time has expired for requesting a trial de novo. The judgment so entered shall be subject to the same provisions of law and shall have the same force and effect as a judgment of the court in a civil action, except that the judgment shall not be subject to review in any other court by appeal or otherwise.

(b) Sealing of arbitration award. The district court shall provide, by local rule adopted under section 2071(a), that the contents of any arbitration award made under this chapter shall not be made known to any judge who might be assigned to the case until the district court has entered final judgment in the action or the action has otherwise terminated.

(c) Trial de novo of arbitration awards.

(1) Time for filing demand. Within 30 days after the filing of an arbitration award with a district court under subsection (a), any party may file a written demand for a trial de novo in the district court.

(2) Action restored to court docket. Upon a demand for a trial de novo, the action shall be restored to the docket of the court and treated for all purposes as if it had not been referred to arbitration.

(3) Exclusion of evidence of arbitration. The court shall not admit at the trial de novo any evidence that there has been an arbitration proceeding, the nature or amount of any award, or any other matter concerning the conduct of the arbitration proceeding, unless:

(A) the evidence would otherwise be admissible in the court under the Federal Rules of Evidence; or

(B) the parties have otherwise stipulated.

§ 658. COMPENSATION OF ARBITRATORS AND NEUTRALS

(a) Compensation. The district court shall, subject to regulations approved by the Judicial Conference of the United States, establish the amount of compensation, if any, that each arbitrator or neutral shall receive for services rendered in each case under this chapter.

(b) Transportation allowances. Under regulations prescribed by the Director of the Administrative Office of the United States Courts, a district court may reimburse arbitrators and other neutrals for actual transportation expenses necessarily incurred in the performance of duties under this chapter.

PART IV. JURISDICTION AND VENUE

CHAPTER 81. SUPREME COURT

§ 1251. ORIGINAL JURISDICTION

(a) The Supreme Court shall have original and exclusive jurisdiction of all controversies between two or more States.

(b) The Supreme Court shall have original but not exclusive jurisdiction of:

(1) All actions or proceedings to which ambassadors, other public ministers, consuls, or vice consuls of foreign states are parties;

(2) All controversies between the United States and a State;

(3) All actions or proceedings by a State against the citizens of another State or against aliens.

§ 1253. DIRECT APPEALS FROM DECISIONS OF THREE-JUDGE COURTS

Except as otherwise provided by law, any party may appeal to the Supreme Court from an order granting or denying, after notice and hearing, an interlocutory or permanent injunction in any civil action, suit or proceeding required by any Act of Congress to be heard and determined by a district court of three judges.

§ 1254. COURTS OF APPEALS; CERTIORARI; CERTIFIED QUESTIONS

Cases in the courts of appeals may be reviewed by the Supreme Court by the following methods:

(1) By writ of certiorari granted upon the petition of any party to any civil or criminal case, before or after rendition of judgment or decree;

(2) By certification at any time by a court of appeals of any question of law in any civil or criminal case as to which instructions are desired, and upon such certification the Supreme Court may give binding instructions or require the entire record to be sent up for decision of the entire matter in controversy.

§ 1257. STATE COURTS; CERTIORARI

(a) Final judgments or decrees rendered by the highest court of a State in which a decision could be had, may be reviewed by the Supreme Court by writ of certiorari where the validity of a treaty or statute of the United States is drawn in question or where the validity of a statute of any State is drawn in question on the ground of its being repugnant to the Constitution, treaties, or laws of the United States, or where any title, right, privilege, or immunity is specially set up or claimed under the Constitution or the treaties or statutes of, or any commission held or authority exercised under, the United States.

(b) For the purposes of this section, the term "highest court of a State" includes the District of Columbia Court of Appeals.

§ 1258. SUPREME COURT OF PUERTO RICO; CERTIORARI

Final judgments or decrees rendered by the Supreme Court of the Commonwealth of Puerto Rico may be reviewed by the Supreme Court by writ of certiorari where the validity of a treaty or statute of the United States is drawn in question or where the validity of a statute of the Commonwealth of Puerto Rico is drawn in question on the ground of its being repugnant to the Constitution, treaties, or laws of the United States, or where any title, right, privilege, or immunity is specially set up or claimed under the Constitution or the treaties or statutes of, or any commission held or authority exercised under, the United States.

CHAPTER 83. COURTS OF APPEALS

§ 1291. FINAL DECISIONS OF DISTRICT COURTS

The courts of appeals (other than the United States Court of Appeals for the Federal Circuit) shall have jurisdiction of appeals from all final decisions of the district courts of the United States, the United States District Court for the District of the Canal Zone, the District Court of Guam, and the District Court of the Virgin Islands, except where a direct review may be had in the Supreme Court. The jurisdiction of the United States Court of Appeals for the Federal Circuit shall be limited to the jurisdiction described in sections 1292(c) and (d) and 1295 of this title.

§ 1292. INTERLOCUTORY DECISIONS

(a) Except as provided in subsections (c) and (d) of this section, the courts of appeals shall have jurisdiction of appeals from:

(1) Interlocutory orders of the district courts of the United States, the United States District Court for the District of the Canal Zone, the District Court of Guam, and the District Court of the Virgin Islands, or of the judges thereof, granting, continuing, modifying, refusing or dissolving injunctions, or refusing to dissolve or modify injunctions, except where a direct review may be had in the Supreme Court;

(2) Interlocutory orders appointing receivers, or refusing orders to wind up receiverships or to take steps to accomplish the purposes thereof, such as directing sales or other disposals of property;

(3) Interlocutory decrees of such district courts or the judges thereof determining the rights and liabilities of the parties to admiralty cases in which appeals from final decrees are allowed.

(b) When a district judge, in making in a civil action an order not otherwise appealable under this section, shall be of the opinion that such order involves a controlling question of law as to which there is substantial ground for difference of opinion and that an immediate appeal from the order may materially advance the ultimate termination of the litigation, he shall so state in writing in such order. The Court of Appeals which would have jurisdiction of an appeal of such action may thereupon, in its discretion, permit an appeal to be taken from such order, if application is made to it within ten days after the entry of the order: Provided, however, That application for an appeal hereunder shall not stay proceedings in the district court unless the district judge or the Court of Appeals or a judge thereof shall so order.

(c) The United States Court of Appeals for the Federal Circuit shall have exclusive jurisdiction:

(1) of an appeal from an interlocutory order or decree described in subsection (a) or (b) of this section in any case over which the court would have jurisdiction of an appeal under section 1295 of this title; and

(2) of an appeal from a judgment in a civil action for patent infringement which would otherwise be appealable to the United States Court of Appeals for the Federal Circuit and is final except for an accounting.

(d) (1) When the chief judge of the Court of International Trade issues an order under the provisions of section 256(b) of this title, or when any judge of the Court of International Trade, in issuing any other interlocutory order, includes in the order a statement that a controlling question of law is involved with respect to which there is a substantial ground for difference of opinion and that an immediate appeal from that order may materially advance the ultimate termination of the litigation, the United States Court of Appeals for the Federal Circuit may, in its discretion, permit an appeal to be taken from such order, if application is made to that Court within ten days after the entry of such order.

(2) When the chief judge of the United States Court of Federal Claims issues an order under section 798(b) of this title, or when any judge of the United States Court of Federal Claims, in issuing an interlocutory order, includes in the order a statement that a controlling question of law is involved with respect to which there is a substantial ground for difference of opinion and that an immediate appeal from that order may materially advance the ultimate termination of the litigation, the United States Court of Appeals for the Federal Circuit may, in its discretion, permit an appeal to be taken from such order, if application is made to that Court within ten days after the entry of such order.

(3) Neither the application for nor the granting of an appeal under this subsection shall stay proceedings in the Court of International Trade or in the Court of Federal Claims, as the case may be, unless a stay is ordered by a judge of the Court of International Trade or of the Court of Federal Claims or by the United States Court of Appeals for the Federal Circuit or a judge of that court.

(4) (A) The United States Court of Appeals for the Federal Circuit shall have exclusive jurisdiction of an appeal from an interlocutory order of a district court of the United States, the District Court of Guam, the District Court of the Virgin Islands, or the District Court for the Northern Mariana Islands, granting or denying, in whole or in part, a motion to transfer an action to the United States Court of Federal Claims under section 1631 of this title.

(B) When a motion to transfer an action to the Court of Federal Claims is filed in a district court, no further proceedings shall be taken in the district court until 60 days after the court has ruled upon the motion. If an appeal is taken from the district court's grant or denial of the motion, proceedings shall be further stayed until the appeal has been decided by the Court of Appeals for the Federal Circuit. The stay of proceedings in the district court shall not bar the granting of preliminary or injunctive relief, where appropriate and where expedition is reasonably necessary. However, during the period in which proceedings are stayed as provided in this subparagraph, no transfer to the Court of Federal Claims pursuant to the motion shall be carried out.

(e) The Supreme Court may prescribe rules, in accordance with section 2072 of this title, to provide for an appeal of an interlocutory decision to the courts of appeals that is not otherwise provided for under subsection (a), (b), (c), or (d).

§ 1294. CIRCUITS IN WHICH DECISIONS REVIEWABLE

Except as provided in sections 1292(c), 1292(d), and 1295 of this title, appeals from reviewable decisions of the district and territorial courts shall be taken to the courts of appeals as follows:

(1) From a district court of the United States to the court of appeals for the circuit embracing the district;

(2) From the United States District Court for the District of the Canal Zone, to the Court of Appeals for the Fifth Circuit;

(3) From the District Court of the Virgin Islands, to the Court of Appeals for the Third Circuit;

(4) From the District Court of Guam, to the Court of Appeals for the Ninth Circuit.

§ 1295. JURISDICTION OF THE UNITED STATES COURT OF APPEALS FOR THE FEDERAL CIRCUIT
(a) The United States Court of Appeals for the Federal Circuit shall have exclusive jurisdiction:

(1) of an appeal from a final decision of a district court of the United States, the United States District Court for the District of the Canal Zone, the District Court of Guam, the District Court of the Virgin Islands, or the District Court for the Northern Mariana Islands, if the jurisdiction of that court was based, in whole or in part, on section 1338 of this title, except that a case involving a claim arising under any Act of Congress relating to copyrights, exclusive rights in mask works, or trademarks and no other claims under section 1338(a) shall be governed by sections 1291, 1292, and 1294 of this title;

(2) of an appeal from a final decision of a district court of the United States, the United States District Court for the District of the Canal Zone, the District Court of Guam, the District Court of the Virgin Islands, or the District Court for the Northern Mariana Islands, if the jurisdiction of that court was based, in whole or in part, on section 1346 of this title, except that jurisdiction of an appeal in a case brought in a district court under section 1346(a)(1), 1346(b), 1346(e), or 1346(f) of this title or under section 1346(a)(2) when the claim is founded upon an Act of Congress or a regulation of an executive department providing for internal revenue shall be governed by sections 1291, 1292, and 1294 of this title;

(3) of an appeal from a final decision of the United States Court of Federal Claims;

(4) of an appeal from a decision of:

(A) the Board of Patent Appeals and Interferences of the United States Patent and Trademark Office with respect to patent applications and interferences, at the instance of an applicant for a patent or any party to a patent interference, and any such appeal shall waive the right of such applicant or party to proceed under section 145 or 146 of title 35;

(B) the Under Secretary of Commerce for Intellectual Property and Director of the United States Patent and Trademark Office or the Trademark Trial and Appeal Board with respect to applications for registration of marks and other proceedings as provided in section 21 of the Trademark Act of 1946 (15 U.S.C. 1071); or

(C) a district court to which a case was directed pursuant to section 145, 146, or 154(b) of title 35;

(5) of an appeal from a final decision of the United States Court of International Trade;

(6) to review the final determinations of the United States International Trade Commission relating to unfair practices in import trade, made under section 337 of the Tariff Act of 1930 (19 U.S.C. 1337);

(7) to review, by appeal on questions of law only, findings of the Secretary of Commerce under U.S. note 6 to subchapter X of chapter 98 of the Harmonized Tariff Schedule of the United States (relating to importation of instruments or apparatus);

(8) of an appeal under section 71 of the Plant Variety Protection Act (7 U.S.C. 2461);

(9) of an appeal from a final order or final decision of the Merit Systems Protection Board, pursuant to sections 7703(b)(1) and 7703(d) of title 5;

(10) of an appeal from a final decision of an agency board of contract appeals pursuant to section 8(g)(1) of the Contract Disputes Act of 1978 (41 U.S.C. 607(g)(1));

(11) of an appeal under section 211 of the Economic Stabilization Act of 1970;

(12) of an appeal under section 5 of the Emergency Petroleum Allocation Act of 1973;

(13) of an appeal under section 506(c) of the Natural Gas Policy Act of 1978; and

(14) of an appeal under section 523 of the Energy Policy and Conservation Act.

(b) The head of any executive department or agency may, with the approval of the Attorney General, refer to the Court of Appeals for the Federal Circuit for judicial review any final decision rendered by a board of contract appeals pursuant to the terms of any contract with the United States awarded by that department or agency which the head of such department or agency has concluded is not entitled to finality pursuant to the review standards specified in section 10(b) of the Contract Disputes Act of 1978 (41 U.S.C. 609(b)). The head of each executive department or agency shall make any referral under this section within one hundred and twenty days after the receipt of a copy of the final appeal decision.

(c) The Court of Appeals for the Federal Circuit shall review the matter referred in accordance with the standards specified in section 10(b) of the Contract Disputes Act of 1978. The court shall proceed with judicial review on the administrative record made before the board of contract appeals on matters so referred as in other cases pending in such court, shall determine the issue of finality of the appeal decision, and shall, if appropriate, render judgment thereon, or remand the matter to any administrative or executive body or official with such direction as it may deem proper and just.

§ 1296. REVIEW OF CERTAIN AGENCY ACTIONS
(a) Jurisdiction.—Subject to the provisions of chapter 179, the United States Court of Appeals for the Federal Circuit shall have jurisdiction over a petition for review of a final decision under chapter 5 of title 3 of—

(1) an appropriate agency (as determined under section 454 of title 3);

(2) the Federal Labor Relations Authority made under part D of subchapter II of chapter 5 of title 3, notwithstanding section 7123 of title 5; or

(3) the Secretary of Labor or the Occupational Safety and Health Review Commission, made under part C of subchapter II of chapter 5 of title 3.

(b) Filing of petition. — Any petition for review under this section must be filed within 30 days after the date the petitioner receives notice of the final decision.

CHAPTER 85. DISTRICT COURTS; JURISDICTION

§ 1330. ACTIONS AGAINST FOREIGN STATES

(a) The district courts shall have original jurisdiction without regard to amount in controversy of any nonjury civil action against a foreign state as defined in section 1603(a) of this title as to any claim for relief in personam with respect to which the foreign state is not entitled to immunity either under sections 1605-1607 of this title or under any applicable international agreement.

(b) Personal jurisdiction over a foreign state shall exist as to every claim for relief over which the district courts have jurisdiction under subsection (a) where service has been made under section 1608 of this title.

(c) For purposes of subsection (b), an appearance by a foreign state does not confer personal jurisdiction with respect to any claim for relief not arising out of any transaction or occurrence enumerated in sections 1605-1607 of this title.

§ 1331. FEDERAL QUESTION

The district courts shall have original jurisdiction of all civil actions arising under the Constitution, laws, or treaties of the United States.

[handwritten annotation: → Liz Taylor → different states NOT of same / states Not of same states]

§ 1332. DIVERSITY OF CITIZENSHIP; AMOUNT IN CONTROVERSY; COSTS

(a) The district courts shall have original jurisdiction of all civil actions where the matter in controversy exceeds the sum or value of $75,000, exclusive of interest and costs, and is between:

    (1) citizens of different States;

[handwritten annotation: # of the Queen]

    (2) citizens of a State and citizens or subjects of a foreign state;

    (3) citizens of different States and in which citizens or subjects of a foreign state are additional parties; and

    (4) a foreign state, defined in section 1603(a) of this title, as plaintiff and citizens of a State or of different States.

For the purposes of this section, section 1335, and section 1441, an alien admitted to the United States for permanent residence shall be deemed a citizen of the State in which such alien is domiciled.

(b) Except when express provision therefor is otherwise made in a statute of the United States, where the plaintiff who files the case originally in the Federal courts is finally adjudged to be entitled to recover less than the sum or value of $75,000, computed without regard to any setoff or counterclaim to which the defendant may be adjudged to be entitled, and exclusive of interest and costs, the district court may deny costs to the plaintiff and, in addition, may impose costs on the plaintiff.

(c) For the purposes of this section and section 1441 of this title:

    (1) a corporation shall be deemed to be a citizen of any State by which it has been incorporated and of the State where it has its principal place of business, except that in any direct action against the insurer of a policy or contract of liability insurance, whether incorporated or unincorporated, to which action the insured is not joined as a party-defendant, such insurer shall be deemed a citizen of the State of which the insured is a citizen, as well as of any State by which the insurer has been incorporated and of the State where it has its principal place of business; and

    (2) the legal representative of the estate of a decedent shall be deemed to be a citizen only of the same State as the decedent, and the legal representative of an infant or incompetent shall be deemed to be a citizen only of the same State as the infant or incompetent.

(d) (1) In this subsection--

    (A) the term "class" means all of the class members in a class action;

    (B) the term "class action" means any civil action filed under rule 23 of the Federal Rules of Civil Procedure or similar State statute or rule of judicial procedure authorizing an action to be brought by 1 or more representative persons as a class action;

    (C) the term "class certification order" means an order issued by a court approving the treatment of some or all aspects of a civil action as a class action; and

    (D) the term "class members" means the persons (named or unnamed) who fall within the definition of the proposed or certified class in a class action.

(2) The district courts shall have original jurisdiction of any civil action in which the matter in controversy exceeds the sum or value of $5,000,000, exclusive of interest and costs, and is a class action in which--

(A) any member of a class of plaintiffs is a citizen of a State different from any defendant;

(B) any member of a class of plaintiffs is a foreign state or a citizen or subject of a foreign state and any defendant is a citizen of a State; or

(C) any member of a class of plaintiffs is a citizen of a State and any defendant is a foreign state or a citizen or subject of a foreign state.

(3) A district court may, in the interests of justice and looking at the totality of the circumstances, decline to exercise jurisdiction under paragraph (2) over a class action in which greater than one-third but less than two-thirds of the members of all proposed plaintiff classes in the aggregate and the primary defendants are citizens of the State in which the action was originally filed based on consideration of--

(A) whether the claims asserted involve matters of national or interstate interest;

(B) whether the claims asserted will be governed by laws of the State in which the action was originally filed or by the laws of other States;

(C) whether the class action has been pleaded in a manner that seeks to avoid Federal jurisdiction;

(D) whether the action was brought in a forum with a distinct nexus with the class members, the alleged harm, or the defendants;

(E) whether the number of citizens of the State in which the action was originally filed in all proposed plaintiff classes in the aggregate is substantially larger than the number of citizens from any other State, and the citizenship of the other members of the proposed class is dispersed among a substantial number of States; and

(F) whether, during the 3-year period preceding the filing of that class action, 1 or more other class actions asserting the same or similar claims on behalf of the same or other persons have been filed.

(4) A district court shall decline to exercise jurisdiction under paragraph (2)--

(A)(i) over a class action in which--

(I) greater than two-thirds of the members of all proposed plaintiff classes in the aggregate are citizens of the State in which the action was originally filed;

(II) at least 1 defendant is a defendant--

(aa) from whom significant relief is sought by members of the plaintiff class;

(bb) whose alleged conduct forms a significant basis for the claims asserted by the proposed plaintiff class; and

(cc) who is a citizen of the State in which the action was originally filed; and

(III) principal injuries resulting from the alleged conduct or any related conduct of each defendant were incurred in the State in which the action was originally filed; and

(ii) during the 3-year period preceding the filing of that class action, no other class action has been filed asserting the same or similar factual allegations against any of the defendants on behalf of the same or other persons; or

(B) two-thirds or more of the members of all proposed plaintiff classes in the aggregate, and the primary defendants, are citizens of the State in which the action was originally filed.

(5) Paragraphs (2) through (4) shall not apply to any class action in which--

(A) the primary defendants are States, State officials, or other governmental entities against whom the district court may be foreclosed from ordering relief; or

(B) the number of members of all proposed plaintiff classes in the aggregate is less than 100.

(6) In any class action, the claims of the individual class members shall be aggregated to determine whether the matter in controversy exceeds the sum or value of $5,000,000, exclusive of interest and costs.

(7) Citizenship of the members of the proposed plaintiff classes shall be determined for purposes of paragraphs (2) through (6) as of the date of filing of the complaint or amended complaint, or, if the case stated by the initial pleading is not subject to Federal jurisdiction, as of the date of service by plaintiffs of an amended pleading, motion, or other paper, indicating the existence of Federal jurisdiction.

(8) This subsection shall apply to any class action before or after the entry of a class certification order by the court with respect to that action.

(9) Paragraph (2) shall not apply to any class action that solely involves a claim--

(A) concerning a covered security as defined under 16(f)(3) of the Securities Act of 1933 (15 U.S.C. 78p(f)(3)) and section 28(f)(5)(E) of the Securities Exchange Act of 1934 (15 U.S.C. 78bb(f)(5)(E));

(B) that relates to the internal affairs or governance of a corporation or other form of business enterprise and that arises under or by virtue of the laws of the State in which such corporation or business enterprise is incorporated or organized; or

(C) that relates to the rights, duties (including fiduciary duties), and obligations relating to or created by or pursuant to any security (as defined under section 2(a)(1) of the Securities Act of 1933 (15 U.S.C. 77b(a)(1)) and the regulations issued thereunder).

(10) For purposes of this subsection and section 1453, an unincorporated association shall be deemed to be a citizen of the State where it has its principal place of business and the State under whose laws it is is organized.

(11)

(A) For purposes of this subsection and section 1453, a mass action shall be deemed to be a class action removable under paragraphs (2) through (10) if it otherwise meets the provisions of those paragraphs.

(B)

(i) As used in subparagraph (A), the term "mass action" means any civil action (except a civil action within the scope of section 1711(2)) in which monetary relief claims of 100 or more persons are proposed to be tried jointly on the ground that the plaintiffs' claims involve common questions of law or fact, except that jurisdiction shall exist only over those plaintiffs whose claims in a mass action satisfy the jurisdictional amount requriements under subsection (a).

(ii) As used in subparagraph (A), the term "mass action" shall not include any civil action in which--

(I) all of the claims in the action arise from an event or occurrence in the State in which the action was filed, and that allegedly resulted in injuries in that State or in States contiguous to that State;

(II) the claims are joined upon motion of a defendant;

(III) all of the claims in the action are asserted on behalf of the general public (and not on behalf of individual claimants or members of a purported class) pursuant to a State statute specifically authorizing such action; or

(IV) the claims have been consolidated or coordinated solely for pretrial proceedings.

(C)

(i) Any action(s) removed to Federal court pursuant to this subsection shall not thereafter be transferred to any other court pursuant to section 1407, or the rules promulgated thereunder, unless a majority of the plaintiffs in the action request transfer pursuant to section 1407.

(ii) This suparagraph will not apply--

(I) to cases certified pursuant to rule 23 of the Federal Rules of Civil Procedure; or

(II) if plaintiffs propose that the action proceed as a class action pursuant to rule 23 of the Federal Rules of Civil Procedure.

(D) The limitations periods on any claims asserted in a mass action that is removed to Federal court pursuant to this subsection shall be deemed tolled during the period that the action is pending in Federal court.

(e) The word "States", as used in this section, includes the Territories, the District of Columbia, and the Commonwealth of Puerto Rico.

§ 1333. ADMIRALTY, MARITIME AND PRIZE CASES

The district courts shall have original jurisdiction, exclusive of the courts of the States, of:

(1) Any civil case of admiralty or maritime jurisdiction, saving to suitors in all cases all other remedies to which they are otherwise entitled.

(2) Any prize brought into the United States and all proceedings for the condemnation of property taken as prize.

§ 1334. BANKRUPTCY CASES AND PROCEEDINGS

(a) Except as provided in subsection (b) of this section, the district courts shall have original and exclusive jurisdiction of all cases under title 11.

(b) Except as provided in subsection (e)(2), and notwithstanding any Act of Congress that confers exclusive jurisdiction on a court or courts other than the district courts, the district courts shall have original but not exclusive jurisdiction of all civil proceedings arising under title 11, or arising in or related to cases under title 11.

(c) (1) Except with respect to a case under chapter 15 of title 11, nothing in this section prevents a district court in the interest of justice, or in the interest of comity with State courts or respect for State law, from abstaining from hearing a particular proceeding arising under title 11 or arising in or related to a case under title 11.

(2) Upon timely motion of a party in a proceeding based upon a State law claim or State law cause of action, related to a case under title 11 but not arising under title 11 or arising in a case under title 11, with respect to which an action could not have been commenced in a court of the United States absent jurisdiction under this section, the district court shall abstain from hearing such proceeding if an action is commenced, and can be timely adjudicated, in a State forum of appropriate jurisdiction.

(d) Any decision to abstain or not to abstain made under subsection (c) (other than a decision not to abstain in a proceeding described in subsection (c)(2)) is not reviewable by appeal or otherwise by the court of appeals under section 158(d), 1291, or 1292 of this title or by the Supreme Court of the United States under section 1254 of this title. Subsection (c) and this subsection shall not be construed to limit the applicability of the stay provided for by section 362 of title 11, United States Code, as such section applies to an action affecting the property of the estate in bankruptcy.

(e) The district court in which a case under title 11 is commenced or is pending shall have exclusive jurisdiction—

(1) of all the property, wherever located, of the debtor as of the commencement of such case, and of property of the estate; and

(2) over all claims or causes of action that involve construction of section 327 of title 11, United States Code, or rules relating to disclosure requirements under section 327.

§ 1335. INTERPLEADER

(a) The district courts shall have original jurisdiction of any civil action of interpleader or in the nature of interpleader filed by any person, firm, or corporation, association, or society having in his or its custody or possession money or property of the value of $500 or more, or having issued a note, bond, certificate, policy of insurance, or other instrument of value or amount of $500 or more, or providing for the delivery or payment or the loan of money or property of such amount or value, or being under any obligation written or unwritten to the amount of $500 or more, if

(1) Two or more adverse claimants, of diverse citizenship as defined in subsection (a) or (d) of section 1332 of this title, are claiming or may claim to be entitled to such money or property, or to any one or more of the benefits arising by virtue of any note, bond, certificate, policy or other instrument, or arising by virtue of any such obligation; and if

(2) the plaintiff has deposited such money or property or has paid the amount of or the loan or other value of such instrument or the amount due under such obligation into the registry of the court, there to abide the judgment of the court, or has given bond payable to the clerk of the court in such amount and with such surety as the court or judge may deem proper, conditioned upon the compliance by the plaintiff with the future order or judgment of the court with respect to the subject matter of the controversy.

(b) Such an action may be entertained although the titles or claims of the conflicting claimants do not have a common origin, or are not identical, but are adverse to and independent of one another.

§ 1337. COMMERCE AND ANTITRUST REGULATIONS; AMOUNT IN CONTROVERSY; COSTS

(a) The district courts shall have original jurisdiction of any civil action or proceeding arising under any Act of Congress regulating commerce or protecting trade and commerce against restraints and monopolies: Provided, however, That the district courts shall have original jurisdiction of an action brought under section 11706 or 14706 of title 49, only if the matter in controversy for each receipt or bill of lading exceeds $10,000, exclusive of interest and costs.

(b) Except when express provision therefor is otherwise made in a statute of the United States, where a plaintiff who files the case under section 11706 or 14706 of title 49, originally in the Federal courts is finally adjudged to be entitled to recover less than the sum or value of $10,000, computed without regard to any setoff or counterclaim to which the defendant may be adjudged to be entitled, and exclusive of any interest and costs, the district court may deny costs to the plaintiff and, in addition, may impose costs on the plaintiff.

(c) The district courts shall not have jurisdiction under this section of any matter within the exclusive jurisdiction of the Court of International Trade under chapter 95 of this title.

§ 1338. PATENTS, PLANT VARIETY PROTECTION, COPYRIGHTS, MASK WORKS, DESIGNS, TRADEMARKS, AND UNFAIR COMPETITION

(a) The district courts shall have original jurisdiction of any civil action arising under any Act of Congress relating to patents, plant variety protection, copyrights and trademarks. Such jurisdiction shall be exclusive of the courts of the states in patent, plant variety protection and copyright cases.

(b) The district courts shall have original jurisdiction of any civil action asserting a claim of unfair competition when joined with a substantial and related claim under the copyright, patent, plant variety protection or trademark laws.

(c) Subsections (a) and (b) apply to exclusive rights in mask works under chapter 9 of title 17, and to exclusive rights in designs under chapter 13 of title 17, to the same extent as such subsections apply to copyrights.

§ 1339. POSTAL MATTERS
The district courts shall have original jurisdiction of any civil action arising under any Act of Congress relating to the postal service.

§ 1340. INTERNAL REVENUE; CUSTOMS DUTIES
The district courts shall have original jurisdiction of any civil action arising under any Act of Congress providing for internal revenue, or revenue from imports or tonnage except matters within the jurisdiction of the Court of International Trade.

§ 1341. TAXES BY STATES
The district courts shall not enjoin, suspend or restrain the assessment, levy or collection of any tax under State law where a plain, speedy and efficient remedy may be had in the courts of such State.

§ 1342. RATE ORDERS OF STATE AGENCIES
The district courts shall not enjoin, suspend or restrain the operation of, or compliance with, any order affecting rates chargeable by a public utility and made by a State administrative agency or a rate-making body of a State political subdivision, where:

(1) Jurisdiction is based solely on diversity of citizenship or repugnance of the order to the Federal Constitution; and,

(2) The order does not interfere with interstate commerce; and,

(3) The order has been made after reasonable notice and hearing; and,

(4) A plain, speedy and efficient remedy may be had in the courts of such State.

§ 1343. CIVIL RIGHTS AND ELECTIVE FRANCHISE
(a) The district courts shall have original jurisdiction of any civil action authorized by law to be commenced by any person:

(1) To recover damages for injury to his person or property, or because of the deprivation of any right or privilege of a citizen of the United States, by any act done in furtherance of any conspiracy mentioned in section 1985 of Title 42;

(2) To recover damages from any person who fails to prevent or to aid in preventing any wrongs mentioned in section 1985 of Title 42 which he had knowledge were about to occur and power to prevent;

(3) To redress the deprivation, under color of any State law, statute, ordinance, regulation, custom or usage, of any right, privilege or immunity secured by the Constitution of the United States or by any Act of Congress providing for equal rights of citizens or of all persons within the jurisdiction of the United States;

(4) To recover damages or to secure equitable or other relief under any Act of Congress providing for the protection of civil rights, including the right to vote.

(b) For purposes of this section:

(1) the District of Columbia shall be considered to be a State; and

(2) any Act of Congress applicable exclusively to the District of Columbia shall be considered to be a statute of the District of Columbia.

§ 1344. ELECTION DISPUTES
The district courts shall have original jurisdiction of any civil action to recover possession of any office, except that of elector of President or Vice President, United States Senator, Representative in or delegate to Congress, or member of a state legislature, authorized by law to be commenced, wherein it appears that the sole question touching the title to office arises out of denial of the right to vote, to any citizen offering to vote, on account of race, color or previous condition of servitude.

The jurisdiction under this section shall extend only so far as to determine the rights of the parties to office by reason of the denial of the right, guaranteed by the Constitution of the United States and secured by any law, to enforce the right of citizens of the United States to vote in all the States.

§ 1345. UNITED STATES AS PLAINTIFF
Except as otherwise provided by Act of Congress, the district courts shall have original jurisdiction of all civil actions, suits or proceedings commenced by the United States, or by any agency or officer thereof expressly authorized to sue by Act of Congress.

§ 1346. UNITED STATES AS DEFENDANT
(a) The district courts shall have original jurisdiction, concurrent with the United States Court of Federal Claims, of:

(1) Any civil action against the United States for the recovery of any internal-revenue tax alleged to have been erroneously or illegally assessed or collected, or any penalty claimed to have been collected without authority or any sum alleged to have been excessive or in any manner wrongfully collected under the internal-revenue laws;

(2) Any other civil action or claim against the United States, not exceeding $10,000 in amount, founded either upon the Constitution, or any Act of Congress, or any regulation of an executive department, or upon any express or implied contract with the United States, or for liquidated or unliquidated damages in cases not sounding in tort, except that the district courts shall not have jurisdiction of any civil action or claim against the United States founded upon any express or implied contract with the United States or for liquidated or unliquidated damages in cases not sounding in tort which are subject to sections 8(g)(1) and 10(a)(1) of the Contract Disputes Act of 1978. For the purpose of this paragraph, an express or implied contract with the Army and Air Force Exchange Service, Navy Exchanges, Marine Corps Exchanges, Coast Guard Exchanges, or Exchange Councils of the National Aeronautics and Space Administration shall be considered an express or implied contract with the United States.

(b)(1) Subject to the provisions of chapter 171 of this title, the district courts, together with the United States District Court for the District of the Canal Zone and the District Court of the Virgin Islands, shall have exclusive jurisdiction of civil actions on claims against the United States, for money damages, accruing on and after January 1, 1945, for injury or loss of property, or personal injury or death caused by the negligent or wrongful act or omission of any employee of the Government while acting within the scope of his office or employment, under circumstances where the United States, if a private person, would be liable to the claimant in accordance with the law of the place where the act or omission occurred.

(2) No person convicted of a felony who is incarcerated while awaiting sentencing or while serving a sentence may bring a civil action against the United States or an agency, officer, or employee of the Government, for mental or emotional injury suffered while in custody without a prior showing of physical injury.

(c) The jurisdiction conferred by this section includes jurisdiction of any set-off, counterclaim, or other claim or demand whatever on the part of the United States against any plaintiff commencing an action under this section.

(d) The district courts shall not have jurisdiction under this section of any civil action or claim for a pension.

(e) The district courts shall have original jurisdiction of any civil action against the United States provided in section 6226, 6228(a), 7426, or 7428 (in the case of the United States district court for the District of Columbia) or section 7429 of the Internal Revenue Code of 1986.

(f) The district courts shall have exclusive original jurisdiction of civil actions under section 2409a to quiet title to an estate or interest in real property in which an interest is claimed by the United States.

(g) Subject to the provisions of chapter 179, the district courts of the United States shall have exclusive jurisdiction over any civil action commenced under section 453(2) of title 3, by a covered employee under chapter 5 of such title.

§ 1350. ALIEN'S ACTION FOR TORT
The district courts shall have original jurisdiction of any civil action by an alien for a tort only, committed in violation of the law of nations or a treaty of the United States.

§ 1351. CONSULS, VICE CONSULS, AND MEMBERS OF A DIPLOMATIC MISSION AS DEFENDANT
The district courts shall have original jurisdiction, exclusive of the courts of the States, of all civil actions and proceedings against:

(1) consuls or vice consuls of foreign states; or

(2) members of a mission or members of their families (as such terms are defined in section 2 of the Diplomatic Relations Act).

§ 1359. PARTIES COLLUSIVELY JOINED OR MADE
A district court shall not have jurisdiction of a civil action in which any party, by assignment or otherwise, has been improperly or collusively made or joined to invoke the jurisdiction of such court.

§ 1361. ACTION TO COMPEL AN OFFICER OF THE UNITED STATES TO PERFORM HIS DUTY
The district courts shall have original jurisdiction of any action in the nature of mandamus to compel an officer or employee of the United States or any agency thereof to perform a duty owed to the plaintiff.

§ 1362. INDIAN TRIBES
The district courts shall have original jurisdiction of all civil actions, brought by any Indian tribe or band with a governing body duly recognized by the Secretary of the Interior, wherein the matter in controversy arises under the Constitution, laws, or treaties of the United States.

§ 1364. DIRECT ACTIONS AGAINST INSURERS OF MEMBERS OF DIPLOMATIC MISSIONS AND THEIR FAMILIES
(a) The district courts shall have original and exclusive jurisdiction, without regard to the amount in controversy, of any civil action commenced by any person against an insurer who by contract has insured an individual, who is, or was at the time of the tortious act or omission, a member of a mission (within the

meaning of section 2(3) of the Diplomatic Relations Act (22 U.S.C. § 254a(3)) or a member of the family of such a member of a mission, or an individual described in section 19 of the Convention on Privileges and Immunities of the United Nations of February 13, 1946, against liability for personal injury, death, or damage to property.

(b) Any direct action brought against an insurer under subsection (a) shall be tried without a jury, but shall not be subject to the defense that the insured is immune from suit, that the insured is an indispensable party, or in the absence of fraud or collusion, that the insured has violated a term of the contract, unless the contract was cancelled before the claim arose.

§ 1367. SUPPLEMENTAL JURISDICTION

(a) Except as provided in subsections (b) and (c) or as expressly provided otherwise by Federal statute, in any civil action of which the district courts have original jurisdiction, the district courts shall have supplemental jurisdiction over all other claims that are so related to claims in the action within such original jurisdiction that they form part of the same case or controversy under Article III of the United States Constitution. Such supplemental jurisdiction shall include claims that involve the joinder or intervention of additional parties.

(b) In any civil action of which the district courts have original jurisdiction founded solely on section 1332 of this title, the district courts shall not have supplemental jurisdiction under subsection (a) over claims by plaintiffs against persons made parties under Rule 14, 19, 20, or 24 of the Federal Rules of Civil Procedure, or over claims by persons proposed to be joined as plaintiffs under Rule 19 of such rules, or seeking to intervene as plaintiffs under Rule 24 of such rules, when exercising supplemental jurisdiction over such claims would be inconsistent with the jurisdictional requirements of section 1332.

(c) The district courts may decline to exercise supplemental jurisdiction over a claim under subsection (a) if:

    (1) the claim raises a novel or complex issue of State law,

    (2) the claim substantially predominates over the claim or claims over which the district court has original jurisdiction,

    (3) the district court has dismissed all claims over which it has original jurisdiction, or

    (4) in exceptional circumstances, there are other compelling reasons for declining jurisdiction.

(d) The period of limitations for any claim asserted under subsection (a), and for any other claim in the same action that is voluntarily dismissed at the same time as or after the dismissal of the claim under subsection (a), shall be tolled while the claim is pending and for a period of 30 days after it is dismissed unless State law provides for a longer tolling period.

(e) As used in this section, the term "State" includes the District of Columbia, the Commonwealth of Puerto Rico, and any territory or possession of the United States.

§ 1369. MULTIPARTY, MULTIFORUM JURISDICTION

(a) In general. The district courts shall have original jurisdiction of any civil action involving minimal diversity between adverse parties that arises from a single accident, where at least 75 natural persons have died in the accident at a discrete location, if:

    (1) a defendant resides in a State and a substantial part of the accident took place in another State or other location, regardless of whether that defendant is also a resident of the State where a substantial part of the accident took place;

    (2) any two defendants reside in different States, regardless of whether such defendants are also residents of the same State or States; or

    (3) substantial parts of the accident took place in different States.

(b) Limitation of jurisdiction of district courts. The district court shall abstain from hearing any civil action described in subsection (a) in which:

    (1) the substantial majority of all plaintiffs are citizens of a single State of which the primary defendants are also citizens; and

    (2) the claims asserted will be governed primarily by the laws of that State.

(c) Special rules and definitions. For purposes of this section:

    (1) minimal diversity exists between adverse parties if any party is a citizen of a State and any adverse party is a citizen of another State, a citizen or subject of a foreign state, or a foreign state as defined in section 1603(a) of this title;

    (2) a corporation is deemed to be a citizen of any State, and a citizen or subject of any foreign state, in which it is incorporated or has its principal place of business, and is deemed to be a resident of any State in which it is incorporated or licensed to do business or is doing business;

(3) the term "injury" means:

(A) physical harm to a natural person; and

(B) physical damage to or destruction of tangible property, but only if physical harm described in subparagraph (A) exists;

(4) the term "accident" means a sudden accident, or a natural event culminating in an accident, that results in death incurred at a discrete location by at least 75 natural persons; and

(5) the term "State" includes the District of Columbia, the Commonwealth of Puerto Rico, and any territory or possession of the United States.

(d) Intervening parties. In any action in a district court which is or could have been brought, in whole or in part, under this section, any person with a claim arising from the accident described in subsection (a) shall be permitted to intervene as a party plaintiff in the action, even if that person could not have brought an action in a district court as an original matter.

(e) Notification of judicial panel on multidistrict litigation. A district court in which an action under this section is pending shall promptly notify the judicial panel on multidistrict litigation of the pendency of the action.

CHAPTER 87. DISTRICT COURTS; VENUE

§ 1391. VENUE GENERALLY

(a) A civil action wherein jurisdiction is founded only on diversity of citizenship may, except as otherwise provided by law, be brought only in (1) a judicial district where any defendant resides, if all defendants reside in the same State, (2) a judicial district in which a substantial part of the events or omissions giving rise to the claim occurred, or a substantial part of property that is the subject of the action is situated, or (3) a judicial district in which any defendant is subject to personal jurisdiction at the time the action is commenced, if there is no district in which the action may otherwise be brought.

(b) A civil action wherein jurisdiction is not founded solely on diversity of citizenship may, except as otherwise provided by law, be brought only in (1) a judicial district where any defendant resides, if all defendants reside in the same State, (2) a judicial district in which a substantial part of the events or omissions giving rise to the claim occurred, or a substantial part of property that is the subject of the action is situated, or (3) a judicial district in which any defendant may be found, if there is no district in which the action may otherwise be brought.

(c) For purposes of venue under this chapter, a defendant that is a corporation shall be deemed to reside in any judicial district in which it is subject to personal jurisdiction at the time the action is commenced. In a State which has more than one judicial district and in which a defendant that is a corporation is subject to personal jurisdiction at the time an action is commenced, such corporation shall be deemed to reside in any district in that State within which its contacts would be sufficient to subject it to personal jurisdiction if that district were a separate State, and, if there is no such district, the corporation shall be deemed to reside in the district within which it has the most significant contacts.

(d) An alien may be sued in any district.

(e) A civil action in which a defendant is an officer or employee of the United States or any agency thereof acting in his official capacity or under color of legal authority, or an agency of the United States, or the United States, may, except as otherwise provided by law, be brought in any judicial district in which (1) a defendant in the action resides, (2) a substantial part of the events or omissions giving rise to the claim occurred, or a substantial part of property that is the subject of the action is situated, or (3) the plaintiff resides if no real property is involved in the action. Additional persons may be joined as parties to any such action in accordance with the Federal Rules of Civil Procedure and with such other venue requirements as would be applicable if the United States or one of its officers, employees, or agencies were not a party.

The summons and complaint in such an action shall be served as provided by the Federal Rules of Civil Procedure except that the delivery of the summons and complaint to the officer or agency as required by the rules may be made by certified mail beyond the territorial limits of the district in which the action is brought.

(f) A civil action against a foreign state as defined in section 1603(a) of this title may be brought:

(1) in any judicial district in which a substantial part of the events or omissions giving rise to the claim occurred, or a substantial part of property that is the subject of the action is situated;

(2) in any judicial district in which the vessel or cargo of a foreign state is situated, if the claim is asserted under section 1605(b) of this title;

(3) in any judicial district in which the agency or instrumentality is licensed to do business or is doing business, if the action is brought against an agency or instrumentality of a foreign state as defined in section 1603(b) of this title; or

(4) in the United States District Court for the District of Columbia if the action is brought against a foreign state or political subdivision thereof.

(g) A civil action in which jurisdiction of the district court is based upon section 1369 of this title may be brought in any district in which any defendant resides or in which a substantial part of the accident giving rise to the action took place.

§ 1392. DEFENDANTS OR PROPERTY IN DIFFERENT DISTRICTS IN SAME STATE

Any civil action, of a local nature, involving property located in different districts in the same State, may be brought in any of such districts.

§ 1395. FINE, PENALTY OR FORFEITURE

(a) A civil proceeding for the recovery of a pecuniary fine, penalty or forfeiture may be prosecuted in the district where it accrues or the defendant is found.

(b) A civil proceeding for the forfeiture of property may be prosecuted in any district where such property is found.

(c) A civil proceeding for the forfeiture of property seized outside any judicial district may be prosecuted in any district into which the property is brought.

(d) A proceeding in admiralty for the enforcement of fines, penalties and forfeitures against a vessel may be brought in any district in which the vessel is arrested.

(e) Any proceeding for the forfeiture of a vessel or cargo entering a port of entry closed by the President in pursuance of law, or of goods and chattels coming from a State or section declared by proclamation of the President to be in insurrection, or of any vessel or vehicle conveying persons or property to or from such State or section or belonging in whole or in part to a resident thereof, may be prosecuted in any district into which the property is taken and in which the proceeding is instituted.

§ 1396. INTERNAL REVENUE TAXES

Any civil action for the collection of internal revenue taxes may be brought in the district where the liability for such tax accrues, in the district of the taxpayer's residence, or in the district where the return was filed.

§ 1397. INTERPLEADER

Any civil action of interpleader or in the nature of interpleader under section 1335 of this title may be brought in the judicial district in which one or more of the claimants reside.

§ 1400. PATENTS AND COPYRIGHTS, MASK WORKS, AND DESIGNS

(a) Civil actions, suits, or proceedings arising under any Act of Congress relating to copyrights or exclusive rights in mask works or designs may be instituted in the district in which the defendant or his agent resides or may be found.

(b) Any civil action for patent infringement may be brought in the judicial district where the defendant resides, or where the defendant has committed acts of infringement and has a regular and established place of business.

§ 1401. STOCKHOLDER'S DERIVATIVE ACTION

Any civil action by a stockholder on behalf of his corporation may be prosecuted in any judicial district where the corporation might have sued the same defendants.

§ 1402. UNITED STATES AS DEFENDANT

(a) Any civil action in a district court against the United States under subsection (a) of section 1346 of this title may be prosecuted only:

(1) Except as provided in paragraph (2), in the judicial district where the plaintiff resides;

(2) In the case of a civil action by a corporation under paragraph (1) of subsection (a) of section 1346, in the judicial district in which is located the principal place of business or principal office or agency of the corporation; or if it has no principal place of business or principal office or agency in any judicial district (A) in the judicial district in which is located the office to which was made the return of the tax in respect of which the claim is made, or (B) if no return was made, in the judicial district in which lies the District of Columbia. Notwithstanding the foregoing provisions of this paragraph a district court, for the convenience of the parties and witnesses, in the interest of justice, may transfer any such action to any other district or division.

(b) Any civil action on a tort claim against the United States under subsection (b) of section 1346 of this title may be prosecuted only in the judicial district where the plaintiff resides or wherein the act or omission complained of occurred.

(c) Any civil action against the United States under subsection (e) of section 1346 of this title may be prosecuted only in the judicial district where the property is situated at the time of levy, or if no levy is made, in the judicial district in which the event occurred which gave rise to the cause of action.

(d) Any civil action under section 2409a to quiet title to an estate or interest in real property in which an interest is claimed by the United States shall be brought in the district court of the district where the property is located or, if located in different districts, in any of such districts.

§ 1404. CHANGE OF VENUE

(a) For the convenience of parties and witnesses, in the interest of justice, a district court may transfer any civil action to any other district or division where it might have been brought.

(b) Upon motion, consent or stipulation of all parties, any action, suit or proceeding of a civil nature or any motion or hearing thereof, may be transferred, in the discretion of the court, from the division in which pending to any other division in the same district. Transfer of proceedings in rem brought by or on behalf of the United States may be transferred under this section without the consent of the United States where all other parties request transfer.

(c) A district court may order any civil action to be tried at any place within the division in which it is pending.

(d) As used in this section, the term "district court" includes the District Court of Guam, the District Court for the Northern Mariana Islands, and the District Court of the Virgin Islands, and the term "district" includes the territorial jurisdiction of each such court.

§ 1406. CURE OR WAIVER OF DEFECTS

(a) The district court of a district in which is filed a case laying venue in the wrong division or district shall dismiss, or if it be in the interest of justice, transfer such case to any district or division in which it could have been brought.

(b) Nothing in this chapter shall impair the jurisdiction of a district court of any matter involving a party who does not interpose timely and sufficient objection to the venue.

(c) As used in this section, the term "district court" includes the District Court of Guam, the District Court for the Northern Mariana Islands, and the District Court of the Virgin Islands, and the term "district" includes the territorial jurisdiction of each such court.

§ 1407. MULTIDISTRICT LITIGATION

(a) When civil actions involving one or more common questions of fact are pending in different districts, such actions may be transferred to any district for coordinated or consolidated pretrial proceedings. Such transfers shall be made by the judicial panel on multidistrict litigation authorized by this section upon its determination that transfers for such proceedings will be for the convenience of parties and witnesses and will promote the just and efficient conduct of such actions. Each action so transferred shall be remanded by the panel at or before the conclusion of such pretrial proceedings to the district from which it was transferred unless it shall have been previously terminated: Provided, however, That the panel may separate any claim, cross-claim, counter-claim, or third-party claim and remand any of such claims before the remainder of the action is remanded.

(b) Such coordinated or consolidated pretrial proceedings shall be conducted by a judge or judges to whom such actions are assigned by the judicial panel on multidistrict litigation. For this purpose, upon request of the panel, a circuit judge or a district judge may be designated and assigned temporarily for service in the transferee district by the Chief Justice of the United States or the chief judge of the circuit, as may be required, in accordance with the provisions of chapter 13 of this title. With the consent of the transferee district court, such actions may be assigned by the panel to a judge or judges of such district. The judge or judges to whom such actions are assigned, the members of the judicial panel on multidistrict litigation, and other circuit and district judges designated when needed by the panel may exercise the powers of a district judge in any district for the purpose of conducting pretrial depositions in such coordinated or consolidated pretrial proceedings.

(c) Proceedings for the transfer of an action under this section may be initiated by:

    (i)   the judicial panel on multidistrict litigation upon its own initiative, or

    (ii)   motion filed with the panel by a party in any action in which transfer for coordinated or consolidated pretrial proceedings under this section may be appropriate. A copy of such motion shall be filed in the district court in which the moving party's action is pending.

The panel shall give notice to the parties in all actions in which transfers for coordinated or consolidated pretrial proceedings are contemplated, and such notice shall specify the time and place of any hearing to determine whether such transfer shall be made. Orders of the panel to set a hearing and other orders of the panel issued prior to the order either directing or denying transfer shall be filed in the office of the clerk of the district court in which a transfer hearing is to be or has been held. The panel's order of transfer shall be based upon a record of such hearing at which material evidence may be offered by any party to an action pending in any district that would be affected by the proceedings under this section, and shall be supported by findings of fact and conclusions of law based upon such record. Orders of transfer and such other orders as the panel may make thereafter shall be filed in the office of the clerk of the district court of the transferee district and shall be effective when thus filed. The clerk of the transferee district court shall forthwith transmit a certified copy of the panel's order to transfer to the clerk of the district court from which the action is being transferred. An order denying transfer shall be filed in each district wherein there is a case pending in which the motion for transfer has been made.

(d) The judicial panel on multidistrict litigation shall consist of seven circuit and district judges designated from time to time by the Chief Justice of the United States, no two of whom shall be from the same circuit. The concurrence of four members shall be necessary to any action by the panel.

(e) No proceedings for review of any order of the panel may be permitted except by extraordinary writ pursuant to the provisions of title 28, section 1651, United States Code. Petitions for an extraordinary writ to review an order of the panel to set a transfer hearing and other orders of the panel issued prior to the order either directing or denying transfer shall be filed only in the court of appeals having jurisdiction over the district in which a hearing is to be or has been held. Petitions for an extraordinary writ to review an order to transfer or orders subsequent to transfer shall be filed only in the court of appeals having jurisdiction over the transferee district. There shall be no appeal or review of an order of the panel denying a motion to transfer for consolidated or coordinated proceedings.

(f) The panel may prescribe rules for the conduct of its business not inconsistent with Acts of Congress and the Federal Rules of Civil Procedure.

(g) Nothing in this section shall apply to any action in which the United States is a complainant arising under the antitrust laws. "Antitrust laws" as used herein include those acts referred to in the Act of October 15, 1914, as amended (38 Stat. 730; 15 U.S.C. 12), and also include the Act of June 19, 1936 (49 Stat. 1526; 15 U.S.C. 13, 13a, and 13b) and the Act of September 26, 1914, as added March 21, 1938 (52 Stat. 116, 117; 15 U.S.C. 56); but shall not include section 4A of the Act of October 15, 1914, as added July 7, 1955 (69 Stat. 282; 15 U.S.C. 15a).

(h) Notwithstanding the provisions of section 1404 or subsection (f) of this section, the judicial panel on multidistrict litigation may consolidate and transfer with or without the consent of the parties, for both pretrial purposes and for trial, any action brought under section 4C of the Clayton Act.

CHAPTER 89. DISTRICT COURTS; REMOVAL OF CASES FROM STATE COURTS

§ 1441. ACTIONS REMOVABLE GENERALLY

(a) Except as otherwise expressly provided by Act of Congress, any civil action brought in a State court of which the district courts of the United States have original jurisdiction, may be removed by the defendant or the defendants, to the district court of the United States for the district and division embracing the place where such action is pending. For purposes of removal under this chapter, the citizenship of defendants sued under fictitious names shall be disregarded.

(b) Any civil action of which the district courts have original jurisdiction founded on a claim or right arising under the Constitution, treaties or laws of the United States shall be removable without regard to the citizenship or residence of the parties. Any other such action shall be removable only if none of the parties in interest properly joined and served as defendants is a citizen of the State in which such action is brought.

(c) Whenever a separate and independent claim or cause of action within the jurisdiction conferred by section 1331 of this title is joined with one or more otherwise non-removable claims or causes of action, the entire case may be removed and the district court may determine all issues therein, or, in its discretion, may remand all matters in which State law predominates.

(d) Any civil action brought in a State court against a foreign state as defined in section 1603(a) of this title may be removed by the foreign state to the district court of the United States for the district and division embracing the place where such action is pending. Upon removal the action shall be tried by the court without jury. Where removal is based upon this subsection, the time limitations of section 1446(b) of this chapter may be enlarged at any time for cause shown.

(e) (1) Notwithstanding the provisions of subsection (b) of this section, a defendant in a civil action in a State court may remove the action to the district court of the United States for the district and division embracing the place where the action is pending if:

(A) the action could have been brought in a United States district court under section 1369 of this title; or

(B) the defendant is a party to an action which is or could have been brought, in whole or in part, under section 1369 in a United States district court and arises from the same accident as the action in State court, even if the action to be removed could not have been brought in a district court as an original matter.

The removal of an action under this subsection shall be made in accordance with section 1446 of this title, except that a notice of removal may also be filed before trial of the action in State court within 30 days after the date on which the defendant first becomes a party to an action under section 1369 in a United States district court that arises from the same accident as the action in State court, or at a later time with leave of the district court.

(2) Whenever an action is removed under this subsection and the district court to which it is removed or transferred under section 1407(j) has made a liability determination requiring further proceedings as to damages, the district court shall remand the action to the State court from which it had been removed

for the determination of damages, unless the court finds that, for the convenience of parties and witnesses and in the interest of justice, the action should be retained for the determination of damages.

(3) Any remand under paragraph (2) shall not be effective until 60 days after the district court has issued an order determining liability and has certified its intention to remand the removed action for the determination of damages. An appeal with respect to the liability determination of the district court may be taken during that 60-day period to the court of appeals with appellate jurisdiction over the district court. In the event a party files such an appeal, the remand shall not be effective until the appeal has been finally disposed of. Once the remand has become effective, the liability determination shall not be subject to further review by appeal or otherwise.

(4) Any decision under this subsection concerning remand for the determination of damages shall not be reviewable by appeal or otherwise.

(5) An action removed under this subsection shall be deemed to be an action under section 1369 and an action in which jurisdiction is based on section 1369 of this title for purposes of this section and sections 1407, 1697, and 1785 of this title.

(6) Nothing in this subsection shall restrict the authority of the district court to transfer or dismiss an action on the ground of inconvenient forum.

(f) The court to which a civil action is removed under this section is not precluded from hearing and determining any claim in such civil action because the State court from which such civil action is removed did not have jurisdiction over that claim.

§ 1442. FEDERAL OFFICERS OR AGENCIES SUED OR PROSECUTED

(a) A civil action or criminal prosecution commenced in a State court against any of the following may be removed by them to the district court of the United States for the district and division embracing the place wherein it is pending:

(1) The United States or any agency thereof or any officer (or any person acting under that officer) of the United States or of any agency thereof, sued in an official or individual capacity for any act under color of such office or on account of any right, title or authority claimed under any Act of Congress for the apprehension or punishment of criminals or the collection of the revenue.

(2) A property holder whose title is derived from any such officer, where such action or prosecution affects the validity of any law of the United States.

(3) Any officer of the courts of the United States, for any act under color of office or in the performance of his duties;

(4) Any officer of either House of Congress, for any act in the discharge of his official duty under an order of such House.

(b) A personal action commenced in any State court by an alien against any citizen of a State who is, or at the time the alleged action accrued was, a civil officer of the United States and is a nonresident of such State, wherein jurisdiction is obtained by the State court by personal service of process, may be removed by the defendant to the district court of the United States for the district and division in which the defendant was served with process.

§ 1442A. MEMBERS OF ARMED FORCES SUED OR PROSECUTED

A civil or criminal prosecution in a court of a State of the United States against a member of the armed forces of the United States on account of an act done under color of his office or status, or in respect to which he claims any right, title, or authority under a law of the United States respecting the armed forces thereof, or under the law of war, may at any time before the trial or final hearing thereof be removed for trial into the district court of the United States for the district where it is pending in the manner prescribed by law, and it shall thereupon be entered on the docket of the district court, which shall proceed as if the cause had been originally commenced therein and shall have full power to hear and determine the cause.

§ 1443. CIVIL RIGHTS CASES

Any of the following civil actions or criminal prosecutions, commenced in a State court may be removed by the defendant to the district court of the United States for the district and division embracing the place wherein it is pending:

(1) Against any person who is denied or cannot enforce in the courts of such State a right under any law providing for the equal civil rights of citizens of the United States, or of all persons within the jurisdiction thereof;

(2) For any act under color of authority derived from any law providing for equal rights, or for refusing to do any act on the ground that it would be inconsistent with such law.

§ 1445. NONREMOVABLE ACTIONS

(a) A civil action in any State court against a railroad or its receivers or trustees, arising under sections 1-4 and 5-10 of the Act of April 22, 1908 (45 U.S.C. 51-54, 55-60), may not be removed to any district court of the United States.

(b) A civil action in any State court against a carrier or its receivers or trustees to recover damages for delay, loss, or injury of shipments, arising under section 11706 or 14706 of title 49, may not be removed to any district court of the United States unless the matter in controversy exceeds $10,000, exclusive of interest and costs.

(c) A civil action in any State court arising under the workmen's compensation laws of such State may not be removed to any district court of the United States.

(d) A civil action in any State court arising under section 40302 of the Violence Against Women Act of 1994 may not be removed to any district court of the United States.

§ 1446. PROCEDURE FOR REMOVAL

(a) A defendant or defendants desiring to remove any civil action or criminal prosecution from a State court shall file in the district court of the United States for the district and division within which such action is pending a notice of removal signed pursuant to Rule 11 of the Federal Rules of Civil Procedure and containing a short and plain statement of the grounds for removal, together with a copy of all process, pleadings, and orders served upon such defendant or defendants in such action.

(b) The notice of removal of a civil action or proceeding shall be filed within thirty days after the receipt by the defendant, through service or otherwise, of a copy of the initial pleading setting forth the claim for relief upon which such action or proceeding is based, or within thirty days after the service of summons upon the defendant if such initial pleading has then been filed in court and is not required to be served on the defendant, whichever period is shorter.

If the case stated by the initial pleading is not removable, a notice of removal may be filed within thirty days after receipt by the defendant, through service or otherwise, of a copy of an amended pleading, motion, order or other paper from which it may first be ascertained that the case is one which is or has become removable, except that a case may not be removed on the basis of jurisdiction conferred by section 1332 of this title more than 1 year after commencement of the action.

(c) (1) A notice of removal of a criminal prosecution shall be filed not later than thirty days after the arraignment in the State court, or at any time before trial, whichever is earlier, except that for good cause shown the United States district court may enter an order granting the defendant or defendants leave to file the notice at a later time.

(2) A notice of removal of a criminal prosecution shall include all grounds for such removal. A failure to state grounds which exist at the time of the filing of the notice shall constitute a waiver of such grounds, and a second notice may be filed only on grounds not existing at the time of the original notice. For good cause shown, the United States district court may grant relief from the limitations of this paragraph.

(3) The filing of a notice of removal of a criminal prosecution shall not prevent the State court in which such prosecution is pending from proceeding further, except that a judgment of conviction shall not be entered unless the prosecution is first remanded.

(4) The United States district court in which such notice is filed shall examine the notice promptly. If it clearly appears on the face of the notice and any exhibits annexed thereto that removal should not be permitted, the court shall make an order for summary remand.

(5) If the United States district court does not order the summary remand of such prosecution, it shall order an evidentiary hearing to be held promptly and after such hearing shall make such disposition of the prosecution as justice shall require. If the United States district court determines that removal shall be permitted, it shall so notify the State court in which prosecution is pending, which shall proceed no further.

(d) Promptly after the filing of such notice of removal of a civil action the defendant or defendants shall give written notice thereof to all adverse parties and shall file a copy of the notice with the clerk of such State court, which shall effect the removal and the State court shall proceed no further unless and until the case is remanded.

(e) If the defendant or defendants are in actual custody on process issued by the State court, the district court shall issue its writ of habeas corpus, and the marshal shall thereupon take such defendant or defendants into his custody and deliver a copy of the writ to the clerk of such State court.

(f) With respect to any counterclaim removed to a district court pursuant to section 337(c) of the Tariff Act of 1930, the district court shall resolve such counterclaim in the same manner as an original complaint under the Federal Rules of Civil Procedure, except that the payment of a filing fee shall not be required in such cases and the counterclaim shall relate back to the date of the original complaint in the proceeding before the International Trade Commission under section 337 of that Act.

§ 1447. PROCEDURE AFTER REMOVAL GENERALLY

(a) In any case removed from a State court, the district court may issue all necessary orders and process to bring before it all proper parties whether served by process issued by the State court or otherwise.

(b) It may require the removing party to file with its clerk copies of all records and proceedings in such State court or may cause the same to be brought before it by writ of certiorari issued to such State court.

(c) A motion to remand the case on the basis of any defect other than lack of subject matter jurisdiction must be made within 30 days after the filing of the notice of removal under section 1446(a). If at any time before final judgment it appears that the district court lacks subject matter jurisdiction, the case shall be remanded. An order remanding the case may require payment of just costs and any actual expenses, including attorney fees, incurred as a result of the removal. A certified copy of the order of remand shall be mailed by the clerk to the clerk of the State court. The State court may thereupon proceed with such case.

(d) An order remanding a case to the State court from which it was removed is not reviewable on appeal or otherwise, except that an order remanding a case to the State court from which it was removed pursuant to section 1443 of this title shall be reviewable by appeal or otherwise.

(e) If after removal the plaintiff seeks to join additional defendants whose joinder would destroy subject matter jurisdiction, the court may deny joinder, or permit joinder and remand the action to the State court.

§ 1448. PROCESS AFTER REMOVAL

In all cases removed from any State court to any district court of the United States in which any one or more of the defendants has not been served with process or in which the service has not been perfected prior to removal, or in which process served proves to be defective, such process or service may be completed or new process issued in the same manner as in cases originally filed in such district court.

This section shall not deprive any defendant upon whom process is served after removal of his right to move to remand the case.

§ 1451. DEFINITIONS

For purposes of this chapter:

(1) The term "State court" includes the Superior Court of the District of Columbia.

(2) The term "State" includes the District of Columbia.

§ 1453. REMOVAL OF CLASS ACTIONS

(a) Definitions. In this section, the terms "class," "class action," "class certification order," and "class member" shall have the meanings given such terms under section 1332(d)(1).

(b) In general. A class action may be removed to a district court of the United States in accordance with section 1446 (except that the 1-year limitation under section 1446(b) shall not apply), without regard to whether any defendant is a citizen of the State in which the action is brought, except that such action may be removed by any defendant without the consent of all defendants.

(c) Review of remand orders.

(1) In general. Section 1447 shall apply to any removal of a case under this section, except that notwithstanding section 1447(d), a court of appeals may accept an appeal from an order of a district court granting or denying a motion to remand a class action to the State court from which it was removed if application is made to the court of appeals not less than 7 days after entry of the order.

(2) Time period for judgment.--If the court of appeals accepts an appeal under paragraph (1), the court shall complete all action on such appeal, including rendering judgment, not later than 60 days after the date on which such appeal was filed, unless an extension is granted under paragraph (3).

(3) Extension of time period.--The court of appeals may grant an extension of the 60-day period described in paragraph (2) if—

(A) all parties to the proceeding agree to such extension, for any period of time; or

(B) such extension is for good cause shown and in the interests of justice, for a period not to exceed 10 days.

(4) Denial of appeal. If a final judgment on the appeal under paragraph (1) is not issued before the end of the period described in paragraph (2), including any extension under paragraph (3), the appeal shall be denied.

(d) Exception. This section shall not apply to any class action that solely involves--

(1) a claim concerning a covered security as defined under section 16(f)(3) of the Securities Act of 1933 (15 U.S.C. 78p(f)(3)) and section 28(f)(5)(E) of the Securities Exchange Act of 1934 (15 U.S.C. 78bb(f)(5)(E));

(2) a claim that relates to the internal affairs or governance of a corporation or other form of business enterprise and arises under or by virtue of the laws of the State in which such corporation or business enterprise is incorporated or organized; or

(3) a claim that relates to the rights, duties (including fiduciary duties), and obligations relating to or created by or pursuant to any security (as defined under section 2(a)(1) of the Securities Act of 1933 (15 U.S.C. 77b(a)(1)) and the regulations issued thereunder).

CHAPTER 97. JURISDICTIONAL IMMUNITIES OF FOREIGN STATES

§ 1602. FINDINGS AND DECLARATION OF PURPOSE

The Congress finds that the determination by United States courts of the claims of foreign states to immunity from the jurisdiction of such courts would serve the interests of justice and would protect the rights of both foreign states and litigants in United States courts. Under international law, states are not immune from the jurisdiction of foreign courts insofar as their commercial activities are concerned, and their commercial property may be levied upon for the satisfaction of judgments rendered against them in connection with their commercial activities. Claims of foreign states to immunity should henceforth be decided by courts of the United States and of the States in conformity with the principles set forth in this chapter.

§ 1603. DEFINITIONS

For purposes of this chapter:

(a) A "foreign state", except as used in section 1608 of this title, includes a political subdivision of a foreign state or an agency or instrumentality of a foreign state as defined in subsection (b).

(b) An "agency or instrumentality of a foreign state" means any entity:

(1) which is a separate legal person, corporate or otherwise, and

(2) which is an organ of a foreign state or political subdivision thereof, or a majority of whose shares or other ownership interest is owned by a foreign state or political subdivision thereof, and

(3) which is neither a citizen of a State of the United States as defined in section 1332(c) and (e) of this title, nor created under the laws of any third country.

(c) The "United States" includes all territory and waters, continental or insular, subject to the jurisdiction of the United States.

(d) A "commercial activity" means either a regular course of commercial conduct or a particular commercial transaction or act. The commercial character of an activity shall be determined by reference to the nature of the course of conduct or particular transaction or act, rather than by reference to its purpose.

(e) A "commercial activity carried on in the United States by a foreign state" means commercial activity carried on by such state and having substantial contact with the United States.

§ 1604. IMMUNITY OF A FOREIGN STATE FROM JURISDICTION

Subject to existing international agreements to which the United States is a party at the time of enactment of this Act a foreign state shall be immune from the jurisdiction of the courts of the United States and of the States except as provided in sections 1605 to 1607 of this chapter.

§ 1605. GENERAL EXCEPTIONS TO THE JURISDICTIONAL IMMUNITY OF A FOREIGN STATE

(a) A foreign state shall not be immune from the jurisdiction of courts of the United States or of the States in any case:

(1) in which the foreign state has waived its immunity either explicitly or by implication, notwithstanding any withdrawal of the waiver which the foreign state may purport to effect except in accordance with the terms of the waiver;

(2) in which the action is based upon a commercial activity carried on in the United States by the foreign state; or upon an act performed in the United States in connection with a commercial activity of the foreign state elsewhere; or upon an act outside the territory of the United States in connection with a commercial activity of the foreign state elsewhere and that act causes a direct effect in the United States;

(3) in which rights in property taken in violation of international law are in issue and that property or any property exchanged for such property is present in the United States in connection with a commercial activity carried on in the United States by the foreign state; or that property or any property exchanged for such property is owned or operated by an agency or instrumentality of the foreign state and that agency or instrumentality is engaged in a commercial activity in the United States;

(4) in which rights in property in the United States acquired by succession or gift or rights in immovable property situated in the United States are in issue;

(5) not otherwise encompassed in paragraph (2) above, in which money damages are sought against a foreign state for personal injury or death, or damage to or loss of property, occurring in the United States and caused by the tortious act or omission of that foreign state or of any official or employee of that foreign state while acting within the scope of his office or employment; except this paragraph shall not apply to:

(A) any claim based upon the exercise or performance or the failure to exercise or perform a discretionary function regardless of whether the discretion be abused, or

(B) any claim arising out of malicious prosecution, abuse of process, libel, slander, misrepresentation, deceit, or interference with contract rights; or

(6) in which the action is brought, either to enforce an agreement made by the foreign state with or for the benefit of a private party to submit to arbitration all or any differences which have arisen or which may arise between the parties with respect to a defined legal relationship, whether contractual or not, concerning a subject matter capable of settlement by arbitration under the laws of the United States, or to confirm an award made pursuant to such an agreement to arbitrate, if (A) the arbitration takes place or is intended to take place in the United States, (B) the agreement or award is or may be governed by a treaty or other international agreement in force for the United States calling for the recognition and enforcement of arbitral awards, (C) the underlying claim, save for the agreement to arbitrate, could have been brought in a United States court under this section or section 1607, or (D) paragraph (1) of this subsection is otherwise applicable.

(7) Repealed.

(b) A foreign state shall not be immune from the jurisdiction of the courts of the United States in any case in which a suit in admiralty is brought to enforce a maritime lien against a vessel or cargo of the foreign state, which maritime lien is based upon a commercial activity of the foreign state: Provided, That--

(1) notice of the suit is given by delivery of a copy of the summons and of the complaint to the person, or his agent, having possession of the vessel or cargo against which the maritime lien is asserted; and if the vessel or cargo is arrested pursuant to process obtained on behalf of the party bringing the suit, the service of process of arrest shall be deemed to constitute valid delivery of such notice, but the party bringing the suit shall be liable for any damages sustained by the foreign state as a result of the arrest if the party bringing the suit had actual or constructive knowledge that the vessel or cargo of a foreign state was involved; and

(2) notice to the foreign state of the commencement of suit as provided in section 1608 of this title is initiated within ten days either of the delivery of notice as provided in paragraph (1) of this subsection or, in the case of a party who was unaware that the vessel or cargo of a foreign state was involved, of the date such party determined the existence of the foreign state's interest.

(c) Whenever notice is delivered under subsection (b)(1), the suit to enforce a maritime lien shall thereafter proceed and shall be heard and determined according to the principles of law and rules of practice of suits in rem whenever it appears that, had the vessel been privately owned and possessed, a suit in rem might have been maintained. A decree against the foreign state may include costs of the suit and, if the decree is for a money judgment, interest as ordered by the court, except that the court may not award judgment against the foreign state in an amount greater than the value of the vessel or cargo upon which the maritime lien arose. Such value shall be determined as of the time notice is served under subsection (b)(1). Decrees shall be subject to appeal and revision as provided in other cases of admiralty and maritime jurisdiction. Nothing shall preclude the plaintiff in any proper case from seeking relief in personam in the same action brought to enforce a maritime lien as provided in this section.

(d) A foreign state shall not be immune from the jurisdiction of the courts of the United States in any action brought to foreclose a preferred mortgage, as defined in section 31301 of title 46. Such action shall be brought, heard, and determined in accordance with the provisions of chapter 313 of title 46 and in accordance with the principles of law and rules of practice of suits in rem, whenever it appears that had the vessel been privately owned and possessed a suit in rem might have been maintained.

(e), (f) Repealed.

(g) Limitation on discovery.

(1) In general.

(A) Subject to paragraph (2), if an action is filed that would otherwise be barred by section 1604, but for section 1605A, the court, upon request of the Attorney General, shall stay any request, demand, or order for discovery on the United States that the Attorney General certifies would significantly interfere with a criminal investigation or prosecution, or a national security operation, related to the incident that gave rise to the cause of action, until such time as the Attorney General advises the court that such request, demand, or order will no longer so interfere.

(B) A stay under this paragraph shall be in effect during the 12-month period beginning on the date on which the court issues the order to stay discovery. The court shall renew the order to stay discovery for additional 12-month periods upon motion by the United States if the Attorney General certifies that discovery would significantly interfere with a criminal investigation or prosecution, or a national security operation, related to the incident that gave rise to the cause of action.

(2) Sunset.

(A) Subject to subparagraph (B), no stay shall be granted or continued in effect under paragraph (1) after the date that is 10 years after the date on which the incident that gave rise to the cause of action occurred.

(B) After the period referred to in subparagraph (A), the court, upon request of the Attorney General, may stay any request, demand, or order for discovery on the United States that the court finds a substantial likelihood would

(i) create a serious threat of death or serious bodily injury to any person;

(ii) adversely affect the ability of the United States to work in cooperation with foreign and international law enforcement agencies in investigating violations of United States law; or

(iii) obstruct the criminal case related to the incident that gave rise to the cause of action or undermine the potential for a conviction in such case.

(3) Evaluation of evidence. The court's evaluation of any request for a stay under this subsection filed by the Attorney General shall be conducted ex parte and in camera.

(4) Bar on motions to dismiss. A stay of discovery under this subsection shall constitute a bar to the granting of a motion to dismiss under rules 12(b)(6) and 56 of the Federal Rules of Civil Procedure.

(5) Construction.--Nothing in this subsection shall prevent the United States from seeking protective orders or asserting privileges ordinarily available to the United States.

§ 1605A. TERRORISM EXCEPTION TO THE JURISDICTIONAL IMMUNITY OF A FOREIGN STATE

(a) In general.

(1) No immunity. A foreign state shall not be immune from the jurisdiction of courts of the United States or of the States in any case not otherwise covered by this chapter in which money damages are sought against a foreign state for personal injury or death that was caused by an act of torture, extrajudicial killing, aircraft sabotage, hostage taking, or the provision of material support or resources for such an act if such act or provision of material support or resources is engaged in by an official, employee, or agent of such foreign state while acting within the scope of his or her office, employment, or agency.

(2) Claim heard. The court shall hear a claim under this section if

(A)(i)(I) the foreign state was designated as a state sponsor of terrorism at the time the act described in paragraph (1) occurred, or was so designated as a result of such act, and, subject to subclause (II), either remains so designated when the claim is filed under this section or was so designated within the 6-month period before the claim is filed under this section; or

(II) in the case of an action that is refiled under this section by reason of section 1083(c)(2)(A) of the National Defense Authorization Act for Fiscal Year 2008 or is filed under this section by reason of section 1083(c)(3) of that Act, the foreign state was designated as a state sponsor of terrorism when the original action or the related action under section 1605(a)(7) (as in effect before the enactment of this section) or section 589 of the Foreign Operations, Export Financing, and Related Programs Appropriations Act, 1997 (as contained in section 101(c) of division A of Public Law 104-208) was filed;

(ii) the claimant or the victim was, at the time the act described in paragraph (1) occurred

(I) a national of the United States;

(II) a member of the armed forces; or

(III) otherwise an employee of the Government of the United States, or of an individual performing a contract awarded by the United States Government, acting within the scope of the employee's employment; and

(iii) in a case in which the act occurred in the foreign state against which the claim has been brought, the claimant has afforded the foreign state a reasonable opportunity to arbitrate the claim in accordance with the accepted international rules of arbitration; or

(B) the act described in paragraph (1) is related to Case Number 1:00CV03110 (EGS) in the United States District Court for the District of Columbia.

(b) Limitations. An action may be brought or maintained under this section if the action is commenced, or a related action was commenced under section 1605(a)(7) (before the date of the enactment of this section) or section 589 of the Foreign Operations, Export Financing, and Related Programs Appropriations Act, 1997 (as contained in section 101(c) of division A of Public Law 104-208) not later than the latter of--

(1) 10 years after April 24, 1996; or

(2) 10 years after the date on which the cause of action arose.

(c) Private right of action.--A foreign state that is or was a state sponsor of terrorism as described in subsection (a)(2)(A)(i), and any official, employee, or agent of that foreign state while acting within the scope of his or her office, employment, or agency, shall be liable to

(1) a national of the United States,

(2) a member of the armed forces,

(3) an employee of the Government of the United States, or of an individual performing a contract awarded by the United States Government, acting within the scope of the employee's employment, or

(4) the legal representative of a person described in paragraph (1), (2), or (3),

for personal injury or death caused by acts described in subsection (a) (1) of that foreign state, or of an official, employee, or agent of that foreign state, for which the courts of the United States may maintain jurisdiction under this section for money damages. In any such action, damages may include economic damages, solatium, pain and suffering, and punitive damages. In any such action, a foreign state shall be vicariously liable for the acts of its officials, employees, or agents.

(d) Additional damages. After an action has been brought under subsection (c), actions may also be brought for reasonably foreseeable property loss, whether insured or uninsured, third party liability, and loss claims under life and property insurance policies, by reason of the same acts on which the action under subsection (c) is based.

(e) Special masters.

(1) In general. The courts of the United States may appoint special masters to hear damage claims brought under this section.

(2) Transfer of funds. The Attorney General shall transfer, from funds available for the program under section 1404C of the Victims of Crime Act of 1984 (42 U.S.C. 10603c), to the Administrator of the United States district court in which any case is pending which has been brought or maintained under this section such funds as may be required to cover the costs of special masters appointed under paragraph (1). Any amount paid in compensation to any such special master shall constitute an item of court costs.

(f) Appeal. In an action brought under this section, appeals from orders not conclusively ending the litigation may only be taken pursuant to section 1292(b) of this title.

(g) Property disposition.

(1) In general.--In every action filed in a United States district court in which jurisdiction is alleged under this section, the filing of a notice of pending action pursuant to this section, to which is attached a copy of the complaint filed in the action, shall have the effect of establishing a lien of lis pendens upon any real property or tangible personal property that is

(A) subject to attachment in aid of execution, or execution, under section 1610;

(B) located within that judicial district; and

(C) titled in the name of any defendant, or titled in the name of any entity controlled by any defendant if such notice contains a statement listing such controlled entity.

(2) Notice. A notice of pending action pursuant to this section shall be filed by the clerk of the district court in the same manner as any pending action and shall be indexed by listing as defendants all named defendants and all entities listed as controlled by any defendant.

(3) Enforceability. Liens established by reason of this subsection shall be enforceable as provided in chapter 111 of this title.

(h) Definitions. For purposes of this section

(1) the term "aircraft sabotage" has the meaning given that term in Article 1 of the Convention for the Suppression of Unlawful Acts Against the Safety of Civil Aviation;

(2) the term "hostage taking" has the meaning given that term in Article 1 of the International Convention Against the Taking of Hostages;

(3) the term "material support or resources" has the meaning given that term in section 2339A of title 18;

(4) the term "armed forces" has the meaning given that term in section 101 of title 10;

(5) the term "national of the United States" has the meaning given that term in section 101(a)(22) of the Immigration and Nationality Act (8 U.S.C. 1101(a)(22));

(6) the term "state sponsor of terrorism" means a country the government of which the Secretary of State has determined, for purposes of section 6(j) of the Export Administration Act of 1979 (50 U.S.C. App. 2405(j)), section 620A of the Foreign Assistance Act of 1961 (22 U.S.C. 2371), section 40 of the Arms Export Control Act (22 U.S.C. 2780), or any other provision of law, is a government that has repeatedly provided support for acts of international terrorism; and

(7) the terms "torture" and "extrajudicial killing" have the meaning given those terms in section 3 of the Torture Victim Protection Act of 1991 (28 U.S.C. 1350 note).

§ 1606. EXTENT OF LIABILITY

As to any claim for relief with respect to which a foreign state is not entitled to immunity under section 1605 or 1607 of this chapter, the foreign state shall be liable in the same manner and to the same extent as a private individual under like circumstances; but a foreign state except for an agency or instrumentality thereof shall not be liable for punitive damages; if, however, in any case wherein death was caused, the law of the place where the action or omission occurred provides, or has been construed to provide, for damages only punitive in nature, the foreign state shall be liable for actual or compensatory damages measured by the pecuniary injuries resulting from such death which were incurred by the persons for whose benefit the action was brought.

§ 1607. COUNTERCLAIMS

In any action brought by a foreign state, or in which a foreign state intervenes, in a court of the United States or of a State, the foreign state shall not be accorded immunity with respect to any counterclaim:

(a) for which a foreign state would not be entitled to immunity under section 1605 or 1605A of this chapter had such claim been brought in a separate action against the foreign state; or

(b) arising out of the transaction or occurrence that is the subject matter of the claim of the foreign state; or

(c) to the extent that the counterclaim does not seek relief exceeding in amount or differing in kind from that sought by the foreign state.

§ 1608. SERVICE; TIME TO ANSWER; DEFAULT

(a) Service in the courts of the United States and of the States shall be made upon a foreign state or political subdivision of a foreign state:

(1) by delivery of a copy of the summons and complaint in accordance with any special arrangement for service between the plaintiff and the foreign state or political subdivision; or

(2) if no special arrangement exists, by delivery of a copy of the summons and complaint in accordance with an applicable international convention on service of judicial documents; or

(3) if service cannot be made under paragraphs (1) or (2), by sending a copy of the summons and complaint and a notice of suit, together with a translation of each into the official language of the foreign state, by any form of mail requiring a signed receipt, to be addressed and dispatched by the clerk of the court to the head of the ministry of foreign affairs of the foreign state concerned, or

(4) if service cannot be made within 30 days under paragraph (3), by sending two copies of the summons and complaint and a notice of suit, together with a translation of each into the official language of the foreign state, by any form of mail requiring a signed receipt, to be addressed and dispatched by the clerk of the court to the Secretary of State in Washington, District of Columbia, to the attention of the Director of Special Consular Services and the Secretary shall transmit one copy of the papers through diplomatic channels to the foreign state and shall send to the clerk of the court a certified copy of the diplomatic note indicating when the papers were transmitted.

As used in this subsection, a "notice of suit" shall mean a notice addressed to a foreign state and in a form prescribed by the Secretary of State by regulation.

(b) Service in the courts of the United States and of the States shall be made upon an agency or instrumentality of a foreign state:

(1) by delivery of a copy of the summons and complaint in accordance with any special arrangement for service between the plaintiff and the agency or instrumentality; or

(2) if no special arrangement exists, by delivery of a copy of the summons and complaint either to an officer, a managing or general agent, or to any other agent authorized by appointment or by law to receive service of process in the United States; or in accordance with an applicable international convention on service of judicial documents; or

(3) if service cannot be made under paragraphs (1) or (2), and if reasonably calculated to give actual notice, by delivery of a copy of the summons and complaint, together with a translation of each into the official language of the foreign state:

(A) as directed by an authority of the foreign state or political subdivision in response to a letter rogatory or request or

(B) by any form of mail requiring a signed receipt, to be addressed and dispatched by the clerk of the court to the agency or instrumentality to be served, or

(C) as directed by order of the court consistent with the law of the place where service is to be made.

(c) Service shall be deemed to have been made:

(1) in the case of service under subsection (a)(4), as of the date of transmittal indicated in the certified copy of the diplomatic note; and

(2) in any other case under this section, as of the date of receipt indicated in the certification, signed and returned postal receipt, or other proof of service applicable to the method of service employed.

(d) In any action brought in a court of the United States or of a State, a foreign state, a political subdivision thereof, or an agency or instrumentality of a foreign state shall serve an answer or other responsive pleading to the complaint within sixty days after service has been made under this section.

(e) No judgment by default shall be entered by a court of the United States or of a State against a foreign state, a political subdivision thereof, or an agency or instrumentality of a foreign state, unless the claimant establishes his claim or right to relief by evidence satisfactory to the court. A copy of any such default judgment shall be sent to the foreign state or political subdivision in the manner prescribed for service in this section.

§ 1609. IMMUNITY FROM ATTACHMENT AND EXECUTION OF PROPERTY OF A FOREIGN STATE

Subject to existing international agreements to which the United States is a party at the time of enactment of this Act the property in the United States of a foreign state shall be immune from attachment arrest and execution except as provided in sections 1610 and 1611 of this chapter.

§ 1610. EXCEPTIONS TO THE IMMUNITY FROM ATTACHMENT OR EXECUTION

(a) The property in the United States of a foreign state, as defined in section 1603(a) of this chapter, used for a commercial activity in the United States, shall not be immune from attachment in aid of execution, or from execution, upon a judgment entered by a court of the United States or of a State after the effective date of this Act, if:

(1) the foreign state has waived its immunity from attachment in aid of execution or from execution either explicitly or by implication, notwithstanding any withdrawal of the waiver the foreign state may purport to effect except in accordance with the terms of the waiver, or

(2) the property is or was used for the commercial activity upon which the claim is based, or

(3) the execution relates to a judgment establishing rights in property which has been taken in violation of international law or which has been exchanged for property taken in violation of international law, or

(4) the execution relates to a judgment establishing rights in property:

(A) which is acquired by succession or gift, or

(B) which is immovable and situated in the United States: Provided, That such property is not used for purposes of maintaining a diplomatic or consular mission or the residence of the Chief of such mission, or

(5) the property consists of any contractual obligation or any proceeds from such a contractual obligation to indemnify or hold harmless the foreign state or its employees under a policy of automobile or other liability or casualty insurance covering the claim which merged into the judgment, or

(6) the judgment is based on an order confirming an arbitral award rendered against the foreign state, provided that attachment in aid of execution, or execution, would not be inconsistent with any provision in the arbitral agreement, or

(7) the judgment relates to a claim for which the foreign state is not immune under section 1605A, regardless of whether the property is or was involved with the act upon which the claim is based.

(b) In addition to subsection (a), any property in the United States of an agency or instrumentality of a foreign state engaged in commercial activity in the United States shall not be immune from attachment in aid of execution, or from execution, upon a judgment entered by a court of the United States or of a State after the effective date of this Act, if

(1) the agency or instrumentality has waived its immunity from attachment in aid of execution or from execution either explicitly or implicitly, notwithstanding any withdrawal of the waiver the agency or instrumentality may purport to effect except in accordance with the terms of the waiver, or

(2) the judgment relates to a claim for which the agency or instrumentality is not immune by virtue of section 1605(a) (2), (3), or (5), 1605(b), or 1605A of this chapter, regardless of whether the property is or was involved in the act upon which the claim is based.

(c) No attachment or execution referred to in subsections (a) and (b) of this section shall be permitted until the court has ordered such attachment and execution after having determined that a reasonable period of time has elapsed following the entry of judgment and the giving of any notice required under section 1608(e) of this chapter.

(d) The property of a foreign state, as defined in section 1603(a) of this chapter, used for a commercial activity in the United States, shall not be immune from attachment prior to the entry of judgment in any action brought in a court of the United States or of a State, or prior to the elapse of the period of time provided in subsection (c) of this section, if

(1) the foreign state has explicitly waived its immunity from attachment prior to judgment, notwithstanding any withdrawal of the waiver the foreign state may purport to effect except in accordance with the terms of the waiver, and

(2) the purpose of the attachment is to secure satisfaction of a judgment that has been or may ultimately be entered against the foreign state, and not to obtain jurisdiction.

(e) The vessels of a foreign state shall not be immune from arrest in rem, interlocutory sale, and execution in actions brought to foreclose a preferred mortgage as provided in section 1605(d).

(f)(1)(A) Notwithstanding any other provision of law, including but not limited to section 208(f) of the Foreign Missions Act (22 U.S.C. 4308(f)), and except as provided in subparagraph (B), any property with respect to which financial transactions are prohibited or regulated pursuant to section 5(b) of the Trading with the Enemy Act (50 U.S.C. App. 5(b)), section 620(a) of the Foreign Assistance Act of 1961 (22 U.S.C. 2370(a)), sections 202 and 203 of the International Emergency Economic Powers Act (50 U.S.C. 1701-1702), or any other proclamation, order, regulation, or license issued pursuant thereto, shall be subject to execution or attachment in aid of execution of any judgment relating to a claim for which a foreign state (including any agency or instrumentality or such state) claiming such property is not immune under section 1605(a)(7) (as in effect before the enactment of section 1605A) or section 1605A.

(B) Subparagraph (A) shall not apply if, at the time the property is expropriated or seized by the foreign state, the property has been held in title by a natural person or, if held in trust, has been held for the benefit of a natural person or persons.

(2)(A) At the request of any party in whose favor a judgment has been issued with respect to a claim for which the foreign state is not immune under section 1605(a)(7) as in effect before the enactment of section 1605A) or section 1605A, the Secretary of the Treasury and the Secretary of State should make every effort to fully, promptly, and effectively assist any judgment creditor or any court that has issued any such judgment in identifying, locating, and executing against the property of that foreign state or any agency or instrumentality of such state.

(B) In providing such assistance, the Secretaries

(i) may provide such information to the court under seal; and

(ii) should make every effort to provide the information in a manner sufficient to allow the court to direct the United States Marshall's office to promptly and effectively execute against that property.

(3) Waiver. The President may waive any provision of paragraph (1) in the interest of national security.

(g) Property in certain actions.

(1) In general. Subject to paragraph (3), the property of a foreign state against which a judgment is entered under section 1605A, and the property of an agency or instrumentality of such a state, including property that is a separate juridical entity or is an interest held directly or indirectly in a separate juridical entity, is subject to attachment in aid of execution, and execution, upon that judgment as provided in this section, regardless of

(A) the level of economic control over the property by the government of the foreign state;

(B) whether the profits of the property go to that government;

(C) the degree to which officials of that government manage the property or otherwise control its daily affairs;

(D) whether that government is the sole beneficiary in interest of the property; or

(E) whether establishing the property as a separate entity would entitle the foreign state to benefits in United States courts while avoiding its obligations.

(2) United States sovereign immunity inapplicable. Any property of a foreign state, or agency or instrumentality of a foreign state, to which paragraph (1) applies shall not be immune from attachment in aid of execution, or execution, upon a judgment entered under section 1605A because the property is regulated by the United States Government by reason of action taken against that foreign state under the Trading With the Enemy Act or the International Emergency Economic Powers Act.

(3) Third-party joint property holders. Nothing in this subsection shall be construed to supersede the authority of a court to prevent appropriately the impairment of an interest held by a person who is not liable in the action giving rise to a judgment in property subject to attachment in aid of execution, or execution, upon such judgment.

§ 1611. CERTAIN TYPES OF PROPERTY IMMUNE FROM EXECUTION

(a) Notwithstanding the provisions of section 1610 of this chapter, the property of those organizations designated by the President as being entitled to enjoy the privileges, exemptions, and immunities provided by the International Organizations Immunities Act shall not be subject to attachment or any other judicial process impeding the disbursement of funds to, or on the order of, a foreign state as the result of an action brought in the courts of the United States or of the States.

(b) Notwithstanding the provisions of section 1610 of this chapter, the property of a foreign state shall be immune from attachment and from execution, if:

(1) the property is that of a foreign central bank or monetary authority held for its own account, unless such bank or authority, or its parent foreign government, has explicitly waived its immunity from attachment in aid of execution, or from execution, notwithstanding any withdrawal of the waiver which the bank, authority or government may purport to effect except in accordance with the terms of the waiver; or

(2) the property is, or is intended to be, used in connection with a military activity and

    (A) is of a military character, or

    (B) is under the control of a military authority or defense agency.

(c) Notwithstanding the provisions of section 1610 of this chapter, the property of a foreign state shall be immune from attachment and from execution in an action brought under section 302 of the Cuban Liberty and Democratic Solidarity (LIBERTAD) Act of 1996 to the extent that the property is a facility or installation used by an accredited diplomatic mission for official purposes.

CHAPTER 99. GENERAL PROVISIONS

§ 1631. TRANSFER TO CURE WANT OF JURISDICTION

Whenever a civil action is filed in a court as defined in section 610 of this title or an appeal, including a petition for review of administrative action, is noticed for or filed with such a court and that court finds that there is a want of jurisdiction, the court shall, if it is in the interest of justice, transfer such action or appeal to any other such court in which the action or appeal could have been brought at the time it was filed or noticed, and the action or appeal shall proceed as if it had been filed in or noticed for the court to which it is transferred on the date upon which it was actually filed in or noticed for the court from which it is transferred.

PART V. PROCEDURE

CHAPTER 111. GENERAL PROVISIONS

§ 1651. WRITS

(a) The Supreme Court and all courts established by Act of Congress may issue all writs necessary or appropriate in aid of their respective jurisdictions and agreeable to the usages and principles of law.

(b) An alternative writ or rule nisi may be issued by a justice or judge of a court which has jurisdiction.

§ 1652. STATE LAWS AS RULES OF DECISION

The laws of the several states, except where the Constitution or treaties of the United States or Acts of Congress otherwise require or provide, shall be regarded as rules of decision in civil actions in the courts of the United States, in cases where they apply.

§ 1653. AMENDMENT OF PLEADINGS TO SHOW JURISDICTION

Defective allegations of jurisdiction may be amended, upon terms, in the trial or appellate courts.

§ 1654. APPEARANCE PERSONALLY OR BY COUNSEL

In all courts of the United States the parties may plead and conduct their own cases personally or by counsel as, by the rules of such courts, respectively, are permitted to manage and conduct causes therein.

§ 1658. TIME LIMITATIONS ON THE COMMENCEMENT OF CIVIL ACTIONS ARISING UNDER ACTS OF CONGRESS

(a) Except as otherwise provided by law, a civil action arising under an Act of Congress enacted after the date of the enactment of this section may not be commenced later than 4 years after the cause of action accrues.

(b) Notwithstanding subsection (a), a private right of action that involves a claim of fraud, deceit, manipulation, or contrivance in contravention of a regulatory requirement concerning the securities laws, as defined in section 3(a)(47) of the Securities Exchange Act of 1934 (15 U.S.C. 78c(a)(47)), may be brought not later than the earlier of:

    (1) 2 years after the discovery of the facts constituting the violation; or

    (2) 5 years after such violation.

CHAPTER 113. PROCESS

§ 1693. PLACE OF ARREST IN CIVIL ACTION

Except as otherwise provided by Act of Congress, no person shall be arrested in one district for trial in another in any civil action in a district court.

§ 1694. PATENT INFRINGEMENT ACTION

In a patent infringement action commenced in a district where the defendant is not a resident but has a regular and established place of business, service of process, summons or subpoena upon such defendant may be made upon his agent or agents conducting such business.

§ 1695. STOCKHOLDER'S DERIVATIVE ACTION

Process in a stockholder's action in behalf of his corporation may be served upon such corporation in any district where it is organized or licensed to do business or is doing business.

§ 1696. SERVICE IN FOREIGN AND INTERNATIONAL LITIGATION

(a) The district court of the district in which a person resides or is found may order service upon him of any document issued in connection with a proceeding in a foreign or international tribunal. The order may be made pursuant to a letter rogatory issued, or request made, by a foreign or international tribunal or upon application of any interested person and shall direct the manner of service. Service pursuant to this subsection does not, of itself, require the recognition or enforcement in the United States of a judgment, decree, or order rendered by a foreign or international tribunal.

(b) This section does not preclude service of such a document without an order of court.

§ 1697. SERVICE IN MULTIPARTY, MULTIFORUM ACTIONS

When the jurisdiction of the district court is based in whole or in part upon section 1369 of this title, process, other than subpoenas, may be served at any place within the United States, or anywhere outside the United States if otherwise permitted by law.

CHAPTER 114. CLASS ACTIONS

§ 1711. DEFINITIONS

In this chapter:

(1) Class. The term "class" means all of the class members in a class action.

(2) Class action. The term "class action" means any civil action filed in a district court of the United States under rule 23 of the Federal Rules of Civil Procedure or any civil action that is removed to a district court of the United States that was originally filed under a State statute or rule of judicial procedure authorizing an action to be brought by 1 or more representatives as a class action.

(3) Class counsel. The term "class counsel" means the persons who serve as the attorneys for the class members in a proposed or certified class action.

(4) Class members. The term "class members" means the persons (named or unnamed) who fall within the definition of the proposed or certified class in a class action.

(5) Plaintiff class action. The term "plaintiff class action" means a class action in which class members are plaintiffs.

(6) Proposed settlement. The term "proposed settlement" means an agreement regarding a class action that is subject to court approval and that, if approved, would be binding on some or all class members.

§ 1712. COUPON SETTLEMENTS

(a) Contingent fees in coupon settlements. If a proposed settlement in a class action provides for a recovery of coupons to a class member, the portion of any attorney's fee award to class counsel that is attributable to the award of the coupons shall be based on the value to class members of the coupons that are redeemed.

(b) Other attorney's fee awards in coupon settlements.

(1) In general. If a proposed settlement in a class action provides for a recovery of coupons to class members, and a portion of the recovery of the coupons is not used to determine the attorney's fee to be paid to class counsel, any attorney's fee award shall be based upon the amount of time class counsel reasonably expended working on the action.

(2) Court approval. Any attorney's fee under this subsection shall be subject to approval by the court and shall include an appropriate attorney's fee, if any, for obtaining equitable relief, including an injunction, if applicable. Nothing in this subsection shall be construed to prohibit application of a lodestar with a multiplier method of determining attorney's fees.

(c) Attorney's fee awards calculated on a mixed basis in coupon settlements.--If a proposed settlement in a class action provides for an award of coupons to class members and also provides for equitable relief, including injunctive relief--

(1) that portion of the attorney's fee to be paid to class counsel that is based upon a portion of the recovery of the coupons shall be calculated in accordance with subsection (a); and

(2) that portion of the attorney's fee to be paid to class counsel that is not based upon a portion of the recovery of the coupons shall be calculated in accordance with subsection (b).

(d) Settlement valuation expertise. In a class action involving the awarding of coupons, the court may, in its discretion upon the motion of a party, receive expert testimony from a witness qualified to provide information on the actual value to the class members of the coupons that are redeemed.

(e) Judicial scrutiny of coupon settlements. In a proposed settlement under which class members would be awarded coupons, the court may approve the proposed settlement only after a hearing to determine whether, and making a written finding that, the settlement is fair, reasonable, and adequate for class members. The court, in its discretion, may also require that a proposed settlement agreement provide for the distribution of a portion of the value of unclaimed coupons to 1 or more charitable or governmental organizations, as agreed to by the parties. The distribution and redemption of any proceeds under this subsection shall not be used to calculate attorneys' fees under this section.

§ 1713. PROTECTION AGAINST LOSS BY CLASS MEMBERS
The court may approve a proposed settlement under which any class member is obligated to pay sums to class counsel that would result in a net loss to the class member only if the court makes a written finding that nonmonetary benefits to the class member substantially outweigh the monetary loss.

§ 1714. PROTECTION AGAINST DISCRIMINATION BASED ON GEOGRAPHIC LOCATION
The court may not approve a proposed settlement that provides for the payment of greater sums to some class members than to others solely on the basis that the class members to whom the greater sums are to be paid are located in closer geographic proximity to the court.

§ 1715. NOTIFICATIONS TO APPROPRIATE FEDERAL AND STATE OFFICIALS
　(a) Definitions
　　　(1) Appropriate Federal official. In this section, the term "appropriate Federal official" means
　　　　　(A) the Attorney General of the United States; or
　　　　　(B) in any case in which the defendant is a Federal depository institution, a State depository institution, a depository institution holding company, a foreign bank, or a nondepository institution subsidiary of the foregoing (as such terms are defined in section 3 of the Federal Deposit Insurance Act (12 U.S.C. 1813)), the person who has the primary Federal regulatory or supervisory responsibility with respect to the defendant, if some or all of the matters alleged in the class action are subject to regulation or supervision by that person.
　　　(2) Appropriate State official. In this section, the term "appropriate State official" means the person in the State who has the primary regulatory or supervisory responsibility with respect to the defendant, or who licenses or otherwise authorizes the defendant to conduct busienss in the State, if some or all of the matters alleged in the class action are subject to regulation by that person. If there is no primary regulator, supervisor, or licensing authority, or the matters alleged in the class action are not subject to regulation or supervision by that person, then the appropriate State official shall be the State attorney general.
　(b) In general. Not later than 10 days after a proposed settlement of a class action is filed in court, each defendant that is participating in the proposed settlement shall serve upon the appropriate State official of each State in which a class member resides and the appropriate Federal official, a notice of the proposed settlement consisting of--
　　　(1) a copy of the complaint and any materials filed with the complaint and any amended complaints (except such materials shall not be required to be served if such materials are made electronically available through the Internet and such service includes notice of how to electronically access such material);
　　　(2) notice of any scheduled judicial hearing in the class action;
　　　(3) any proposed or final notification to class members of--
　　　　　(A)
　　　　　　　(i) the members' rights to request exclusion from the class action; or
　　　　　　　(ii) if no right to request exclusion exists, a statement that no such right exists; and
　　　　　(B) a proposed settlement of a class action;
　　　(4) any proposed or final class action settlement;
　　　(5) any settlement or other agreement contemporaneously made between class counsel and counsel for the defendants;
　　　(6) any final judgment or notice of dismissal;
　　　(7)(A) if feasible, the names of class members who reside in each State and the estimated proportionate share of the claims of such members to the entire settlement to that State's appropriate State official; or
　　　　　(B) if the provision of information under subparagraph (A) is not feasible, a reasonable estimate of the number of class members residing in each State and the estimated proportionate share of the claims of such members to the entire settlement; and
　　　(8) any written judicial opinion relating to the materials described under subparagraphs (3) through (6).
　(c) Depository institutions notification.
　　　(1) Federal and other depository institutions. In any case in which the defendant is a Federal depository institution, a depository institution holding company, a foreign bank, or a non-depository institution subsidiary of the foregoing, the notice requirements of this section are satisfied by serving the notice required under subsection (b) upon the person who has the primary Federal regulatory or supervisory responsibility with respect to the defendant, if some or all of the matters alleged in the class action are subject to regulation or supervision by that person.
　　　(2) State depository institutions. In any case in which the defendant is a State depository institution (as that term is defined in section 3 of the Federal Deposit Insurance Act (12 U.S.C. 1813)), the notice

requirements of this section are satisfied by serving the notice required under subsection (b) upon the State bank supervisor (as that term is defined in section 3 of the Federal Deposit Insurance Act (12 U.S.C. 1813)) of the State in which the defendant is incorporated or chartered, if some or all of the matters alleged in the class action are subject to regulation or supervision by that person, and upon the appropriate Federal official.

(d) Final approval. An order giving final approval of a proposed settlement may not be issued earlier than 90 days after the later of the dates on which the appropriate Federal official and the appropriate State official are served with the notice required under subsection (b).

(e) Noncompliance if notice not provided.

(1) In general. A class member may refuse to comply with and may choose not to be bound by a settlement agreement or consent decree in a class action if the class member demonstrates that the notice required under subsection (b) has not been provided.

(2) Limitation. A class member may not refuse to comply with or to be bound by a settlement agreement or consent decree under paragraph (1) if the notice required under subsection (b) was directed to the appropriate Federal official and to either the State attorney general or the person that has primary regulatory, supervisory, or licensing authority over the defendant.

(3) Application of rights. The rights created by this subsection shall apply only to class members or any person acting on a class member's behalf, and shall not be construed to limit any other rights affecting a class member's participation in the settlement.

(f) Rule of construction. Nothing in this section shall be construed to expand the authority of, or impose any obligations, duties, or responsibilities upon, Federal or State officials.

CHAPTER 115. EVIDENCE; DOCUMENTARY

§ 1738. STATE AND TERRITORIAL STATUTES AND JUDICIAL PROCEEDINGS; FULL FAITH AND CREDIT

The Acts of the legislature of any State, Territory, or Possession of the United States, or copies thereof, shall be authenticated by affixing the seal of such State, Territory or Possession thereto.

The records and judicial proceedings of any court of any such State, Territory or Possession, or copies thereof, shall be proved or admitted in other courts within the United States and its Territories and Possessions by the attestation of the clerk and seal of the court annexed, if a seal exists, together with a certificate of a judge of the court that the said attestation is in proper form.

Such Acts, records and judicial proceedings or copies thereof, so authenticated, shall have the same full faith and credit in every court within the United States and its Territories and Possessions as they have by law or usage in the courts of such State, Territory or Possession from which they are taken.

§ 1738A. FULL FAITH AND CREDIT GIVEN TO CHILD CUSTODY DETERMINATIONS.

(a) The appropriate authorities of every State shall enforce according to its terms, and shall not modify except as provided in subsections (f), (g), and (h) of this section, any custody determination or visitation determination made consistently with the provisions of this section by a court of another State.

(b) As used in this section, the term:

(1) "child" means a person under the age of eighteen;

(2) "contestant" means a person, including a parent or grandparent, who claims a right to custody or visitation of a child;

(3) "custody determination" means a judgment, decree, or other order of a court providing for the custody of a child, and includes permanent and temporary orders, and initial orders and modifications;

(4) "home State" means the State in which, immediately preceding the time involved, the child lived with his parents, a parent, or a person acting as parent, for at least six consecutive months, and in the case of a child less than six months old, the State in which the child lived from birth with any of such persons. Periods of temporary absence of any of such persons are counted as part of the six-month or other period;

(5) "modification" and "modify" refer to a custody or visitation determination which modifies, replaces, supersedes, or otherwise is made subsequent to, a prior custody or visitation determination concerning the same child, whether made by the same court or not;

(6) "person acting as a parent" means a person, other than a parent, who has physical custody of a child and who has either been awarded custody by a court or claims a right to custody;

(7) "physical custody" means actual possession and control of a child;

(8) "State" means a State of the United States, the District of Columbia, the Commonwealth of Puerto Rico, or a territory or possession of the United States; and

(9) "visitation determination" means a judgment, decree, or other order of a court providing for the visitation of a child and includes permanent and temporary orders and initial orders and modifications.

(c) A child custody or visitation determination made by a court of a State is consistent with the provisions of this section only if:

(1) such court has jurisdiction under the law of such State; and

(2) one of the following conditions is met:

(A) such State (i) is the home State of the child on the date of the commencement of the proceeding, or (ii) had been the child's home State within six months before the date of the commencement of the proceeding and the child is absent from such State because of his removal or retention by a contestant or for other reasons, and a contestant continues to live in such State;

(B) (i) it appears that no other State would have jurisdiction under subparagraph (A), and (ii) it is in the best interest of the child that a court of such State assume jurisdiction because (I) the child and his parents, or the child and at least one contestant, have a significant connection with such State other than mere physical presence in such State, and (II) there is available in such State substantial evidence concerning the child's present or future care, protection, training, and personal relationships;

(C) the child is physically present in such State and (i) the child has been abandoned, or (ii) it is necessary in an emergency to protect the child because the child, a sibling, or parent of the child has been subjected to or threatened with mistreatment or abuse;

(D) (i) it appears that no other State would have jurisdiction under subparagraph (A), (B), (C), or (E), or another State has declined to exercise jurisdiction on the ground that the State whose jurisdiction is in issue is the more appropriate forum to determine the custody or visitation of the child, and (ii) it is in the best interest of the child that such court assume jurisdiction; or

(E) the court has continuing jurisdiction pursuant to subsection (d) of this section.

(d) The jurisdiction of a court of a State which has made a child custody or visitation determination consistently with the provisions of this section continues as long as the requirement of subsection (c)(1) of this section continues to be met and such State remains the residence of the child or of any contestant.

(e) Before a child custody or visitation determination is made, reasonable notice and opportunity to be heard shall be given to the contestants, any parent whose parental rights have not been previously terminated and any person who has physical custody of a child.

(f) A court of a State may modify a determination of the custody of the same child made by a court of another State, if:

(1) it has jurisdiction to make such a child custody determination; and

(2) the court of the other State no longer has jurisdiction, or it has declined to exercise such jurisdiction to modify such determination.

(g) A court of a State shall not exercise jurisdiction in any proceeding for a custody or visitation determination commenced during the pendency of a proceeding in a court of another State where such court of that other State is exercising jurisdiction consistently with the provisions of this section to make a custody or visitation determination.

(h) A court of a State may not modify a visitation determination made by a court of another State unless the court of the other State no longer has jurisdiction to modify such determination or has declined to exercise jurisdiction to modify such determination.

§ 1738B. FULL FAITH AND CREDIT FOR CHILD SUPPORT ORDERS

(a) General rule. The appropriate authorities of each State:

(1) shall enforce according to its terms a child support order made consistently with this section by a court of another State; and

(2) shall not seek or make a modification of such an order except in accordance with subsections (e), (f), and (i).

(b) Definitions. In this section:

"child" means:

(A) a person under 18 years of age; and

(B) a person 18 or more years of age with respect to whom a child support order has been issued pursuant to the laws of a State.

"child's State" means the State in which a child resides.

"child's home State" means the State in which a child lived with a parent or a person acting as parent for at least 6 consecutive months immediately preceding the time of filing of a petition or comparable pleading for support and, if a child is less than 6 months old, the State in which the child lived from birth with any of them. A period of temporary absence of any of them is counted as part of the 6-month period.

"child support" means a payment of money, continuing support, or arrearages or the provision of a benefit (including payment of health insurance, child care, and educational expenses) for the support of a child.

"child support order":

(A) means a judgment, decree, or order of a court requiring the payment of child support in periodic amounts or in a lump sum; and

(B) includes:

(i) a permanent or temporary order; and

(ii) an initial order or a modification of an order.

"contestant" means:

(A) a person (including a parent) who:

(i) claims a right to receive child support;

(ii) is a party to a proceeding that may result in the issuance of a child support order; or

(iii) is under a child support order; and

(B) a State or political subdivision of a State to which the right to obtain child support has been assigned.

"court" means a court or administrative agency of a State that is authorized by State law to establish the amount of child support payable by a contestant or make a modification of a child support order.

"modification" means a change in a child support order that affects the amount, scope, or duration of the order and modifies, replaces, supersedes, or otherwise is made subsequent to the child support order.

"State" means a State of the United States, the District of Columbia, the Commonwealth of Puerto Rico, the territories and possessions of the United States, and Indian country (as defined in section 1151 of title 18).

(c) Requirements of child support orders. A child support order made by a court of a State is made consistently with this section if:

(1) a court that makes the order, pursuant to the laws of the State in which the court is located and subsections (e), (f), and (g):

(A) has subject matter jurisdiction to hear the matter and enter such an order; and

(B) has personal jurisdiction over the contestants; and

(2) reasonable notice and opportunity to be heard is given to the contestants.

(d) Continuing jurisdiction. A court of a State that has made a child support order consistently with this section has continuing, exclusive jurisdiction over the order if the State is the child's State or the residence of any individual contestant unless the court of another State, acting in accordance with subsections (e) and (f), has made a modification of the order.

(e) Authority to modify orders. A court of a State may modify a child support order issued by a court of another State if:

(1) the court has jurisdiction to make such a child support order pursuant to subsection (i); and

(2) (A) the court of the other State no longer has continuing, exclusive jurisdiction of the child support order because that State no longer is the child's State or the residence of any individual contestant; or

(B) each individual contestant has filed written consent with the State of continuing, exclusive jurisdiction for a court of another State to modify the order and assume continuing, exclusive jurisdiction over the order.

(f) Recognition of child support orders. If 1 or more child support orders have been issued with regard to an obligor and a child, a court shall apply the following rules in determining which order to recognize for purposes of continuing, exclusive jurisdiction and enforcement:

(1) If only 1 court has issued a child support order, the order of that court must be recognized.

(2) If 2 or more courts have issued child support orders for the same obligor and child, and only 1 of the courts would have continuing, exclusive jurisdiction under this section, the order of that court must be recognized.

(3) If 2 or more courts have issued child support orders for the same obligor and child, and more than 1 of the courts would have continuing, exclusive jurisdiction under this section, an order issued by a court in the current home State of the child must be recognized, but if an order has not been issued in the current home State of the child, the order most recently issued must be recognized.

(4) If 2 or more courts have issued child support orders for the same obligor and child, and none of the courts would have continuing, exclusive jurisdiction under this section, a court having jurisdiction over the parties shall issue a child support order, which must be recognized.

(5) The court that has issued an order recognized under this subsection is the court having continuing, exclusive jurisdiction under subsection (d).

(g) Enforcement of modified orders. A court of a State that no longer has continuing, exclusive jurisdiction of a child support order may enforce the order with respect to nonmodifiable obligations and unsatisfied obligations that accrued before the date on which a modification of the order is made under subsections (e) and (f).

(h) Choice of law:

(1) In general. In a proceeding to establish, modify, or enforce a child support order, the forum State's law shall apply except as provided in paragraphs (2) and (3).

(2) Law of State of issuance of order. In interpreting a child support order including the duration of current payments and other obligations of support, a court shall apply the law of the State of the court that issued the order.

(3) Period of limitation. In an action to enforce arrears under a child support order, a court shall apply the statute of limitation of the forum State or the State of the court that issued the order, whichever statute provides the longer period of limitation.

(i) Registration for modification. If there is no individual contestant or child residing in the issuing State, the party or support enforcement agency seeking to modify, or to modify and enforce, a child support order issued in another State shall register that order in a State with jurisdiction over the nonmovant for the purpose of modification.

§ 1738C. CERTAIN ACTS, RECORDS, AND PROCEEDINGS AND THE EFFECT THEREOF
No State, territory, or possession of the United States, or Indian tribe, shall be required to give effect to any public act, record, or judicial proceeding of any other State, territory, possession, or tribe respecting a relationship between persons of the same sex that is treated as a marriage under the laws of such other State, territory, possession, or tribe, or a right or claim arising from such relationship.

§ 1739. STATE AND TERRITORIAL NONJUDICIAL RECORDS; FULL FAITH AND CREDIT
All nonjudicial records or books kept in any public office of any State, Territory, or Possession of the United States, or copies thereof, shall be proved or admitted in any court or office in any other State, Territory, or Possession by the attestation of the custodian of such records or books, and the seal of his office annexed, if there be a seal, together with a certificate of a judge of a court of record of the county, parish, or district in which such office may be kept, or of the Governor, or secretary of state, the chancellor or keeper of the great seal, of the State, Territory, or Possession that the said attestation is in due form and by the proper officers.

If the certificate is given by a judge, it shall be further authenticated by the clerk or prothonotary of the court, who shall certify, under his hand and the seal of his office, that such judge is duly commissioned and qualified; or, if given by such Governor, secretary, chancellor, or keeper of the great seal, it shall be under the great seal of the State, Territory, or Possession in which it is made.

Such records or books, or copies thereof, so authenticated, shall have the same full faith and credit in every court and office within the United States and its Territories and Possessions as they have by law or usage in the courts or offices of the State, Territory, or Possession from which they are taken.

§ 1746. UNSWORN DECLARATIONS UNDER PENALTY OF PERJURY
Wherever, under any law of the United States or under any rule, regulation, order, or requirement made pursuant to law, any matter is required or permitted to be supported, evidenced, established, or proved by the sworn declaration, verification, certificate, statement, oath, or affidavit, in writing of the person making the same (other than a deposition, or an oath of office, or an oath required to be taken before a specified official other than a notary public), such matter may, with like force and effect, be supported, evidenced, established, or proved by the unsworn declaration, certificate, verification, or statement, in writing of such person which is subscribed by him, as true under penalty of perjury, and dated, in substantially the following form:

(1) If executed without the United States: "I declare (or certify, verify, or state) under penalty of perjury under the laws of the United States of America that the foregoing is true and correct. Executed on (date). (Signature)".

(2) If executed within the United States, its territories, possessions, or commonwealths: "I declare (or certify, verify, or state) under penalty of perjury that the foregoing is true and correct. Executed on (date). (Signature)".

CHAPTER 117. EVIDENCE; DEPOSITIONS

§ 1781. TRANSMITTAL OF LETTER ROGATORY OR REQUEST

(a) The Department of State has power, directly, or through suitable channels —

(1) to receive a letter rogatory issued, or request made, by a foreign or international tribunal, to transmit it to the tribunal, officer, or agency in the United States to whom it is addressed, and to receive and return it after execution; and

(2) to receive a letter rogatory issued, or request made, by a tribunal in the United States, to transmit it to the foreign or international tribunal, officer, or agency to whom it is addressed, and to receive and return it after execution.

(b) This section does not preclude —

(1) the transmittal of a letter rogatory or request directly from a foreign or international tribunal to the tribunal, officer, or agency in the United States to whom it is addressed and its return in the same manner; or

(2) the transmittal of a letter rogatory or request directly from a tribunal in the United States to the foreign or international tribunal, officer, or agency to whom it is addressed and its return in the same manner.

§ 1782. ASSISTANCE TO FOREIGN AND INTERNATIONAL TRIBUNALS AND TO LITIGANTS BEFORE SUCH TRIBUNALS

(a) The district court of the district in which a person resides or is found may order him to give his testimony or statement or to produce a document or other thing for use in a proceeding in a foreign or international tribunal, including criminal investigations conducted before formal accusation. The order may be made pursuant to a letter rogatory issued, or request made, by a foreign or international tribunal or upon the application of any interested person and may direct that the testimony or statement be given, or the document or other thing be produced, before a person appointed by the court. By virtue of his appointment, the person appointed has power to administer any necessary oath and take the testimony or statement. The order may prescribe the practice and procedure, which may be in whole or part the practice and procedure of the foreign country or the international tribunal, for taking the testimony or statement or producing the document or other thing. To the extent that the order does not prescribe otherwise, the testimony or statement shall be taken, and the document or other thing produced, in accordance with the Federal Rules of Civil Procedure.

A person may not be compelled to give his testimony or statement or to produce a document or other thing in violation of any legally applicable privilege.

(b) This chapter does not preclude a person within the United States from voluntarily giving his testimony or statement, or producing a document or other thing, for use in a proceeding in a foreign or international tribunal before any person and in any manner acceptable to him.

§ 1783. SUBPOENA OF PERSON IN FOREIGN COUNTRY

(a) A court of the United States may order the issuance of a subpoena requiring the appearance as a witness before it, or before a person or body designated by it, of a national or resident of the United States who is in a foreign country, or requiring the production of a specified document or other thing by him, if the court finds that particular testimony or the production of the document or other thing by him is necessary in the interest of justice, and, in other than a criminal action or proceeding, if the court finds, in addition, that it is not possible to obtain his testimony in admissible form without his personal appearance or to obtain the production of the document or other thing in any other manner.

(b) The subpoena shall designate the time and place for the appearance or for the production of the document or other thing. Service of the subpoena and any order to show cause, rule, judgment, or decree authorized by this section or by section 1784 of this title shall be effected in accordance with the provisions of the Federal Rules of Civil Procedure relating to service of process on a person in a foreign country. The person serving the subpoena shall tender to the person to whom the subpoena is addressed his estimated necessary travel and attendance expenses, the amount of which shall be determined by the court and stated in the order directing the issuance of the subpoena.

§ 1784. CONTEMPT

(a) The court of the United States which has issued a subpoena served in a foreign country may order the person who has failed to appear or who has failed to produce a document or other thing as directed therein to show cause before it at a designated time why he should not be punished for contempt.

(b) The court, in the order to show cause, may direct that any of the person's property within the United States be levied upon or seized, in the manner provided by law or court rules governing levy or seizure under execution, and held to satisfy any judgment that may be rendered against him pursuant to subsection (d) of this section if adequate security, in such amount as the court may direct in the order, be given for any damage that he might suffer should he not be found in contempt. Security under this subsection may not be required of the United States.

(c) A copy of the order to show cause shall be served on the person in accordance with section 1783(b) of this title.

(d) On the return day of the order to show cause or any later day to which the hearing may be continued, proof shall be taken. If the person is found in contempt, the court, notwithstanding any limitation upon its power generally to punish for contempt, may fine him not more than $100,000 and direct that the fine and costs of the proceedings be satisfied by a sale of the property levied upon or seized, conducted upon the notice required and in the manner provided for sales upon execution.

§ 1785. SUBPOENAS IN MULTIPARTY, MULTIFORUM ACTIONS

When the jurisdiction of the district court is based in whole or in part upon section 1369 of this title, a subpoena for attendance at a hearing or trial may, if authorized by the court upon motion for good cause shown, and upon such terms and conditions as the court may impose, be served at any place within the United States, or anywhere outside the United States if otherwise permitted by law.

CHAPTER 119. EVIDENCE; WITNESSES

§ 1826. RECALCITRANT WITNESSES

(a) Whenever a witness in any proceeding before or ancillary to any court or grand jury of the United States refuses without just cause shown to comply with an order of the court to testify or provide other information, including any book, paper, document, record, recording or other material, the court, upon such refusal, or when such refusal is duly brought to its attention, may summarily order his confinement at a suitable place until such time as the witness is willing to give such testimony or provide such information. No period of such confinement shall exceed the life of —

(1) the court proceeding, or

(2) the term of the grand jury, including extensions,

before which such refusal to comply with the court order occurred, but in no event shall such confinement exceed eighteen months.

(b) No person confined pursuant to subsection (a) of this section shall be admitted to bail pending the determination of an appeal taken by him from the order for his confinement if it appears that the appeal is frivolous or taken for delay. Any appeal from an order of confinement under this section shall be disposed of as soon as practicable, but not later than thirty days from the filing of such appeal.

(c) Whoever escapes or attempts to escape from the custody of any facility or from any place in which or to which he is confined pursuant to this section or section 4243 of title 18, or whoever rescues or attempts to rescue or instigates, aids, or assists the escape or attempt to escape of such a person, shall be subject to imprisonment for not more than three years, or a fine of not more than $10,000, or both.

CHAPTER 121. JURIES; TRIAL BY JURY

§ 1861. DECLARATION OF POLICY

It is the policy of the United States that all litigants in Federal courts entitled to trial by jury shall have the right to grand and petit juries selected at random from a fair cross section of the community in the district or division wherein the court convenes. It is further the policy of the United States that all citizens shall have the opportunity to be considered for service on grand and petit juries in the district courts of the United States, and shall have an obligation to serve as jurors when summoned for that purpose.

§ 1862. DISCRIMINATION PROHIBITED

No citizen shall be excluded from service as a grand or petit juror in the district courts of the United States or in the Court of International Trade on account of race, color, religion, sex, national origin, or economic status.

§ 1863. PLAN FOR RANDOM JURY SELECTION

(a) Each United States district court shall devise and place into operation a written plan for random selection of grand and petit jurors that shall be designed to achieve the objectives of sections 1861 and 1862 of this title, and that shall otherwise comply with the provisions of this title. The plan shall be placed into operation after approval by a reviewing panel consisting of the members of the judicial council of the circuit and either the chief judge of the district whose plan is being reviewed or such other active district judge of that district as the chief judge of the district may designate. The panel shall examine the plan to ascertain that it complies with the provisions of this title. If the reviewing panel finds that the plan does not comply, the panel shall state the particulars in which the plan fails to comply and direct the district court to present within a reasonable time an alternative plan remedying the defect or defects. Separate plans may be adopted for each division or combination of divisions within a judicial district. The district court may modify a plan at any time and it shall modify the plan when so directed by the reviewing panel. The district court shall promptly notify the panel, the Administrative Office of the United States Courts, and the Attorney General of the United States, of the initial adoption and future modifications of the plan by filing copies therewith. Modifications of the plan made at the instance of the district court shall become effective after approval by the panel. Each district court shall submit a report on the jury selection process within its jurisdiction to the Administrative Office of the United States Courts in such form and at such times as the Judicial Conference of the United States may specify. The Judicial Conference of the United States may, from time to time, adopt rules and regulations governing the provisions and the operation of the plans formulated under this title.

(b) Among other things, such plan shall—

(1) either establish a jury commission, or authorize the clerk of the court, to manage the jury selection process. If the plan establishes a jury commission, the district court shall appoint one citizen to serve with the clerk of the court as the jury commission: Provided, however, That the plan for the District of Columbia may establish a jury commission consisting of three citizens. The citizen jury commissioner shall not belong to the same political party as the clerk serving with him. The clerk or the jury commission, as the case may be, shall act under the supervision and control of the chief judge of the district court or such other judge of the district court as the plan may provide. Each jury commissioner shall, during his tenure in office, reside in the judicial district or division for which he is appointed. Each citizen jury commissioner shall receive compensation to be fixed by the district court plan at a rate not to exceed $50 per day for each day necessarily employed in the performance of his duties, plus reimbursement for travel, subsistence, and other necessary expenses incurred by him in the performance of such duties. The Judicial Conference of the United States may establish standards for allowance of travel, subsistence, and other necessary expenses incurred by jury commissioners.

(2) specify whether the names of prospective jurors shall be selected from the voter registration lists or the lists of actual voters of the political subdivisions within the district or division. The plan shall prescribe some other source or sources of names in addition to voter lists where necessary to foster the policy and protect the rights secured by sections 1861 and 1862 of this title. The plan for the District of Columbia may require the names of prospective jurors to be selected from the city directory rather than from voter lists. The plans for the districts of Puerto Rico and the Canal Zone may prescribe some other source or sources of names of prospective jurors in lieu of voter lists, the use of which shall be consistent with the policies declared and rights secured by sections 1861 and 1862 of this title. The plan for the district of Massachusetts may require the names of prospective jurors to be selected from the resident list provided for in chapter 234A, Massachusetts General Laws, or comparable authority, rather than from voter lists.

(3) specify detailed procedures to be followed by the jury commission or clerk in selecting names from the sources specified in paragraph (2) of this subsection. These procedures shall be designed to ensure the random selection of a fair cross section of the persons residing in the community in the district or division wherein the court convenes. They shall ensure that names of persons residing in each of the counties, parishes, or similar political subdivisions within the judicial district or division are placed in a master jury wheel; and shall ensure that each county, parish, or similar political subdivision within the district or division is substantially proportionally represented in the master jury wheel for that judicial district, division, or combination of divisions. For the purposes of determining proportional representation in the master jury wheel, either the number of actual voters at the last general election in each county, parish, or similar political subdivision, or the number of registered voters if registration of voters is uniformly required throughout the district or division, may be used.

(4) provide for a master jury wheel (or a device similar in purpose and function) into which the names of those randomly selected shall be placed. The plan shall fix a minimum number of names to be placed initially in the master jury wheel, which shall be at least one-half of 1 per centum of the total number of persons on the lists used as a source of names for the district or division; but if this number of names is believed to be cumbersome and unnecessary, the plan may fix a smaller number of names to be placed in the master wheel, but in no event less than one thousand. The chief judge of the district court, or such other district court judge as the plan may provide, may order additional names to be placed in the master jury wheel from time to time as necessary. The plan shall provide for periodic emptying and refilling of the master jury wheel at specified times, the interval for which shall not exceed four years.

(5) (A) except as provided in subparagraph (B), specify those groups of persons or occupational classes whose members shall, on individual request therefor, be excused from jury service. Such groups or classes shall be excused only if the district court finds, and the plan states, that jury service by such class or group would entail undue hardship or extreme inconvenience to the members thereof, and excuse of members thereof would not be inconsistent with sections 1861 and 1862 of this title.

(B) specify that volunteer safety personnel, upon individual request, shall be excused from jury service. For purposes of this subparagraph, the term "volunteer safety personnel" means individuals serving a public agency (as defined in section 1203(6) of title I of the Omnibus Crime Control and Safe Streets Act of 1968) in an official capacity, without compensation, as firefighters or members of a rescue squad or ambulance crew.

(6) specify that the following persons are barred from jury service on the ground that they are exempt: (A) members in active service in the Armed Forces of the United States; (B) members of the fire or police departments of any State, the District of Columbia, any territory or possession of the United States,

or any subdivision of a State, the District of Columbia, or such territory or possession; (C) public officers in the executive, legislative, or judicial branches of the Government of the United States, or of any State, the District of Columbia, any territory or possession of the United States, or any subdivision of a State, the District of Columbia, or such territory or possession, who are actively engaged in the performance of official duties.

(7) fix the time when the names drawn from the qualified jury wheel shall be disclosed to parties and to the public. If the plan permits these names to be made public, it may nevertheless permit the chief judge of the district court, or such other district court judge as the plan may provide, to keep these names confidential in any case where the interests of justice so require.

(8) specify the procedures to be followed by the clerk or jury commission in assigning persons whose names have been drawn from the qualified jury wheel to grand and petit jury panels.

(c) The initial plan shall be devised by each district court and transmitted to the reviewing panel specified in subsection (a) of this section within one hundred and twenty days of the date of enactment of the Jury Selection and Service Act of 1968. The panel shall approve or direct the modification of each plan so submitted within sixty days thereafter. Each plan or modification made at the direction of the panel shall become effective after approval at such time thereafter as the panel directs, in no event to exceed ninety days from the date of approval. Modifications made at the instance of the district court under subsection (a) of this section shall be effective at such time thereafter as the panel directs, in no event to exceed ninety days from the date of modification.

(d) State, local, and Federal officials having custody, possession, or control of voter registration lists, lists of actual voters, or other appropriate records shall make such lists and records available to the jury commission or clerks for inspection, reproduction, and copying at all reasonable times as the commission or clerk may deem necessary and proper for the performance of duties under this title. The district courts shall have jurisdiction upon application by the Attorney General of the United States to compel compliance with this subsection by appropriate process.

§ 1864. DRAWING OF NAMES FROM THE MASTER JURY WHEEL; COMPLETION OF JUROR QUALIFICATION FORM

(a) From time to time as directed by the district court, the clerk or a district judge shall publicly draw at random from the master jury wheel the names of as many persons as may be required for jury service. The clerk or jury commission may, upon order of the court, prepare an alphabetical list of the names drawn from the master jury wheel. Any list so prepared shall not be disclosed to any person except pursuant to the district court plan or pursuant to section 1867 or 1868 of this title. The clerk or jury commission shall mail to every person whose name is drawn from the master wheel a juror qualification form accompanied by instructions to fill out and return the form, duly signed and sworn, to the clerk or jury commission by mail within ten days. If the person is unable to fill out the form, another shall do it for him, and shall indicate that he has done so and the reason therefor. In any case in which it appears that there is an omission, ambiguity, or error in a form, the clerk or jury commission shall return the form with instructions to the person to make such additions or corrections as may be necessary and to return the form to the clerk or jury commission within ten days. Any person who fails to return a completed juror qualification form as instructed may be summoned by the clerk or jury commission forthwith to appear before the clerk or jury commission to fill out a juror qualification form. A person summoned to appear because of failure to return a juror qualification form as instructed who personally appears and executes a juror qualification form before the clerk or jury commission may, at the discretion of the district court, except where his prior failure to execute and mail such form was willful, be entitled to receive for such appearance the same fees and travel allowances paid to jurors under section 1871 of this title. At the time of his appearance for jury service, any person may be required to fill out another juror qualification form in the presence of the jury commission or the clerk or the court, at which time, in such cases as it appears warranted, the person may be questioned, but only with regard to his responses to questions contained on the form. Any information thus acquired by the clerk or jury commission may be noted on the juror qualification form and transmitted to the chief judge or such district court judge as the plan may provide.

(b) Any person summoned pursuant to subsection (a) of this section who fails to appear as directed shall be ordered by the district court forthwith to appear and show cause for his failure to comply with the summons. Any person who fails to appear pursuant to such order or who fails to show good cause for noncompliance with the summons may be fined not more than $100 or imprisoned not more than three days, or both. Any person who willfully misrepresents a material fact on a juror qualification form for the purpose of avoiding or securing service as a juror may be fined not more than $100 or imprisoned not more than three days, or both.

§ 1865. QUALIFICATIONS FOR JURY SERVICE

(a) The chief judge of the district court, or such other district court judge as the plan may provide, on his initiative or upon recommendation of the clerk or jury commission, or the clerk under supervision of the court if the court's jury selection plan so authorizes, shall determine solely on the basis of information provided on the juror qualification form and other competent evidence whether a person is unqualified for, or exempt, or to be excused from jury service. The clerk shall enter such determination in the space provided on the juror qualification form and in any alphabetical list of names drawn from the master jury wheel. If a person did not appear in response to a summons, such fact shall be noted on said list.

(b) In making such determination the chief judge of the district court, or such other district court judge as the plan may provide, or the clerk if the court's jury selection plan so provides, shall deem any person qualified to serve on grand and petit juries in the district court unless he —

(1) is not a citizen of the United States eighteen years old who has resided for a period of one year within the judicial district;

(2) is unable to read, write, and understand the English language with a degree of proficiency sufficient to fill out satisfactorily the juror qualification form;

(3) is unable to speak the English language;

(4) is incapable, by reason of mental or physical infirmity, to render satisfactory jury service; or

(5) has a charge pending against him for the commission of, or has been convicted in a State or Federal court of record of, a crime punishable by imprisonment for more than one year and his civil rights have not been restored.

§ 1866. SELECTION AND SUMMONING OF JURY PANELS

(a) The jury commission, or in the absence thereof the clerk, shall maintain a qualified jury wheel and shall place in such wheel names of all persons drawn from the master jury wheel who are determined to be qualified as jurors and not exempt or excused pursuant to the district court plan. From time to time, the jury commission or the clerk shall publicly draw at random from the qualified jury wheel such number of names of persons as may be required for assignment to grand and petit jury panels. The jury commission or the clerk shall prepare a separate list of names of persons assigned to each grand and petit jury panel.

(b) When the court orders a grand or petit jury to be drawn, the clerk or jury commission or their duly designated deputies shall issue summonses for the required number of jurors. Each person drawn for jury service may be served personally, or by registered, certified, or first-class mail addressed to such person at his usual residence or business address. If such service is made personally, the summons shall be delivered by the clerk or the jury commission or their duly designated deputies to the marshal who shall make such service. If such service is made by mail, the summons may be served by the marshal or by the clerk, the jury commission or their duly designated deputies, who shall make affidavit of service and shall attach thereto any receipt from the addressee for a registered or certified summons.

(c) Except as provided in section 1865 of this title or in any jury selection plan provision adopted pursuant to paragraph (5) or (6) of section 1863(b) of this title, no person or class of persons shall be disqualified, excluded, excused, or exempt from service as jurors: Provided, That any person summoned for jury service may be (1) excused by the court, or by the clerk under supervision of the court if the court's jury selection plan so authorizes, upon a showing of undue hardship or extreme inconvenience, for such period as the court deems necessary, at the conclusion of which such person either shall be summoned again for jury service under subsections (b) and (c) of this section or, if the court's jury selection plan so provides, the name of such person shall be reinserted into the qualified jury wheel for selection pursuant to subsection (a) of this section, or (2) excluded by the court on the ground that such person may be unable to render impartial jury service or that his service as a juror would be likely to disrupt the proceedings, or (3) excluded upon peremptory challenge as provided by law, or (4) excluded pursuant to the procedure specified by law upon a challenge by any party for good cause shown, or (5) excluded upon determination by the court that his service as a juror would be likely to threaten the secrecy of the proceedings, or otherwise adversely affect the integrity of jury deliberations. No person shall be excluded under clause (5) of this subsection unless the judge, in open court, determines that such is warranted and that exclusion of the person will not be inconsistent with sections 1861 and 1862 of this title. The number of persons excluded under clause (5) of this subsection shall not exceed one per centum of the number of persons who return executed jury qualification forms during the period, specified in the plan, between two consecutive fillings of the master jury wheel. The names of persons excluded under clause (5) of this subsection, together with detailed explanations for the exclusions, shall be forwarded immediately to the judicial council of the circuit, which shall have the power to make any appropriate order, prospective or retroactive, to redress any misapplication of clause (5) of this subsection, but otherwise exclusions effectuated under such clause shall not be subject to challenge under the provisions of this title. Any person excluded from a particular jury under clause (2), (3), or (4) of this subsection shall be eligible to sit on another jury if the basis for his initial exclusion would not be relevant to his ability to serve on such other jury.

(d) Whenever a person is disqualified, excused, exempt, or excluded from jury service, the jury commission or clerk shall note in the space provided on his juror qualification form or on the juror's card drawn from the qualified jury wheel the specific reason therefor.

(e) In any two-year period, no person shall be required to (1) serve or attend court for prospective service as a petit juror for a total of more than thirty days, except when necessary to complete service in a particular case, or (2) serve on more than one grand jury, or (3) serve as both a grand and petit juror.

(f) When there is an unanticipated shortage of available petit jurors drawn from the qualified jury wheel, the court may require the marshal to summon a sufficient number of petit jurors selected at random from the voter registration lists, lists of actual voters, or other lists specified in the plan, in a manner ordered by the court consistent with sections 1861 and 1862 of this title.

(g) Any person summoned for jury service who fails to appear as directed shall be ordered by the district court to appear forthwith and show cause for his failure to comply with the summons. Any person who fails to show good cause for noncompliance with a summons may be fined not more than $100 or imprisoned not more than three days, or both.

§ 1867. CHALLENGING COMPLIANCE WITH SELECTION PROCEDURES

(a) In criminal cases, before the voir dire examination begins, or within seven days after the defendant discovered or could have discovered, by the exercise of diligence, the grounds therefor, whichever is earlier, the defendant may move to dismiss the indictment or stay the proceedings against him on the ground of substantial failure to comply with the provisions of this title in selecting the grand or petit jury.

(b) In criminal cases, before the voir dire examination begins, or within seven days after the Attorney General of the United States discovered or could have discovered, by the exercise of diligence, the grounds therefor, whichever is earlier, the Attorney General may move to dismiss the indictment or stay the proceedings on the ground of substantial failure to comply with the provisions of this title in selecting the grand or petit jury.

(c) In civil cases, before the voir dire examination begins, or within seven days after the party discovered or could have discovered, by the exercise of diligence, the grounds therefor, whichever is earlier, any party may move to stay the proceedings on the ground of substantial failure to comply with the provisions of this title in selecting the petit jury.

(d) Upon motion filed under subsection (a), (b), or (c) of this section, containing a sworn statement of facts which, if true, would constitute a substantial failure to comply with the provisions of this title, the moving party shall be entitled to present in support of such motion the testimony of the jury commission or clerk, if available, any relevant records and papers not public or otherwise available used by the jury commissioner or clerk, and any other relevant evidence. If the court determines that there has been a substantial failure to comply with the provisions of this title in selecting the grand jury, the court shall stay the proceedings pending the selection of a grand jury in conformity with this title or dismiss the indictment, whichever is appropriate. If the court determines that there has been a substantial failure to comply with the provisions of this title in selecting the petit jury, the court shall stay the proceedings pending the selection of a petit jury in conformity with this title.

(e) The procedures prescribed by this section shall be the exclusive means by which a person accused of a Federal crime, the Attorney General of the United States or a party in a civil case may challenge any jury on the ground that such jury was not selected in conformity with the provisions of this title. Nothing in this section shall preclude any person or the United States from pursuing any other remedy, civil or criminal, which may be available for the vindication or enforcement of any law prohibiting discrimination on account of race, color, religion, sex, national origin or economic status in the selection of persons for service on grand or petit juries.

(f) The contents of records or papers used by the jury commission or clerk in connection with the jury selection process shall not be disclosed, except pursuant to the district court plan or as may be necessary in the preparation or presentation of a motion under subsection (a), (b), or (c) of this section, until after the master jury wheel has been emptied and refilled pursuant to section 1863(b)(4) of this title and all persons selected to serve as jurors before the master wheel was emptied have completed such service. The parties in a case shall be allowed to inspect, reproduce, and copy such records or papers at all reasonable times during the preparation and pendency of such a motion. Any person who discloses the contents of any record or paper in violation of this subsection may be fined not more than $1,000 or imprisoned not more than one year, or both.

§ 1868. MAINTENANCE AND INSPECTION OF RECORDS

After the master jury wheel is emptied and refilled pursuant to section 1863(b)(4) of this title, and after all persons selected to serve as jurors before the master wheel was emptied have completed such service, all records and papers compiled and maintained by the jury commission or clerk before the master wheel was emptied shall be preserved in the custody of the clerk for four years or for such longer period as may be ordered by a court, and shall be available for public inspection for the purpose of determining the validity of the selection of any jury.

§ 1869. DEFINITIONS

For purposes of this chapter —

(a) "clerk" and "clerk of the court" shall mean the clerk of the district court of the United States, any authorized deputy clerk, and any other person authorized by the court to assist the clerk in the performance of functions under this chapter;

(b) "chief judge" shall mean the chief judge of any district court of the United States;

(c) "voter registration lists" shall mean the official records maintained by State or local election officials of persons registered to vote in either the most recent State or the most recent Federal general election, or, in the case of a State or political subdivision thereof that does not require registration as a prerequisite to voting, other official lists of persons qualified to vote in such election. The term shall also include the list of eligible voters maintained by any Federal examiner pursuant to the Voting Rights Act of 1965 where the names on such list have not been included on the official registration lists or other official lists maintained by the appropriate State or local officials. With respect to the districts of Guam and the Virgin Islands, "voter registration lists" shall mean the official records maintained by territorial election officials of persons registered to vote in the most recent territorial general election;

(d) "lists of actual voters" shall mean the official lists of persons actually voting in either the most recent State or the most recent Federal general election;

(e) "division" shall mean: (1) one or more statutory divisions of a judicial district; or (2) in statutory divisions that contain more than one place of holding court, or in judicial districts where there are no statutory divisions, such counties, parishes, or similar political subdivisions surrounding the places where court is held as the district court plan shall determine: Provided, That each county, parish, or similar political subdivision shall be included in some such division;

(f) "district court of the United States", "district court", and "court" shall mean any district court established by chapter 5 of this title, and any court which is created by Act of Congress in a territory and is invested with any jurisdiction of a district court established by chapter 5 of this title;

(g) "jury wheel" shall include any device or system similar in purpose or function, such as a properly programed electronic data processing system or device;

(h) "juror qualification form" shall mean a form prescribed by the Administrative Office of the United States Courts and approved by the Judicial Conference of the United States, which shall elicit the name, address, age, race, occupation, education, length of residence within the judicial district, distance from residence to place of holding court, prior jury service, and citizenship of a potential juror, and whether he should be excused or exempted from jury service, has any physical or mental infirmity impairing his capacity to serve as juror, is able to read, write, speak, and understand the English language, has pending against him any charge for the commission of a State or Federal criminal offense punishable by imprisonment for more than one year, or has been convicted in any State or Federal court of record of a crime punishable by imprisonment for more than one year and has not had his civil rights restored. The form shall request, but not require, any other information not inconsistent with the provisions of this title and required by the district court plan in the interests of the sound administration of justice. The form shall also elicit the sworn statement that his responses are true to the best of his knowledge. Notarization shall not be required. The form shall contain words clearly informing the person that the furnishing of any information with respect to his religion, national origin, or economic status is not a prerequisite to his qualification for jury service, that such information need not be furnished if the person finds it objectionable to do so, and that information concerning race is required solely to enforce nondiscrimination in jury selection and has no bearing on an individual's qualification for jury service.

(i) "public officer" shall mean a person who is either elected to public office or who is directly appointed by a person elected to public office;

(j) "undue hardship or extreme inconvenience", as a basis for excuse from immediate jury service under section 1866(c)(1) of this chapter, shall mean great distance, either in miles or traveltime, from the place of holding court, grave illness in the family or any other emergency which outweighs in immediacy and urgency the obligation to serve as a juror when summoned, or any other factor which the court determines to constitute an undue hardship or to create an extreme inconvenience to the juror; and in addition, in situations where it is anticipated that a trial or grand jury proceeding may require more than thirty days of service, the court may consider, as a further basis for temporary excuse, severe economic hardship to an employer which would result from the absence of a key employee during the period of such service;

(k) "publicly draw", as referred to in sections 1864 and 1866 of this chapter, shall mean a drawing which is conducted within the district after reasonable public notice and which is open to the public at large under the supervision of the clerk or jury commission, except that when a drawing is made by means of electronic data processing, "publicly draw" shall mean a drawing which is conducted at a data processing center located in or out of the district, after reasonable public notice given in the district for which juror names are being drawn, and which is open to the public at large under such supervision of the clerk or jury commission as the Judicial Conference of the United States shall by regulation require; and

(l) "jury summons" shall mean a summons issued by a clerk of court, jury commission, or their duly designated deputies, containing either a preprinted or stamped seal of court, and containing the name of the issuing clerk imprinted in preprinted, type, or facsimile manner on the summons or the envelopes transmitting the summons.

§ 1870. CHALLENGES

In civil cases, each party shall be entitled to three peremptory challenges. Several defendants or several plaintiffs may be considered as a single party for the purposes of making challenges, or the court may allow additional peremptory challenges and permit them to be exercised separately or jointly.

All challenges for cause or favor, whether to the array or panel or to individual jurors, shall be determined by the court.

§ 1872. ISSUES OF FACT IN SUPREME COURT

In all original actions at law in the Supreme Court against citizens of the United States, issues of fact shall be tried by a jury.

§ 1875. PROTECTION OF JURORS' EMPLOYMENT

(a) No employer shall discharge, threaten to discharge, intimidate, or coerce any permanent employee by reason of such employee's jury service, or the attendance or scheduled attendance in connection with such service, in any court of the United States.

(b) Any employer who violates the provisions of this section—

(1) shall be liable for damages for any loss of wages or other benefits suffered by an employee by reason of such violation;

(2) may be enjoined from further violations of this section and ordered to provide other appropriate relief, including but not limited to the reinstatement of any employee discharged by reason of his jury service; and

(3) shall be subject to a civil penalty of not more than $1,000 for each violation as to each employee.

(c) Any individual who is reinstated to a position of employment in accordance with the provisions of this section shall be considered as having been on furlough or leave of absence during his period of jury service, shall be reinstated to his position of employment without loss of seniority, and shall be entitled to participate in insurance or other benefits offered by the employer pursuant to established rules and practices relating to employees on furlough or leave of absence in effect with the employer at the time such individual entered upon jury service.

(d) (1) An individual claiming that his employer has violated the provisions of this section may make application to the district court for the district in which such employer maintains a place of business and the court shall, upon finding probable merit in such claim, appoint counsel to represent such individual in any action in the district court necessary to the resolution of such claim. Such counsel shall be compensated and necessary expenses repaid to the extent provided by section 3006A of title 18, United States Code.

(2) In any action or proceeding under this section, the court may award a prevailing employee who brings such action by retained counsel a reasonable attorney's fee as part of the costs. The court may tax a defendant employer, as costs payable to the court, the attorney fees and expenses incurred on behalf of a prevailing employee, where such costs were expended by the court pursuant to paragraph (1) of this subsection. The court may award a prevailing employer a reasonable attorney's fee as part of the costs only if the court finds that the action is frivolous, vexatious, or brought in bad faith.

CHAPTER 123. FEES AND COSTS

§ 1914. DISTRICT COURT; FILING AND MISCELLANEOUS FEES; RULES OF COURT

(a) The clerk of each district court shall require the parties instituting any civil action, suit or proceeding in such court, whether by original process, removal or otherwise, to pay a filing fee of $350, except that on application for a writ of habeas corpus the filing fee shall be $5.

(b) The clerk shall collect from the parties such additional fees only as are prescribed by the Judicial Conference of the United States.

(c) Each district court by rule or standing order may require advance payment of fees.

§ 1915. PROCEEDINGS IN FORMA PAUPERIS

(a) (1) Subject to subsection (b), any court of the United States may authorize the commencement, prosecution or defense of any suit, action or proceeding, civil or criminal, or appeal therein, without prepayment of fees or security therefor, by a person who submits an affidavit that includes a statement of all assets such prisoner possesses that the person is unable to pay such fees or give security therefor. Such affidavit shall state the nature of the action, defense or appeal and affiant's belief that the person is entitled to redress.

(2) A prisoner seeking to bring a civil action or appeal a judgment in a civil action or proceeding without prepayment of fees or security therefor, in addition to filing the affidavit filed under paragraph (1), shall submit a certified copy of the trust fund account statement (or institutional equivalent) for the prisoner for the 6-month period immediately preceding the filing of the complaint or notice of appeal, obtained from the appropriate official of each prison at which the prisoner is or was confined.

(3) An appeal may not be taken in forma pauperis if the trial court certifies in writing that it is not taken in good faith.

(b) (1) Notwithstanding subsection (a), if a prisoner brings a civil action or files an appeal in forma pauperis, the prisoner shall be required to pay the full amount of a filing fee. The court shall assess and, when funds exist, collect, as a partial payment of any court fees required by law, an initial partial filing fee of 20 percent of the greater of:

(A) the average monthly deposits to the prisoner's account; or

(B) the average monthly balance in the prisoner's account for the 6-month period immediately preceding the filing of the complaint or notice of appeal.

(2) After payment of the initial partial filing fee, the prisoner shall be required to make monthly payments of 20 percent of the preceding month's income credited to the prisoner's account. The agency having custody of the prisoner shall forward payments from the prisoner's account to the clerk of the court each time the amount in the account exceeds $10 until the filing fees are paid.

(3) In no event shall the filing fee collected exceed the amount of fees permitted by statute for the commencement of a civil action or an appeal of a civil action or criminal judgment.

(4) In no event shall a prisoner be prohibited from bringing a civil action or appealing a civil or criminal judgment for the reason that the prisoner has no assets and no means by which to pay the initial partial filing fee.

(c) Upon the filing of an affidavit in accordance with subsections (a) and (b) and the prepayment of any partial filing fee as may be required under subsection (b), the court may direct payment by the United States of the expenses of (1) printing the record on appeal in any civil or criminal case, if such printing is required by the appellate court; (2) preparing a transcript of proceedings before a United States magistrate judge in any civil or criminal case, if such transcript is required by the district court, in the case of proceedings conducted under section 636(b) of this title or under section 3401(b) of title 18, United States Code; and (3) printing the record on appeal if such printing is required by the appellate court, in the case of proceedings conducted pursuant to section 636(c) of this title. Such expenses shall be paid when authorized by the Director of the Administrative Office of the United States Courts.

(d) The officers of the court shall issue and serve all process, and perform all duties in such cases. Witnesses shall attend as in other cases, and the same remedies shall be available as are provided for by law in other cases.

(e) (1) The court may request an attorney to represent any person unable to afford counsel.

(2) Notwithstanding any filing fee, or any portion thereof, that may have been paid, the court shall dismiss the case at any time if the court determines that:

(A) the allegation of poverty is untrue; or

(B) the action or appeal:

   (i)   is frivolous or malicious;

   (ii)   fails to state a claim on which relief may be granted; or

   (iii)   seeks monetary relief against a defendant who is immune from such relief.

(f) (1) Judgment may be rendered for costs at the conclusion of the suit or action as in other proceedings, but the United States shall not be liable for any of the costs thus incurred. If the United States has paid the cost of a stenographic transcript or printed record for the prevailing party, the same shall be taxed in favor of the United States.

(2) (A) If the judgment against a prisoner includes the payment of costs under this subsection, the prisoner shall be required to pay the full amount of the costs ordered.

(B) The prisoner shall be required to make payments for costs under this subsection in the same manner as is provided for filing fees under subsection (a)(2).

(C) In no event shall the costs collected exceed the amount of the costs ordered by the court.

(g) In no event shall a prisoner bring a civil action or appeal a judgment in a civil action or proceeding under this section if the prisoner has, on 3 or more prior occasions, while incarcerated or detained in any facility, brought an action or appeal in a court of the United States that was dismissed on the grounds that it is frivolous, malicious, or fails to state a claim upon which relief may be granted, unless the prisoner is under imminent danger of serious physical injury.

(h) As used in this section, the term "prisoner" means any person incarcerated or detained in any facility who is accused of, convicted of, sentenced for, or adjudicated delinquent for, violations of criminal law or the terms and conditions of parole, probation, pretrial release, or diversionary program.

§ 1915A. SCREENING

(a) Screening. The court shall review, before docketing, if feasible or, in any event, as soon as practicable after docketing, a complaint in a civil action in which a prisoner seeks redress from a governmental entity or officer or employee of a governmental entity.

(b) Grounds for dismissal. On review, the court shall identify cognizable claims or dismiss the complaint, or any portion of the complaint, if the complaint:

(1) is frivolous, malicious, or fails to state a claim upon which relief may be granted; or

(2) seeks monetary relief from a defendant who is immune from such relief.

(c) Definition. As used in this section, the term "prisoner" means any person incarcerated or detained in any facility who is accused of, convicted of, sentenced for, or adjudicated delinquent for, violations of criminal law or the terms and conditions of parole, probation, pretrial release, or diversionary program.

§ 1919. DISMISSAL FOR LACK OF JURISDICTION

Whenever any action or suit is dismissed in any district court, the Court of International Trade, or the Court of Federal Claims for want of jurisdiction, such court may order the payment of just costs.

§ 1920. TAXATION OF COSTS

A judge or clerk of any court of the United States may tax as costs the following:

(1) Fees of the clerk and marshal;

(2) Fees of the court reporter for all or any part of the stenographic transcript necessarily obtained for use in the case;

(3) Fees and disbursements for printing and witnesses;

(4) Fees for exemplification and copies of papers necessarily obtained for use in the case;

(5) Docket fees under section 1923 of this title;

(6) Compensation of court appointed experts, compensation of interpreters, and salaries, fees, expenses, and costs of special interpretation services under section 1828 of this title.

A bill of costs shall be filed in the case and, upon allowance, included in the judgment or decree.

§ 1924. VERIFICATION OF BILL OF COSTS

Before any bill of costs is taxed, the party claiming any item of cost or disbursement shall attach thereto an affidavit, made by himself or by his duly authorized attorney or agent having knowledge of the facts, that such item is correct and has been necessarily incurred in the case and that the services for which fees have been charged were actually and necessarily performed.

§ 1927. COUNSEL'S LIABILITY FOR EXCESSIVE COSTS

Any attorney or other person admitted to conduct cases in any court of the United States or any Territory thereof who so multiplies the proceedings in any case unreasonably and vexatiously may be required by the court to satisfy personally the excess costs, expenses, and attorneys' fees reasonably incurred because of such conduct.

CHAPTER 125. PENDING ACTIONS AND JUDGMENTS

§ 1961. INTEREST

(a) Interest shall be allowed on any money judgment in a civil case recovered in a district court. Execution therefor may be levied by the marshal, in any case where, by the law of the State in which such court is held, execution may be levied for interest on judgments recovered in the courts of the State. Such interest shall be calculated from the date of the entry of the judgment, at a rate equal to the weekly average 1-year constant maturity Treasury yield, as published by the Board of Governors of the Federal Reserve System, for the calendar week preceding [ ] the date of the judgment. The Director of the Administrative Office of the United States Courts shall distribute notice of that rate and any changes in it to all Federal judges.

(b) Interest shall be computed daily to the date of payment except as provided in section 2516(b) of this title and section 1304(b) of title 31, and shall be compounded annually.

(c) (1) This section shall not apply in any judgment of any court with respect to any internal revenue tax case. Interest shall be allowed in such cases at the underpayment rate or overpayment rate (whichever is appropriate) established under section 6621 of the Internal Revenue Code of 1986.

(2) Except as otherwise provided in paragraph (1) of this subsection, interest shall be allowed on all final judgments against the United States in the United States Court of Appeals for the Federal [C]ircuit, at the rate provided in subsection (a) and as provided in subsection (b).

(3) Interest shall be allowed, computed, and paid on judgments of the United States Court of Federal Claims only as provided in paragraph (1) of this subsection or in any other provision of law.

(4) This section shall not be construed to affect the interest on any judgment of any court not specified in this section.

§ 1963. REGISTRATION OF JUDGMENTS FOR ENFORCEMENT IN OTHER DISTRICTS

A judgment in an action for the recovery of money or property entered in any court of appeals, district court, bankruptcy court, or in the Court of International Trade may be registered by filing a certified copy of the judgment in any other district or, with respect to the Court of International Trade, in any judicial district, when the judgment has become final by appeal or expiration of the time for appeal or when ordered by the court that entered the judgment for good cause shown. Such a judgment entered in favor of the United States may be so registered any time after judgment is entered. A judgment so registered shall have the same effect as a judgment of the district court of the district where registered and may be enforced in like manner.

A certified copy of the satisfaction of any judgment in whole or in part may be registered in like manner in any district in which the judgment is a lien.

The procedure prescribed under this section is in addition to other procedures provided by law for the enforcement of judgments.

§ 1964. CONSTRUCTIVE NOTICE OF PENDING ACTIONS

Where the law of a State requires a notice of an action concerning real property pending in a court of the State to be registered, recorded, docketed, or indexed in a particular manner, or in a certain office or county or parish in order to give constructive notice of the action as it relates to the real property, and such law authorizes a notice of an action concerning real property pending in a United States district court to be registered, recorded, docketed, or indexed in the same manner, or in the same place, those requirements of the State law must be complied with in order to give constructive notice of such an action pending in a United States district court as it relates to real property in such State.

CHAPTER 131. RULES OF COURTS

§ 2071. RULE-MAKING POWER GENERALLY

(a) The Supreme Court and all courts established by Act of Congress may from time to time prescribe rules for the conduct of their business. Such rules shall be consistent with Acts of Congress and rules of practice and procedure prescribed under section 2072 of this title.

(b) Any rule prescribed by a court, other than the Supreme Court, under subsection (a) shall be prescribed only after giving appropriate public notice and an opportunity for comment. Such rule shall take effect upon the date specified by the prescribing court and shall have such effect on pending proceedings as the prescribing court may order.

(c) (1) A rule of a district court prescribed under subsection (a) shall remain in effect unless modified or abrogated by the judicial council of the relevant circuit.

(2) Any other rule prescribed by a court other than the Supreme Court under subsection (a) shall remain in effect unless modified or abrogated by the Judicial Conference.

(d) Copies of rules prescribed under subsection (a) by a district court shall be furnished to the judicial council, and copies of all rules prescribed by a court other than the Supreme Court under subsection (a) shall be furnished to the Director of the Administrative Office of the United States Courts and made available to the public.

(e) If the prescribing court determines that there is an immediate need for a rule, such court may proceed under this section without public notice and opportunity for comment, but such court shall promptly thereafter afford such notice and opportunity for comment.

(f) No rule may be prescribed by a district court other than under this section.

§ 2072. RULES OF PROCEDURE AND EVIDENCE; POWER TO PRESCRIBE

(a) The Supreme Court shall have the power to prescribe general rules of practice and procedure and rules of evidence for cases in the United States district courts (including proceedings before magistrate judges thereof) and courts of appeals.

(b) Such rules shall not abridge, enlarge or modify any substantive right. All laws in conflict with such rules shall be of no further force or effect after such rules have taken effect.

(c) Such rules may define when a ruling of a district court is final for the purposes of appeal under section 1291 of this title.

§ 2073. RULES OF PROCEDURE AND EVIDENCE; METHOD OF PRESCRIBING

(a) (1) The Judicial Conference shall prescribe and publish the procedures for the consideration of proposed rules under this section.

(2) The Judicial Conference may authorize the appointment of committees to assist the Conference by recommending rules to be prescribed under sections 2072 and 2075 of this title. Each such committee shall consist of members of the bench and the professional bar, and trial and appellate judges.

(b) The Judicial Conference shall authorize the appointment of a standing committee on rules of practice, procedure, and evidence under subsection (a) of this section. Such standing committee shall review each recommendation of any other committees so appointed and recommend to the Judicial Conference rules of practice, procedure, and evidence and such changes in rules proposed by a committee appointed under subsection (a)(2) of this section as may be necessary to maintain consistency and otherwise promote the interest of justice.

(c) (1) Each meeting for the transaction of business under this chapter by any committee appointed under this section shall be open to the public, except when the committee so meeting, in open session and with a majority present, determines that it is in the public interest that all or part of the remainder of the meeting on that day shall be closed to the public, and states the reason for so closing the meeting. Minutes of each meeting for the transaction of business under this chapter shall be maintained by the committee and made available to the public, except that any portion of such minutes, relating to a closed meeting and made available to the public, may contain such deletions as may be necessary to avoid frustrating the purposes of closing the meeting.

(2) Any meeting for the transaction of business under this chapter, by a committee appointed under this section, shall be preceded by sufficient notice to enable all interested persons to attend.

(d) In making a recommendation under this section or under section 2072 or 2075, the body making that recommendation shall provide a proposed rule, an explanatory note on the rule, and a written report explaining the body's action, including any minority or other separate views.

(e) Failure to comply with this section does not invalidate a rule prescribed under section 2072 or 2075 of this title.

§ 2074. RULES OF PROCEDURE AND EVIDENCE; SUBMISSION TO CONGRESS; EFFECTIVE DATE

(a) The Supreme Court shall transmit to the Congress not later than May 1 of the year in which a rule prescribed under section 2072 is to become effective a copy of the proposed rule. Such rule shall take effect no earlier than December 1 of the year in which such rule is so transmitted unless otherwise provided by law. The Supreme Court may fix the extent such rule shall apply to proceedings then pending, except that the Supreme Court shall not require the application of such rule to further proceedings then pending to the extent that, in the opinion of the court in which such proceedings are pending, the application of such rule in such proceedings would not be feasible or would work injustice, in which event the former rule applies.

(b) Any such rule creating, abolishing, or modifying an evidentiary privilege shall have no force or effect unless approved by Act of Congress.

§ 2075. BANKRUPTCY RULES

The Supreme Court shall have the power to prescribe by general rules, the forms of process, writs, pleadings, and motions, and the practice and procedure in cases under title 11. Such rules shall not abridge, enlarge, or modify any substantive right. The Supreme Court shall transmit to Congress not later than May 1 of the year in which a rule prescribed under this section is to become effective a copy of the proposed rule. The rule shall take effect no earlier than December 1 of the year in which it is transmitted to Congress unless otherwise provided by law. The bankruptcy rules promulgated under this section shall prescribe a form for the statement required under section 707(b)(2)(C) of title 11 and may provide general rules on the content of such statement.

§ 2077. PUBLICATION OF RULES; ADVISORY COMMITTEES

(a) The rules for the conduct of the business of each court of appeals, including the operating procedures of such court, shall be published. Each court of appeals shall print or cause to be printed necessary copies of the rules. The Judicial Conference shall prescribe the fees for sales of copies under section 1913 of this title, but the Judicial Conference may provide for free distribution of copies to members of the bar of each court and to other interested persons.

(b) Each court, except the Supreme Court, that is authorized to prescribe rules of the conduct of such court's business under section 2071 of this title shall appoint an advisory committee for the study of the rules of practice and internal operating procedures of such court and, in the case of an advisory committee appointed by a court of appeals, of the rules of the judicial council of the circuit. The advisory committee shall make recommendations to the court concerning such rules and procedures. Members of the committee shall serve without compensation, but the Director may pay travel and transportation expenses in accordance with section 5703 of title 5.

PART VI.　PARTICULAR PROCEEDINGS

CHAPTER 151.　DECLARATORY JUDGMENTS

§ 2201. CREATION OF REMEDY

(a) In a case of actual controversy within its jurisdiction, except with respect to Federal taxes other than actions brought under section 7428 of the Internal Revenue Code of 1986, a proceeding under section 505 or 1146 of title 11, or in any civil action involving an antidumping or countervailing duty proceeding regarding a class or kind of merchandise of a free trade area country (as defined in section 516A(f)(10) of the Tariff Act of 1930), as determined by the administering authority, any court of the United States, upon the filing of an appropriate pleading, may declare the rights and other legal relations of any interested party seeking such declaration, whether or not further relief is or could be sought. Any such declaration shall have the force and effect of a final judgment or decree and shall be reviewable as such.

(b) For limitations on actions brought with respect to drug patents see section 505 or 512 of the Federal Food, Drug, and Cosmetic Act.

§ 2202. FURTHER RELIEF

Further necessary or proper relief based on a declaratory judgment or decree may be granted, after reasonable notice and hearing, against any adverse party whose rights have been determined by such judgment.

CHAPTER 155. INJUNCTIONS; THREE-JUDGE COURTS

§ 2283. STAY OF STATE COURT PROCEEDINGS

A court of the United States may not grant an injunction to stay proceedings in a State court except as expressly authorized by Act of Congress, or where necessary in aid of its jurisdiction, or to protect or effectuate its judgments.

§ 2284. THREE-JUDGE COURT; WHEN REQUIRED; COMPOSITION; PROCEDURE

(a) A district court of three judges shall be convened when otherwise required by Act of Congress, or when an action is filed challenging the constitutionality of the apportionment of congressional districts or the apportionment of any statewide legislative body.

(b) In any action required to be heard and determined by a district court of three judges under subsection (a) of this section, the composition and procedure of the court shall be as follows:

(1) Upon the filing of a request for three judges, the judge to whom the request is presented shall, unless he determines that three judges are not required, immediately notify the chief judge of the circuit, who shall designate two other judges, at least one of whom shall be a circuit judge. The judges so designated, and the judge to whom the request was presented, shall serve as members of the court to hear and determine the action or proceeding.

(2) If the action is against a State, or officer or agency thereof, at least five days' notice of hearing of the action shall be given by registered or certified mail to the Governor and attorney general of the State.

(3) A single judge may conduct all proceedings except the trial, and enter all orders permitted by the rules of civil procedure except as provided in this subsection. He may grant a temporary restraining order on a specific finding, based on evidence submitted, that specified irreparable damage will result if the order is not granted, which order, unless previously revoked by the district judge, shall remain in force only until the hearing and determination by the district court of three judges of an application for a preliminary injunction. A single judge shall not appoint a master, or order a reference, or hear and determine any application for a preliminary or permanent injunction or motion to vacate such an injunction, or enter judgment on the merits. Any action of a single judge may be reviewed by the full court at any time before final judgment.

CHAPTER 159. INTERPLEADER

§ 2361. PROCESS AND PROCEDURE

In any civil action of interpleader or in the nature of interpleader under section 1335 of this title, a district court may issue its process for all claimants and enter its order restraining them from instituting or prosecuting any proceeding in any State or United States court affecting the property, instrument or obligation involved in the interpleader action until further order of the court. Such process and order shall be returnable at such time as the court or judge thereof directs, and shall be addressed to and served by the United States marshals for the respective districts where the claimants reside or may be found.

Such district court shall hear and determine the case, and may discharge the plaintiff from further liability, make the injunction permanent, and make all appropriate orders to enforce its judgment.

CHAPTER 161. UNITED STATES AS PARTY GENERALLY

§ 2401. TIME FOR COMMENCING ACTION AGAINST UNITED STATES

(a) Except as provided by the Contract Disputes Act of 1978, every civil action commenced against the United States shall be barred unless the complaint is filed within six years after the right of action first accrues. The action of any person under legal disability or beyond the seas at the time the claim accrues may be commenced within three years after the disability ceases.

(b) A tort claim against the United States shall be forever barred unless it is presented in writing to the appropriate Federal agency within two years after such claim accrues or unless action is begun within six months after the date of mailing, by certified or registered mail, of notice of final denial of the claim by the agency to which it was presented.

§ 2402. JURY TRIAL IN ACTIONS AGAINST UNITED STATES

Subject to chapter 179 of this title, any action against the United States under section 1346 shall be tried by the court without a jury, except that any action against the United States under section 1346(a)(1) shall, at the request of either party to such action, be tried by the court with a jury.

§ 2403. INTERVENTION BY UNITED STATES OR A STATE; CONSTITUTIONAL QUESTION

(a) In any action, suit or proceeding in a court of the United States to which the United States or any agency, officer or employee thereof is not a party, wherein the constitutionality of any Act of Congress affecting the public interest is drawn in question, the court shall certify such fact to the Attorney General, and shall permit the United States to intervene for presentation of evidence, if evidence is otherwise admissible in the case, and for argument on the question of constitutionality. The United States shall, subject to the applicable provisions of law, have all the rights of a party and be subject to all liabilities of a party as to court costs to the extent necessary for a proper presentation of the facts and law relating to the question of constitutionality.

(b) In any action, suit, or proceeding in a court of the United States to which a State or any agency, officer, or employee thereof is not a party, wherein the constitutionality of any statute of that State affecting the public interest is drawn in question, the court shall certify such fact to the attorney general of the State, and shall permit the State to intervene for presentation of evidence, if evidence is otherwise admissible in the case, and for argument on the question of constitutionality. The State shall, subject to the applicable provisions of law, have all the rights of a party and be subject to all liabilities of a party as to court costs to the extent necessary for a proper presentation of the facts and law relating to the question of constitutionality.

§ 2412. COSTS AND FEES

(a) (1) Except as otherwise specifically provided by statute, a judgment for costs, as enumerated in section 1920 of this title, but not including the fees and expenses of attorneys, may be awarded to the prevailing party in any civil action brought by or against the United States or any agency or any official of the United States acting in his or her official capacity in any court having jurisdiction of such action. A judgment for costs when taxed against the United States shall, in an amount established by statute, court rule, or order, be limited to reimbursing in whole or in part the prevailing party for the costs incurred by such party in the litigation.

(2) A judgment for costs, when awarded in favor of the United States in an action brought by the United States, may include an amount equal to the filing fee prescribed under section 1914(a) of this title. The preceding sentence shall not be construed as requiring the United States to pay any filing fee.

(b) Unless expressly prohibited by statute, a court may award reasonable fees and expenses of attorneys, in addition to the costs which may be awarded pursuant to subsection (a), to the prevailing party in any civil action brought by or against the United States or any agency or any official of the United States acting in his or her official capacity in any court having jurisdiction of such action. The United States shall be liable for such fees and expenses to the same extent that any other party would be liable under the common law or under the terms of any statute which specifically provides for such an award.

(c) (1) Any judgment against the United States or any agency and any official of the United States acting in his or her official capacity for costs pursuant to subsection (a) shall be paid as provided in sections 2414 and 2517 of this title and shall be in addition to any relief provided in the judgment.

(2) Any judgment against the United States or any agency and any official of the United States acting in his or her official capacity for fees and expenses of attorneys pursuant to subsection (b) shall be paid as provided in sections 2414 and 2517 of this title, except that if the basis for the award is a finding that the United States acted in bad faith, then the award shall be paid by any agency found to have acted in bad faith and shall be in addition to any relief provided in the judgment.

(d) (1) (A) Except as otherwise specifically provided by statute, a court shall award to a prevailing party other than the United States fees and other expenses, in addition to any costs awarded pursuant to subsection (a), incurred by that party in any civil action (other than cases sounding in tort), including proceedings for judicial review of agency action, brought by or against the United States in any court having jurisdiction of that action, unless the court finds that the position of the United States was substantially justified or that special circumstances make an award unjust.

(B) A party seeking an award of fees and other expenses shall, within thirty days of final judgment in the action, submit to the court an application for fees and other expenses which shows that the party is a prevailing party and is eligible to receive an award under this subsection, and the amount sought, including an itemized statement from any attorney or expert witness representing or appearing in behalf of the party stating the actual time expended and the rate at which fees and other expenses were computed. The party shall also allege that the position of the United States was not substantially justified. Whether or not the position of the United States was substantially justified shall be determined on the basis of the record (including the record with respect to the action or failure to act by the agency upon which the civil action is based) which is made in the civil action for which fees and other expenses are sought.

(C) The court, in its discretion, may reduce the amount to be awarded pursuant to this subsection, or deny an award, to the extent that the prevailing party during the course of the proceedings engaged in conduct which unduly and unreasonably protracted the final resolution of the matter in controversy.

(D) If, in a civil action brought by the United States or a proceeding for judicial review of an adversary adjudication described in section 504(a)(4) of title 5, the demand by the United States is substantially in excess of the judgment finally obtained by the United States and is unreasonable when compared with such judgment, under the facts and circumstances of the case, the court shall award to the party the fees and other expenses related to defending against the excessive demand, unless the party has committed a willful violation of law or otherwise acted in bad faith, or special circumstances make an award unjust. Fees and expenses awarded under this subparagraph shall be paid only as a consequence of appropriations provided in advance.

(2) For the purposes of this subsection:

(A) "fees and other expenses" includes the reasonable expenses of expert witnesses, the reasonable cost of any study, analysis, engineering report, test, or project which is found by the court to be necessary for the preparation of the party's case, and reasonable attorney fees (The amount of fees awarded under this subsection shall be based upon prevailing market rates for the kind and quality of the services furnished, except that (i) no expert witness shall be compensated at a rate in excess of the highest rate of compensation for expert witnesses paid by the United States; and (ii) attorney fees shall not be awarded in excess of $125 per hour unless the court determines that an increase in the cost of living or a special factor, such as the limited availability of qualified attorneys for the proceedings involved, justifies a higher fee.);

(B) "party" means (i) an individual whose net worth did not exceed $2,000,000 at the time the civil action was filed, or (ii) any owner of an unincorporated business, or any partnership, corporation, association, unit of local government, or organization, the net worth of which did not exceed $7,000,000 at the time the civil action was filed, and which had not more than 500 employees at the time the civil action was filed; except that an organization described in section 501(c)(3) of the Internal Revenue Code of 1986 (26 U.S.C. 501(c)(3)) exempt from taxation under section 501(a) of such Code, or a cooperative association as defined in section 15(a) of the Agricultural Marketing Act (12 U.S.C. 1141j(a)), may be a party regardless of the net worth of such organization or cooperative association or for purposes of subsection (d)(1)(D), a small entity as defined in section 601 of Title 5;

(C) "United States" includes any agency and any official of the United States acting in his or her official capacity;

(D) "position of the United States" means, in addition to the position taken by the United States in the civil action, the action or failure to act by the agency upon which the civil action is based; except that fees and expenses may not be awarded to a party for any portion of the litigation in which the party has unreasonably protracted the proceedings;

(E) "civil action brought by or against the United States" includes an appeal by a party, other than the United States, from a decision of a contracting officer rendered pursuant to a disputes clause in a contract with the Government or pursuant to the Contract Disputes Act of 1978;

(F) "court" includes the United States Court of Federal Claims and the United States Court of Appeals for Veterans Claims;

(G) "final judgment" means a judgment that is final and not appealable, and includes an order of settlement;

(H) "prevailing party", in the case of eminent domain proceedings, means a party who obtains a final judgment (other than by settlement), exclusive of interest, the amount of which is at least as close to the highest valuation of the property involved that is attested to at trial on behalf of the property owner as it is to the highest valuation of the property involved that is attested to at trial on behalf of the Government; and

(I) "demand" means the express demand of the United States which led to the adversary adjudication, but shall not include a recitation of the maximum statutory penalty (i) in the complaint, or (ii) elsewhere when accompanied by an express demand for a lesser amount.

(3) In awarding fees and other expenses under this subsection to a prevailing party in any action for judicial review of an adversary adjudication, as defined in subsection (b)(1)(C) of section 504 of title 5, United States Code, or an adversary adjudication subject to the Contract Disputes Act of 1978, the court shall include in that award fees and other expenses to the same extent authorized in subsection (a) of such section, unless the court finds that during such adversary adjudication the position of the United States was substantially justified, or that special circumstances make an award unjust.

(4) Fees and other expenses awarded under this subsection to a party shall be paid by any agency over which the party prevails from any funds made available to the agency by appropriation or otherwise.

(e) The provisions of this section shall not apply to any costs, fees, and other expenses in connection with any proceeding to which section 7430 of the Internal Revenue Code of 1986 applies (determined without regard to subsections (b) and (f) of such section). Nothing in the preceding sentence shall prevent the awarding under subsection (a) of section 2412 of title 28, United States Code, of costs enumerated in section 1920 of such title (as in effect on October 1, 1981).

(f) If the United States appeals an award of costs or fees and other expenses made against the United States under this section and the award is affirmed in whole or in part, interest shall be paid on the amount of the award as affirmed. Such interest shall be computed at the rate determined under section 1961(a) of this title, and shall run from the date of the award through the day before the date of the mandate of affirmance.

CHAPTER 171. TORT CLAIMS PROCEDURE

§ 2671. DEFINITIONS

As used in this chapter and sections 1346(b) and 2401(b) of this title, the term "Federal agency" includes the executive departments, the judicial and legislative branches, the military departments, independent establishments of the United States, and corporations primarily acting as instrumentalities or agencies of the United States, but does not include any contractor with the United States.

"Employee of the government" includes (1) officers or employees of any federal agency, members of the military or naval forces of the United States, members of the National Guard while engaged in training or duty under section 115, 316, 502, 503, 504, or 505 of title 32, and persons acting on behalf of a federal agency in an official capacity, temporarily or permanently in the service of the United States, whether with or without compensation, and (2) any officer or employee of a Federal public defender organization, except when such officer or employee performs professional services in the course of providing representation under section 3006A of title 18.

"Acting within the scope of his office or employment", in the case of a member of the military or naval forces of the United States or a member of the National Guard as defined in section 101(3) of title 32, means acting in line of duty.

§ 2672. ADMINISTRATIVE ADJUSTMENT OF CLAIMS

The head of each Federal agency or his designee, in accordance with regulations prescribed by the Attorney General, may consider, ascertain, adjust, determine, compromise, and settle any claim for money damages against the United States for injury or loss of property or personal injury or death caused by the negligent or wrongful act or omission of any employee of the agency while acting within the scope of his office or employment, under circumstances where the United States, if a private person, would be liable to the claimant in accordance with the law of the place where the act or omission occurred: Provided, That any award, compromise, or settlement in excess of $25,000 shall be effected only with the prior written approval of the Attorney General or his designee. Notwithstanding the proviso contained in the preceding sentence, any award, compromise, or settlement may be effected without the prior written approval of the Attorney General or his or her designee, to the extent that the Attorney General delegates to the head of the agency the authority to make such award, compromise, or settlement. Such delegations may not exceed the authority delegated by the Attorney General to the United States attorneys to settle claims for money damages against the United States. Each Federal agency may use arbitration, or other alternative means of dispute resolution under the provisions of subchapter IV of chapter 5 of title 5, to settle any tort claim against the United States, to the extent of the agency's authority to award, compromise, or settle such claim without the prior written approval of the Attorney General or his or her designee.

Subject to the provisions of this title relating to civil actions on tort claims against the United States, any such award, compromise, settlement, or determination shall be final and conclusive on all officers of the Government, except when procured by means of fraud.

Any award, compromise, or settlement in an amount of $2,500 or less made pursuant to this section shall be paid by the head of the Federal agency concerned out of appropriations available to that agency. Payment of any award, compromise, or settlement in an amount in excess of $2,500 made pursuant to this section or made by the Attorney General in any amount pursuant to section 2677 of this title shall be paid in a manner similar to judgments and compromises in like causes and appropriations or funds available for the payment of such judgments and compromises are hereby made available for the payment of awards, compromises, or settlements under this chapter.

The acceptance by the claimant of any such award, compromise, or settlement shall be final and conclusive on the claimant, and shall constitute a complete release of any claim against the United States and against the employee of the government whose act or omission gave rise to the claim, by reason of the same subject matter.

§ 2674. LIABILITY OF UNITED STATES

The United States shall be liable, respecting the provisions of this title relating to tort claims, in the same manner and to the same extent as a private individual under like circumstances, but shall not be liable for interest prior to judgment or for punitive damages.

If, however, in any case wherein death was caused, the law of the place where the act or omission complained of occurred provides, or has been construed to provide, for damages only punitive in nature, the United States shall be liable for actual or compensatory damages, measured by the pecuniary injuries resulting from such death to the persons respectively, for whose benefit the action was brought, in lieu thereof.

With respect to any claim under this chapter, the United States shall be entitled to assert any defense based upon judicial or legislative immunity which otherwise would have been available to the employee of the United States whose act or omission gave rise to the claim, as well as any other defenses to which the United States is entitled.

With respect to any claim to which this section applies, the Tennessee Valley Authority shall be entitled to assert any defense which otherwise would have been available to the employee based upon judicial or legislative immunity, which otherwise would have been available to the employee of the Tennessee Valley Authority whose act or omission gave rise to the claim as well as any other defenses to which the Tennessee Valley Authority is entitled under this chapter.

§ 2675. DISPOSITION BY FEDERAL AGENCY AS PREREQUISITE; EVIDENCE

(a) An action shall not be instituted upon a claim against the United States for money damages for injury or loss of property or personal injury or death caused by the negligent or wrongful act or omission of any employee of the Government while acting within the scope of his office or employment, unless the claimant shall have first presented the claim to the appropriate Federal agency and his claim shall have been finally denied by the agency in writing and sent by certified or registered mail. The failure of an agency to make final disposition of a claim within six months after it is filed shall, at the option of the claimant any time thereafter, be deemed a final denial of the claim for purposes of this section. The provisions of this subsection shall not apply to such claims as may be asserted under the Federal Rules of Civil Procedure by third party complaint, cross-claim, or counterclaim.

(b) Action under this section shall not be instituted for any sum in excess of the amount of the claim presented to the federal agency, except where the increased amount is based upon newly discovered evidence not reasonably discoverable at the time of presenting the claim to the federal agency, or upon allegation and proof of intervening facts, relating to the amount of the claim.

(c) Disposition of any claim by the Attorney General or other head of a federal agency shall not be competent evidence of liability or amount of damages.

§ 2676. JUDGMENT AS BAR

The judgment in an action under section 1346(b) of this title shall constitute a complete bar to any action by the claimant, by reason of the same subject matter, against the employee of the government whose act or omission gave rise to the claim.

§ 2677. COMPROMISE

The Attorney General or his designee may arbitrate, compromise, or settle any claim cognizable under section 1346(b) of this title, after the commencement of an action thereon.

§ 2678. ATTORNEY FEES; PENALTY

No attorney shall charge, demand, receive, or collect for services rendered, fees in excess of 25 per centum of any judgment rendered pursuant to section 1346(b) of this title or any settlement made pursuant to section 2677 of this title, or in excess of 20 per centum of any award, compromise, or settlement made pursuant to section 2672 of this title.

Any attorney who charges, demands, receives, or collects for services rendered in connection with such claim any amount in excess of that allowed under this section, if recovery be had, shall be fined not more than $2,000 or imprisoned not more than one year, or both.

§ 2679. EXCLUSIVENESS OF REMEDY

(a) The authority of any federal agency to sue and be sued in its own name shall not be construed to authorize suits against such federal agency on claims which are cognizable under section 1346(b) of this title, and the remedies provided by this title in such cases shall be exclusive.

(b) (1) The remedy against the United States provided by sections 1346(b) and 2672 of this title for injury or loss of property, or personal injury or death arising or resulting from the negligent or wrongful act or omission of any employee of the Government while acting within the scope of his office or employment is exclusive of any other civil action or proceeding for money damages by reason of the same subject matter against the employee whose act or omission gave rise to the claim or against the estate of such employee. Any other civil action or proceeding for money damages arising out of or relating to the same subject matter against the employee or the employee's estate is precluded without regard to when the act or omission occurred.

(2) Paragraph (1) does not extend or apply to a civil action against an employee of the Government:

(A) which is brought for a violation of the Constitution of the United States, or

(B) which is brought for a violation of a statute of the United States under which such action against an individual is otherwise authorized.

(c) The Attorney General shall defend any civil action or proceeding brought in any court against any employee of the Government or his estate for any such damage or injury. The employee against whom such civil action or proceeding is brought shall deliver within such time after date of service or knowledge of service as determined by the Attorney General, all process served upon him or an attested true copy thereof to his immediate superior or to whomever was designated by the head of his department to receive such papers and such person shall promptly furnish copies of the pleadings and process therein to the United States attorney for the district embracing the place wherein the proceeding is brought, to the Attorney General, and to the head of his employing Federal agency.

(d) (1) Upon certification by the Attorney General that the defendant employee was acting within the scope of his office or employment at the time of the incident out of which the claim arose, any civil action or proceeding commenced upon such claim in a United States district court shall be deemed an action against the United States under the provisions of this title and all references thereto, and the United States shall be substituted as the party defendant.

(2) Upon certification by the Attorney General that the defendant employee was acting within the scope of his office or employment at the time of the incident out of which the claim arose, any civil action or proceeding commenced upon such claim in a State court shall be removed without bond at any time before trial by the Attorney General to the district court of the United States for the district and division embracing the place in which the action or proceeding is pending. Such action or proceeding shall be deemed to be an action or proceeding brought against the United States under the provisions of this title and all references thereto, and the United States shall be substituted as the party defendant. This certification of the Attorney General shall conclusively establish scope of office or employment for purposes of removal.

(3) In the event that the Attorney General has refused to certify scope of office or employment under this section, the employee may at any time before trial petition the court to find and certify that the employee was acting within the scope of his office or employment. Upon such certification by the court, such action or proceeding shall be deemed to be an action or proceeding brought against the United States under the provisions of this title and all references thereto, and the United States shall be substituted as the party defendant. A copy of the petition shall be served upon the United States in accordance with the provisions of Rule 4(d)(4) of the Federal Rules of Civil Procedure. In the event the petition is filed in a civil action or proceeding pending in a State court, the action or proceeding may be removed without bond by the Attorney General to the district court of the United States for the district and division embracing the place in which it is pending. If, in considering the petition, the district court determines that the employee was not acting within the scope of his office or employment, the action or proceeding shall be remanded to the State court.

(4) Upon certification, any action or proceeding subject to paragraph (1), (2), or (3) shall proceed in the same manner as any action against the United States filed pursuant to section 1346(b) of this title and shall be subject to the limitations and exceptions applicable to those actions.

(5) Whenever an action or proceeding in which the United States is substituted as the party defendant under this subsection is dismissed for failure first to present a claim pursuant to section 2675(a) of this title, such a claim shall be deemed to be timely presented under section 2401(b) of this title if:

(A) the claim would have been timely had it been filed on the date the underlying civil action was commenced, and

(B) the claim is presented to the appropriate Federal agency within 60 days after dismissal of the civil action.

(e) The Attorney General may compromise or settle any claim asserted in such civil action or proceeding in the manner provided in section 2677, and with the same effect.

§ 2680. EXCEPTIONS

The provisions of this chapter and section 1346(b) of this title shall not apply to:

(a) Any claim based upon an act or omission of an employee of the Government, exercising due care, in the execution of a statute or regulation, whether or not such statute or regulation be valid, or based upon the exercise or performance or the failure to exercise or perform a discretionary function or duty on the part of a federal agency or an employee of the Government, whether or not the discretion involved be abused.

(b) Any claim arising out of the loss, miscarriage, or negligent transmission of letters or postal matter.

(c) Any claim arising in respect of the assessment or collection of any tax or customs duty, or the detention of any goods, merchandise, or other property by any officer of customs or excise or any other law enforcement officer, except that the provisions of this chapter and section 1346(b) of this title apply to any claim based on injury or loss of goods, merchandise, or other property, while in the possession of any officer of customs or excise or any other law enforcement officer, if:

(1) the property was seized for the purpose of forfeiture under any provision of Federal law providing for the forfeiture of property other than as a sentence imposed upon conviction of a criminal offense;

(2) the interest of the claimant was not forfeited;

(3) the interest of the claimant was not remitted or mitigated (if the property was subject to forfeiture); and

(4) the claimant was not convicted of a crime for which the interest of the claimant in the property was subject to forfeiture under a Federal criminal forfeiture law.

(d) Any claim for which a remedy is provided by chapter 309 or 311 of Title 46 relating to claims or suits in admiralty against the United States.

(e) Any claim arising out of an act or omission of any employee of the Government in administering the provisions of sections 1-31 of Title 50, Appendix.

(f) Any claim for damages caused by the imposition or establishment of a quarantine by the United States.

[(g) Repealed. Sept. 26, 1950, c. 1049, § 13(5), 64 Stat. 1043.]

(h) Any claim arising out of assault, battery, false imprisonment, false arrest, malicious prosecution, abuse of process, libel, slander, misrepresentation, deceit, or interference with contract rights: Provided, That, with regard to acts or omissions of investigative or law enforcement officers of the United States Government, the provisions of this chapter and section 1346(b) of this title shall apply to any claim arising, on or after the date of the enactment of this proviso, out of assault, battery, false imprisonment, false arrest, abuse of process, or malicious prosecution. For the purpose of this subsection, "investigative or law enforcement officer" means any officer of the United States who is empowered by law to execute searches, to seize evidence, or to make arrests for violations of Federal law.

(i) Any claim for damages caused by the fiscal operations of the Treasury or by the regulation of the monetary system.

(j) Any claim arising out of the combatant activities of the military or naval forces, or the Coast Guard, during time of war.

(k) Any claim arising in a foreign country.

(l) Any claim arising from the activities of the Tennessee Valley Authority.

(m) Any claim arising from the activities of the Panama Canal Company.

(n) Any claim arising from the activities of a Federal land bank, a Federal intermediate credit bank, or a bank for cooperatives.

TITLE 42, THE PUBLIC HEALTH AND WELFARE

CHAPTER 21. CIVIL RIGHTS

§ 1981. EQUAL RIGHTS UNDER THE LAW

(a) Statement of equal rights

All persons within the jurisdiction of the United States shall have the same right in every State and Territory to make and enforce contracts, to sue, be parties, give evidence, and to the full and equal benefit of all laws and proceedings for the security of persons and property as is enjoyed by white citizens, and shall be subject to like punishment, pains, penalties, taxes, licenses, and exactions of every kind, and to no other.

(b) "Make and enforce contracts" defined

For purposes of this section, the term "make and enforce contracts" includes the making, performance, modification, and termination of contracts, and the enjoyment of all benefits, privileges, terms, and conditions of the contractual relationship.

(c) Protection against impairment

The rights protected by this section are protected against impairment by nongovernmental discrimination and impairment under color of State law.

§ 1982. PROPERTY RIGHTS OF CITIZENS

All citizens of the United States shall have the same right, in every State and Territory, as is enjoyed by white citizens thereof to inherit, purchase, lease, sell, hold, and convey real and personal property.

§ 1983. CIVIL ACTION FOR DEPRIVATION OF RIGHTS

Every person who, under color of any statute, ordinance, regulation, custom, or usage, of any State or Territory or the District of Columbia, subjects, or causes to be subjected, any citizen of the United States or other person within the jurisdiction thereof to the deprivation of any rights, privileges, or immunities secured by the Constitution and laws, shall be liable to the party injured in an action at law, suit in equity, or other proper proceeding for redress, except that in any action brought against a judicial officer for an act or omission taken in such officer's judicial capacity, injunctive relief shall not be granted unless a declaratory decree was violated or declaratory relief was unavailable. For the purposes of this section, any Act of Congress applicable exclusively to the District of Columbia shall be considered to be a statute of the District of Columbia.

§ 1985. CONSPIRACY TO INTERFERE WITH CIVIL RIGHTS

(1) Preventing officer from performing duties

If two or more persons in any State or Territory conspire to prevent, by force, intimidation, or threat, any person from accepting or holding any office, trust, or place of confidence under the United States, or from discharging any duties thereof; or to induce by like means any officer of the United States to leave any State, district, or place, where his duties as an officer are required to be performed, or to injure him in his person or property on account of his lawful discharge of the duties of his office, or while engaged in the lawful discharge thereof, or to injure his property so as to molest, interrupt, hinder, or impede him in the discharge of his official duties;

(2) Obstructing justice; intimidating party, witness, or juror

If two or more persons in any State or Territory conspire to deter, by force, intimidation, or threat, any party or witness in any court of the United States from attending such court, or from testifying to any matter pending therein, freely, fully, and truthfully, or to injure such party or witness in his person or property on account of his having so attended or testified, or to influence the verdict, presentment, or indictment of any grand or petit juror in any such court, or to injure such juror in his person or property on account of any verdict, presentment, or indictment lawfully assented to by him, or of his being or having been such juror; or if two or more persons conspire for the purpose of impeding, hindering, obstructing, or defeating, in any manner, the due course of justice in any State or Territory, with intent to deny to any citizen the equal protection of the laws, or to injure him or his property for lawfully enforcing, or attempting to enforce, the right of any person, or class of persons, to the equal protection of the laws;

(3) Depriving persons of rights or privileges

If two or more persons in any State or Territory conspire or go in disguise on the highway or on the premises of another, for the purpose of depriving, either directly or indirectly, any person or class of persons of the equal protection of the laws, or of equal privileges and immunities under the laws; or for the purpose of preventing or hindering the constituted authorities of any State or Territory from giving or securing to all persons within such State or Territory the equal protection of the laws; or if two or more persons conspire to prevent by force, intimidation, or threat, any citizen who is lawfully entitled to vote, from giving his support or advocacy in a legal manner, toward or in favor of the election of any lawfully qualified person as an elector for President or Vice President, or as a Member of Congress of the United States; or to injure any citizen in person or property on account of such support or advocacy; in any case of conspiracy set forth in this section, if one or more persons engaged therein do, or cause to be done, any act in furtherance of the object of such conspiracy, whereby another is injured in his person or property, or deprived of having and exercising any right or privilege of a citizen of the United States, the party so injured or deprived may have an action for the recovery of damages occasioned by such injury or deprivation, against any one or more of the conspirators.

§ 1986. ACTION FOR NEGLECT TO PREVENT

Every person who, having knowledge that any of the wrongs conspired to be done, and mentioned in section 1985 of this title, are about to be committed, and having power to prevent or aid in preventing the commission of the same, neglects or refuses so to do, if such wrongful act be committed, shall be liable to the party injured, or his legal representatives, for all damages caused by such wrongful act, which such person by reasonable diligence could have prevented; and such damages may be recovered in an action on the case; and any number of persons guilty of such wrongful neglect or refusal may be joined as defendants in the action; and if the death of any party be caused by any such wrongful act and neglect, the legal representatives of the deceased shall have such action therefor, and may recover not exceeding $5,000 damages therein, for the benefit of the widow of the deceased, if there be one, and if there be no widow, then for the benefit of the next of kin of the deceased. But no action under the provisions of this section shall be sustained which is not commenced within one year after the cause of action has accrued.

§ 1987. PROSECUTION OF VIOLATION OF CERTAIN LAWS

The United States attorneys, marshals, and deputy marshals, the United States magistrate judges appointed by the district and territorial courts, with power to arrest, imprison, or bail offenders, and every other officer who is especially empowered by the President, are authorized and required, at the expense of the United States, to institute prosecutions against all persons violating any of the provisions of section 1990 of this title or of sections 5506 to 5516 and 5518 to 5532 of the Revised Statutes, and to cause such persons to be arrested, and imprisoned or bailed, for trial before the court of the United States or the territorial court having cognizance of the offense.

§ 1988. PROCEEDINGS IN VINDICATION OF CIVIL RIGHTS

(a) Applicability of statutory and common law

The jurisdiction in civil and criminal matters conferred on the district courts by the provisions of titles 13, 24, and 70 of the Revised Statutes for the protection of all persons in the United States in their civil rights, and for their vindication, shall be exercised and enforced in conformity with the laws of the United States, so far as such laws are suitable to carry the same into effect; but in all cases where they are not adapted to the object, or are deficient in the provisions necessary to furnish suitable remedies and punish offenses against law, the common law, as modified and changed by the constitution and statutes of the State wherein the court having jurisdiction of such civil or criminal cause is held, so far as the same is not inconsistent with the Constitution and laws of the United States, shall be extended to and govern the said courts in the trial and disposition of the cause, and, if it is of a criminal nature, in the infliction of punishment on the party found guilty.

(b) Attorney's fees

In any action or proceeding to enforce a provision of sections 1981, 1981a, 1982, 1983, 1985, and 1986 of this title, title IX of Public Law 92-318 [20 U.S.C.A. § 1681 et seq.], the Religious Freedom Restoration Act of 1993 [42 U.S.C.A. § 2000bb et seq.], the Religious Land Use and Institutionalized Persons Act of 2000 [42 U.S.C.A. § 2000cc et seq.], title VI of the Civil Rights Act of 1964 [42 U.S.C.A. § 2000d et seq.], or section 13981 of this title, the court, in its discretion, may allow the prevailing party, other than the United States, a reasonable attorney's fee as part of the costs, except that in any action brought against a judicial officer for an act or omission taken in such officer's judicial capacity such officer shall not be held liable for any costs, including attorney's fees, unless such action was clearly in excess of such officer's jurisdiction.

(c) Expert fees

In awarding an attorney's fee under subsection (b) of this section in any action or proceeding to enforce a provision of section 1981 or 1981a of this title, the court, in its discretion, may include expert fees as part of the attorney's fee.

EXAMPLES OF STATE LONG-ARM STATUTES

CALIFORNIA

Cal. Civ. Proc. § 410.10. Jurisdiction. Basis.

A court of this state may exercise jurisdiction on any basis not inconsistent with the Constitution of this state or of the United States.

FLORIDA

Fla. Stat. Ann. § 48.193. Acts subjecting person to jurisdiction of courts of state.

(1) Any person, whether or not a citizen or resident of this state, who personally or through an agent does any of the acts enumerated in this subsection thereby submits himself or herself and, if he or she is a natural person, his or her personal representative to the jurisdiction of the courts of this state for any cause of action arising from the doing of any of the following acts:

(a) Operating, conducting, engaging in, or carrying on a business or business venture in this state or having an office or agency in this state.

(b) Committing a tortious act within this state.

(c) Owning, using, possessing, or holding a mortgage or other lien on any real property within this state.

(d) Contracting to insure any person, property or risk located within this state at the time of contracting.

(e) With respect to a proceeding for alimony, child support, or division of property in connection with an action to dissolve a marriage or with respect to an independent action for support of dependents, maintaining a matrimonial domicile in this state at the time of the commencement of this action or, if the defendant resided in this state preceding the commencement of the action, whether cohabiting during that time or not. This paragraph does not change the residency requirement for filing an action for dissolution of marriage.

(f) Causing injury to persons or property within this state arising out of an act or omission by the defendant outside this state, if, at or about the time of the injury, either:

1. The defendant was engaged in solicitation or service activities within this state; or

2. Products, materials, or things processed, serviced, or manufactured by the defendant anywhere were used or consumed within this state in the ordinary course of commerce, trade, or use.

(g) Breaching a contract in this state by failing to perform acts required by the contract to be performed in this state.

(h) With respect to a proceeding for paternity, engaging in the act of sexual intercourse within this state with respect to which a child may have been conceived.

(2) A defendant who is engaged in substantial and not isolated activity within this state, whether such activity is wholly interstate, intrastate, or otherwise, is subject to the jurisdiction of the courts of this state, whether or not the claim arises from that activity.

(3) Service of process upon any person who is subject to the jurisdiction of the courts of this state as provided in this section may be made by personally serving the process upon the defendant outside this state, as provided in Section 48.194. The service shall have the same effect as if it had been personally served within this state.

(4) If a defendant in his or her pleadings demands affirmative relief on causes of action unrelated to the transaction forming the basis of the plaintiff's claim, the defendant shall thereafter in that action be subject to the jurisdiction of the court for any cause of action, regardless of its basis, which the plaintiff may by amendment assert against the defendant.

(5) Nothing contained in this section limits or affects the right to serve any process in any other manner now or hereinafter provided by law.

ILLINOIS

735 Ill. Comp. Stat. 5/2-209. Act submitting to jurisdiction--Process.

(a) Any person, whether or not a citizen or resident of this state, who in person or through an agent does any of the acts hereinafter enumerated, thereby submits such person, and, if an individual, his or her personal representative, to the jurisdiction of the courts of this State as to any cause of action arising from the doing of any such acts:

(1) The transaction of any business within this State;

(2) The commission of a tortious act within this State;

(3) The ownership, use or possession of any real estate situated in this State;

(4) Contracting to insure any person, property or risk located within this State at the time of contracting;

(5) With respect to actions of dissolution of marriage, declaration of invalidity of marriage and legal separation, the maintenance in this State of a matrimonial domicile at the time this cause of action arose or the commission in this State of any act giving rise to the cause of action;

(6) With respect to actions brought under the Illinois Parentage Act of 1984, as now or hereafter amended, the performance of an act of sexual intercourse within this State during the possible period of conception;

(7) The making or performance of any contract or promise substantially connected with this State;

(8) The performance of sexual intercourse within this State which is claimed to have resulted in a the conception of a child who resides in this State;

(9) The failure to support a child, spouse or former spouse who has continued to reside in this State since the person either formerly resided with them in this State or directed them to reside in this State;

(10) The acquisition of ownership, possession or control of any asset or thing of value present within this State when ownership, possession or control was acquired;

(11) The breach of any fiduciary duty within this State;

(12) The performance of duties as a director or officer of a corporation organized under the laws of this State or having its principal place of business within this State;

(13) The ownership of an interest in any trust administered within this State; or

(14) The exercise of powers granted under the authority of this State as a fiduciary.

(b) A court may exercise jurisdiction in any action arising within or without this State against any person who:

(1) Is a natural person present within this State when served;

(2) Is a natural person domiciled or resident within this State when the cause of action arose, the action was commenced, or process was served;

(3) Is a corporation organized under the laws of this State; or

(4) Is a natural person or corporation doing business within this State.

(c) A court may also exercise jurisdiction on any other basis now or hereafter permitted by the Illinois Constitution and the Constitution of the United States.

(d) Service of process upon any person who is subject to the jurisdiction of the courts of this State, as provided in this Section, may be made by personally serving the summons upon the defendant outside this State, as provided in this Act, with the same force and effect as though summons had been personally served within this State.

(e) Service of process upon any person who resides or whose business address is outside the United States and who is subject to the jurisdiction of the courts of this State, as provided in this Section, in any action based upon product liability may be made by serving a copy of the summons with a copy of the complaint attached upon the Secretary of State. The summons shall be accompanied by a $5 fee payable to the Secretary of State. The plaintiff shall forthwith mail a copy of the summons, upon which the date of service upon the Secretary is clearly shown, together with a copy of the complaint to the defendant at his or her last known place of residence or business address. Plaintiff shall file with the circuit clerk an affidavit of the plaintiff or his or her attorney stating the last known place of residence or the last known business address of the defendant and a certificate of mailing a copy of the summons and complaint to the defendant at such address as required by this subsection (e). The certificate of mailing shall be prima facie evidence that the plaintiff or his or her attorney mailed a copy of the summons and complaint to the defendant as required. Service of the summons shall be deemed to have been made upon the defendant on the date it is served upon the Secretary and shall have the same force and effect as though summons had been personally served upon the defendant within this State.

(f) Only causes of action arising from acts enumerated herein may be asserted against a defendant in an action in which jurisdiction over him or her is based upon subsection (a).

(g) Nothing herein contained limits or affects the right to serve any process in any other manner now or hereafter provided by law.

Louisiana

La. Rev. Stat. Ann. § 13:3201. Personal jurisdiction over nonresidents.

A. A court may exercise jurisdiction over a nonresident, who acts directly or by an agent, as to a cause of action arising from any one of the following activities performed by the nonresident:

(1) Transacting any business in this state.

(2) Contracting to supply services or things in this state.

(3) Causing injury or damage by an offense or quasi offense committed through an act or omission in this state.

(4) Causing injury or damage in this state by an offense or quasi offense committed through an act or omission outside of this state if he regularly does or solicits business, or engages in any other persistent course of conduct, or derives revenue from goods used or consumed or services rendered in this state.

(5) Having an interest in, using or possessing a real right on immovable property in this state.

(6) Non-support of a child, parent, or spouse or a former spouse domiciled in this state to whom an obligation of support is owed and with whom the nonresident formerly resided in this state.

(7) Parentage and support of a child who was conceived by the nonresident while he resided in or was in this state.

(8) Manufacturing of a product or component thereof which caused damage or injury in this state, if at the time of placing the product into the stream of commerce, the manufacturer could have foreseen, realized, expected, or anticipated that the product may eventually be found in this state by reason of its nature and the manufacturer's marketing practices.

B. In addition to the provisions of Subsection A, a court of this state may exercise personal jurisdiction over a nonresident on any basis consistent with the constitution of this state and of the Constitution of the United States.

Massachusetts

Mass. Gen. Laws Ch. 223A, § 3. Transactions or conduct for personal jurisdiction.

A court may exercise personal jurisdiction over a person, who acts directly or by an agent, as to a cause of action in law or equity arising from the person's

(a) transacting any business in this commonwealth;

(b) contracting to supply services or things in this commonwealth;

(c) causing tortious injury by an act or omission in this commonwealth;

(d) causing tortious injury in this commonwealth by an act or omission outside this commonwealth if he regularly does or solicits business, or engages in any other persistent course of conduct, or derives substantial revenue from goods used or consumed or services rendered, in this commonwealth;

(e) having an interest in, using or possessing real property in this commonwealth;

(f) contracting to insure any person, property or risk located within this commonwealth at the time of contracting;

(g) maintaining a domicile in this commonwealth while a party to a personal or marital relationship out of which arises a claim for divorce, alimony, property settlement, parentage of a child, child support or child custody; or the commission of any act giving rise to such a claim; or

(h) having been subject to the exercise of personal jurisdiction of a court of the commonwealth which has resulted in an order of alimony, custody, child support or property settlement, notwithstanding the subsequent departure of one of the original parties from the commonwealth, if the action involves modification of such order or orders and the moving party resides in the commonwealth, or if the action involves enforcement of such order notwithstanding the domicile of the moving party.

New York

N.Y. C.P.L.R. § 302. Personal jurisdiction by acts of non-domiciliaries.

(a) Acts which are the basis of jurisdiction. As to a cause of action arising from any of the acts enumerated in this section, a court may exercise personal jurisdiction over any non-domiciliary, or his executor or administrator, who in person or through an agent:

1. transacts any business within the state or contracts anywhere to supply goods or services in the state; or

2. commits a tortious act within the state, except as to a cause of action for defamation of character arising from the act; or

3. commits a tortious act without the state causing injury to person or property within the state, except as to a cause of action for defamation of character arising from the act, if he

      (i) regularly does or solicits business, or engages in any other persistent course of conduct, or derives substantial revenue from goods used or consumed or services rendered, in this state, or

      (ii) expects or should reasonably expect the act to have consequences in the state and derives substantial revenue from interstate or international commerce; or

    4. owns, uses, or possesses any real property situated within the state.

(b) Personal jurisdiction over non-resident defendant in matrimonial actions or family court proceedings. A court in any matrimonial action or family court proceeding involving a demand for support, alimony, maintenance, distributive awards or special relief in matrimonial actions may exercise personal jurisdiction over the respondent or defendant notwithstanding the fact that he or she no longer is a resident or domiciliary of this state, or over his or her executor or administrator, if the party seeking support is a resident of or domiciled in this state at the time such demand is made, provided that this state was the matrimonial domicile of the parties before their separation, or the defendant abandoned the plaintiff in this state, or the claim for support, alimony, maintenance, distributive awards or special relief in matrimoniial actions accrued under the laws of this state or under an agreement executed in this state. The family court may exercise personal jurisdiction over a non-resident respondent to the extent provided in sections one hundred fifty-four and one thousand thirty-six and article five-B of the family court act and article five-A of the domestic relations law.

(c) Effect of appearance. Where personal jurisdiction is based solely upon this section, an appearance does not confer such jurisdiction with respect to causes of action not arising from an act enumerated in this section.

Ohio

Ohio R. Civ. P. 4.3. Process: out-of-state service.

(a) When service permitted

Service of process may be made outside of this state, as provided in this rule, in any action in this state, upon a person who, at the time of service of process, is a nonresident of this state or is a resident of this state who is absent from this state. "Person" includes an individual, an individual's executor, administrator, or other personal representative, or a corporation, partnership, association, or any other legal or commercial entity, who, acting directly or by an agent, has caused an event to occur out of which the claim that is the subject of the complaint arose, from the person's:

    (1) Transacting any business in this state;

    (2) Contracting to supply services or goods in this state;

    (3) Causing tortious injury by an act or omission in this state, including, but not limited to, actions arising out of the ownership, operation, or use of a motor vehicle or aircraft in this state;

    (4) Causing tortious injury in this state by an act or omission outside this state if the person regularly does or solicits business, engages in any other persistent course of conduct, or derives substantial revenue from goods used or consumed or services rendered in this state;

    (5) Causing injury in this state to any person by breach of warranty expressly or impliedly made in the sale of goods outside this state when the person to be served might reasonably have expected the person who was injured to use, consume, or be affected by the goods in this state, provided that the person to be served also regularly does or solicits business, engages in any other persistent course of conduct, or derives substantial revenue from goods used or consumed or services rendered in this state;

    (6) Having an interest in, using, or possessing real property in this state;

    (7) Contracting to insure any person, property, or risk located within this state at the time of contracting;

    (8) Living in the marital relationship within this state notwithstanding subsequent departure from this state, as to all obligations arising for spousal support, custody, child support, or property settlement, if the other party to the marital relationship continues to reside in this state;

    (9) Causing tortious injury in this state to any person by an act outside this state committed with the purpose of injuring persons, when the person to be served might reasonably have expected that some person would be injured by the act in this state;

    (10) Causing tortious injury to any person by a criminal act, any element of which takes place in this state, that the person to be served commits or in the commission of which the person to be served is guilty of complicity.

(b) Methods of service

(1) Service by certified or express mail.

Evidenced by return receipt signed by any person, service of any process shall be by certified or express mail unless otherwise permitted by these rules. The clerk shall place a copy of the process and complaint or other document to be served in an envelope. The clerk shall address the envelope to the person to be served at the address set forth in the caption or at the address set forth in written instructions furnished to the clerk with instructions to forward. The clerk shall affix adequate postage and place the sealed envelope in the United States mail as certified or express mail return receipt requested with instructions to the delivering postal employee to show to whom delivered, date of delivery, and address where delivered.

The clerk shall forthwith enter the fact of mailing on the appearance docket and make a similar entry when the return receipt is received. If the envelope is returned with an endorsement showing failure of delivery, the clerk shall forthwith notify, by mail, the attorney of record or, if there is no attorney of record, the party at whose instance process was issued and enter the fact of notification on the appearance docket. The clerk shall file the return receipt or returned envelope in the records of the action. If the envelope is returned with an endorsement showing failure of delivery, service is complete when the attorney or serving party, after notification by the clerk, files with the clerk an affidavit setting forth facts indicating the reasonable diligence utilized to ascertain the whereabouts of the party to be served.

All postage shall be charged to costs. If the parties to be served certified or express mail are numerous and the clerk determines there is insufficient security for costs, the clerk may require the party requesting service to advance an amount estimated by the clerk to be sufficient to pay the postage.

(2) Personal service.

When ordered by the court, a "person" as defined in division (A) of this rule may be personally served with a copy of the process and complaint or other document to be served. Service under this division may be made by any person not less than eighteen years of age who is not a party and who has been designated by an order of the court. On request, the clerk shall deliver the summons to the plaintiff for transmission to the person who will make the service.

Proof of service may be made as prescribed by Civ. R. 4.1(B) or by order of the court.

VIRGINIA

Va. Code Ann. § 8.01-328.1. When personal jurisdiction over person may be exercised.

A. A court may exercise personal jurisdiction over a person, who acts directly or by an agent, as to a cause of action arising from the person's:

1. Transacting any business in this Commonwealth;

2. Contracting to supply services or things in this Commonwealth;

3. Causing tortious injury by an act or omission in this Commonwealth;

4. Causing tortious injury in this Commonwealth by an act or omission outside this Commonwealth if he regularly does or solicits business, or engages in any other persistent course of conduct, or derives substantial revenue from goods used or consumed or services rendered, in this Commonwealth;

5. Causing injury in this Commonwealth to any person by breach of warranty expressly or impliedly made in the sale of goods outside this Commonwealth when he might reasonably have expected such person to use, consume, or be affected by the goods in this Commonwealth, provided that he also regularly does or solicits business, or engages in any other persistent course of conduct, or derives substantial revenue from goods used or consumed or services rendered in this Commonwealth;

6. Having an interest in, using, or possessing real property in this Commonwealth;

7. Contracting to insure any person, property, or risk located within this Commonwealth at the time of contracting;

8. Having (i) executed an agreement in this Commonwealth which obligates the person to pay spousal support or child support to a domiciliary of this Commonwealth, or to a person who has satisfied the residency requirements in suits for annulments or divorce for members of the armed forces pursuant to Section 20-97 provided proof of service of process on a nonresident party is made by a law-enforcement officer or other person authorized to serve process in the jurisdiction where the nonresident party is located, (ii) been ordered by pay spousal support or child support pursuant to an order entered by any court of competent jurisdiction in this Commonwealth having in personam jurisdiction over such person, or (iii) shown by personal conduct in this Commonwealth, as alleged by affidavit, that the person conceived or fathered a child in this Commonwealth;

9. Having maintained within this Commonwealth a matrimonial domicile at the time of separation of the parties upon which grounds for divorce or separate maintenance is based, or at the time a cause of action arose for divorce or separate maintenance or at the time of commencement of such suit, if the other party to the matrimonial relationship resides herein; or

10. Having incurred liability for taxes, fines, penalties, interest, or other charges to any political subdivision of the Commonwealth.

Jurisdiction in subdivision 9 is valid only upon proof of service of process pursuant to Section 8.01-296 on the nonresident party by a person authorized under the provisions of Section 8.01-320. Jurisdiction under subdivision 8(iii) of this subsection is valid only upon proof of personal service on a nonresident pursuant to Section 8.01-320.

B. Using a computer or computer network located in the Commonwealth shall constitute an act in the Commonwealth. For purposes of this subsection, "use" and "computer network" shall have the same meanings as those contained in Section 18.2-152.2.

C. When jurisdiction over a person is based solely upon this section, only a cause of action arising from acts enumerated in this section may be asserted against him; however, nothing contained in this chapter shall limit, restrict or otherwise affect the jurisdiction of any court of this Commonwealth over foreign corporations which are subject to service of process pursuant to the provisions of any other statute.

EXAMPLES OF STATE VENUE STATUTES

CALIFORNIA

Cal. Civ. Proc. § 392. Real property actions; proper court.

(a) Subject to the power of the court to transfer actions and proceedings as provided in this title, the superior court in the county where the real property that is the subject of the action, or some part thereof, is situated, is the proper court for the trial of the following actions:

(1) For the recovery of real property, or of an estate or interest therein, or for the determination in any form, of that right or interest, and for injuries to real property.

(2) For the foreclosure of all liens and mortgages on real property.

(b) In the court designated as the proper court in subdivision (a), the proper court location for trial of a proceeding for an unlawful detainer, as defined in Section 1161, is the location where the court tries that type of proceeding that is nearest or most accessible to where the real property that is the subject of the action, or some part thereof, is situated. Otherwise any location of the superior court designated as the proper court in subdivision (a) is a proper court location for the trial. The court may specify by local rule the nearest or most accessible court location where the court tries that type of case.

Cal. Civ. Proc. § 393. Actions to recover penalty or forfeiture; actions against public officers; proper court.

Subject to the power of the court to transfer actions and proceedings as provided in this title, the county in which the cause, or some part of the cause, arose, is the proper county for the trial of the following actions:

(a) For the recovery of a penalty or forfeiture imposed by statute, except, that when it is imposed for an offense committed on a lake, river, or other stream of water, situated in two or more counties, the action may be tried in any county bordering on the lake, river, or stream, and opposite to the place where the offense was committed.

(b) Against a public officer or person especially appointed to execute the duties of a public officer, for an act done by the officer or person in virtue of the office, or against a person who, by the officer's command or in the officer's aid, does anything touching the duties of the officer.

Cal. Civ. Proc. § 394. Actions by or against a city, county, city and county or local agency; transfer of cases; proper court.

(a) An action or proceeding against a county, or city and county, a city, or local agency, may be tried in the county, or city and county, or the county in which the city or local agency is situated, unless the action or proceeding is brought by a county, or city and county, a city, or local agency, in which case it may be tried in any county, or city and county, not a party thereto and in which the city or local agency is not situated. Except for actions initiated by the local child support agency pursuant to Section 17400, 17402, 17404, or 17416 of the Family Code, any action or proceeding brought by a county, city and county, city, or local agency within a certain county, or city and county, against a resident of another county, city and county, or city, or a corporation doing business in the latter, shall be, on motion of either party, transferred for trial to a county, or city and county, other than the plaintiff, if the plaintiff is a county, or city and county, and other than that in which the plaintiff is situated, if the plaintiff is a city, or a local agency, and other than that in which the defendant resides, or is doing business, or is situated. Whenever an action or proceeding is brought against a county, city and county, city, or local agency, in any county, or city and county, other than the defendant, if the defendant is a county, or city and county, or, if the defendant is a city, or local agency, other than that in which the defendant is situated, the action or proceeding must be, on motion of that defendant, transferred for trial to a county, or city and county, other than that in which the plaintiff, or any of the plaintiffs, resides, or is doing business, or is situated, and other than the plaintiff county, or city and county, or county in which that plaintiff city or local agency is situated, and other than the defendant county, or city and county, or county in which the defendant city or local agency is situated; provided, however, that any action or proceeding against the city, county, city and county, or local agency for injury occurring within the city, county, or city and county, or within the county in which the local agency is situated, to person or property or person and property caused by the negligence or alleged negligence of the city, county, city and county, local agency, or its agents or employees, shall be tried in that county, or city and county, or if a city is a defendant, in the city or in the county in which the city is situated, or if a local agency is a defendant, in the county in which the local agency is situated. In

379

that action or proceeding, the parties thereto may, by stipulation in writing, or made in open court, and entered in the minutes, agree upon any county, or city and county, for the place of trial thereof. When the action or proceeding is one in which a jury is not of right, or in case a jury is waived, then in lieu of transferring the cause, the court in the original county may request the chairperson of the Judicial Council to assign a disinterested judge from a neutral county to hear that cause and all proceedings in connection therewith. When the action or proceeding is transferred to another county for trial, a witness required to respond to a subpoena for a hearing within the original county shall be compelled to attend hearings in the county to which the cause is transferred. If the demand for transfer is made by one party and the opposing party does not consent thereto, the additional costs of the nonconsenting party occasioned by the transfer of the cause, including living and traveling expenses of the nonconsenting party and material witnesses, found by the court to be material, and called by the nonconsenting party, not to exceed five dollars ($5) per day each in excess of witness fees and mileage otherwise allowed by law, shall be assessed by the court hearing the cause against the party requesting the transfer. To the extent of that excess, those costs shall be awarded to the nonconsenting party regardless of the outcome of the trial. This section shall apply to actions or proceedings now pending or hereafter brought.

(b) For the purposes of this section, "local agency" shall mean any governmental district, board, or agency, or any other local governmental body or corporation, but shall not include the State of California or any of its agencies, departments, commissions, or boards.

Cal. Civ. Proc. § 395. Actions generally; proper court; waiver.

(a) Except as otherwise provided by law and subject to the power of the court to transfer actions or proceedings as provided in this title, the superior court in the county where the defendants or some of them reside at the commencement of the action is the proper court for the trial of the action. If the action is for injury to person or personal property or for death from wrongful act or negligence, the superior court in either the county where the injury occurs or the injury causing death occurs or the county where the defendants, or some of them reside at the commencement of the action, is a proper court for the trial of the action. In a proceeding for dissolution of marriage, the superior court in the county where either the petitioner or respondent has been a resident for three months next preceding the commencement of the proceeding is the proper court for the trial of the proceeding. In a proceeding for nullity of marriage or legal separation of the parties, the superior court in the county where either the petitioner or the respondent resides at the commencement of the proceeding is the proper court for the trial of the proceeding. In a proceeding to enforce an obligation of support under Section 3900 of the Family Code, the superior court in the county where the child resides is the proper court for the trial of the action. In a proceeding to establish and enforce a foreign judgment or court order for the support of a minor child, the superior court in the county where the child resides is the proper court for the trial of the action. Subject to subdivision (b), if a defendant has contracted to perform an obligation in a particular county, the superior court in the county where the obligation is to be performed, where the contract in fact was entered into, or where the defendant or any defendant resides at the commencement of the action is a proper court for the trial of an action founded on that obligation, and the county where the obligation is incurred is the county where it is to be performed, unless there is a special contract in writing to the contrary. If none of the defendants reside in the state or if they reside in the state and the county where they reside is unknown to the plaintiff, the action may be tried in the superior court in any county that the plaintiff may designate in his or her complaint, and, if the defendant is about to depart from the state, the action may be tried in the superior court in any county where either of the parties reside or service is made. If any person is improperly joined as a defendant or has been made a defendant solely for the purpose of having the action tried in the superior court in the county where he or she resides, his or her residence shall not be considered in determining the proper place for the trial of the action.

(b) Subject to the power of the court to transfer actions or proceedings as provided in this title, in an action arising from an offer or provision of goods, services, loans or extensions of credit intended primarily for personal, family or household use, other than an obligation described in Section 1812.10 or Section 2984.4 of the Civil Code, or an action arising from a transaction consummated as a proximate result of either an unsolicited telephone call made by a seller engaged in the business of consummating transactions of that kind or a telephone call or electronic transmission made by the buyer or lessee in response to a solicitation by the seller, the superior court in the county where the buyer or lessee in fact signed the contract, where the buyer or lessee resided at the time the contract was entered into, or where the buyer or lessee resides at the commencement of the action is the proper court for the trial of the action. In the superior court designated in this subdivision as the proper court, the proper court location for trial of a case is the location where the court tries that type of case that is nearest or most accessible to where the buyer or lessee resides, where the buyer or lessee in fact signed the contract, where the buyer or lessee resided at the time the contract was entered into, or where the buyer or lessee resides at the commencement of the action. Otherwise, any location of the superior court designated as the proper court in this subdivision is a proper court location for the trial. The court may specify by local rule the nearest or most accessible court location where the court tries that type of case.

(c) Any provision of an obligation described in subdivision (b) waiving that subdivision is void and unenforceable.

Cal. Civ. Proc. § 395.1. Executor, administrator, guardian, conservator, or trustee in official or representative capacity.

Except as otherwise provided in Section 17005 of the Probate Code pertaining to trustees, when a defendant is sued in an official or representative capacity as executor, administrator, guardian, conservator, or trustee on a claim for the payment of money or for the recovery of personal property, the county which has jurisdiction of the estate which the defendant represents shall be the proper county for the trial of the action.

Cal. Civ. Proc. § 395.2. Unincorporated associations.

If an unincorporated association has filed a statement with the Secretary of State pursuant to statute, designating its principal office in this state, the proper county for the trial of an action against the unincorporated association is the same as it would be if the unincorporated association were a corporation and, for the purpose of determining the proper county, the principal place of business of the unincorporated association shall be deemed to be the principal office in this state listed in the statement.

Cal. Civ. Proc. § 395.5. Actions against corporations or associations; place of trial.

A corporation or association may be sued in the county where the contract is made or is to be performed, or where the obligation or liability arises, or the breach occurs; or in the county where the principal place of business of such corporation is situated, subject to the power of the court to change the place of trial as in other cases.

MASSACHUSETTS

Mass. G.L. c. 223 § 1. Transitory actions; general provisions.

A transitory action shall, except as otherwise provided, if any one of the parties thereto lives in the commonwealth, be brought in the county where one of them lives or has his usual place of business; provided, however, that if the instrument of the crime is a forged check, credit card, or other negotiable instrument, intending on its face to be presented for payment at another place in another county and the value of the money, goods or services involved is in excess of one hundred dollars, the action may be brought in the county where the instrument was presented or at the place where the instrument was presented for payment, if such place of payment is located in the commonwealth; and provided, further, that except in actions upon negotiable instruments if the plaintiff is an assignee of the cause of action, it shall be brought only in a county where it might have been brought by the assignor thereof. If neither party lives in the commonwealth, the action may be brought in any county. If an action is dismissed because the defendant has raised timely objection to venue, the defendant shall be allowed double costs.

Mass. G.L. c. 223 § 2. Transitory actions; district courts.

Except as provided in section twenty-one of chapter two hundred and eighteen, a transitory action in a district court shall be brought in a court in the judicial district where one of the parties lives or has his usual place of business or in a court, the judicial district of which is adjacent to the judicial district where one of the parties lives or has his usual place of business or, if in connection with the commencement of such an action the approval of trustee process is sought, that action shall be brought in a court in the judicial district where one of the parties or any person alleged to be trustee lives or has a usual place of business, or in a court the judicial district of which adjoins the judicial district where one of the parties or one of the alleged trustees lives or has a usual place of business; provided, however, that an action may be brought in the municipal court of the city of Boston as provided in section fifty-four of chapter two hundred and eighteen.

Said courts shall have jurisdiction of a transitory action against a defendant who is not an inhabitant of the commonwealth, if personal service or an effectual attachment of property is made within the commonwealth; and such action may be brought in any of said courts in the county where the service or attachment was made.

Mass. G.L. c. 223 § 3. Transitory actions; enumeration.

Every action for rent, use and occupation or breach of covenant shall be considered a transitory action.

Mass. G.L. c. 223 § 4. Replevin actions.

An action brought pursuant to chapter two hundred and forty-seven shall be brought in the county where the goods or beasts are detained.

Mass. G.L. c. 223 § 5. Actions by the commonwealth.

A civil action in which the commonwealth is plaintiff or in which money due to the commonwealth is sought to be recovered may be brought in the county where the defendant lives or has his usual place of business, or in Suffolk county.

Mass. G.L. c. 223 § 6. Counties; actions by or against.

A local or transitory action by a county shall be brought in the county where the defendant lives or in a county adjoining the plaintiff county. If the defendant lives in the plaintiff county, it shall be brought in an adjoining county. Such action against a county shall, at the election of the plaintiff, be brought in the county where he lives, in the defendant county or in an adjoining county.

Mass. G.L. c. 223 § 7. Defective ways, etc.; negligence actions.

An action against a town or person to recover for injury or damage received by reason of a defect, want of repair or of an insufficient railing in or upon a public way shall be brought in the county where said town is situated or in the county where the plaintiff lives, except that such action against the city of Boston may be brought in Middlesex county, in Norfolk county or in the county where the plaintiff lives, and such action against the town of Nantucket or against any town in Dukes county may be brought in Bristol county. An action against a town or person to recover for injury or damage received in the commonwealth by reason of negligence other than that relating to such defect, want of repair or insufficient railing shall be brought in the county where the plaintiff lives or has his usual place of business, or in the county where the alleged injury or damage was received. This section shall not apply to actions that may be brought in a district court.

Mass. G.L. c. 223 § 8. Corporations; actions by or against.

Transitory actions, except those mentioned in the preceding section, to which a corporation, other than a county or the city of Boston, is a party, may be brought as follows:

(1) If both parties are cities, towns or parishes, in the county where either party is situated.

(2) If both parties are corporations, other than a city, town or parish, in any county in which either corporation has a usual place of business, or in which it held its last annual meeting, or usually holds its meetings.

(3) If one party is a city, town or parish, and the other a corporation named in clause (2), in any county in which either party might sue or be sued.

(4) If one party is a corporation named in clause (1) or (2), and the other an individual, in any county in which the corporation might sue or be sued, or in the county in which the individual lives or has a usual place of business.

Mass. G.L. c. 223 § 9. Transitory actions by or against city of Boston.

An action by or against the city of Boston, except actions mentioned in section seven and actions by the collector of said city under sections thirty-five and thirty-six of chapter sixty, may be brought in Suffolk, Essex, Middlesex or Norfolk county, or in the county in which the plaintiff lives.

Mass. G.L. c. 223 § 11. Executors or administrators; transitory actions by or against.

A transitory action by or against an executor or administrator may be brought in a county in which it might have been brought by or against the testator or intestate at the time of his decease.

Mass. G.L. c. 223 § 12. Land title actions.

If a tract of land lies in two or more counties, an action relative to it, to which neither a county, the city of Boston nor any corporation named in section eight is a party, may be brought in any of said counties, and the complaint shall be so drawn as to include the whole tract.

New York

N.Y. C.P.L.R. § 501. Contractual provisions fixing venue.

Subject to the provisions of subdivision two of section 510, written agreement fixing place of trial, made before an action is commenced, shall be enforced upon a motion for change of place of trial.

N.Y. C.P.L.R. § 502. Conflicting venue provisions.

Where, because of joinder of claims or parties, there is a conflict of provisions under this article, the court, upon motion, shall order as the place of trial one proper under this article as to at least one of the parties or claims.

N.Y. C.P.L.R. § 503. Venue based on residence.

(a) Generally. Except where otherwise prescribed by law, the place of trial shall be in the county in which one of the parties resided when it was commenced; or, if none of the parties then resided in the state, in any county designated by the plaintiff. A party resident in more than one county shall be deemed a resident of each such county.

(b) Executor, administrator, trustee, committee, conservator, general or testamentary guardian, or receiver. An executor, administrator, trustee, committee, conservator, general or testamentary guardian, or receiver shall be deemed a resident of the county of his appointment as well as the county in which he actually resides.

(c) Corporation. A domestic corporation, or a foreign corporation authorized to transact business in the state, shall be deemed a resident of the county in which its principal office is located; except that such a corporation, if a railroad or other common carrier, shall also be deemed a resident of the county where the cause of action arose.

(d) Unincorporated association, partnership, or individually-owned business. A president or treasurer of an unincorporated association, suing or being sued on behalf of the association, shall be deemed a resident of any county in which the association has its principal office, as well as the county in which he actually resides. A partnership or an individually-owned business shall be deemed a resident of any county in which it has its principal office, as well as the county in which the partner or individual owner suing or being sued actually resides.

(e) Assignee. In an action for a sum of money only, brought by an assignee other than an assignee for the benefit of creditors or a holder in due course of a negotiable instrument, the assignee's residence shall be deemed the same as that of the original assignor at the time of the original assignment.

(f) Consumer credit transaction. In an action arising out of a consumer credit transaction where a purchaser, borrower or debtor is a defendant, the place of trial shall be the residence of a defendant, if one resides within the state or the county where such transaction took place, if it is within the state, or, in other cases, as set forth in subdivision (a).

N.Y. C.P.L.R. § 504. Actions against counties, cities, towns, villages, school districts and district corporations.

Notwithstanding the provisions of any charter heretofore granted by the state and subject to the provisions of subdivision (b) of section 506, the place of trial of all actions against counties, cities, towns, villages, school districts and district corporations or any of their officers, boards or departments shall be, for:

1. a county, in such county;

2. a city, except the city of New York, town, village, school district or district corporation, in the county in which such city, town, village, school district or district corporation is situated, or if such school district or district corporation is situated in more than one county, in either county; and

3. the city of New York, in the county within the city in which the cause of action arose, or if it arose outside of the city, in the county of New York,

N.Y. C.P.L.R. § 505. Actions involving public authorities.

(a) Generally. The place of trial of an action by or against a public authority constituted under the laws of the state shall be in the county in which the authority has its principal office or where it has facilities involved in the action.

(b) Against New York city transit authority. The place of trial of an action against the New York city transit authority shall be in the county within the city of New York in which the cause of action arose, or, if it arose outside of the city, in the county of New York.

N.Y. C.P.L.R. § 506. Where special proceeding commenced.

(a) Generally. Unless otherwise prescribed in subdivision (b) or in the law authorizing the proceeding, a special proceeding may be commenced in any county within the judicial district where the proceeding is triable.

(b) Proceeding against body or officer. A proceeding against a body or officer shall be commenced in any county within the judicial district where the respondent made the determination complained of or refused to perform the duty specifically enjoined upon him by law, or where the proceedings were brought or taken in the course of which the matter sought to be restrained originated, or where the material events otherwise took place, or where the principal office of the respondent is located, except that

1. a proceeding against a justice of the supreme court or a judge of a county court or the court of general sessions shall be commenced in the appellate division in the judicial department where the action, in the course of which the matter sought to be enforced or restrained originated, is triable, unless a term of the appellate division in that department is not in session, in which case the proceeding may be commenced in the appellate division in an adjoining judicial department; and

2. a proceeding against the regents of the university of the state of New York, the commissioner of education, the commissioner of taxation and finance, the tax appeals tribunal except as provided in section two thousand sixteen of the tax law, the public service commission, the commissioner or the department of transportation relating to articles three, four, five, six, seven, eight, nine or ten of the transportation law or to the railroad law, the water resources board, the comptroller or the department of agriculture and markets, shall be commenced in the supreme court, Albany county.

3. notwithstanding the provisions of paragraph two of this subdivision, a proceeding against the commissioner of education pursuant to section forty-four hundred four of the education law may be commenced in the supreme court in the county of residence of the petitioner.

4. a proceeding against the New York city tax appeals tribunal established by section one hundred sixty-eight of the New York city charter shall be commenced in the appellate division of the supreme court, first department.

N.Y. C.P.L.R. § 507. Real property actions.

The place of trial of an action in which the judgment demanded would affect the title to, or the possession, use or enjoyment of, real property shall be in the county in which any part of the subject of the action is situated.

N.Y. C.P.L.R. § 508. Actions to recover a chattel.

The place of trial of an action to recover a chattel may be in the county in which any part of the subject of the action is situated at the time of the commencement of the action.

NORTH CAROLINA

N.C. G.S.A. § 1-76. Where subject of action situated.

Actions for the following causes must be tried in the county in which the subject of the action, or some part thereof, is situated, subject to the power of the court to change the place of trial in the cases provided by law:

(1) Recovery of real property, or of an estate or interest therein, or for the determination in any form of such right or interest, and for injuries to real property.

(2) Partition of real property.

(3) Foreclosure of a mortgage of real property.

(4) Recovery of personal property when the recovery of the property itself is the sole or primary relief demanded.

N.C. G.S.A. § 1-76.1. Where deficiency debtor resides or where loan was negotiated.

Subject to the power of the court to change the place of trial as provided by law, actions to recover a deficiency, which remains owing on a debt after secured personal property has been sold to partially satisfy the debt, must be brought in the county in which the debtor or debtor's agent resides or in the county where the loan was negotiated.

N.C. G.S.A. § 1-77. Where cause of action arose.

Actions for the following causes must be tried in the county where the cause, or some part thereof, arose, subject to the power of the court to change the place of trial, in the cases provided by law:

(1) Recovery of a penalty or forfeiture, imposed by statute; except that, when it is imposed for an offense committed on a sound, bay, river, or other body of water, situated in two or more counties, the action may be brought in any county bordering on such body of water, and opposite to the place where the offense was committed.

(2) Against a public officer or person especially appointed to execute his duties, for an act done by him by virtue of his office; or against a person who by his command or in his aid does anything touching the duties of such officer.

N.C. G.S.A. § 1-78. Official bonds, executors and administrators.

All actions against executors and administrators in their official capacity, except where otherwise provided by statute, and all actions upon official bonds must be instituted in the county where the bonds were given, if the principal or any surety on the bond is in the county; if not, then in the plaintiff's county.

N.C. G.S.A. § 1-79. Domestic corporations, limited partnerships, limited liability companies, and registered limited liability partnerships.

(a) For the purpose of suing and being sued the residence of a domestic corporation, limited partnership, limited liability company, or registered limited liability partnership is as follows:

(1) Where the registered or principal office of the corporation, limited partnership, limited liability company, or registered limited liability partnership is located, or

(2) Where the corporation, limited partnership, limited liability company, or registered limited liability partnership maintains a place of business, or

(3) If no registered or principal office is in existence, and no place of business is currently maintained or can reasonably be found, the term "residence" shall include any place where the corporation, limited partnership, limited liability company, or registered limited liability partnership is regularly engaged in carrying on business.

(b) For purposes of this section, the term "domestic" when applied to an entity means:

(1) An entity formed under the laws of this State, or

(2) An entity that (i) is formed under the laws of any jurisdiction other than this State, and (ii) maintains a registered office in this State pursuant to a certificate of authority from the Secretary of State.

N.C. G.S.A. § 1-80. Foreign corporations.

An action against a corporation created by or under the law of any other state or government may be brought in the appropriate trial court division of any county in which the cause of action arose, or in which the corporation usually did business, or has property, or in which the plaintiffs, or either of them, reside, in the following cases:

(1) By a resident of this State, for any cause of action.

(2) By a nonresident of this State in any county where he or they are regularly engaged in carrying on business.

(3) By a plaintiff, not a resident of this State, when the cause of action arose or the subject of the action is situated in this State.

N.C. G.S.A. § 1-81. Actions against railroads.

In all actions against railroads the action must be tried either in the county where the cause of action arose or where the plaintiff resided at that time or in some county adjoining that in which the cause of action arose, subject to the power of the court to change the place of trial as provided by statute.

N.C. G.S.A. § 1-81.1. Venue in apportionment or redistricting cases

(a) Venue in any action concerning any act of the General Assembly apportioning or redistricting State legislative or congressional districts lies exclusively with the Wake County Superior Court.

(b) Any action brought concerning an act of the General Assembly apportioning or redistricting the State legislative or congressional districts shall be filed in the Superior Court of Wake County.

N.C. G.S.A. § 1-82. Venue in all other cases.

In all other cases the action must be tried in the county in which the plaintiffs or the defendants, or any of them, reside at its commencement, or if none of the defendants reside in the State, then in the county in which the plaintiffs, or any of them, reside; and if none of the parties reside in the State, then the action may be tried in any county which the plaintiff designates in his summons and complaint, subject to the power of the court to change the place of trial, in the cases provided by statute; provided that any person who has resided on or been stationed in a United States army, navy, marine corps, coast guard or air force installation or reservation within this State for a period of one (1) year or more next preceding the institution of an action shall be deemed a resident of the county within which such installation or reservation, or part thereof, is situated and of any county adjacent to such county where such person stationed at such installation or reservation lives in such adjacent county, for the purposes of this section. The term person shall include military personnel and the spouses and dependents of such personnel.

Finality & Preclusion

Res Judicata: A thing decided → Claim Preclusion = A final judgment on the merits percludes the same parties from litigating the same claim in a subsequent law suit.
: Requires π to assert all matters arising out of the same transaction or occurance against the same party

Claim Perclusion Elements: 1) prior suit that proceeded to a final judgment on the merits
2) the present suit arises out of the same claim as the prior suit.
3) the parties in both suits are the same or in privity

1) The same Claim: Valid & final judgment against the Δ w/ respect to all or any part of the transaction.
: cannot split the claim → what wasn't brought in A1 is gone
: Arithmetical split = 1) theory of recovery 2) kind of relief
: exception → subrogation → issurance company (property damage)

Rush v. City of Maple Heights: (moto-cycle accident A1: property A2 injury)
: All rights π had in A1 are precluded in subsequent actions.
: No claim splitting (except subrogation)

Car Carriers v. Ford Moter: (Sherman Act)
: transactional test: Is there a single core of operative facts?
1) Idenity of parties + privitys 2) identity of cause of action:
3) final judgment on the merits

Jones v. Morris Plan Bank: (car under installment plan)
: 1 K, 1 breach ∴ must bring all damages together
Where same evidence will support both COA then just bring 1.

Federated Dept Stores v. Moitie: (anti-trust, price fixing women's clothing)
: courts are required to apply res judicata even when simple justice may suggest its abandonment. Bigger picture of Justice.
: Litigant can't use the claim as a defense in one suit & then bring it as a π in A2. If claim is a defense use it & also counter-claim

Mitchell v. Federated credit Bank: (Potatos)
: a Δ in A1 must file a counter-claim in A1 any claim he has against the π which arose out of the same transaction or occurance

2) Valid Final Judgment on the merits: Restatement 2d of Judgments §20

3) Parties the Same or in Privity: Strangers to a prior adjudication can neither bind nor be bound by claim perclusion

Gonzales v. Banco Central: (FL swamp property)
: Parties need not be named in A1 to be subject to claim perclussion
: if the parties are substantially related.
: Privity Requires (1) substantial control in A1 (same lawyer or financing is not enough.) Look for participation throughout suit.
(2) virtual representation in A1. Look for non-party to have constructive notice, express/implied legal relationship + adequacy of representation. (identity of interest is necessary but not enough)

Issue Perclusion: Collateral Estoppel
: does not require a final judgment on the merits. But the issue must be litigated
: Extinguishes issues that were already litigated which were necessary to the judgment
: Less weight than claim perclusion

Issue Perclusion Elements: 1) Idenity of issues 2) issue must have been litigated and determined 3) the determination of the issue must have been necessary for the judgment.

Cromwell v. County of Sac: (bond case)
: If the issue was litigated + decided + helps to explain the judgment in A1 then that issue is percluded in subsequent actions

386

Russel v. Place: (infringment) (majority rule)
: 2 issues + don't know on which the court used to determine the guilty verdict then neither gets perclussive effect